Commercial Liability Risk Management and Insurance

Volume I

Commercial Liability Risk Management and Insurance

Volume I

DONALD S. MALECKI, CPCU
Editor, Property and Casualty Publications
The National Underwriter Company

JAMES H. DONALDSON, LL.B., LL.M.
of the New York and New Jersey Bar

RONALD C. HORN, Ph.D., CPCU, CLU
Professor of Insurance and Chairholder of Insurance Studies
Eastern Kentucky University

First Edition • 1978

AMERICAN INSTITUTE FOR
PROPERTY AND LIABILITY UNDERWRITERS
Providence and Sugartown Roads, Malvern, Pennsylvania 19355

Third Printing • December 1981

Library of Congress Catalog Number   78-67497
International Standard Book Number   0-89463-007-5

Printed in the United States of America

Foreword

The American Institute for Property and Liability Underwriters and the Insurance Institute of America are companion, nonprofit, educational organizations supported by the property-liability insurance industry. Their purpose is to provide quality continuing education programs for insurance personnel.

The Insurance Institute of America offers programs leading to the Certificate in General Insurance, the Associate in Insurance Adjusting Diploma, the Associate in Management Studies Diploma, the Associate in Risk Management Diploma, and the Associate in Underwriting Diploma. The American Institute develops, maintains, and administers the educational program leading to the Chartered Property Casualty Underwriter (CPCU) professional designation.

Throughout the history of the CPCU program, an annual updating of parts of the course of study took place. But as changes in the insurance industry came about at an increasingly rapid pace and as the world in which insurance operates grew increasingly complex, it became clear that a thorough, fundamental revision of the CPCU curriculum was necessary.

The American Institute began this curriculum revision project by organizing a committee of academicians, industry practitioners, and Institute staff members. This committee was charged with the responsibility of determining and stating those broad goals which should be the educational aims of the CPCU program in contemporary society. With these goals formulated, the curriculum committee began writing specific educational objectives which were designed to achieve the stated goals of the program. This was a time-consuming and difficult task. But this process made certain that the revised CPCU curriculum would be based on a sound and relevant foundation.

Once objectives were at least tentatively set, it was possible to outline a new, totally revised and reorganized curriculum. These outlines were widely circulated and the reactions of more than 1,800 educators and industry leaders were solicited, weighed, and analyzed. These outlines were then revised and ultimately became the structure of the new, ten-course curriculum.

With the curriculum design in hand, it was necessary to seach for study materials which would track with the revised program's objectives and follow its design. At this stage of curriculum development, the Institute reached the conclusion that it would be necessary for the Institute to prepare and publish study materials specifically tailored to the revised program. This conclusion was not reached hastily. After all, for the Institute to publish textbooks and study materials represents a significant broadening of its traditional role as an examining organization. But the unique educational needs of CPCU candidates, combined with the lack of current, suitable material available through commercial publishers for use in some areas of study, made it necessary for the Institute to broaden its scope to include publishing.

Throughout the development of the CPCU text series, it has been—and will continue to be—necessary to draw on the knowledge and skills of Institute staff members. These individuals will receive no royalties on texts sold and their writing responsibilities are seen as an integral part of their professional duties. We have proceeded in this way to avoid any possibility of conflicts of interests.

All Institute textbooks have been—and will continue to be—subjected to an extensive review process. Reviewers are drawn from both industry and academic ranks.

We invite and will welcome any and all criticisms of our publications. It is only with such comments that we can hope to provide high quality educational texts, materials, and programs.

Edwin S. Overman, Ph.D., CPCU
President

Preface

This text, which is designed for the fourth course in the ten-semester Chartered Property Casualty Underwriter program, is devoted primarily to the legal *liability* loss exposures faced by modern *business firms*. Additionally, in keeping with the desires of the curriculum planners, the text includes sections on surety exposures, aircraft and motor vehicle physical damage exposures, and the liability exposures of charitable, educational, and governmental entities. In each of these areas, to the extent that space permits, emphasis is placed upon the legal nature of the exposures and the corresponding insurance coverages or bonds, followed by a brief description of the noninsurance techniques which may be efficacious.

The first chapter of Volume I is a general review of the basic legal concepts which govern the legal liability of business firms for their acts and omissions. In the remaining six chapters, these concepts are applied to the specific liability exposures and insurance coverages that are associated with premises and operations, products and completed operations, contractual and protective agreements, and employers' liability and workers' compensation.

Volume II of the text examines the liability and physical damage loss potential, as well as the relevant insurance coverages, for a business firm which owns or operates motor vehicles or aircraft. It also considers the liability exposures associated with professional persons, corporate officers and directors, environmental pollution, employee benefit programs, data processing, the foreign operations of domestic companies, and the unique legal and insurance implications for charitable, educational, and governmental entities. One full chapter is devoted to suretyship exposures and their treatment. Then, in the concluding two chapters, the student is provided with some comprehensive case studies and illustrative risk management programs. These survey cases are' based upon the text material in both CPCU 3 and 4, and their purpose is to give the student the simulated experience of applying the text material to a variety of factual situations.

No review or discussion questions appear in this text. These are included in a companion study aid—the CPCU 4 Course Guide. The Course Guide contains educational objectives, outlines of the study material, key terms and concepts, review questions, discussion questions, and sample questions and answers of the type which may be encountered on a national examination.

Because of the extensive range of complicated subject matter and the imposing publication deadlines, completion of this text would not have been possible without the assistance of a great many dedicated professionals. We are especially grateful to the contributing authors, acknowledged separately following this preface, for writing or rewriting manuscripts upon which a number of the chapters are based. Their specialized knowledge, writing and research skills, and cooperative attitudes significantly enhanced the overall quality of the text.

For reviewing various sections of the text and providing us with constructive suggestions and comments, our thanks also go to the following persons: Warren G. Brockmeier, J.D., CPCU, Director, Risk Management Services, The Wyatt Company; Frank A. Gahren, Jr., CPCU, Manager, Rochester Branch Office, General Accident Group; Edward D. Gladstone, CPCU, Assistant Director, Policy Accounting and Audit Services, The Travelers Insurance Companies; David Gustafson, CPCU, Branch Manager, Employee Benefits Insurance Company; Roger L. Huss, CPCU, CLU, Assistant Vice President, Marsh & McLennan, Incorporated; Grant L. Miller, LL.B., Assistant General Counsel, Employers Insurance of Wausau; Robert Needle, J.D., Harvey, Pennington, Herting & Renneisen, Ltd.; Frances M. Pommer, CPCU, University Extension Division, Rutgers University; Alfred E. Reichenberger, LL.D., Utica Mutual Insurance Company; Gary K. Stone, Ph.D., CLU, Professor of Insurance, Michigan State University; Rollyn L. Storey, J.D., CPCU, CSP, CHCM, ARM, AIM, AIC, Director of Risk Management, SCM Corporation; Harold Uhrig, LL.B., Claim Supervisor, United States Fidelity & Guaranty Company; Donald L. Very, J.D., Tucker Arensburg Very & Ferguson; Paul B. Wever, J.D., Attorney at Law; Numan A. Williams, Ph.D., CPCU, Associate Professor of Insurance, Ball State University.

We are also sincerely grateful to all of the American Institute staff members who patiently coordinated our efforts, provided us with encouragement and counsel, and assisted in every phase of the project. Because we share with the Institute staff the common goal of making this text an effective learning device, we welcome suggestions on how subsequent editions may be improved.

Finally, it happens that the Malecki, Donaldson, and Horn families were involved in cross-country moves during the writing of this text. The usual frustrations of authorship were compounded by the tensions of relocation. For responding with a full measure of love and understanding, our wives and children deserve very special recognition. They are very special people.

Donald S. Malecki
James H. Donaldson
Ronald C. Horn

Contributing Authors

The American Institute for Property and Liability Underwriters and the authors acknowledge, with deep appreciation, the work of the following contributing authors whose manuscripts in their areas of expertise helped make this text possible:

John R. F. Baer, J.D.
Keck, Cushman, Mahin & Cate

Martin R. Cohen, J.D.
Attorney at Law

Clement J. DeMichelis, LL.B.
McCaslin, Imbus & McCaslin

Donald J. Hirsch, J.D.
Associate Research Director
Defense Research Institute

Alan M. Kramer, J.D.
Anthony M. Lanzone & Associates

Anthony M. Lanzone, LL.B.
Anthony M. Lanzone & Associates

Douglass F. Rohrman, J.D.
Keck, Cushman, Mahin & Cate

Edward S. Silber, J.D.
Keck, Cushman, Mahin & Cate

Bernard L. Webb, CPCU, FCAS
Professor of Actuarial Science and Insurance
Georgia State University

George I. Whitehead, Jr., LL.B.
Corporate Director
Piper Aircraft

Table of Contents

Chapter 2—Premises and Operations Liability Exposures and Their Treatment...................... 61

Premises and Operations Exposures ~ *Premises Liability Exposures in General; Duties of the Possessor of Land; Operations Liability Exposures in General; Premises and Operations Liability as to Specific Business Entities*

Premises and Operations Liability Insurance ~ *Standard Liability Forms; Nonstandard Liability Forms; Nature and Scope of Standard Policy Provisions; Comprehensive General Liability Coverage Part; Owners, Landlords, and Tenants Coverage Part; Manufacturers and Contractors Coverage Part; Garage Liability Forms; Storekeepers Liability Form; Guidelines for Use of Coverages and Forms Discussed*

Broad Form CGL Endorsement ~ *Limited Worldwide Liability Coverage; Extended Bodily Injury Coverage; Newly Acquired Organizations—Automatic Coverage; Additional Persons Insured; Blanket Contractual Liability Coverage; Personal Injury Liability Coverage; Advertising Injury Liability Coverage; Premises Medical Payments Coverage; Host Liquor Liability Coverage; Fire Legal Liability Coverage—Real Property; Broad Form Property Damage Liability Coverage (Including Completed Operations); Incidental Medical Malpractice Liability Coverage; Nonowned Watercraft Liability Coverage*

Commercial Umbrella Liability Insurance ~ *Nature of Commercial Umbrella Liability Insurance; Coverages, Policy Provisions, and Rationale; Use of Commercial Umbrella Liability Insurance*

Noninsurance Techniques for Handling Premises and Operations Liability Exposures ~ *Avoidance; Noninsurance Transfer Agreements; Loss Control; Retention*

Chapter 3—Products and Completed Operations Liability Exposures....................................159

Products Liability Exposures ~ *Grounds for the Imposition of Products Liability; Statutory Influences; Duties and Vulnerability of Those Exposed; Problem Areas; Defenses to Product Actions; Examples of Losses Which May Arise from Products*

CHAPTER 1

Commercial Liability Loss Exposures

INTRODUCTION

Commercial liability loss exposures arise out of legal duties. Consequently, much of CPCU 4 will analyze the legal principles that give rise to a potential for liability losses. This course also will analyze both insurance and noninsurance risk management techniques for treating the exposures. Emphasis will be placed on insurance, but not to the exclusion of the other risk management techniques—avoidance, control, noninsurance transfer, and retention.

Chapter 1 introduces this course with a general analysis of commercial liability loss exposures. Later chapters will expand on the principles presented here, and relate them specifically to the exposures arising out of premises and operations, products and completed operations, contractual and protective liability, employers' liability and workers' compensation, motor vehicles, professional liability, and other miscellaneous exposures. Surety exposures and their treatment will be analyzed in detail, and the course will conclude with several survey cases which tie together the analyses of both property and liability loss exposures and their treatment.

Chapter 1 will describe first the general nature of legal liability exposures of business firms. Subsequent sections of the chapter will discuss more specifically liability for intentional interference torts, liability for negligent torts, strict liability, *res ipsa loquitur*, and vicarious liability. Each of these areas of discussion identifies potential commercial liability loss exposures which must be identified and evaluated if the proper risk management technique is to be applied.

GENERAL NATURE OF LEGAL LIABILITY
EXPOSURES OF BUSINESS FIRMS

Legal Liability

Nature of Legal Obligations or Duties The English common law, which was adopted by American courts, recognized that each individual was endowed with certain rights the law was bound to protect. These legally protected rights included the right to security of person, property, and reputation, as well as to the services of an unemancipated child and wife. Over the years, as a result of the judicial modification of the common law and by the enactment of statutes, other rights of individuals have been established, such as the right of privacy and the right to vote. Like an individual, a business organization has certain legally protected rights, such as the right to the security of its property and its good reputation, and the right to be free from malicious interference. Any wrongful invasion of such legally protected rights entitles the business organization to bring an action against the wrongdoer for damages or other relief that the court may deem appropriate. The general rule is that where there is a right which has been invaded, there is a remedy.

In a legal sense, a *duty* is the correlative of a right.[1] Where there is a right, there is a duty on the part of others to respect that right and to refrain from any action or omission which will impair or damage that right. In the case of any wrongful act or omission which deprives the individual or a business firm of a right, the injured party may bring an action at law to recover money damages for the loss which has been sustained. In certain cases, other forms of recovery, such as injunctive relief, are possible. Similarly, duties which are imposed upon individuals with respect to the rights of others are likewise imposed upon business firms. For example, business entities are under a duty to maintain their premises in a reasonably safe condition, to exercise care in their operations, both on and off their premises, to exercise care in the manufacture of any product, and to operate their motor vehicles in a reasonably safe manner. If a business entity is guilty of a wrongful act or omission which causes damages, the business firm may be held legally liable to the injured party to the extent of the damage caused. However, the extent of a business entity's liability depends on the type of business organization involved.

Organization of Business Firms. Business entities assume one of the following forms: (1) individual proprietorship, (2) partnership, (3) corporation, or (4) association.

INDIVIDUAL PROPRIETORSHIP. In the individual proprietorship form, one individual is the sole owner and has the right of management of a business enterprise. The individual proprietor is *personally* liable for the debts of the business. Thus, in the case of an unsatisfied judgment, not only is the property of the business subject to execution, but the individual's property also is subject to execution.

PARTNERSHIP. The partnership type of organization is formed by a contract between two or more individuals, and it contemplates that the individuals involved will use their capital and labor in lawful commerce or business with the understanding that there shall be a proportional sharing of the profits and losses between them. When all the partners are jointly and severally liable for the debts of the partnership, the arrangement is referred to as a *general partnership.*

A *limited partnership* is a partnership consisting of one or more general partners, jointly and severally liable as ordinary partners, and by whom the business is conducted, and one or more special partners, who contribute a specific amount of capital and who are not liable for the debts of the partnership beyond the amount so contributed. The special partners participate in the profits on an agreed basis. Since the special partners have no voice in the management of the business, in essence they may be regarded as nothing more than financial backers.

A *joint enterprise* is an undertaking somewhat similar to that of the partnership, but is formulated to accomplish some specific purpose rather than being a permanent arrangement. All persons engaged in the joint enterprise, sometimes called a *joint venture* or *joint adventure,* must have a voice in its management. All joint adventurers are liable to third persons, and the negligence of one member of the joint enterprise is imputable to the others.

CORPORATION. A corporation may be defined as an artificial person or entity which is created by or under the authority of the laws of a state or nation, has a capacity for perpetual existence, and is able to act only through agents. It is an entity which exists solely apart from its individual directors, officers, and/or shareholders.

A corporation may exist pursuant to the terms of its articles of incorporation, either for a fixed period of time or perpetually. Changes among the individuals who are on a corporation's board of directors, who are corporate officers, or who are shareholders can be and are consummated regularly without affecting the corporation's continuing existence. The owners of a corporation, the shareholders, are normally shielded from any personal liability for corporate acts.

A *public corporation* is one created by the state to act as an agency in the administration of civil government, generally within a particular territory or subdivision of the state, and usually invested with local powers of legislation. Some such corporations administer an entire county, city, town, or school district, whereas others are created for a single purpose, such as a turnpike authority or a port authority.

A *private corporation* is one which is founded by private individuals for private purposes. The principal distinction between public and private corporations is that the former are organized for some governmental purpose, while the latter are not.

While private corporations are liable for their negligent acts, public corporations are sometimes shielded from liability for their negligent acts by the *doctrine of sovereign immunity*. This doctrine, it should be noted, is under severe attack.

Public service corporations are private corporations in the sense that they are owned and managed by private individuals, but their operations serve the needs of the general public or contribute to the comfort and convenience of an entire community. Examples of public service corporations are railroads and gas, water, and electric companies. Because the business of such companies is said to be "affected with the public interest," they are subject to legislative regulation and control to a greater extent than other types of private corporations. Most public service corporations are treated like private corporations insofar as their tort liability is concerned.

The creation of various other types of corporations is often specifically authorized by statute. These others include medical insurance corporations, banking corporations, and professional corporations. The personal liability of the shareholders, officers, and/or directors of these types of corporations is sometimes mandated by law. In many states, for example, lawyers or doctors practicing as agents of a professional corporation remain personally liable for their acts, if said acts constitute professional "malpractice."

The words "company" and "corporation" are commonly used interchangeably. Strictly speaking, "& Company" denotes a partnership. Thus, Jones & Company would refer to a partnership consisting of Jones, the nominal partner, and one or more unnamed partners. On the other hand, some corporations have included the word "company" in the corporate title, such as the National Broadcasting Company. Therefore, due to common usage, the word "company" can refer to either a partnership or a corporation.

ASSOCIATION. An association is formed when a number of persons unite for some special purpose or business. It is fundamentally a large partnership, but it differs from the usual partnership in that it is not bound by the acts of the individual partners, but only by the acts of its manager(s) or trustee(s). The shares in it are transferable, and it is not dissolved by the retirement, death, or bankruptcy of its individual members.

Vicarious Liability of Business Firms. A general rule of agency law is that when an individual does something by means of an agent or employee under his or her control, it is legally as if that individual does it personally. Therefore, the negligence of the agent or employee is imputed to the principal or employer, and the principal or employer must respond in damages to the injured person even though the principal or employer was otherwise blameless. The liability imposed upon the principal or employer is called *vicarious liability,* and the doctrine under which it is applied is called *respondeat superior* (let the master answer). However, the employer is not vicariously liable when the employee or agent is acting outside the scope of his or her employment or authority.

Vicarious liability may be applied not only to individuals but also to business entities. Thus, if an employee or agent is driving a motor vehicle on the business premises of the employer and negligently causes injury to a person or to property, the employer will usually be held vicariously liable to the injured person. This rule would apply regardless of whether the employee was operating the motor vehicle on the premises or on the public highway. The motor vehicle could be of any type, such as a truck and trailer unit, a private passenger automobile, or a hi-lo loader designed for use on the premises. The same rule is applicable to all acts done in the course and scope of the agency or employment.

In situations where an employee is negligent, commits an intentional assault, and/or has unreasonably failed to conform to the employer's supervision while doing the act that causes the injury, the employee may be held liable personally. In most cases, however, it is the employer who will pay the damages.

Liability of Business Firms for Criminal Acts. The common law recognized that in order for the community to live in harmony, each member of the community, whether a private individual or a business entity, had certain duties with respect to both the rights of the community as a whole and the rights of its members. Thus, the individuals in a community hope to live without fear with respect to their persons and property. An action which disturbs the basic norms of the community is considered a *crime.* Crimes can consist of murder, mayhem, assault, manslaughter, rape, burglary, robbery, bribery, larceny, embezzlement, receiving stolen property, or perjury. The commission of a crime will subject the perpetrator to criminal liability and, upon conviction, will subject him or her to punishment in the form of a fine, imprisonment for a term of years, or (in capital cases) execution. It should be noted that in some situations (e.g., antitrust violations, improper manufacture of drugs for human consumption, issuing of false statements with reference to the sale of securities), a statute may prescribe civil (monetary) liability on both a corporation and its agents and criminal (e.g., imprisonment) liability on certain directors and/or agents of the improperly acting corporate entity.

Broad Sources of Legal Liability. Legal liability, whether criminal, civil, or both, is imposed by either (1) common law or (2) statute.

COMMON LAW. The common law consists of a body of principles and rules of conduct which derive their authority mainly from custom. It is unwritten law in the sense that it has never been codified and can be found only by referring to the decisions of the courts.

During the colonial period, American courts were bound to apply the English common law as the rule of decision in all cases, both civil and criminal. With the Declaration of Independence, the courts were freed from any direction or obligation to follow the English rules. However, since the new nation had no legal rules of its own, the courts continued to apply the English common law as it existed on July 4, 1776. They refused to be bound by any later decisions of the English courts, preferring to develop a common law of their own.

Since the common law reflects the customs and usages of society, one would expect the law to change with the customs or attitudes of society. Where the reason for a rule no longer exists, the courts generally will abandon it. Where a new rule is necessary, the courts will provide one. For example, the original common-law rule with regard to the ownership of land was that the owner owned not only the land on the surface but also the airspace to the heavens above. With the advent of aircraft, the courts abandoned the old rule and fabricated a legal construct which established three zones above the land. The first zone consists of that part of the airspace which had been reduced to possession by the owner by his or her buildings. Thus, regardless of the size of the building, whether it be a 2-story house or a 100-story office building, the owner is entitled to sole and exclusive possession of the airspace occupied by the building. The second zone consists of the space above the buildings which the owner requires for the peaceful enjoyment of his or her property. To this zone also the owner is entitled to sole and exclusive possession. Any intrusion into either of these areas is a trespass and is actionable. The third zone, which is above the other two, is regarded as being in the public domain and may be used by any type of private, public, or commercial aircraft.

STATUTES. A statute consists of the written enactment of a legislative body. A statute is thus an expression of the will of the people as enacted by their elected representatives. It can alter or amend the common law or it can create liabilities which never existed at common law. For example, the enactment of workers' compensation laws created an entirely new basis of liability for the employer. "No-fault" automobile statutes partially changed the common-law concept of recovery based on fault, and comparative negligence laws have changed the common-law rule that contributory negligence is a complete defense to a negligence action.

Nature of Criminal Liability Early in the development of the common law, the courts decided that certain acts and/or omissions were offensive to the peace and dignity of the community. Such acts and/or omissions were designated as crimes. All states have codified their criminal law by enacting penal statutes which set forth the elements of each crime and prescribe the punishments which should be imposed. These statutes also set forth the procedures to be followed in arresting accused persons, arraigning them before a magistrate at which time they are informed of the charges against them and asked to plead to them, the filing of a district attorney's information in minor cases, and the indictment by a grand jury in cases involving major offenses. In addition, the states and the federal government have enacted various statutes which require actions on the part of individuals, firms, and corporations and provide penalties for the violation thereof.

A crime will often be described as a "felony," a "misdemeanor," or a "minor offense." These terms cannot be given precise definitions as their meanings vary from one jurisdiction to the next; however, the more serious crimes such as murder, armed robbery, and rape are considered felonies.

Criminal Liability of Business Firms. The general rule is that where an agent commits a crime, even though it is in the course and scope of his or her agency, the principal is not criminally liable unless the principal aids, abets, or compels the commission of the crime. If the principal does so aid, abet, or conspire in the commission of the crime, he or she is just as guilty as the perpetrator. A corporation cannot be imprisoned, however, but it can be fined, be enjoined from committing illegal acts, and/or be stripped of its license to do business.

Insurance. Generally an insurance contract which purports to hold a criminal harmless from the consequences of his or her criminal acts is for illegal purpose, is against public policy *(contra bonos mores)*, and is void. Obviously it is in the public interest to avoid the commission of crimes. Therefore, any type of insurance which would cover a criminal for the commission of a crime is against public policy and void.

On the other hand, to protect against situations where an entirely blameless business firm may be subject to civil liability as a consequence of the acts of another for whom it is responsible, the business may obtain liability insurance for its own protection. Such policies to some extent cover the firm's legal liability to the injured victim, even though the injuries were acquired as a result of a crime. However, as will be discussed in subsequent chapters, liability policies generally do not cover the business in the case of an assault committed by or at its direction. In any case, there is no insurance available to the criminal who commits the act.

Clearly, punishment in the form of a fine, injunction, or loss of a license can have an unfavorable influence on the future of a business firm. There is no type of insurance, however, that will protect a business from this type of loss.

Crime and Tort. It sometimes happens that the same act has both public and private consequences, in that it is an offense against the peace and dignity of the community and also invades the rights of an individual. In such a case, the offender is subject to both criminal and civil liability. Such an offender is answerable to the public for violation of his or her public duty, and is also answerable to the injured person for wrongful invasion of the latter's private right. These are separate and distinct actions brought in different courts. Whereas the criminal action brought by the state to punish and deter will be tried in a criminal court, the action for compensatory damages will be brought in a civil court. For example, assume that a man drove an automobile in a wantonly careless manner, causing the death of another. He is indicted for automobile homicide and brought to trial in a criminal court. Thereafter a civil action for wrongful death is brought against him. The verdict in the criminal case will not control the disposition of the civil cause of action. Nevertheless, a formally sworn admission of improper driving by an individual in a criminal case could be used in a civil case, for purposes of cross-examination, in order to establish improper driving. However, a showing that the defendant has violated a criminal standard regarding the operation of a motor vehicle does not in itself win a civil case. There must also be a showing of proximate causation and lack of contributory negligence on the part of the injured party. Thus, the accused may be convicted in the criminal court and win the case in the civil court. The opposite also could be true or, in a third situation, the offender could win or lose both cases. Some of these results may seem to be inconsistent, but they are arrived at in two separate cases and two separate courts. There have been cases where persons convicted of setting fire to their own buildings in order to collect the insurance brought actions on their fire insurance contracts and obtained judgments against the insurance companies. The difference in part results from the fact that the verdicts were rendered by different juries in different criminal and civil courts and, in most cases, the parties were represented by different counsel.

Nature of Civil Liability Civil liability, as opposed to criminal liability, arises out of a breach of some private or individualized duty which is owed to a member of the community. A person or business entity that breaches such a duty is subject to an action for damages. These duties are either imposed by the common law or civil statutes, or voluntarily assumed by contract.

Common Law and Statutes. At common law a party is under a duty to exercise reasonable care for the safety of others. Thus, a business firm must exercise such care in the operation and maintenance of its premises, in the manufacture and design of its products, in the use of dangerous chemicals or explosives, and in the operation and use of its motor vehicles. Since statutes modify and define the extent of the duty to be undertaken, a violation of a statute will be considered a breach of the duty. For example, a local ordinance will define the speed limit at which trucks and automobiles may be driven. Since the owner is under a duty to exercise reasonable care in the operation of the motor vehicle, a violation of the statute would constitute the failure to exercise reasonable care. The same thing would apply to the use and storage of dangerous or inflammable material. A violation of the requirements of a statute would constitute a breach of the duty of care.

Contract. If one party to a contract fails to perform his or her obligations thereunder and the failure results in injury or damage to the other party, the aggrieved party may bring legal action against the defaulting party to recover the damages incurred. The duties imposed by the common law and statutes with regard to the safety of others cannot be avoided by a contracting party. In a contract the obligations are voluntarily assumed. A party could avoid the obligations by not making a contract at all.

Legal Action. Whether the duties arise in contract, statute, or common law, if there is a breach of a private duty, the aggrieved or injured party may initiate a civil action against the allegedly responsible party. The party bringing the suit is called the plaintiff and the party against whom action is taken is called the defendant. Action is begun by the service of a legal document called a writ of summons. This is a document issued by the clerk of the court and directed to the sheriff or other proper officer, requiring the officer to notify the person named in the action by serving a copy of the writ of summons on him or her personally or in the manner prescribed by law. The complaint, which is a statement of the plaintiff's claim and a demand for damages, is usually served with the writ of summons. In that way the defendant knows that a suit has been filed against him or her, and also has knowledge of the specific claim being asserted. The costs of having the writ of summons issued and the service of the summons and complaint on the defendant are borne by the plaintiff.

The defendant, after service of the writ of summons and complaint, is required to appear and answer the complaint within a certain period of time (usually twenty days). Failure to appear and answer will result in a default judgment for the relief demanded in the complaint. After a defendant has properly answered, a substantial period of time may elapse for the purposes of allowing discovery procedures (formalized fact investigation by parties) and for the court's disposition of any outstanding pre-trial motions (e.g., motion to dismiss, motion for summary judgment). After these matters have been completed, the case will, if not settled by agreement, be listed for trial.

At the option of the parties, depositions may be taken from adverse witnesses before trial. These are called discovery procedures. Each witness is examined before a notary public and the questions and answers are recorded by a court reporter. The expense of taking depositions is borne by the party requiring the examination. These include attorney's fees, the court reporter's fee, and the cost of transcribing the record, a copy of which must be served on the other party and also made a part of the court record. Depending upon the length of the deposition, these costs can be considerable.

The costs of litigation, including attorney's fees, depositions, witness fees, and filing fees, are borne by the defendant. Even though the defendant is successful in obtaining a favorable verdict, the amount of statutory costs which will be awarded to him or her are small and will not compensate fully for the defense attorney's fees or other actual expenses incurred. Therefore, even where there is a successful defense of the suit, the defendant may sustain a large monetary loss (in the absence of liability insurance). If the plaintiff obtains the verdict, he or she will be awarded interest and costs. It should be pointed out that in bodily injury claims the injured person may be able to employ an attorney on a contingent fee basis under which the attorney receives as his or her fee a percentage of the verdict or settlement. In the event of no recovery by means of a settlement or verdict, the attorney receives nothing. The usual fee arrangement is that the attorney will receive from one-third to one-half of the net recovery if there is one. This type of arrangement is to the advantage of the plaintiff in that he or she has little or no money at risk and is more likely to press a dubious claim than if his or her own money were at stake.

Legal actions against a defendant may consist of (1) an action at law for money damages, or (2) a suit in equity for one of the many forms of equitable relief.

ACTION AT LAW. An action at law is brought solely to recover money damages. The damages claimed may arise out of bodily injury or property damage caused by the defendant's failure to exercise reasonable care for the safety of the person or property of others, or they may arise out of losses sustained by others due to the failure of the defendant to meet the obligations of a contract to which he or she was a party. In all such actions there are certain pre-trial provisional remedies which are available to the plaintiff in the form of (1) attachment and (2) arrest.

An *attachment* is a writ issued by the court, on the motion of the plaintiff, which directs the sheriff to take possession of specified property of the defendant and hold it in custody (so that it may be used to satisfy the defendant's debt to the plaintiff if and when said debt is established). The attachment may be released only if a proper bond with good and sufficient surety is substituted in place of the attached property.

Arrest is the attachment of the person of the defendant rather than his or her property. It is a writ granted by the court in the same way as an attachment of property. It is an order directed to the sheriff to take the defendant into custody and to produce the body in court in order to meet the demands of the plaintiff. Upon application to the court and the filing of a proper bond, the defendant may be granted the "liberties of the jail," which are usually fixed by the court and limit the defendant's freedom of movement to one or two counties.

The purpose of both of these remedies is to provide the plaintiff with some means of satisfying his or her judgment, if and when one is obtained. Either could be a substantial business expense to the defendant. However, many liability policies, under the supplementary payments agreements, obligate the insurer to pay for the premium on bonds to release attachments or bail bonds. The insurer usually has no obligation to obtain the bond but merely to pay the premium.

SUIT IN EQUITY. The law courts have jurisdiction to award only money damages. There are some cases where the award of money damages is not adequate, and in early England it became the custom for an aggrieved party in such cases to appeal to the king or queen, asking that the other party be prevented from continuing a nuisance or that a certain contract be reformed or rescinded. Ultimately, the monarch turned these matters over to the chancellor, the keeper of his or her conscience; and under the chancellor, courts of chancery or equity were established. Courts of equity in this country functioned for many years as a separate judicial system independent of the law courts, but at the present time, both systems are combined and administered by the same judges.

It should be emphasized that if there is an adequate remedy at law, equity jurisdiction may not be invoked. In other words, if the payment of money damages available "at law" will properly compensate the plaintiff, the plaintiff would have no standing in equity. Suppose a business organization begins to operate a glue factory near the plaintiff's residence. Malodorous fumes are blown into the plaintiff's residence, thus impairing the use and enjoyment of the property. At law, the plaintiff would have a cause of action against the factory each time the fumes entered the premises, and an amount of damages could be assessed on each such occasion. However, because such damages would not necessarily terminate the harmful intrusion, the plaintiff has a cause of action in equity to enjoin the factory from creating the nuisance. In such a case, equity is empowered to grant an injunction which orders the factory to cease and desist from such harmful operations.

Equity jurisdiction may also be invoked to compel the performance of a contract, to release an innocent party from a contract which was entered into because of fraudulent inducement, or to reform the contract terms so as to conform with the intention of the parties. The corresponding equity remedies are (1) injunction, (2) specific performance of contracts, (3) rescission of contracts, and (4) reformation of contracts.

An *injunction* is a prohibitive writ issued by a court of equity, at the suit of the party complainant and directed to the party defendant, which forbids the latter or his or her agents to do some act, such act being unjust, inequitable, and injurious to the plaintiff. For example, a developer who intends to build an apartment house in an area which is zoned for one-family dwellings can, by means of an injunction, be restrained from doing any act in furtherance of this intention.

An action for *specific performance* may be brought when suit for damages would not be an adequate remedy. Generally, where one party to a contract fails to meet the obligations of the contract, a cause of action for damages for breach of contract will accrue to the other party. In some cases the payment of money damages will not compensate the aggrieved party for his or her actual loss. In these cases equity can compel the defaulting party to honor the commitments of the contract. For example, a corporation owns a factory which it wishes to enlarge. It therefore contracts with the owner of an adjoining parcel of land for an outright purchase of the land. The corporation tenders the purchase price on the due date but the owner refuses to sell. Clearly, the corporation could proceed at law for the damages it has sustained, such damages being the difference in the cost of the property it had contracted to purchase and the cost of another parcel of land similarly situated in the same general area. However, another parcel of land in the same area would not suit the purpose for which the corporation wanted the land. The adjoining parcel was particularly suited to that purpose. Under such circumstances, a court of equity would compel the owner to transfer the land to the corporation in accordance with the terms of the contract. Such an action is termed an action for specific performance.

A suit for *rescission* calls upon the court of equity to exercise its power to abrogate, annul, or cancel a contract and to declare the contract void from its inception. The decision of the court will not merely terminate the contract and release the parties from any further obligations thereunder but will abrogate it from the beginning and restore the parties to the same position they would have occupied if the contract had never come into existence. For example, *A* induces *X*, an insurance company, to issue a liability insurance policy covering his automobile. *A* represents that no other insurance had been canceled by an insurance company. This is untrue and *X* soon thereafter acquires knowledge of its falsity. *X* then has the option of waiving the misrepresentation or rescinding the policy by notice to *A* and returning to *A* the premium paid. In the latter case, the position of the parties is the same as if no contract of insurance had ever come into existence. The theory behind this type of rescission is that if the insurer had known the truth concerning the prior cancellation, it would not have entered into the contract in the first place. Since the insurer was induced to enter the contract by a fraudulent representation, it can avoid the contract from its inception.

On the other hand, if *X* opts to waive the misrepresentation, coverage could be said to be effective from that moment in time when *X* clearly demonstrates a willingness to grant such coverage to *A* even though *A* in fact had experienced a prior cancellation. Such willingness might be demonstrated by the failure of *X* to communicate at all with *A* after the discovery of the prior cancellation.

The courts of equity have the power to *reform* a contract which has been incorrectly drawn so that the contract will conform to the original intention of the parties. Such an act of reforming a contract is called *reformation*. For example, a business firm sustained a fire loss to one of its buildings on March 5. Not having fire insurance, it immediately purchased a policy which was to be effective on March 11. Through a clerical error, the inception date of the policy was recorded as March 1. Thereafter a claim was made for the loss which occurred prior to the time the policy was ordered. The insurer can apply to a court of equity and have the policy reformed to reflect the intention of the parties, which was that the policy should be effective from March 11.

Litigation Exposures. It has been said that one way to avoid a lawsuit is not to deserve one. Unfortunately, this is not entirely true. There are a number of suits filed which are false, fraudulent, or groundless. Since the failure to defend a suit will result in a default judgment, all suits, regardless of their merit, must be defended. The defendant must thus engage an attorney and pay whatever attorney and filing fees are required. If the case goes to trial, the defendant must pay for subpoena fees, witness fees and, if a jury is demanded by the defendant, the jury fee. If the defendant should obtain a verdict in his or her favor, he or she is entitled to reimbursement for statutory costs. Statutory costs usually include only the filing fees incurred (approximately $10 to $50), statutory witness fees (approximately $10 per day), public notary fees, and subpoena fees. It should be noted, for example, that an expert witness for the defendant might charge $1,000 per day and only a $10 per day statutory witness fee would be recoverable by a successful defendant from the plaintiff. Unfortunately, the statutory costs which are reimbursed are small and in no case will fully reimburse the defendant for the defense attorney's fees or the other expenses incurred. This is one reason why many suits are compromised in advance of trial, usually for an amount approximating the cost of trial, even though liability is specifically denied.

The mere fact that a suit has been filed does not necessarily mean that the defendant is liable. The burden of proof is ordinarily on the shoulders of the party asserting the claim, who must sustain this burden in order to recover. If he or she does not, there will be a verdict for the defendant.

Regardless of the outcome of the suit, the defendant may sustain other indirect losses as a result. These will include any uninsured costs of bonds to release attachments, the impairment of business operations caused by injunctions and the like, the loss of executive time, the cost of answering interrogatories, the possible impairment of the firm's credit standing, and the loss of customers (particularly in products cases) from the adverse publicity surrounding a lawsuit.

Sources of Civil Liability. Business organizations are subject to civil liability in (1) tort, (2) contract, or (3) a combination of both.

LAW OF TORTS. This branch of the law deals with the relationship of the members of the community to one another and establishes duties which are imposed by the general law. A violation of a duty thus imposed is actionable.

LAW OF CONTRACTS. This branch of the law relates to the enforcement of contracts, which are agreements voluntarily made by the parties and supported by adequate consideration. It establishes the rules governing contracts generally, sets forth the causes of action which arise out of contract breaches, and prescribes the rules to establish the damages therefor.

COMBINATION OF BOTH. There are some circumstances under which the aggrieved party may elect between suing in contract (*ex contractu*) or in tort (*ex delicto*). For example, a woman drives away in a car which was parked in an automobile dealer's lot and puts it to her own use. The dealer may assume that the woman intended to buy the car and, if payment is not made, sue her for the purchase price. The assumption here is that the woman's actions constituted a contract of sale. On the other hand, the dealer may sue her in tort for conversion (wrongful taking of the property of another) and seek damages for the wrongful taking.

Combinations of Criminal and Civil Liability As noted earlier, certain acts have both public and private consequences. They are crimes against the peace and dignity of the community and, in addition, they wrongfully invade the rights of other persons. The person doing the acts is subject to both criminal and civil liability and is answerable to the community and subject to punishment in the form of a fine, imprisonment, or death. Such a person is also liable to his or her victim for damages. These are separate actions, one by the public prosecutor for the crime against the community and the other a cause of action in tort for the damages sustained by the victim. The disposition of one action will have no effect on the other. Two examples with insurance implications are assault and battery, and homicide.

Assault and Battery. A threat to use force to injure another is an assault. The actual use of force to injure another is a battery. A battery always includes an assault. Hence, the two terms are combined in the phrase "assault and battery." Assault and battery can then be defined as any nonconsensual infliction of physical harm on a human being. One convicted of this crime is answerable both to the community and to the injured person.

Any person who aids and abets in the commission of a crime is a principal and, upon conviction, is liable to the same penalty as if he or she personally had committed the crime. Therefore, where one directs that an assault be committed, that individual is just as guilty as the one who actually committed the act.

There are also situations where an employer could be vicariously liable in damages for an assault committed by an employee. In such situations the employer might be held civilly liable, while the employee might be civilly and criminally liable. For example, the owner of an apartment house employs a janitor, who by being supplied with master keys, has access to all parts of the building. The janitor enters the apartment of a female tenant and assaults her. On these facts alone the owner would not be liable to the tenant for her injuries. However, suppose we add one additional fact; namely, that the janitor had been discharged from his previous position because of complaints from female tenants that he had entered their apartments without authorization and attempted to molest them. These facts were not known to the janitor's current employer, but a reasonable inquiry would have unearthed them. The employer's failure to exercise care in the selection of employees, with resulting injury to the tenants to whom he or she had a duty of care, constitutes negligence and would make the landlord liable for the injuries sustained. It must be pointed out that the landlord's liability arises from failure to exercise care. He or she is guilty of negligence but not assault.

Homicide. Homicide may be defined as the killing of one human being by the act, procurement, or omission of another. Homicide is not necessarily a crime. Homicide is a necessary ingredient of the crimes of murder and manslaughter, but there are other cases in which homicide may be committed without criminal intent or criminal consequences, such as when it is done in the lawful execution of a judicial sentence or in self-defense, or when it is done accidentally by a lawful act without any intention of injuring another. The criminal aspects of homicide are murder and manslaughter.

Murder is the unlawful killing of another with malice aforethought, or in other words, a premeditated slaying. Murder also includes any killing which occurs during the commission or attempted commission of certain felonies, such as arson, rape, burglary, or robbery. In addition to the criminal liability for such an act, the guilty person is also answerable in damages to the estate of the deceased person.

Manslaughter is the unlawful killing of another human being without any deliberation. Manslaughter may be involuntary or voluntary. In manslaughter, the elements of premeditation and occurrence in the course of the commission of a felony are lacking. For example, an automobile driver who operates his or her car in such a willful and wanton manner as to endanger the lives of others and whose action results in the death of a human being, is guilty of manslaughter. He or she can be indicted, tried, and sentenced for that offense. In addition, that driver has a civil liability to the estate or personal representative of the deceased person. In such a case, automobile liability insurance would probably be involved.

Statutory Criminal and Civil Liability It is the congressional practice to enact legislation which sets forth certain objectives to be attained and which creates an agency in the form of a commission. Legislative power to make and enforce regulations for carrying out the objectives of the original act is delegated to the commission. The following are illustrative of various statutes which may impose criminal and/or civil penalties on violators. Often statutes, such as those described below, are actually codifications of principles (rules) which have already been articulated by courts in prior cases decided in conformity with a common-law methodology. After such a codification has taken place, a violation of a statutory standard may lead to the imposition of sanctions by a governmental agency, *whether or not* the actions in question could lead to a verdict pursuant to a purely common-law based action in tort. Likewise, an entity could still be found liable at common law for actions which do not violate any existing statutory standard.

Occupational Safety and Health Act (OSHA). Under this act Congress declared that the public policy of the United States is to guarantee every worker in industry a safe place to work. In furtherance of this act, Congress created a commission to which was delegated the power and duty to make and enforce safety regulations with respect to all industries, make inspections, make recommendations, enforce such regulations, and impose sanctions on violators.

Consumer Product Safety Act. This act has as its purpose the protection of the consumer from the use or consumption of hazardous products. It creates a federal agency, the Consumer Products Safety Commission, whose duty it is to examine products for defects and to determine which defects produce a substantial hazard. It has the power to ban all products which do not conform to appropriate safety standards and to impose sanctions when the orders to ban a product are not observed.

Food, Drug and Cosmetic Act. This act creates the federal Food and Drug Administration, whose duty it is to regulate the quality of certain products which move in interstate commerce. The products include every variety of foodstuffs, as well as all types of drugs and cosmetics. It likewise has the power to penalize the manufacturer for any violation of the regulations. In addition, the regulations require that all drugs be submitted for approval before they are placed in interstate commerce.

Environmental Protection Laws. Many states have passed environmental protection laws which refer not only to the pollution of bodies of water but also to the pollution of the air. These laws establish standards, and any pollution which is in excess of the standards is punishable by fine and makes the manufacturer subject to an injunction restraining the manufacturer from continuing the operation. In addition, Congress passed the National Environmental Policy Act which establishes the Environmental Protection Administration. It requires federal agencies to prepare statements on proposed actions, detailing environmental effects, proposed alternatives, and irreversible resource commitments involved in the proposed action should it be implemented. The Environmental Protection Administration would then consider this impact statement and approve or disapprove of the proposed action.

The polluter is answerable in damages to those whose interests have been invaded by the pollution. This type of action has been brought to public attention in recent years by the occurrence of oil spills and the damage to private interests which has resulted. For example, in the Santa Barbara oil spill in 1969, commercial fishermen sustained an economic loss as a result of the damage to aquatic life. In an action at law based on the negligence of the oil company, the court held that the fishermen, in sustaining lost profits from this negligently caused ecological damage, had suffered a legally compensable injury. The polluter is also liable for negligently violating the environmental laws. For example, the state environmental laws will establish the maximun air pollution which will be permitted and any air pollution which exceeds the maximum is actionable. It must be noted in passing that in some cases of emergency these restrictions have been relaxed for specific periods of time, such as when power companies were allowed to burn certain types of coal when oil or other fuels were in short supply. Pollution during the emergency period was not actionable.

Contractual Liability Exposures

A contract is defined as a promise supported by adequate consideration, for the breach of which the law gives a remedy, or the performance of which the law in some way recognizes as a duty.

A contract may be discharged by the full performance of both parties. A contract is breached when one party has performed and the other has not performed within the time limit in the contract (or, if no time is expressed, within a reasonable time). The party who has performed then has a cause of action for damages for breach of contract. The damages which may be claimed are such amounts as the aggrieved party would have received had the contract been fully performed by the other, sometimes referred to as the "benefit of the bargain."

When a contract has been breached, the innocent party may consider the contract at an end, and, should an action be begun by the adverse party, he or she may interpose the nonperformance of the other as a complete defense. On the other hand, the performing party may seek specific performance, that is, an order from a court of equity which directs the delinquent party to perform the contract.

Where there has been no breach of contract but one party discovers that he or she has been induced to enter the contract through fraud or duress or some form of mistake, that party may have the remedy of rescission or reformation, as previously discussed.

The size of the potential losses under an action for breach of contract are largely determined by the nature of the contract and the original terms. However, in some cases the breach of a contract may give rise to an action in tort. For example, assume that an employee has a contract of employment which, among other things, provides that he or she will not engage in the same trade or business within 500 miles of the employer's place of business at the termination of employment. The employee breaches the contract and is hired by the employer's competitor who operates in the same city. The employer has a cause of action against the former employee for breach of the restrictive covenant in the contract and may have a possible cause of action in tort against the new employer for wrongful interference with a business advantage.

Tort Liability Exposures

Tort Defined A tort may be defined as follows:

A tort is a wrongful act or omission, arising in the course of social relationships, other than contracts, which violates a person's legally protected right, and for which the law provides a remedy in the form of an action for damages.[2]

Under this definition, the elements of a tort are the following:

1. a legally protected right,
2. a wrongful invasion of that right, and
3. damages as a proximate result.

Some authors recognize a fourth element of any tort—absence of any justification for the act involved. In CPCU 4, however, the presence of any affirmative justification for the act will be considered as a defense to a tort action. The person committing a tort is called a wrongdoer or a *tortfeasor*. When two or more persons unite in causing the tort they are called *joint tortfeasors*. However, to be joint tortfeasors they must act together in committing the wrong, or their acts, if independent of each other, must unite in causing a single injury. For example, a motorist negligently injures a pedestrian. While the pedestrian is still lying on the road he is run over by another motorist. The motorists are joint tortfeasors, even though the act of the second motorist was not concurrent with the act of the first motorist. In another situation, motorist *A* collides with the car of motorist *B*, driving his car on to the sidewalk where he strikes *C*, a pedestrian. *A* and *B* are *concurrent joint tortfeasors*, since their acts together resulted in the single injury to *C*. In any case, where there are joint tortfeasors involved, whether concurrent or not, they are both equally liable to the injured party.

The legally protected rights recognized by the early common law included the rights of safety of person, property, and reputation, and the right to the services of an unemancipated child and wife. To these protected rights, either by statute or court decision, other rights have been added. These include the right of privacy, the right to vote, the right to earn a living, and the right to an education.

Wrongful invasions of legally protected rights include not only acts which are negligent or intentional, but also acts which subject the actor to liability apart from negligence or intent. Examples of the latter are the possession and maintenance of dangerous instrumentalities and the conducting of ultrahazardous operations, both of which expose others to unreasonable risks of harm.

The damages recoverable are those which are directly caused by the wrongful act. There must be an unbroken chain of causation from the act to the injury. Injuries which are not proximately caused by the wrongful act are not recoverable.

Grounds for Imposition of Tort Liability   Torts can be divided into the following three groups, according to their nature and origin:

1. *Intentional.* If a person intends the reasonable consequences of his or her tortious act, the tort is said to be intentional. The act does not necessarily have to be committed with malicious or hostile intent. If it is the result of a voluntary action, it will come within this classification.
2. *Strict Liability.* Strict liability is liability imposed by law without any regard to negligence or intent.
3. *Negligent.* A negligent tort occurs when the wrongdoer exposes others to an unreasonable risk of harm through his or her failure to exercise that degree of care which the law requires for the safety of others.

LIABILITY FOR INTENTIONAL INTERFERENCE TORTS

Nature of Intentional Interference

The wrongful invasion of the rights of others by a voluntary intentional act which produces injury is an actionable tort, and the tortfeasor is answerable in damages to the injured person. While intention refers to the state of mind of the actor, the courts will infer his or her intent from the nature and quality of the act. In some cases in this category, a hostile or malicious intent is not a necessary element. In others, malice is a necessary element which must be proved in order for there to be a recovery. In still other cases, there is no intent to do any harm whatsoever but, because of the nature of the act, the actor is held liable as if he or she had so intended.

There are situations in which a legally protected right may be waived. For example, a landowner may permit members of the public to cross his or her land. Evidence of this waiver may be the existence of a footpath which has been used by others without any protest from the landowner. However, if any of the persons crossing the land pick fruit from the trees, remove topsoil, or remove vegetables from the garden, they are considered trespassers, and they may be charged with conversion. The landowner waived his or her right of exclusive possession only to the extent of allowing others to cross the land, but did not waive ownership of the soil or the growing crops.

An individual is entitled to safety of his or her person. One may waive this right by agreeing to engage in a boxing bout. If one should be injured in such competition, his or her opponent will not be liable for such injuries. However, the individual waived his or her right only for the limited purpose of engaging in boxing and did not waive his or her right with respect to all injuries that may be sustained from any source. Thus, if his or her opponent becomes incensed and hits the individual with an ax, there will be a wrongful invasion of the right of safety of person, which is actionable.

Representative Intentional Torts

Defamation—Libel and Slander Because an individual is entitled to security of reputation, any untrue statement which is published and which damages that reputation is actionable, the wrongdoer having committed an intentional tort referred to as defamation (or defamation of character). The elements of defamation consist of the following:

1. a false and malicious statement tending to subject the plaintiff to public ridicule or censure,
2. publication, and
3. damages.

A False Statement.   A false statement may be defined as an untrue statement which, if believed, would hold the plaintiff up to hatred, contempt, or ridicule, or which would cause him or her to be shunned and avoided. Malice or evil intent can be inferred from the utterance. It is thus defamatory to say, if untrue, that a man will not pay his just debts, is immoral, a coward, a crook, a bastard, or a eunuch, or that he has committed an act which is morally reprehensible or dishonorable.

A false statement also can be inferred from an action taken. For example, the action of a bank in refusing to pay a check drawn on a perfectly solvent bank account is considered to be defamation in the sense that the bank is making a false statement that the drawer of the check has issued a check drawn against insufficient funds.

Frequently bill collection agencies adopt methods of collection which may involve defamation. They will park a truck in front of the debtor's house which exhibits a sign, such as "bad debt collector," or will interview the neighbors telling them that the debtor is a "deadbeat" or that he or she is attempting to avoid the payment of just bills. If the account is current and these actions and statements are untrue, the so-called debtor has been defamed.

Publication.   The statement must be published or brought to the attention of one or more persons other than the person defamed. Merely to call a person a crook, a shyster, or a "deadbeat" when no other person is present is not defamatory. However, to dictate a letter containing defamatory statements to a secretary amounts to publication, even though no other person sees it.

Damages.   Generally, damages must be alleged and proved by the plaintiff. Even though the words were offensive and did result in injured feelings or insult, unless some actual damage came about as a result, the most that the plaintiff would be able to recover would be nominal damages. In some aggravated cases (defamation per se) damages are presumed, and the jury can return a verdict without any specific proof of damages in the form of monetary loss. Such cases are:

1. imputation of serious crimes;
2. imputation of a loathsome disease, such as leprosy or syphilis; and
3. imputations adversely affecting the plaintiff in his or her business, trade, or profession, such as calling a surgeon a butcher, or a lawyer a shyster or a crook.

In some states there is an additional category in which damages are presumed. This is the imputation of unchastity to a person. In most states this presumption is restricted only to women, but in some states it is applied to both sexes.

Defamation may take one of two forms, libel or slander. Originally libel consisted of anything of a defamatory nature which was written or printed, whereas slander consisted of defamation of an oral nature conveyed by speech alone. Libel has recently been held to include pictures, cartoons, moving pictures, signs, and statues. Because of the permanent nature of a libel and the fact that the statement can be seen by many people, it is considered the greater offense and capable of inflicting the greater damage. On the other hand, a slanderous statement is usually heard by a few. Generally, therefore, libel causes of action obtain larger verdicts.

There is an open question as to whether a broadcast by radio or television is libel or slander. The courts are divided on the question. Some courts have taken the middle ground, holding that if the broadcaster reads from a written script, it is libel, whereas if he or she does not, it is slander. In any case, great damage can be inflicted by broadcasting, either by television or radio and, in the case of a verdict, the damages can be substantial.

Punitive damages are not part of the essential elements of the defamation tort but may be demanded upon a showing that the defendant's conduct was outrageous, malicious, fraudulent, or evil and that it was a conscious and deliberate disregard of the interests of others. Punitive damages are awarded to the plaintiff against the defendant as punishment for the nature and quality of the latter's conduct. It is sometimes called "smart money" because it is intended to make the defendant "smart," and it is also intended to act as a deterrent to others who may consider following the same course of conduct. Punitive damages are not based on any particular loss which is suffered by the plaintiff; hence, they are actually a windfall to the successful plaintiff. The amount of punitive damages is subject to a jury determination. In many cases the amount of punitive damages far exceeds the amount awarded as compensatory damages.

Defenses to Libel and Slander. The defenses to actions for libel or slander are (1) truth and (2) privilege.

TRUTH. Clearly, since one of the elements to be established by the plaintiff is the existence of a false and malicious statement, the fact that the statement is true goes to the heart of the matter. If the plaintiff cannot establish that the statement is false, then he or she has no cause of action and the suit must be dismissed. Regardless of the motives which impelled the defendant to publish the true statement, the fact that it is true will insulate the defendant from liability.

PRIVILEGE. Privilege, as a complete defense to actions for libel and slander, may be (1) absolute or (2) qualified.

Statements made in the course of judicial or legislative proceedings, executive communications between the chief executive of a corporation or of the United States and officials of the executive department, and statements between husband and wife are *absolutely privileged*. Statements made in the course of any of these proceedings or relationships, even if untrue and damaging, are not actionable.

A qualified type of conditional privilege exists with reference to the publication of information in the discharge of some public or private duty. Thus, if a credit reporting service issues to its principal a statement concerning the credit status of an individual, the report is subject to a *qualified privilege*. Even if the information is untrue, if it can be shown that the credit agency made its inquiry fairly and as completely as was possible under the circumstances, the information is privileged. However, should the credit agency disclose the contents of the report to another person who has no connection or interest in the matter, the privilege is lost.

Qualified privilege also attaches to replies to inquiries made where the subject has applied for a position. The reply could come from former employers or from neighbors and friends. The person giving the information and the person collecting it are subject to a qualified privilege. Again, if the information is untrue and it is disclosed to one who has no interest in the matter, the privilege is lost.

Physicians who report to prospective employers with respect to the applicant's physical condition enjoy the benefits of a qualified privilege, even though the information may disclose that the applicant is suffering from some loathsome disease. This qualified privilege exists only as to reports made to prospective employers. If such a report is disclosed to another having no interest in the matter, the privilege is lost.

Finally, there is a qualified privilege attached to fair comment on matters of public concern, even though the comment may be critical of a public official for acts undertaken in his or her public capacity.

Right of Privacy The right of privacy has been defined as the right of an individual to be let alone, to live a life of seclusion, or to be free from unwarranted publicity. A wrongful invasion of this right will give rise to an action for damages. An individual has a right to have his or her private affairs, as well as his or her photograph, free from unwarranted publicity. However, when an individual applies for credit, it is reasonable to expect that some inquiry will be made as to his or her past dealings and eligibility for credit. Or, when an individual makes a claim for bodily injury, he or she puts his or her physical condition and ability to work in issue. It is reasonable to expect that the defendant or his or her insurance carrier will make some inquiry to verify the allegations of the injury sustained. Therefore, such inquiries do not constitute an invasion of the right of privacy.

Individuals such as politicians, actors, athletes, and others who, because of their prominence are commented upon and photographed by the news media have, as a result, a more restricted right of privacy than individuals who do not attract public attention because of their position in society.

Assault and Battery Assault consists of an intentional, unlawful threat of bodily harm to another under such circumstances as to create a well-founded fear of imminent peril, coupled with the apparent present ability to inflict bodily harm if not prevented. Battery consists of any unlawful touching of or other physical injury inflicted on a human being without his or her consent. Usually these two torts are coupled under the heading of assault and battery. An individual is entitled to the legally protected right of safety of person. Therefore, an assault and/or battery is an invasion of said right.

Defenses to Assault and Battery. The defenses which may be interposed to an action for damages for assault and battery are (1) self-defense, (2) defense of property, and (3) defense of others.

SELF-DEFENSE. The individual is entitled to use reasonable force to prevent injury to himself or herself. He or she may use whatever force is necessary under the circumstances, even to the extent of taking the life of the attacker. The amount of force necessary will, of course, differ with the circumstances, and in some cases it might mean that seemingly excessive force was used. However, since the Supreme Court has said, "Detached reflection is not required in the face of an uplifted knife," the benefit of the doubt usually is given to the possible victim. The individual does not have to wait until the first blow is struck. If the individual has reason to believe under the circumstances that he or she is about to be attacked, he or she may take such measures as are necessary for self-protection. The individual has this privilege of self-defense, even though he or she may be under a misapprehension as to the facts and even where the other party has no intention of doing bodily harm. If the circumstances are such that a reasonable person would expect an attack, the individual is within his or her rights in taking such measures as he or she deems appropriate for self-protection. This is true even though he or she is mistaken as to the ultimate fact. In the final analysis, the question of whether or not the individual acted reasonably under the circumstances will be a question for the jury to decide.

DEFENSE OF PROPERTY. The owner of real property, be it an individual, firm, or corporation, is entitled to the sole and peaceful possession of the property without the intrusion of others. When a trespasser is on the property, the owner has the right to exercise reasonable force to eject him or her. The owner may not, however, erect spring guns, traps, or other devices to injure the trespasser. The owner may employ a guard to act as his or her agent in ejecting unwanted visitors, but the guard must use reasonable force to accomplish such ejections.

It has been the custom of many business firms to maintain a watchdog on the premises to discourage any unwelcome visitors. However, such firms are under the duty to refrain from maintaining a vicious dog on the premises solely for the purpose of intentionally injuring known trespassers. This is true even though notice of the presence of a dog on the premises is posted and brought to the attention of potential trespassers.

DEFENSE OF OTHERS. While there is no duty on the part of an individual to come to the aid of a person he or she believes is being attacked, the individual may do so, in which case the same rules that apply to self-defense are applicable. In going to the defense of another, the individual may mistakenly believe that he or she is aiding the person attacked when in truth and in fact the individual is aiding the attacker. Therefore, the person that the individual is defending might not be privileged to defend himself or herself in the same manner. The majority of the courts hold that the intermeddler takes his or her chances. If he or she does mistakenly defend the attacker, he or she is guilty of assault and battery, since there is no privilege of self-defense.

False Arrest and Wrongful Detention One of the legally protected rights which every individual has is the right of liberty of movement. Any wrongful act which deprives him or her of that right is an actionable tort. Placing a person in a locked room or a locked part of a premises amounts to false imprisonment or wrongful detention. In addition, a person on crutches may be wrongfully detained when the tortfeasor takes away his or her crutches. If a store or other type of commercial enterprise tries to keep a woman confined by taking her purse, this likewise is a case of wrongful detention.

It sometimes happens that a store has reasonable cause to suspect a customer of stealing merchandise or "shoplifting." In such a case the procedure is often to let the customer leave the store and to make an arrest (or detain the customer) outside of the premises. If the arrest (detention) was made on the premises, the customer could claim that he or she expected to pay for the merchandise before leaving the store, in which case there would be a cause of action for wrongful detention. When the customer is first allowed to leave the store, there is little question that the customer intended to leave the store without paying for the merchandise.

Malicious Prosecution Malicious prosecution involves the legally protected right of safety of reputation. When a criminal proceeding is brought against a person, it is published to all that he or she has been accused of a certain crime. The damage to that person's reputation, as well as the damage to his or her business and credit rating, can be considerable.

The elements of an action for malicious prosecution are the following:

1. a criminal proceeding instituted or continued by the defendant against the plaintiff,
2. termination of the proceeding in favor of the accused,
3. absence of probable cause for the proceeding, and
4. "malice" or a primary purpose other than bringing an offender to justice.

Criminal Prosecution. The actual criminal prosecution must be commenced. Merely because the defendant has sworn out a warrant or has testified before a grand jury is not enough. The criminal prosecution must have actually been instituted and the resultant publicity must have been damaging to the plaintiff's reputation.

Termination in Favor of the Accused. The accused must be found not guilty. If he or she is found guilty, such a verdict is a bar to an action for malicious prosecution.

Absence of Probable Cause. The plaintiff must show that the facts and circumstances were such that no reasonable person would have concluded that the plaintiff was guilty. The law generally encourages citizens to come forward where there has been a crime committed about which the citizen has knowledge. Therefore, the burden of proof on this issue is on the plaintiff. Also, the fact that the defendant has instigated the criminal proceedings on advice of counsel is some evidence of probable cause. It should be pointed out that a conviction in a criminal proceeding must be supported by evidence beyond a reasonable doubt. In civil cases the plaintiff or defendant must sustain the burden of proof by a preponderance of evidence. Therefore, despite the criminal acquittal, the defendant of the civil case can show, by a preponderance of evidence, that the plaintiff was in fact guilty of the crime. The quality of evidence needed to establish a preponderance of the evidence is much less than that which would be required to establish the crime beyond a reasonable doubt.

Malice. Malice can be defined as ill will. Where the primary purpose in bringing the proceeding was to give vent to motives of ill will, malice will be established. Another means of establishing malice is where the evidence will show that the defendant initiated the criminal proceedings to extort money, to collect a debt, or to recover property. The cases hold, however, that even though the defendant felt hatred, resentment, or indignation toward the plaintiff, if the proceeding was otherwise a proper one, the feelings of the defendant would not establish malice.

Trespass The owner or occupier (renter) of land has the legally protected right to the exclusive possession and use of the land. A trespasser is a person who is on the premises without the actual or constructive consent of the owner. The trespass may be on the surface of the land, beneath it, or over it within the airspace required by the owner for the peaceful enjoyment of his or her property. Though he or she may not physically be on the land itself, a person who dumps garbage on the land is a trespasser, even if the garbage is dumped in an area which the owners use for their own garbage. A person likewise may not encroach by building a structure which is partly on another's land. That person has trespassed by such a positioning of the structure. The person is also guilty of a trespass if he or she constructs on his or her own land a dam which backs up water on another's land. The dam owner is a trespasser, even though he or she personally was never physically on the other's land.

A continuing trespass and a series of separate trespasses have the same legal consequences, but in some ways they are different. Thus, if the possessor of land should consent to one person's leaving an automobile on the land and to another's dumping ashes on it, the death of the possessor will terminate the consent in both cases. The owner of the automobile would have a reasonable time to remove the automobile, whereas the person who dumped ashes on the day after the death would be a trespasser. Furthermore, if possible, the person who dumped ashes would be expected to remove said ashes within a reasonable amount of time.

A trespass may be accomplished by means of an increase in the lateral pressure which causes upheavals on the neighboring land. For example, A, a neighboring landowner, erects a huge structure on his land. The weight of the building causes an increase in the lateral pressure which damages B's land and the buildings thereon. A is therefore a trespasser.

Trespass is an intentional tort and the trespasser is liable for any damage which his or her wrongful intrusion may cause. The amounts of such damage may be slight and only call for an award of nominal damages, or they may be substantial, such as for a building encroachment, in which case the owner of the building would be required to relocate the building on to his or her own land.

Conversion Conversion is an intentional tort which occurs when one person commits the act of appropriating the property of another to his or her own beneficial use and enjoyment, or of destroying it or altering its nature. Since conversion involves only personal property, it is sometimes referred to as a trespass to chattels. The Restatement, Second, Torts Section 222A defines conversion as follows:[3]

(1) Conversion is an intentional exercise of dominion or control over a chattel which so seriously interferes with the right of another to control it that the actor may justly be required to pay the full value of the chattel.

(2) In determining the seriousness of the interference and the justice of requiring the actor to pay the full value, the following factors are important:
    (a) the extent and duration of the actor's exercise of dominion or control;
    (b) the actor's intent to assert a right in fact inconsistent with the other's right of control;
    (c) the actor's good faith;
    (d) the extent and duration of the resulting interference with the other's right of control;
    (e) the harm done to the chattel;
    (f) the inconvenience and expense caused to the other.

A classic example of conversion is the case where an automobile owner entrusted his automobile to a dealer for the purpose of sale, and the dealer used the car for a ten-mile trip on his own business. This was not a conversion. The use was minimal and did not cause any harm to the automobile. On the other hand, if the dealer had used the car on his own business for a trip exceeding 2,000 miles, it would have been a conversion. The owner would have been deprived of the use of the car, and driving 2,000 miles would have reduced its value to some extent.

Similarly, suppose A, on leaving a restaurant, takes B's hat from the rack, believing it to be his own. When he reaches the sidewalk, A puts the hat on and discovers that it is not his own. He immediately reenters the restaurant and returns the hat to the rack. This is not a conversion. There was no intent to deprive B of the ownership of the hat. A's good faith is evidenced by the fact that he immediately returned the hat.

The relationship of bailor and bailee offers opportunities for unauthorized use of the bailed property. For example, a woman takes a dress to a dry cleaner for cleaning. The dry cleaner's wife wears the dress to a dance and the dress is soiled and damaged beyond repair. This is a conversion. The dry cleaner is liable for the value of the dress.

A car is parked in a garage for storage. The garage owner uses the car for the illegal transportation of narcotics. He is arrested and the car is confiscated by the federal government. This is a conversion and the garage owner is liable for the value of the car.

Nuisance   The owner or occupier of real property is entitled to the undisturbed enjoyment of the premises. Neighboring landowners or occupiers have the duty of making reasonable use of their premises so as not to invade the other's rights of enjoyment. Activity of neighbors which impairs the right of the landowner or occupier is a private nuisance which may be abated by an action for damages, an injunction, or both.

There is a fine line of distinction between trespass and nuisance, and in some cases the difference is almost indiscernible. Trespass is the wrongful intrusion on to the lands of another by an individual or by things under his or her control, such as water or cattle. Thus, trespass invades the right of exclusive and peaceful possession of the land. On the other hand, nuisance invades the owner's right to enjoyment of his or her property.

What constitutes a nuisance will in many cases be governed by the area in which the activity is being carried on. For example, the operation of a factory, a dog boarding kennel, or a slaughterhouse in a residential area would constitute a nuisance. However, since it is socially advantageous to have such things, they are not nuisances when conducted in an area set aside for that purpose. Thus, if a person purchases a residence in the gashouse district, he or she cannot complain about the smell of gas. The gashouse in such a case is not a nuisance, even though its presence does interfere with the owner's enjoyment of his or her land. The owner will have to tolerate the condition for the good of others in the community. The same reasoning applies to the operation of airports, railroad yards, and other places maintained for use by the public.

Remedies Available. As with any other tort, an action for damages will lie for a private nuisance. The elements of the damages claimed would include the value of the use and enjoyment of the property of which the owner has been deprived; the rental loss, if any, caused by the nuisance; and the future diminution in value which will occur if the nuisance is continued. In addition, where the property involved has a business use, the loss of business caused by the nuisance will be an additional element. If the nuisance is such that it causes injury to the health of the owner or members of his or her family, any personal injury that may have proximately resulted from the nuisance may also be claimed as damages. A suit for an injunction restraining the defendant from continuing the nuisance may also be brought, together with a plea for the damages which have been incurred up to the time of the granting of the injunction.

It is possible for the landowner to abate the nuisance by what is known as "self-help." This includes such activity as going on the land of the other and taking such steps as will end the nuisance. This might mean the killing of a barking dog, cutting off the power to a factory, or taking other summary means. This is a dangerous method which exposes the actor to an action for damages, if it should later be decided that the thing complained of was not in fact a nuisance. Therefore, the method of self-help is seldom undertaken.

Defenses. The only complete defense to an action based on nuisance is that the defendant's actions did not amount to a nuisance but represented only a reasonable use of the premises. As a partial defense, it could be shown that the plaintiff could have avoided some of the consequences of the nuisance and, thus, was not entitled to recover for the full damages claimed. For example, the plaintiff is under a duty to prevent cattle from drinking water which he or she knows is poisoned by the defendant's activity. Likewise, the plaintiff cannot hold the defendant liable for the stench from an unburied dead animal, where he or she could have buried the animal so as to prevent further damage to the enjoyment of his or her property. The defendant would, however, be liable for any inconvenience which occurred prior to the time that the plaintiff was made aware of the cause of the difficulty. Thus, the defendant is not liable for the avoidable consequences of maintaining a nuisance when some action on the part of the plaintiff would have reduced the amount of damages.

Wrongful Interference with a Business Advantage   The privilege of competition is enjoyed by all in the business community. As long as it is bona fide competition, there is no tort liability involved, even though one firm may claim that its goods or products are superior to those of a competitor, that they will last longer, that they contain better or different ingredients, or that they will lead to a better result. On the other hand, a firm may not advertise falsely that the competitor's food products are not fit for human consumption or that other products contain dangerous ingredients. Moreover, a firm may not seek to obtain trade secrets from a competitor or encourage its employees to commit sabotage. It may not engage in any type of harassment which will annoy customers or employees or prevent such persons from having a means of access to the competitor's premises. The Sherman Anti-Trust Act mandates against a conspiracy in restraint of trade and provides for an action by the U.S. Department of Justice to enjoin same. The victim of the conspiracy has a cause of action in tort for such damages as have been sustained as a result. Pursuant to federal law, of course, labor unions are given certain rights to interfere with another's business (strike), as well as to form combinations in restraint of trade (collective bargaining units).

LIABILITY FOR NEGLIGENT TORTS

Concept of Negligence in Tort Law

Negligence is the failure to exercise that standard of care for the safety of others which the law imposes on an individual, firm, or corporation. The exercise of care might consist of doing an act, such as maintaining a building in reasonably safe condition for the safety of others, or it may consist of not doing certain acts which would endanger others, such as storing explosives or harboring a wild animal on the premises. In short, negligence contemplates the failure to do what ought to have been done or the doing of an act which should not be done. In the first instance it is referred to as an act of omission, and in the second, as an act of commission.

Essential Elements of Negligence Liability

Legal liability for negligence will be imposed only in situations where there is (1) a legally protected right; (2) a duty owed to the individual, firm, or corporation possessing the right; (3) conduct which falls below the standard of care required by law to meet the duty; and (4) damages as a consequence thereof. Thus, these are referred to as the essential elements of negligence liability.

A Legally Protected Right The law contemplates that every man has certain rights, including the right to safety of person, property, and reputation, and the right to the services of an unemancipated child and wife. A wrongful invasion of any of these rights is actionable.

A Duty Owed A legal duty may be defined as an obligation to act in conformity with law. A legal duty arises out of social relationships and requires that each party exercise reasonable care for the safety of others. However, where there is no social relationship, no duty will arise. For example, suppose a thief steals a truck from a company parking lot and the truck has a defective braking system. Due to the faulty brakes, the thief has an accident and is injured. There is no social relationship between the owner of the truck and thief from which a duty of care on the part of the owner would arise for the benefit of the thief.

In another situation, suppose a thief breaks into a store after hours intending to steal merchandise. He picks up a bottle of perfume which explodes in his hand and cuts him severely. Or he pulls on a light and the entire fixture falls on him, causing injuries. In neither instance does the store owner owe any duty to the thief. On the other hand, the store owner does owe a duty to persons legitimately on the premises. He or she must maintain the premises in reasonably safe condition for their safety. Failure to do so constitutes negligence. There is a social relationship between the store owner and the customers in the store.

Some statutes require compliance with their terms for the safety of others and their property. For example, statutes and local ordinances require sprinkler systems in certain types of buildings, particularly warehouses. Suppose a fire breaks out in a warehouse which has not complied with the statute, and the building, its contents, and the adjoining building are burned. The evidence indicates that all the property could have been saved if there was a properly functioning sprinkler system in operation. The building owner is liable not only to the owners of the property stored in his or her building but also to the adjoining building owners. Failure to comply with the statute was the proximate cause of the loss of property, even though he had no responsibility for the origin of the fire.

Standard of Care   The law requires that where there is a duty owed, the person, firm, or corporation owing the duty must exercise reasonable care in the performance of the duty. Since the amount of care necessary will vary with the circumstances, the courts have evolved the "reasonably prudent man" test to be applied to the conduct of the person owing the duty. In essence, it consists of the omission of something which a reasonable person, guided by those considerations which ordinarily regulate human affairs would do, or the doing of something which a reasonable and prudent person would not do. For example, the reasonably prudent person will operate an automobile or truck within the speed limits. Therefore, one who operates such a motor vehicle in excess of that speed is negligent. If the speed results in an accident and injury or property damage to others, that person is answerable in damages to the persons injured.

Damages as a Consequence   It is possible that there could be a legally protected right, a duty owed, and conduct which had fallen below said standard, but there would be no chain of causation running from the duty and the failure to meet it to the damages which occurred. In such a case there is no recovery. If the damages are proximately caused by the wrongdoer's action or omission, there is a recovery.

Defenses to Negligence Actions

Contributory Negligence   Contributory negligence consists of the failure of a person to exercise care for his or her own safety or the safety of his or her property, which failure helps to cause his or her own injury. It is also defined as any want of ordinary care on the part of the person injured which combined and/or concurred with the defendant's negligence, was a proximate cause of his or her own injury, and without which the injury would not have occurred.

The common-law rule is that if the conduct of the injured person falls below the standard of care which he or she is required to exercise for his or her own safety and if such conduct was a contributing cause of the injury, that person may not recover. This is true even though the negligence of the defendant was much greater than that of the plaintiff. In other words, if the jury should find that the plaintiff was 1 percent contributorily negligent and the defendant was 99 percent negligent, theoretically the plaintiff may not recover anything, in the absence of judicial or statutory modifications of common-law contributory negligence doctrine.

It should be emphasized that contributory negligence is a defense only in negligence cases. It does not apply to intentional torts, such as assault, mayhem, and murder.

Assumption of Risk A person who knowingly and voluntarily exposes himself or herself to the danger of injury is said to have assumed the risk and, as a result, may not recover. This is on the theory that that to which a person assents is not actionable in law.

To interpose the defense of assumption of risk, two elements must be established as follows:

1. knowledge or awareness of the existence of the risk, with a corresponding appreciation of the extent of the danger; and
2. a voluntary exposure to the danger.

Knowledge of the Risk. The individual must understand the nature of the risk and the extent of it. For example, *A* has a learner's permit to drive an automobile. *B*, knowing this, agrees to teach her to drive. An accident occurs due to *A*'s inexperience. *B* has assumed the risk of driving with an inexperienced driver, since she knew before she got into the car that the driver was only learning to drive. On the other hand, suppose *A* asked *B* to go for a drive with her without telling *B* that she, *A*, had only a learner's permit. *B* did not assume any risks in such a case. However, suppose *A* tells *B* that she has only a learner's permit. *B* offers to teach her to drive. The car has a defective axle which breaks during the course of the ride and *B* is injured. *B* has not assumed this particular risk, since she had no prior knowledge of the condition of the axle.

Voluntary Exposure to the Danger. For the assumption of risk defense to apply, the exposure to danger also must be voluntary. For instance, suppose *A* is a patron of a moving picture theater. Upon entering the theater, A assumes the risk of injury which is occasioned by the darkness within the theater which he expects to find and to which he voluntarily exposes himself. However, the theater owner has the duty to maintain the theater in reasonably safe condition. The patron trips over a loose rug in the aisle. He voluntarily assumed the risk of the darkness, but he did not assume the risk of faulty maintenance. In attending a baseball game, A is aware of the fact that there are seats in a screened part of the park, but the view from that section is not satisfactory. Therefore, A chooses to sit in an unscreened part of the park. He is struck by a batted ball. He has assumed the risk of such injury.

Exculpatory Contracts   Closely related to the defense of assumption of risk is the defense that the plaintiff has by contract exonerated the defendant from any liability arising out of the defendant's negligence. For example, a railroad issues a pass to A with the understanding that, in consideration of the free ticket, A will absolve the railroad from any liability for the negligence of its employees, agents, or contractors. Under such circumstances, A has assumed all the risks of the journey, including those which arise out of the negligence of the railroad.

However, in order for an exculpatory contract to be effective, it must be established that the contract was accepted with full knowledge of its terms. For example, A goes on an amusement ride. On the back of the ticket was printed an exculpatory contract where it was agreed that in consideration of the issuance of the ticket, A assumed all the risks of injury, including those caused by the negligence of the operator. A does not read the ticket. There are no signs calling attention to the contract. Obviously, A could not accept the terms of the contract without having some knowledge of such terms. Therefore, the exculpatory contract is not effective. In the same case, let us assume that A did read the contract on the back of the ticket, but nevertheless did take the ride. In that case, the exculpatory contract is a complete defense, should A be injured due to the negligence of the operator.

The proof of a signed exculpatory agreement is easily established. In most cases it is admitted in evidence, even though the plaintiff denies having read it. This type of exculpatory agreement is found most frequently in leases where the tenant agrees to exculpate the landlord from any liability arising out of the failure of the landlord to maintain the premises in reasonably safe condition. If both the landlord and the tenant bargained on equal terms, there are no public policy considerations which would be violated by such an agreement.

On the other hand, the public has an interest in the operation of utility companies, express companies, and telegraph and telephone companies. Such companies exist as a consequence of a franchise granted by the public, which in most cases is an exclusive franchise. Public interest demands that such companies deal reasonably with each member of the public. Therefore, an exculpatory contract demanded and received as a condition for the rendering of the franchised service is against the public interest and void. The company may not take advantage of its superior bargaining power to exact such a contract. For example, an electric company refused to supply electricity to a householder unless the householder would agree in advance that the electric company be exonerated from any liability arising from the negligent acts of its employees, servants, or agents. Even if the householder did sign such an agreement, it would be void as it is against public policy. Public policy would demand that the utility furnish service to the householder without any conditions, except that reasonable bills for the service be paid.

Intervening Negligence One of the elements which must be established in order to make out a prima facie case based on negligence is that the negligence of the defendant was the proximate or nearest cause of the injury or property damage sustained. If the plaintiff fails to establish an unbroken chain of causation between the accident or the event and the resultant injury, he or she cannot recover. For example, suppose a motorist is driving at a speed of eighty miles per hour, which is in excess of the posted speed limit and also excessive in view of the driving conditions. A passenger grabs the wheel to turn the car away from an oncoming vehicle with the result that the car goes out of control, turns over, and injures the driver and passengers. The original act of negligence, driving at an excessive speed, has been superseded by another cause; namely, the action of the passenger. It cannot be established that the excessive speed would have caused an accident. The driver could have slowed down or could have controlled the vehicle so that no accident would have occurred. In a such a case the action of the passenger was the proximate cause of the accident.

Statute of Limitations For the interests of business, as well as individuals, the legislatures of the various states decided that there must be some point in time when the threat of possible litigation must cease. They accordingly enacted statutes that set forth the periods of time within which various types of actions must be brought. Such statutes are called statutes of limitation. Failure to bring the action within the time set forth in the statute deprives the plaintiff of the right to enforce his or her claim.

It should be noted that the running of the time period of the statute does not nullify or void the cause of action. It merely makes it unenforceable. In most states, the defense of the statute of limitations must be pleaded by the defendant. If it is not pleaded, it is waived, and the trial will proceed just as if the suit were brought within the time limitation.

The statutes also provide that the time limitation will not run against certain classes of persons. It will not run against a minor during the period of minority. The minor is usually granted an additional period of time after attaining majority within which the action may be initiated. In addition, in the case of insane persons, the statute will not run during the period of insanity or during the period in which the insane person is not represented by a guardian.

The time periods in these statutes differ state by state. In tort cases the applicable statute of limitations is that of the state in which the accident took place, regardless of where the action is brought. For example, if an accident occurred in New Jersey where the tort cause of action for personal injuries is limited to two years and the action is brought in New York, which has a three-year statute of limitations applicable to bodily injury claims, the applicable limitation would be two years. If not brought within that time, the claim would be barred (unless the defense was not pleaded by the defendant, as noted above).

Minority   The general rule is that a minor is liable for his or her own torts. As to negligence, some courts have taken the arbitrary position that a minor under the age of seven years is incapable of negligence or contributory negligence; between seven and fourteen he or she is presumed to be incapable of negligence, but the contrary may be proved; and between the ages of fourteen and twenty-one he or she is presumed to be capable of negligence, but evidence to the contrary may be asserted. Other courts have not supported this arbitrary method but have taken the position that whether a minor is capable of negligence or not is a matter of proof of capacity. It would seem that a child under the age of seven would not have such capacity.

When the minor engages in an adult activity, such as driving a car or flying an airplane, he or she usually is treated as an adult and is liable for negligent acts, regardless of age or capability. The reason for this ruling is that the responsibility for the injury or damage should fall on the minor rather than the innocent victim.

Contrary to the popular belief, parents are not automatically responsible for torts committed by their children, unless the child or children are clearly acting as agents for the parent at the time. The agency could come about where the parents instruct the child to do a certain act, and in obedience to that direction, the child does the act. Parents, however, may be liable for their own negligent supervision. For example, a parent leaves a loaded revolver in a place where it is accessible to a child. The child is unfamiliar with its use. The child takes the gun and injures another person by firing it. Under those circumstances the parent would be liable, not for the child's negligent act, but for his or her own negligence in making the gun available to the child who he or she knew was unfamiliar with its use. Parents are under a duty to adequately supervise the activities of their children.

Some states have enacted statutes which changed the common law and made the parents liable, within certain monetary limitations, for the torts of the child. Most of these statutes cover only property damage, and the amount of liability is usually less than $500. Such statutes have generally been enacted at the request of the various highway departments, to cover the cost of replacing street and traffic signs which seem to be particularly attractive to children.

Effect of Automobile Reparations Laws

As will be discussed in Chapter 8, the so-called "no-fault" automobile reparations statutes have substituted new systems for dealing with the problem of automobile bodily injury accidents. Under these new systems, the injured person generally is entitled to recover specified benefits from his or her own insurer, and is deprived of his or her common-law action against the responsible party, except where the injuries exceed the "threshold" amounts or fall within other exceptions set forth in the statutes. The cases in which the injured person retains his or her common-law rights are usually defined as those in which the medical treatment exceeds a certain amount (usually $500 or more), or the injury causes extensive temporary disability, disfigurement, permanent injury, or death. Most of said statutes do not abolish common-law actions to recover damages to property or those arising from intentional torts.

As to business organizations which may be involved in such accidents, the new legislation should reduce the number of (auto) bodily injury suits which will be brought by injured persons. However, in the case of payment by the injured person's insurer, some statutes provide that the company making such payments may sue the third-party tortfeasor to recover the payments actually made. Even in that situation, since the required payment does not encompass noneconomic losses, such as pain and suffering, the ultimate liability of the tortfeasor should be much less than the recoveries under the old common-law system. As to the cases which come over the "threshold," the liability of the tortfeasor will remain the same as it has been.

Comparative Negligence

Definition There has been widespread dissatisfaction with the common-law rule that the contributory negligence of the plaintiff, no matter how slight, will defeat his or her recovery. Comparative negligence applies the rule that the contributory negligence of the plaintiff will not defeat recovery but will be taken into account by the jury in reducing the amount of recovery.

Comparative negligence is not new to the law. It had its origin in cases of admiralty and maritime torts, and it continues to be applied in such cases. The same rule has been adopted in several federal statutes, such as the Federal Employers Liability Act (45 USCA 51 et seq.); the Jones Act (46 USCA 688), which applies to the injury or death of seamen; and the Death on the High Seas by Wrongful Act statute (46 USCA 761-768), which applies to a death sustained on American vessels on the high seas.

Application By the time of this writing, thirty-two jurisdictions had adopted the rule of comparative negligence, either by judicial modification of the common law or by statute passed by the legislature. These states or territories are shown in Table 1-1. The dates given in Table 1-1 refer to the years of the latest legislation and/or court cases on the subject of comparative negligence.

Forms of Comparative Negligence While the jurisdictions listed in Table 1-1 are uniform in accepting the principle of comparative negligence, they are not in agreement as to the implementation of the rule. The statutes or court decisions will fall into one of the following categories: (1) pure form, (2) modified form, and (3) slight versus gross negligence.

Pure Form. Under the pure form, the plaintiff may recover if the defendant was in some degree negligent, regardless of the percentage of contributory negligence which is applicable to the plaintiff. Theoretically the plaintiff could recover some part of the damages if he or she were 99 percent negligent and the defendant 1 percent. The amount of the plaintiff's damages would be reduced by the percentage of contributory negligence of which he or she is guilty. Therefore, if the plaintiff was 75 percent contributorily negligent and the defendant 25 percent negligent, the plaintiff would recover 25 percent of his or her damages. If the plaintiff's provable damages amounted to $50,000 and the defendant's damages were $500, the plaintiff would recover 25 percent of $50,000 or $12,500. On the other hand, the defendant would recover 75 percent of $500 or $375. Thus, the odds are in favor of the party who has sustained the greater damage.

Table 1-1

Jurisdictions Which Have Adopted the Rule of Comparative Negligence

Jurisdiction	Statute or Court Decision
Alaska	Kaatz v. Alaska, 540 p. 2d 1037 (1975)
Arkansas	Ark. Stat. Ann. 27.1763 (1955)
California	Nga Li v. Yellow Cab Co., 532 Pac. 2d 1226 (1975)
Colorado	Colo. Rev. Stat. Ann. 41-2-14 (1971)
Connecticut	Conn. Stat. Ann. 52-572h (1975)
Florida	Hoffman v. Jones, 280 So. 2d 431 (1973)
Georgia	Ga. Code Ann. 105-603 (1968)
Hawaii	Hawaii Rev. Stat. 663-31 (1974)
Idaho	Idaho Code 6-801 (1974)
Kansas	Kan. Stat. Ann. 60-258a (1974)
Maine	Me. Rev. Stat. Ann. Title 14, Sec. 156 (1974)
Massachusetts	Mass. Ann. Laws, Ch. 231, Sec. 85 (1974)
Minnesota	Minn. Stat. Ann. 604.01 (1975)
Mississippi	Miss. Code Ann. 11-7-15 (1972)
Montana	Mont. Rev. Codes 58-607 (1947)
Nebraska	Neb. Rev. Stat. 25-1151 (1964)
Nevada	Nev. Rev. Stat. 41.141 (1973)
New Hampshire	N.H. Rev. Stat. Ann. 507.7a (1973)
New Jersey	N.J. Stat. Ann. 2A 15-5.1 (1975)
New York	CPLR 1411-13 (1976)
North Dakota	N.D. Cent. Code 9-10-07 (1975)
Oklahoma	Okla. Stat. Ann. Title 23, Sec. 11 (1974)
Oregon	Ore. Rev. Stat. 18.470 (1973)
Puerto Rico	Puerto Rico Laws Ann. Title 31 Sec. 5141 (1968)
Rhode Island	R.I. Gen. Laws Ann. 9-20-4 (1974)
South Dakota	S.D. Comp. Laws Ann. 20-9-2 (1967)
Texas	Tex. Civ. Stat. Art. 2212a (1974)
Utah	Utah Code Ann. 78-27-32 (1975)
Vermont	Vt. Stat. Ann. Title 12 Sec. 1036 (1973)
Washington	Wash. Rev. Code 4.22-010-190 (1973)
Wisconsin	Wis. Stat. Ann. 895-045 (1975)
Wyoming	Wyo. Stat. Ann. 1-7.2 (1975)

Six states have adopted the pure form. They are Alaska, California, Florida, Mississippi, Rhode Island, and Washington.

Modified Form. The modified type of statute allows a recovery by the plaintiff only where his or her negligence did not exceed that of the defendant. If the plaintiff's negligence exceeds that of the defendant, there is no recovery by the plaintiff. There are two variations of this form. The first requires that the plaintiff's contributory negligence be *less than* the negligence of the defendant for a recovery by him to be allowed. Thus, if the plaintiff's contributory negligence equals or exceeds that of the defendant, he or she cannot recover. The states which have adopted this form are Arkansas, Colorado, Georgia, Hawaii, Idaho, Maine, Massachusetts, Minnesota, North Dakota, Oklahoma, Oregon, Utah, and Wyoming.

The second variation permits a recovery as long as the plaintiff's negligence is *not greater than* the defendant's negligence. Thus, if the plaintiff's negligence equals that of the defendant, he or she may recover. If the plaintiff's negligence exceeds that of the defendant, he or she cannot recover at all. The states which follow this form are Connecticut, Montana, Nevada, New Hampshire, New Jersey, New York, Texas, Vermont, and Wisconsin.

Slight Versus Gross Negligence.   Some states by statute apply the principle of comparative negligence only to cases where the court finds that the plaintiff's negligence was slight and the defendant's negligence was gross. Since no guidelines or definition of the terms "slight and gross" are set forth in the statute, courts have had to grapple with the problem of determining the legislative intent. As a result, although there has been substantial litigation, no clear-cut definitions of the terms have been arrived at. Fortunately, only two states, Nebraska and South Dakota, have adopted this form. The chances of other states following this form are very slim.

Multiple Defendants   Some cases involve more than one defendant. The effect of the joinder of one or more defendants will vary in accordance with the law applicable to comparative negligence, whether it be the pure form or one of the types of the modified form.

Pure Form.   Under the pure form, the addition of other defendants will not affect the plaintiff's right to recover or the extent of his or her recovery. It will affect the apportionment of the fault to each defendant. For example, let us assume that the jury found that the plaintiff was 40 percent contributorily negligent and that the two defendants were guilty of negligence to the extent of 45 percent and 15 percent, respectively. The plaintiff would still recover 60 percent of his or her damages, which would be apportioned between both defendants in proportion to their percentage of fault. Thus, if the plaintiff's damages amounted to $10,000, he or she would recover $6,000. This amount would be apportioned between the defendants so that the first defendant (45 percent) would pay $4,500 (45 percent of $10,000), and the second defendant (15 percent) would pay $1,500 (15 percent of $10,000).

Modified Form.   The statutes and decisions are divided as to the disposition of multiple defendant claims under the modified form. Two possibilities are (1) based on the combined negligence of the defendants, or (2) based on the individual negligence of the defendants.

COMBINED NEGLIGENCE OF THE DEFENDANTS. The contributory negligence of the plaintiff will be compared with the aggregate negligence of all defendants. Therefore, if the plaintiff's negligence is less than that of the total negligence in the case, the plaintiff may recover. In states subscribing to the rule that the plaintiff may recover if his or her negligence is not greater than that of the defendant, the plaintiff may recover if his or her negligence is equal to that of the combined negligence of the defendants. For example, the Nevada statute provides:

> The plaintiff may not recover if his contributory negligence has contributed more to the injury than the negligence of the defendant or the combined negligence of multiple defendants.[5]

Returning to the hypothetical case, the combined negligence of defendant one (45 percent) and defendant two (15 percent) amounts to 60 percent. The plaintiff's negligence was 40 percent. Since the plaintiff's negligence has not contributed more to the injury than the combined negligence of both defendants, the plaintiff can recover from both defendants.

INDIVIDUAL NEGLIGENCE OF THE DEFENDANTS. An example of this type of statute is the Minnesota statute (Minn. Stat. Ann. 604.01). The legislative comment to this statute provides:

> In cases involving more than one defendant, the plaintiff's negligence is to be compared to that of each defendant separately and he can recover only from the defendant or defendants whose negligence exceeds his own.

The application of this statute to the hypothetical case gives a far different result. The plaintiff, whose contributory negligence is 40 percent, can recover from defendant one whose negligence is 45 percent, because the plaintiff's negligence is less than that of defendant one. On the other hand, since the plaintiff's contributory negligence exceeds that of defendant two (15 percent), the plaintiff cannot recover from defendant two.

Unfortunately, many of the comparative negligence statutes are not specific as to exactly what comparisons are to be made in multiple defendant cases. Therefore, until the courts have had the opportunity of ruling on the issue, the question must be considered open.

STRICT LIABILITY

Nature of Strict or Absolute Liability—Early Concepts

The common-law courts originally held the view that whenever there was an injury sustained, the person, firm, or corporation causing the injury was liable for damages. This liability was imposed regardless of the kind and type of act involved, i.e., regardless of whether it involved a lack of care or an intentional act. In short, the courts awarded damages whenever an injury was sustained.

As time passed and life became more complex with the introduction of machinery of various kinds, social progress demanded that the courts adopt the fault concept. Under this theory, the person, firm, or corporation charged with causing an injury to person or property would be answerable in damages only if due care for the safety of others was not exercised. Otherwise there was no liability. Clearly, if everyone, including business organizations, were required to respond in damages every time an injury or property damage was sustained, businesses and individuals would be seriously hampered.

The courts did, however, retain certain rules with respect to cases which arose out of the use and operation of the defendant's premises, as well as to cases involving dangerous or defective products placed in the stream of commerce. In such cases, the rule of strict liability or liability without fault was retained on the theory that liability is imposed for the doing of the act or acts, even though great care was exercised.

Strict Liability Under Common Law

The common-law view on cases of strict liability is that by doing the act or acts of manufacturing a dangerous or defective product, the defendant has exposed others to an unreasonable risk of harm, regardless of the amount of care which was exercised. The liability thus imposed will fall into one of the following three categories: (1) dangerous instrumentality doctrine, (2) the inherently dangerous operations doctrine, or (3) strict products liability doctrine.

Dangerous Instrumentality Doctrine An owner or occupier of land who possesses, maintains, or stores a dangerous instrumentality on his or her premises is strictly liable to anyone who is injured because of its presence. Such a dangerous instrumentality might consist of dynamite, gasoline, noxious chemicals, explosives, or any type of firearms. Liability is imposed because the abnormal use of the property exposes the community to an unreasonable risk of harm. The community, on the other hand, is under no duty to anticipate that the owner of land will use his premises for that purpose. Therefore, members of the community are under no duty to guard against the possible results by boarding up their windows or evacuating the area. In fact, under strict liability, the defense of contributory negligence is not available.

The dangerous instrumentality might also consist of animals which are kept on the premises. These animals could be wild or domestic.

Wild Animals. The rule is that all wild animals (including untamed or atypical domestic animals) are dangerous instrumentalities, and the mere ownership thereof imposes strict liability on the owner whenever an injury or damage occurs. The mere fact that the owner exercised great care in confining the animal will not insulate him or her from liability.

Domestic Animals. Most typical domestic animals are regarded as harmless, since they do not pose any particular danger to the community. But certain animals are capable of doing damage or causing injury. As a result, the owner or harborer of such animals is subject to strict liability for any damage or injury which they might cause. Such animals fall into one of the following three classes:

1. livestock (animals which, because of their size or habits, are known to cause damage when they intrude on another's property);
2. animals in which dangerous propensities are normal, such as Brahman bulls, etc.; or
3. abnormally dangerous domestic animals, such as a vicious dog, known to the owner to have previously exhibited such propensities.

An owner or occupier of land who harbors or possesses such animals is subject to strict liability should the animals cause injury or damage to others.

Inherently Dangerous Operations Doctrine This is also referred to as the ultra-hazardous operations doctrine. It is closely related to the dangerous instrumentality doctrine in that it refers to abnormal use of the premises by the owner or occupier. If the owner or occupier should conduct operations on his or her land which are unreasonably dangerous to others in the vicinity, he or she is strictly liable to others for any injury or property damage which may result. Such operations could consist of blasting, oil well drilling, mining, or the production of dangerous chemicals.

Strict Products Liability As will be discussed fully in Chapter 3, the rule of strict liability in tort is applied to the sale of products where the seller sells any product in a defective condition unreasonably dangerous to users or consumers or to their property. Under such circumstances, the seller is subject to strict liability, and mere proof of the defect and consequent damages will be sufficient to support a cause of action against the seller. This rule is imposed even though the seller has exercised all possible care in the preparation of the product.

Strict Liability Imposed by Statute

Strict liability may be imposed by statute, as well as by the common law. The following statutes create strict liability where no liability existed before.

Workers' Compensation Statutes These statutes are described in some detail in Chapter 6. Briefly, the statutes abolished the common-law rule in most master and servant cases and substituted a system whereby the injured employee would receive specified benefits if he or she sustained a work-related injury. These benefits consist of weekly compensation payments and medical, surgical, and hospital expenses.

The statutes imposed strict liability on the employer for the payment of benefits set forth in the statute. Insurance against such liability may be obtained either through a state-managed compensation fund or private insurance. (In some cases, a funded retention program may be used in lieu of insurance.)

Disability Benefits Laws Several states have statutes which require the employer to provide for insurance against nonoccupational injuries sustained by employees. These statutes require that a form of accident insurance be obtained in order to compensate the employee in the case of accidents which do not occur in the course of employment. The statutes create a liability on the part of the employer which never existed at common law, and it can be viewed as a form of strict liability.

Uniform State Law for Aeronautics This statute, which is recommended by the Commissioners on Uniform State Laws, provides for a rule of absolute or strict liability on the part of the owner of any aircraft for injuries (to persons or property on the land or water underneath) which are caused by the ascent, descent, or flight of the aircraft. The statute was adopted in only nine states—Delaware, Hawaii, Minnesota, Montana, New Jersey, North Dakota, South Carolina, Tennessee, and Wyoming. Other states passed legislation establishing a presumption of negligence in such cases, and still others did not legislate at all, and this left these fact situations to be dealt with under common-law precedents.

At the present time, the commissioners have withdrawn the recommendation for this uniform law, and they are in the process of reconsidering the provisions thereof in the light of the safety progress which the aviation industry has made. In addition, the states which have adopted the uniform act are considering either repeal or a substitute act.

Federal Aviation Act of 1958   This act created the Federal Aviation Administration, whose duty it is to formulate and enforce safety regulations relating to aircraft, both commercial and private. Strict liability is imposed where there has been a violation of such regulations, which proximately caused injury to persons or damage to property.

International Flights   The Warsaw Convention, to which the United States declared its adherence, provides for the imposition of strict liability unless the airline can establish its freedom from negligence. It further provides for a $75,000 limitation of liability on the part of the airline for bodily injury. The limitation does not apply if the passenger can establish that the accident or injury was caused by the willful misconduct of the carrier.

This convention applies, as far as the United States is concerned, to any international transportation by air which, according to the relevant contract of carriage, includes a place in the United States as a point of origin, point of destination, or agreed stopping place.

Dram Shop Acts   A number of states have passed "dram shop acts" or "civil damage acts" which impose strict liability on the seller of intoxicating beverages who, by illegally selling, bartering, or giving intoxicating beverages, causes the intoxication of a person whose intoxication in turn causes injury to the person or property of another.

An illegal sale would consist of a sale to a minor or an obviously intoxicated person in violation of the Alcoholic Control Act of the particular state involved.

Interstate Commerce Act   Under this act the Interstate Commerce Commission was created to supervise the transportation of persons and freight by land or water. The commission has the power to make rules governing interstate transportation and to impose regulations which the carrier must meet.

The commission is also empowered to regulate the amount of insurance to be carried, if any, as well as the rules relating to the filing and cancellation of policies of insurance. The ICC does permit a carrier to limit the dollar amount of its liability.

RES IPSA LOQUITUR

Nature of *Res Ipsa Loquitur* (The Thing Speaks for Itself)

This rule of evidence raises the presumption of negligence from the presentation of certain facts. It all began back in 1863 when a barrel of flour rolled out of the second-story window of a warehouse and fell on the plaintiff. It was conceded that the barrel was in the custody of the warehouseman and was under his control. However, these were the only facts in evidence. In disposing of the issue of negligence, the court said that the facts speak for themselves, i.e., the accident could not have happened if the warehouseman had exercised due care. Therefore, the plaintiff was not obligated to establish any specific acts of negligence. In making this decision, the court used the Latin words, *res ipsa loquitur* (Byrne v. Boadle, 2 H.&C. 722). This phrase has been repeated in thousands of cases since.

Generally, *res ipsa loquitur* is applied where the plaintiff can establish the following elements:

1. The instrumentality which caused the accident must be in the exclusive control of the defendant.
2. The accident must be one which does not happen in the ordinary course of things if those who have control have exercised proper care.
3. The accident must not have been due to any voluntary contribution (contributory negligence) on the part of the plaintiff.

Res ipsa loquitur, once established, creates only a rebuttable presumption of negligence. This presumption can be overcome by the defendant if he or she is able to convince the court either that he or she was not negligent or that the plaintiff was guilty of contributory negligence.

Application of *Res Ipsa Loquitur*

The application of the rule gives the plaintiff an initial advantage. He or she must merely offer proof of the facts of the event while the defendant, in order to defend successfully, must offer evidence to negate the presumption of negligence. The defendant ordinarily has greater access to the facts concerning his or her control of the instrumentality than the plaintiff and therefore is generally in a position, if it is possible, to refute the presumption of negligence. To return to the flour barrel case, if the warehouseman could have shown that the barrel was started on its way to the window by a trespasser and that the warehouseman had no control over it, there would have been a verdict for the warehouseman. Or, if it could have been shown that the barrel had never been in the custody of the warehouseman and had fallen from some window other than the one in his warehouse, then a defendant's verdict might also have been possible.

The fact that the offending instrumentality must have been in the control of one of several defendants will not entitle the plaintiff to the benefit of *res ipsa loquitur*, unless he or she can establish which one of the possible defendants actually had control of the instrumentality. For example, in Wolf v. American Tract Society (58 NE 31, New York) a brick fell from a building in the course of construction and injured a passerby. Many workers under the control of various contractors were working on the building. Under those circumstances, while the evidence established that someone had been negligent, the failure of the plaintiff to establish exactly who had control of the brick precluded the application of *res ipsa loquitur*.

Res Ipsa Loquitur *and Strict Liability* Under both of these doctrines the burden of establishing the facts of the accident or event is on the plaintiff. In both instances the proof of the facts and nothing more will insure a verdict for the plaintiff. However, in the application of *res ipsa loquitur*, the defendant has the privilege of going forward with the evidence to establish either that he or she was not negligent or that the plaintiff had failed to exercise care for his or her own safety. Should the defendant be successful in establishing either of these positions, the presumption of negligence disappears. On the other hand, in cases involving strict liability, the defendant has no such defense. The mere happening of the event will be sufficient to charge him or her with liability. There is no burden on the plaintiff to prove negligence on the part of the defendant.

VICARIOUS LIABILITY

Agency

Agency may be defined as every relationship where one party acts for or represents another pursuant to the latter's orders and directions. It is a relationship created by express or implied contract or by law, whereby one party delegates the transaction of another who agrees to undertake said activity as directed. The relationship could involve principal and agent, employer and employee. In some cases an alleged proprietor and his or her independent contractor are actually acting as principal and agent, respectively. Business firms are particularly involved in agency relationships and, as a result, are responsible for the acts of their agents done within the scope of authority delegated to said agents.

Imputed Negligence

The fundamental rule in agency is that where a party does an act through an agent, he or she does it personally. Therefore, if the agent is negligent in the performance of the act, which negligence results in injury or property damage to another, the principal is also liable as if he or she had done the act personally. Thus, the agent's negligence is imputed to the principal, and the principal is answerable jointly and severally in damages to the injured person.

Scope of Agency

The agent is limited in his or her activity to the authority to act given to the agent by the principal. The principal is not responsible for any activity of the agent which is undertaken outside of the scope of the authority granted to him or her. Therefore, if the agent is acting for his or her own purposes, the principal is not subject to liability. For example, a truck driver is employed to bring the employer's products to a depot south of town. On the way he meets a friend who asks him to drive to her home north of town. While on the trip north there is an accident caused by the truck driver's negligence. The employer is not liable for the accident. Assume further that the friend had arrived at her home and the truck driver had resumed his trip to the depot when the accident happened. There are two schools of thought as to the liability of the employer. If the truck driver was back on the usual route to the depot, the employer is liable. If the truck driver had not yet returned to the normal route, some courts hold that he was in the course of employment, because he was engaged in furthering the interest of the master in transporting the goods in the direction of the depot. Other courts hold that he is not back in the course of his employment until he actually arrives at a point where the deviation had ended and he is back on the usual route. Thus, according to these courts, the employer should not be responsible until the deviation is completely over and the driver is back on the usual route.

Intentional Torts

As to intentional torts, the general rule is that if the intentional tort is committed in the scope of agency while serving the interests of the principal, the principal is jointly and severally liable to the injured person. This is true no matter how much of a mistake in judgment was made by the agent. For example, in a District of Columbia case, an assault occurred when the plaintiff told the defendant's employee that his hamburger contained unground meat. It was the employee's duty to adjust any disputes or complaints with customers. The court held that he was acting within the scope of his employment when he violently resented the complaint and attacked the customer (Dilli v. Johnson, 107 Fed. 2d 609).

Relationships Which May Result in Vicarious Liability

The following fact situations may expose the principal to liability for the acts of his agents.

Principal and Agent   The principal confides certain matters to the agent who will act for him or her within the scope of the authority granted. The agent may represent more than one principal, and the liability of the principal will depend upon whether or not the acts complained of were done in his or her interest and within the scope of the agent's authority.

Employees in the Course of Employment   Generally, an employee is the agent of the employer while in the course of employment and doing the particular job assigned to him or her. If the employee exceeds this authority the employer is not liable, unless the employer clothed said agent with "apparent authority" to act as he or she did and said apparent authority was relied on justifiably by the person subsequently injured.

Partners   A partnership is a business enterprise which comes into being as a result of a contract entered into by the parties. It may consist of two or more partners. The parties agree to invest their money, efforts, labor, and skill in a lawful enterprise with the understanding that the profits or losses shall be shared among them. Each partner is an agent of the partnership and because of the nature of the business, he or she represents all of the individuals comprising the partnership including himself or herself. Thus, each partner is both a principal and an agent in all acts.

Independent Contractors   Normally, independent contractors are not agents and are not subject to the control and direction of the employer. However, in some situations, the employer may exercise control, in which case the independent contractor is no longer independent and becomes the agent of the employer.

Ratification of Unauthorized Acts

Under some circumstances, the agent may exceed his or her authority, and his or her act or acts may be for the benefit of the principal. If the principal accepts the beneficial results of these acts, the rule is that there is a ratification, and the principal accepts the act or acts as his or her own.

FINANCIAL LOSS POTENTIAL FROM TORT LIABILITY

Determination of Damages

Compensatory Damages   Where it has been established that the defendant is responsible for the injury or damage, the plaintiff is entitled to damages which will reasonably compensate him or her for the loss suffered. These consist of special damages and general damages.

Special Damages.   Special damages generally consist of the out-of-pocket expenses which the plaintiff has incurred as a result of the injury or damage. In cases involving bodily injury, such damages consist of the following:

1. Loss of earnings. This is the amount that the plaintiff otherwise would have been capable of earning but for the injury. The mere fact that the plaintiff's employer continued his or her salary during the disability will not be taken into account. The actual loss will consist of the money that he or she was prevented from earning because of the injury, projected over the plaintiff's lifetime, in the case of a permanent disability.
2. Medical expenses. These will include the costs of medical, hospital, surgical, and nursing services and, where appropriate, the costs of crutches, artificial limbs, glasses, and all types of prostheses.

In cases involving property damage, the plaintiff normally is entitled to the lesser of the cost of repair or the replacement cost of property of like kind and quality. The losses from being unable to use certain property (e.g., a building) during the replacement period are also compensable.

General Damages. In bodily injury cases the plaintiff is entitled to recover for the pain and suffering which he or she sustained. The amount will be awarded by the jury on the basis of the medical testimony and the plaintiff's own testimony as to the extent of the suffering and the length of time during which it continued.

Death of the Plaintiff or Defendant

At common law the death of a person ended his or her legal as well as earthly existence. He or she could not sue or be sued. If an action was pending trial, the death of either the plaintiff or defendant abated the action, calling for a dismissal. In addition, where the injured person's death was caused through the negligence or default of the defendant, there was no cause of action accruing to the heirs or dependents. This common-law rule has been changed by statute in all states by providing for (1) abatement and survival actions, and (2) wrongful death actions.

Abatement and Survival. The statutes provide that the death of an injured person shall not abate the action, but that the action may be brought or continued by his or her personal representative for the benefit of the injured person's heirs at law. This statute refers only to a cause of action which the deceased person had while alive, and the damages recoverable are those which he or she would have been able to recover had he or she lived.

Where the defendant is deceased, the statutes provide that his or her death will not abate the action, whether brought by the personal representative of a deceased plaintiff or by the plaintiff personally. The action may be continued against the estate of the deceased defendant.

Wrongful Death. Where the death of a person is caused by a wrongful act, neglect, or default, such as would have entitled the injured person to maintain an action for damages, if death had not ensued, the statutes provide that an action may be brought by the executor or administrator of the estate to recover damages for the benefit of his or her dependents. Other statutes provide for a recovery based on the loss to the estate of the deceased.

Punitive Damages

In addition to compensatory damages, some states allow the jury to award an additional amount by way of punishment where the defendant's conduct has been intentional, malicious, or outrageous. The award is made to the plaintiff, over and above the amount of compensatory damages, to provide solace for mental anguish, injured feelings, shame, degradation, or other aggravations of the original wrong and also to punish the defendant for outrageous behavior and prevent him or her from repeating the same acts. These damages are sometimes referred to as exemplary damages or "smart money."

A principal may be subject to an award of punitive damages for the acts of his or her agent where it is shown that the principal either encouraged or ratified the outrageous behavior of the agent or employee.

Determination of the Amount of Damages Generally, the question of the amount of damages to be awarded is one for the jury to decide pursuant to instructions from the judge. The judge has no role in determining damages in a jury case. The matter is entirely within the province of the jury. However, the judge does have the power to set aside a verdict which is so large or so small that it "shocks the conscience of the court," in which case he or she will either order a new trial or attempt to compromise by having the parties agree to an *"additur* or *remittitur,"* which means that in spite of the verdict, the parties will agree to pay more or take less than the amount brought in by the jury. In cases where a jury is waived by the parties, the court acts as judge and jury and makes the determination of the amount of the damages to be awarded.

The amount that will be awarded is, of course, in the hands of the jury in most cases. There is usually no dollar maximum beyond which the jury may not go, so that the potential loss to a business firm is governed by the extent of the injury or damage and the view taken by the jury as to the value thereof. While the court will usually instruct the jury that the wealth of the defendant is not to be taken into account in determining the amount of damages, it stands to reason that, since the jury is composed of human beings, they will be more likely to award a large amount of damages when the business firm is large and is well known. It is true that the court may set aside a verdict as excessive or insufficient, but the court exercises this power very sparingly.

Even after all the evidence has been presented, it is difficult to forecast the dollar amount the jury might award in a given case. The jury is usually impressed by such things as the extent of the injuries, the manner in which the injury was caused, and the conduct of the defendant both before and after the accident. For example, in a recent California case (Rosendin v. Trans-Exec. Co., Superior Court, Santa Clara County) the plaintiff and his wife flew in a company-owned plane with an experienced pilot from San Jose to Lake Tahoe. In making the approach to the Lake Tahoe airport, the right engine stalled but the left engine was still working. In attempting to get the right engine started, the pilot went beyond the airstrip for about a mile over the lake. In making a left turn to the base leg at an altitude of 500 feet, the stall horn sounded and the pilot gave the good engine full power. The plane flipped over and crashed. The plaintiff's wife was killed, as was the pilot. The plaintiff himself lost both legs and the use of one arm in addition to other injuries. The plaintiff alleged that not only the manufacturers of the engine and its magnetos were negligent, but further that they had willfully violated federal air regulations governing the rebuilding of the same kind of engines as the one which failed. The evidence further indicated that the manufacturer did not act on reports of magneto failures until a certain percentage of failures had occurred. The jury verdict awarded the plaintiff over a million dollars for his injuries and in the wrongful death action for his wife's death, he and his five children were awarded $1.2 million. Because of the defendant's conduct with regard to ignoring the federal standards in the rebuilding of the engine and their failure to heed the reports of magneto failures, the jury also awarded the plaintiff $10.5 million in punitive damages. The defendant is currently appealing the punitive damages award. However, with this jury verdict, the defendant is still exposed to other claims to be made by the estate of the pilot and some friends who were also passengers in the plane and were killed.

In another claim involving the crash of an aircraft (Pease v. Beech Aircraft Corp. 38 Cal. App. 3d 450), claims were brought by the estates of four passengers who were killed when the aircraft malfunctioned and crashed. The jury brought in a verdict of $4 million for compensatory damages and $17.5 million in punitive damages. The trial court granted a new trial on the issue of punitive damages, but both of these high-verdict cases are illustrative of the extent to which a jury might go in determining damages.

Where a life insurance company sold hospital care insurance with a $5,000 limit, one would not anticipate that the liability of the company would exceed $5,000. However, in one case (Silberg v. California Life Insurance Company, 521 P. 2d 1103) the facts indicated the plaintiff had bought such a policy and, after an injury for which the plaintiff incurred over $7,000 in medical expenses, the company refused to pay, because Silberg had also filed a compensation claim for the same injury. For two years no payments were made either by the life insurance company or the compensation insurer. During this time the life insurance company advised the plaintiff's hospitals that benefits would not be paid. During this time the plaintiff's condition deteriorated and he had second, third, and fourth operations by different surgeons (and in different hospitals, because the first hospital and surgeon had not been paid). Ultimately, the plaintiff lost his business and had to borrow money to meet his medical and living expenses. In an action against the life insurance company in which allegations were made of fraud, bad faith, and malicious conduct, the jury awarded the plaintiff $75,000 in compensatory damages and $500,000 in punitive damages. The compensatory damage award was upheld on appeal, but the trial court's ruling in granting a new trial on the punitive damage issue was upheld. This case is illustrative of the possible tort exposures which can result from a particular manner of conducting a business.

Thus, the problem of deciding what liability insurance limits should be recommended to a business entity is not free from difficulty. The ideal situation would be where the business organization purchases limits which are sufficient to meet any possible contingency. But, as will be explained in Chapter 2, this frequently poses problems of availability and price.

When a verdict is rendered and the defendant does not have adequate insurance, the successful plaintiff can levy execution on the defendant's property, including bank accounts, thus preventing the defendant from selling or otherwise disposing of these assets. In addition, a sheriff's sale may have to be conducted to satisfy the judgment. Where an appeal is taken from the verdict, the appellant must furnish a bond with good and sufficient surety to guarantee not only the payment of the verdict but an excess amount as well. In some states this amounts to a bond for twice the amount of the verdict. If the appeal is unsuccessful, the defendant will be liable not only for the amount of the verdict, but the interest which has accrued from the rendering of the original verdict until said amount is actually paid.

Defense Costs

Attorneys' Fees The amount for which the defendant will be liable to his or her attorneys will include the per diem costs of the actual trial, and will also include all preliminary costs, including discovery proceedings, motions, interviews with expert witnesses, and such conferences with the defendant as are required. The amount of the attorneys' fees will differ with the type of case, the amount of preliminary trial preparation which is required, and the actual amount of time involved in the trial. Attorneys' fees can often be high enough to influence a decision to settle a case and can easily reach $500 to $1,000 a day during a trial.

Witnesses' Fees These include not only the fee for the initial report of findings (for expert witnesses) but will also cover the length of time spent in court and testifying. Witnesses will include fact witnesses who could testify as to the facts of the event which is the subject matter of the suit, as well as expert witnesses, such as physicians, surgeons, engineers, and so on, who could not only testify as to the facts but also give opinions in answer to hypothetical questions. The amounts to be paid as witness fees will vary with the kind and type of witness involved, as well as the amount of preliminary research which may be necessary to be prepared for the trial. Many experts, such as surgeons, receive $1,000 a day.

Court Costs   The defendant will be liable for the payment of all costs imposed by the court in which the action is pending. These include jury fees, filing fees, and the like. Court fees (about $50 to $100) are comparatively low.

Bond Premiums   Costs would also include the premiums on bonds to release attachments, as well as the cost of bail bonds required because of an accident or violation involving the use of a motor vehicle.

In liability policies all of the above items of expense are generally covered in full or in part under the defense and supplementary payments provisions.

Other Costs Involved with Defense

When a lawsuit is initiated, its existence is publicized. The allegations may be detrimental to the business organization or its products and substantial business losses can be incurred. In addition, the business organization invariably will have to spend some money in order to overcome any unfavorable public reaction which there may be as a consequence of the lawsuit. The following review of trial procedures highlights the cost involved.

A lawsuit is begun by the service of a summons and complaint. The summons merely establishes the jurisdiction of the court to try the case, but the complaint will set forth the allegations of the plaintiff upon which he or she seeks to establish the right to the recovery of damages. The defendant has the obligation of filing an answer to the complaint within a certain period of time (usually twenty days from the date of service, exclusive of the day of service). Failure on the part of the defendant to file an answer within the time limit will subject him or her to a default judgment which may be entered by the plaintiff.

After issue is joined by the service of the complaint and answer, both sides have the right to conduct discovery proceedings under which either side may seek to establish the facts upon which the adversary will rely in the trial of the case. This means that the testimony of witnesses may be taken by deposition, which is a question and answer procedure conducted under oath, usually in the office of the attorney requiring the deposition. The defendant may have to submit the testimony of his or her witnesses, including executives of the company, to this deposition procedure. Clearly, the loss of time on the part of its executives is costly and may hamper the operations of a business organization.

When the deposition is taken by the defendant, he or she will have to provide the notary public, as well as the stenographer who will record the testimony so taken. In addition, the opposing party will have to be supplied with a copy of the deposition so taken. When the case comes to trial the defendant will have to present its witnesses, whether they be executives, employees of the company, or others. The latter could include eyewitnesses, police officers, experts, and all others who can support the defenses offered by the defendant. Again, the loss of time of the executives and other employees will result in a business loss, and the other witnesses will have to be paid a fee for testifying, which in the case of the experts could be substantial, and which in the case of others generally will consist of the expenses incurred in traveling to the courthouse and reimbursement for any loss of salary which might have been incurred because of the witness's absence from work. Usually the losses which accrue to the defendant because of bad publicity and the loss of executive time are not paid under the defendant company's defense and supplementary payment clause in its insurance contract. However, some policies do pay for a limited amount of lost wages or salary up to a nominal amount such as $25 or $50 per day.

Supplementary payment agreements indicate the insurer typically will pay for other "reasonable expenses." What is "reasonable" depends on the circumstances, but the term could include travel and hotel expenses, legal expenses, stenographic expenses, copying expenses, and so forth.

TORTS AND LIABILITY INSURANCE

Insurability

Liability insurance policies had their origins in the maritime law. Vessel owners were indemnified against loss arising out of damages claimed by others in a collision of two or more vessels. Such policies found their way into maritime operations in the early 1800s. About 1880, similar policies were issued to employers to indemnify them against claims by employees arising out of work-connected accidents in which it was claimed that the employer was negligent.

When liability insurance was first introduced in the United States, the objection was made that policies which indemnified or held harmless an individual, firm, or corporation from the tort consequences of their actions were against public policy. The argument was advanced that an insured would be less likely to exercise care for the safety of others when an insurer responded by paying the damages for his or her negligence. On the other hand, it was urged that the existence of liability insurance was for the benefit of the accident victim in that the injured person could be guaranteed a recovery, regardless of whether the insured personally was financially able to meet the judgment. Without liability insurance, there would be a large number of uncompensated victims, and this prospect balanced the scale and led to the view that such contracts of indemnity were not against public policy.

The modern version of the liability contract pays on behalf of the insured, or indemnifies the insured, for legal liability which arises out of the particular operations covered by the contract. These could include the operation of motor vehicles, the operation of a factory, store, or other premises, and/or the manufacture and sale of products.

Torts which will come within the scope of the insuring agreement and for which the insured is entitled to protection are (1) intentional torts, (2) strict liability in tort, and (3) negligent torts.

Intentional Torts Most liability policies exclude from their terms any liability for bodily injury or property damage caused intentionally by the insured. But they do not exclude the intentional acts of others for which the insured is only vicariously liable. Therefore, if an employee driving the insured's automobile or truck intentionally ran over a person or struck a building or other property, the insured might be vicariously liable for the acts of his or her employee. In such a case, unless the insured directed the employee to commit these acts, the insured's vicarious liability would be within the scope of the liability coverage.

Strict Liability in Tort Under the usual insuring agreements, the insured is protected against tort liability imposed upon him or her by law. Therefore, if the law imposes strict liability on the insured, whether as a result of the manufacture of a defective or dangerous product or the hazardous use of his or her premises, such acts usually come within the insuring agreement.

Negligence Negligent torts occur when the insured has failed to exercise that degree of care for the safety of others which the law requires. Since damages are imposed upon him or her for such failure, this type of action normally comes within the scope of the insuring agreement.

Effect of Insurance on Tort Judgments

When liability insurance first came into being, the courts decided that in the trial of a tort action, the fact that the defendant was insured was not admissible as evidence. The rationale behind this ruling was that the jury was required to decide the issues on the merits. They should not be influenced in any degree by the presence or absence of insurance. Theoretically the jury would be more likely to bring in a large verdict if they knew that the defendant would not have to pay it. Conversely, if they knew that the defendant had no insurance, they would be more likely to reduce the amount for the benefit of the defendant.

While the existence of liability insurance is not admissible evidence, some states have by statute or rules of court permitted the plaintiff to ascertain both the existence of insurance and the actual policy limits. This is done in discovery proceedings with the limitation that the information thus discovered would not be admissible evidence. Thus, where the plaintiff knows the policy limits, he or she can tailor demands accordingly. In states where such a rule has not been adopted, the plaintiff will usually be in the dark as to whether or not the demands exceed the policy limits. This is an advantage to the defendant, especially where the defendant is not possessed of property which can be reached by execution after judgment.

With the coming of compulsory automobile insurance, the advantages to the defendant with regard to the nondisclosure of the policy limits began to disappear. In automobile cases the jury knows that the defendant very probably has insurance with at least the minimum limits mandated by law. In addition, where a large corporation is the defendant, the jury may not be concerned with the amount of insurance at all. Whether the defendant is an individual or a large corporation, juries are now bringing in verdicts for larger amounts than was the case before insurance became a factor. Because of this threat, people are buying higher limits of insurance, creating a spiraling effect.

Chapter Notes

1. Many of the definitions and concepts in this chapter are based on James H. Donaldson, *Casualty Claims Practice*, rev. ed. (Homewood, IL: Richard D. Irwin, 1969).
2. Donaldson, p. 17.
3. *The Restatement (Second) of Torts* is one of a series of essential and authoritative legal reference works published as an ongoing project by the American Law Institute. It articulates the basic rules of law in the field of torts, supplementing its statement of rules with detailed commentary.
4. States having adopted some form of comparative negligence in previous years are Georgia (1855), Nebraska (1913), Mississippi (1919), South Dakota (1941), and Wisconsin (1931).
5. Nev. Rev. Stat. 41.141 (2)(a). To the same effect is Conn. Gen. Stat. Ann. 52-572(h).

CHAPTER 2

Premises and Operations Liability Exposures and Their Treatment

PREMISES AND OPERATIONS EXPOSURES[1]

Exposures to loss can arise out of either the premises owned or utilized by a firm, or out of the operations conducted at or away from those premises. The first section of this chapter analyzes the exposures arising out of a firm's premises and operations. Later sections discuss insurance and noninsurance techniques which may be used in treating these premises and operations exposures.

Premises Liability Exposures in General

The "possessor of land" owes to others certain common-law duties which arise out of the possessor's use and occupancy of the land. The possessor may be the owner or a tenant, since the tenant is deemed to have attributes of ownership during the period of the lease. The possessor could also include one whose occupancy is in a representative or fiduciary capacity, such as a trustee in bankruptcy or a mortgagee in possession.

The term "possessor of land" might also include an executor under the last will and testament of a deceased person, or an administrator *cum testamento annexo* (with will attached) appointed by the probate court. Where the executor or administrator assumes the occupancy and control of premises which are part of the estate, such person will be subject to liability to others for any negligent acts. Likewise, a life tenant who has legal occupancy and control of the premises is subject to

61

the same liability. In any case, for the purposes of determining the duties owed, the person in possession and control of the land is required to exercise care for the safety of others, and, except as hereafter discussed, is liable in damages where the failure to exercise care results in injury or property damage to others.

"Land," as used in this context, refers not only to the earth but also to things of a permanent nature affixed thereto, such as buildings, fixtures, fences, walls and bridges, as well as works constructed for the use of water (e.g., dikes and canals).

Generally, the extent of the care which must be exercised is "reasonable care" and is measured by the use to which the premises are put and the injured person's relationship to them. For example, where the owner occupies an empty lot surrounded by an anchor fence with "No Trespassing" signs displayed, it would appear that the owner's duty of care would be practically nil with respect to others who may come on the premises. On the other hand, if the owner maintains a retail store to which the public is invited, his or her duty of care in keeping the premises in reasonably safe condition would be much greater.

The owner or occupier of land must exercise reasonable care with respect to the activities which he or she conducts or allows others to conduct on the premises. These common-law duties are imposed regardless of whether the owner or occupier is an individual or a business enterprise.

The legal grounds for the imposition of premises liability may consist of (1) negligence, (2) intentional interference, or (3) strict liability.

Negligence The failure to exercise reasonable care under the circumstances is negligence. This failure might consist of an act of commission or an act of omission. An act of commission might consist of creating an unsafe condition, such as using an excessive amount of wax on the floors of a store, operating unsafe machinery with knowledge of the presence of others, or even employing incompetent individuals to work on the premises. On the other hand, an act of omission might consist of the failure to correct an unsafe condition when it is known to the occupier, or the failure to provide a sufficient number of employees for the protection of the patrons in places such as bars, baseball parks, or boxing arenas.

Intentional Interference Intentional interference torts involving premises liability are trespass and nuisance. These two types of intentional torts will be reviewed in the following paragraphs.

Trespass. The owner or possessor of the premises may undertake some affirmative act or acts with respect to the alteration, repairs, or additions to the property, and may undertake some construction thereon and, as long as it does not interfere with the rights of others to enjoy their property, the owner or occupier is within his or her rights in taking such action. On the other hand, the owner or occupier may not interfere with the natural drainage of the land. Thus, if the construction so undertaken does cause damage to other owners as a result of interfering with the drainage, the owner is liable.

As to abutting buildings and property, the adjoining owner is entitled to lateral support from an owner or occupier excavating on his or her premises. If such excavation causes the adjoining building to suffer damage, this constitutes a trespass and the party doing the excavating is liable. The necessity of providing lateral support to the neighbor acts as a restriction on the use to which the owner may be able to utilize his or her own property. In any case, a major excavation may deprive the neighbor of his or her right to lateral support, and in that respect, the excavation is a wrongful act. The duty to furnish lateral support to the neighboring owner becomes especially onerous when the neighbor will not permit the owner to enter upon his or her land to erect safeguards to prevent any damage. As a result, some states have enacted statutes which modify the common-law rule and enable the owner, under certain circumstances, to proceed with the construction regardless of whether the neighbor gives permission to enter his or her land to erect safeguards. Such statutes are undoubtedly in the public interest in that they encourage construction and improvements upon land.

Typical of the aforementioned statutes and the form they take is the law in the state of New Jersey, NJSA 46:10-1, which reads as follows:

> Whenever excavations for buildings or other purposes on any lot or piece of land shall be intended to be carried to a depth of more than 8 feet below the curb or grade of the street, and there shall be any party or other wall wholly or partly on adjoining land, and standing upon or near the boundary lines of such lot or piece of land, the person causing such excavations to be made, if afforded the necessary license to enter on the adjoining land, but not otherwise, shall, at all times, from the commencement until the completion of such excavations, preserve, at his own expense, such party or other wall from injury, and so support the same by proper foundation, that it shall remain as stable as before such excavations were commenced.

Note that in New Jersey the owner may undertake an excavation which the owner deems necessary, regardless of whether permission is granted to enter the adjoining land or not. However, even where permission is so granted, the owner will be liable for any damage caused by the lack of lateral support.

Nuisance. The action taken by the possessor of land may constitute a nuisance. A nuisance may be any thing, action, or condition which is dangerous to health, indecent or offensive to the senses, an obstruction to the free use of property so as to interfere with the comfortable enjoyment of life or property, or anything which obstructs the free passage or use, in the customary manner, of any lake, river, square, street, or highway. Where the condition is adjudged to be a nuisance, an aggrieved person may bring an action for damages sustained, or may ask for an injunction requiring that the possessor of the land cease and desist from further maintenance of the nuisance. Or, the aggrieved person may ask for both forms of relief in the same action. Thus, the action may demand damages which have already been incurred and may also require that the nuisance be abated so that there will be no future damages sustained.

In actions for an injunction to abate a nuisance, the jury is usually instructed that a nuisance consists of any condition which arises out of the unreasonable, unwarranted, or unlawful use (by a person, firm or corporation) which produces material annoyance, inconvenience, discomfort, or injury to others.

In actions for damages, the plaintiff will ask for an amount which will reasonably compensate him or her for the inconvenience and the interference with his comfortable enjoyment of his property. The following are examples of actions constituting a nuisance: placing a dam across a stream so as to deprive lower riparian owners of their rights to the use of the water; obstructing the public street so as to prevent neighboring owners from having access to their property; burying dead animals on the premises which causes obnoxious fumes to be dissipated in the air; the operation of a house of prostitution, and other actions or activities which interfere with other people's enjoyment of their property.

It should be noted that an action based on nuisance differs from an action for negligence. In a negligence action, the plaintiff must establish that there was a duty on the part of the defendant, that the defendant failed to meet the duty, and that the plaintiff suffered damage as a result. To this action, the defendant may interpose the defense of contributory negligence, by showing that the plaintiff had failed to exercise reasonable care for his or her own safety. In an action based on nuisance, the defense of contributory negligence is not available to the defendant. The plaintiff must establish only that the condition complained of is a nuisance and that he or she has sustained damages as a result of its existence. The only defenses available to the defendant are that the condition is not a nuisance or that he or she did not create or maintain it.

Where damages will not properly or adequately compensate the complaining party and the facts entitle that party to an order forbidding the continuance of the defendant's acts or actions, an injunction will be issued by the court. This is a prohibitive writ directed to the defendant forbidding him or her to do some act or to permit his or her servants and employees to do so. The writ may restrain the defendant from continuing some act or actions undertaken. Such writs are obtainable only where the payment of damages will not adequately compensate the injured person. For example, a defendant begins to operate a slaughterhouse in a residential neighborhood. Action is brought for the damages already sustained and for an injunction restraining the defendant from continuing to operate the slaughterhouse. While the neighbors would have a separate cause of action every time their homes were invaded by noxious fumes from the slaughterhouse, damages for such intrusion would not be an adequate remedy. The only way the neighbors could be assured of the enjoyment of their property would be for the elimination of the slaughterhouse.

Strict Liability   Under certain circumstances, where the activities undertaken by the possessor on his or her property may expose others to an unreasonable risk of harm, strict liability will be imposed. That is to say, regardless of negligence or wrongful intent, the possessor will be strictly and absolutely liable to anyone injured because of such activity. The primary common-law doctrines under which liability is thus imposed are (1) the dangerous instrumentality doctrine, and (2) the ultra-hazardous operations doctrine.

Dangerous Instrumentality Doctrine.   The general rule is that where the owner or occupier possesses, stores, uses, or maintains a "dangerous instrumentality" on his or her premises, that owner has exposed the community to an unreasonable risk of harm, and is therefore strictly liable for any damage which may be caused by the presence of the dangerous instrumentality, regardless of whether a lack of care on the owner's part contributed to the causation of the accident or not. Dangerous instrumentalities could consist of dynamite, gasoline, explosives, and firearms. In storing such things, the owner or occupier has exposed the neighborhood to an unreasonable risk of harm.

ANIMALS AS DANGEROUS INSTRUMENTALITIES.   An owner or occupier of land who owns or harbors a hostile animal is subject to the dangerous instrumentality doctrine. This is again on the theory that in bringing such an animal into the neighborhood, the owner has exposed the neighborhood to an unreasonable risk of harm. Such animals would include a lion, tiger, elephant, or bear, as well as certain snakes not indigenous to the neighborhood.

A dog known to the owner to have vicious tendencies, as well as cattle (such as Brahman bulls) in which vicious tendencies are normal, is likewise considered a dangerous instrumentality for the purpose of imposing strict or absolute liability on the owner.

An exception to the rule of absolute liability concerns persons and business enterprises who exercise possession of a wild and dangerous animal in response to a public duty. Such persons or corporations are liable only for their own negligence in allowing such an animal to escape. Such parties could include a municipality operating a public zoo, its employees, or a railroad or express company which is required by law to transport wild animals.

The doctrine of strict liability in respect to the actions of wild animals has been applied to persons or organizations other than the owners or possessors of the wild animals. For example, in Abrevaya v. Palace Theater & Realty Co., 197 N.Y.S. 2d 27, the plaintiff was attending a performance at the defendant's theatre when a monkey, which was part of a performing act, came down into the audience and bit him. Strict liability was imposed on the theatre owner even though he did not own or possess the animal. Also, in Smith v. Jalbert, 221 N.E. 2d 744, a licensor of premises upon which an exposition was conducted was held strictly liable for property damage caused by an escaped zebra owned by one of the exhibitors.

In recent years, it has become a practice among business firms to utilize guard dogs for the purposes of protecting the premises, especially at night. These dogs may be owned by the business firm or by a guard service. Where a person is attacked by the dog and sustains injuries, the injured person, in order to recover, must establish that the dog was vicious. The fact that the dog had previously bitten someone else will be sufficient to establish this. The common-law rule is that a dog is "entitled to one bite." Until the dog has demonstrated vicious tendencies by biting someone else, the owner is not on notice of the vicious character of the animal.

Some states have modified the common-law rule with legislation that imposes on the owner or harborer of the dog strict liability for injuries caused by the dog, regardless of whether the owner knew of the vicious tendencies of the animal or not. These statutes are one of two types. One imposes strict liability only where the dog actually bit a person. The other type applies the rule when a person sustained injuries from an attack by the dog, whether he or she was bitten or not. However, under most statutes, the person injured must establish that he was "peaceably conducting himself in any place where he may lawfully be." This would seem to exclude trespassers from the application of the statute.

Inherently Dangerous Operations Doctrine. The inherently dangerous operations doctrine, which is related to the dangerous instrumentality doctrine, imposes strict liability where the owner or occupier conducts operations on his or her premises which expose the neighbors to an unreasonable chance of harm. An example would be the conducting of blasting operations. Regardless of whether he or she is negligent, the owner or occupier is strictly liable for any injury or damage caused. This is true even though the owner employed a competent contractor to do the work. Since the duty on the part of the owner or occupier is in law nondelegable, the owner or occupier is still strictly liable.

In summary, premises liability may be imposed on the legal grounds of negligence, intentional interference, or strict liability. The application of these principles can be better understood with reference to the specific legal duties which the law requires of the possessor.

Duties of the Possessor of Land

The owner or occupier of land must exercise reasonable care in the maintenance and use of his or her premises and must avoid interfering with the rights of others and subjecting such others to unreasonable risks of harm. The persons to whom these duties are owed will come within one of two general classes: (1) those outside the premises, and (2) those on the premises.

Duties to Those Outside the Premises The duty of care which the possessor of land owes to persons outside the premises consists of maintaining the premises in a manner which will protect such persons from all chance of harm arising from the use of the premises. The persons "outside" the premises include all those who are in the vicinity, either neighboring owners or those using the public streets and sidewalks. Among the specific hazards for which the owner may be liable, in the event of an accident and due to the owner's creation and defective maintenance, are the following.

Signs. In the conduct of certain enterprises, it is necessary for business organizations to erect advertising signs. Some signs are attached to the building itself while others are suspended over the public sidewalk. In erecting the sign, the owner or occupier of the property must exercise care for the safety of others. His or her failure to do so will constitute negligence. In addition, some municipalities regulate the placing of such signs by a city ordinance. Where the owner fails to erect the sign in accordance with the regulations of the city ordinance, and where such failure is the cause of an injury, the owner is negligent and is liable for the injury.

Where a sign is suspended over the public sidewalk or is erected on its own pedestal, the question which always arises is whether or not the sign was erected in such a way that it will withstand the effects of weather. Generally, if the sign will withstand the effects of storms and winds which are prevalent in the area, the owner has met the duty of care. If an unprecedented hurricane or storm should occur and a dislodged sign causes bodily injury or property damage, the unprecedented storm is usually regarded as an "act of God" and the owner is thus insulated from liability. On the other hand, if the sign were erected in the "huricane belt," the owner will be deemed negligent unless the sign can withstand hurricane force winds.

Streets and Sidewalks. The general rule is that the owner or occupier of the abutting premises has no common-law duty to maintain or repair the public streets or the sidewalks adjacent to his or her premises. He or she is liable, however, if he or she creates an unsafe condition on a street or sidewalk and an accident ensues as a result of that condition. Defects in the sidewalk could be caused by subjecting the pavement to extremely heavy weight, as where a truck is driven over the sidewalk or where the delivery of building material obstructs the sidewalk or street. Where the street or sidewalk has been damaged by the owner or occupier, he or she is under a legal duty to correct the defect, and in correcting the defect, must exercise care to be certain that the corrections meet the proper standards. A negligently repaired defect remains a defect which will subject the owner or occupier to liability for any resulting accidents.

As to defects in the streets or sidewalks which are not due to the activity of the owner or occupier, he or she is not subject to liability. Usually, the state or political subdivision having the responsibility will be answerable in damages for such defects, provided that the state, county, township, or municipality has notice of the defect and fails either to repair it or erect barricades which would prevent injury and damage to users of the street or sidewalk.

Snow and Ice. The same rules which apply to defects in the public streets and sidewalks apply to the accumulation of snow and ice thereon. The state or municipality is responsible for the maintenance of the streets and sidewalks; accordingly, the abutting owner or occupier has no responsibility to remove the snow and ice. As a matter of business practice, most business organizations will remove the snow and ice, at least from the sidewalks, and in some cases, they will clear the snow and ice from the street. Having voluntarily assumed the job of such removal, the business is under a duty to exercise care in so doing. Should its removal result in a worsening of the condition, it will be responsible for the worsened condition. The rationale behind this conclusion is that the municipality is responsible for the condition of the streets and sidewalks and their safe condition. Merely to require the abutting owner or occupier to clear the snow under the penalty of a fine for his or her failure to do so does not insulate the municipality from its responsibility.

Should the occupier create an unsafe condition by placing an abnormal amount of water on the street or sidewalk, such as with the use of a poorly located downspout or by operating a car wash, the occupier will be answerable in damages should such unsafe condition result in injury.

In some municipalities there are ordinances which require the abutting owner or occupier to remove the snow and ice from the public sidewalk within twenty-four hours after the snow has stopped falling. In case of the failure of the owner or occupier to so remove the snow and ice, the municipality may do so at the expense of the owner and, in some cases, may also impose a fine. The existence of such ordinances does not change the abutting owner's responsibilities to others who are using the sidewalk and are injured because of the accumulation of snow and ice. The owner or occupier still has no duty to such persons and liability will not be imposed. In a word, the ordinance will not create a liability on the part of the owner or occupier where none existed before.

Parking Lots. Many business enterprises maintain private parking lots for the convenience of their customers. Since these lots are on the premises of the business, and since the business has invited its customers to use such facilities, the business is under a duty to maintain not only the parking lot itself but also the entrance-way. Liability will be imposed where the business has failed to maintain the lot, as well as the entrance-ways from the lot to the main building, in a safe condition. If the business is a tenant, it has all the attributes and responsibilities of an owner.

Pollution. Where the owner intentionally pollutes the air or an adjoining water-way, in violation of the rights of others, or in violation of environmental protection standards, he or she may be guilty of creating and maintaining a nuisance. The persons affected thereby may bring an action for damages, as well as an action for injunctive relief. For a more complete discussion, see Chapter 11.

Natural Conditions of the Land. The general rule is that the owner is not responsible for the existence of natural conditions on his or her land, regardless of whether such conditions interfere with a neighbor's enjoyment of his or her property. Thus, the existence of a swamp or a pond which serves as a breeding ground for insects would not involve any responsibility on the part of the owner to correct or remove the conditions. Likewise, where there is a natural lake on the premises which is used by children or adults for swimming, the owner is under no obligation to provide safeguards or to make any provisions to assure the safety of those using the lake. On the other hand, if the owner is in the business of providing swimming facilities for a charge, then he or she must exercise reasonable care for the safety of the patrons. This duty, which includes the maintenance of all facilities, might even require some dredging of the lake in certain areas.

As to running streams and percolating water (swamps and water under the surface of the land) the owner is under no obligation to others to divert or otherwise dispose of such water even though its existence might impair the use of another's property. The owner may not, however, impair the natural drainage of the land, or he or she will be liable for any damage that such action may cause.

As to trees, the early common-law rule regarded them as natural to the land. Whether they were planted by the occupier or not, there was no liability imposed upon the occupier for any damage their presence may cause. However, there seems to be a different rule emerging, especially as to trees in the city areas. It is probably safe to say now that the original common-law rule has been modified so as to place a duty on the occupier with respect to dangerous trees. Therefore, where a tree is dead or diseased and where it abuts the street and sidewalk or the neighbor's land, the occupier is under a duty to remove it or to take such steps as will avoid the danger of injury or property damage which might ensue should the tree fall.

In some municipalities there are local ordinances with respect to trees which abut the highway. If such trees are in a dangerous condition, the occupier is under a duty to remove them. If he or she fails to do so, the municipality is empowered by the ordinance to remove them at the expense of the occupier.

A different rule seems to be applied to trees in rural areas. Unless the owner or occupier has actual knowledge of the dangerous condition of a tree abutting the highway, he or she is not liable for any injury or property damage which it may cause. The theory behind this ruling is that it would be an extremely heavy burden for the occupier to make periodic inspections of the trees located in large acreages and, therefore, unless the occupier has actual knowledge of the dangerous condition of the tree, he or she is not obligated to remove it or take any remedial steps to avoid the danger.

Duties to Those on the Premises   At common law, persons entering or remaining on the premises of another would fall into one of the three following categories recognized by the majority of courts: (1) business invitees, (2) licensees, or (3) trespassers.

Business Invitees.   The general rule is that a business invitee is one who enters the premises for the business advantage of the occupier and has an express or implied invitation to be there. The visit may also be to the invitee's advantage as well, but the essential ingredient which must be present to classify him or her as an invitee is that the occupier must derive some business advantage from the visit. To an invitee, the occupier owes the following duties:

1. the duty to exercise reasonable care for the safety of the invitee;
2. the duty to warn the invitee of any dangerous conditions which are not open and obvious and of which the owner has knowledge; and
3. the duty to make inspections at reasonable intervals to discover and remedy dangerous conditions which such inspections should reveal.

The failure of the occupier to meet any one of these conditions is negligence, and, in the event of injury, is actionable.

The most common example of an invitee is a person who visits a retail store for the purpose of making a purchase. Regardless of whether a purchase is made, the person is considered an invitee. Persons who accompany a possible purchaser are also invitees in relation to the store owner, on the theory that if such persons were not within the area of invitation, the purchaser might not even enter the store. In all cases of this sort, the courts hold that the store makes an implied invitation for members of the public to enter, examine the goods, and make a purchase, if the goods meet their requirements.

Likewise, persons who enter the premises at the request of the occupier in order to perform some service are all invitees. These could include people making deliveries, mail carriers, meter readers employed by gas, electric, and water companies, garbage collectors, and even tax appraisers and tax collectors. Persons who enter the premises to do repair or alteration work are also invitees. The courts have been extremely liberal in construing the circumstances under which a person can be classified as an invitee. If there is the slightest business advantage which may accrue to the owner as a result of their presence, they are invitees. Thus, friends who visit a tenant in an apartment house are invitees as to the landlord when they are in that portion of the premises under the landlord's control, the theory being that it is to the business advantage of the landlord to have tenants. If they were not permitted to have guests, they would not want to rent the premises. Also, persons who attend free public lectures, church services, or the opening of stores where free gifts are given are all invitees as to the occupier of the premises.

There are certain necessary services which are required by business firms. The business must receive mail, merchandise, and other materials, and also in some cases need to send their finished products by means of a parcel service or express. Persons who render these types of services are all invitees.

Employees of catering firms who provide meals and other food to employees, either under contract or with the permission of the employer, are invitees. Employees of vending machine companies who service the machines on the premises are likewise invitees.

Licensees. A licensee is a person who enters or remains on the premises with the express or implied consent of the owner or occupier and for the licensee's own personal benefit, convenience, or pleasure. To the licensee, the occupier owes no duty of care with respect to correcting a condition of the premises. The licensee takes the premises as he or she finds them and is voluntarily exposed to the same conditions and the same dangers to which the occupier is exposed. The occupier is under no duty to inspect the premises to discover and remedy unsafe conditions, but the occupier does have the duty to warn the licensee of any unsafe or dangerous conditions of which the occupier has knowledge.

Licensees include door-to-door salespersons, solicitors of charitable contributions, persons entering to borrow tools or to pick up refuse and garbage for their own benefit, tourists visiting a plant at their own request, and persons who take a short cut across the land when not specifically prohibited from doing so. A social guest is a licensee, no matter how cordial the invitation may be, and this same rule applies to friends who call on employees of the business firm for purely social purposes.

Trespassers. A trespasser is a person who is making illegal use of another's real property. The possessor has a legally protected right to the exclusive use of his or her property, and no one may enter the premises without his or her consent. Thus, the possessor ordinarily has no duty to make the property safe for the trespasser. Nor does the possessor have any duty to discover the presence of the trespasser, but if the possessor has knowledge of the trespasser's presence, he or she may not take action for the purpose of injuring the trespasser beyond the use of such reasonable force as is necessary to expel him or her from the premises.

In the event that the trespasser sustains injury or death and litigation ensues, the ultimate decision as to whether or not the force which was exerted was reasonable under the surrounding circumstances will be made by the court and jury. If excessive force were used and an injury has been sustained, there will be a verdict in favor of the trespasser. On the other hand, if the jury finds that the amount of force used was reasonable under the circumstances, the trespasser will not recover.

The possessor also may not erect booby traps or other devices which are calculated to injure a trespasser. He or she is liable to the trespasser if such a trap injures the trespasser, even though the trespasser had no legal right to be on the premises. Therefore, the duty of care which might be owed to a trespasser is largely a negative one in the sense that the possessor must refrain from willful, wanton, and intentional misconduct which is calculated to injure the trespasser. However, as discussed later, the degree of care owed to a child trespasser may be rather high under certain circumstances.

Exceptions to the Common-Law Rules. There is some evidence in the reported cases that some states have abandoned the common-law distinction among invitees, licensees, and trespassers, and substituted in its place one duty of reasonable care on the part of the possessor for the safety of all.

In 1968, for example, the Supreme Court of California decided that there was no logical reason for the application of the common-law distinction. In Rowland v. Christian, 70 Cal. Reptr. 97, the court held that, "Everyone is responsible for an injury occasioned to another by his want of ordinary care and skill in the management of his property." The court refused to follow the rigid classifications of licensee, invitee, and trespasser, and substituted instead the following:

> The proper test to be applied to the liability of the possessor of land . . . is whether in the management of his property he has acted as a reasonable man in view of the probability of injury to others, and, although the plaintiff's status as a trespasser, or as a licensee or invitee may in the light of the facts giving rise to such status have some bearing on the question of liability, the status is not decisive.

In 1975, the Supreme Court of Rhode Island in Mariorenzi v. Joseph DiPonte, Inc., 333 Atl. 2d 127, decided to follow the reasoning of the California court. In a case involving a minor trespasser, the court abandoned the classifications of trespasser, licensee, and invitee. The court said:

> As we assign the trichotomy to the historical past, we substitute in its place the basic tort test of reasonableness. Hereafter, the common-law status of an entrant onto the land of another will no longer be determinative of the degree of care owed by the owner, but rather the question to be resolved will be whether the owner has used reasonable care for the safety of all persons reasonably expected to be upon his premises. Evidence of the status of the invitee may have some relevance to the question of liability but it no longer will be conclusive. The traditional tort question of foreseeability will become important.

Other courts have not gone so far as to change the status of a trespasser, but have abandoned the distinction between licensee and invitee, holding that the rule of reasonable care should be applied. The cases involving this rule are: Pickard v. City of Honolulu 452 Pac. 2d 445 (Hawaii); Alexander v. General Ins. Co. 98 So. 2d 730 (Louisiana);

Mounsey v. Ellard 297 NE 2d 43 (Massachusetts); and Genessee Bank v. Payne 148 NW 2d 503 (Michigan).

Connecticut has by statute abolished the distinction between invitees and licensees and substituted the rule of reasonable care for their safety, but has made no change in the rule with relation to trespassers (Conn. Gen. Stat. Ann. 52-557a).

Children. A child may be an invitee, a licensee, or a trespasser, depending upon the circumstances of his or her entry onto the land. If a child of tender years (normally under sixteen years of age) should accompany an adult into a store, the child would have the same status as the adult. If the adult is a patron, both the adult and the child would be classified as invitees. If the adult were a licensee on the premises, the child would have the same status. Where a child is old enough to be out without guidance, he or she could be an invitee, licensee, or trespasser, in the same manner and to the same extent as any adult.

As to trespassing children of tender years, there is one important exception to the general rules, where the owner maintains on the premises artificial conditions which are highly dangerous to children. This is sometimes referred to as the "attractive nuisance" doctrine. The theory is that where the owner creates a condition on his or her premises which the owner knows (or in the exercise of due care, should know) is attractive to children, he or she is under a duty to eliminate the danger. This can sometimes be accomplished by the posting of guards, the erection of fences of sufficient height to keep the children away from the condition, or the removal of the dangerous condition entirely.

The Restatement of the Law of Torts, 2d, Section 339, states the rule as follows:

> A possessor of land is subject to liability for physical harm to children trespassing thereon caused by an artifical condition upon the land if
> (a) the place where the condition exists is one upon which the possessor knows or has reason to know that children are likely to trespass, and
> (b) the condition is one which the possessor knows or has reason to know and which he realizes or should realize will involve an unreasonable risk of death or serious bodily harm to children, and
> (c) the children because of their youth do not discover the condition or realize the risk involved in intermeddling with it or coming within the area made dangerous by it, and
> (d) the utility to the possessor of maintaining the condition and the burden of eliminating them are slight as compared to the risk to children involved, and
> (e) the possessor fails to exercise reasonable care to eliminate the danger or otherwise protect the children.

Note that the doctrine involves a dangerous condition created or maintained by the owner and an injury to trespassing children so young that they are incapable of appreciating the danger. If either element is not present, the doctrine does not apply. Likewise, the doctrine does not apply to natural conditions on the land, regardless of how dangerous such natural conditions may be.

Landlord and Tenant. The landlord and the tenant are both possessors of land, and, as such, have legally recognized duties to the public, to each other, and to any other tenants.

Where the tenant has leased an entire building for a term of years, the tenant is subject to all the duties and liabilities which an owner might have during the term of the lease. On the other hand, where the landlord leases only part of a building and retains other portions of the building, the duties and responsibilities of each are limited to the portions of the building which are under their individual control. For example, where the landlord retains those portions of the building which are not leased, he or she is subject to liability to the general public for any failure to maintain those portions of the premises in reasonably safe condition. Such portions of the building could consist of the roof, the common stairway, entrance-ways, private sidewalks leading to the building, and parking lots if they are the subject matter of the lease. On the other hand, the tenant must maintain his or her own premises in reasonably safe condition for the safety of others who may legally be on his or her part of the premises.

A lease is an instrument in which two parties agree to the occupancy by the tenant of property owned by the landlord in consideration of the payment of rent. A "bare" lease merely transfers possession and nothing more, but the landlord is under a duty to disclose to the tenant any dangerous conditions on the premises of which the landlord has knowledge and which are not open and obvious. However, most leases contain conditions in the agreement which may, in some instances, exculpate the landlord from liability in all matters, create an assumption by the tenant of all liability to the public, and relieve the landlord of any liability the landlord may have to the tenant. In addition, some leases require that the tenant carry public liability insurance listing the landlord as a named insured.

It should be pointed out that the existence of an indemnity agreement between the landlord and tenant, wherein the tenant agrees to indemnify and save harmless the landlord, would have no effect upon the cause of action brought by the injured person against the landlord. The landlord is still liable to the injured person and the judgment will be taken against the landlord. All the typical indemnity agreement does is to provide the landlord with an indemnitor, who will in his or her place defend the action and pay whatever damages are awarded (other types of indemnity agreements are discussed in Chapter 5). If it should happen that the indemnitor-tenant were insolvent, the landlord's liability to the injured person would remain. If judgment were taken, the landlord would be obligated to satisfy it. The only redress available to the landlord would be an action against the tenant for breach of the contract of indemnity.

In the absence of conditions in which the tenant assumes the landlord's liability, the landlord is responsible to the tenant for the maintenance of the roof and the electric and water conduits in the walls and elsewhere, as well as for the safe maintenance of the elevators, stairways, halls, and entrance doors. In addition, the landlord is responsible for the safe maintenance of the private sidewalks, if any, leading to the building, including repair and the clearing of snow and ice.

As to the liability of the tenant to the landlord, the tenant is restricted to whatever uses of the premises are described in the lease. At the termination of the lease, the tenant is obligated to return the premises to the landlord in the same condition as they were received, less ordinary wear and tear. Therefore, under this type of arrangement, the tenant is responsible for repairs to the premises.

In some cases, the landlord will want to make repairs on notice from the tenant that such is necessary. Under those circumstances, the lease will provide that the landlord has a right of entry for the purpose of making such repairs, since ordinarily the landlord has no right to enter the premises for any purpose, during the period of the lease, without the tenant's consent.

As to the tenant's liability to other tenants, ordinarily, there is none unless the tenant is negligent or violates the lease by using the premises for purposes other than provided therein. For example, if a tenant should store flammable material on the premises, either in violation of the lease or in violation of the fire laws, he or she would be liable to other tenants whose property was destroyed should a fire ensue. Clearly, if an accident should occur on one tenant's premises and it is caused solely by the negligence of the tenant, the offending tenant would be subject to liability not only for injury or damage suffered by other tenants, but by the landlord and members of the public as well.

Operations Liability Exposures in General

A business firm is exposed to liability for its operations, whether conducted on the premises or away from the premises. It is under a duty to conduct the operations with reasonable care to avoid injury or property damage to others. Since the duty of care will vary depending upon the type of operations which are being conducted, what might be considered as reasonable care in one type of situation might not be so considered in some others. For example, in the case of a fireworks manufacturer, reasonable care might demand that (1) extreme caution be exercised in order to prevent fire, and (2) fire fighting equipment be readily at hand in case a fire does break out. However, there might be no such requirements in the case of a grocery store operator. Likewise, the construction of a new office building might require the erection of barricades and other safety devices for the protection of the public. Thus, the degree of care which must be exercised is governed by the extent of the risk of harm to which others are exposed. Since many of these duties of care must be delegated to agents or employees, their negligence, if any, is imputed to the principal or employer under the doctrine of *respondeat superior* (let the superior party answer).

Where the operations are conducted away from the premises, such as frequently would be the case with contracts of repair, maintenance, or alteration, the employer is subject to liability for any negligence on the part of its employees if it arises out of and during the progress of the work.

Passenger elevators which are maintained in buildings open to the public, such as apartment houses, stores, hotels, and office buildings, create certain liability problems, largely because it has been held that an elevator is a common carrier of passengers. As such, the owner or operator of the elevator is charged with the duty of exercising the highest degree of care for the safety of the passengers. Therefore, it is almost axiomatic that where the elevator falls, starts suddenly, or stops abruptly, the owner is liable for the resulting injuries. This is especially true when the owner or lessee contracts with a company to install, inspect, or maintain an elevator because the elevator company usually requires a hold harmless agreement from the owner or lessee as a condition precedent to performing such work or service.

In addition to the liability exposures incidental to the use and occupancy of the premises and the operations conducted thereon, as well as those conducted outside of the premises, a business firm may be subject to liability in the following areas.

Operation of Automobiles The business firm may be subject to liability for the negligent operation of automobiles, regardless of whether they are private passenger automobiles or trucks or whether they are owned by or rented to the business firm. For example, an executive or employee of the business organization uses his or her own private passenger automobile on the business of the employer. In the event of an accident, the business firm may be exposed to liability under the doctrine of *respondeat superior*.

Products   Where the firm places a defective product in the stream of commerce, it may be subject to liability if the defect causes injury or property damage to others.

Other possible liability exposures include causes of action arising from slander and libel, unfair competition or the infringement of a copyright or patent.

Premises and Operations Liability as to Specific Business Entities

In applying the general principles of premises and operations liability, the extent of the care which must be exercised differs according to the kind and type of premises and the use to which it is put. The following are illustrative.

Retail Stores   Retail stores which are engaged in the sale of goods and merchandise have various legal duties and are subject to liability in cases where such duties are not met. These duties are owed to all persons who come upon the premises, but the extent of the duty rests on the classification into which the person in question belongs. The great majority of persons who come upon the premises of retail stores are invitees. As previously discussed, invitees are defined as persons who by invitation, express or implied, have been induced by the owner or operator to come upon the premises. To an invitee, remember, the owner owes the duty of (1) maintaining the premises in reasonably safe condition, (2) warning the invitee of any dangerous conditions which are not open and obvious, and (3) making periodic inspections of the premises at reasonable intervals to discover any defects which might cause injury. This third duty is subject to variations. What would be a reasonable interval in one type of store might be unreasonable in others. For example, where the store sells millinery, perhaps once or twice a day might be sufficient to meet this duty. On the other hand, in a vegetable store or a vegetable department of a supermarket where leaves and other debris might fall to the floor on wet spots, then once an hour might be a reasonable interval between inspections. As a matter of practice, many stores keep a record of the time the inspection was made and the name of the employee who made it. Clearly, the floors, aisles, and shelves cannot be kept in safe condition every second. The actions of customers, especially children, may create conditions which are unsafe. For example, a child drops her ice cream cone on the floor and a customer immediately following slips and falls. There ordinarily would be no liability on the part of the store. However, if the ice cream had remained on the floor for an unreasonable period of time, the store would be liable.

In any case, the burden of proof as to the period of time during which the unsafe condition was present is on the person asserting the claim.

The invitee exposure applies only to those portions of the premises which are set aside for the use of customers. It does not apply to areas limited to the use of employees, such as spaces behind counters, employees' rest rooms, or the storage part of the store, which are set apart by doors marked "No Admittance" or "Employees Only." As to those portions of the premises, the customer is a trespasser or at best a bare licensee.

Contractors and Subcontractors A contractor may be defined as one who, for a fixed price, undertakes to procure the performance of works on a large scale for the public, a company, or an individual. He or she may subcontract part of the work to others, but his or her responsibility for the performance of the work to the owner or principal remains the same. Where subcontractors are involved, the first contractor is usually referred to as the "prime" or "general" contractor. The general contractor is one who, in the pursuit of an independent business, undertakes to perform a job or a piece of work, and retains control of the means, method, and manner of accomplishing the desired result. In any case, the general contractor is responsible to the owner or principal for the result, and the owner or principal has no right to interfere with the methods and means of accomplishing the result. Thus, it is the general contractor, not the owner, who is usually liable to others for any injury or property damages sustained as a result of his or her operations and caused by his or her negligence. Similarly, subcontractors are responsible for any injuries or property damage caused by their negligence or the negligence of their employees. This responsibility runs not only to the general public but also to employees of the general contractor and employees of other subcontractors.

The general contractor, having taken possession of the job site and having assumed general supervision over the activities of the subcontractors, is responsible for the maintenance of the job site in reasonably safe condition. This is for the safety of all who are authorized to come on the job, including employees of all subcontractors. His or her failure to meet this duty is actionable if it results in an injury.

The owner of the land, having delegated the authority to the general contractor to complete the job, generally has no responsibility to others as a result of any conditions created by the contractors or the subcontractors, but there are two exceptions. These are the liabilities created by the dangerous instrumentality doctrine and the ultra-hazardous operations doctrine. The first is that the owner who stores (or permits to be stored) on his or her land any dangerous instrumentality such as dynamite, blasting caps, or gasoline, is liable to others who might be injured by the presence of such instrumentalities. Also, if the owner conducts (or authorizes to be conducted) any ultra-hazardous operations on his or her land, such as blasting, the owner is likewise liable to others who may suffer injury or property damage as a consequence of such activity.

In the interests of self-protection, the owner or principal usually insists that the contract contain hold harmless provisions under which the general contractor agrees not only to indemnify the owner or principal, but also agrees to defend any action brought against him or her arising out of such operations, even though such actions may be false, fraudulent, or without merit. Hold harmless arrangements are discussed in detail in Chapter 5.

Manufacturers Not only must the manufacturer maintain his or her premises in reasonably safe condition for the safety of all who may be permitted to enter therein, the manufacturer must also conduct his or her operations in ways which will not interfere with the right of others in the neighborhood to enjoy their property. If he or she should invade the legally protected right of the neighboring property owners, he or she could be held to strict liability for the consequent damage which such may cause. Such invasion might consist of noxious odors, noise, or other types of pollution. The manufacturer is subject to liability for the damages so caused, but may also be enjoined from continuing the operation by means of an action in equity praying for an injunction.

Warehousemen A warehouseman is a bailee for hire. Under his or her contract with the owner of goods, he or she agrees to store and protect the goods for a period in time and to return the goods in the same condition as received. Failure to so return the goods may subject the warehouseman to liability.

The warehouseman is not liable for the safe return of the goods where they have been destroyed or damaged by (1) an act of God, (2) an act of the common enemy, or (3) because of the inherent vice of the goods. An act of God consists of an unusual and unprecedented act of nature which could not be foreseen, such as a tornado in a place not usually subject to tornadoes, or a windstorm of unprecedented velocity. An act of the common enemy would consist of an invasion by hostile forces. Inherent vice refers to the tendency of some goods to deteriorate with the passage of time. The warehouseman is not an insurer of the property and is not liable for the natural and normal deterioration of the goods due to the passage of time.

In spite of the foregoing, there are certain presumptions which are applicable to bailment cases. It is presumed that where the goods are not returned, or are returned in a damaged condition, the bailee was negligent in dealing with the goods. Thus, the bailor or owner of the goods need only to establish (1) the delivery of the goods to the bailee, and (2) the failure of the bailee to return the goods or the bailee's failure to return the goods in the same condition in which they were received. The proof of these two elements makes out a prima facie case, and the burden of establishing that the loss or damage was not due to his or her negligence is on the bailee. Failing in proving that the loss or damage to the goods was not due to his or her negligence will result in a recovery of damages by the owner or bailor.

Recreation Centers   Recreation centers can take various forms. They include amusement parks, bathing beaches, swimming pools, parks for viewing competitive sports, and places of public recreation. Consideration will be given to the duties of possessors in each of these illustrative types of recreation centers.

Amusement Parks.   The owner or operator of an amusement park is under a duty to the public to make thorough and periodic inspections of his or her premises and equipment and to make such prompt repairs as are necessary to insure the safety of patrons. Such an owner also must warn or instruct customers of the dangers which are not open and apparent and, in other situations, he or she must provide warning signs, guard rails, barricades, and a sufficient number of attendants to safeguard the customers. The owner must also have available the proper appliances to rescue patrons from positions of danger. And, finally, he or she must refrain from any acts of negligence on his or her part or on the part of the employees which may cause injury to those properly on the premises.

In amusement park liability situations, there is one departure from the usual imposition of the duties on the owner. In cases where a part of the premises is leased to others, the owner is not liable for injuries which occur after he or she has relinquished control. However, in some states, the owner of the amusement park has been held liable to patrons of the park for injuries caused by the improper maintenance of amusement devices operated by others, as well as a premature explosion of fireworks in charge of an independent operator. Therefore, an injured person may have a cause of action against both the operator of the amusement device and the owner of the amusement park as well. The patron, however, in making use of amusement devices, assumes the chances of injury which might occur during normal operation of the device. The chances are so open and obvious that thrill-seeking customers can reasonably expect to be tossed about or even fall when using the devices.

Bathing Beaches.   The duty of the operator of a bathing beach extends to the proper maintenance of the buildings, bathhouses, and other structures, as well as to maintenance of the depth and purity of the water and the condition of the bottom or things thereon. The operator must also provide warnings, lifeguards, and attendants in sufficient number.

Professional Services and Premises A physician or dentist, in undertaking the treatment of a patient, warrants that he or she will employ skill for the best interests of the patient and that the treatment or operative procedure will meet the standards of medical practice.

When the treatment or operation is conducted at a hospital or sanitarium, it is the duty of the hospital or sanitarium to provide proper medical equipment and facilities for the use of the physician or dentist.

Where defective equipment is furnished and is used by the doctor to the detriment of the patient, the responsibilities of the doctor and the medical institution overlap. Damages could be sought from either.

PREMISES AND OPERATIONS LIABILITY INSURANCE

In view of the nature and the scope of premises and operations liability exposures confronting business entities, it is not difficult to understand why corresponding insurance is so commonly purchased to cover the losses which may result. Indeed, a firm which does not properly diagnose and handle such exposures eventually may be confronted with a loss large enough to impair its very existence.

However, the business or commercial liability insurance contracts in use today are very seldom confined to covering only the "pure" premises and operations liability exposures discussed earlier. To do so would be not only unwise but also impractical, because there is more to premises and liability insurance, in a broader sense, than that which the law imposes upon possessors of land. First of all, products, completed operations, contractual agreements, motor vehicles, aircraft, and workers' compensation exposures are as much a part of the activities of entities in furthering their business interests as the exposures associated with the physical hazards of premises per se. Moreover, in spite of the fact that exposures such as those attributable to products, motor vehicles, and contractual agreements are treated by the insurance industry under separate, ratable insurance coverages, it is often difficult to isolate such exposures from premises and operations exposures, in the pure or narrower sense.

For example, premises and operations liability insurance, as provided under most commercial liability policies, includes a certain amount of coverage for liability stemming from products. Normally, a given loss is considered by insurers to be one of "products" liability (1) if loss occurs after physical possession of the product has been relinquished, and (2) if the injury occurs away from premises of the vendor (except in the case of restaurants, where it is required only that the products have been physically relinquished). So, a store owner would be protected under premises and operations liability insurance if a customer were injured by a product on the store premises. But the off-premises products liability exposure of entities is covered by separate products liability insurance, which is available for an additional charge.

Premises and operations liability insurance also provides at least some coverage, necessarily, for exposures such as completed operations, contractual liability, motor vehicles, aircraft, and professional liability, which overlap with the premises exposure, in some respects, but which will be dealt with in later chapters.[2]

Standard Liability Forms

Various liability forms are available to fit the needs of commercial entities.[3] Some are standard, whereas others are nonstandard in nature. Standard forms are sometimes referred to as bureau forms because their provisions are drafted by an organization such as the Insurance Services Office (ISO) and are recommended for use by insurers which are members or subscribers to the organization.[4] They are "standard" in the sense that the language of the policy provisions is the same regardless of insurer. For example, the same standard liability policy written by an insurer of a hotel in Kentucky can be used by another insurer of a hotel in Arizona. In each instance, the "basic" standard provisions of these two policies, i.e., insuring agreements, exclusions and conditions, are the same.[5]

Advantages of Standard Forms and Provisions A number of advantages are derived by insurers, regulatory officials, and insurance buyers from standard forms and provisions. Standard forms provide the benefits of court-tested language, written by bureau personnel who have expertise in the matter of policy language. When premium and loss statistics are compiled from a variety of insurers using the same form, they form a meaningful basis for rate adjustments. The provisions of two or more standard forms applying to one business firm are more compatible and less likely to create nonconcurrencies of coverage or so-called "coverage gaps" than a mix of standard and nonstandard forms written for one business. In addition, the use of standard forms greatly simplifies the selling of insurance.

Disadvantages of Standard Forms and Provisions Standard forms are somewhat inflexible. Despite a variety of broad, standard coverages suitable to some businesses, many increasingly sophisticated corporate risk managers and large brokerage and consulting firms desire special coverage to meet their special needs. Most insurers are unwilling to modify the coverage of standard forms by making special concessions, such as deleting the fellow employee exclusion. Insurers selling standard forms find that their product is the same as that of the competition, and they find themselves forced to compete on the basis of price and service.

For such reasons, there is a trend today toward increased use of nonstandard liability forms. Producers and risk managers are demanding broader coverage; companies find it advantageous to compete by offering broader coverage.

Nonstandard Liability Forms

Nonstandard liability forms are especially prevalent among commercial package policy programs independently filed by domestic insurers. Although such policies may contain much of the language used in standard forms, there may be notable differences. Other nonstandard liability forms are used by domestic insurers to fulfill special needs, such as products withdrawal coverage, discussed in Chapter 4, or data processing errors and omissions coverage, discussed in Chapter 11.

Nonstandard liability forms are also available through the excess and surplus market. Such coverage is not necessarily broad in scope, but may afford the opportunity to obtain special forms of protection, excess limits of liability, or certain coverages which are not available through normal markets. Besides offering variations of the OL&T, M&C, and CGL policies discussed later in this chapter, the excess and surplus market makes available coverage for such exposures as professional liability of accountants, architects, hospitals, engineers, pension trustees, and a host of other professions; products liability and products warranty coverage; off-shore drilling, oil well, and petroleum refinery liability; pollution liability; advertisers' liability for radio and television stations; patent infringement liability; directors' and officers' liability; and railroad liability.

"Manuscript" policies are sometimes drafted from scratch by the buyer and insurer for larger corporate accounts. Some such manuscript policies contain a mix of new and older versions of standard liability provisions. Others include provisions and terminology which are entirely foreign to standard forms.

Nature and Scope of Standard Policy Provisions

Despite the growing importance of nonstandard liability forms, the bulk of this discussion will be devoted to the nature and the scope of premises and operations coverages of standard liability forms. A basic understanding of standard forms is important in its own right. It also will be a good foundation for grasping the underlying nature and purpose for nonstandard forms of coverage, and it will set the stage for noting such major differences in the nonstandard forms as space limitations will permit.

Essential Components of a Standard Liability Policy A standard liability policy comprises two essential components: a policy jacket and a coverage part. The policy jacket contains a declarations page which describes pertinent information about the nature of the insured business. The jacket also contains the following provisions which are common to all liability coverages: (1) a supplementary payments section, which includes coverage agreements concerning defense costs and other kindred expenses incurred by an insured following loss; (2) definitions of the common terms; and (3) general conditions on such matters as other insurance, cancellation, and the duties of an insured in the event of loss. The coverage part contains a so-called "schedule of hazards" which lists appropriate manual classifications of liability exposures, the rating basis, rates, and premiums. The coverage part also contains the insuring agreements, exclusions, additional definitions, and conditions which are peculiar to the coverage being provided. Among the coverage parts available to business firms are comprehensive general liability (CGL), owners, landlords, and tenants (OL&T), manufacturers and contractors (M&C), owners and contractors protective (OCP), completed operations and products liability, storekeepers liability (SL), and garage liability (GL).[6]

As a basis for a more uniform discussion of liability coverage provisions in this chapter and in subsequent ones, the approach chosen here is to describe the major sections of the policy jacket.

Standard Policy Jacket Provisions The provisions of the policy jacket which are explained in subsequent pages are the supplementary payments, conditions, and definitions of terms which have a direct bearing on *premises and operations coverages*. As the discussion of other liability provisions, such as contractual and products liability, proceeds in subsequent chapters, pertinent definitions of terms and other provisions of the policy jacket will be handled as they appear.

Supplementary Payments. The insurer agrees, under the supplementary payments provision of the policy jacket, to pay the following expenses and other costs in addition to the applicable limits of liability of the policy:

1. All expenses incurred by the insurer and all costs assessed against the insured in any suit which is defended by the insurer. Also, all interest which accrues on the entire amount of any court award, after such an award is made but before the insurer pays, tenders or deposits that part of the award which does not exceed the limit of the insurer's liability. (Note that the interest is payable on the entire judgment, even if the judgment exceeds the limit of liability. However, the ultimate judgment amount payable by the insurer is confined to its limit of liability.)

2. Premiums on appeal bonds which may be required in any suit, and premiums on bonds to release attachments, provided the bond penalty does not exceed the applicable limits of liability.[7] Also, the costs of any bail bonds required of the insured following an accident or a traffic violation and arising out of the use of any vehicle to which this policy applies. However, compensable costs are limited to $250 per bail bond, and the insurer is under no obligation *to apply for or to furnish* the bail bonds or the appeal and release of attachment bonds.

3. Expenses incurred by the insured for first aid to others at the time of an accident for bodily injury which is covered by the policy. (If a restaurant is without products liability insurance and its owner incurs first aid expenses because a customer is taken ill following the consumption of food on premises, such expenses are not covered.)

4. Reasonable expenses incurred by the insured in assisting the insurer in the investigation or the defense of any claim or suit. Such expenses must be incurred at the insurer's request and they include actual loss of an insured's earnings up to a maximum of $25 per day.

While some of the supplementary payments discussed above involve expenses which are incurred in the defense of an insured, the basic obligation of an insurer to defend an insured appears within the insuring agreements of each coverage part. The purpose of this format is to relate the insurer's defense obligations more closely to the coverages in question.

Definitions. The terms which are defined in the definitions section of the policy jacket often appear in boldface type within the policy jacket and within appropriate provisions of the coverage parts. Thus, when a boldface term appears within the provisions of a coverage part, one need only refer to the definition of the term in the policy jacket to determine its meaning.

The terms which must be understood in any analysis of premises and operations coverages of the CGL, OL&T, M&C, SL, and GL coverage parts are: automobile, mobile equipment, bodily injury, property damage, elevator, incidental contract, insured, named insured, occurrence, and policy territory. Each of these terms will be defined and explained below and, as necessary, in appropriate areas of later pages.

AUTOMOBILE. The meaning of automobile is especially important to the premises and operations provisions of the coverage parts, because almost all automobile liability exposures are excluded. The term "automobile" is defined as "a land motor vehicle, trailer or semitrailer designed for travel on public roads (including any machinery or apparatus attached thereto), but does not include mobile equipment."[8] While the precise meaning of an automobile hinges on the definition of "mobile equipment," note that an automobile, as a land motor vehicle designed for public road travel, does not include aircraft, watercraft, locomotives operated on rails, and self-propelled equipment not designed for road travel, such as contractors' cranes and bulldozers, even though the latter equipment travels on public roads. On the other hand, the term "automobile" is not limited to four-wheel vehicles, as is the case under many personal automobile policies which are designed to cover private passenger automobiles. Thus, an automobile, as defined in the policy jacket, can consist of vehicles with one or more wheels, as well as land vehicles operated on treads if they do not otherwise qualify as mobile equipment. Note, finally, that machinery or apparatus which is attached (towed or carried) to a land motor vehicle is deemed to be as much a part of the automobile liability exposure as the powered unit that conveys such machinery or apparatus.

MOBILE EQUIPMENT. The definition of "mobile equipment" is important, because the liability exposure of any land vehicle which qualifies as such equipment is automatically covered under the premises and operations provisions of the various coverage parts. To qualify as mobile equipment, a land vehicle, whether or not self-propelled, must come within *one* of four categories, as follows:

1. land vehicles not subject to motor vehicle registration;
2. land vehicles which are maintained for use exclusively on owned or rented premises of the named insured, including the ways immediately adjoining such premises;
3. land vehicles which are designed for use principally off public roads; or
4. land vehicles which are designed or maintained for the sole purpose of conveying equipment which either forms an integral part of the land vehicle or is permanently attached to such vehicle.

Among the types of equipment specifically listed in the definition are power cranes, shovels, concrete mixers (other than the mix-in-transit type), road construction equipment, welding and building cleaning equipment, and well servicing equipment.

To illustrate how the definition of mobile equipment works, assume a firm is in the business of sandblasting buildings. It owns a truck which is used for transporting building cleaning equipment that is permanently attached to the truck. The truck is licensed and is operated on public roads while going from one job site to another. If this vehicle is to qualify as mobile equipment, it must fall into one of the four categories above. Note that because the truck is licensed and is operated on public roads, it does not meet the first three categories. But, because that truck is designed or maintained for the sole purpose of conveying building cleaning equipment, it qualifies as mobile equipment. Accordingly, the liability insurance for the truck, as mobile equipment, is provided by the premises and operations coverage under the various coverage parts, and automobile liability insurance on the truck is not necessary.

BODILY INJURY. The term "bodily injury" is defined, in brief, to mean bodily injury, sickness, or disease sustained by any person during the policy period, including death which results at any time. An important point about this definition is that bodily injury, sickness, or disease must occur during the policy period, while any death resulting from injury, sickness or disease is covered whenever it occurs, even after expiration of the policy term. The only criterion for coverage is that such death result from an injury, sickness or disease which occurred during the policy period. However, damages resulting from such things as invasion of privacy or slander are not encompassed by the definition of bodily injury liability. Coverage for the latter kinds of intentional interference torts is obtainable by purchasing "personal injury" liability insurance, which may be added to almost any type of commercial liability policy.[9]

PROPERTY DAMAGE. Covered losses to others resulting from "property damage," as defined in the policy jacket, include those involving (1) physical injury to or destruction of tangible property that occurs during the policy period, (2) any loss of use of tangible property resulting from property that is physically damaged, regardless of when it occurs, and (3) loss of use of tangible property which has not been physically damaged or destroyed, provided the loss of use is "caused by an occurrence" during the policy period.

An example of a property damage loss of the first type is the demolition contractor who physically damages an adjoining building. Following damage, it is discovered that the adjoining building was rendered structurally unsound and has to be repaired over a period of one year. Any loss of use resulting therefrom, such as the interruption of business sustained by occupants of that building, also is considered to be a property damage loss. An example of a loss involving the third type of covered loss is the demolition contractor whose crane topples onto a main thoroughfare. Although the accident does not physically damage any property, access to several businesses is prohibited or inhibited until the crane can be removed. Any interruption of business sustained by those affected by the incident is considered to be loss of use of tangible property (the business establishments) that has not been physically injured or destroyed. However, the covered loss in this third situation must be "sudden and accidental" and occur during the policy period.

Note that in all three examples the property was tangible in nature. To be covered, any physical injury or any loss of use giving rise to damages must first involve tangible property. Loss to intangible property, such as loss of goodwill or loss of profits, is not covered, unless tangible property somehow is involved in the loss.

ELEVATOR. The definition of "elevator" is treated at length in the policy jacket. In brief, an elevator means any hoisting or lowering device to connect floors or landings, including its appliances, such as any car, platform, stairway, power equipment, or machinery. However, an elevator does not include (1) an automobile servicing hoist, (2) a hoist without mechanical power and without a platform which is used outside a building, (3) a material hoist which is used in alteration, construction, or demolition operations, (4) an inclined conveyor used exclusively for conveying property, and (5) a dumbwaiter which has a compartment height not exceeding four feet.

The meaning of "elevator" is not as important as it once was to insurers, especially since coverage on the liability exposures of elevators is now automatically provided under the premises and operations feature of most coverage parts. Nonetheless, its definition is pertinent for three reasons. First, the almost universal exclusion of liability for damage to property in the care, custody, or control of an insured does not apply to accidents occurring on elevators.[10] Second, the definition is broad enough to include passenger escalators; however, passenger escalators are subject to an additional premium if coverage is desired against their liability exposures. And third, state laws usually require the safety inspection of elevators at certain specified intervals. While state inspectors can perform that service, some insurers also will inspect them for an additional charge.

INCIDENTAL CONTRACT. Generally, protection for liability contractually assumed by a firm must be separately covered for an additional premium. However, certain of the contractual liability exposures that will be discussed in Chapter 5—the so-called incidental contracts—are automatically covered under most commercial liability forms. The term incidental contract is defined in the policy jacket to mean any *written* (1) lease agreement; (2) easement agreement, except one concerning construction or demolition work on or adjacent to railroad property; (3) agreement required by municipalities, except an agreement required in connection with work for municipalities; (4) railroad sidetrack agreement; or (5) elevator maintenance agreement. The following are specific illustrations of the types of written agreements considered to be incidental contracts and therefore covered under premises and operations insurance.

1. Lease of premises. Landlords commonly require tenants to enter into written leases before the tenant is permitted to occupy the property. Leases not only specify conditions dealing with rental or lease arrangements, but also specify the respective responsibilities of landlords and of tenants for such obligations as alterations, repairs, general upkeep, the payment of utilities, and damages caused by neglect. For example, a firm, as a tenant or a lessee, may agree to hold the landlord harmless, under a written lease agreement, for any bodily injury or property damage arising from any physical defects of the premises or from any negligent operations within that firm's control.[11] The liability so assumed by the tenant automatically would be covered under its premises and operations liability insurance (and most other commercial liability forms).

2. Easements. Although easements involve a variety of legal complexities, they can be simply defined as limited rights to use land belonging to others. Such rights can benefit owners and users, or only users. An example of the former are owners who contribute portions of their land to construct a common thoroughfare to be used by them. An example of the latter is the right-of-way on property owned by a township that gives the public access to a body of water. Another is the use of private land by a public utility for maintenance of an underground natural gas pipeline. When an entity agrees, in writing, to hold an owner of property harmless for any liability that may result from the user's negligence, any such negligence resulting in loss is automatically covered under virtually any commercial liability policy the entity carries. This is unless the easement agreement is required in connection with any construction or demolition operations on or adjacent to any railroad, in which case additional contractual liability coverage must be obtained.

3. Agreements required by municipalities. Municipalities often have ordinances requiring other entities to hold the municipali-

ties harmless for any liability stemming from devices or obstructions which can cause bodily injury or property damage to members of the public. A store owner, for example, often will be required to enter into an agreement if he or she desires to erect a sign or a canopy which will hang over a public walkway. The owner agrees, in writing, to hold the city harmless for any claims that may arise because of that sign or canopy.[12] Such assumed liability automatically is covered as long as the indemnification is required by a municipal ordinance. However, if work is to be performed for a municipality and a hold harmless agreement is required, separate contractual liability insurance must be purchased to cover the work exposure.

4. Sidetrack agreements. Railroads often require business firms, as a condition precedent to installing sidetracks or spurs to facilitate private operations, to hold them harmless from losses arising from the use of such railroad property. Such agreements also may hold firms responsible for any damage to the property itself. A wholesale distribution firm, for example, that desires a railroad sidetrack to its premises in order to load or unload goods from boxcars is automatically covered against the assumption of such liability as it may have assumed under a written contract.

5. Elevator maintenance agreements. Building owners or lessees are frequently required to hold harmless firms which install and/or service elevators, in the event of any claim stemming from an elevator. The resulting contractual liability of the owner or lessee is covered automatically, having been assumed under an incidental contract. Note that escalator maintenance agreements would also be considered incidental contracts because of the broad definition of "elevator."

INSURED. As defined in the policy jacket, insured means any person or entity which qualifies as an insured within the "persons insured" provisions of the respective coverage parts. While each of the liability coverage parts has its own "persons insured" provisions, they are identical for the CGL, OL&T, and M&C coverage parts.

The term "persons insured" means the following persons and/or firms:

1. An individual, when such person is designated in the policy declarations as the named insured, but only to the extent of that person's business conducted as a sole proprietorship.

2. A partnership or joint venture, when such firm is designated in the policy declarations as the named insured, including any partner's or member's liability during the conduct of a partnership or joint venture.

3. Any organization other than a sole proprietorship, partnership, or joint venture, such as a corporation or unincorporated association, when such organization is designated in the policy declarations as the named insured, including the liability of any executive officer, director, or stockholder while such person is acting within the scope of his or her duties.[13]
4. Any person or organization while acting as a real estate manager for the named insured, other than employees of the named insured.[14]

The "persons insured" provision also contains a so-called "omnibus clause" which designates those who are and are not considered to be insureds while operating mobile equipment registered under any motor vehicle registration law for purposes of locomotion upon public highways.[15] Those who are considered as persons insured in these circumstances are:

(A) any employee of the named insured while operating such mobile equipment in the course of his or her employment, and
(B) any other person who is operating such mobile equipment of the named insured, as well as any person or organization which is legally responsible for such operation, but only when such person or organization in the latter circumstance has no valid *and* collectible insurance, whether on a primary or excess basis.

However, a person is not considered to be an insured while operating mobile equipment of the named insured on public highways in circumstances involving:

(A) bodily injury to any fellow employee who is injured during the course of his or her employment, or
(B) property damage to property owned by, rented to, in the charge of, or occupied by the named insured or by an employer of any person who is operating such mobile equipment of the named insured.[16]

Coverage of the CGL form (or whatever form applies) does not apply to bodily injury or property damage which arises out of the conduct of any partnership or joint venture of which an insured is a partner or member, when such partnership or joint venture is not designated in the policy as the named insured. The purpose of this provision, as noted earlier, is to prevent covering a liability exposure which is not contemplated by the basic premium charge of the policy. If coverage is desired for additional partnerships or joint ventures that arise during the policy period, they must be specifically declared and added to the policy by endorsement.

The definition of the term "insured" in the policy jacket also states:

"The insurance afforded applies separately to each insured against whom claim is made or suit is brought, except with respect to the limits of the company's liability."[17] This quoted provision, commonly referred to as the "severability" clause, serves to clarify that each person or entity which seeks protection, as an insured, will be protected as if each of them has separate coverage under the policy. So, if one insured is determined to be without coverage, this has no effect on other insureds seeking protection. However, the limits of liability are not cumulative, regardless of the number of different insureds which may be involved in any one claim or suit.[18]

NAMED INSURED. The term "named insured" means the person or entity named in the policy declarations. The named insured can include an individual, a partnership, a corporation, or an unincorporated association. It could also include two or more partnerships which are involved in a joint venture, a parent company and its subsidiaries, or a corporation and the individual shareholders who have a controlling interest.[19] The important point is that each such person or entity must be specifically designated in the policy declarations if they are to be covered as named insureds. If a corporation acquires a subsidiary company during the policy period, for example, the subsidiary is not automatically protected. The subsidiary must be declared to the insurer and listed on the policy as an additional named insured.

OCCURRENCE. "Occurrence" is defined to mean "an accident, including continuous or repeated exposure to conditions, which results in bodily injury or property damage neither expected nor intended from the standpoint of the insured."[20] Note that an occurrence can be any adverse condition that continues over a long period and eventually results in bodily injury or property damage, or it can be an event that occurs suddenly. In either case, the resulting bodily injury or property damage must be "neither expected nor intended from the standpoint of the insured." Thus, if a firm has a serious premises liability hazard and fails to take steps to eliminate it, any subsequent bodily injury or property damage loss could conceivably be denied as not coming within the definition of an occurrence.[21]

POLICY TERRITORY. The policy jacket definition of "policy territory" consists of three sections. The first two concern the territorial scope of all liability exposures. The third one is limited to the policy territory of products liability exposures, which will be discussed fully in Chapter 4.

As defined in the first two sections, "policy territory" means: "the United States of America, its territories, possessions, or Canada, or international waters or air space, provided the bodily injury or property damage does not occur in the course of travel or transportation to or from any other country, state or nation."[22]

The quoted definition makes coverage applicable while an insured is upon international waters or in air space between the United States and its territories, possessions, or Canada, between the continental United States and Hawaii or Alaska, or between the United States, its territories, possessions, or Canada and off-shore towers, regardless of their location in international waters. However, no coverage applies during the course of travel or transportation between two foreign countries, between the United States and a foreign country, other than Canada, or between Canada and a foreign country.

Policy Jacket Conditions. There are twelve conditions within the policy jacket. They are all important, but space limitations will permit only a brief summary of each.

PREMIUM. In the premium condition, the statement is made that all premiums are to be computed in accordance with the insurer's rules, rates, rating plans, premiums, and minimum premiums. The named insured also must maintain such records as are necessary for premium computations. Also, the "advance premium" is merely a deposit premium. The final earned premium is to be determined by audit at the end of the policy period.

INSPECTION AND AUDIT. The inspection and audit condition puts special stress on disclaiming any implication that an inspection constitutes an undertaking, on behalf of or for the benefit of the insured or others, to determine or warrant that property or operations are safe. It also stipulates that the insurer shall be permitted to examine and audit the named insured's books and records at any time during the policy period.

FINANCIAL RESPONSIBILITY LAWS. The purpose of the condition entitled "financial responsibility laws" is to certify that the policy will meet the requirements of any motor vehicle responsibility law which requires proof of financial responsibility. For example, a firm whose automobile is involved in an out-of-state accident may be required to show proof of insurance for at least the minimum limits of liability required by the state wherein the accident occurred. If the financial responsibility limits to be certified are higher than the limits specified on the firm's policy, the higher limits nonetheless shall apply. However, it is further stipulated that the insured shall reimburse the insurer for any payment which is made in excess of the specified policy limits. There are two reasons why the financial responsibility condition appears in the policy jacket per se. A coverage part concerning automobile liability insurance may be attached to the policy jacket, and there may be times when an insured needs certification of financial responsibility for mobile equipment that is operated on public roads.

INSURED'S DUTIES IN THE EVENT OF OCCURRENCE, CLAIM OR SUIT.   It is a condition of the policy that in the event of an occurrence, the insured will give the insurer written notice as soon as practicable, as well as particulars concerning time, place, and circumstances of any loss. In the event of claim or suit, the insured agrees to forward every demand, notice, or summons immediately to the insurer, and to cooperate and assist the insurer in attending hearings and in making settlements.

ACTION AGAINST COMPANY.   Sometimes an insured may wish to bring an action against his or her own insurer. This is not permissible until the insured is in full compliance with all terms of the policy, or until the amount of the insured's obligations have been determined, either by judgment after trial or by written agreement of the insured, claimant or insurer. The condition also makes it clear that bankruptcy or insolvency of the insured or of the insured's estate will not relieve the insurer of its obligations.

OTHER INSURANCE.   The purpose of the condition entitled "other insurance" is to specify how an insurer will contribute to the payment of loss when an insured has more than one applicable policy. When the insurance of the coverage part attached to the policy jacket is on a "primary basis," the applicable limit will be paid without requiring any contribution from another insurer whose limits are stated to be excess or contingent upon the absence of other applicable insurance. But, if all policies are written on the same basis, i.e., all primary, all excess, or all contingent, settlement will be made in one of the following two ways:

1. If all policies provide for "contribution by equal shares," each insurer will contribute equally to the loss until the limit of liability of the lowest policy is reached or the loss is paid. For example, assume Company Y provides limits of $100/100/300 ($100,000 per occurrence bodily injury, $100,000 per occurrence property damage, $300,000 aggregate property damage).[23] Company Z provides limits of $50/50/100, and a $25,000 bodily injury liability judgment is rendered against the insured who has insurance with the aforementioned companies. Under contribution by equal shares, each insurer will contribute equally up to the lowest applicable limit or the amount of loss, whichever is the lesser of the two. In this case, since the $25,000 loss is less than the lowest applicable limit ($50,000), each insurer will contribute $12,500. Going one additional step, assume the same limits as above but a bodily injury liability judgment of $125,000. In this situation, Company Z will pay $50,000, which is

its maximum limit, and Company Y will pay the remaining $75,000.

2. If all policies do not provide for contribution by equal shares, e.g., one policy provides for contribution by equal shares and the other provides for contribution by limits, settlement will be made on the basis of "contribution by limits." This means that each insurer's contribution will be calculated on the basis of the ratio between its limit and the total limit of all valid and collectible insurance. For example, assume that Company A provides limits of $50/25/50 and Company B provides limits of $100/100/300. The judgment amount for a bodily injury liability loss is $54,000. The apportionment is as follows: since Company A's limit is $50,000 and the total limit of both policies for bodily injury is $150,000 ($50,000 Company A and $100,000 Company B), Company A is liable for $50,000/$150,000 of the $54,000 loss or $18,000. Company B, on the other hand, is liable for the remainder of the loss or $36,000.

SUBROGATION. In the event that any payment is made by the insurer in a situation where another person's tortious conduct contributed to the loss, it is a condition of the subrogation clause that the insurer may, to the extent of its payment, take over its insured's right of recovery against that negligent third party. If a judgment award were to exceed the insurer's limit of liability, the insurer may exercise its right of subrogation in an attempt to recover the amount of its payment, and the insured also may proceed against the negligent third party in an attempt to recover at least a portion of any amount the insured had to pay in excess of the insurer's limit of liability.

CHANGES. It is a further condition that the terms of the policy may not be waived or changed except by endorsement attached to the policy. Also, any notice to or knowledge by the agent or any other person concerning a change has no effect on the policy and does not prevent the insurer from exercising any of its rights.

ASSIGNMENT. It is a condition of the "assignment" clause that any assignment of interest under this policy is not binding without the insurer's consent. However, in the event of the named insured's death, coverage applies to the named insured's legal representative or to a person who has temporary custody of the named insured's property until a legal representative is appointed and qualifies for that role.

THREE YEAR POLICY. The "three year policy" condition is to the effect that if a policy is written for a period of three years, any limit stated in the policy as an "aggregate" shall apply separately to each consecutive annual period.[24]

CANCELLATION. Under the "cancellation" provision, the named insured is given the right to cancel his or her policy at any time by mailing notice to the insurer and specifying when cancellation is to be effective. The insurer also has a right of cancellation, if not otherwise prohibited by law. However, the insurer must specify when, not less than ten days following the mailing of its notice to the named insured, cancellation is to be effective. When the named insured requests cancellation, the insurer's earned premium is calculated on a "short-rate" basis, and when the insurer requests cancellation, its earned premium is calculated on a pro rata basis. The difference between a short-rate and a pro rata cancellation is that the former includes a penalty.

DECLARATIONS. The named insured agrees, under the final condition in the policy jacket, that (1) all statements made in the policy declarations are considered to be the named insured's agreements and representations, and (2) the policy is issued in reliance of those representations.

With an understanding of the policy jacket provisions, one now can gain a better insight into the provisions of the various liability coverage parts. Since the CGL coverage part is considered to be the broadest of the standard liability coverages for nonautomobile liability exposures, its basic characteristics, premises and operations coverages, and exclusions will be discussed first. Then, the basic characteristics of the OL&T, M&C, storekeepers, and garage liability coverage parts will be described briefly, as will the differences among the premises and operations features of the various coverage parts.

Comprehensive General Liability Coverage Part

The CGL coverage part, though not an all-encompassing form of coverage, has two general characteristics which make it the broadest of all standard liability forms currently available. First, it automatically provides coverage for more liability exposures than most other coverage parts. The covered exposures are (1) premises and operations, (2) owners and contractors protective, meaning the vicarious liability of a business owner or a contractor for the negligent acts or omissions of others, (3) products liability, and (4) completed operations. Second, it not only covers whatever insurable exposures are known and specified at policy inception, but it also covers any insurable exposures that may arise during the policy period, within the policy territory.

The two principal determinants of the CGL coverage part's scope are its insuring agreement and its exclusions (the latter of which are discussed later). An insurer basically makes two promises under the CGL insuring agreement:

(1) to pay on behalf of the insured all sums which the insured shall become legally obligated to pay as damages because of bodily injury or property damage to which this insurance applies, caused by an occurrence, and

(2) to defend any suit against the insured seeking damages on account of such bodily injury or property damage, even if any of the allegations of the suit are groundless, false or fraudulent, and may make such investigation and settlement of any claim or suit as it deems expedient.[25]

Of importance in (1) above is the phrase "to which this insurance applies," because an insurer does not have to fulfill its promise if the loss otherwise is excluded. And, in (2) above, an insurer is obligated to defend its insured even if any of the allegations are "groundless, false or fraudulent," so long as the claimant alleges a commission of a tort which is covered. For example, if a claimant were to allege damages because of an insured's slanderous remarks, no defense need be provided, since slander is an intentional tort which is not encompassed by the term "bodily injury." In order to have defense coverage here, an insured needs personal injury liability coverage of the type which is discussed later. However, if a claimant alleges a commission of a tort which is covered, an insurer is obligated to provide the defense.

The insuring agreement of the CGL coverage part (and all the other coverage parts, for that matter) also contains a provision which states that an insurer is not obligated to pay any claim or to defend any suit after the insurer's limit of liability has been exhausted by the payment of any judgments or settlements. Thus, suppose an insured is confronted with two concurring premises bodily injury liability suits brought by separate claimants but for damages arising from a single covered occurrence. If settlement of the first suit exhausts the limit of liability, the second suit need not be defended by the insurer. But, if the two bodily injury liability suits were to arise from separate occurrences, both would have to be defended, even if the first suit exhausts the limit of liability, because there is no provision in liability coverage parts which requires a reduction of limits following the payment of any claim, suit or settlement.[26]

Since the CGL insuring agreement (and the insuring agreements of other coverage parts) applies only to insurance which is provided, and premises and operations coverage is automatically included, the next step is to determine the extent of premises and operations protection under the CGL coverage part.

Premises and Operations Coverages Despite the fact that premises and operations coverages are automatically included in the

CGL coverage part, it is necessary that the premises or the operations exposure, as it is known to exist at policy inception, be indicated in the declarations. While bodily injury coverage may be purchased without property damage coverage (the latter cannot be purchased without the former), most insureds obtain both coverages.

Because the insurer makes the promise, under the insuring agreement of the CGL coverage part, to protect the insured for all damages involving bodily injury or property damage which is caused by an occurrence, without defining the terms "premises" or "operations," there is no limit to the number and kinds of premises or operations liability exposures which can be covered during the course of the policy period. In fact, an advantageous feature of the CGL policy is that any expansion of operations, during the policy period, is covered automatically, so long as an operation is within the policy territory. Furthermore, it makes no difference whether the additional exposures are related to the type of business that is initially insured or not. A firm can go into an entirely different business and still have coverage for its newly acquired premises and operations exposures under the CGL policy. Additional premiums, of course, will be required at policy expiration upon audit. Thus, if a store owner acquires additional locations during the policy period, these locations must be specified in the policy at renewal, but the premiums on them will be charged retroactively to the time when they were acquired. In the meantime, coverage is provided automatically without the necessity of reporting or describing the newly acquired locations until policy renewal. When a business is rated on a payroll basis, the premium charges likewise will reflect any additional payrolls during the expiring policy period for new operations. Also, the additional payroll and the locations of new operations must be declared on the renewal policy.

The coverage of the CGL policy, for premises and operations liability exposures which are known to exist at policy inception and which may arise during the policy period, is considered to be broad in scope, because all such exposures are considered to be covered, unless they otherwise are excluded. This coverage approach of the CGL policy (and other commercial liability policies) therefore corresponds to the way coverage is provided by property insurance policy which is written on an "all-risks" basis. Accordingly, the exclusions are of special importance in understanding the coverages that may apply.

Reasons for Exclusions Basically, exclusions under general liability policy provisions apply for three reasons.

1. They eliminate exposures that require additional premiums, such as those associated with most contractual liability assumptions and liquor liability.

2. They eliminate exposures that are customarily covered under other policies. Examples are most automobile, aircraft, and watercraft, workers' compensation and employers' liability, nuclear energy, and products recall exposures.
3. They eliminate exposures which normally are not considered insurable, such as fellow employee suits, war, insurrection, pollution or contamination, and faulty workmanship.

Exclusions of the CGL Coverage Part. The CGL coverage part contains more exclusions than most other liability coverage parts, with the possible exception of the garage liability form, because the CGL form covers more exposures. While space does not permit a comprehensive examination of each exclusion and exception under the CGL coverage part, all of them will at least be noted in summary fashion. The exclusions which apply to other liability exposures, e.g., products liability, completed operations, and workers' compensation, will be referenced to the appropriate chapters of this text, where they are discussed more fully.

CONTRACTUAL LIABILITY EXCLUSION. The purpose of the contractual liability exclusion is twofold. First, it excludes all liability contractually assumed by the insured under any contract or agreement, except an incidental contract of the type described earlier. (Contractual liability insurance, discussed in Chapter 5, is available under separate coverage parts which can be added to the CGL policy to cover the liability assumed under contracts which are not incidental in nature.) The second purpose of the exclusion is to clarify that any "warranty" concerning the fitness or quality of the named insured's products or performance of work is not to be considered a contractual assumption. The implications of such warranties are explored, along with products and completed operations insurance, in Chapter 4.

EXCLUSION OF AUTOMOBILES AND AIRCRAFT. The reason for the automobile and aircraft exclusion is to eliminate exposures which are customarily covered under other policies. Automobile liability insurance is discussed in Chapter 9, and aircraft is discussed in Chapter 12.

The CGL automobile and aircraft exclusion precludes coverage for bodily injury or property damage claims that arise from the ownership, maintenance, operation, use, or loading or unloading of automobiles or aircraft, when they are owned, operated, rented, or loaned to any insured. Also excluded is liability from vehicles and aircraft which are operated by any person who is employed by an insured. However, it can be inferred from these provisions that an insured is protected, under premises and operations coverage, if the insured becomes implicated in a claim involving the loading or unloading of any such nonowned vehicle or conveyance. There also is coverage for claims involving the use of nonowned automobiles and aircraft operated by independent contractors or by some other person or firm that is not employed by the insured—but used, nevertheless, in the furtherance of the insured's business.

Additional coverage specifically is granted by way of exceptions. Coverage applies, for example, to the insured's parking of any nonowned vehicle on premises owned, rented, or controlled by the insured, as well as the ways immediately adjoining. Restaurants, hotels, and office complexes that provide parking for their customers or clients and provide attendants to park them have coverage under their premises and operations insurance for any bodily injury or property damage arising from the parking of such automobiles. Damage to the vehicles themselves is not covered, however, because of the "care, custody, or control exclusion" mentioned later. A business that desires physical damage insurance for such automobiles must purchase garagekeepers' insurance.

EXCLUSION OF LIABILITY FOR THE USE OF MOBILE EQUIPMENT DURING HAZARDOUS ACTIVITIES. While most mobile equipment liability exposures are covered automatically by the CGL policy, the following two circumstances are excluded, unless they are specifically added to the policy for an additional cost. The first circumstance is when bodily injury or property damage arises out of the ownership, maintenance, operation, use, loading or unloading of any mobile equipment "while being used in any prearranged or organized racing, speed or demolition contest or in any stunting activity or in the practice or preparation for any such contest or activity."[27] Note that since this exclusion contains a so-called "while clause," bodily injury or property damage is excluded only "while" mobile equipment is being used for those activities. The second situation which is excluded is bodily injury or property damage arising out of the operation or use of any snowmobile or any trailer designed for use with a snowmobile.

EXCLUSION OF MOBILE EQUIPMENT BEING TRANSPORTED BY AUTOMOBILE. The CGL coverage part excludes bodily injury or property damage arising from any mobile equipment being transported by an automobile which is owned, operated, rented or loaned to any insured. The reason for this exclusion is that mobile equipment in this circumstance is considered to be part of the automobile and, therefore, covered as part of the automobile liability exposure (discussed in Chapter 9).

WATERCRAFT EXCLUSION. The exclusion of bodily injury or property damage arising from the ownership, maintenance, operation, use, loading or unloading of owned and nonowned watercraft is similar to the exclusion of automobiles mentioned previously. There is a difference in that the watercraft exclusion does not apply to any bodily injury or property damage arising from owned or nonowned watercraft while ashore and on premises owned, rented, or controlled by the insured. However, there is no coverage for damage to owned or nonowned watercraft because of the care, custody, or control exclusion.

POLLUTION AND CONTAMINATION EXCLUSION. The pollution and contamination exclusion is a broadly worded provision which precludes coverage for pollution and contamination claims, except those which are attributable to sudden and accidental pollution or contamination. The exclusion reads:

> To bodily injury or property damage arising out of the discharge, dispersal, release or escape of smoke, vapors, soot, fumes, acids, alkalis, toxic chemicals, liquids or gases, waste materials or other irritants, contaminants or pollutants into or upon land, the atmosphere or any water course or body of water; but this exclusion does not apply if such discharge, dispersal, release or escape is sudden and accidental.[28]

This pollution exclusion, as explained in more detail in Chapter 11, is considered necessary (1) to provide firms with an additional incentive to observe existing state and federal environmental protection laws and to take measures to prevent and control pollution, and (2) to avoid insuring potentially catastrophic losses of a nonaccidental and nonsudden nature.

EXCLUSION OF CONTRACTUAL LIABILITY AND FIRST AID EXPENSES DUE TO WAR AND ALLIED PERILS. No coverage applies for liability assumed by the insured under any incidental contract or for first aid expenses incurred by the insured (as provided in the supplementary payments provision of the policy jacket) for bodily injury or property damage due to war, whether or not declared, civil war, insurrection, rebellion, revolution, or to any act which is incident to these perils. The rationale of this exclusion is that war and allied perils present (1) catastrophic loss potentials which are beyond the control of an insured, and (2) potentially large claims for first aid expenses, particularly since first aid coverage is provided without dollar limitation. The reason incidental contracts are singled out in this exclusion is that they are the only contracts automatically covered by the CGL policy provisions. When other types of contractual agreements are insured under separate coverage parts, this same exclusion applies to them.

LIQUOR LIABILITY EXCLUSION. The so-called "liquor liability exclusion" is aimed at firms which are engaged in the business of manufacturing, distributing, selling, or serving alcoholic beverages, as well as owners and lessees of premises which are used for those purposes. The exclusion has wide application, because it precludes bodily injury and property damage coverages for losses for which those firms may be held liable for selling, serving, or giving any alcoholic beverage:

1. in violation of any statute, ordinance, or regulation which is concerned with alcoholic beverages,
2. to a minor,
3. to a person under the influence of alcohol, or
4. which causes or contributes to the intoxication of any person.

The laws mentioned in (1) above, which apply in varying degrees in many states, are sometimes referred to as "dram shop acts" or "alcoholic beverage control acts." While the application and scope of these laws vary by state, their general purpose is to give a person, when injured by an intoxicated adult or by a minor who is served alcoholic beverages, a right of action against the vendor of the beverages. A vendor confronted with any such suit by an injured person is without protection under the CGL policy.

The circumstances in (2), (3), and (4) above, which do not apply to owners or lessees of premises used by others for liquor businesses, are excluded because they are violations for which a common law cause of action sometimes may be maintained against a vendor of liquor.

Exclusion of Obligations Under Workers' Compensation and Similar Laws. The CGL policy (and virtually all commercial liability policies) excludes any obligation for which the insured or its insurer may be held liable under any workers' compensation, unemployment compensation, disability benefits, or similar law. The purpose of the exclusion is to avoid duplicating, with the CGL policy, benefits which are more appropriately provided under forms and statutes specifically designed for such employee protection.

Bodily Injury to Any Employee Exclusion. No CGL coverage applies for bodily injury sustained by any employee of the insured when such injury arises out of and in the course of an employee's work. However, specifically excepted from this exclusion is any liability for bodily injury to any employee of the insured which the insured assumes under any incidental contract. The reason for the exclusion is to make workers' compensation or employers' liability insurance (a retention or "self-insurance" program), rather than the CGL policy, the exclusive source of benefits for an employee's injury. The rationale of the exception to the exclusion is to narrow a coverage gap which would otherwise apply. The workers' compensation and employers' liability policy excludes liability assumed by an employer under any contract or agreement. The CGL policy partially fills in the gap by covering liability an employer assumes under an incidental contract. Contractual liability insurance is needed for any kind of contractual assumption which is not incidental in nature.

CARE, CUSTODY, OR CONTROL EXCLUSION. The exclusion of damage to property in the care, custody, or control of an insured business enterprise applies under all standard liability forms. The exclusion is not only broad in scope, but also is a common source of argument. Its purpose is to preclude any coverage for damage to property that is best handled through the exercise of care or by insuring the exposure under some form of property or inland marine insurance. As such, the exclusion concerns itself with (1) property owned, occupied by, or rented to the insured, (2) property used by the insured, and (3) property in the care, custody, or control of the insured.

The care, custody, or control exclusion, however, does not apply to liability claims under *written sidetrack agreements* for property categories (2) or (3) above. This means that the CGL policy provides a business with protection for any liability stemming from the use of a sidetrack spur, under the so-called incidental contract provisions, as well as protection for any liability because of damage to the sidetrack spur itself. Another exception to the care, custody, or control exclusion is property within category (3) above, which is damaged through the negligent use of elevators at premises owned, rented, or controlled by an insured. Damage to the elevators is not covered, however. If coverage is desired for the elevators themselves, it is necessary to purchase elevator collision insurance.

PREMISES ALIENATED (SOLD) EXCLUSION. The so-called "premises alienated exclusion" precludes coverage for property damage to premises sold by a firm which is negligent in not informing the purchaser about latent premises defects and the property damage arises out of and is confined to the sold premises. Say, for example, a firm sells its building which is known to have a latent electrical defect and the seller, as a matter of oversight, does not make the defect known to the purchaser. If, after the property is sold, the latent defect causes a fire which damages that building, the seller has no protection in the event of suit instituted by the purchaser. The policy is not designed to cover the results of any dangerous condition which should have been corrected by the seller before the sale or should have been communicated to the purchaser. However, it can be inferred from this exclusion that coverage does apply to any bodily injury emanating from defective, sold premises, as well to property damage to other than the sold premises. If the fire, in the previous example, were to spread to an adjoining building, the seller would have protection, provided it has a liability policy in force at the time of bodily injury or property damage and the loss is determined to have been caused by an occurrence. Because it is of special importance to a firm in the business of constructing buildings or dwellings for sale, the subject of the premises alienated exclusion also is discussed at some length under completed operations insurance in Chapter 4.

FAILURE TO PERFORM EXCLUSION. The so-called "failure to perform exclusion" is aimed at precluding coverage for loss of use of undamaged tangible property which results from failure of the named insured's work or product to perform as the named insured warrants or represents. While this exclusion is discussed more fully in Chapter 4, one segment of it is related to premises and operations coverage; namely, there is no coverage for another's loss of use of tangible property which has not been physically injured or destroyed, resulting from a delay or lack of performance of any contract or agreement by the named insured or by someone who is performing work or a service on the named insured's behalf. By way of illustration, consider a construction firm which promises to complete a building within a certain period but does not fulfill that promise. As a result of the lack of performance by the construction firm, the owner is unable to use the new building as anticipated and, thereby, loses a certain amount of business. Any subsequent claim by the owner against the contractor for loss of use of the unfinished building is excluded. The promise of the contractor is more appropriately handled by performance (surety) bonds, which are discussed in Chapter 13.

EXCLUSION OF DAMAGE TO THE NAMED INSURED'S PRODUCTS. The exclusion of property damage to the named insured's products prevents an insurer from having to pay for the repair or the replacement of a product which is incorrectly designed or defectively produced. This exclusion is discussed in depth in Chapter 4.

INJURY TO WORK PERFORMED EXCLUSION. The exclusion of property damage to work performed by or on behalf of the named insured has essentially the same purpose as the preceding exclusion concerning damage to the named insured's products. The injury to work performed exclusion, in other words, prevents an insurer from having to pay for redoing faulty work performed by the named insured. This exclusion is discussed later in these pages in relation to completed operations insurance.

SISTERSHIP EXCLUSION. The so-called "sistership liability exclusion" is another important provision that directly affects products liability and completed operations insurance. The exclusion, which is treated in Chapter 4, is directed at the costs incurred by a firm for the withdrawal, inspection, repair, or replacement of its products or work, if such products or work must be withdrawn from the market or from use because either is known or suspected of being defective.

EXPLOSION, COLLAPSE, AND UNDERGROUND EXCLUSIONS. Another set of exclusions sometimes used on the CGL policy, unless they are deleted for an additional premium, are commonly referred to as the "XCU exclusions." Many of the classifications listed in the ISO *Manuals of Liability Insurance* involve business operations particularly exposed to the explosion, collapse, and underground hazards (defined in the policy). For such firms, the classification code incorporates one or more of the letters "X, C, and U." For example, for "Excavation" the classification code is 15111XCU, and for "Irrigation or Drainage System Construction" the code is 16255XU. The classification code for the operations performed by a firm is shown in the declarations of the general liability policy, and the presence of the letters X, C, or U indicates that the X, C, or U exclusions apply. These exclusions preclude coverage for property damage liability claims included within the explosion, collapse, and underground property damage hazards, as those three hazards are defined in the policy jacket or by endorsement. Firms affected by the exclusions include those involved in blasting work, excavating, grading of land, oil and gas pipe line construction, pile driving, plumbing, sewer construction, tunneling, welding, or cutting.

It should be noted that some insurers automatically incorporate the aforementioned exclusions into the CGL form, while others do not. Insurers which do not incorporate the exclusions do so nonetheless, if an insured declares such an exposure at policy inception, but does not desire to insure it. In the latter case, if an insured does not declare such an exposure and an operation involving a classification with the symbols X, C, or U arises during the course of the policy period, coverage will apply, since neither the exclusion nor the appropriate classification and symbols have been incorporated into the policy. Yet, even when the exclusion is automatically incorporated into the policy, it does not apply (coverage is not excluded), unless the schedule of hazards specifically lists an excluded classification and the appropriate symbol or symbols after it. To avoid providing automatic coverage, some insurers add a schedule of operations, i.e., a descriptive list of all hazardous operations and their symbols, at policy inception, along with the exclusionary provision. This has the net effect of excluding any property damage claim that ultimately arises from operations listed in the schedule.[29]

Based upon all of the exclusions which may apply and the different claim circumstances which may involve them, it is sometimes difficult to ascertain precisely what is covered until a claim occurs. Nevertheless, it is possible to determine many of the premises and operations liability exposures which may be covered if one has a basic understanding of the exclusions and policy jacket definitions.

Having first discussed many of the important CGL policy provisions, it is now easier to explain various characteristics of the OL&T,

M&C, storekeepers, and garage liability coverage parts and how they differ from the CGL policy.

Owners, Landlords, and Tenants Coverage Part

The owners, landlords, and tenants (OL&T) form is one of the earlier contracts that was devised to provide liability coverages to individuals and firms whose exposures are centered primarily on premises. The only coverages automatically provided by the basic OL&T coverage part are premises and operations, including contractual liability for "incidental contracts" and liability for structural alterations performed by or on behalf of the named insured, provided alterations *do not* involve changing the size of or moving an existing structure or building. However, the OL&T form is not intended for use when an exposure exists for either products or completed operations. This form therefore is suited only for persons or firms which do not have a products or completed operations exposure, such as lessors and lessees of building office complexes, firms which operate automobile parking lots, municipal exposures concerning firehouses, golf courses, street signs and banners, and individuals who rent one or more private dwellings or apartment houses to others.

The OL&T form's premises and operations coverages, which are much narrower in scope than the same coverages of the CGL policy, are best understood by examining the definition of insured premises, the operations liability coverage, and the exclusions.

Insured Premises Defined The premises coverage of the OL&T form is limited to the ownership, maintenance, or use of the insured premises. In brief, the term "insured premises," as used in the OL&T form means:

1. Premises designated in the policy declarations. (Whether the premises is designated as a store, an office located within a building complex, or a building leased in whole or in part to others, the owner, tenant, lessee or whoever purchases the OL&T policy will have protection for any liability suits arising from the physical exposures of such premises as are described in the form.)

2. Premises alienated (sold) to others—other than those constructed for sale. (Premises constructed for sale are not covered under the OL&T policy, because they are insurable exposures customarily covered under completed operations insurance, and the OL&T policy cannot be written to include completed operations insurance.)

3. Newly acquired premises and the ways immediately adjoining on land, provided notice is given to the insurer within thirty days following any acquisition. (A firm that acquires a new building can be at a disadvantage under the OL&T policy if it fails to report such acquisition. Note that there is no similar restriction under the CGL policy.)

Operations Liability Coverage Coverage for operations under the OL&T policy is limited to operations that are specified in the policy declarations, plus those which are necessary or incidental to the insured premises. What is "necessary or incidental" could very well be a source of argument. It is clear, however, that a firm will not be automatically covered under the OL&T policy (whereas it would be covered under the CGL) if it decides to expand its operations to an entirely different type of business venture. Furthermore, the fact that completed operations insurance is not available under this form means that only operations in progress are covered, subject, of course, to the applicable exclusions.

Exclusions All of the exclusions which apply to premises and operations coverages of the CGL policy also are contained in the OL&T policy. However, the OL&T policy has two additional exclusions which are not found in the CGL form.

The first of these excludes bodily injury or property damage arising out of operations on or from premises owned, rented, or controlled by the named insured—other than insured premises, as the latter term is defined in the OL&T coverage part. This exclusion merely reinforces the intent that the only premises and operations covered are those which are reported and insured. Thus, if a store owner obtains a second location and sustains a liability claim thirty-one days after acquiring the new premises, it will not be covered unless its location has been reported and insured within thirty days of its acquisition.

The second exclusion peculiar to the OL&T policy precludes coverage for claims arising out of (1) structural alterations which involve changing the size of or moving an existing structure or building, and (2) new construction or demolition operations, regardless of their nature, whether all such operations in (1) and (2) above are performed by or for the named insured. The purpose of this exclusion is to require that such hazardous exposures be specifically declared and insured for an additional premium. Although demolition and new construction operations are easily defined, such is not the case on operations dealing with structural alterations. Based upon the court decisions thus far rendered, there is very little agreement on the meaning of the term "structural alterations."[30] Although much depends on the nature of the work being performed at the time of injury or damage, examples of alterations which are not considered to change the size of a structure or building include the replacement of an old heating system, the rewiring of electrical outlets, the resurfacing of floors, and the paneling of office walls. Examples of alterations which involve changing the size of an existing structure or building include the construction of an additional room onto a dwelling or a new wing to a building office complex, the construction of new interior walls to make additional offices, and the construction of a new dormer on a dwelling. While, as mentioned later, structural alterations which involve a change in size of a structure or building are not covered, whether they are performed by the named insured or by an independent contractor, such exposure can be covered for an additional premium.

Whereas the OL&T policy is predominately a premises-oriented coverage which includes operations coverage of an incidental nature, the M&C policy is just the reverse, because the liability exposures of manufacturers and contractors are generally concentrated away from their premises.

Manufacturers and Contractors Coverage Part

The manufacturers and contractors (M&C) form is one of the earlier contracts that was devised to provide various liability coverages to individuals and commercial enterprises whose exposures are predominately away from premises. Among those for whom coverage may be written under the M&C form are auctioneers, marine divers, funeral directors, fire fighters, and sales and service organizations.[31] The M&C policy at one time provided a means for including somewhat similar coverages as are now provided by the CGL policy. Presently, the only coverages automatically provided by the basic M&C coverage part are (1) premises coverage, (2) contractual liability for "incidental contracts," (3) liability for operations performed by the named insured away from its premises, and (4) liability for operations performed by the named insured or by independent contractors involving maintenance and repairs at premises owned by or rented to the named insured, and structural alterations at the named insured's owned or rented premises which do not involve changing the size of or moving buildings or other structures. The fact that the M&C policy cannot be written to include products liability and completed operations insurance, as once was possible, makes this policy unsuitable to manufacturers and contractors, since the former usually requires products coverage and the latter usually requires completed operations coverage.

While the scope of the M&C form's premises and operations coverages is much narrower than the same coverages of the CGL policy, the premises and operations coverages of the M&C policy are somewhat broader than those of the OL&T policy.

Premises and Operations Coverage The premises coverage of the M&C form encompasses exposures relating to premises without restricting the premises by definition, as is the case with the OL&T form. The reason the premises coverage of the M&C policy is not defined is that the primary exposures of firms written on an M&C form seldom are concerned with the physical nature of the insured's own premises. Instead, the primary exposures are associated with operations emanating from premises, as well as away from premises.

Construction contractors, for example, ordinarily have comparatively little exposure to liability loss on their own premises. Most liability losses occur at construction sites of others. However, if a premises liability claim were to occur at a construction contracting firm's office or grounds or at a construction site to which the firm holds title until work is completed, the firm has coverage for its negligence. An OL&T form rated on an area basis would not properly price the off-premises exposure of a contractor or other firm whose exposure is predominately away from its premises, nor would the coverage of the OL&T form suffice, since it is designed for the on-premises exposures of the insured. The M&C form rated on the basis of payroll or receipts is more appropriate.

Manufacturers, on the other hand, seldom operate from premises other than their own, but it is not the premises exposure to the public that is hazardous. It is the potential vicarious liability of manufacturers, resulting from the negligent acts and omissions of its employees who work away from the manufacturing premises, which is the major exposure to liability loss. Hence, an M&C policy rated on the basis of payroll more clearly and fairly reflects the exposure than would an OL&T policy rated on the basis of area.

Coverage of the M&C policy applies to all operations, i.e., the operations are not in any way limited to those which are necessary or incidental to the insured business. If a firm decides to undertake an unrelated type of operation, it will be covered. However, the scope of such coverage again depends upon the exclusions. The exclusions of the M&C form are virtually identical to those of the OL&T form, with the following two exceptions.

The first exclusion peculiar to the M&C policy precludes bodily injury or property damage arising out of (1) operations performed for the named insured by independent contractors and, (2) acts or omissions stemming from the general supervision of such operations by the named insured. It makes no difference whether such claims occur on the premises of the named insured or on the premises of others. If an insured anticipates using independent contractors and decides that insurance is desirable or necessary, independent contractors coverage must be specifically added to the M&C policy and an additional premium paid.

Specifically excepted from the foregoing exclusion is bodily injury or property damage that occurs in the course of (1) maintenance and repairs at premises owned by or rented to the insured, or (2) structural alterations at such premises which do not involve changing the size of or moving buildings or other structures.

Two points of coverage can be inferred from the two exceptions. First, claims emanating from maintenance and repair work at premises of the named insured are covered under premises and operations coverage of the M&C policy, whether they are performed by the named insured or by independent contractors. Second, structural alterations which do not involve significant changes or do not involve the moving of buildings or other structures are covered by the M&C form, whether they are performed by independent contractors or not. More important, claims stemming from alterations which involve changing the size of or moving a building or structure also are covered by the M&C premises and operations coverage part when they are performed by the named insured or by the named insured's employees. But when they are performed by an independent contractor, additional coverage is required, whether such operations take place on premises of the named insured or on premises of others.

Figure 2-1 illustrates the coverage differences of the OL&T, M&C, and CGL forms for structural alterations, new construction, and demolition exposures.

The second exclusion applicable to the M&C form (also identical to that of the CGL form) excludes property damage including the explosion, collapse, and underground property damage hazards, unless a firm doing work within the scope of those hazards has the appropriate x, c, or u exclusion deleted from the policy for an additional cost.

Garage Liability Forms

Garage liability insurance is basically a package of coverages suited for such firms as automobile and equipment dealers, repair shops, and parking lot operators. It consists of premises and operations coverages including coverage for the operation of service hoists and elevators, contractual liability coverage for "incidental contracts," independent contractors coverage somewhat like that offered as an addition to the M&C form, products and completed operations coverages, premises medical payments insurance, and some automobile liability coverage,

Figure 2-1
Coverage for Structural Alterations, New Construction, and Demolition Exposures

Exposures	OL&T Form	M&C Form	CGL Form
Structural alterations changing the size of or moving buildings or structures	Not covered whether performed by the named insured or independent contractor	Covered only when performed by the named insured	Covered without exception
Structural alterations which do not involve changing the size of or moving buildings or structures	Covered whether performed by the named insured or independent contractor	Covered whether performed by the named insured or independent contractor	Covered without exception
New construction or demolition work	Not covered whether performed by the named insured or independent contractor	Covered only when performed by the named insured	Covered without exception
Ordinary repairs at owned or rented premises of the named insured	Covered whether performed by the named insured or independent contractor	Covered whether performed by the named insured or independent contractor	Covered
Acts or omissions of independent contractors	Covered, unless work involves structural alterations which change the size of or move buildings or structures	Not covered, except for maintenance and ordinary repairs, including structural alterations which do not change the size of or move buildings or structures	Covered without exception

depending upon the nature of the operations. Garagekeepers' coverage, which is a form of bailee liability insurance, also can be added to cover physical damage losses to automobiles in the care, custody, or control of an insured.

Two garage liability forms are available to those who meet the eligibility requirements. The principal difference between the forms concerns the extent to which automobile liability insurance is provided. The first form, "garage operations and automobile hazard 1," includes coverage for all owned and nonowned automobiles. Those eligible for hazard 1 coverage are franchised dealers, nonfranchised dealers, and equipment and implement dealers. The second form, "garage operations and automobile hazard 2," covers only automobiles which are neither owned nor hired by the garage firm or by partners of a partnership. Owned and hired automobiles of the named insured therefore must be specifically insured under private passenger or commercial automobile liability policies, as the case may be. Repair shops, service stations, and storage garages are eligible only for hazard 2 coverage. A repair shop, in other words, cannot purchase the form that provides automobile hazard 1 coverage, unless the repair shop forms a part of an automobile dealership.

Since garage liability forms have some of the coverage features of the CGL form, as well as the more limited OL&T and M&C forms, the discussion of the garage forms' premises and operations coverages is based upon the differences between the garage forms and the other forms.

Premises and Operations Coverages The premises and operations coverages of the garage liability forms are very similar to those provided by the OL&T form. Such coverages apply when bodily injury or property damage arises out of "garage operations." As that term is defined in the provisions, it means the "ownership, maintenance, or use of the premises for purposes of a garage and all operations necessary or incidental thereto."[32] The word, "premises " as used in that definition, is further defined as meaning "premises where the named insured conducts garage operations, and including the ways immediately adjoining, but does not include any part of such premises upon which business operations are conducted by any other person or organization."[33] It appears clear from the definitions that if a service station decides to sell household appliances or to operate a small restaurant, such operations are not likely to be considered as necessary or incidental operations. It may very well be an expensive question if a court ultimately must rule upon it. It is important, therefore, for such matters to be cleared with the insurer prior to commencing them. If the service station owner or operator desires products liability insurance for the exposures of the household appliances it sells or, if a restaurant, the food which is consumed on and off its premises, the best approach is to combine a CGL coverage part with the garage liability form. However, if products liability insurance is not desired and the owner or operator of the service station is not planning on expanding operations to other locations, the appropriate form for use with the garage liability form is the OL&T coverage part.

The exclusions and exceptions also are of importance in determining the extent of premises and operations coverages under the garage liability forms. Most exclusions are not too different from those which apply under the CGL, M&C, and OL&T forms.

Exclusions Liability assumed by these entities under written contracts or agreements, for example, automatically are covered if they are defined as incidental contracts. On the other hand, claims stemming from automobile servicing hoists and elevators are covered, since there is no other exclusion that applies to them. Furthermore, there is coverage for damage to property in the insured's care, custody, or control when it arises out of the use of an automobile servicing hoist designed to raise an entire automobile. The hoist coverage is specifically given as an exception to the care, custody, or control exclusion found in most other liability forms.

Under the garage liability forms there is no coverage for property damage *to* work performed by or on behalf of the insured and arising out of work, or any portion of such work, or out of any materials, parts, or equipment that may be furnished for such work. If a repair garage asks another garage specialist to repair an automobile generator for one of its customers and it fails to function properly, for example, the repair garage has no coverage under its garage liability form if such work has to be performed on it again. It does not matter whether the insured performed such work or an independent contractor performed it.

An exclusion of structural alterations, new construction, or demolition operations applies, but somewhat differently than it does under either the M&C and OL&T forms. Under the garage liability forms, there is a stipulation that coverage applies when such operations are performed by independent contractors, provided the insurer receives written notice within thirty days of their commencement. By inference, then, work performed by independent contractors is not covered if no written notice is given to the insurer as specified. Furthermore, coverage does apply, without restriction, if such operations are performed by the insured or by its employees.

Those who qualify as insured persons or firms under garage liability forms differ somewhat from those who are insured persons under other liability coverage parts.

Persons Insured Under Garage Forms Although the person and/or firm listed as the named insured of a garage liability form is covered as an insured without qualification, the insured status of others varies according to whether the coverage is for garage operations or the automobile hazard. The following are insureds with respect to *garage operations only*:

1. any employee, director, or stockholder of the named insured while such person is acting within the scope of his or her duties;
2. an individual, when such person is designated in the policy declarations as the named insured, but only with respect to that person's business activities as a sole proprietorship, including the spouse of the named insured in the conduct of business affairs;
3. a partnership or joint venture, when such firm is designated in the policy declarations as the named insured, including any partner's or member's liability during the conduct of such partnership or joint venture; and
4. any person or organization which has a financial interest in the named insured's garage operations.

Those who are insureds with respect to the *automobile hazard* (essentially the same persons and firms which usually are included under the "omnibus clause" of commercial automobile liability policies) are as follows:

1. any person while using an automobile which is covered under the automobile hazard of the garage form with the permission of the named insured as to the automobile's operation and scope of use;
2. a borrower of the covered automobile or a partner, member, or employee of the named insured or borrower, but only with respect to bodily injury or property damage arising out of the loading or unloading of such automobile; or
3. any other person or organization which becomes vicariously liable because of the acts or omissions of the named insured, or the named insured's employee, director, or stockholder while acting within the scope of his or her duties.

As is usual with the provisions of "omnibus clauses," certain persons and firms are not considered to be insureds under any circumstances. Those in this category are:

1. any person, while engaged in the business of his or her employer, who causes bodily injury to a fellow employee in the course of his or her employment;
2. any person or organization which performs operations for the named insured as an independent contractor;

3. any person or firm, other than the named insured, with respect to any automobile owned by such firm or person, including a member of that person's household; or whose possession has been transferred to another by the named insured under the terms of any agreement or sale; or

4. any partner, member, or employee of the named insured, including a spouse of such person concerning property damage to property owned, rented, or held for sale by the named insured, as well as property in the care, custody, or control of, or transported by the named insured.

Finally, the persons insured provision of garage liability forms, usually, does not provide coverage for bodily injury or property damage arising out of the conduct of any partnership or joint venture which is not designated in the policy as a named insured.

Storekeepers Liability Form

The storekeepers liability form is an indivisible package of liability coverages designed for retail stores which meet the eligibility requirements prescribed in the OL&T Manual. Retail stores which sell more than 50 percent of their goods by mail order are not eligible. Nor are auction stores, barber shops, beauty salons, chain stores having more than ten locations, cleaning and dyeing establishments, certain department stores, drug stores, mail-order houses, and open-air markets. Stores in the supermarket class are also ineligible if their total sales annually exceed $500,000 and their store area exceeds 3,000 square feet.

The storekeepers liability form provides premises and operations coverage and exclusions that are almost identical to those of the OL&T form. The form also includes coverage for the elevator liability exposure, premises medical payments, products and completed operations, and independent contractors coverage, excluding only the demolition hazard.

However, since firms covered under the storekeepers form are less likely to have off-premises mobile equipment liability exposures than firms which are covered by CGL, OL&T, and M&C forms, the persons insured provision of the storekeepers form is considerably shorter than the other forms.

Persons Insured Under the Storekeepers Form In brief, the term "persons insured," as it appears in the storekeepers liability form, means:

1. An individual, when such person is designated in the policy declarations as the named insured, but only to the extent of that person's business activities as a sole proprietor.
2. A partnership or joint venture, when such firm is designated in the policy declarations as the named insured, and including any partner's or member's liability during the conduct of a partnership or joint venture activity.
3. Any organization, other than a sole proprietorship, partnership, or joint venture, such as a corporation, when such organization is designated in the policy declarations as the named insured, including the liability of any executive officer, director, or stockholder while such person is acting within the scope of his or her duties.
4. Any person or organization while acting as a real estate manager for the named insured, other than employees of the named insured.

An understanding of the basic provisions of the CGL, OL&T, M&C, storekeepers, and garage liability forms should provide a sound basis for decisions concerning when each form can best be used.

Guidelines for Use of Coverages and Forms Discussed

Whether one liability form should be recommended over another depends upon the needs and qualifications of the firm. For example, if a commercial establishment needs products liability or completed operations insurance or it needs somewhat fluid coverage for its expanding operations, its choice should be the CGL policy, since the CGL policy provides a number of coverages, including products liability and completed operations, as well as automatic coverage for new exposures that arise during the policy period. As a matter of fact, the CGL policy is recommended for any firm, except those eligible for garage liability forms, even if products liability or completed operations coverage is not desired or is unavailable, because the CGL policy's principal advantage is its automatic coverage for newly acquired exposures. Furthermore, the cost of a CGL policy without products liability and completed operations coverages is the same as an OL&T or an M&C policy.

If a store has a relatively small growth pattern and it requires products liability insurance, the storekeepers liability policy should seriously be considered as an alternative to the CGL policy. This is because products liability insurance is automatically included as part of the storekeepers package premium without the requirement of an audit on product sales. However, when a store does not qualify for the latter form, it should select the CGL policy.

Automobile dealers, repair shops, and other similar operations should select one of the garage liability forms because they contain coverages for exposures usual to those businesses. In addition, garage liability forms provide the convenience of automatic coverage.

Both the OL&T and the M&C forms are so limited in scope that they should be used only when operations are so limited that coverage is needed simply for premises or operations. The OL&T form is suited for individuals whose dwellings do not qualify for the homeowners program or for separate CPL policies, for individuals and commercial entities whose rental properties do not qualify for the commercial multi-peril package programs, or for firms which do not need the broader coverage provided by the CGL policy, particularly products and/or completed operations insurance, such as lessors of apartment houses or mercantile or office buildings. The M&C form, on the other hand, may be suited for the supervisory exposures of architects and engineers, detective agencies, and fire fighters who have no need for products and/or completed operations insurance.

At one time, the M&C form was commonly written for the individual contractor who specialized in small operations. But with the broad insurance requirements now demanded by owners of projects, the M&C appears not to serve a useful purpose. Therefore, it would be better for a contractor to purchase a CGL policy with or without products and/or completed operations coverage, rather than an OL&T or M&C form, to get the extra benefits provided at little, if any, additional cost.

BROAD FORM CGL ENDORSEMENT

Up to this point, the discussion of general liability policy provisions has dealt with coverages which automatically apply under the various coverage parts of the standard policies, without the addition of endorsements to broaden protection.[34] Many broadening endorsements have been available over the years and their use has gradually increased. During the mid-1970s, some insurers introduced their own independently filed packages of coverage extensions for use with CGL forms which included the broadening coverages commonly sought by insureds. Prior to this, each coverage extension required a separate endorsement. More recently, ISO has introduced a "broad form comprehensive general liability insurance endorsement" which is similar to many of those independent filings.

The standard broad form CGL endorsement provides the following twelve coverage extensions for a premium equal to a fixed percentage of the premiums for basic limits of the bodily injury and property damage liability coverage: (1) blanket contractual liability, (2) personal injury liability and advertising injury liability, (3) premises medical payments, (4) host liquor liability, (5) fire legal liability on real property, (6) broad form property damage, including completed operations, (7) incidental medical malpractice, (8) nonowned watercraft liability, (9) limited worldwide coverage, (10) additional persons insured, (11) extended bodily injury coverage, and (12) automatic coverage on newly acquired organizations.[35] Space limitations will permit only a very brief explanation of each coverage (although several are elaborated upon in subsequent chapters). Since coverages (9), (10), (11), and (12) have an important effect on the scope of the other coverages of the endorsement, they will be explained first.

Limited Worldwide Liability Coverage

The sole purpose of limited worldwide liability coverage is to extend the scope of "policy territory" to anywhere in the world. However, this broadened territorial scope only applies if bodily injury, property damage, personal injury, or advertising injury liability arises from activities of any insured who is permanently domiciled in the United States of America, and the original suit for damages is brought within the United States, its territories, possessions, or in Canada.

For example, if an employee of a firm negligently injures someone while on a business trip to the Far East, both the employer and the employee will be protected in the event a suit against them is filed within the United States, its territories, possessions, or in Canada.[36] If the *suit* is instituted in the foreign country of injury, neither the employer nor employee will be protected. However, an insurer is obligated to investigate and to settle a claim, if it can, in order to prevent a suit, since there is no provision in the broad form endorsement which precludes that obligation of the insurer.

Finally, limited worldwide liability coverage does not apply to (1) premises medical payments coverage, and (2) bodily injury or property damage arising from the named insured's products or completed operations.

Extended Bodily Injury Coverage

Extended bodily injury coverage amends the definition of occurrence to include any intentional act by or at the direction of the insured which results in bodily injury, but only if such bodily injury results solely from the use of "reasonable" force for purposes of protecting persons or property. Were it not for this amendment, an insured would not have such protection, because the standard, unamended definition of occurrence refers to "bodily injury . . . neither expected nor intended from the standpoint of the insured." While extended bodily injury coverage can be viewed as a distinct advantage to insureds, the question of whether force exercised by an insured is "reasonable" may be a troublesome one to answer until a court has resolved the matter. In the meantime, the insured at least has defense protection.

Newly Acquired Organizations—Automatic Coverage

A commercial firm which is acquired or formed by the named insured is automatically protected as a named insured under the extension of coverage for newly acquired organizations, until the new firm is specifically added to the policy or for no longer a period than ninety days, whichever occurs first. If a newly acquired or a newly formed firm is not added to the policy at the expiration of the ninetieth day, such firm is without further protection. The only conditions that must be met under this extension are that (1) the named insured either must own or have a majority interest in such newly acquired organization, (2) the insurance of the endorsement does not apply for bodily injury, property damage, personal injury liability and advertising injury liability if such new organization is an insured under any other similar liability or indemnity policy, and (3) the newly acquired organization must not be part of a joint venture with the named insured. The extension may be viewed as an advantage to firms that acquire subsidiaries from time to time, in the sense that the standard CGL policy does not cover such acquisitions until they are added to the policy.

Additional Persons Insured

By addition of the broad form endorsement, the persons insured provision of the CGL coverage part includes as insureds (1) any spouse of a partner concerning business activities of the partnership, and (2) any employee of the named insured while acting within the scope of his or her duties. But the insurance as to any such employee does not apply:

1. to bodily injury or personal injury sustained by a fellow-employee which occurs during the course of employment;

2. to personal injury or advertising injury to the named insured or, if the named insured is a partnership or joint venture, to any partner, member, or spouse of such partnership or joint venture; or,

3. to damage to property owned by, occupied, or used by, rented to, in the care, custody, or control of, or over which physical control is being exercised by (a) an employee of the named insured, (b) the named insured, or (c) any partner or member of a partnership or joint venture and a spouse of such partner or member.

While (3) above is similar to the care, custody, or control exclusion of commercial liability coverage parts, there is one difference. The exclusion under the broad form endorsement also precludes damage to property which is in the care, custody, or control of any employee nor spouse of any partner or member. The CGL policy does not contain this same exclusion because neither employees nor spouses are covered as insureds under the basic provisions of the CGL policy.

By keeping in mind the persons who are insured, the territorial scope of coverage, the provisions of extended bodily injury coverage, and the automatic coverage of newly acquired organizations, readers will gain a better perspective of the other coverages provided by the broad form endorsement.

Blanket Contractual Liability Coverage

Briefly, the broad form CGL endorsement automatically includes blanket contractual liability coverage as an extension of the term "incidental contract" as that term is defined in the policy jacket. What is particularly advantageous about blanket contractual liability coverage is that it applies to both written and oral agreements relating to the named insured's business. The coverage also applies to contractual agreements made by principals of the named insured's newly acquired organizations, if the latter firms are specifically added to the CGL at the time of any claim or a claim occurs during the ninety-day grace period for reporting such newly acquired organizations.

Personal Injury Liability Coverage

The personal injury liability coverage of the broad form endorsement corresponds, in many respects, to that which is available under the conventional endorsement to the CGL policy. In order to convey how the personal injury liability coverage of the broad form endorsement differs from the coverage which is available under the conventional endorsement, features of the latter coverage will be discussed first.

Personal Injury Liability Coverage Under the Conventional Endorsement In the conventional endorsement to the CGL policy, the insuring agreement for personal injury liability coverage stipulates that an insured is protected against damage for which the insured is legally obligated to pay, because of personal injury sustained by any person or organization which arises out of one or more of the following "offenses" that are committed by the named insured during the policy period:

A. False arrest, detention or imprisonment, or malicious prosecution.
B. The publication or utterance of a libel or slander or other defamatory or disparaging material, or a publication or utterance in violation of an individual's right of privacy, except publications or utterances in the course of or related to advertising, broadcasting or telecasting activities conducted by or on behalf of the named insured.
C. Wrongful entry or eviction, or other invasion of the right of private occupancy.[37]

An insured can purchase coverage against the offenses in any one group above or in all groups, so long as a premium charge is made for each group selected. In addition to its promise to pay, on behalf of an insured, such damages as are attributable to a covered offense, the insurer also promises to defend the insured against the allegation of a covered offense, i.e., to defend, even if the allegations of the suit are groundless, false, or fraudulent.

The personal injury liability coverage of the conventional endorsement also contains a so-called "participation clause" in which a percentage is applied somewhat like a deductible. Although the participation clause is not mandatory, its use permits a reduction in the cost of the endorsement. If a participation percentage applies, the insurer's liability is stated to be for no "greater proportion of any loss than the difference between such percentage and one hundred percent," with the balance of the loss to be borne by the insured.[38] For purposes of illustration, assume that a participation of 15 percent applies and a $50,000 judgment is rendered against the insured. The insured would have to pay $7,500 (15 percent of $50,000) and the insurer would have to pay the balance or $42,500 subject, of course, to the applicable "each person aggregate" limit. Note, also, that the "general aggregate" limit for the rest of the policy year would be reduced by the $42,500 payment of the insurer.

Five exclusions normally apply to the personal injury liability coverage of the conventional endorsement. Coverage does not apply to:

(a) Liability assumed by the insured under any contract or agreement.

(b) Personal injury which arises out of the willful violation of any penal statute or ordinance and which is committed by any insured or with the insured's knowledge or consent. Any act which is committed in violation of a penal statute is too hazardous an undertaking to insure.[39]

(c) Personal injury sustained by any person as a result of an offense by the named insured which is directly or indirectly related to the employment of any person. This exclusion can be deleted (usually for an additional premium equal to 5 percent of the total premium). It is directed at personal injury claims of an employer who slanders an employee, for example, or who informs someone about privileged information of an employee whose employment has been terminated.

(d) Offenses within group B, if any personal injury arises out of any publication or utterance which was made prior to the effective date of the coverage endorsement.

(e) Offenses in group B, if any personal injury is caused by an insured or at the insured's direction with the knowledge that the insured's publication or statement is false. The rationale of this exclusion is to avoid covering a person who knows what he or she is doing is untrue.

The foregoing explanation of personal injury liability coverage under the conventional endorsement makes it easier to describe the corresponding coverage of the broad form endorsement.

Conventional Endorsement Coverage Versus Broad Form Endorsement Coverage Personal injury liability coverage under the broad form endorsement differs from the provisions of the conventional endorsement in the following respects. Personal injury liability coverage of the broad form endorsement:

1. does not contain exclusion (c) of the conventional endorsement concerning employment-related offenses,
2. covers employees as insureds,
3. covers personal injury liability claims arising out of the conduct of the named insured's business on a worldwide basis (as previously defined in the discussion of limited worldwide coverage), and
4. does not include a participation clause.

Advertising Injury Liability Coverage

Advertising injury liability coverage is provided in combination with personal injury liability coverage under the broad form endorsement. This means that everything which has been said about the latter coverage, i.e., the insuring agreement, exclusions, persons insured, and limits of liability, also applies to advertising injury liability, except that advertising injury liability coverage lists its own set of covered offenses and is subject to additional exclusions.

It should be made clear at the outset that advertising injury liability coverage, as provided by the broad form endorsement, is not intended for a firm which is in the business of advertising, broadcasting, publishing, or telecasting.[40] Instead, the coverage is directed at the normal activities of firms which buy advertising in order to sell their own products or services. For purposes of the coverage, "advertising injury" is defined in the broad form endorsement as:

> injury arising out of an offense committed during the policy period occurring in the course of the named insured's advertising activities, if such injury arises out of libel, slander, defamation, violation of right of privacy, piracy, unfair competition, or infringement of copyright, title or slogan.[41]

However, no coverage applies for advertising injury arising out of:

(a) failure of contract performance, except the unauthorized appropriation of ideas based upon an alleged breach of an implied warranty, or

(b) infringement of trademark, service mark or trade name, other than titles or slogans, by use thereof on or in connection with goods, products or services sold, offered for sale or advertised, or

(c) incorrect description or mistake in advertised price of goods, products or services sold, offered for sale or advertised, or

(d) with respect to "advertising injury," as defined, to any injury arising out of any act committed by the insured with actual malice.[42]

Premises Medical Payments Coverage

The premises medical payments coverage which is included in the broad form CGL endorsement is virtually identical to the coverage which can be purchased separately as an endorsement to commercial liability policies.[43] In either case, premises medical payments coverage is not a form of liability insurance in the strict sense, because negligence of the insured need not be established as a condition precedent to payment by the insurer. Premises medical payments are made if there is reason to believe that the resulting injury would not have occurred but for some condition on the insured premises or operations conducted by the insured. Specifically, payments are made for medical expenses which are incurred by members of the public who sustain injuries arising out of (1) a condition in "insured premises," meaning "all premises owned by or rented to the named insured with respect to which the named insured is afforded coverage for bodily injury liability under [the] policy, and including the ways immediately adjoining on land," and (2) operations for which the named insured is covered for bodily injury liability under the policy to which the endorsement forms a part.[44] Note that if the named insured does not have bodily injury liability coverage for the circumstances under which injury occurs, the named insured is not covered for the claimant's medical bills.

Host Liquor Liability Coverage

Host liquor liability coverage, which only applies to firms not engaged in the business of manufacturing, distributing, selling, or serving alcoholic beverages, takes the form of a coverage clarification. That is to say, host liquor liability coverage, as provided by the broad form endorsement (or by separate endorsement for an additional cost), makes it clear that the liquor liability exclusion, which otherwise applies to all commercial liability policies, does not apply to the liability of the named insured or to someone whose liability is assumed by the named insured, "arising out of the giving or serving of alcoholic beverages at functions incidental to the named insured's business."

For example, a firm which serves alcoholic beverages at a company picnic for its employees and their families is covered if some third party sustains bodily injury or property damage because of a participant's intoxication. If the distributor of the beverages requires the employer to agree under contract to hold the distributor harmless for any liability stemming from such activities involving the serving of alcoholic beverages, the distributor also is protected. Coverage, of course, is subject to all the exclusions which apply to the CGL policy. For example, if an employee injures others while operating the employer's owned watercraft, the employer is not protected.

Fire Legal Liability Coverage—Real Property[45]

Fire legal liability coverage, as provided by the broad form endorsement, is intended for the tenant or lessee of a commercial building who agrees under contract to be responsible for the building or for that part of the building which is in its care, custody, or control. The coverage is for property damage liability caused by one peril, fire, when fire is the result of an insured's negligence.

Only one exclusion applies to fire legal liability coverage, and it pertains to liability which is assumed by the insured under any contract or agreement. The exclusion precludes coverage for claims which arise solely from a contractual obligation that is not grounded in real or alleged negligence on the part of the insured. For example, the coverage will not protect an insured for his or her failure to keep the rented or leased premises in good repair or in as good a condition as when it was received. But any fire damage to property in the insured's care, custody, or control is covered if the insured is found to be legally liable, whether or not such liability is assumed under any contract or agreement.

Under the broad form endorsement, fire legal liability coverage is excess insurance over any other valid and collectible property insurance which is available to the insured, such as fire, extended coverage, builders' risk, or an installation floater. The coverage is limited to $50,000 per occurrence, moreover, unless the limit is increased for an additional cost.

Broad Form Property Damage Liability Coverage (Including Completed Operations)

Broad form property damage liability coverage, including completed operations, is identical to coverage which is available by separate endorsement to the CGL policy. The coverage, intended for firms which perform work or services rather than produce or sell products, is treated in depth in Chapter 4.

Briefly, broad form property damage liability coverage modifies both the care, custody, or control exclusion and the injury to work performed exclusion of commercial liability policy provisions. The result of such exclusionary modifications is to give an insured liability protection for damage to property in its care, custody, or control, except that part of any property on which the insured is performing work at the time of an occurrence. And, since coverage for completed operations is included as a part of broad form property damage, an insured has liability protection for damage to work which was performed on behalf of the insured by someone such as an independent contractor.

Incidental Medical Malpractice Liability Coverage

It is not entirely clear whether the standard CGL policy would cover an insured who inadequately administers medical treatment to a business invitee who sustains bodily injury while on the insured's premises, or an insured who fails to render such immediate medical treatment as may be warranted by the circumstances. Incidental medical malpractice liability coverage clarifies such questions of coverage by extending the term "bodily injury" to mean "injury arising out of the rendering of or failure to render, during the policy period, the following services: (A) medical, surgical, dental, x-ray or nursing service or treatment or the furnishing of food or beverages in connection therewith, or (B) the furnishing or dispensing of drugs or medical, dental or surgical supplies or appliances."[46]

However, incidental medical malpractice liability coverage *does not apply* to any insured who (1) provides any of the medical and kindred services in (A) or (B) above as part of its business or occupation, such as a hospital or municipal rescue unit; (2) incurs any expenses for the treatment of first aid to others at the time of accident; and (3) causes an injury for which it has assumed liability under any contract or agreement, if the insured is engaged in the business or occupation of providing any medical and related services in (A) or (B) above. The fact that a firm in (1), (2), or (3) above does not receive incidental medical malpractice liability coverage does not make that firm ineligible for the broad form package. A firm may still purchase the package for the other extended coverages which are provided by the form.

Nonowned Watercraft Liability Coverage

The final extension of coverage under the broad form endorsement modifies the CGL policy exclusion of bodily injury or property damage arising out of the ownership, maintenance, operation, use, loading, or unloading of any watercraft (1) owned or operated by or rented or loaned to any insured, or (2) operated by any person during the course of his or her employment by the insured. The net effect of the modification is to provide coverage for liability which arises from any watercraft under twenty-six feet in length, so long as the watercraft is not owned by the named insured or is not used to carry passengers for a charge. Note that the latter limitation is directed, in part, to watercraft owned by the *named* insured. There is coverage for liability which arises from watercraft under twenty-six feet, if owned by a partner of a partnership, an employee, or an executive officer of a corporation (if they are not listed as named insured). Thus, if an employee or executive officer uses his or her own watercraft (under twenty-six feet in length) to entertain customers of the company, both the named insured and the owner of such watercraft are protected in the event the customers are injured, assuming the customers were not charged anything. However, if any such insured is covered under another policy, the extension of nonowned watercraft liability coverage does not apply, even though the other policy ultimately is determined to have inadequate limits.

While some coverages of the broad form endorsement may not be required by a particular firm, the endorsement provides the twelve coverages and extensions at a price which is lower than if all the coverages were purchased separately.

COMMERCIAL UMBRELLA LIABILITY INSURANCE

Commercial umbrella liability insurance applies to a wide range of liability loss exposures, including not only premises and operations but also products, completed operations, automobile and aircraft, contractual, and employers' liability loss exposures. However, in order to avoid unnecessary repetition, the nature and scope of commercial umbrella liability insurance will be discussed only in this, the first of the chapters to which it applies.

Umbrella liability, umbrella excess liability, broad form excess liability, blanket catastrophe excess liability, and bumbershoot liability are some of the many terms used to describe forms which provide firms with excess liability protection. In a strict sense, however, there is a distinct difference between "true umbrella" liability insurance and excess liability insurance.

Commercial umbrella liability policies serve two basic purposes: (1) they provide excess liability limits over any underlying liability coverage that may apply, and (2) they cover many (but not all) of the liability exposures excluded by the underlying liability policies, subject to deductibles or so-called "self-insured retention" or "SIR."

Excess liability policies, on the other hand, provide excess limits on exposures which are covered in underlying policies. They normally do not cover exposures excluded by the underlying policies. The difference between commercial liability policies and excess liability policies is illustrated in Figure 2-2. The primary disadvantage of an excess liability policy, as compared to an umbrella liability policy, is that the excess limits of the former apply only to the exposures selected. If a wrong selection of exposures is made, a firm may be without excess protection.

Bumbershoot liability policies serve to provide excess liability limits on certain ocean marine-oriented coverages, such as protection and indemnity, collision (running down clause), and stevedores' liability.

There is no standard form of umbrella liability insurance, even though many of the provisions of such policies are similar. Nor can one rely on the name of the form alone in determining whether it is an umbrella or an excess liability policy. The policy provisions must be examined carefully to determine the scope of coverage. Furthermore, insurance companies and underwriters at Lloyd's of London promulgate their own rates, mostly on a judgment basis. Prospective purchasers,

Figure 2-2

Excess Liability Policies Versus Commercial Umbrella Policies

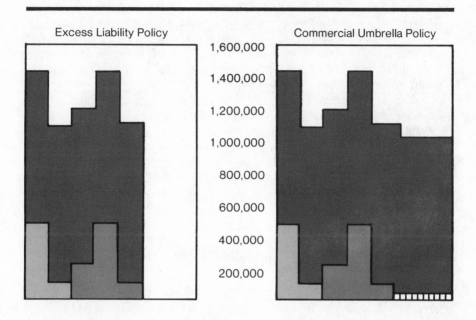

Key:

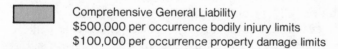

Comprehensive General Liability
$500,000 per occurrence bodily injury limits
$100,000 per occurrence property damage limits

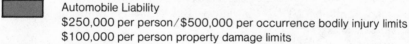

Automobile Liability
$250,000 per person/$500,000 per occurrence bodily injury limits
$100,000 per person property damage limits

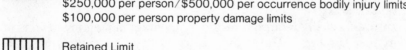

Retained Limit
$25,000

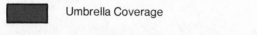

Umbrella Coverage

In this example, both the excess liability policy and the commercial umbrella policy provide $1,000,000 of additional liability coverage for the same losses covered by underlying policies. In addition, the commercial umbrella policy covers some losses not covered by underlying insurance, subject to a retained limit of $25,000.

therefore, should compare their costs against the coverages they provide. Important considerations not only include what may be specifically covered, but also what may be specifically precluded from coverage, as well as what coverages and limits may be required on underlying policies. Another important point to consider is the language of excess and umbrella liability policies. If the wording of excess or umbrella policy provisions varies from that of underlying coverage provisions, gaps may be created which can turn out to be costly in the event of large losses.[47]

Unless otherwise noted, the remainder of this discussion will be devoted solely to "true" umbrella liability policies, i.e., those which provide excess liability limits over underlying coverage, as well as coverage of liability exposures excluded by underlying policies, subject to retention amounts. The adjective "true" will be dropped for convenience, and the policies simply will be referred to as umbrella policies or contracts, umbrella liability policies or contracts, or umbrella liability insurance.

Nature of Commercial Umbrella Liability Insurance

Umbrella liability insurance is meant to be a catastrophe type coverage. It does not provide primary insurance, nor is it a panacea for all losses. It is designed first to be used for the protection of losses which exceed primary (underlying) insurance limits. Second, it is intended for the less frequent losses which usually are not covered by primary insurance or intentionally retained. Third, the commercial umbrella policy provides coverage that automatically replaces underlying policies whose aggregate limits are reduced or used up by losses. Generally, the higher the limits of primary insurance and the higher the deductibles (retained limit or SIR), the lower the costs of umbrella liability insurance will be.

Insurers usually require insureds to maintain minimum amounts of underlying coverage. Until the early 1970s, the minimum limits generally were $100,000 per person BI, $300,000 per occurrence BI, $100,000 PD for comprehensive general liability and comprehensive automobile liability, $1 million for comprehensive aviation liability, $200,000 for bailee liability, and $100,000 for employers' liability.[48] Losses excluded by primary liability policies and covered by umbrella liability often required retained limits of $10,000. But, because of changing legal concepts, the growth of consumerism and claim consciousness, the increase in size of awards by juries, and the overall net losses sustained by insurers, requirements have changed. The same basic coverages still are required, but minimum primary limits have more than doubled for all coverages except bailee and employers' liability. Today, the required minimum retentions are often $25,000, $100,000 or more.

It is important to understand how the policy limits and retained limits are applied in relation to (1) covered losses of underlying liability policies, (2) excluded losses of underlying policies, and (3) excluded losses of both the umbrella and underlying policies, and (4) the application of loss settlements involving aggregate limits.

When an underlying liability policy covers a loss exposure which also is covered by an umbrella policy, the umbrella policy, subject to its limits, generally pays for that part of the covered loss which exceeds the limits of an underlying liability policy, without application of the retained limit. For example, if an insured with $100,000 aggregate property damage limits under a CGL policy sustained a $110,000 property damage liability loss, the primary or underlying insurer would pay up to its $100,000 limit and the umbrella liability insurer would pay the remaining $10,000. [49] However, if the loss in the preceding example were covered by the umbrella policy but not covered by the underlying policy, the umbrella insurer would only pay for that amount of the loss, subject to its limit, which exceeds the retained limit. If the umbrella policy had a $25,000 retained limit, the umbrella insurer would pay $85,000 of the property damage liability loss. If the retained limit was $100,000 instead, the umbrella policy would only pay the excess over the retained limit or $10,000. But when an umbrella policy contains an exclusion which also is found in the underlying insurance, the insured obviously has no insurance protection whatsoever.

When an aggregate limit of an underlying liability policy is reduced by the payment of a loss, the umbrella liability policy, subject to its limits, will pay any excess of the reduced underlying aggregate limit for the duration of the annual policy period.[50] For example, if a $500,000 bodily injury aggregate limit for the products liability coverage of an underlying policy is reduced by $200,000 as the result of a loss, the insured only has $300,000 of underlying products liability coverage remaining for the duration of the annual policy period. If the insured were to sustain another products liability loss involving bodily injury and amounting to $400,000, the insured would be required to retain $100,000 of that loss in absence of an umbrella liability policy. But if the insured has an umbrella liability policy which covers the loss, it would "drop down" and cover the additional $100,000 of loss. More important, the umbrella liability policy would continue to provide coverage, as if it were the primary source of coverage, in the event that the aggregate limit of the underlying liability policy is exhausted by the payment of losses. Thus, after the payment of the second loss in this example, the umbrella policy would continue to provide the insured with protection for the remainder of the annual policy period, subject to the aggregate limit of the umbrella policy.

Coverages, Policy Provisions, and Rationale

So much diversity exists among umbrella liability policies that it is difficult to summarize them accurately in a brief discussion. For the most part, the policies are indemnity contracts in the sense that insurers agree to *reimburse* insureds for amounts they ultimately are obligated to pay claimants, within the specified limits, rather than to *pay on behalf of* insureds. However, the difference between these two payment arrangements is not nearly as significant as it first may appear, because an umbrella policy which is written as an indemnity contract usually does not require the insured to pay a claim as a condition to reimbursement. Instead, the criterion is that the insured must be legally obligated to pay the settlement or judgment amount. Once that obligation is established, an insurer of an umbrella policy usually will make the payment on behalf of the insured. The real difference between these two payment arrangements is that an umbrella policy written on an indemnity basis gives the insured more control in handling the negotiation and litigation of any claims than an umbrella policy that contains the agreement to pay on behalf of the insured.

Insuring Clauses—Defense The insuring clauses of most umbrella policies state that the insurer will indemnify the insured for the ultimate net loss in excess of the retained limit. Thus, of obvious importance are the definitions of "ultimate net loss" and "retained limit."

Although the definition of "ultimate net loss" varies by policy, it usually means the amount actually paid or payable for the settlement of a claim for which the insured is liable (sometimes including and sometimes excluding the defense costs) after deductions are made for all recoveries and salvage.

When the term "ultimate net loss" is defined to *include* defense costs, the insured can be somewhat at a disadvantage, because the defense costs are not payable in addition to the umbrella policy limit. Thus, if an insured's umbrella policy has a limit of $1 million, the court imposes a judgment of $1 million and the defense costs are $200,000, the ultimate net loss is $1.2 million or $200,000 more than the umbrella policy limit. In a case such as this, the umbrella insurer would pay its $1 million limit—$800,000 of the judgment amount and $200,000 for defense costs. The insured therefore would be required to pay $200,000, which represents the difference between the ultimate net loss of $1.2 million and the $1 million actually paid by the umbrella insurer.

When "ultimate net loss" is defined to *exclude* defense costs, the insured normally receives protection for its defense costs in addition to the applicable limit of the umbrella liability policy. In fact, most such umbrella policies contain a supplementary payments provision similar to the one found in the standard policy jacket used with commercial liability forms. If an insured in the preceding example had an umbrella liability policy which covered defense costs in addition to the applicable limit of liability, the umbrella insurer would have paid the $1 million judgment, as well as the $200,000 defense costs. Furthermore, many umbrella contracts contain provisions which give the insurer the right to participate in or take over the defense of any claim, even when there is no underlying insurance (i.e., even when a loss is within the insured's retained limit).

The "retained limit" can represent either the amount recoverable under any valid and collectible underlying insurance or the amount stated in the umbrella policy declarations as the insured's retention, but in either case the loss must be sustained by the insured because of liability (for covered torts) imposed by law or assumed under any contract. The three groups of coverages normally provided are personal injury, property damage, and advertising liability.[51] And many of the differences among commercial umbrella policies are differences in the scope of these three coverages.

Personal Injury. While personal injury is not defined uniformly among umbrella contracts, virtually all such contracts define personal injury to include the term "bodily injury" as the latter is defined in the standard policy jacket for use with commercial liability forms. Strictly speaking, the term "personal injury" refers only to torts of intentional interference. But, since the personal injury coverage is defined to include bodily injury, coverage also applies for bodily injury stemming from the negligence of the insured.

Whatever else is included within the definition of "personal injury" varies significantly from one umbrella contract to the next. Some umbrella contracts define "personal injury" to include essentially the same so-called "offenses" as are commonly covered by the personal injury coverage endorsement for use with standard liability policies (as well as by the broad form CGL endorsement, which was mentioned earlier); namely, false arrest, detention, malicious prosecution, wrongful entry or eviction, libel, and slander. Other umbrella contracts define personal injury to include mental injury, shock, and disease. And sometimes it includes discrimination based on race, religion, sex, or age, when insurance for such is not otherwise prohibited by law.

Property Damage. The scope of property damage liability coverage generally corresponds to the definition of that term in the standard policy jacket.

Advertising Liability. Advertising liability coverage refers to coverage for acts committed or alleged to have been committed in any advertisement, publicity article, broadcast, or telecast, and arising out of the advertising activities of the insured. Any damages arising out of such advertising activities are generally covered when caused by libel or slander; infringement of copyright, title, or slogan; privacy or unfair competition or idea misappropriation under an implied contract; or invasion of privacy rights. The umbrella coverage of advertising liability resembles the corresponding coverage which is provided by the broad form CGL endorsement, except that umbrella contracts do not preclude coverage of firms which are in the advertising or broadcasting business.

Exclusions What is or is not specifically covered under umbrella liability policies depends largely upon the applicable exclusions.

There is little uniformity among the exclusions used by the various umbrella insurers, but the following, which are replicas of the exclusions that apply under the standard CGL policy, are at least representative of the more common exclusions in use: obligations of an employer which are payable under workers' compensation and similar laws; liability arising from the ownership, maintenance, use, loading, or unloading of all aircraft, and any watercraft over certain lengths, such as twenty-five or fifty feet; pollution and/or contamination losses, other than those which are sudden *and* accidental; injury to work performed by or on behalf of the named insured, as well as damage to the named insured's products; expenses for recalling products because they are known or suspected to be defective; the so-called failure to perform exclusion, which precludes coverage for loss of use of undamaged tangible property that results from the failure of the named insured's work or product to perform as the named insured warrants or represents; and damage to property which is owned by, or in the care, custody or control of the named insured.[52]

The foregoing are some of the more common exclusions that apply under umbrella liability policies currently in use. Virtually all umbrella contracts also contain the same broad form nuclear energy liability exclusion that is found in other commercial liability forms. On the other hand, the treatment of war and allied perils varies considerably. Some umbrella contracts specifically exclude liability of an insured due to war and allied perils, while other policies do not contain any war exclusion whatsoever.[53]

Despite all of the preceding exclusions, umbrella liability contracts do provide a valuable range of protection for firms. For example, readers who examine one or two umbrella contracts will find that they usually do not exclude, and therefore cover subject to a retention, such exposures as liquor liability; blanket explosion, collapse, or underground property damage; blanket contractual for oral and written agreements; and property damage to alienated premises, other than an insured's work performance or products.[54]

Use of Commercial Umbrella Liability Insurance

It bears repeating that commercial umbrella liability insurance is designed to provide protection against large, catastrophic losses. What constitutes a "large" or "catastrophic" loss depends upon the size of the firm, its financial capacity and willingness to withstand losses, and other such considerations. A $100,000 loss may be catastrophic to one firm and comparatively minor to another, but firms of all sizes purchase substantial amounts of commercial umbrella liability insurance protection.

In some instances, umbrella coverage may be the only form of liability insurance available to a business firm, since insurance on a primary basis (especially for certain exposures) may be difficult or impossible to obtain, or economically unfeasible to purchase. Firms in these circumstances may be able to obtain at least some protection in the form of umbrella contracts over large retentions.

However, some firms are not always able to obtain umbrella liability insurance without encountering difficulty. One problem area is in obtaining sufficient underlying limits of primary coverage in order to qualify for umbrella liability insurance. It is not uncommon for an umbrella insurer to demand high underlying limits of a firm that poses an unusual loss exposure or a poor loss record. For example, the customary underlying limit for CGL coverage may be $500,000 BI/$100,000 PD. But, because of a firm's extraordinary products liability exposure, an umbrella insurer may demand underlying limits of $1 million BI/$500 PD. When a firm's primary insurer cannot provide the minimum limits to qualify for umbrella coverage, the firm will have to seek another insurer to provide all or part of the required limits, if the firm still feels that the umbrella liability coverage is essential. But, while there are insurers willing to provide intermediate levels of limits, commonly referred to as "buffer layers" or "gap" insurance, the major drawback is the price. For example, a manufacturer of machinery with a catastrophic products liability exposure may be required to pay as much as $100,000 for an annual buffer layer limit of $500,000, just to qualify for umbrella liability protection. The manufacturer also undoubtedly would be subject to a high retention limit between the underlying limit and the umbrella limit.

Another problem confronting some firms is that it is not always easy to obtain the desired upper limits on umbrella liability insurance. A firm may only be able to obtain an umbrella policy with $10 million limits, for example, when in reality it desires limits of $50 million or more. In order to obtain the higher limits, the firm may have to purchase excess limits through the process of "layering."

To layer means to "stack" successive amounts of excess limits from as many insurers as may be required to reach the combined or total limit desired. For example, a firm with an umbrella liability policy for limits of $10 million from one insurer may be able to obtain an additional $10 million in limits from each of five different insurers. The arrangement normally specifies that the second layer does not become effective until the first $10 million limit is exhausted, and the third layer of $10 million does not become effective until the second layer is exhausted, and so on. On the other hand, it may take two or more insurers to provide the limits of a particular layer. An insurer may be receptive to writing one-fourth of the second layer and half of the fifth layer. Although each layer becomes effective only when the preceding layer is exhausted, where two or more insurers participate in the writing of a given layer, each contributes to losses within that layer on a pro rata basis. As an illustration, assume Insurer A provides the first $10 million umbrella limit and the second layer of $10 million is shared one-fourth by Insurer B and three-fourths by Insurer C. In the event of a $20 million court verdict against the insured, Insurer A will pay its limit of $10 million, Insurer B will pay one-fourth of the second layer or $2.5 million and Insurer C will pay the remaining three-fourths or $7.5 million.

The Adequacy of Dollar Limits   Umbrella liability insurance, along with layering, no doubt permits many firms to obtain high levels of protection. But whether the limits are truly "adequate" is another matter entirely. Though a number of writers have shed some light on the matter, asking how much liability insurance is "enough" is still very much like asking how high is up.[55]

It sometimes is said that a proprietor or a partner stands to lose his or her personal worth and a shareholder no more than his or her investment, a corporation can lose no more than its assets.[56] These observations contain an important element of truth, but they do not answer the question of how much liability insurance should be purchased. Liability insurance merely increases the size of a judgment that would be large enough to bankrupt a firm.

Consider a corporation with $1 million of assets, for instance. If it carries $1 million of liability insurance, a $2 million court judgment could cause bankruptcy. It if carries $2 million of liability insurance, a $3 million judgment could cause bankruptcy. Moreover, even a smaller uninsured verdict of, say, $500,000, could bankrupt or seriously impair the firm's financial condition, particularly when we acknowledge the possibility of several such losses in a single fiscal period.

How should risk managers determine the adequacy of liability insurance limits? Unfortunately, there is no truly satisfactory answer to that question. We do know that jury awards are getting larger and larger and that, as a practical matter, there is no upper dollar limit on the amount a jury might award. What makes matters even worse is that many firms today are experiencing difficulties in finding markets for the liability insurance limits they desire, at least at prices they are willing and/or able to pay.

In fact, a number of risk managers buy the highest limits they *can* obtain in the worldwide market and hope that they will be adequate. This approach does not guarantee that the available limits will be high enough, of course, nor does it address the matter of whether the successively higher layers of protection are obtained at reasonable prices. But it does underscore the nature of the current dilemma. Even firms that are willing and able to pay for available jumbo limits often do not feel they are adequate. Some firms feel the need for jumbo limits but are not willing or able to pay for them; some find that higher limits are unavailable; and nearly all firms face the formidable loss potential which has become very difficult to determine in a rapidly changing legal environment.

Given the problem of growing loss potential, insurance availability, and price, it is all the more important for firms to coordinate their insurance-purchasing decisions with careful consideration of available alternatives. If a firm retains the smaller losses which are so costly to insure and concentrates its premium dollars on the purchase of the higher limits needed, which are less expensive to insure, on the margin; and if it implements effective loss controls; it should be in a much better position to obtain catastrophic protection at economically feasible costs. In short, firms can get the most from insurance only when it is properly combined with noninsurance techniques, a subject which will now be discussed in the context of premises and operations liability loss exposures.

NONINSURANCE TECHNIQUES FOR HANDLING PREMISES AND OPERATIONS LIABILITY EXPOSURES

Every business firm should utilize appropriate noninsurance

techniques for handling premises and operations liability exposures, as a complement to adequate liability insurance. Insurance should not be viewed as a substitute for exercising special precautions to reduce, control, and otherwise deal with potential losses. Indeed, firms that rely entirely on insurance eventually will find it unavailable or economically unfeasible to obtain.

Before firms can effectively utilize any risk management technique, they must first identify their loss exposures. In this regard, firms can study (1) existing insurance contracts, which can reveal exposures that presently are covered, partially covered, and not covered; (2) loss records, which may indicate certain exposures that are the source for high loss frequencies; and (3) rental, lease, purchase-order and other contractual agreements, which specify the terms, conditions and liabilities of those contracts. Surveys which require visual inspections also are extremely beneficial in identifying liability exposures, as are various coverage checklists. While there are many such exposure-identification aids from which to choose (some are available for sale and others are provided by insurers), many of the aids, particularly the coverage checklists, are directed principally at the common and insurable exposures of businesses. To avoid overlooking loss exposures which are uninsurable, or insurable but peculiar to a business operation, a risk manager, insurance buyer, agent, consultant, or whoever has the responsibility for managing a firm's loss exposures, may wish to obtain and study several such surveys and coverage checklists. In any case, the need for an exhaustive and painstaking search for loss exposures cannot be overemphasized, if only because oversights can have such severe consequences for the firm.

Upon completion of the identification process, the next step is to analyze the loss-producing capabilities of the exposures which have been identified. Estimating the maximum loss potential of third-party liability exposures is especially problematical, for reasons noted earlier, but the difficulty of that task should not obscure the need for other kinds of loss analysis. When firms make no effort to determine and analyze their loss costs, insurance can become an overused and "abused link" in the risk management process, particularly when such insurance is required by statute or is readily available at an affordable price (such as premises and operations liability coverage).

Yet, in a survey on the attitudes toward risk management of 1,143 businesses in six industrial classifications, Hogue and Olson found that only a slight majority (50.9 percent) of the businesses attempt to obtain valuations of "expected loss costs" for at least some portion of their premises liability exposures.[57] However, the estimates apparently deal mostly with "slips and trips," exposures of a type which produce high frequency and low severity losses. To make estimates on the loss costs of any other premises and operations liability exposures would be too difficult, the authors conclude, because there are too many variables involved.

What is particularly interesting about this survey are the reasons given, by the other 49.1 percent of the businesses surveyed, for not conducting any loss cost estimates for their premises and operations liability exposures. The authors state that firms with $25 million or more in sales (17.4 percent of the respondents) that do not attempt such loss cost estimates "were inclined to state that it was 'not worth the effort'," while firms with sales ranging from $1 to $25 million in sales (25.1 percent of the respondents) "were more inclined to say 'didn't consider it, since insurance company will pay'." On the other hand, small firms of less than $1 million in sales (44.7 percent of the respondents) stated their reason as being the "company is too small to make such an estimate meaningful." Two other groups not broken down by sales volume (comprising 12.8 percent of the respondents) either gave no reason for not obtaining loss cost estimates or they stated that they "lacked the expertise and they could not obtain reliable outside help."

Hogue and Olson take issue with the respondents who do not make any special effort to analyze the loss-producing capabilities of their premises and operations liability exposures.[58] The authors' principal arguments, which seem particularly persuasive with respect to the medium and large-size firms that have the resources to make loss-cost estimates, are that (1) a business which relies upon its insurance as a crutch for the payment of all losses, large and small, rather than as a device for handling a firm's catastrophic losses is merely "trading dollars"; and (2) a business which properly identifies and analyzes its loss-producing exposures and uses insurance, along with other perhaps more appropriate noninsurance techniques, would find the time and effort rewarding.[59]

In any event, once a business concern identifies and analyzes its liability loss exposures, the third step in the risk management process is to decide how best to handle the exposures. It may be possible for a business to avoid some of its exposures altogether. If not, virtually every business may retain at least a portion of its losses. Some exposures may be transferred to others through such devices as lease, purchase-order, and hold harmless agreements. And loss prevention and control techniques are always highly desirable, if not essential, to supplement and complement all of insurance and noninsurance methods a firm decides to use.

Avoidance

Avoidance, as a noninsurance technique, is a method by which an individual or firm (1) refuses to assume a loss exposure, even momentarily, such as when a firm decides to forgo the purchase of another business location; or (2) abandons an existing exposure to loss which is capable of producing catastrophic results, such as when a demolition contracting firm decides to liquidate its business following several large losses and sharp increases in its insurance premiums.

Since the operation of a business necessarily involves some chances of loss, it should be obvious that a firm which successfully avoids all loss exposures would not be in business at all. Moreover, to avoid many exposures would be impractical, because to do so the business would have to forgo opportunities to make profits. Although avoidance is not a particularly common tool for the treatment of premises and operations liability exposures, since most firms rely upon their insurance, avoidance of some narrowly-defined liability exposures may be desirable, and it may even be essential when liability insurance is either unavailable or unaffordable.

Isolating the "pure" premises and operations liability exposures confronting businesses, i.e., distinguishing the purely physical exposures of business premises and their maintenance from automobile, aircraft, completed operations, products liability and workers' compensation exposures, for purposes of citing examples of situations which some-times can be avoided effectively, is not an easy task. However, among the "pure" premises and operations liability exposures which might need to be avoided are the exposures excluded by the various liability insurance coverage provisions discussed earlier in this chapter.

Examples of avoiding such exposures include the owner of a business premises who refuses to lease the premises to an operator of a restaurant or bar for fear of the liability implications created by various liquor liability or dram shop acts; the appliance dealer who sells but refuses to install goods in order to avoid losses to a purchaser's property which may be in the care, custody, or control of the seller during the actual course of installing such appliances; and the landscape contractor who refuses the offer to perform certain excavation work in areas of underground piping or wiring. An example of a more broadly defined exposure which may be avoided through abandonment is the firm which decides to go out of business because it does not have the financial resources either to meet federal and/or state environmental standards concerning pollution or contamination controls or to survive potentially catastrophic losses of the uninsurable type.

So, while avoidance is sometimes the proper method for handling narrowly defined aspects of a firm's premises and operations liability exposures, it is impossible to use it for all exposures if the firm wants to stay in business. To deal with the many important exposures which invariably remain, the firm must look to other methods and combinations of methods.

Noninsurance Transfer Agreements

Almost all businesses have opportunities, under the terms of contracts, to transfer some part of their losses to others.[60] Conversely, there are occasions when almost all firms will agree, sometimes reluctantly, to accept responsibility for the losses of others. Circumstances arise, moreover, when a firm will be a transferee (assuming losses of another) under some agreements, and a transferor (delegating responsibility for losses to another) under other agreements.

One can readily understand why a firm might seek to *transfer* losses to another. A contractual transfer can be a convenient and economical method of handling the transferor's loss exposures. Less apparent is why a firm would ever go so far as to *assume* the losses of another. The answer, in many cases, is that the transferee has little choice. Unless the transferee is able to modify a proposed agreement, it must either accept all of its terms, including the assumption provision, or forgo the business advantage sought by entering into the contract in the first place. A great deal depends upon the relative bargaining strength of the parties.

Types of Noninsurance Transfers Noninsurance transfers generally are of two types.[61] The first type concerns the transfer of property or operations which are the source of losses, as for example, the sale of a building or business or the employment of a subcontractor to perform a portion of a construction project.[62] The second type of noninsurance transfer concerns itself with shifting the financial consequences of loss to another, rather than the transfer of property or operations, as for example, the provisions of leases which transfer certain financial losses from lessor to lessee or from landlord to tenant and sometimes vice versa. Since risk management is concerned primarily with the second type of noninsurance transfer, the remainder of the subject matter is confined to noninsurance transfer agreements which concern themselves with the shifting of financial consequences of losses.

Classes of Loss Transfers Loss transfers may be classified, according to their purpose, as (1) hold harmless agreements, (2) exculpatory agreements, and (3) indemnity agreements.

Hold Harmless Agreements. When the subject of transfer concerns itself with the assumption of another's legal obligations under a suit by a third party, the arrangement commonly is referred to as a hold harmless agreement.[63] The hold harmless agreement becomes effective when one party (the indemnitor) agrees to hold another party (the indemnitee) harmless from tort liability under third-party actions. An example is the contractor who agrees to hold harmless the owner of a project for any negligent act or omission by the contractor which results in bodily injury or property damage to third persons. Such assumption by the indemnitor (the contractor) can become effective (1) when liability of the indemnitee (the project owner) is established, i.e., following court proceedings handled by the indemnitee for his or her own defense and any court award; or (2) when the indemnitee first becomes involved in a suit. The circumstances of (2) above involve a true hold harmless arrangement, in the sense that the indemnitor takes over the entire defense of the indemnitee and pays any judgment to a third party as rendered against the indemnitee by a court or as agreed upon in any settlement outside of a court proceeding. The arrangement in (1) above, on the other hand, merely requires the indemnitor to reimburse (indemnify) the other party to the extent of any court judgment which may be rendered or any settlement which is reached prior to court proceedings. Whether the indemnitor is obligated to pay for the defense and other costs incurred by the indemnitee depends upon the terms of the contract.

However, it should be understood that neither of the above two contractual arrangements really absolves the indemnitee (property owner) from its tort liability. The arrangements merely give an indemnitee a contractual right to seek recovery from the indemnitor. If an indemnitor is uninsured or insolvent or a court does not uphold the terms of the contract, the indemnitee then is obligated to settle the matter with the third party.[64]

Exculpatory Agreements. An exculpatory agreement is an arrangement whereby one party agrees to absolve another party from any blame when the latter causes loss to the former. Exculpatory agreements commonly are used in various lease agreements. Here, a lessee (the firm which desires to occupy all or part of another's premises) who sustains a loss caused by the lessor (property owner) nevertheless agrees to vindicate the lessor from blame. Thus, the lessee accepts all the consequences, just as though loss were caused by it, if the agreement is not otherwise held to be invalid by statute or by a court of law. Note the difference between a hold harmless agreement and an exculpatory agreement. In a hold harmless arrangement, the indemnitor takes over the defense of and/or reimburses the indemnitee for any judgment (and, perhaps, other costs) rendered against the indemnitee which are assumed under contract. In an exculpatory agreement, the exculpator accepts the entire blame caused by the other party, and it handles the entire matter just as if the other party were nonexistent.

Indemnity Agreements. The term "indemnity agreement" sometimes is used interchangeably with the term "hold harmless agreement."
But in a strict sense, an indemnity agreement concerns itself with
bailments, rather than with the assumption of another's liability for
negligence or another tort that results in loss to some third party, as is
the case with hold harmless agreements. Thus, an indemnity agreement
is a contractual undertaking involving the owner of personal property
(the bailor) and the individual or firm which has temporary possession of
such property (the bailee), whereby the bailee agrees to pay for any
physical damage losses to the bailor's property stemming from the acts
or omissions of the bailee. An example is when a firm leases electronic
data processing equipment from its owner and agrees to indemnify the
owner in the event any such equipment is physically damaged while it is
in the care, custody, or control of the bailee or user.

Noninsurance Transfer Agreements—Points to Consider

Hold harmless and other transfer agreements can be effective in dealing
with a firm's loss exposures, if such contracts are reasonable in scope and
unambiguously worded, and, then, only if transferees are financially
able to handle the agreed upon consequences. However, this is not
always the case. Loss transfer agreements often present problems, not
only for those who are to assume the losses, but also for those who are
attempting to transfer them.

Some transfer agreements are plainly against public policy or in
violation of statute, particularly those which seek to hold indemnitors
responsible for *all* losses, regardless of the nature of losses or whose
negligence may cause losses. Others are so ambiguously worded that
their true intent is unclear, in which case the courts often are called
upon to settle the issues. When the contract wording is ambiguous to the
courts, the courts generally construe them strongly against the draftors.
And the fact that many contracts are subject to court interpretation also
means that valuable time and expense is wasted pending final
settlements. Moreover, there are occasions when the losses to be
assumed not only are beyond the scope of any insurance that an
intended transferee may have, but also of such a magnitude that losses
ultimately could not be assumed financially by the transferee. Hence,
contrary to what was intended, the party seeking to transfer the losses
ends up bearing the ultimate consequences.

It is important for those seeking to transfer losses via contract to
consult with competent legal counsel. The agreements need to be
worded very carefully if they are to conform to applicable statutes and
court decisions and to achieve, within the legal constraints, the desired
results. Sometimes the desired results clearly will not be enforceable at
law. But even when competent legal counsel believes that the desired

results are enforceable, that alone does not necessarily mean that the transfer will be effective.[65] Care also should be exercised to make sure that the intended transferee is financially able to pay for the losses which may occur.

One common way to support the legal agreement with financial security is for the transferor to insist that the transferee purchase and maintain adequate insurance. However, the amount of insurance that would be "adequate" is difficult to determine. Though the underlying agreement is contractual in nature, the dollar size of losses will be determined in accordance with tort law concepts. Consequently, it is as problematical to evaluate the adequacy of the transferee's insurance as it is with any other form of liability insurance.[66] Ideally, therefore, some effort should also be made to ascertain the transferee's general financial capacity, apart from its insurance. While this is not always easy, determining the transferee's experience in terms of years it has been in business and locating other firms, architects, engineers, or contractors who will attest to the transferee's reputation, integrity, and experience are alternative sources of evidence which may prove to be helpful. Furthermore, evidence of surety bonds, while not necessarily guaranteeing the financial capabilities of a bond holder, at least signifies such bond holder as having the qualities which are necessary to meet the conditions of contracts.[67]

Where the proposed transfer would be both legally enforceable and supported by adequate insurance and general financial capacity on the part of the proposed transferee, the transfer agreement is likely to be effective. But it still may not be *desirable* from a risk management point of view. Whether a transfer agreement is desirable depends largely upon (1) its effectiveness, and (2) its cost, if any, relative to alternative methods of handling the exposure.

It is conceivable that a firm with overwhelmingly superior bargaining strength might be able to impose a transfer agreement upon another party, very much at will, in which case the agreement might not involve any real or hidden "cost" to the transferor. But the courts are sometimes reluctant to enforce hold harmless and exculpatory agreements unless the parties are of relatively equal bargaining strength. And the relative bargaining strength of the parties frequently does not differ that much, in any event. Furthermore, the true costs of transfer are sometimes hidden. If Firm A forces Firm B to assume Firm A's liability, for example, Firm B might charge a higher price for its services. Or, a subcontractor forced to carry insurance and to hold harmless the general contractor might well include a dollar allowance in its bid price. The point here is simply that contractual transfers often involve some "cost" to the transferor. What makes the point all the more significant is that the residual uncertainties of transfer agreements sometimes lead a firm to carry its own insurance anyway, as an added precaution.

Costs of Transfers   That some hidden costs may have to be assumed by a transferor in spite of its imposition of a hold harmless agreement cannot be dispelled. And, while the cost of the transferor's liability insurance is not directly reduced simply because it requires contracts to transfer losses to others, there nonetheless are indirect methods for reducing the transferor's insurance costs.

The first transaction of the transferor is to obtain proof that the transferee's liability insurance includes coverage of the former's contractual agreement. Although this proof of insured transfer does not in any way reduce the direct insurance costs of the transferor, it may enable the transferor to escape any adverse loss experience, if the validity of the contract is upheld, including any additional costs which might otherwise apply to the transferor's experience rating or retrospective rating plan. The second thing the transferor could do is to request the transferee to purchase a separate owners and contractors protective liability policy from the latter's insurer and list the transferor as the named insured.[68] There are several reasons for such a request.

1. By obtaining a separate policy, the exposure need not be reported nor a charge made for it under the transferor's owners and contractors protective liability insurance, which is an automatic coverage of the CGL policy.
2. The transferor is obtaining defense protection under that separate policy at the expense of the transferee in the event the former is drawn into a claim stemming from the transferee's negligence.
3. Any loss which is handled by the transferee's insurer does not affect the transferor's loss experience, and, particularly, the transferor's experience rating or retrospective rating plan.

So, in spite of the transferor's assumption of certain hidden costs which may form a part of a contract bid, there are some very real offsetting costs (savings) which can accrue to the transferor in any event. However, if the hold harmless or other agreement is held to be unenforceable, the transferor can then rely upon its own premises and operations insurance for protection. Or, if the owners and contractors protective liability policy is found to have deficient limits against any judgment, the transferor's owners and contractors protective liability insurance will pay for any excess, if the loss is covered. Of course, if either of the two situations were to arise, the costs of effecting the transfers would all but be nullified.

Loss Control

While any number of insurance and noninsurance techniques can be utilized at any given time to handle premises and operations liability exposures, a program of loss prevention and control is virtually indispensable. Regardless of its size or the nature and scope of its operations, a firm always should take the initiative to adopt and administer a workable program of loss prevention and control.

Loss control can be effected in several ways. It can take the form of loss control which is aimed at reducing the frequency and/or the severity of losses, and, hence, the financial consequences which may otherwise result. Separation and combination are two other methods of control. The former separates loss exposures into many units so that losses can be better predicted. Decentralizing the locations of a firm's branches is an example. By maintaining separate responsibility for the exposures of the branches, it may be easier to implement loss control measures, to predict areas of high frequency and severity, and to pinpoint responsibility for taking corrective measures in reducing or controlling losses. Combination, as a form of control, takes the opposite approach to separation. Here, the procedure is to combine or centralize many units of exposure (branches) in order to enhance the predictability of losses and to obtain better controls in taking corrective measures.

Whatever the method, loss prevention and control programs should not be viewed as alternative tools to be used in lieu of other risk management techniques. Instead, they should be viewed as tools to supplement and complement other methods of handling liability loss exposures. A firm cannot simultaneously be in business and successfully avoid very many types of liability losses. Nor should a firm place undue reliance on its ability to transfer losses to others. Even a firm which combines adequate insurance with effective contractual transfers and sound retention procedures will be better off, in the final analysis, by anticipating and seeking to prevent and control losses. But when firms choose to ignore various control measures, they not only may find their principal source of insurance protection difficult to obtain at an affordable price, but also may find some of their uninsured exposures difficult to retain without depleting their cash flows.

In recognition of the foregoing, large and sophisticated firms have long since employed full-time risk managers and loss prevention specialists. Smaller firms may not be able to employ such expertise on a full-time basis, but they can obtain satisfactory results by seeking and following the advice of part-time consultants and qualified representatives of insurers.

Premises and Operations Liability Exposures Subject to Prevention and Control Measures Generally, most premises liability exposures stem from physical defects of buildings, structures, and grounds, and from the manner in which the premises are maintained. Examples of such hazards include sidewalks in need of repair, defective stairways, unmarked glass door panels, exposed floor plugs and wiring, poor lighting, insufficient means of egress from buildings, sidewalks which are not properly and promptly cleared of ice and snow, signs and billboards which are weakened through weathering and not periodically inspected, and sidewalk canopies that are not raised during closing hours or during severe weather conditions. These and other hazards can be reduced or controlled by making sufficiently frequent inspections and timely corrections and repairs.

Since most structural hazards of premises are relatively fixed in time and place, they can be eliminated or controlled, in most cases, through the exercise of foresight and care. An automobile repair shop, for example, may be able to reduce bodily injury claims emanating from accidents within its work areas by strictly enforcing rules which preclude access to customers within these areas. Or a commercial firm may be able to reduce or control certain liability losses by fencing its premises.

Less easy for firms to handle, generally speaking, are the liability exposures which arise out of business operations away from premises owned, maintained, or used by them, particularly those which stem from operations performed on premises of others. Whereas many hazards *on* the firm's own premises stem from defective conditions which usually can be sought out and corrected, hazards *away from* the firm's premises are actively created as work is performed and, by their nature, are often more difficult to anticipate and control.

A manufacturing plant which is not open to the public, for example, may have little in the way of an on-premises liability exposure. But its operations stemming from those premises can produce a variety of costly losses, particularly of a vicarious nature, i.e., where an employer is imputedly responsible for its employees' negligent acts or omissions arising out of and during the course of their employment. Most liability policies, as a practical matter, do not automatically include employees as insureds, and, since few employees realize that they also can be held personally accountable for their own acts and omissions, they should be informed about how they should conduct themselves in business matters.

Construction contracting firms, unlike those who operate predominately from fixed locations, may be confronted with somewhat different hazards at every location. Work in many instances is conducted in populated areas over which contractors have little control. A demolition contractor, for example, is not always permitted to disrupt the flow of traffic during its operations, in which case it should proceed with special caution and take care not to injure members of the public or damage adjoining buildings or structures. An excavation contractor, on the other hand, must be careful in determining the location of underground hazards such as telephone cables and natural gas lines. It also must see to it that properly lighted barriers are installed to warn pedestrians and motorists of hazardous conditions.

In all likelihood, businesses will not establish programs of loss prevention and control solely for purposes of handling their premises and operations liability exposures. Well-managed firms with loss control programs encompassing all facets of their liability exposures, e.g., automobile, products, completed operations, and workers' compensation may, as a practical matter, incorporate certain measures in controlling their premises and operations liability exposures, particularly when they have been experiencing a high frequency of losses. Smaller firms, on the other hand, may simply look to outside advice, e.g., agents, consultants and/or insurers, for whatever corrective measures may be necessary to prevent or control losses. However, no loss control program, however structured, or no amount of warning from outside sources concerning hazards will produce results unless management and personnel seriously give their support in becoming more safety conscious. Such support can range from sophisticated loss control programs which are established with objectives drawn up and supported by top management, including safety committees comprised of top management personnel of all departments, to instances when no formal program of loss prevention or control is maintained, but loss control nevertheless is communicated to be *everyone's* responsibility and is enforced by top management.

Thus, it is only through the implementation of prevention and control measures, buttressed by the support of top management and all personnel, that firms may be able to reduce their premises and operations, as well as other liability losses, and, hence, their insurance and/or retention costs.

Retention

Types of Retention Retention of losses can come about unknowingly (passively) or knowingly (actively). A *passive* retention is one whereby a firm has no other choice but to retain a loss which has already occurred, having failed to identify the loss exposure in the first place. Passive retention is worth mentioning, if only to stress the potential consequences of ignorance or oversight, but it is obviously not a rational approach. Thus, throughout the balance of this text, the discussions of retention will implicitly focus on *active* retention, i.e., that technique whereby a firm is aware of an exposure and consciously decides in advance to retain or bear loss, if and when it occurs.

Active retention may be either partial or total. Retention is said to be *partial* when a portion of every loss (or an aggregate of losses) is retained or borne by a firm, while a portion is transferred to another. Most often, the transferee is an insurer, and the amount of loss transferred is an amount in excess of a deductible. Retention is *total*, on the other hand, when every loss or aggregate of losses is fully retained or borne by the firm itself, i.e., no portion of loss is transferred to another.

Arrangements for Handling Retained Losses Whether retention is partial or total, losses which actually materialize may be *unfunded* or *funded*. The retention is unfunded when no special monetary fund is earmarked or set aside in advance to handle the losses retained. Thus, as and when it becomes necessary, losses are paid from the firm's "cash flow" (i.e., from the excess of operating revenue over operating expenses). However, when the firm's cash flow is inadequate in relation to the losses which occur, it may be necessary for the firm to liquidate some or all of its assets, depending on the seriousness of the situation and the availability of credit, in order to obtain the necessary funds. Asset liquidation might still be necessary, even if the firm maintains a bookkeeping "reserve" for such losses, since a mere bookkeeping entry does not in itself assure that liquid funds will be available when they are needed.

Under a *funded* retention program, losses are paid from funds or liquid assets which have been earmarked in advance for the specific purpose. Some firms create such funds through an initial appropriation. Others attempt to accumulate the funds over time, hopefully from the difference between the previous insurance premiums and the actual losses and expenses under the retention program. In either case, the mere fact that a retention program is funded does not necessarily mean that it is "fully" funded. Ultimately, it is fully funded only if the fund is large enough to pay, over the longer term, all of the losses which have been retained. It therefore follows that determining the adequacy of a retention fund, at any point in time, necessarily requires that losses be forecasted within tolerable degrees of accuracy. Though sophisticated actuarial techniques are beyond the scope of this text, the reader is reminded that no such technique will mystically reveal the future. The frequency and severity of liability losses, in particular, are difficult to predict. And this, in turn, poses some special problems for the retention approach.

It should also be noted that in practice "self-insurance" is *not necessarily* a program of funded retention. Indeed, in the jargon of the insurance industry, "self-insurance" is used in so many different ways that it suffers from a primary equivocation of terms. "Self-insurance" is frequently used, for example, when the speaker or author really means "planned uninsurance" (herein referred to as "unfunded retention"). And the matter should not be dismissed summarily as a mere game of semantics; to the contrary, there are some very important practical implications associated with the careless use of such labels, especially where "self-insurance" is used in a way which erroneously implies "adequate funding." Among those who could be seriously misled, as a consequence, are stockholders, potential investors, actual or potential creditors, injured workers, auditors, and regulators. Thus, in the absence of a universally agreed-upon definition of "self-insurance", the term probably should be avoided. Herein, the term "retention" will be used to refer to that generic class of risk management techniques which subsumes all of the various ways a firm might finance losses with its own resources, rather than transferring the losses to others. The generic class may be subdivided into two major subclasses—partial retention and total retention—and the losses which materialize under either approach may be funded or unfunded.

In recent years, a number of firms have formed or acquired so-called "captive insurers" to handle some or all of the firms' loss exposures. This approach could be thought of as an insurance transfer, perhaps, but there is a sense in which it is a form of funded retention.

Apart from captive insurers, the extent to which firms actively retain liability losses is difficult to quantify. From the limited data available, it is apparent that a number of firms do at least partially retain some of their liability losses, whether by choice or otherwise, and it is also apparent that many such firms have retention programs of an unfunded nature. Although there are some obvious potential dangers inherent in the unfunded retention approach, these dangers must be weighed against tax, accounting, and other financial considerations, including the firm's capacity to absorb unfunded losses. Management often finds particularly compelling the argument that unfunded retention avoids "tying up" funds which can be used more profitably in the firm's normal business activities. While this argument is not without merit for financially strong firms with adequate excess insurance, for others it is at least debatable.

Retention of Premises and Operations Liability Exposures As a general rule, tort liability losses should never be *fully* retained, assuming the firm has a realistic alternative. There are situations where a particular liability exposure can not be avoided, the noninsurance transfer technique is unavailable, and the exposure is either uninsurable or insurable only for a premium which is larger than management is able and/or willing to pay, in which case total retention, funded or otherwise, may be the only practical short-run alternative. But in so doing, a sole proprietor or general partner is risking all of his or her personal assets. And corporate shareholders, while risking only their investments, should at least be made to understand the implications of an uninsured tort liability exposure. Tort liability exposures, by their very nature, can give rise to a single loss which is virtually unlimited in amount (and multiple losses can and do occur within a given fiscal period). Larger firms may be better able to absorb liability losses, but they are also vulnerable to larger jury verdicts, as a practical matter. Moreover, if a particular firm has difficulty obtaining reasonably priced insurance available to other firms of the same type, this strongly suggests the need for changes in the firms' operations.

Fortunately, since there are only a few uninsurable aspects of the premises and operations liability exposure per se (e.g., nonaccidental pollution), there are likewise few losses which must be totally retained. Partial retention is sometimes forced upon an insured, by the imposition of a mandatory deductible on certain property damage liability exposures (e.g., spray painting operations outside buildings), or when a mandatory retention becomes effective because an umbrella policy covers a loss which is not covered by underlying insurance. Various experience rating plans also have features which effectively amount to partial retention when the insured has unfavorable loss experience. Otherwise, the partial retention of premises and operations liability exposures is not as common as it is in connection with property exposures.

In the context of primary insurance for premises and operations liability exposures, smaller deductibles seldom offer the insured enough premium savings to make them attractive. And larger deductibles are beyond the financial capacity of many firms to absorb, especially since deductibles are often applicable on a per occurrence basis (and there can be multiple occurrences in a single fiscal period). Accordingly, the active partial retention of premises and operations liability exposures is not a viable alternative for many firms, with the possible exception of larger firms which include such exposures in an overall retention program.

The incentives for retention can be substantial, but the potential benefits can be realized only if the retention technique is properly applied. At a minimum, effective loss prevention and control techniques should be utilized to complement every well-conceived retention program.

Chapter Notes

1. The definitions and concepts in the exposures section of this chapter are based on James H. Donaldson, *Casualty Claim Practice*, rev. ed. (Homewood, IL: Richard D. Irwin, 1969).
2. Premises and operations exposures of educational, charitable, and governmental entities are discussed separately in Chapter 12, because of their special nature.
3. Such terms as "form," "policy," "contract," and "coverage part" are commonly used interchangeably in insurance parlance. For example, reference sometimes is made to a comprehensive general liability form, to a comprehensive general liability coverage part, or to a comprehensive general liability policy.
4. ISO is a nonprofit organization whose functions are to gather statistics, promulgate rates, draft various property-liability policies and coverage provisions, conduct inspections for rate-making purposes, and perform other related services for the benefit of member insurance companies, as well as subscriber companies. Another somewhat smaller organization is the American Association of Insurance Services (AAIS), which serves similar purposes.
5. However, there may be occasions when certain standard provisions for commercial liability policies will vary from state to state. For example, the standard cancellation provisions of these liability policies sometimes must be amended in certain states, such as Michigan, to reflect the requirements of that state's cancellation provisions. Also, the standard liquor liability exclusion of commercial liability policies, which is mentioned later, must be amended in South Carolina to reflect the provisions of that state's alcoholic beverage control law.
6. Owners and contractors protective liability insurance is discussed in Chapter 5, whereas products and completed operations insurance is discussed in Chapter 4.
7. Appeal bonds and bonds to release attachments are discussed in Chapter 13.
8. Insurance Services Office, 1973 edition.
9. Personal injury liability insurance is discussed later in this chapter.
10. However, collision damage to the elevators themselves is not covered, unless an insured purchases elevator collision insurance for an additional cost.
11. A full discussion of hold harmless agreements appears in Chapter 5.
12. The owner also will be required to obtain and file a license and permit bond which guarantees the city that any claims will be paid by the owner if it is required to do so. License and permit bonds are discussed in Chapter 13.
13. Note that employees are not included as insureds either in (2) or (3) above. If employees are to be protected, additional coverage for them, as insureds, must be purchased by endorsement for an additional premium.
14. Although the term "real estate manager" is not defined in the policy jacket

or in the coverage parts, it presumably includes any person or firm that manages the real property (buildings and grounds) of the named insured. Such duties could involve maintaining the general upkeep of the premises, making minor repairs, collecting rents, advertising and filling vacancies to prospective tenants, and answering complaints.

15. An "omnibus clause" is another term for the "persons insured" provision. The former commonly is used in reference to automobile liability policies and is explained in Chapter 9.

16. What may be startling to most employees is that they are not covered under general liability policy provisions in the event they are sued for negligently injuring fellow employees during the course of their employment. This same exclusion in question even applies when employees are added as insureds under various liability coverage parts, and no insurer willingly offers insurance protection to employees for that type of an exposure. The rationale for the exclusion is to make workers' compensation insurance the exclusive remedy to an injured employee. However, if a negligent employee who causes a compensable injury to a fellow employee is sued for his or her personal assets, the defense costs and judgment against the negligent employee must be assumed by such employee.

17. Insurance Services Office, 1973 edition.

18. The "severability clause" is discussed more fully, along with automobile liability insurance, in Chapter 9.

19. A joint venture, as noted earlier, is not automatically covered under commercial liability policies. If coverage is desired, a joint venture must be specifically declared to the insurer and listed as the named insured on the policy.

20. Insurance Services Office, 1973 edition.

21. Whether an insurer will succeed in denying a loss of that nature is open to question. However, if a second bodily injury claim were to result from an unsafe condition of premises, an insurer probably could successfully deny that claim.

22. Insurance Services Office, 1973 edition.

23. The limits of liability shown as $100/100/300 are referred to as "dual limits," because separate limits apply to bodily injury and property damage coverages. The first amount shown means that $100,000 is available for payment to one or more persons who sustain bodily injuries in any *one* occurrence. The second amount means that $100,000 is the maximum amount payable to all persons who sustain property damage in any one occurrence, and the third amount, $300,000, represents the "aggregate limit" or the maximum amount payable by the insurer for all property damage claims in a one-year policy period. As an example of how these limits work, assume two persons sustain severe bodily injuries as the result of an insured's negligent operations. Each claimant seeks and is awarded $50,000 judgments by a court. Both amounts will be paid by the insurer, including the payment of the insured's defense costs, even though the latter costs may exceed the insured's limit of liability. On the other hand, if one person is awarded a bodily injury judgment of $60,000 and the other is awarded $50,000 for injuries in one occurrence, the former will only receive $50,000 from the

insurer, because $100,000 is the maximum amount which is payable under the insured's policy to one or more persons in any one occurrence. Now assume that a person is awarded a property damage claim of $50,000. This amount will be paid because $100,000 is available for each such occurrence. But, because $300,000 is the annual aggregate limit for property damage liability, the insured only has $250,000 of property damage liability coverage available for the remainder of the current policy year. The property damage liability aggregate limit, in other words, is reduced by the amount of a property damage claim which is paid by the insurer. (When an insured has products liability and/or completed operations coverage, a bodily injury liability aggregate limit also applies to those two coverages. Technically, therefore, the CGL policy could show four limits rather than three. Bodily injury liability aggregate limits for products liability and completed operations are discussed in Chapter 4.)

Limits of liability also are commonly available on a "single limit" basis, meaning that only one limit, such as $300,000, applies to all bodily injury and property damage liability claims in any one occurrence, subject to an annual aggregate for products, completed operations, premises and operations rated on a payroll or receipts basis, and independent contractors coverage. Technically, the single limit can be more advantageous to the insured than the dual limits. For example, if an insured had a single limit of $300,000 in the earlier example involving a bodily injury judgment of $60,000 for one person and $50,000 for the other, the claimant who was awarded the $60,000 would have been paid in full, making it unnecessary for the insured to retain $10,000 of that judgment (as he or she would have, if dual limits of $100/100 had been applicable).

24. Aggregate limits generally apply to bodily injury limits for products liability and completed operations, and to property damage limits for premises and operations rated on payroll or receipts, independent contractors coverage, and for contractual liability under "incidental contracts."
25. Insurance Services Office, 1973 edition.
26. There is an exception. The limits *are* reduced by the payment of claims when the limits are stated to apply as "aggregate" amounts.
27. Insurance Services Office, 1973 edition.
28. Ibid.
29. For a comprehensive discussion of the xcu exclusions, readers are referred to *FC&S Bulletins*, Casualty and Surety Volume, pp. Public Liability Xcu-1 to 19.
30. For more details on this subject, see David A. Johns, "Construction of Provision of Liability Insurance Policy Excluding Injuries in Connection with 'Structural Alterations' of Premises," 37 *A.L.R.* 3rd 1421.
31. When marine divers need completed operations insurance or sales and service organizations need products liability insurance, the CGL policy should be purchased. Funeral directors who have limited operations are suited for the M&C form, because they automatically receive completed operations coverage as part of their premises and operations cover. What is ironic about the M&C form, today, is that it is not suited for manufacturers

or contractors, because the former almost always need products liability insurance and the latter require completed operations insurance.

32. Insurance Services Office, 1974 edition.
33. Ibid.
34. Endorsements are the principal forms which are used to modify the provisions of an existing policy. To this end, endorsements can be used to broaden the scope of a policy, for example, by adding personal injury liability coverage, to limit the scope of coverage, for example, by deleting products liability and/or completed operations coverage, or by changing the address of the named insured or by adding an additional insured to the policy.
35. The basic limits are $25,000 per occurrence for bodily injury liability and $5,000 per occurrence for property damage liability. Fire legal liability insurance is discussed in CPCU 3. However, brief mention of this coverage is made in this chapter.
36. Such injury sustained by a person must be of the type which is otherwise covered under premises and operations liability coverage of the CGL policy. Injury caused by an employee while operating a rented automobile would not be covered, because the automobile liability exposure of the named insured is covered by automobile liability insurance and not the CGL policy.
37. Insurance Services Office, 1976 edition.
38. Insurance Services Office, 1973 edition.
39. William S. Anderson, ed. *Ballantine's Law Dictionary with Pronunciations*, 3rd ed. (Rochester, NY: Lawyers Co-Operative Publishing Co., 1969), defines a "penal statute" as a "statute which imposes a penalty or creates a forfeiture as the punishment for the neglect of some duty, or the commission of some wrong that concerns the good of the public and is commanded or prohibited by law."
40. Firms which are in the business of advertising, broadcasting, telecasting, or publishing must purchase special coverage against their exposures of libel, slander, copyright, piracy, and plagiarism, although much of this coverage is provided by commercial umbrella excess liability policies, discussed later in this chapter.
41. Insurance Services Office, 1976 edition.
42. Ibid.
43. Premises medical payments coverage is automatically included as part of the storekeepers liability package policy without additional cost.
44. Quoted portion from Insurance Services Office, 1976 edition.
45. Fire liability insurance is discussed in greater detail in CPCU 3, Chapter 3.
46. Insurance Services Office, 1976 edition.
47. For an insight into some of the problems of coverage gaps concerning umbrella liability policies, readers are referred to the article of Thomas F. Sheehan, J.D., CPCU, "Beware of the Broad Form Excess or Umbrella Excess Policies," *The CPCU Annals*, The Society of Chartered Property and Casualty Underwriters, June 1969, Vol. 22, No. 2 pp. 165-174.
48. Prior to 1973, most general liability policies were written with two limits for bodily injury liability. The first limit was the maximum that could be paid to a single person injured in a given occurrence. The second limit was the

maximum amount that could be paid for bodily injury in a given occurrence regardless of the number of persons injured, subject to the per person limit in the case of each individual. Since 1973, most general liability policies do not have a "per person" liability limit for bodily injury.

49. The above example does not take defense costs into consideration. If an umbrella liability policy includes defense costs as part of its total liability, instead of in addition to its total liability, the $10,000 amount could be reduced by the amount of any defense costs incurred by the umbrella insurer. Defense cost provisions of umbrella liability policies are discussed later in this chapter.

50. However, most umbrella liability policies also commonly contain aggregate limits for various coverages, so that if an insured's underlying aggregate limit is exhausted early in a policy period and additional losses should occur within that same policy period, the insured may be without protection if the aggregate limit of the umbrella policy also is exhausted.

51. While many umbrella liability policies list advertising liability as a separate coverage, others simply include it in the personal injury coverage.

52. When an umbrella liability policy contains an exclusion which also applies to an underlying policy, a firm has no coverage under either contract.

53. However, there is nothing to prevent an insurer from amending its renewal and newly insured umbrella liability contracts to incorporate a war exclusion, if the insurer deems it necessary.

54. Moreover, when an insured has underlying coverage for liquor liability or any one of the above-mentioned exposures, or the insured has a broad form CGL endorsement (which also includes all of these exposures), the umbrella liability policy will apply *without* the prerequisite of a retention amount.

55. For example, see Bernard J. Daenzer, "Excess Liability, Umbrella Aggregates, and Deductibles," *Property and Liability Insurance Handbook*, John D. Long and Davis W. Gregg, eds. (Homewood, IL: Richard D. Irwin, 1965), p. 165.

56. Some contend that a corporation can lose only its surplus or net worth, but that is not really true because a court judgment is a very high priority lien and other creditors would still have to be paid, even if it takes liquidation of assets to pay off all the debts.

57. Michael E. Hogue and Douglas G. Olson, *Business Attitudes Toward Risk Management, Insurance and Related Social Issues*, 1976, Wharton School, University of Pennsylvania, p. 76.

58. This study also includes numerous other third-party and first-party exposures to loss.

59. The phrase "trading dollars" refers to situations where firms purchase insurance needlessly, i.e., where the protection they receive could have been safely retained at a significant savings, because the losses are so highly predictable that the insured ends up paying them anyway, and retention would save the insured from paying the insurer's profit margin, as well as some of the expenses in the premium loading, Hogue and Olson, p. 78.

60. Although insurance may be thought of as a form of transfer, a noninsurance transfer is a technique whereby financial consequences of loss are transferred to another individual or firm other than an insurance company. The

transfer to another of one's negligence liability, under a hold harmless provision, is an example. And, since corporate suretyship is not really insurance, it, too, can be viewed as a form of noninsurance transfer. But suretyship is treated separately in Chapter 13.

61. C. A. Williams, Jr., and R. M. Heins, *Risk Management and Insurance*, 2nd ed. (New York: McGraw-Hill, 1971), p. 189.

62. Though the effect can be the same, there is a difference between a noninsurance transfer and the technique of avoidance. In a noninsurance transfer, the property or activity, its potential loss exposures, and financial consequences continue to exist, but the exposure and its financial consequences now confront the individual or firm which accepts the transfer. With avoidance, the exposure either is not created in the first place, or the exposure is eliminated in its entirety, such as when a firm liquidates its business.

63. Hold harmless and kindred agreements are discussed here principally from the viewpoint of the transferor. The methods by which these agreements can be handled, including insurance considerations, are treated more fully in Chapter 5.

64. However, if the indemnitor (transferee) has appropriate contractual liability insurance and the hold harmless agreement is deemed to be enforceable, the insurer is obligated to settle the matter.

65. This point should not be overlooked, since legal counsel is not infallible. If an outside attorney gives the wrong advice, he or she conceivably could be confronted with an errors and omissions action. However, if an in-house, i.e., attorney employee, gives the wrong advice, the resulting action could be the subject of a directors' and officers' liability action. The employer may be forced to pay the defense costs and judgment, if any, unless it has lawyers errors and omissions insurance (which is discussed in Chapter 10) or directors' and officers' liability insurance (discussed in Chapter 11) with the attorney as an insured.

66. An even more problematical circumstance is when a transferor has many contracts of a similar nature outstanding, such as a general contractor who imposes hold harmless agreements upon all of its subcontractors, and an argument results from one occurrence involving several such transferees. If the transferor's contracts ultimately are construed by a court to be unenforceable, the transferor's premises and operations liability insurance limits may be inadequate to settle all such losses which it had hoped to transfer to others. Transferors should take account of this rather common circumstance in evaluating the adequacy of their liability limits.

67. Surety bonds are discussed in Chapter 13.

68. Owners and contractors protective liability insurance is discussed in Chapter 5. Briefly, its purpose is to protect a firm, principally with defense, when it becomes implicated in a suit for its vicarious liability, i.e., its liability for having hired incompetent persons to perform certain work or services which result in injury or damage to others.

CHAPTER 3

Products and Completed Operations Liability Exposures

PRODUCTS LIABILITY EXPOSURES

Products liability is the term applied to the legal responsibility of the manufacturer, distributor, or retailer to the user or consumer of a product. The liability arises out of the manufacture, distribution, or sale of an unsafe, dangerous, or defective product, and the failure of the manufacturer, distributor, or retailer to meet the legal duties imposed with respect to the particular product. If the user or consumer sustains an injury or property damage caused by the product, liability may be imposed.

The term "products" includes all species of movable personal property and, under special circumstances, real property, as well. A sale of a product in violation of a criminal statute or ordinance may expose the seller to the possibility of criminal liability. For example, in most states the sale of firearms or intoxicating beverages to minors is prohibited, and such sales are subject to criminal penalties. Criminal liability also may attach to sales of narcotics, some poisons, and certain drugs without a valid prescription. However, the term "products liability" is used almost always in the context of civil liability.

In early cases, negligence usually was the basis of the relatively rare actions which could be described as products cases. But contract law eventually blended with negligence concepts as courts regularly examined the presence or absence of contractual relationships between parties. The absence of a direct contractual relationship between manufacturer and user consistently resulted in a finding of nonliability. Thus, initially, the courts construed a sales transaction as a contract

159

between buyer and seller. All of the contract elements, including the inducements of representations and warranties, were applicable. In the case of a breach of warranty, the buyer had a cause of action against the immediate seller. Since the buyer and the manufacturer usually were not contracting parties, and since they were rarely in privity of contract with each other, early cases held that the buyer had no cause of action against the manufacturer.

Grounds for the Imposition of Products Liability

If an injury is caused by a defective product, the injured user or consumer may bring one of several types of actions against the seller, alleging either contractual liability or tort liability. As has been noted, in early cases the presence or absence of contractual relationships between parties determined whether a products liability claim could be sustained.

Privity and Its Erosion   In the early years of the industrial age, the courts reasoned that only the contracting parties—the buyer and seller—were in privity with each other or able to assert a cause of action one against the other. One who was not a party to the contract of sale had no legal status and could not maintain an action based on the contract. This was true even though third parties stood in some relationship to the buyer—such as members of the buyer's family, or the buyer's employees or agents. The rule originally was laid down in 1842 in the case of Winterbottom v. Wright,[1] in which the injured driver of a mail coach brought an action against one who had contracted to sell the coach and keep it in repair. In holding that the driver had no maintainable cause of action, the court said:

> There is no privity of contract between these parties; and if the plaintiff can sue, every passenger, or even a person passing along the road who was injured by the upsetting of the coach, might bring similar action. Unless we confine the operation of such contracts as this to the parties who entered into them, the most absurd and outrageous consequences, to which I can see no limit, would ensue.[2]

The privity doctrine, historically, developed as a means by which a manufacturer or remote seller could avoid liability, based upon express or implied warranty, to a person with whom the manufacturer or seller had no contractual relationship.

A landmark decision in 1916 resulted in the virtual extinction of the privity rule, leading the courts to recognize that a buyer can have a cause of action in tort against a manufacturer, where the product is negligently manufactured and the negligence results in damage to the buyer. In MacPherson v. Buick Motor Co.,[3] the buyer of an automobile brought an action against the manufacturer, alleging that he was injured as a result of the negligence of the manufacturer in placing a defective automobile in the stream of commerce. The court sustained the cause of action, holding that the manufacturer was under a duty of exercising reasonable care in the production of its automobiles. Its failure to meet that duty was negligence. There was no contractual relationship between the buyer and the manufacturer, because the car was bought from a retail dealer. Yet, the buyer was allowed to recover on the tort theory of negligence. This theory will be discussed later in more detail, but this introductory reference, by way of MacPherson, should help to put into proper historical perspective our subsequent discussions of the negligence theory—as well as the theories of warranty and strict liability.

Few jurisdictions still adhere to the privity requirement as an element to be established in a products action grounded on contract. The doctrine has been steadily eroded by courts, which have placed restrictions and limitations on the rule's application, and by legislatures.

Contract Action Under the Uniform Commercial Code, a buyer has a cause of action based on breach of either express or implied warranties. Various measures have been used to determine the amount of damages resulting from breach of warranty.

The Uniform Commercial Code. Adoption of the Uniform Commercial Code in forty-nine states and the District of Columbia has had a great impact on the rules governing contractual liability. The Code, a body of law governing sales and other commercial transactions, is "uniform" in the sense that the same provisions are applicable in most states. The Code provisions relating to sales constitute a restatement of the common-law rights and duties of the parties to a contract of sale, with some clarification of areas where differences of opinion have existed between the states. The object of this legislation is to bring the applicable rules of law of the several states into conformity with each other, enhancing the predictability of the rules to be applied to business transactions. A further effect of this legislation is to overrule prior court decisions which are inconsistent with the Code and to substitute its provisions as the rule of decision in future cases.

The Code further abolishes the privity requirement in contract actions based on sales. Therefore, if a state has adopted the Uniform Commercial Code, it would follow that it has abandoned the privity rule, regardless of whether there are outstanding court decisions which have applied the rule. Section 2-318 of the Code, as drafted, provides three alternative forms of abolishing privity. Alternative A, adopted by a majority of jurisdictions, provides:

A seller's warranty whether express or implied extends to any natural person who is in the family or household of his buyer or who is a guest in his home if it is reasonable to expect that such person may use, consume or be affected by the goods, and who is injured in person by breach of the warranty. A seller may not exclude or limit operation of this section.

Alternatives B and C, adopted in about thirteen jurisdictions, vary slightly but are of similar import.

Express Warranties. With respect to the sale of personal property, a warranty may be described as a statement or representation—having reference to the character or quality of the goods sold—made by the seller of goods to induce the sale, and relied on by the buyer. It usually, but not necessarily, arises as an incident of the contract of sale. If the warranty is breached and the buyer sustains injury to his person or property as a result of his reliance on it, the seller is liable in an action for damages.

Prior to the Uniform Commercial Code, a buyer, in order to recover for the breach of an express warranty, had to establish that there was reliance on the express warranty. Under the Code, the element of reliance by the buyer on the express warranty is no longer necessary in order to maintain an action for the breach. The applicable section of the Uniform Commercial Code (2-313) reads as follows:

(1) Express warranties by the seller are created as follows:
  (a) Any affirmation of fact or promise made by the seller to the buyer which relates to the goods and becomes the basis of the bargain creates an express warranty that the goods shall conform to the affirmation or promise.
  (b) Any description of the goods which is made part of the basis of the bargain creates an express warranty that the goods shall conform to the description.
  (c) Any sample or model which is made part of the basis of the bargain creates an express warranty that the goods will conform to the sample or model.
(2) It is not necessary to the creation of an express warranty that the seller use formal words such as "warrant" or "guarantee" or that there be specific intention to make a warranty, but an affirmation of value of the goods or a statement purporting to be merely the seller's opinion or commendation of the goods does not create a warranty.

Under the Code, the "seller" includes anyone who places the goods in the stream of commerce. Therefore, under the statute, the term includes not only the immediate retailer but the manufacturer as well. Both may make an express warranty, in which case either or both may be held liable if the warranty is breached. Where one makes an express warranty and the other does not, then the seller making the warranty may be held liable for the breach. But one seller's express warranty does not automatically become the warranty of another farther down in the chain of distribution. In one case, for example, the manufacturer affixed a label to each can of antifreeze attesting to its quality and safety; the purchase in issue was made in reliance upon the truth of the warranty.[4] In an action against the distributor, the court held that the distributor had neither made a warranty nor adopted the manufacturer's warranty, and therefore was not liable to the purchaser. The purchaser would have probably prevailed, if the action had been brought against the manufacturer. However, it is certainly possible for a seller to adopt a manufacturer's warranty, thus binding the seller as if the seller had made the warranty.

Under Section 2-313 of the Code, "any affirmation of fact or promise" may give rise to an express warranty, although a statement that is "merely the seller's opinion or commendation of the goods does not create a warranty." This last quoted language of Section 2-313 seems to countenance "puffing" by the seller to induce a sale, and the distinction between puffery and warranty is certain to create difficulties. The nature of the product and the assertion made are relevant factors. A mere expression of opinion will not expose the seller to liability, but courts may resolve in favor of a buyer any doubt as to whether an expression was a warranty. There are cases going both ways, holding either that an expression was (1) a mere opinion not constituting a warranty[5] or (2) a representation amounting to an express warranty.[6] Such assertions, particularly concerning safety or suitability for a specific purpose, can be expected to be construed as warranties if such a construction is possible. Similarly, liability for breach of express warranty can result from statements made in advertisements, sales brochures, and catalogs. The plaintiff may allege that assurances of safety or quality caused a justifiable reliance upon what turned out to be a material misrepresentation and that the plaintiff's injury resulted from that reliance.

Promotional statements made by manufacturers through the advertising media can give rise to an express warranty, as explained in the *Restatement of Torts:*

> One engaged in the business of selling chattels who, by advertising, labels, or otherwise makes to the public a misrepresentation of a material fact concerning the character or quality of a chattel sold by him is subject to liability for physical harm to a consumer of the chattel caused by justifiable reliance upon the misrepresentation, even though (a) it is not made fraudulently or negligently, and (b) the consumer has not bought the chattel from or entered into any contractual relation with the seller.[7]

Advertising representations, particularly with regard to safety, have been found to be "material misrepresentations" which created express warranties to injured plaintiffs. A classic case involving a hunting and fishing knife illustrates the concepts of "material fact" and "justifiable reliance." An advertisement described the knife this way: "Handfitting Swedish Birch handle—it cannot slip or turn in the hand. No hilt to get in the way of cutting action. Knife is of such perfect design the hand cannot slip." The plaintiff purchased the knife and when he was using it to clean fish, his hand slipped down the handle and was cut severely. The court found that the plaintiff had offered sufficient evidence for the jury to find misrepresentation of a material fact and justifiable reliance.[8]

Implied Warranties. The parties to a contract of sale may agree upon any terms and conditions which are mutually acceptable. Both parties will be bound by the agreed terms. Where a contract of sale is made unconditionally, the courts have recognized that the seller has superior knowledge as to the ownership of the article, the ingredients of the article, and its quality with respect to its salability and fitness for a particular purpose. Therefore, the courts impose, "by operation of law," an obligation on the part of the seller to warrant or guarantee these things about the article. The obligation is deemed to arise out of the nature of the transaction and is implied without any specific agreement between the parties. The implied warranties are (1) warranty of title, (2) warranty of merchantability, and (3) warranty of fitness for a particular purpose.

WARRANTY OF TITLE. When an article is offered for sale, the seller warrants that the seller has title and ownership or that the seller has been authorized by the owner to pass title to another. This warranty of title has no great significance to our consideration of products liability, but the other types of implied warranties require detailed discussion.

WARRANTY OF MERCHANTABILITY. This means that the seller warrants that the goods are of such quality that they will be reasonably fit for the ordinary uses to which such products are put. The Uniform Commercial Code, in Section 2-314, describes the warranty of merchantability:

(1) Unless excluded or modified, a warranty that the goods shall be merchantable is implied in a contract for their sale if the seller is a merchant with respect to goods of that kind. Under this section the serving for value of food or drink to be consumed either on the premises or elsewhere is a sale.

(2) Goods to be merchantable must be at least such as
    (a) pass without objection in the trade under the contract description; and
    (b) in the case of fungible goods, are of fair average quality within the description; and
    (c) are fit for the ordinary purposes for which such goods are used; and

    (d) run within the variations permitted by the agreement, of even kind, quality and quantity within each unit and among all units involved; and

    (e) are adequately contained, packaged and labeled as the agreement may require; and

    (f) conform to the promises or affirmations of fact made on the container, or label, if any.

Generally speaking, the warranty of merchantability means that a product is of medium quality or goodness, is reasonably fit for the purposes for which such products are ordinarily used, and will compare favorably with other products of like kind and description that are on the market.

Most breach of warranty cases are brought under the theory of breach of implied warranty of merchantability. These cases generally relate to Section 2-314(2)(c) of the Code, just quoted, alleging that the product was not fit for the ordinary purpose for which it was intended, or, in other words, that the product did not do what it was supposed to do. For example, the collapse of a ladder under a person of average weight was a breach of this implied warranty.[9]

WARRANTY OF FITNESS FOR A PARTICULAR PURPOSE. A warranty of fitness for a particular purpose means generally that, if the seller sells a commodity, knowing the purpose for which it is purchased, the seller is understood to warrant it to be reasonably fit for the purpose for which it was bought. This warranty arises out of the nature of the transaction. It must be one in which the buyer can establish that the seller knew the purpose for which the product was bought and that the buyer relied on the judgment of the seller in selecting the particular product. The seller's knowledge of the purpose for which the article is bought can sometimes be inferred from the facts and circumstances of the sale.

Section 2-315 of the Uniform Commercial Code provides:

> Where the seller at the time of contracting has reason to know any particular purpose for which the goods are required and that the buyer is relying on the seller's skill or judgment to select or furnish suitable goods, there is unless excluded or modified under the next section an implied warranty that the goods shall be fit for such purpose.

The rule was applied in a case involving a bumper jack.[10] The plaintiff went to the defendant's store and asked for a bumper jack for a 1957 Buick. The salesman sold the plaintiff a jack which the salesman said would do the job. When the plaintiff was using it, it slipped and the plaintiff's car fell and injured him. The court held that the plaintiff did not have to prove that the jack was defective and its ability to lift cars of different makes was immaterial. The plaintiff established a breach of an implied warranty of fitness because he proved *reliance* on the defendant's *judgment,* the defendant's *knowledge* of the purpose for which the product was required, and that the product did not fulfill that purpose.

Damages for Breach of Warranty. Damages for breach of warranty which may be assessed against the seller consist of such amounts as will place the user or consumer in the same condition as he would have occupied if the breach had not occurred. This might consist only of the return of the purchase price or, more commonly in litigated cases, it could consist of damages for injury to property caused by the use of the product or damages for bodily injury sustained by the user or consumer.

PROPERTY DAMAGE. In one property damage case, defective oil, which was sold under an express warranty for use in the manufacture of carpets, caused considerable property damage to the carpets being manufactured. Damages were awarded, based on the difference in value of the carpets made with the defective oil and the value of the carpets if they had been of merchantable quality.[11] In another case, a roof leak in a mobile home made it unfit for its intended purpose. The damages awarded consisted of the difference between the reasonable market value at the time of purchase and the original market price.[12] The same principle has been applied to sales of defective seed or animal feed. The measure of damages in such cases is the difference between the value of the crop or herd actually produced and the crop or herd which ordinarily would have been produced, less the cost of production.[13]

Therefore, in property damage claims, the measure of damages will be an amount which will reasonably compensate the user or consumer for the loss which has been sustained. The plaintiff may be able to recover for loss of profits, loss of customers or damage to goodwill because of the defendant's breach, *if* it can be shown that these were within the parties' contemplation in entering into a contract of sale and adequate proof of such losses can be offered.[14]

BODILY INJURY. Where the user or consumer suffers bodily injury as a result of using the product which is the subject of a warranty, the measure of damages will be the same as those allowable in any tort cause of action. These consist of an amount which will reasonably compensate the injured person for out-of-pocket expenses, loss of wages, pain and suffering, and permanent injury, if any.

A manufacturer was held liable for breach of warranty for injuries to the plaintiff's hair (adhesion of gluey substance which hardened and could not be removed) when the plaintiff established that the product contained a substance not found in another purchased sample.[15] Another manufacturer was held liable for head injuries caused by a "Golfing Gizmo," an apparatus for unskilled golfers which struck the plaintiff during use. The manufacturer had warranted its safety and claimed it would not strike the user.[16]

WRONGFUL DEATH. There is a difference of opinion among the states as to whether or not a breach of warranty can form the basis of a wrongful death claim. Recovery of damages for wrongful death is a purely statutory remedy. The wrongful death statutes generally allow a recovery where the death was caused, for example, by the "wrongful act, neglect or default" of the defendant. In some states the courts hold that a breach of warranty is not a "wrongful act, neglect or default" so as to meet the requirements of proof necessary under the wrongful death statute.

Tort Action   The user or consumer of a product may bring a tort action against a seller, including the retailer or the manufacturer, if it can be established that the seller failed in one of the duties owed to the user or consumer. The seller's tort liability may be based on intentional deceit, negligence, or strict liability. Increasing emphasis is being placed on strict liability.

Intentional Deceit, Fraud, or Misrepresentation.   A seller who makes untrue statements to the buyer, either through general advertising or by direct statements, is liable to the user or consumer if the product does not meet the standards of quality which were claimed for it and the user or consumer has suffered injury to person or property through the use of the product.

In deciding cases of this nature, most courts apply the rule set forth in *Restatement (Second) of Torts*, Sec. 402B.

402B Misrepresentation by Seller of Chattels to Consumer

> One engaged in the business of selling chattels who, by advertising, labels or otherwise makes to the public a misrepresentation of a material fact concerning the character or quality of a chattel sold by him is subject to liability for physical harm to a consumer caused by justifiable reliance upon the the misrepresentation.

Sellers, especially manufacturers, are considered to be experts when it comes to the ingredients and the properties of the article which they sell. The user or consumer is not such an expert, and usually relies on the statements or advertising of the seller. Therefore, if the article does not conform to the statements or the advertising, a user or consumer who is injured may bring action in tort against the offending seller for damages, assuming justifiable reliance by the user on a misrepresentation of material fact. A good example of a case illustrating traditional concepts of fraud and misrepresentation involved the prescription drug triparanol, manufactured and sold under the name MER/29. A user of the drug who developed cataracts brought an action against the manufacturer for fraud and misrepresentation. The manufacturer untruthfully represented, both orally and through advertisements in medical journals and other promotional literature, that the drug was nontoxic, safe, and remarkably free of side effects. In fact, the manufacturer had knowledge through animal experiments that the drug caused blood changes and vision changes in most of the animals tested.[17]

Negligence. As noted earlier, the law of products liability developed in its earlier stages as a curious mixture of tort and warranty concepts. Courts were reluctant to find manufacturers liable for negligence to persons with whom they had no direct contractual relationships. But this privity of contract rule was rejected in the landmark MacPherson case.[18]

The allegation that a manufacturer was negligent may be raised with respect to the manufacturer's violation of a duty in (1) the product's design; (2) the construction or assembly or packaging of the product; and/or (3) the warnings, labels, and instructions which accompanied or should have accompanied the product.

DUTY OF A SAFE DESIGN. A plaintiff in a products liability suit frequently does not contest that the product may have been manufactured and put together perfectly, may have been made of good quality material, and may be functioning just as it was intended to function. The plaintiff, instead, attacks the very concept or design of the product and alleges that, by reason of a design defect, particular articles manufactured in accord with that design were dangerous for their intended use.

A manufacturer has a duty to design a product that is reasonably fit for its intended use and free from hidden defects which could make it unsafe for its intended use. The design defect claim usually is based upon one of several theories. In one case involving a *concealed defect*, the plaintiff sat on a lawn chair and placed his fingers close to the folding mechanism under the arm. One finger was traumatically amputated when his weight on the chair caused the mechanism to shift. The court found that the chair was defectively designed by reason of a concealed defect which rendered it unsafe for its intended use. The court found that the mechanism should have been covered with a housing to prevent the possibility of such an injury.[19]

A second theory advanced as a basis for design defect liability is failure on the part of the manufacturer to incorporate *guards or other safety devices* into products. A widely accepted rule has developed that the absence of guards or safety devices does not necessarily, in and of itself, create liability. Numerous cases have held that, if a manufacturer does everything necessary to make a product function properly for the purpose for which it is designed, if it contains no hidden or latent hazards, and if its functioning creates no danger or peril that is unknown to the user, then the manufacturer has met its duty to design a product that is reasonably safe for its intended use. In the leading case in this area,[20] a worker was injured when his hands were caught in moving parts of a machine. The court held that the machine had no latent defects, that the manufacturer had done everything possible to make the machine function properly for the purpose for which it was designed, and that the danger of placing one's hands near the moving parts of the machine was an open and obvious hazard. Some courts, however, on similar facts, may find that the manufacturer has a duty to design guards or safety devices into its product to protect users from even open and obvious hazards.[21]

A third theory used as the basis of design defect claims relates to the *nature of the material* specified in the design. A manufacturer was held liable for an injury caused by a nail which shattered as a result of the type of steel (and the treatment of the steel) specified for use in the product.[22] The court held that there was a defect in the design which rendered the product unsafe for the purpose for which it was intended.

A fourth theory used as the basis of an alleged design defect claim is that a manufacturer has a duty, not only to design a product that is reasonably safe for its intended use, but also to foresee and design against possible *unintended uses* of a product that are reasonably likely to occur. This issue has arisen often in the "crashworthiness" or "second collision cases," usually involving the design of automobiles. In such litigation, the claim is often made that the design of a vehicle increased or enhanced injuries occurring in an accident, and that a manufacturer has a duty to foresee that automobile accidents occur and therefore has a duty to design a vehicle which is relatively safe in a collision. The majority of cases which have considered this issue have concluded that a collision is a reasonably *foreseeable* (although unintended) use of an automobile and that a manufacturer has a duty to design its vehicles so as to avoid or minimize the consequences of collisions.[23] A substantial minority of jurisdictions has held that, because a collision is not one of the intended purposes of an automobile, a manufacturer has no duty to design a motor vehicle so that it will be a completely safe vehicle in which to participate in a collision.[24]

DUTY TO SAFELY MANUFACTURE, CONSTRUCT, ASSEMBLE, AND PACKAGE. The issue, with respect to manufacture, construction, and assembly of a product, is generally whether some error in the production of the product in question caused the defect which resulted in the injury to the plaintiff. The focus is upon a specific defect or production error which occurred with respect to a specific product, rather than calling into question a design which has been embodied in a large number of products following that particular design. In such a case, the plaintiff commonly alleges that, in the manufacture of a particular product alleged to have caused the injury, the manufacturer was responsible for some act which constituted a failure to exercise care, which should be recognized as creating an unreasonable risk of causing harm to a user. Such negligence may consist of any number of problems caused by human or mechanical error or breakdown in the course of manufacture and assembly of a product, such as failure to tighten a bolt, failure to prevent foreign matter from getting into food or medical products, failure to securely attach a safety device, and so on. It is often difficult for a plaintiff to establish that an alleged product defect was caused by specific and identifiable negligent acts or omissions in the course of the manufacturing process.

The seller has a duty to properly package (as well as to design and manufacture) its product. This duty means that the seller must exercise reasonable care in adopting a method of packaging which is safe, not only for the user or consumer, but which also protects those who are concerned with transporting or storing the product while awaiting sale. For example, in one case, the consumer (a physician conducting experiments) suffered severe hand burns when a caustic chemical which he was pouring out of a bottle gushed out when the entire bakelite cap came off. The court held that the packaging was defective and that the defendant failed to exercise care commensurate with the risk of harm in packaging a dangerous chemical.[25]

The duty to properly package is often closely related to a duty to warn (which will be discussed in more detail in a subsequent section of this chapter). In certain cases, the method of packaging may be safe if the product is carefully handled, but the absence of instructions or warnings about improper handling may constitute negligence on the part of the seller.

DUTY TO TEST AND INSPECT. Manufacturers have a duty to conduct such tests and inspections—in the course of product development, manufacture, and distribution—as are reasonably necessary to assure production of a safe product. This duty should be carried out with a degree of care commensurate with the foreseeable risk of harm. The manufacturer of a potentially dangerous prescription drug, for example, is expected to comply with tough government regulations, as well as procedures that are customary in the industry. Such compliance will constitute evidence of reasonable care.

A manufacturer of grinding wheels was held liable to a worker injured by a wheel which disintegrated while it was being operated. The accident, the court held, was caused by internal flaws which would have been discovered by a standard method of testing employed by other manufacturers in the industry.[26]

Generally, a retailer is under no duty to inspect or test products of a reputable manufacturer, unless the retailer has reason to believe that a product is dangerously defective or has some special opportunity or competence as a seller of such products. (The relative duties of retailers and others in the chain of distribution of products will be discussed in a subsequent section of this chapter.)

DUTY TO WARN AND INSTRUCT. A manufacturer or seller of a product which is inherently dangerous when used for its intended purpose owes a duty to give adequate warning of that dangerous propensity to the prospective user. The same rule applies to a product which is not inherently dangerous, but may in certain circumstances cause a foreseeable injury.

A general rule has developed, however, that there is no duty to warn of "open and obvious" dangers. This rule is exemplified by a case in which a plaintiff was injured by the open rollers of a farm machine. The court found no affirmative duty to warn on the part of the manufacturer and denied recovery, because "the very nature of the article gives notice and warning of the consequences to be expected, of the injuries to be suffered."[27] Although this rule is still followed in many jurisdictions, it must be noted that a danger may appear obvious—thus evoking no duty to warn—to the courts in one jurisdiction. But other courts, considering similar facts, may minimize the obviousness factor, finding a duty to warn and imposing liability for negligent breach of that duty. The primary thrust of the duty is that the manufacturer must warn of hidden (or latent) danger or hazardous limitations of a product, when used for reasonably foreseeable uses, if the danger would not be reasonably apparent to the average user of the product. One court, for example, held the manufacturer liable for failing to anticipate and warn against the possibility that children might drink from a bottle of furniture polish.[28] The court also emphasized that a warning will be sufficient to shift the risk of harm from the manufacturer to the user if it could reasonably be expected to catch the attention of the user, to be understandable to the average user, and to convey to him "a fair indication of the nature and extent of the danger."

The issue of the adequacy and intensity of a warning generally will be judged on the basis of the facts of a given case. The chance for a successful defense by the manufacturer seems to decrease in proportion to the smallness of the print on the warning—or in inverse proportion to the danger of the product. Thus, the manufacturer was held liable for failing to warn that a bottle of nail polish would explode if the plaintiff smoked as she applied the nail polish. The bottle was labeled in small red type: "Do not heat or use near fire." Such a warning, held to be insufficiently clear and intense to warn of the nature and seriousness of the hazard, was as much a violation of the manufacturer's duty as a complete failure to warn.[29]

Although *instructions* relative to use or maintenance differ from *warnings*, they too may have a strong bearing on safe use of a product. In one such case, the boom of a crane fell and killed a worker. It was found that the failure was due to the fact that a "safety ratchet" had not been lubricated for seventeen months and had become frozen with rust. The manufacturer's guide to proper lubrication failed to mention the safety ratchet. The court held that, by undertaking to give lubricating instructions, the manufacturer was under the duty to make them complete and all-inclusive. Its failure to do so was a breach of that duty, leading to imposition of liability for negligence.[30]

Negligence—Res Ipsa Loquitur. In negligence actions against the manufacturer, the plaintiff has the burden of establishing that the accident was caused by the negligence of the manufacturer in failing to exercise care, for example, in the production, design, packaging or inspection of the product before it left the manufacturer's possession. Since the entire production process is in the control of the manufacturer, the plaintiff is faced with a problem of proof which may be difficult (and sometimes virtually impossible) to sustain.

In some cases the courts have applied the rule of *res ipsa loquitur*, which means "the thing speaks for itself." It is a rule of evidence which eases the plaintiff's burden of proof by creating an inference or a presumption of negligence where certain basic elements have been established. These elements are: (1) the accident must be one which normally would not occur unless the defendant was negligent; (2) the instrumentality which caused the accident must be within the exclusive control of the defendant; and (3) the plaintiff must not have contributed in any way to the causation of the accident.[31] Obviously, in products cases the instrumentality which causes the accident is not in the physical control of the defendant at the time of the accident, since possession has been relinquished to the plaintiff. The courts have reasoned that, because the negligent act must have occurred while the product was in the hands of the manufacturer, that possession is sufficient to satisfy the requirements of the rule. Thus, if a bottler overfills a bottle (subjecting it to pressure beyond its capacity) or uses a defective bottle, and the bottle explodes, causing injury to the buyer or consumer, the application of the rule would be sufficient to establish a presumption or inference that the manufacturer was negligent. The plaintiff would not have to prove facts establishing any specific act of negligence, because the circumstances of the accident would provide the evidence of negligence.

However, to invoke the application of the rule, the plaintiff would have to show that the bottle or other product was in the same condition when received by the plaintiff as it was when it left the manufacturer's hands. This would require evidence that the product had not been mishandled en route to the consumer. The failure of the plaintiff to negate any possibility of mishandling of the product while en route will deny the plaintiff the advantage of the rule.

The rule creates only an inference or presumption of negligence. This may be overcome by evidence offered by the manufacturer that the product was not defective or, if there was a defect, it did not occur through the negligence of the manufacturer. Once these facts have been established, the rule drops out of play and the plaintiff must prove specific acts of negligence on the part of the manufacturer in order to recover.

The courts have applied the rule of *res ipsa loquitur* sparingly in products cases, but generally have been willing to apply the rule to cases involving (1) exploding bottles, (2) foreign substances in bottled goods or goods in sealed containers, and (3) foreign substances in drugs or cosmetics. The doctrine has generally been found inapplicable to such products as heavy equipment, vehicles, and major appliances, since such products have often been used safely for an extended period of time prior to an accident giving rise to a lawsuit.

Strict Liability in Tort. It is possible to speak of "strict liability" in terms of warranty. The theory of implied warranty without privity, applied by some courts, is very similar to the doctrine which is the subject of this section. It serves little purpose, however, to focus on the warranty language, since the main point of the doctrine of strict liability in tort is to provide a theory of recovery in products cases which is unfettered by statutory restrictions on warranty.

The doctrine was first applied in the key 1963 decision in Greenman v. Yuba Power Products, Inc.[32] The plaintiff was a worker injured by a power lathe, which had been purchased from the manufacturer by his employer. Upon suing the manufacturer, he was confronted by prior decisions refusing to extend warranty without privity beyond food products cases, as well as his failure to give timely notice of the manufacturer's "breach of warranty," as required by the applicable statute, the Uniform Sales Act. The California Supreme Court cut this Gordian knot of difficulties by holding that the case did not really involve warranty but could be resolved by imposing strict liability in tort.

The concept was adopted as Section 402A of the *Restatement (Second) Torts.* The writers also saw no need to speak of warranty at all, considering it as inappropriate borrowing from the contract law of sales.

They discarded warranty terminology and adopted Section 402A as follows:

(1) One who sells any product in a defective condition unreasonably dangerous to the user or consumer or to his property is subject to liability for physical harm thereby caused to the ultimate user or consumer, or his property, if
  (a) the seller is engaged in the business of selling such a product, and
  (b) it is expected to and does reach the user or consumer without substantial change in the condition in which it is sold.
(2) The rule stated in Subsection (1) applies although
  (a) the seller has exercised all possible care in the preparation and sale of his product, and
  (b) the user or consumer has not bought the product from or entered into any contractual relation with the seller.

In order to understand the rule of strict liability, certain of the above terms must be defined—"seller," "user or consumer," and "defective condition unreasonably dangerous."

SELLER. The rule of strict liability in tort is applied against a seller engaged in the business of selling the type of product in question. The term "seller" is defined in Comment f (an explanatory note) to Section 402A as including an entity which is engaged in the business of selling products for use or consumption, but not including a person who makes a casual or occasional sale. One who is engaged in the business of selling products may include the manufacturer, as well as others in the chain of production or distribution, including component part manufacturers and suppliers, wholesale distributors, and retailers.

If, for example, a woman is injured when a bicycle wheel breaks and collapses while she is riding the bicycle in a normal way, she may have a cause of action against one or a number of sellers. These might include: the wheel manufacturer; the component supplier who supplied the wheels to the bicycle manufacturer; the manufacturer who fabricated the bicycle; the wholesale distributor; and the retail store which sold the bicycle which it purchased from the distributor. All these parties are sellers and subject to imposition of liability under the strict liability doctrine. However, if the plaintiff had borrowed the bicycle from a neighbor who, in turn, had purchased it second hand from a friend, neither of these persons would be subject to a strict liability action since they are not sellers "engaged in the business of selling such a product." A few jurisdictions have applied the rule to defendants who would not traditionally be considered sellers, such as: bailors and lessors; building developers and builders of homes; testing companies; a hospital supplying blood to a patient; and a landlord renting a furnished apartment.

USER OR CONSUMER. The terms "user" or "consumer" are not limited to actual purchasers or owners of the products. The categories of user or consumer include those who are ultimately benefiting from the use of product, such as passengers in a vehicle, a hospital patient who is given a drug, or a worker who is repairing an appliance for the ultimate purchaser.

A few decisions have extended the doctrine of strict liability in tort to permit recovery by "bystanders" who were neither users nor consumers of the product but who suffered injury through being in the vicinity of a defective product which was in use. Examples include eye damage caused by fumes from contact cement circulated throughout a building through an air conditioning system;[33] and injuries to passengers in a vehicle which was struck by another, allegedly defective, automobile which went out of control.[34]

DEFECTIVE CONDITION UNREASONABLY DANGEROUS. A plaintiff, to recover under the theory of strict liability in tort, must establish that the injury was caused by a product which was in a defective condition unreasonably dangerous to the user or consumer when it left the control of the defendant. A "defective condition" is one which would not be contemplated by the average consumer and which would be unreasonably dangerous to that consumer. "There is no all-embracing definition of defect. What is in back of most decisions, however, is what may be called the consumer expectation test: did the product perform as a reasonable consumer would have expected?"[35] "Unreasonably dangerous" means that the article sold must be dangerous to an extent beyond that which would be contemplated by the ordinary consumer who purchases it, with the ordinary knowledge common to the community. The fact that a product is dangerous does not automatically mean that strict liability is applicable. "Objects such as guns and dynamite are dangerous but can be said, based upon ordinary consumer understanding, to be reasonably so. At the other end of the spectrum, it can be said that some products, even if they have produced personal injury, are not 'dangerous'...."[36]

A hammer was found to be in a "defective and unreasonably dangerous condition" because it became "work hardened" or brittle as a result of use over a prolonged period of time. A piece of metal chipped from the hammer head and struck the plaintiff in the eye while he was using the hammer. The court found that the product was in a defective condition and unreasonably dangerous because it could not stand up under repeated, foreseeable stresses which would accord with reasonable "consumer expectations."[37] Nearly every product—from food to light bulbs or plastic toys—is capable of causing injury. However, the mere fact that injury occurred in connection with the use of a product does not prove that the product was defective, since the law does not require that the product be accident-proof or foolproof.

Some courts have liberalized still further the concept of strict liability by applying it without the need for the plaintiff to establish that the product was "unreasonably dangerous." This further eases the plaintiff's burden of proof, requiring only a showing that the product was in a "defective condition." He need not show that it was more dangerous than the average consumer would ordinarily expect.[38]

Issues such as causation and foreseeability are important to the application of the strict liability concept. However, it seems more appropriate to consider these factors later in this chapter in the context of defenses to products cases.

IMPACT OF STRICT LIABILITY. Strict liability in tort certainly has not been unanimously and uniformly accepted in all jurisdictions, and the rule remains subject to certain limitations. However, it has substantially altered the law of products liability in several respects. For example, it has eliminated from tort liability all vestiges of contractual privity, so that any user or consumer of a defective product can sue the manufacturer or retailer of the product (or, for that matter, any other seller in the chain of distribution) without regard to any question of whether any of the sellers contracted with or extended a warranty to the user or consumer. Moreover, the rule has eliminated any necessity on the part of the user or consumer to prove negligent acts on the part of the manufacturer or other seller. Thus, the defendant may be held liable for an injury caused by a defective product, although he has exercised all possible care in connection with the product. Negligence is not a prerequisite to liability.

Therefore, the doctrine has dispensed with two of the more troublesome elements which sometimes have afflicted plaintiffs in products cases: the need to prove either negligence on the part of the seller or privity of contract with the seller.

Statutory Influences

In response to pressures generated by consumer groups, Congress has passed a number of statutes regulating the manufacture and sale of consumer goods. Among these statutes are the Consumer Product Safety Act; the Pure Food, Drug and Cosmetic Act; the Federal Hazardous Substances Act; the Federal Insecticide, Fungicide and Rodenticide Act; the Occupational Safety and Health Act; the Federal Flammable Fabrics Act; and the National Traffic and Motor Vehicle Safety Act.

Penal statutes, such as those cited above, may be adopted or applied in products liability suits, and can theoretically be the basis of a "negligence per se" holding. Section 286 of the *Restatement* codifies the current existing law. In essence, it provides that a plaintiff is barred from recovering on a negligence per se or prima facie evidence theory unless the plaintiff can show (1) that the plaintiff belonged to a particular class of persons which the legislature sought to protect; (2) that the particular interest which was invaded was of a type which the legislature intended to safeguard; (3) that the legislature sought to protect that interest from a particular type of harm which occurred; and (4) that the statute was designed to guard against the kind of harm exemplified by this injury.

As to the effect of a violation of a penal statute on a civil suit, there is much confusion and disparity among the various jurisdictions. Basically, there are three recognized positions concerning such a violation and its immediate consequences. They are: (1) the violation constitutes negligence per se,[39] or negligence as a matter of law and unless some justifiable excuse can be shown,[40] the violation is conclusive as to the issue of breach of duty; (2) the violation is prima facie evidence of negligence or presumptive negligence which shifts the burden to the defendant to explain, justify or rebut the violation; and (3) the violation is merely evidence of negligence and it is to be weighed by the jury along with all the other evidence.

The first two positions have the effect of creating a kind of strict liability for the product's failure to comply with statutory standards.

It is almost universally held that the defendant's compliance with a statutory standard will not insulate the defendant from potential liability.[41] Courts have consistently held that a legislative enactment merely designates the minimum standard of care and that, in any particular case, the common law standard may exceed that of the statute.[42] However, the admission into evidence of the defendant's compliance with a statutory mandate is still beneficial and efficacious to the defense. First and most important, such a showing frees the defendant from the immediate effects of a negligence per se finding.[43] Second, such compliance is admissible to indicate the exercise of due care. Moreover, in some rare instances, a showing of compliance will be sufficient to show that the defendant executed his duty of due care (e.g., where the situation calls for only minimum due care and compliance with the statute fulfills that minimum).[44]

The fact that a defendant may be found liable despite compliance can create real policy problems for the judiciary. In one such case, a child ingested a roach killer which resulted in his death. In the subsequent negligence action the defendant introduced evidence showing that his product and its label were both properly registered under the Federal

Insecticide, Fungicide and Rodenticide Act as well as the Texas Hazardous Substances Act. In addition, the approval of the Federal Department of Agriculture and the State Department of Health was introduced to supplement this showing. Upon this proof the defendant (unsuccessfully) urged: "that the label was approved by proper authorities, state and federal, and he was by law *required* to use this labeling and as a matter of law he cannot be guilty of negligence. His position is that he could not market his product without the precise label, and if he did so, he would be guilty of violating the law."[45]

Although the rationale may have been inapplicable to the case at hand, it should be noted that as federal and state standards become more stringent, allowing for less deviation, this dilemma and its consequent defense will have more appeal. Despite this possibility, the Consumer Product Safety Act expressly provides that compliance will not be proof of due care nor will the act affect common-law negligence actions.

Consumer Product Safety Act[46]   Of all the federal statutes which may have an impact concerning products liability actions, the Consumer Product Safety Act stands supreme. This comprehensive act, enacted in 1972, empowers one central federal commission to regulate the burgeoning field of consumer products. Specifically, the commission is empowered to promulgate mandatory safety standards; prohibit the sale or production of products which it bans; require the identification of distributors and labelers, and the manufacturer of their products; and require labelers, manufacturers or distributors to notify the public of defects or to replace the goods. Several of the more pertinent sections will be discussed.

Section 2052 indicates the scope of the CPSA. In essence, the act covers all possible consumer products, excluding such products as food, drugs, automobiles, and so on, which are otherwise federally regulated.

Section 2054 mandates the creation of an Injury Information Clearinghouse. Pursuant to the mandate, the Consumer Product Safety Commission created NEISS (National Electronic Information Surveillance System), which collects and organizes information concerning consumer injuries by consumer products. In a negligence action against a manufacturer, the admission into evidence of prior accidents collected by NEISS would be highly helpful to the plaintiff to show the existence of a defect or dangerous condition, notice or knowledge of the defect and the element of causation. Unfortunately for the defense, until the system becomes more comprehensive and complete, the admission into evidence of a lack of reported accidents will be most improbable.

Section 2063 provides for the labeling and certification of certain specified products. Once an applicable safety standard has been promulgated by the commission for a specific product, the manufacturer is then required to certify its compliance with the standard. This certification must either accompany the product or be furnished to all retailers and distributors. Furthermore, the commission may require the manufacturer to provide clearly visible labels identifying the manufacturer and the place of production. Their labels and certificates should alleviate plaintiffs' tasks in locating and identifying a particular manufacturer of a uniform or unidentifiable product, and these certificates or labels may well be used as the basis of a breach of express warranty action.

Closely analogous to the labeling and certification requirements is Section 2076(e) of the act, authorizing the commission to require manufacturers to furnish performance and technical data to prospective purchasers. In complying with such a requirement, it would appear the manufacturer would once again be making an express warranty, thereby becoming exposed to possible breach of warranty actions.

Section 2064 requires manufacturers and others in the chain of distribution to inform the commission of any product which fails to conform to safety standards or contains a defect which would create a substantial product hazard. It is still undecided whether such a notification would be admissible in a negligence action to show the existence of a defect or of causation. Conversely, Section 2055(B)(1) and (C), states that the commission must notify the *manufacturer* of any defect which it discovers.

Section 2065 provides that the commission may require the maintenance of records to implement the statute. Such records may be of great assistance to a plaintiff's attorney who wishes to trace the distribution of products.

As mentioned earlier, Section 2072 provides that an injured party may bring a cause of action against any party who knowingly or willfully violates this statute. Subsection B goes on to indicate that this remedy does not limit or preclude any of the common-law remedies. It should be noted that Section 2072 has a severe limitation (i.e., in order to invoke the remedy the violation must be willful or with knowledge). Moreover, this legislative cause of action is subject to a $10,000 jurisdictional amount.

Although Section 2072 is somewhat weakened by the "knowing or willful" limitation, Section 2073 greatly enhances the plaintiff's position in any type of products liability action. This section provides that for any violation of a safety standard an "interested person" may file a suit and obtain "injunctive relief." It would appear that the threat of an injunctive action under Section 24 could give a plaintiff substantial settlement leverage, since, if successful, he conceivably could close down a manufacturer's entire production.

Section 2074 merely codifies existing common law in relation to compliance with a statutory mandate. Under this section, "compliance with consumer product safety rules ... shall not relieve any person from liability at common law...." Subsection B provides that the commission's inaction in regulating a product is not admissible to show an absence of defect or other dangerous condition.

Section 2075 creates a federal preemption. Basically, no state standard will be permitted to stand once a properly promulgated federal safety standard is established. However, this only applies negatively. States are free to adopt standards which create *higher* requirements than that of CPSA.

Since CPSA has only been in effect since 1972, very little case law has been decided based upon the act. More importantly, since the CPSC has only promulgated one safety standard (concerning swimming pool slides) the current possibility of actions based upon violations of the statute are limited. However, as time goes on and more standards are enacted, this trend should reverse.

Pure Food, Drug and Cosmetic Act[47]   The federal Food, Drug and Cosmetic Act provides a standard with which all food and drugs must comply. In reference to food, the act stipulates that food which contains deleterious particles or adulterated foodstuffs must not be manufactured, distributed, or sold. A violation of this statute (and others like it) has been held to be either negligence per se or presumptive negligence, depending upon the particular rule of the jurisdiction. Likewise, compliance has been held to be merely evidence of due care and not a conclusive defense.

The importance of the act is not so much in creating statutory standards in per se actions, but rather in serving as a prototype or example for state legislation. Rather than apply the federal statute, state courts usually rely upon state statutes modeled upon the federal prototype as the basis for a negligence per se finding.

In any event, it should be noted that neither the state law nor the federal law creates any greater standard of care than that of the common law. However, the fact that the standards are in statutory form eases the plaintiff's burden of proof.

Federal Hazardous Substances Act[48]   The Federal Hazardous Substances Act is an enactment designed to (1) require appropriate cautionary labels on products defined as hazardous substances; (2) prohibit the manufacture and sale in interstate commerce of products which do not comply with labeling requirements; and (3) prohibit the manufacture and sale of products which are so hazardous that even a cautionary label will not protect the consumer.

The heart of the FHSA is the labeling requirement. Failure to properly label a product pursuant to the act constitutes "misbranding" and thereby results in a violation of the statute and negligence per se. Once again, compliance with the statute is only some evidence of due care and does not exonerate the defendant from liability. The defendant's duty may go beyond that required by the act. However, in special circumstances, a showing of compliance is sufficient to defeat recovery. Similarly, failure to show a causal relationship between the violation and the injury defeats recovery.

Before the statute can be invoked, a plaintiff must show the presence of three conditions: first, the substance must have been in a container intended for household use; second, the article must be toxic, a strong sensitizer, an irritant, corrosive, flammable, or capable of generating pressure or heat through decomposition; and third, the product must be of a kind which could cause substantial injury or substantial illness during or as a proximate result of any foreseeable handling or use.

The FHSA was substantially amended and expanded by the Child Protection Act and Toy Safety Act of 1969 and the Child Protection Act of 1966. All three of the above acts are now administered by the Consumer Product Safety Commission. Under the Toy Safety Act of 1969, hazardous substances now include "any toy or other article intended for use by children which ... presents an electrical, mechanical or thermal hazard." No cases have been decided concerning a breach of this statute in a negligence per se products liability case. However, since the act is designed to protect a specified group from a specific type of harm, there is no reason why it could not be the basis of such an action.

Federal Insecticide, Fungicide and Rodenticide Act[49]   Similar to the previous statutes, the Federal Insecticide, Fungicide and Rodenticide Act creates a statutory duty to warn of dangerous substances, as well as a duty to register certain products with the Environmental Protection Agency. Failure to properly label a product under the act has been held to be negligence per se, while compliance has been held to be mere evidence of due care.[50]

If a product falls within the terms of the act, the label must contain: name and address of the manufacturer; trademark under which the product is sold; weight and measure; skull and crossbones; the word "poison" (in red); statement of an antidote; and, when required, the registration number assigned under this act. It is interesting to note the extremes to which liability has been carried, despite compliance with the statutory standards. The manufacturer of a roach killer properly submitted his label to the appropriate federal and state authorities. Because there was no known antidote for the poison, the defendant merely stated the pertinent first aid measures rather than an antidote.

In finding the manufacturer causally negligent, the court held that, when there is no known antidote, that fact must be stated on the label.[51] Another manufacturer was found liable when two farm workers died of insecticide poisoning. The insecticide did not have the skull and crossbones and other indications of poison. Although the defendant had fully stated the dangers of the poison on the package and, in addition, had fully complied with all federal requirements, the court nevertheless found the defendant liable. The absence of the crossbones and the word "poison" (in red) was sufficient to find liability.[52]

Occupational Safety and Health Act[53] Little case law has been decided based upon the Occupational Safety and Health Act. However, two cases worth noting have been decided in reference to the act.

The first held that the violation of an OSHA standard was negligence per se. The case arose when an employee of the National Cargo Bureau, Inc., boarded the ship owned by the defendant, in order to inspect the vessel for grain loading. Due to low water conditions, the vessel utilized a "brow gangway" instead of the traditional gangway. The substitute gangway did not have a handrail as dictated by OSHA standards. While attempting to board the ship, the plaintiff fell and injured himself. In affirming the negligence per se instruction, the court used the "statutory purpose" doctrine in analyzing the cause of action. The court found that the plaintiff (a business frequenter) was within the class of persons sought to be protected by the regulation and that his injury was of a sort which OSHA sought to prevent.[54]

The second case came about when an employee was electrocuted by a crane which had come in contact with some electrical lines. In the subsequent suit against the crane operator, the defendant manufacturer offered, as a defense, evidence of OSHA standards pertaining to the operation of cranes near power lines. The court held that the evidence was irrelevant and hence inadmissible. The defendant wanted to introduce the evidence so as to shift the blame for failing to provide safety devices to the employer and employee (i.e., contributory negligence). The court ruled that, since the accident would not have occurred had the defendant fulfilled his original duty to install safety devices, the defendant would be precluded from using a contributory negligence defense. Hence, neither the contributory negligence defense nor evidence of the OSHA standards were allowed.[55]

Federal Flammable Fabrics Act[56] The Federal Flammable Fabrics Act was enacted to inhibit the introduction of highly flammable apparel into the stream of interstate commerce. Pursuant to this end, a flammability standard was established to which all clothing must conform.

Due to the success of the standard (or its liberality), little case law has developed in which a violation was involved. Usually the act has been invoked by the defendant as a defense. However, if the plaintiff meets all the "statutory purpose" requirements, violation thereof should result in negligence per se. In regard to compliance, courts have consistently held that compliance with the act will not protect the defendant from a higher standard of care.[57] Moreover, courts have held that the federal act does not preempt higher state statutory or common-law requirements.

Until a higher standard of flammability is enacted, it is unlikely that much future case law will involve violation of this statute.

The National Highway Traffic and Motor Vehicle Safety Act of 1966 [58]   This act was designed to reduce the incidence of deaths and injuries resulting from auto accidents. Under the act, the Secretary of Commerce was authorized to establish motor vehicle safety standards with which auto manufacturers must comply. There are presently no cases to support a finding of negligence per se as a result of a violation of this act. However, there is a good argument for finding some violation of the act (e.g., noncompliance with federal safety standards) to be negligence per se, because the purpose of the act is to protect the public against unreasonable risk of accidents occurring as a result of design, construction, or performance of motor vehicles or equipment and against unreasonable risk of death or injury to persons in the event accidents occur.

In reference to compliance, one important decision held that compliance with the National Highway Traffic and Motor Vehicle Safety Act would not exempt the defendant from liability. The case arose when the plaintiff was injured while driving a Chevrolet Corvair, manufactured by the defendant. The plaintiff contended that the steering wheel and its placement was defectively designed and that the defect aggravated his injuries. The defendant contended that any safety standards in design and equipment should be restricted to those envisioned by the National Highway Traffic and Motor Vehicle Safety Act, not imposed on a case by case basis by the courts. In refusing to accept the defendant's contentions, the court held that the federal act would not preclude or preempt state common-law requirements and that a showing of compliance would not be sufficient to grant summary judgment for the defendant.[59]

Duties and Vulnerability of Those Exposed

Many parties may find themselves defendants in a products liability suit, based on the contract actions and tort actions previously discussed.

Where penal statutes are applicable, they may also have a bearing on the suit. Having explored the various grounds for imposition of products liability and statutory influences, we will now proceed to examine the impact on manufacturers, assemblers, component suppliers, wholesalers and distributors, distributors who adopt products as their own, retailers, bailors and lessors, and testing companies. As we shall see, all of these parties are exposed to products liability claims.

Manufacturers Previous sections of this chapter presented illustrations of manufacturers' duties and vulnerabilities. The manufacturer is most frequently the target defendant in products litigation.

The manufacturer's general duty is to use reasonable care in the design, construction, and assembly of products to keep them free from latent defects. Liability may be imposed if there is a design defect caused by inadequate or defective specifications or material chosen. The manufacturer is also subject to liability if production methods used are conducive to the manufacture of defective products. The duty extends to inspecting and testing during and after completion of the manufacturing process, if the tests are reasonably necessary for production of a safe product.

The manufacturer's duty also includes ordinary care in warning the user of facts known to the manufacturer, and unknown to the user, which are likely to make the product dangerous. The manufacturer's duty is commensurate with the risk of harm involved. Its duty is to keep the product free from latent or hidden defects so as to avoid an unreasonable risk of harm to users and others. The manufacturer discharges the duty of care if the product functions properly and creates no peril not known to the user. The manufacturer is liable, in the language of negligence, if it manufactures a product that is foreseeably dangerous when used for a foreseeable purpose. Or, to put it in the language of strict liability, a manufacturer is liable if it sells a defective product unreasonably dangerous to the user or consumer.

But the trend of products liability is to hold liable, for product defects, any and all suppliers and sellers in the chain of distribution from manufacturer to consumer. Before moving on to consideration of these various suppliers, one or two points relative to the manufacturer's relationships to suppliers may be noted.

A manufacturer may be held liable for a defective component part of its product. It has a duty to test and inspect component parts, and failure to do so (or negligence in performing the duty) may result in liability. With regard to the terminal point of the manufacturing process, it has been held (in cases involving motorcycles and automobiles) that a manufacturer cannot avoid liability by purporting to delegate to vehicle dealers a duty to inspect and adjust vehicles. In one such case, a manufacturer was held liable for injuries caused by a defective master brake cylinder.[60]

Assemblers   Assemblers are manufacturers who make up finished products from parts or components furnished by others. Assemblers of products have been held subject to liability on both negligence and strict liability theories. In the area of negligence, the majority view is that assemblers must inspect and test to discover latent defects. This duty exists even if the assembler purchases the components making up the finished product from reputable manufacturers who do their own testing, if the assembler's tests are reasonably necessary to put a safe product into the stream of commerce.

There is authority holding the assembler of a product (made of components and put out under the assembler's own name) liable only if the assembler's inspection or process of manufacture is done negligently, and not for latent defects resulting from negligence of suppliers.[61] However, in another case, the assembler was found responsible for the negligence of those who supplied the components. This was because by incorporating the parts into the final product the supplier adopted them as his own and assumed responsibility for them. This is the theory applicable to "ostensible manufacturers," where the assembler is subject to the same liability as if the assembler had manufactured the component.[62]

In a case involving a machine, an operating valve obtained from another manufacturer malfunctioned, causing injury. The plaintiff recovered from the machine assembler for the negligent failure to discover the defect before incorporating it into its product.[63]

Under a strict liability theory the importance diminishes of determining whether the supplier or the assembler caused the defect. It has been held that strict liability encompasses defects regardless of their origin. Thus, an assembler-defendant cannot escape liability by tracing the defect to a supplier, because the assembler is liable for unreasonably dangerous conditions in component parts without inquiry into who may have been at fault.[64]

An assembler of a truck which included component parts manufactured by others was held strictly liable for the plaintiff's injuries. The court said that an assembler who sells the completed product as its own and represents to the public that it is the manufacturer *is* the manufacturer for purposes of liability.[65]

Component Suppliers   A component part supplier and/or manufacturer furnishes parts to be used in the makeup of a finished product. Component part suppliers have been found liable under negligence and strict liability theories.

Within the framework of negligence, the duty imposed on this type of manufacturer includes utilizing its special competence to furnish a safe product. If an injury-causing component is supplied and incorporated into a finished product, the negligence of the supplier may create an unreasonable risk of harm and subject it to liability. The supplier must exercise ordinary care in design, construction and assembly to keep the product free from latent or hidden defects.[66] In one case, liability for a fire caused by a defectively welded electrical resistance heater was imposed on the component supplier who furnished the unit manufacturer with a defective part.[67] Another case involved a manufacturer of an ingredient of a water repellant compound that exploded. The court found the component manufacturer liable for negligence for the defect.[68]

In the area of strict liability, *Restatement (Second) Torts* Section 402A, Comment p reiterates that the authors of the *Restatement* make no comment respecting strict liability of a seller of a product that is expected to be processed or otherwise substantially changed prior to reaching the ultimate user. The question, then, is whether responsibility to discover and prevent danger shifts to the intermediate party. The Comments suggest that strict liability carries from the component supplier to the ultimate user if there is no change in the part itself and it is merely incorporated into another product.

Wholesalers and Distributors Wholesalers and distributors generally act as intermediaries who sell products for resale. As with others in the chain of distribution, there are certain duties arising out of such a transaction. The duty is one of reasonableness, and a negligent wholesaler or distributor is subject to liability for injury due to foreseeable dangers. It is difficult to prove a negligence case against a wholesaler or distributor, as illustrated by a decision allowing no recovery because the plaintiff did not prove negligence based on knowledge. The court held that a wholesaler is liable for negligence only if it knew or had reason to know of a defect.[69]

Strict liability is the most commonly used theory against these parties in the chain of distribution. However, one court refused to impose strict liability on the wholesaler and retailer of wearing apparel. The decision was based on reasoning that the court could not put the duty of inspection for latent defects on these parties because of the volume of merchandise they handle as a sales conduit. The conclusion was that such a ruling would result in these parties acting as insurers of items handled.[70]

Section 402A of the *Restatement*, Comment f, includes wholesalers in the definition of sellers. Cases which apply this section have found the wholesaler and/or distributor strictly liable under some very peculiar circumstances. One court found the wholesaler strictly liable, despite the fact that he never had possession of the dynamite fuse involved and merely passed on the order to the manufacturer, who shipped the goods directly to the customer.[71] Another decision imposed strict liability on the wholesaler/distributor, although it neither manufactured nor possessed the defective product.[72] The reasoning in another case was that, although the distributor never had possession of the defective machine, it was strictly liable because it ordered the machine for the purchaser and got a commission on the sale.[73] However, this type of economic argument was rebuffed by another court, and a defendant wholesaler prevailed against a plaintiff who was alleging strict liability against the wholesaler for innocently passing along a defective product. The court rejected the plaintiff's argument that the wholesaler should be held responsible solely because he derived economic gain from the sale.[74]

Distributors Who Adopt Products as Their Own Distributors who adopt a product as their own and retailers who label and sell products under their own name, or otherwise represent products as their own, can be considered together for the purpose of determining duties and vulnerability. These entities in the chain of distribution, like assemblers, are often termed ostensible manufacturers or sponsors. They may be subject to liability on either a negligence or a strict liability theory. Potential exposure to negligence liability for ostensible manufacturers may range from negligence on the part of the actual manufacturer to exposure for their own negligence as, for example, in failing to inspect for defects. One who labels a product with his own name or represents it as his own is treated on the same basis as if he had manufactured it and so is liable for the manufacturer's negligence, even if the sponsor could not have discovered the defect. Thus, a meat company was held liable for the death of a consumer caused by a piece of metal in canned beef, because the defendant, Armour, sold the product under its brand name. Liability was imposed despite the defense that a South American company packed the beef and Armour could not have discovered the defect.[75]

Another court held the doctrine of strict liability applicable to one who vouches for a product manufactured by another; by selling the product as his own, the seller makes the responsibility for defects his own. The court found it just as proper to impose strict liability on middlemen as it is to impose it on retailers. The case involved a supplier which distributed nails under its own supplier's trade name. As an ostensible manufacturer, it was held strictly liable for damages for the defective product.[76]

Liability of a retailer is dealt with in three important decisions in this area, all involving causes of action in negligence. In a floor polisher case, citing the *Restatement* Section 400, the court found the retailer warranted merchantability and assumed responsibility for injuries resulting from defects arising in the course of manufacture when it sold the product under its trade name.[77] A second case rejected the defendant's contention that he was not liable because he had not manufactured the product and was not in privity with the injured party. The court recognized liability based on the reasoning that it was in keeping with the current trend in products liability to afford broad protection to the consumer.[78] In a third case, the approach was somewhat different. Here the court recognized that in order to recover, the plaintiff must fasten liability on the manufacturer (not just the retailer) for a defect arising during manufacture. The court held that this, in effect, was what the plaintiff was doing by holding the retailer responsible, because it had held the product out as its own.[79]

Retailers Retailers of products ordinarily are exposed to different vulnerability than are manufacturers. Unless a retailer is in effect a manufacturer (e.g., a restaurant operator or other person engaged in preparation of a product for immediate use), or ostensible manufacturer, the retailer is ordinarily not chargeable with negligence occurring in the design or manufacture of a product. Retailers that are required to assemble a product they sell, however, are held to a standard of care comparable to that of an assembler.

Retailers who buy products from competent manufacturers ordinarily are not liable, in the absence of knowledge of defectiveness. However, a retailer is required to guard against or to warn users of known dangers in use of a product. This duty may be discharged by product labeling and instruction. A seller of a mobile home purchased from a reputable manufacturer a furnace to place in the home. When the furnace exploded, the seller was liable for the loss because the retailer's duty includes reasonable care to protect the buyer from dangers that were or should have been known and here, the court ruled, the seller should have known of the defect.[80]

Retailers who are merely conduits of products made by reputable manufacturers may sell the product without subjecting it to extensive inspection and testing to discover latent defects. This is because the burden on the retailer outweighs the risk of the product being defective, and it is impractical to force retailers to test everything they sell. In a case in which a ladder collapsed while in use by the plaintiff, because of latent manufacturing defects, the court said there was no cause of action in negligence against the retailer, because the defects were unascertainable without expert examination.[81] However, a retailer who sells products of an unknown manufacturer or one whose reputation is unknown has a duty to inspect.[82]

A retailer may be subject to liability if, though unaware of the dangerous character of the product, a retailer could have discovered it based on the competence the retailer has or should have as a dealer in such products. An example is a used car dealer, because the general character of the business requires inspection and repair. In one such case, the seller was responsible for negligent failure to inspect an auto prior to delivery when the defect could have been discovered by a proper predelivery inspection.[83]

Retailers are generally sued on a strict liability or warranty theory. These theories are used because often the plaintiff cannot establish the retailer's negligence since many products come from the supplier in sealed containers without giving the retailer an opportunity to inspect. The "sealed container" doctrine is still sometimes used, although it appears incompatible with strict liability. Essentially it holds retailers and sellers other than the manufacturer not strictly liable for injury caused by products purchased in sealed containers if there is nothing in the appearance of the container to put the seller on notice of anything being amiss. The "sealed container" doctrine prevented imposition of strict liability against the seller of a floor coat, sold in a sealed can, because the defect was undiscoverable.[84] Likewise, in a case in which a cookie containing a wire caused injury, the seller was not strictly liable because it was sold in a sealed package.[85]

Bailors and Lessors　A lessor or bailor for hire may be subject to liability if, when the article is turned over, the bailor knows of a defect or fails to make a reasonable inspection to discover possible defects. Cases finding a bailor negligent generally impose liability for a failure to inspect; thus a rental firm was found negligent for failure to inspect. The court noted that one who is engaged in the business of leasing items (in this case, autos) for hire, does not by that fact become an insurer of the article, but he must exercise reasonable diligence to know the condition of items before renting them out. Liability extends to damages from known defects as well as from defects he could have discovered in the exercise of reasonable care. Finally, the supplier has a duty to use reasonable care to inspect items for hire and protect against creating an unreasonable risk of harm.[86] As another example, an injured golfer had a good cause of action because the bailor failed to warn that a golf cart had no brakes while in reverse.[87]

Cases applying strict liability to bailors and lessors are becoming more common. The general rule is that strict liability applies to lessors if the lessor is in the commercial business of leasing items or the lease transaction is of a commercial nature. The reason for this is that leasing is increasingly being used as a substitute for purchasing. The main issue in the lease of an item on a continuing basis is whether the defect arose before the item left the possession of the bailor.[88] In a leading case, the court held that lessors of personal property (in this case a ladder) are like manufacturers and retailers in that they are engaged in the business of distributing goods to the public, are an integral part of the overall marketing process and should bear the same liability.[89] Two other important cases have held that the nature of a lessor's business (renting vehicles) necessitated that a representation be implied that the vehicles were fit.[90] These decisions have recognized that the bailor is not an insurer of leased items but must use reasonable care to see that the chattel is safe and suitable for the purpose for which it is hired. However, one of these decisions likened a bailor to a manufacturer and retailer in that the bailor can be strictly liable for placing an item on the market knowing that it will be used without inspection.[91]

Testing Companies The exposure to liability of testing companies is relatively new. The theories under which these entities may be held liable for damages due to defective products include traditional tort doctrines. These are exemplified in *Restatement* Section 324A, which imposes liability for injury due to negligent performance of an undertaking and Section 311, which imposes liability for physical harm due to negligent misrepresentation. Strict liability and warranty theories have seen little or no application.

It should be noted at the outset that there are different kinds of testing companies. They have been divided into three categories: (1) *Visible testing agencies* can be subdivided into (a) self-publicizing agencies which actively seek public recognition by self-advertisement, and (b) approving agencies which rely on the manufacturer to make the public aware of their existence via use of their seal of approval. Reliance by the consumer is seen most clearly in this category. (2) *Consumer testing agencies* release the results of tests performed on products after they are on the market. These agencies have no input into the manufacture of products and merely grade the product without solicitation from manufacturers. In this case, reliance by the consumer appears nonexistent. (3) *Invisible testing agencies* prohibit the employing manufacturer from using the testing agency name or results of tests in advertisement. Here, too, reliance is nonexistent.[92]

In a case involving an issue of liability for negligent performance of an undertaking, a fire extinguisher being used by the plaintiff exploded, causing injury. The plaintiff sought to hold Underwriters Laboratories, an independent testing agency employed by the manufacturer, liable for damages. U.L. moved for summary judgment and the motion was denied, so the court did not decide any issue other than that U.L. *could* be liable *if* the plaintiff proved the allegations of negligent approval of a dangerous design and proximate cause.[93] In a case involving an issue of negligent misrepresentation, the plaintiff shoe purchaser sought recovery based on the "Good Housekeeping's Consumer's Guaranty Seal" which she alleged she believed signified the product had been inspected, tested, examined by the defendant, and found safe for the use intended. She slipped and fell while wearing shoes bearing the seal. The issue, as the court framed it, was whether one who endorses a product for economic gain, and to induce the public to buy it, may be liable to a purchaser who in reliance on the endorsement buys the product and is injured because it is not as represented in the endorsement. The court answered affirmatively, on grounds of public policy. There is not a privity requirement, and liability of the defendant depends on balancing several factors, including the extent to which the transaction was intended to affect the plaintiff, the foreseeability of harm to him, and the closeness of connection between the defendant's conduct and the injury. The defendant's duty was defined as exercising ordinary care in issuance of the seal and certification of quality so that the public is not unreasonably exposed to the risk of harm.[94]

On the other hand, another action against U.L. was dismissed although it had endorsed a misrepresentation by the manufacturer. The reasoning was that there was no physical injury to the ultimate user and the balancing of the kinds of factors noted in the preceding case did not warrant imposition of liability.[95]

Problem Areas

The preceding section, discussing duties and vulnerabilities of those potentially exposed to products liability, suggests several problem areas in which the law has not developed fully or where even the applicability of the law of products liability is uncertain. There are several other problem areas which deserve brief discussion.

Unavoidably Unsafe Products The *Restatement* recognizes that the doctrine of strict liability in tort should not be applied to "unavoidably unsafe products." There are some products which, in the present state of human knowledge, cannot be made safe for their intended and ordinary use. These are especially common in the field of drugs. Comment a notes that the vaccine for the Pasteur treatment of rabies sometimes leads to serious, damaging consequences. But, since the disease itself invariably leads to a terrible death, the marketing and use of the vaccine are justified, notwithstanding the unavoidably high degree of risk which they involve. "Such a product, properly prepared, and accompanied by proper direction and warning, is not defective, nor is it *unreasonably* dangerous. The same is true of many other drugs, vaccines, and the like, many of which for this very reason cannot legally be sold except to physicians, or under the prescription of a physician." The same is true of experimental drugs, where experience justifies the marketing and use of the drug despite a medically recognizable risk.

The seller of such products has a duty to properly prepare and market them and to give appropriate warnings, but is not to be held to strict liability for injuries connected with their use. The rationale is that the seller has undertaken to supply the public with a useful and desirable product, attended with a known but apparently reasonable risk. It is generally accepted that situations involving products which cannot be made safe for their ordinary uses, but which are necessary for the protection or preservation of life, should not be subject to the rule of strict liability. The law of negligence is a more appropriate and flexible instrument for deciding cases involving such products, since the utility of the product, the reasonableness of the consequences of the use, and the seller's care can all be considered in relation to the standard of care applicable in negligence actions. An example of misapplication of the strict liability doctrine can be seen in a case involving a hospital which supplied blood to a patient. After receiving the transfusion, the patient developed serum hepatitis. The court avoided the difficult questions of whether blood is a "product" and whether a hospital is a "seller," and determined that strict liability was to be applied. Since strict liability was invoked, it became irrelevant whether the seller exercised all possible care in the preparation of the product, and the impossibility under the current state of medical knowledge of determining the presence of hepatitis virus could not be a factor in the case.[96]

In an interesting legislative response to this and similar "blood" cases, legislatures in many states have passed statutes subjecting suppliers of blood to liability only for negligence, abolishing a cause of action for strict liability in cases involving similar circumstances.

Is a "Service" a "Sale"? The problem of service versus sale which was implicit in the above case has also been touched upon in the preceding section on duties and vulnerabilities. However, it is worth mentioning as a problematical gray area in the field of products liability.

A number of courts have struggled with the task of determining the essence of a transaction and its effect, attempting to formulate rational distinctions between transactions of a commercial nature (essentially "sales") and professional transactions (essentially "services"). Before a court can submit to a jury the issue of whether a product allegedly injuring the plaintiff was in a defective condition unreasonably dangerous at the time it left the defendant's control, the court must decide as a matter of law whether the case is one for the application of the rule of strict liability at all. "That is, was the defendant's participation in the manufacturing or supplying of the product to the general public (and the plaintiff in particular) a transaction of such a commercial nature as to sustain the use of such a procedural shortcut (as strict liability)?"[97] Some courts have extended the application of strict liability to various types of transactions, or expanded the concept of "sale," far beyond the intent of Section 402A. Some have argued that the term "sale" is really a general description of the types of situations by which products are transmitted to consumers and that use of the word "sells" is not a deliberate limitation of the principle to cases in which a product is specifically sold.[98] Other courts have found that strict liability can apply to any transaction by which a product is transmitted to a consumer, such a transaction being considered "essentially commercial in character."[99]

There are numerous activities or transactions in which the person providing a service may also provide or use a product in the course of rendering the service. One case held that a dentist was not strictly liable for injuries caused to a patient by the breaking of a defective hypodermic needle in the patient's jaw. The court noted that a dentist (or other professional person) performs a service that is essentially professional, rather than engaging in the business of supplying a product to a consumer.[100] Similarly, a hospital where a defective drug was administered and a doctor who prescribed a defective drug have been held not to be subject to application of the doctrine of strict liability.[101] Strict liability would apply only to manufacturers and distributors of those products, since the dentist or doctor or hospital was engaged in essentially professional services and the supplying or use of a product was strictly incidental to the professional services. The opposite result was reached in the blood transfusion case noted in the previous section, since the court minimized the distinction between sale and service and found to its satisfaction that the hospital in effect was engaged in the business of "selling" a "product."

In another case, the defendant was a professional architect who contracted to design, engineer, and supervise construction of a plant. The plaintiff was a worker who was exposed to harmful chemical dust during the construction. The court found that the essence of the transaction was the performance of professional services. The furnishing of some tangible products was entirely incidental and was not analogous to a true sale. The court also found that the defendant, in supplying his services, had no impact on the public as a whole since there was no question of mass production or large scale marketing of products. This type of reasoning appears to "limit the rule of strict liability to cases in which the policy considerations often cited in products liability actually apply; that is, where substantial injustice would be done by requiring the plaintiff to trace his injury to some specific misconduct and where the defendant is able to spread the risk of economic loss through commercial processes."[102]

Class Actions   Although the issue is still somewhat unsettled, it seems probable that class action suits in federal court can not be maintained in products liability cases involving personal injury. The reasons behind this fact are twofold. First, since most class action suits are based upon federal statutes, such as the antitrust and securities acts, federal courts are reluctant to ground product class action suits solely upon diversity (residency of plaintiffs and defendants in different states). Secondly, the fact that personal injuries are so subjective in nature necessarily negates the mandatory requirement of class "issue" predominance. In relation to the latter cause, the Advisory Committee's Note to the 1966 Amendment to Federal Rule 23 states:

> A "mass accident" resulting in injuries to numerous persons is ordinarily not appropriate for a class action because of the likelihood that significant questions, not only of damages but of liability and defenses to liability, would be present, affecting the individual in different ways. In these circumstances an action conducted nominally as a class action would degenerate in practice into multiple lawsuits separately tried.[103]

In a similar vein, a federal district court rejected the plaintiff's desire to maintain a class action:

> It is clear that each claimant in this situation may properly be regarded as having a legitimate interest in litigating independently. Not only do the claims vitally affect a significant aspect of the lives of the claimants (unlike the usual class action, where individual claims are usually somewhat peripheral to the lives of the claimants), but there is a wide range of choice of the strategy and tactics of the litigation.[104]

In contrast to personal injury class action suits, products liability class action suits involving economic losses should be maintainable in federal courts. For example, a federal court permitted a group of convention exhibitors to maintain a class action suit after a fire destroyed their materials. Since the fire was caused by faulty wiring, rather than by a product, this was not a products liability case. However, since the suit was analogous in most respects to a products case, the court presumably would have reached the same result had a defective product caused the fire. In permitting the suit, the court found that the four elements of Federal Rule of Civil Procedure 23(A) (governing class actions) were satisfied (i.e., numerosity, common question, typical claims, adequate representation). The court also noted that a common question of fact or law predominated over any issue affecting only individual members (i.e., each case would require identical evidence to show the fire's origin, the parties' responsibility, and proximate causation). Secondly, the court found that a class action suit would be superior to any other available method for the adjudication of the controversy.[105]

If federal courts are somewhat reluctant to allow consumer product class action suits, state courts are even less disposed to allow such suits. Except for those states which pattern their rules of procedure after the Federal Rules of Civil Procedure, many state courts follow the rationale espoused in a New York case: "Separate wrongs to separate persons, though committed by similar means and even pursuant to a single plan, do not alone create a common or general interest in those who are wronged."[106]

Multiple Litigation There are two methods by which an entire industry (or its trade association) may be held liable for a single injury caused to a plaintiff. First, the defendants may be held liable on simple causation principles if the plaintiff can show that each defendant was a substantial factor in bringing about the plaintiff's injuries. Secondly, a court may invoke *Restatement* Rule 433(B)(3).

In a case which best exemplifies the former method, an industrial insulation worker sued eleven asbestos manufacturers after the worker contracted asbestosis from thirty years of exposure to asbestos. In holding that each defendant's conduct was a substantial factor in bringing about the plaintiff's damages, the court said:

> In the instant case, it is impossible as a practical matter, to determine with absolute certainty which particular exposure to asbestos dust resulted in injury to Borel. It is undisputed, however, that Borel contracted the asbestosis from inhaling asbestos dust and that he was exposed to the products of all defendants on many occasions.[107]

As to method two, a New York district court used *Restatement* Rule 433(B)(3) to find the entire blasting cap industry liable for damages caused to a single plaintiff by a single blasting cap. The manufacturer of the specific cap could not be identified. The rule states:

> Where the conduct of two or more actors is tortious, and it is proved that harm has been caused to the plaintiff by only one of them, but there is uncertainty as to which one has caused it the burden is upon each such actor to prove that he has not caused the harm.[108]

In addition to using this rule to support its holding, the court also mentioned two other theories on which the defendants could be held liable: (1) the joint control of a common risk or the joint creation of a common risk; and (2) the enterprise theory, whereby the foreseeable costs of an activity are assigned to those who are in the best strategic position to prevent or reduce them.

While such decisions are most disturbing to manufacturers, it must be noted that they are isolated. Enterprise liability is not typical of the law of products liability.

Defenses to Product Actions

The plaintiff in a products liability case must establish the facts and circumstances essential to the elements of the plaintiff's theory of liability. Failure to do so should lead to a successful defense in the form of a nonsuit or a directed verdict at the close of the plaintiff's proof. Even if the defendant is not so fortunate, certain substantive or affirmative defenses to the plaintiff's cause of action may be available, depending upon the plaintiff's theory of liability.

Contributory Negligence, or Assumption of Risk Conduct on the part of the plaintiff may prove to be one of the most useful sources of effective products defense. Contributory negligence on the part of the plaintiff (that is, negligence which contributes to causation of the injury) is a valid defense to an action based upon negligence. However, the courts and commentators have had difficulty with the application of the concept of contributory negligence to actions grounded in warranty and strict liability. Yet, conduct amounting to voluntary exposure to a known risk by the plaintiff has been widely accepted as a defense in both warranty and strict liability tort actions. Dean Prosser, the principal drafter of the *Restatement*, explained the subtle differences between the concepts of contributory negligence and voluntary exposure to a known risk in the context of products liability:

> Contributory negligence of the plaintiff is not a defense when such negligence consists merely in a failure to discover a defect in a product, or to guard against the possibility of its existence. On the other hand, a form of contributory negligence which consists of involuntarily and unreasonably proceeding to encounter a known danger, and commonly passes under the name of assumption of risk, is a defense.[109]

The same commentator elsewhere described available defenses to warranty actions in very similar terms to the defense available under strict liability in tort.

Assumption of risk, of the kind where a person proceeds unreasonably in the face of a known risk, is illustrated by two cases involving auto brakes. In one, a passenger in a car which he knew to have defective brakes was found to have assumed the risk of the injuries he sustained in a single car accident. He was knowledgeable about brakes in general (and the brakes of this car in particular) but rode in the car in disregard of the risk.[110] In another case, a truck driver was found to have assumed the risk of a steering failure, because he had experienced similar failures on several occasions prior to the accident in question.[111] Another court held that a bulldozer used to gather trees and brush was not defective when operated without a canopy guard. The plaintiff, who was injured when a tree fell across the bulldozer he was operating, had full knowledge of the machine and of the hazards of operation without the guard. He was held to have assumed the risk of the injury.[112]

One court has strongly reaffirmed its minority view that contributory negligence is a viable defense in strict liability cases. The plaintiff brought an action against the defendant tire retailer and manufacturer on the grounds that the auto accident in which he was injured was caused by the manner in which metal studs had been inserted in the tires, causing him to lose control of his car. The court accepted the defense contention that the proximate cause of the accident was actually the negligence of the plaintiff in operating his car at eighty mph and switching lanes abruptly while rounding a curve. Analyzing the principle of contributory negligence closely, the court noted that when it had adopted the doctrine of strict liability in tort, the rule of contributory negligence in tort actions was well settled in the jurisdiction. After analyzing some of the difficulties that courts and commentators have had with the application of contributory negligence as a defense to an action based upon strict liability, it concluded that most apparent conflicts reflect differences in terminology rather than fundamental disagreement over applicable legal principles. It saw no reason why long-established principles in tort law (including contributory negligence) should not apply in strict liability actions, since "there is nothing to justify holding the seller for the consequences for the user's own contributory fault or breach of duty in the use of the product, which conduct is a proximate cause of the injury he has incurred."[113]

Since most courts, however, have not viewed contributory negligence in strict liability actions in so favorable a light to the defense, it is probably more useful to use the generic term, product misuse, to cover a broad range of conduct on the part of plaintiffs which may form the basis for a defense.

Product Misuse Products liability claims, whatever the theory of liability, are all concerned in some way with a question of intended, expected, or normal uses of the product. Under a negligence test, the manufacturer has a duty to manufacture a product that will be safe for a purpose for which the manufacturer should expect it to be used. The warranty test is that the product must be fit for the ordinary purpose for which such products are used. The strict liability test is that a product must be safe for normal handling and consumption and free of defects unreasonably dangerous to the user. In determining what is intended, expected, normal, or ordinary use, the issue of foreseeability will come into play. In one case, a plaintiff garage owner sued the lessor and manufacturer of gasoline pumping equipment for damages caused by a fire. The court found that the fire was caused, not by a product defect, but by the negligence of a cab driver who drove off with the nozzle of the pump inserted in the gas tank. The violent stress upon the hose caused a component part of the pump to rupture and leak, leading to the subsequent fire. The court held that the misuse of the product was the cause of the damage and that the manufacturer could not reasonably be expected to foresee and guard against such a misuse.[114]

In recent years, there has developed a long line of cases in which automobile manufacturers have been sued by plaintiffs who were involved in collisions and claimed that the manufacturer, in effect, should have designed a vehicle in which it was safe to have a collision. Defendant manufacturers have consistently contended that collisions are not an expected, ordinary, or normal use of an automobile. One line of decisions had adopted the view that the intended purpose does not include participation in collisions, despite the manufacturer's ability to foresee that such collisions will sometimes occur.[115] Another line of decisions, on the contrary, has stressed foreseeability aspects rather than focusing on normal use. These decisions have held that a manufacturer should foresee the possibility that collisions will occur and that this concept carries with it the duty to design the product to minimize the consequences of a collision. In these cases, it is not claimed that an allegedly defective design caused the injury-producing collision in the first instance. The claim is that the design created an "unsafe environment" for an accident, in that some object in the interior of the vehicle or some change in structure as a result of collision forces *enhanced* the injuries the plaintiff received in the accident.[116]

The latter line of decisions has tended to ignore the fact that, in a second collision case, it is the collision itself and not the design of the product which causes displacement and damage to the plaintiff's body. These courts ignore an important tenet of strict liability—that a product is not defective when it leaves the hands of the seller in a safe condition, and subsequent mishandling or other causes (such as a collision) render it harmful.

For all practical purposes, the manufacturer today must evaluate carefully the total environment in which its product will be used, and attempt to anticipate the ways in which it foreseeably may be misused. Realistically, the manufacturer must attempt to anticipate unintended, as well as intended uses of its product and safeguard the product accordingly. Needless to say, the insistence of some courts that a seller must foresee unintended uses of its product can lead to some strange results which, fortunately, are not necessarily representative of majority law in this country. For example, a manufacturer of cologne was held liable for burns sustained by a girl who attempted to spray the cologne directly into the flame of a lighted candle in order to scent the candle.[117] It can be hoped that most courts would not impose upon the manufacturer the obligation to guard against, or even to realize the possibility, of such a bizarre abuse of the product.

It is a general rule that use with knowledge of a hazard will constitute a valid defense. Although a few recent decisions have retreated from this widely accepted general rule, it is still the law in many jurisdictions. The concept of open and obvious danger comes into play here, since these are often the types of cases in which "the very nature of the article gives notice and warning of the consequences to be expected, of the injuries to be suffered."[118] A good example is a recent case in which the plaintiff suffered injuries when his arm was caught in a pipe cutting machine. The plaintiff brought suit against the manufacturer for negligent design in the location of the stop switch. Because the plaintiff was an experienced master plumber and had used the same type of machine many times, the court reasoned that the location of the switch created an open and obvious condition. The manufacturer, thus, had not breached any duty owed to the defendant. The user in this case was a member of a particular trade whose members are skilled in the use of such products and are generally aware of attendant hazards. The court concluded that the machine was reasonably safe for its intended use, taking into account the training and experience of the persons for whose use the machine was intended.[119]

Another common aspect of product misuse consists of using the product in disregard of warnings or contrary to instructions. Use of a product in disregard of specific warnings may be a defense as long as the warnings are adequate to reasonably alert a person to a hazard. While warnings have been discussed in detail previously in this chapter, one more example will illustrate the potential for a sound defense. In this case, the issues of adequacy and disregard of the warning were resolved in favor of the manufacturer. The plaintiff was using contact cement in connection with his carpentry work. The container had a label which clearly and specifically warned against smoking and warned that all fires and flames must be extinguished and sparking must be prevented by turning off electric motors. An explosion occurred when the plaintiff used the cement within a few inches of a gas stove where the pilot light was left burning. The court held that the plaintiff used the product in disregard of a warning which was adequate to give notice of the hazard.[120]

Directions and warnings serve somewhat different purposes: directions are given to assure effective use and warnings to assure safe use.[121] The two may overlap, however, since a statement directing that something be done or not be done is at least partially cautionary in nature. In a case in which the plaintiff sustained skin injuries while apparently using home permanent solution for normal purposes, the court found that she misused the product in the sense of failing to follow instructions regarding the making of a test curl. The court held that a consumer may not knowingly violate the unambiguous instructions and ignore the information supplied by the manufacturer, and then attempt to hold the manufacturer liable for resulting injuries.[122]

It should be evident from this discussion of defenses based upon misuse by the plaintiff that there is a considerable amount of overlap among the various defenses. For example, the conduct of a plaintiff in a single case may involve an unintended use of a product, as well as disregard of a warning and use with full knowledge of a potential hazard. One or more aspects of his conduct may constitute, in the terminology of a particular court, either a voluntary assumption of a known risk or contributory negligence. In short, the labels are used as convenient categories. The key point is that the types of conduct discussed above may form the basis for a tenable defense through which the defendant can attempt to establish that either the product was not defective or, even if defective, the plaintiff's conduct, rather than the defect, was the real cause of the plaintiff's injuries.

Alteration or Modification of Product by Plaintiff or Third Party Conduct on the part of a person other than the plaintiff or the defendant may enter into the consideration of a products case and may constitute the basis for a defense.

The conduct of a third person may be the actual cause of the plaintiff's injury. In one case, a successful defense resulted from proof that the negligence of a prescribing doctor in failing to follow instructions for the use of a drug caused a patient's injury. Since the drug itself was safe in the absence of the doctor's negligence, the drug company was held to be not liable.[123] A common example of conduct on the part of the third person causing an otherwise safe product to become dangerous or defective occurs in industrial settings. It is in such settings, involving capital goods (products such as machines used in industry) that a large proportion of product-connected injuries occurs. A third person such as the owner of a machine may render inoperable a safety device, either by removing the device or modifying the machine to bypass it, allowing operation without the safety device functioning. In such cases, the manufacturer may be relieved of liability if it can establish that such conduct was, in fact, the cause of an injury. In one such case, an inspection of a machine after an accident indicated that a switch, installed by the owner of the machine, allowed it to be operated without the safety gate in place. In addition, it was established that the plaintiff's employer did not properly maintain the machine and its related safety equipment. The manufacturer was relieved from liability on the grounds that the negligence of the owner of the machine was the cause of his own employee's injuries.[124] Other types of activity, short of such drastic modifications of a product, may form the basis of a defense: these may include mishandling, or failure to follow cautionary instructions.[125] A manufacturer is not an insurer of its product, warranting that it will never deteriorate in spite of mishandling or improper maintenance.

State of the Art Defense A number of cases have held that the manufacturer's or seller's liability is to be determined solely on the basis of circumstances existing at a time of a product's design or manufacture.[126] This state of the art defense is well recognized in the law of products liability and is applicable to actions under both negligence and strict liability, since such concepts as foreseeability and reasonableness are important to the application of both theories.

It is not unreasonable for a manufacturer to follow a design or method of manufacture customary in the industry, although through the use of hindsight when a products liability lawsuit is filed, other possible designs or methods may be conceived of as safer. In determining whether a product or its design was unreasonably dangerous or defective, it is relevant for the court to consider the conformity of the defendant's practice to that of other manufacturers in the industry at the time of the design or the manufacturing process.[127] In a lawnmower case, the plaintiff's expert witness testified as to alternative designs which would have made the machine safer. The defense expert, however, established that the mower met or exceeded all safety standards, that it embodied the most advanced technology known to the industry, and that the plaintiff's alternatives would create further functional and safety problems.[128] In a case involving the crash of a chartered airplane, the injuries of the plaintiffs were allegedly enhanced because seats broke loose from the floor, blocking an exit. The plaintiffs attempted to introduce evidence of improvements in standards for installation of seats between the time the plane was manufactured in 1952 and the time of the 1970 crash. The court held that the plane was not defective, because it was in accord with the state of the art within the aircraft industry when designed, manufactured, and first sold. It held that proof that improved seats were available eighteen years after the manufacture of the plane was not relevant to the determination of reasonable care at the time the plane was designed.[129] On the question of reasonableness, some courts may admit into evidence proof of alternative designs or processes, but restrict admissibility to alternatives which were available at the time the defendant's product was designed and manufactured.[130]

Disclaimers   Whatever the surface attraction of disclaimers in the context of products liability, it must be remembered that the law will construe them *very* strictly. A reference to Section 2-719 of the Uniform Commercial Code indicates the narrowness with which disclaimers will be interpreted:

> . . . consequential damages may be limited or excluded unless the limitation or exclusion is unconscionable. Limitation of consequential damages or injury to the person in the case of consumer goods is prima facie unconscionable but limitation of damages where the loss is commercial is not.

In short, disclaimers may be effective in cases involving purely commercial loss. But a disclaimer is useless in an attempt to avoid liability for personal injuries resulting from a defective product. While some courts are willing to accept disclaimers as reasonable in commercial settings, they have found them to be totally inapplicable to personal injury situations.[131]

Statutes of Limitations   In certain circumstances, a defense may be based on a statute of limitations, asserting that the defendant is no longer subject to suit because the statutory time in which to bring an action has expired. Most jurisdictions have differing statutes for torts (including negligence and strict liability) and contracts (including breach of warranty). There may be two basic questions involved in this defense to products actions: first, what statute (tort or contract) is to be used. And second, when does the action arise and when does the time begin to run? Assuming an action in tort, the question of which statute applies may be relatively simple, but a more difficult question is, when does the action accrue?

Some courts have held that the time begins to run at the time of the injury.[132] In other words, if the tort statute is three years, then the plaintiff will have three years from the time of the injury to bring an action. A few courts have held that the cause of action accrues at the time the product is sold, since, if an actionable defect exists, it must be present when the product leaves the seller's control.[133] Therefore, assuming again a three year statute, if the injury does not occur until thirty-five months after the product is manufactured and sold, then the plaintiff must act with great dispatch to avoid seeing his action barred. The latter is definitely a minority view, although a number of state statutes enacted by legislatures in recent years have altered statutes of limitations for the benefit of manufacturers.

Examples of Losses Which May Arise from Products

A collection of examples of product-connected losses (including property damage and personal injury) could be almost as extensive as a listing of the products cases which have been litigated. The recovery or denial of recovery will depend, in many cases, upon often subtle differences of facts.

The following examples are collected in the hope of presenting the reader with a broad cross section of types of injuries or damage and types of recoveries either awarded or denied.

Bodily Injury and/or Property Damage An automobile driver, injured in an intersection collision brought suit against the owner and operator of a truck and the manufacturer of his own automobile. The allegation against the manufacturer was that it had used defective window glass in the left side window of the car. This was alleged to be the direct and proximate cause of his injuries, even though the manufacturer was not responsible for the initial collision. The driver sustained eye lacerations as a result of the accident, leading to blindness. In addition to the plaintiff's settlement with the owner and operator of the truck, the court determined that the plaintiff was entitled to a damage award of $500,000 against the manufacturer.[134]

Two plaintiffs, a child and his father, recovered $840,000 for the injuries sustained by the child when he became entangled in the sharp blades of the auger of a cattlefeeder. The device was assembled by the father from parts provided by the manufacturer. The parts were sold without a cover for the auger and without a warning to use a cover. An issue in the case was whether the manufacturer of the machine should have foreseen that young children would use the machine to play a game and step across the uncovered auger while the machine was operating. The court found that this was a question for the jury, which resolved it against the manufacturer, partly upon the basis of the fact that the manufacturer advertised the machine as so simple to operate that "even a child can do your feeding." The defense contention that a cattlefeeder is obviously dangerous and that the open and obvious danger should relieve the manufacturer of an obligation to warn was rejected by the court. It emphasized that the full danger of the machine, with the uncovered blades sharpening themselves rather than dulling in the course of time, might not have been fully appreciated by the users. The fact that the injured twelve-year-old boy might have not understood any warning also did not relieve the manufacturer of a duty to warn, since the child's father would have been put on notice by a warning. The court held that it was proper for the trial court to permit the jury to consider evidence of the plaintiff's post-traumatic personality disorder, as well as his severe physical injuries, in arriving at its assessment of damages against the manufacturer.[135]

On the other hand, a court ordered a new trial on the issue of damages for the purchaser and drinker of a can of contaminated soft drink. The new trial was ordered on the basis that, while there was proof that the plaintiff had a preexisting condition of the gums, there was no proof of her main contention, that the drinking of the contaminated soda aggravated that condition.[136]

In a case involving telephone equipment, it was held that a telephone user who suffered permanent hearing impairment as a result of excessive noise from a telephone was entitled to recover $10,000 in damages. The court allowed the theory of *res ipsa loquitur* to be applied. Although the injured party had physical possession of the telephone, this did not prevent a finding that the instrumentality was controlled and managed by the telephone company, which was held to have a duty to use known devices and methods to prevent the passage of dangerous sound levels.[137]

An action was brought against a manufacturer of a heating/air-conditioning unit in a new house which was destroyed by fire. A negligence recovery for the plaintiff was allowed on a theory of *res ipsa loquitur*, since the evidence showed that the fire started in the general area of the unit, which was new and had just left the control of the manufacturer.[138]

Loss of Use or Failure of Product to Serve Its Purpose or Perform Its Function Cases in this category generally involve property damage or injury to economic interests of the plaintiff. In a case involving defective carpeting, the plaintiff sought recovery for carpeting which was not of the quality claimed by the seller. Recovery of the difference between market value and what the market value should have been was allowed on the basis that the manufacturer had placed a worthless article in the hands of the purchaser.[139]

An action was brought against the seller of an insecticide for loss of the market value of a crop when, because of new, more sophisticated testing methods, the crop was made unmarketable due to discovery of a residue on the crop from the insecticide. Strict liability was imposed for the product's failure to perform its intended function, despite the seller's unawareness of newer testing methods.[140]

Loss of Use of Property Due to Product's Failure to Perform Its Function The owner of a parcel of real estate sought damages for depreciation of property value, as a result of a defective septic system. The court held that the depreciation of property value was not a proper element of damages in a negligence cause of action against the supplier of a product.[141] On the other hand, it was held that a commercial fisherman had a good cause of action in negligence against a diesel engine manufacture. He sought and recovered damages for economic loss resulting from several engine failures which disabled his boat for extended periods of time during the fishing season.[142]

Another plaintiff sought damages for depreciation in vehicles which he owned. The alleged damages were due to cost of inspection, cost of repairs and replacements, and loss of use prior to and during inspection and repair. The court found that the first and last allegations of damages listed were not compensable because they did not flow from compensable physical damage. The second allegation was moot because the plaintiff had already been reimbursed for that element of damages.[143]

Damage to the Product The owner of a mobile home sued the manufacturer and assembler of the unit and the manufacturer of the truck on which it was mounted, for damages resulting when wheels sheered away from the vehicle because the truck did not maintain the manufacturer's torque requirements. The court noted that there is a split among jurisdictions as to whether damage to a product itself is recoverable under the doctrine of strict liability, but concluded that recovery should be allowed. Since, under Section 402A, the burden of placing a defective product into the stream of commerce falls upon the manufacturer, it appears inconsistent, the court held, to limit his responsibility to bodily injury or to injury to property other than the product sold. However, in relation to the plaintiff's claim for loss of business use of the vehicle, the court declined to extend strict liability to commercial or business loss. This view is in accord with the views of several jurisdictions which have limited recovery for strict liability to "physical harm caused to the ultimate user or consumer, or to his property." This latter statement was the holding of an important California case, which allowed recovery for product damage in an accident caused by a truck brake failure, but refused to extend strict liability recovery to commercial or business losses.[144]

Another court held that there was a cause of action in strict liability for an alleged defect in fan blades contained in an electric motor. The cause of action included recovery for damage to components of the motor other than that portion containing the defect, because the defect in the blades was found to create an unreasonable danger to the other components of the motor.[145] Another purchaser recovered under strict liability for damages to a trailer that occurred when the spare tire rack came loose as a result of broken welds.[146]

Loss of Income When a Product Fails A nursery owner brought an action against the manufacturer and distributor of an herbicide for damages to his azalea crop caused by use of the product. The attempt of the sellers to disclaim warranties as to the effects of the use of the chemical, the court held, did not expressly or fairly warn the purchaser that they were attempting to deny responsibility for the particular side effects which occurred. The sellers had represented the product specifically to be safe for the purpose for which it was used. However, the damages award for loss of part of the azalea crop on which the herbicide was used was limited to the amount specifically expended ($8,323) in digging up and disposing of the plants. Nothing was awarded for the commercial value of the lost plants, because the owner failed to offer any evidence as to the value.[147]

Another case (going to the opposite extreme) dealt with loss of income caused by product failure, including damage to the product. It involved defective propellers for a commercial vessel. The producer of an alloy used for the propellers was held liable not only for the value of the defective propellers, but for the loss of the plaintiff's ship and (upon proper proof) for its resultant economic loss.[148]

A commercial fisherman was held to have a good cause of action in negligence against a diesel engine manufacturer for economic loss resulting from several engine failures during the fishing season. The plaintiff offered competent evidence of the value of the fish that could have been expected to have been caught during the period that the boat was being repaired. The court held that:

> ... a manufacturer intending and foreseeing that its product would eventually be purchased by persons operating commercial ventures, owes such persons the duty not to impair the purchaser's commercial operations by a faulty product. The negligent manufacturer of such an article sold, poses the foreseeable risk that the output of the entire enterprise would be diminished or temporarily halted. The type of harm generated by such work stoppage (lost profits) is well within the zone of danger created and foreseen by the negligent act.[149]

As was pointed out previously, the courts which have considered the issue have been reluctant to apply the doctrine of strict liability in tort to commercial losses. In effect, these cases have placed a limitation on the scope of the manufacturer's strict liability in tort. The manufacturer, according to the court,

> ... can appropriately be held liable for physical injuries caused by defects by requiring his goods to match a standard of safety defined in terms of conditions that create unreasonable risks of harm. He cannot be held for the level of performance of his products in the consumer's business unless he agrees that the product was designed to meet the consumer's demands. A consumer should not be charged at the will of the manufacturer with bearing the risk of physical injury when the consumer buys a product on the market. He can, however, be fairly charged with the risk that the product will not match his economic

expectations unless the manufacturer agrees [warrants] that it will. If the plaintiff is suing "solely because the product was not up to the expected standard, and he did not receive what he contracted for, then the essence of his action is contract, not tort."[150]

Aside from commercial loss liability, it should be noted that there is no question that a plaintiff suffering bodily injury caused by a hazardous product may recover for his personal economic loss, such as lost earnings or impaired future earning capacity, regardless of the theory of liability. For example, a plumbing employee recovered damages of $540,000 from the manufacturer of a gas control valve on a furnace which permitted gas vapors to escape and explode when the worker lit his propane torch to solder a water pipe. A substantial amount of the recovery was for loss of future earnings as a result of impaired earning capacity due to his injury.[151] In another case, the plaintiff was killed when an automobile head restraint not only failed to provide protection but (due to defective materials) allegedly enhanced head injuries suffered in a rear end collision. The court allowed $2,024,710 in damages. The decedent was a young psychologist with a young family, and expert testimony from an economist as to future growth rates of earnings was held admissible. The damages were based upon the evidence of loss of future earnings.[152] This type of testimony, by economic experts, is common in wrongful death and severe injury cases.

Expenses to Withdraw, Inspect, Repair, or Replace a Defective Component or Whole Product This section deals, in part, with another aspect of cases cited in previous sections. For example, the nursery owner, who was denied recovery for the loss of commercial value of his azaleas, was allowed damages limited to the amount expended in digging up and disposing of damaged plants.[153] Similarly, although the truck owner was not allowed to recover for commercial loss caused by the fact that the product was not up to the expected standard, he was allowed damages for the inspection and repair of the truck which was damaged in an accident caused by a brake failure.[154]

In another case, contravening the majority rule on strict liability for commercial losses, the plaintiff was allowed to recover lost profits, as well as the cost of repairs and cleanup, due to a fire caused by a gas heater which destroyed the plaintiff's variety store building and contents.[155] In another case, the plaintiff was entitled to recover his expenses of inspecting and removing the defective product, a piece of drilling equipment, from the drill hole in which it broke.[156]

Expenses of a product withdrawal would ordinarily be incurred by a product manufacturer or seller and would not be an element of damages sought by a plaintiff in a products case. Although appellate cases involving product withdrawal are few, if any, it is conceivable that a manufacturer or seller might attempt to recover from a supplier who was responsible for a defect requiring a product withdrawal campaign. Or, such a supplier might become the defendant in a subrogation action by an insurer who has indemnified the manufacturer for its withdrawal expenses.

Because few cases have been decided involving product withdrawal, the exposure can best be discussed by examining both the coverage and exclusions of a nonstandard insurance coverage often called "recall" insurance. The coverage will indemnify for the reasonable and necessary cost of:

1. telephone and telegraphic communications, radio, or television announcements, newspaper advertising;
2. stationery, envelopes, production of announcements and postage;
3. remuneration paid to regular employees of the insured for necessary overtime;
4. the cost of hire of persons other than regular employees;
5. the actual cost of disposal of the products, if normal methods of trash disposal will not eliminate the hazard. Disposal costs must be related exclusively to the withdrawal of the product....

Several types of withdrawal situations are excluded from coverage. Although excluded from "recall" insurance coverage, many of these items serve to illustrate additional loss exposures of a manufacturer. Not covered are product withdrawals occasioned by:

1. failure of the products to accomplish their intended purpose; or
2. improper, inadequate, or faulty formulae or specifications (domestic policies differ in this respect from the Lloyd's form); or
3. breach of warranties of fitness, quality, efficacy or efficiency; or
4. deterioration, decomposition, or transformation of chemical structure unless a result of error or omission in the manufacturing; or
5. withdrawals of kindred products of the insured; or
6. withdrawals of products bearing the same trade or brand name but of different batches from the batch suspected to be harmful, but only if the insured has represented in his application that the products are identifiable by batches; or
7. withdrawals occasioned simply by a lack of consumer acceptance of a product, or the expense of regaining good will, or other consequential loss; or
8. redistribution or replacement of the withdrawn products; or
9. caprice or whim of the insured; or

10. knowledge prior to policy inception of a preexisting condition likely to cause a loss under the policy.[157]

COMPLETED OPERATIONS EXPOSURES

Whereas products liability exposures arise out of goods which have been manufactured, sold, handled, or distributed by a business enterprise, completed operations exposures arise out of services performed by a firm, after the performance of such services has been completed.

A contractor who agrees to undertake an operation for another who may be liable to that other person, as well as to third persons, for injuries and/or property damage arising out of and during the progress of the work. The work could consist of the erection of an entire building, an alteration, or minor repairs. In each case, the liability of the contractor remains the same. The contractor is liable for any negligence during the operation. This rule of liability applies to contractors doing original work, repairpersons, employees who install parts, and supervising architects and engineers.[158]

In insurance and legal circles, however, the phrase "completed operations liability exposures" refers specifically to the liability, if any, of the contractor which remains *after all of the work has been completed and abandoned* by the contractor.[159]

Legal Foundations of Exposures

Accepted Work Doctrine The original concept adopted by the courts was that, once the work was completed and accepted by the owner, the liability of the contractor was at an end, regardless of whether the work had been negligently performed or not. This rule of nonliability was based on the theory that, in the absence of privity of contract, the contractor owed no duty to anyone other than the contractee.[160] The rationale was that, in accepting the work, and in exercising control over it, the owner adopted the completed work and was thereafter liable to any third person who might be injured or suffer property damage due to the negligence of the owner in owning or maintaining an unsafe condition.[161] Thus, a contractor was engaged to remove equipment from a job site under the employer's direction. The court held that the injured third-party plaintiff had no cause of action against the contractor in negligence, because the defendant owed no duty at the time and place of injury. The court followed the general rule that the contractor is not liable after the work is completed, turned over to the owner, and accepted; the owner is then substituted as the responsible party.[162] Another case involved an action by the first subcontractor's employee against the second subcontractor's insurer for injuries caused by a fall into an unmarked hole in a concrete pit in which the second subcontractor had done work. The court held that the action could not be sustained, because the subcontractor had surrendered control of the pit several months previously.[163] As is pointed out in the above cases, if the subcontractor retains some control over the project, he or she may not be free of liability.[164]

In the absence of an express or implied agreement to the contrary, there is no duty to inspect after the work is completed and accepted unless, in the exercise of reasonable care, there is or should be knowledge that a defect is likely to develop making the project imminently dangerous. Just such an agreement to the contrary was the key to a case in which a contractor was held liable for failing to fulfill a continuing duty of inspection.[165] Another qualification of the rule of nonliability is acceptance by other than the owner or employer. For example, a contractor was not relieved of liability by his argument that the work (removal of a telephone pole according to a contract with the telephone company) was accepted by an employee of the user of the property on which the pole had been located. The plaintiff was injured when he fell into the hole left by the removal. The court rejected the defense because there was no proof the employee had actual or apparent authority to accept the work.[166]

The general rule, therefore, is that if there is a valid acceptance of the contractor's work, at the time of acceptance the liability of the contractor to third persons ceases. The responsibility for maintaining or using the property in its defective state then shifts to the proprietor.

Exceptions to Accepted Work Doctrine Exceptions to the doctrine are numerous. The fact that there is some overlap among exceptions is unimportant because the end result of each exception is the same—the contractor will be held liable to third parties injured by the contractor's negligence even after acceptance of the work by the owner. Exceptions to the general rule of nonliability include projects where the work to be performed contemplates a completed operation which is inherently dangerous, if negligently performed. For example, liability may be imposed where a third party is injured as a direct result of an inherently dangerous act, or where the act results in a dangerous situation, the natural and probable consequence of which would be injury to a third party. A highway repair contractor's act in leaving a deep depression in the shoulder of the road is an example of such a situation.[167]

Another (related) exception arises where the thing dealt with is imminently dangerous in kind, such as explosives, poisonous gases, and the like. This exception was applied and rendered the contractor liable for negligent construction of a chimney to serve a furnace using propane gas as fuel. The defective chimney allowed carbon monoxide to escape into living quarters and created an imminently dangerous condition.

The question arises, what is meant by imminently dangerous? The nature of the instrumentality is of primary importance. It is usually necessary for the contractor to have some knowledge that a danger is probable. This requirement causes this exception to merge with the exception that, if there is knowledge of the danger, the contractor is liable. For example, a general contractor was sued when the ductwork in a supermarket fell, striking the plaintiff (a shopper in the store) three years after completion of construction. The defense was raised that the defendant could not, and did not know of, or discover, the improper installation. The defense was rejected because the defendants designed the building, supervised construction, and had the opportunity to know of the danger. Furthermore, the danger could have been anticipated from the method of construction, and the court found the danger inherent, although the injury was not immediate.[168]

Where the subject matter of the project is to be used for a particular purpose, requiring security for the protection of life or limb (such as a stairway), the courts recognize an exception to the accepted work doctrine. A contractor who improperly attached an attic stairway was liable for injuries when the plaintiff, while using the stairway, was injured by its becoming detached.[169] Another exception is recognized where the thing is rendered dangerous by a defect which the contractor knows about, but deceitfully or deliberately conceals, and which causes an accident when the thing is used for the particular purpose for which it was constructed.[170]

A final exception is applied where the work completed constitutes a nuisance. The contractor may be liable to third parties who come in contact with the nuisance and are injured by it, as in the case of a contractor who created a nuisance on a public highway and was liable for resulting injuries.[171]

Abandonment of Accepted Work Doctrine The numerous exceptions to the accepted work doctrine eventually led to abandonment of it by about one half the jurisdictions. The modern view adopts the doctrine of MacPherson v. Buick Motor Co. (discussed in connection with products liability exposures), applying it to independent contractors.[172] The duty owed to third parties after completion is the same as that owed by manufacturers to users and consumers of their products, despite the absence of privity. The rationale for the rule is that there is no reason to distinguish between the negligence of a manufacturer and that of a contractor.[173] The emphasis under the modern view is the probability of injury, which gives rise to a duty, rather than the fact of completion and acceptance. Representative of the cases rejecting the doctrine of nonliability is a case in which a minor plaintiff was burned by exposed hot piping leading to the radiator in her room.[174] The court was ready to abandon the old view and did not even consider the patency (or openness) of the defect a defense. The defendants in the case included the heating contractor, the architects, and the builder. The court could see no reason why the principles of negligence should not apply to all builders and contractors involved in mass housing developments. Liability may be imposed on the architects and engineers on the basis of negligent design and on the contractors for defective materials and workmanship. As is true under MacPherson, the lack of privity is not a bar. Thus, a general contractor was liable for injuries caused to a longshoreman due to the collapse of a boom, rigging and mast the defendants had remodeled for the plaintiff's employer.[175]

However, where the owner maintains the work in an unsafe condition, and knows (or should have known by reasonable inspection) of the dangerous condition, the owner is not insulated from liability because the work has been negligently performed by the contractor. The owner is liable as a joint tortfeasor, and the injured person may maintain an action against the owner, against the contractor, or both.[176] A question of intervening and superseding cause arises in this context in the defendant's effort to avoid joint liability. An owner's negligence may supersede the contractor's or repairer's negligence if the owner knew of the defect when the owner accepted the work or if, by reasonable care, the owner should have discovered it and avoided the accident. Acceptance of completed work is not an intervening cause, automatically. Failure of the owner to inspect adequately may not be foreseeable, and the contractor may be found not liable if his negligence as the cause of the accident cannot be established. In one case, summary judgment was denied because just such a proximate cause issue had to be decided by a jury. The repairman failed to connect the left headlight and failed to warn that the light did not work. The issue to be decided was whether the driver's action of failing to inspect the headlight himself, and edging into the adjacent oncoming lane to check for traffic prior to passing, was an intervening cause of the collision with the plaintiff, where it was alleged the accident could have been avoided if the headlight had been lit.[177]

Where the owner is not aware of the unsafe condition and could not have discovered it by inspection, he or she clearly is not subject to liability. For example, the unsafe condition might be concealed in such a way that it could not be discovered by reasonable inspection. The owner is not required to dismantle the work in order to ascertain whether or not the contractor has used safe and satisfactory materials. A sun deck constructed by an independent contractor collapsed and injured a social guest on the owner's premises. The work had been completed and accepted by the owner. In an action against the contractor, he interposed the defense of the accepted work doctrine; the defense was rejected and the contractor was held liable for injuries to third persons proximately caused by his negligence.[178] Therefore, the rule which has been adopted in several states is that liability is imposed on the contractor for injuries to a third person occurring after the completion of the work and its acceptance by the contractee, where the work is reasonably certain to endanger third persons if it has been negligently performed. This is true despite the fact that a subcontractor is responsible for the negligent act. In such a case, the court said that, because the defendant contractor prepared the plans and specifications, it was the defendant's responsibility to construct the house (in which the decedent was asphyxiated due to a faulty gas heater) with adequate subcontractors' work. This duty could not be delegated or shifted.[179] However, in another situation, the tile work contracted to the subcontractor was not inherently dangerous, so there was no recovery against the general contractor for the subcontractor's negligence.[180] The distinguishing feature between the cases is the inherent danger involved in the subcontractor's work. In the first case, the court said one who installs a dangerous instrumentality is charged with knowledge of the dangerous characteristics and with a nondelegable duty to use a degree of care commensurate with the danger that is likely to eventuate into actual harm, and to guard against it.

It should be noted that the doctrine of *res ipsa loquitur* (discussed in connection with products liability exposures) is applicable to a negligence cause of action against a contractor. The same rules apply as to any negligence theory. For example, a court instructed the jury on *res ipsa loquitur* because the defendant had removed, repaired, and replaced a wheel which came off fifteen days later, rolled down the highway, and collided with a tractor-trailer, causing injury.[181]

Strict Liability In completed operations cases, a few courts have applied the strict liability in tort rule in much the same way as in holding the product manufacturer liable to the ultimate consumer or user. In one such decision, the defendant was held liable to a minor tenant of the owner who was injured by a defectively designed hot water system, which was installed without a mixing valve. The house was built for the owner and accepted by him. The court refused to adopt the accepted work doctrine and went even further, in applying the strict liability rule to the facts of this case.

The New Jersey Supreme Court could see no difference between the sale of a house and the sale of a chattel (such as a tool or an appliance or a prescription drug) and imposed strict liability on a developer who was also the architect, builder, and vendor. The injury resulted from defective construction and the court was of the opinion that the cost should be borne by the one who created the danger.[182]

In an effort to stem the increased exposure to liability this decision created in conjunction with the same court's decision abandoning the accepted work doctrine discussed above, the New Jersey legislature responded with a statute that provided that no action, whether in contract or tort, could be brought to recover for injury from a deficiency in design, planning, supervision, or construction of an improvement to real property more than ten years after the services were furnished.[183] This statute was later construed by the court as an attempt to limit the increased liability created by these decisions, and the court responded in accord with the apparent will of the legislature.[184]

Another plaintiff, the injured user of a meat grinding machine, attempted to use the strict liability approach against a contractor. The plaintiff alleged that the electrician who did the wiring was negligent in that he located the on-off switch outside the operator's reach. The court denied the plaintiff's claims and granted the electrician's motion for summary judgment, holding that the electrician had no duty to the plaintiff because he was not obliged to inquire what the function of the machine was prior to wiring it, and thus, the plaintiff's injury was unforeseen.[185]

Effect of the Passage of Time As it does in the sale of a chattel, the question sometimes arises as to what effect, if any, the passage of time should have on the liability of the contractor for defective work. It has been argued that the passage of a long period of time should insulate the contractor from liability, especially in cases where the owner was aware of the defective workmanship, made no claims against the contractor, and continued to maintain the premises in their defective condition. The courts have generally held that the effect of the passage of time is a question of fact for the jury to decide and that it does not involve a question of law for the court. In other words, the jury would have to decide whether the negligence of the contractor—however remote in time—was the cause of the accident. Lapse of time is considered as a factor in determining whether work was done negligently. Safe use without incident over a period of time may preclude an inference of negligence, but it does not foreclose a finding of liability as a matter of law. For example, a taxi was operated for two weeks and 1,200 miles before the brakes malfunctioned. There the jury was allowed to find that the defendant negligently repaired the brakes and the passage of time did not control.[186] In another case, the mere fact that the employer, for six months, used the equipment which the defendant had installed and which caused the plaintiff's injury, did not relieve the contractor of liability.[187] The court held that the passage of time between the construction and the injury was only a factor for jury consideration. Finally, the time span of two and one-half years did not relieve the contractor of liability for a porch roof he had attached with nails that did not penetrate the studding because they were too short. There the court held that the action was immediately and inherently dangerous and the lapse of time did not alter that.[188] Thus, there is no standard of measurement as to when the contractor can be certain that he will not be required to defend an action based on his negligence.

It should be noted that the statute of limitations against these kinds of negligence actions generally begins to run from the date of the accident and not from the date that the negligent act was committed. For example, it was held that a cause of action for the negligent repair of an automobile accrued when the brakes failed and caused injury to a third person, not on the date the repairs were made.[189] In another case, the injury due to the falling of the marble facing of a fireplace installed by the defendant started the one year statute of limitations for personal injury.[190]

Another question, not yet considered in our discussion, is the liability of a contractor or worker who constructs something from defective plans or materials not furnished by him but by another. Whether the accepted work doctrine is followed or not, the usual rule is not to impose liability for following plans that are not obviously defective. For example, a defendant constructed grandstand seats through which a four-year-old child fell. The work was done according to plans and specifications supplied by the owner. The court found the contractor was not liable to the child because he met the owner's plans. The court added that, had he failed to follow the plans, then a question of negligence would arise.[191] The same rule was applied to the use of materials supplied by the contractor's employer,[192] as well as where another contractor carefully carried out the plans he was given.[193] In the latter decision, the court relieved the contractor of liability where the plans were not so obviously defective and dangerous that no reasonable man would follow them. Finally, the plaintiffs brought a negligence action against the state highway department and the contractor who completed a highway, alleging that the construction was negligent in that it permitted an oil slick to develop, which caused their automobile to go out of control. It was agreed that the contractor had constructed the highway in accordance with the plans and specifications published by the highway department and that, prior to the accident, the state highway engineer had accepted the work as completed. In granting summary judgment for the contractor, the court held that the contractor had followed the plans and specifications and that under those circumstances he could not be held liable for any defects which could develop. He would be liable for faulty workmanship or a failure to complete the work in accordance with the plans and specifications, but not otherwise.[194]

The courts have generally held the contractor to be liable in cases of negligent construction and—where the owner was aware of the defective condition—have held him liable as a joint tortfeasor. (See discussion above.) But the *Restatement (Second) Torts*, Section 452(2) suggests that the rule be amended to provide for an escape route for the contractor where the owner is aware of the defect and does nothing to prevent harm to another. The rule provides that the original actor who created an unreasonable risk of harm by his or her negligence is relieved of liability if a third person (presumably the owner in the case of contractors or repairpersons) can prevent any harm flowing from that act by his own affirmative action. This shifting of the duty implies that the action, if taken, would prevent the harm. The *Restatement Comments* suggest how the duty may shift. This may be because of a contract between the actor and the third party, a gratuitous promise, or it may be implied from the agreement between the parties. Factors in favor of the duty shifting in the case of contractors include the character and position of the third party, his or her knowledge of the danger, and the lapse of time. Factors that may prevent the duty from shifting include the degree of danger and the magnitude of the risk of harm. The *Restatement*, therefore, suggests that where the owner continues to maintain the premises in an unsafe condition which causes injury to another, and has knowledge of the unsafe condition, his or her negligence then becomes the cause of the accident, absolving from liability the contractor whose original negligence created the condition. This rule would not, however, apply where the danger is extreme, as in the case of dangerous instrumentalities.

The *Restatement* rule was applied in a case in which the plaintiff was injured as a result of electric current coming over a wire installed by one defendant and maintained by a village. The court examined the defendant's negligence in construction, but concluded that the village followed this initial negligence with serious and wrongful inaction in failing to maintain and inspect the electrical wires, as it had agreed to do in the original contract. This constituted a superseding cause of the plaintiff's injury, relieving the contractor of liability.[195]

Examples of Losses
Which May Result from Completed Operations

Bodily Injury and/or Property Damage to the User Caused by Completed Work If the completed work collapses and injures a person, whether a third party or the owner, the contractor is subject to liability for damages for the injuries sustained. In addition, the contractor is liable for the damage to other property on the premises which may be damaged by the collapse. The contractor will also be liable to the owner for breach of contract and subject to an award of damages for his or her failure to do the work in a workmanlike manner. This is true despite the fact that the underlying cause of the loss was created while operations were still in progress.

The supermarket falling ductwork case, the chimney case, the loose stairway case, and the hot radiator piping case (discussed earlier) are all examples of bodily injuries caused by completed operations.

Loss of Use of Property Caused by the Failure of the Completed Work to Serve Its Purpose or Function Defective work may make the property on which it is done unusable. In such a case, the contractor is not only liable for the defective workmanship but also for the loss of use of the property during the time that the property could not be used.

The damages caused by loss of use may be enormous, especially where the defective work causes a business use to be suspended. For example, a contract was granted to erect a tramway system. Later the subcontract for fabrication of the towers and saddles for the system was granted. As a result of defective saddles, the entire tramway system was rendered inoperative.[196]

Damages for loss of use may also be sustained as a result of defective plumbing, explosion of gas, or defective wiring in the building.[197] The faulty or defective installation or repair of manufacturing machinery might deprive the owner of the use of the machinery during the period while the defective workmanship is being corrected. Thus, the damages would amount to the loss of profits which would have been realized if the machinery had been operating.[198]

Damage to Completed Work (Arising Out of the Work or Out of the Materials or Equipment Furnished) Defective work may cause damage to other work completed by the same contractor or by a different contractor. In one case, for example, a contractor was constructing a library building and doing all the work except for the heating and air conditioning system, which was subcontracted. Before the building was completed, but after partial occupancy, the air conditioning system malfunctioned and caused water to condense and damage the walls and ceiling, which were the work of the insured. In this case, the library walls and ceiling were the work product of the contractor, and the damage was caused by the work of the subcontractor.[199]

Expenses to Withdraw, Inspect, Repair, or Replace Any Work Which Has Been Completed Where the owner claims that the work or equipment is defective, the contractor will normally make an inspection to determine the validity of the claim. Even if the claim is untenable, the contractor ordinarily will have to absorb the cost of the inspection as a business expense. Where the work is defective and must be repaired, or equipment must be replaced, this also is a business expense.

In the tramway case discussed above, the cost of removing the defective tramway became an issue in a dispute between the contractor and the insurer.[200]

Loading and Unloading of Vehicles Where the subject matter of the contract contemplates the pickup and delivery of articles, merchandise or materials, the contractor may be held liable for any loss or damage to the load which is transported, from the time the pickup is made until the load reaches its ultimate destination. The decision that stated this rule noted that the trend of modern authority accepts this view.[201] No distinction is made between loading and preparatory action at the beginning of the operation, or between unloading and delivery at the end. Thus, the liability of the contractor continues throughout the entire operation until it is completed. Likewise, the contractor is liable to third persons, to the consignor and/or consignee for any bodily injury or property damage which is caused through the contractor's negligence. Bodily injury claims sometimes arise when members of the public are injured during the loading or unloading operation. Injuries often occur when the pickup or delivery is made by crossing the public sidewalk. For example, a contractor was liable to a pedestrian who was injured when he fell into an open manhole on the sidewalk, which had been opened in preparation for delivery of beer kegs to a storeowner.[202]

In another typical loading and unloading situation, the activity of a chemical manufacturer in loading anhydrous ammonia solution into a defective tank car for shipment to the purchaser was considered a delivery onto the railroad car and thus was an operation which was complete when the tank car was delivered. The manufacturer loaded the chemical and subleased the tank car to the purchaser. On arrival, the car was used for storage for the chemical and was unloaded as needed. An employee of the purchaser, injured when disconnecting the apparatus used to unload the chemical, sought to hold the chemical manufacturer liable for his injury due to the negligent loading of the chemical into the defective tank car.[203]

Differences and Similarities Between Products and Completed Operations Exposures

In products liability cases, we are dealing with an article of personal property, which reaches the user or consumer through the chain of distribution from the original manufacturer.[204] Completed operations refers to erection, repair, or alteration, usually of real property. There usually are two parties to the contract and there are no intermediates (e.g., assemblers or distributors) who have any responsibility for the result. The products hazard involves losses resulting from goods or products that are manufactured, sold, handled, or distributed by an entity. The completed operations hazard, however, includes situations in which an entity is engaged in rendering services rather than in the business of handling goods or products. The service may be performed incorrectly, or it may fail to serve its purposes as warranted by the one who completes the operation.

The completed operations hazard has at least two criteria that must be met for a loss to have occurred. *First*, bodily injury or property damage must arise from improper performance of a completed task; from the contractor's use of defective materials, parts, or equipment; or from an operation which—while not performed erroneously or with inappropriate materials—is not as warranted by the contractor. The *second* necessary element of a completed operations hazard is that the performance giving rise to the injury be completed or abandoned by the contractor at premises other than those owned by or rented to the contractor.

The Meaning of "Completed Operations"

Controversy over the meaning of a "completed" operation arises in numerous instances. What constitutes "completion" is that the work undertaken has been substantially finished even though minor details of performance may remain. However, there is no completion while something remains yet to be done by the contractor in the performance of a contract. For example, an insurer (relying on a completed operations exclusion) denied liability because it claimed the operation of installing revolving doors was complete. The court agreed with the opposite view of the insured contractor. The decision of incompleteness was based on the evidence adduced at trial and the contract itself. The contract provided there was no completion until the adjustments and testing were complete, that there was no acceptance of the work until the adjustments were made, and that acceptance would constitute completion. The court construed the contract to say that the work was incomplete as long as the workers omitted or altogether failed to perform some substantial requirement essential to its functioning, the performance of which the owner still had a contractual right to demand.[205]

In the event the contract provides for inspection of minor phases of performance or periodic servicing of goods, it is generally held that there is a completion of operations. For example, a contractor agreed to make monthly inspections under the contract. The court construed each inspection as a separate and complete transaction, thus precluding the allegation that the work was incomplete.[206]

In an action by an injured motorist against a state highway department, the reappearance of painted lines on a state highway, put there originally to reroute traffic during construction, rendered the accident (caused by the confusion of the lines) an occurrence on the premises of the insured because of the state ownership of the highway.[207]

To summarize briefly, the product manufacturer, distributor, and retailer are regarded as sellers of a product, and each may have a liability to an injured user or consumer. However, as has been noted, the contractor and owner are the sole parties to the contract in a completed operations context.

The completed operation represents the "work product" of the contractor, whereas the chattel or product in the products liability sense is that which is produced by the manufacturer and sold by intermediaries in the chain of distribution.[208] In the case of a defective product, the user or consumer is entitled to the repair or replacement of the product or a refund of the purchase price.[209] Similarly, in the case of completed operations, the owner is entitled to the replacement or repair of a defective work product. In both cases, where injuries or property damage are caused by a defect in the product or work product, the seller of the product or performer of the operation is ultimately liable in damages, as seen in many examples throughout this chapter.

Chapter Notes

1. CCH Prod. Liab. Rptr. 4501 (Eng. 1842).
2. Ibid.
3. 111 NE 1050 (NY 1916).
4. Cochran v. McDonald, 161 P. 2d 305 (WA 1945).
5. Carpenter v. Alberto Culver Co., 184 NW 2d 547 (Mich. App. 1970).
6. Senter v. B. F. Goodrich Co., 127 F. Supp. 705 (D. Colo. 1954).
7. Sec. 402B.
8. Pfeiffer v. Empire Merch. Co., 305 NYS 2d 245 (App. Div. 1969).
9. Handrigan v. Apex Warwick, Inc., 275 A. 2d 262 (RI 1971).
10. Austin v. Western Auto Supply Co., 421 SW 2d 203 (MO 1967).
11. Wait v. Borne, 25 NE 1053 (NY 1890).
12. Nobility Homes v. Shivers, 539 SW 2d 190 (TX 1976).
13. Atlanta Tallow Co., Inc. v. John W. Eshelman & Sons, Inc., 140 SE 2d 118 (GA 1964).
14. Schutler Candy Co. v. Stein Bros. Paper Box Co., 338 F. 2d 558 (7 Cir. 1964).
15. West v. Alberto Culver Co., 486 F. 2d 459 (10 Cir. 1973).
16. Hauter v. Zogarts, 534 P. 2d 377 (CA 1975).
17. Toole v. Richardson-Merrell, Inc., 60 Cal. Rptr. 398 (Cal. App. 1967).
18. CCH Prod. Liab. Rptr. 4501 (Eng. 1842). Note 1 above at 1053.
19. Matthews v. Lawnlite Co., 88 So. 2d 299 (FL 1956).
20. Campo v. Scofield, 95 NE 2d 802 (NY 1950).
21. Moren v. Samuel M. Langston Co., 237 NE 2d 759 (Ill. App. 1968).
22. Independent Nail & Packing Co., Inc. v. Mitchell, 343 F. 2d 819 (1 Cir. 1965).
23. Larsen v. General Motors Corp., 391 F. 2d 495 (8 Cir. 1968).
24. Evans v. General Motors Corp., 359 F. 2d 822 (7 Cir. 1966).
25. Lorenc v. Chemirad Corp., 179 A. 2d 401 (NJ 1962).
26. Trowbridge v. Abrasive Co. of Phila., 190 F. 2d 825 (3 Cir. 1951).
27. Campo v. Scofield, note 20 above at 804.
28. Spruill v. Boyle-Midway, Inc., 308 F. 2d 79 (4 Cir. 1962).
29. Whitehurst v. Revlon, Inc., 307 F. Supp. 918 (D VA 1969).
30. Jackson v. Baldwin-Lima-Hamilton Corps., 252 F. Supp. 529 (ED PA 1966).
31. William L. Prosser, *Handbook of the Law of Torts*, 4th ed. (St. Paul: West Publishing Co., 1971), pp. 211-228.
32. 377 P. 2d 897 (Cal. 1963).
33. Tucson Industries, Inc. v. Schwartz, 487 P. 2d 12 (Ariz. App. 1971).
34. Elmore v. American Motors Corp., 451 P. 2d 84 (CA 1969).
35. Rheingold, "The Expanding Liability of the Product Supplier. A Primer," 2 *Hofstra. L. Rev.* 521, 525-6, citing Ford Motor Co. v. Lonon, 398 SW 2d 240 (TN 1966).
36. Ibid., p. 523.
37. Dunham v. Vaughn & Bushnell Mfg. Co., 247 NE 2d 401 (IL 1969).
38. Cronin v. J. B. E. Olson Corp., 501 P. 2d 1153 (CA 1972).

39. See, e.g., among many cases, Roberts v. Burlington Northern R.R., 556 P. 2d 1243 (MT 1976); Ward v. Thompson Heights Swim Club, 219 SE 2d 73 (NC App. 1975).
40. Prosser, p. 228.
41. Sherman v. M. Lowenstein & Sons, Inc., 282 NYS 2d 142 (App. Div. 1967); Campbell & Vargo, "The Flammable Fabrics Act and Strict Liability in Tort," 9 *Ind. L. Rev.* 395 (1976).
42. Stevens v. Parke, Davis & Co., 507 P. 2d 653 (CA 1973).
43. Wolford v. General Cable Co., 58 FRD 583 (ED PA 1973); Burch v. Amsterdam Corp., 366 A. 2d 1079 (DC. Cir. 1976).
44. Ibid.
45. Rumsey v. Freeway Manor, 423 SW 387, 391-92 (Tex. Civ. App. 1968).
46. 15 USC 2051 et seq.
47. 21 USC 331 et seq.
48. 15 USC 1261 et seq.
49. 7 USC 135 et seq.
50. Gonzales v. Virginia-Carolina Chem. Co., 239 F. Supp. 567 (ED SC 1965); Rumsey v. Freeway Manor, note 62 above; Hubbard-Hall Chem. Co. v. Silverman, 340 F. 2d 402 (1 Cir. 1965).
51. Rumsey v. Freeman Manor, note 45 above.
52. Hubbard-Hall Chem. Co. v. Silverman, note 50 above.
53. 15 USCA 1191 et seq.
54. Arthur v. Flota Merchante Gran Centro Americana, S.A., 487 F. 2d 561 (5 Cir. 1973).
55. Jasper v. Skyhook Corp., 547 P. 2d 1140 (NM 1976).
56. 15 USC 1191 et seq.
57. Sherman v. M. Lowenstein & Sons, Inc., note 58 above; La Gorga v. Kroger Co., 275 F. Supp. 373 (WD PA 1967).
58. 15 USC 1381 et seq.
59. Larsen v. General Motors Corp., note 20 above.
60. Fish v. Ford Motor Co., 346 SW 2d 469 (AR 1961).
61. Martin v. Studebaker Corp., 133 A 385 (NJ 1926).
62. Ford Motor Co. v. Mathes, 322 F. 2d 267 (5 Cir. 1963).
63. Di Meo v. Minster Machine Co., Inc., 388 F. 2d 18 (2 Cir. 1968).
64. Vandermark v. Ford Motor Co., 391 P. 2d 168 (CA 1964).
65. Favors v. Firestone Tire & Rubber Co., CCH Prod. Liab. Rptr. 7397 (FL 1975).
66. CCH Prod. Liab. Rptr. 1500 et seq.
67. Continental Cas. Co. v. Westinghouse Elec. Corp., CCH Prod. Liab. Rptr. 6628 (D MI 1970).
68. E. I. du Pont de Nemours & Co. v. McCain, 414 F. 2d 369 (5 Cir. 1969).
69. Willey v. Fyrogas Co., 251 SW 2d 635 (MO 1952).
70. Sam Shainberg Co. v. Barlow, 258 So 2d 242 (MS 1972).
71. Canifax v. Hercules Powder Co., 46 Cal. Rptr. 552 (Cal. App. 1965).
72. Barth v. B. F. Goodrich Tire Co., 71 Cal. Rptr. 306 (Cal. App. 1968).
73. Little v. Maxam, Inc., 301 F. Supp. 875 (D IL 1970).
74. Price v. Gatlin, 405 P. 2d 502 (OR 1965).
75. Burkhardt v. Armour & Co., 161 A 385 (CT 1932).

76. Schwartz v. MacRose Lumber & Trim Co., Inc., 270 NYS 2d 875 (NY Sup. 1966).

77. Smith v. Regina Mfg. Corp., 396 F. 2d 826 (4 Cir. 1968).

78. Moody v. Sears, Roebuck & Co., 324 F. Supp. 844 (SD GA 1971).

79. Carney v. Sears, Roebuck & Co., 309 F. 2d 300 (4 Cir. 1962).

80. Cadillac Corp. v. Moore, CCH Prod. Liab. Rptr. 7506 (MS 1975).

81. Utley v. Standard Mag. & Chem. Co., 478 P. 2d 953 (OK 1970).

82. CCH Prod. Liab. Rptr. 2180.

83. Ford v. Flaherty, CCH Prod. Liab. Rptr. 6928 (MA 1972).

84. Walker v. Decora, Inc., 471 SW 2d 778 (TN 1971).

85. Bowman Biscuit Co. v. Hines, 251 SW 2d 153 (TX 1952).

86. Bassons v. Hertz Corp., 176 NW 2d 882 (MN 1970).

87. Roberts v. Reynolds Mem. Park, 187 SE 2d 721 (NC 1972).

88. Annot, Products Liability: Application of strict liability in tort doctrine to lessor of personal property, 52 ALR 3d 121 (1973).

89. McClaflin v. Bayshore Equip. Rental Co., 79 Cal. Rptr. 337 (Cal. App. 1969).

90. Cintrone v. Hertz Truck Leasing & Rental Service, 212 A. 2d 767 (NJ 1965); Price v. Shell Oil Co., 466 P. 2d 722 (CA 1970).

91. Price v. Shell Oil Co.

92. Note, "Tort Liability of Independent Testing Agencies," 22 *Rutgers L. Rev.* 299 (1968).

93. Hempstead v. General Fire Ext. Corp., 269 F. Supp. 109 (D DE 1967).

94. Hanberry v. Hearst Corp., 81 Cal. Rptr. 519 (Cal. App. 1969).

95. Benco Plastics Inc. v. Westinghouse Elec. Corp., 387 F. Supp. 772 (ED TN 1974).

96. Cunningham v. MacNeal Mem. Hosp., 266 NE 2d 897 (IL 1970).

97. Phipps, "When Does a 'Service' Become a 'Sale?' " in Defense Research Institute monograph *Products Liability: Practical Defense Problems,* 23, 31 (1972).

98. Ibid. at 26. Citing Delaney v. Towmotor Corp., 339 F. 2d 4 (2 Cir. 1964); Dunham v. Vaughn & Bushnell Mfg. Co., 247 NE 2d 401 (IL 1969).

99. Hill, "How Strict Is Strict?" 32 *Texas Bar J* 759 (Nov. 1969).

100. Magrine v. Krasnica, 250 A. 2d 129 (NJ 1969).

101. Carmichael v. Reitz, 95 Cal. Rptr. 381 (Cal. App. 1971).

102. Phipps, note 121 supra at 30.

103. The Advisory Committee Notes to the Federal Rules of Civil Procedures are, in effect, comments on the meanings of these Rules which govern practice and procedure in the federal courts.

104. Hobbs v. Northeast Airlines, Inc., 50 FRD 76 (ED PA 1970).

105. American Trading & Prod. Corp. v. Fischbach & Moore, Inc., 47 FRD 155 (ND IL 1969).

106. Gaynor v. Rock, 204 NE 2d 627, 631 (NY 1965).

107. Borel v. Fibreboard Paper Prod., 493 F. 2d 1076 (5 Cir. 1974).

108. Hall v. E. I. du Pont de Nemours & Co., 345 F. Supp. 353 (ED NY 1972).

109. Prosser, p. 402.

110. Sperling v. Hatch, 88 Cal. Rptr. 704 (Cal. App. 1970).

111. Kirby v. General Motors Corp., 229 NE 2d 777 (IL App. 1973).

112. Orfield v. International Harvester Co., 535 F. 2d 959 (6 Cir. 1976).

113. Hoelter v. Mohawk Service, Inc., CCH Prod. Liab. Rptr. 7674 (CT 1976).
114. Speyer, Inc. v. Humble Oil Co. & A. O. Smith, 275 F. Supp. 861 (WD PA 1967), aff'd 403 F. 2d 766.
115. The leading case is Evans v. General Motors Corp., 359 F. 2d 822 (7 Cir. 1966), cert den 385 US 836 (1966).
116. The leading case is Larsen v. General Motors Corp., 391 F. 2d 495 (8 Cir. 1968).
117. Moran v. Faberge, Inc., 332 A. 2d 11 (MD 1975).
118. Campo v. Scofield, 95 NE 2d 802, 804 (NY 1950).
119. Collins v. Ridge Tool Co., 520 F. 2d 591 (7 Cir. 1975).
120. Borowicz v. Chicago Mastic Co., 367 F. 2d 751 (7 Cir. 1966).
121. Louis R. Frumer and Melvin I. Friedman, *Products Liability*, vol. 3 (New York: Matthew Bender Co., 1973), sec. 805[1]. p. 186.4.
122. Pinto v. Clairol, Inc., 324 F. 2d 608 (6 Cir. 1963).
123. Carmichael v. Reitz, 95 Cal. Rptr. 381 (Cal. App. 1971).
124. Santiago v. Package Machinery Co., 260 NE 2d 89 (Ill. App. 1970).
125. Ulrich v. Kasco Abrasives Co., 532 SW 2d 197 (KY 1976).
126. Day v. Barber-Colman Co., 135 NE 2d 231 (Ill. App. 1956).
127. Ibid. See also Ward v. Hobart Mfg. Co., 450 F. 2d 1176 (5 Cir. 1971).
128. Welch v. Outboard Marine Corp., 481 F. 2d 252 (5 Cir. 1973).
129. Bruce v. Martin-Marietta Corp., 544 F. 2d 442 (10 Cir. 1976).
130. George v. Morgan Constr., 389 F. Supp. 253 (ED PA 1975).
131. See, e.g., Henningsen v. Bloomfield Motors, Inc., 161 A. 2d 69 (NJ 1960).
132. See, e.g., Victorson v. Block Laundry Machine Co., 37 NY 2d 398 (NY 1975).
133. See, e.g., Prokolkin v. General Motors Corp., CCH Prod. Liab. Rptr. 7629 (CT 1976).
134. General Motors Corp. v. Simmons, 545 SW 2d 502 (TX 1976).
135. De Santis v. Parker Feeders, Inc., 547 F. 2d 357 (NY 1976).
136. De Mento v. Nehi Beverages, Inc., 398 NYS 2d 909 (NY 1976).
137. McDowell v. Southwestern Bell Telephone Co., 546 SW 2d 160 (MO 1976).
138. American Security Ins. Co. v. Griffith's Air Cond., 317 So 2d 256 (LA 1975).
139. Santor v. Karagheusian, Inc., 207 A. 2d 305 (NJ 1965).
140. Suncheck v. I. M. Young & Co., 363 NYS 2d 619 (App. Div. 1975).
141. McDonough v. Whalen, 313 NE 2d 435 (MA 1973).
142. Berg v. General Motors Corp., 555 P. 2d 818 (WA 1976).
143. Anthony v. Kelsey-Hayes Co., 102 Cal. Rptr. 113 (Cal. App. 1972).
144. Seely v. White Motors, 403 P. 2d 145 (CA 1965).
145. Air Products & Chemical, Inc. v. Fairbanks, Morse, Inc., 206 NW 2d 414 (WI 1973).
146. Trailmobile v. Higgs, 297 NE 2d 598 (IL 1973).
147. Casadaban v. Bel Chem. & Supply Co., Inc., 322 S. 2d 854 (LA 1975).
148. States S. S. Co. v. Stone Manganese Marine, Ltd., 371 F. Supp. 500 (D NJ 1973).
149. Berg v. General Motors Corp., note 142 above.
150. Seely v. White Motors, note 144 above.
151. Raney v. Honeywell, Inc., CCH Prod. Liab. Rptr. 7802 (ND IA 1976).
152. Huddell v. Levin, 395 F. Supp. 64, reversed 537 F. 2d 726 (D NJ 1975).
153. Casadaban v. Bel Chem. & Supply Co., note 147 above.

154. Seely v. White Motors, note 144 above.
155. Hales v. Green Colonial, Inc., 490 F. 2d 1015 (8 Cir. 1974).
156. Drilling & Service, Inc. v. Cato Enterprises, 191 NE 2d 114 (IN 1963).
157. Robert Buell, "Product Withdrawal Expense Insurance," in Defense Research Institute monograph, *Products Liability: Practical Defense Problems II* p. 41 (1976).
158. Prosser, pp. 680-681.
159. George J. Couch, *Couch on Insurance*, 2nd ed. (Rochester: The Lawyers Cooperative Publishing Co., 1971), 44:434.
160. DelGaudio v. Ingerson, 115 A. 2d 665 (CT 1955).
161. Russell v. Arthur Whitcomb, Inc., 121 A. 2d 781 (NH 1956).
162. Hannefin v. Cahill-Mooney Co., 498 P. 2d 1214 (MT 1972).
163. Scheyxneydre v. Travelers Ins. Co., 172 So 2d 719 (LA 1965).
164. Bauer v. Harris Intertype Corp., 316 NYS 2d 593 (NY 1970).
165. Axland v. Pacific Heating Co., 293 P. 2d 466 (WA 1930).
166. Smith v. Fitton & Pittman, Inc., 212 SE 2d 925 (SC 1975).
167. Reynolds v. Manley, 265 So 2d 714 (AR 1954).
168. Andrews v. DelGuzzi, 353 P. 2d 422 (WA 1960).
169. Littleton v. B & R Constr. Co., 266 So 2d 560 (La. App. 1972).
170. Roush v. Johnson, 80 SE 2d 857 (WV 1954).
171. Brown v. Welsbach Corp., 93 NE 2d 640 (NY 1950).
172. MacPherson v. Buick Motor Co., 111 NE 1050 (NY 1916).
173. Hunter v. Quality Homes, 68 A 2d 620 (DE 1949).
174. Totten v. Gruzen, 245 A. 2d 1 (NJ 1968).
175. Standholm v. General Constr. Co., 382 P. 2d 843 (OR 1963).
176. Annot. Negligence of builder or construction contractor as grounds of liability upon his part for injury or damages to third persons occurring after completion and acceptance of the work, 58 ALR 2d 865 (1958).
177. Clausen v. Ed Fanning Chevrolet, Inc., 291 NE 2d 202 (Ill. App. 1972).
178. Hilla v. Gross, 204 NW 2d 712 (MI 1972).
179. Dow v. Holly Mfg. Co., 321 P. 2d 736 (CA 1958).
180. Johnson v. Central Tile & Terrazzo Co., 207 NE 2d 160 (Ill. App. 1965).
181. Martino v. Barra, 293 NE 2d 745 (Ill. App. 1973).
182. Schipper v. Levitt & Sons, Inc., 207 A. 2d 314 (NJ 1965).
183. NJSA 2A:14-1.1 (1967).
184. O'Connor v. Altus, 334 A. 2d 545 (NJ 1975).
185. Olich v. John E. Smith Sons Co., Inc., 367 A. 2d 1216 (NJ 1976).
186. Royal Motors v. Murray, 275 F. 2d 3 (DC Cir. 1960).
187. Standholm v. General Constr. Co., supra note 175.
188. Leigh v. Wadsworth, 361 P. 2d 849 (OK 1961).
189. Konar v. Monroe Muffler Shops, Inc., 280 NYS 2d 812 (NY 1967).
190. Leyen v. Dunn, 461 SW 2d 41 (TN 1970).
191. Barnthouse v. California Steel Building Co., 29 Cal. Rptr. 835 (Cal. App. 1963).
192. Johnson v. City of Leandro, 4 Cal. Rptr. 404 (Cal. App. 1960).
193. Massei v. Lettunich, 56 Cal. Rptr. 232 (Cal. App. 1967).
194. Black v. Peter Kiewit Sons Co., 497 P. 2d 1056 (ID 1972).

195. Goar v. Village of Stephen, 196 NW 171 (MN 1923).

196. Pittsburgh Bridge & Iron Works v. Liberty Mut. Ins. Co., 444 F. 2d 1286, 1288 (3 Cir. 1971).

197. Dickert v. Allstate Ins. Co., 175 SE 2d 98 (GA 1970) (plumbing); Nielson v. Travelers Indem. Co., 174 F. Supp. 648 (D IA 1959) (gas); General Cas. Co. v. Larson, 196 F. 2d 170 (8 Cir. 1952) (wiring).

198. Berger Bros. Electric Motors, Inc. v. New Amsterdam Cas. Co., 58 NE 2d 717 (NY 1945).

199. B. A. Green Construction Co. v. Liberty Mutual Insurance Co., 517 Pac (2nd) 563 (1973).

200. Pittsburgh Bridge & Iron Works v. Liberty, Mut. Ins. Co., supra note 197.

201. Home Indem. Co. v. Allstate Ins. Co., 393 F. 2d 593 (9 Cir. 1968).

202. Butte Brewing Co. v. District Ct., 100 P. 2d 932 (MT 1940).

203. Ketona Chem. Corp. v. Globe Indem. Co., 404 F. 2d 181 (5 Cir. 1969).

204. Prosser, p. 641.

205. Arnold v. Edelman, 392 SW 2d 231 (MO 1965).

206. Hartford v. Coolidge-Lochner Co., 314 SW 2d 445 (TX 1958).

207. Baca v. New Mexico State Highway Dept., 486 P. 2d 625 (NM 1971).

208. Prosser, p. 663; Rowland H. Long, *Law of Liability Insurance* (New York: Matthew Bender Co., 1976), sec. 7.09.

209. Prosser, pp. 665-667.

CHAPTER 4

Treatment of Products and Completed Operations Liability Exposures

PRODUCTS LIABILITY INSURANCE

Forms Available

Various standard and nonstandard forms are used in providing products liability insurance. Among the more common standard forms (i.e., those formulated by the Insurance Services Office for use by its member and subscriber companies) are the comprehensive general liability, storekeepers liability, garage liability, druggists liability, hospital liability, special multi-peril package, and businessowners package policies. Among the nonstandard forms are manuscript policies geared for large entities, independently filed policies of insurers, various policies offered by excess and surplus lines insurers, and commercial liability excess and commercial umbrella liability policies.

Standard Forms The comprehensive general liability (CGL) policy automatically includes products liability insurance on exposures that exist at policy inception as well as exposures that develop during the policy term. The premium initially is based upon known exposures at policy inception, and the final premium is determined by audit at policy expiration. When products liability insurance is not desired or is unavailable, the CGL policy must be amended by endorsement with a products liability exclusion; otherwise, coverage would apply whether a premium is charged or not.

The storekeepers liability policy basically is a package of liability coverages designed for retail outlets meeting certain eligibility requirements. Since products liability insurance automatically is included in that package of liability coverages and the total package premium does not identify the separate costs of each coverage, none of the coverages, including products liability, can be excluded. The garage liability policy, designed for automobile and equipment dealers, repair shops, and parking lot operators, also provides products liability insurance as a built-in feature without requiring an additional premium. The products liability coverage in the garage liability policy applies not only to automobiles, tires, and batteries, but also to any other products incidental to the aforementioned businesses.

The druggists liability policy, on the other hand, is a combination of products and professional liability insurance written for one premium. The products liability insurance provides the insured with protection against claims arising from not only drugs and medicines, but also any type of goods or sundries usually handled by drug stores. The hospital liability policy also includes products liability insurance as an automatic coverage. However, the coverage is limited to products liability claims stemming from food, beverages, drugs, supplies, and appliances which are furnished to patients. A hospital that operates a cafeteria or a restaurant for its visitors and/or staff must obtain separate products liability insurance against that particular exposure.

Under the SMP program, any of the standard general liability coverage parts and endorsements may be used. Form MP-200, which may also be used, includes coverage for products and completed operations, although these coverages may be excluded by endorsement.

Products liability insurance of the businessowners package policy is also comprehensive in scope, to the same extent as the conventional CGL policy. The businessowners policy, however, includes products insurance as part of one package with an indivisible premium. Thus, the products coverage cannot be excluded.

With the exception of the CGL and SMP policies, all other standard liability forms that include products liability insurance do so automatically and without additional premium, regardless of the exposure. A certain amount of coverage stemming from products also is provided under the premises and operations coverages of the various standard forms. An example is the customer who is injured by a product while on the store premises. And, as described in more detail later, certain OL&T and M&C manual classifications, such as funeral directors, engravers, data processing centers, and theaters other than the drive-in type, automatically include products liability insurance as part of the premises and operations coverages.

Nonstandard Forms The products liability coverages of non-standard forms vary greatly. Manuscript policies, for example, often contain products liability insurance provisions completely foreign to those normally provided under standard policy versions. Some manuscript policies, however, do contain combinations of ISO provisions which apply today, as well as older provisions that applied under former standard policy editions. Most independently filed policies follow standard products liability provisions to a degree but otherwise deviate from them, particularly with respect to the exclusions.

Products liability insurance offered in the excess and surplus lines markets usually is purchased by entities unable to obtain that coverage through regular domestic markets. Lloyd's of London handles most such insurance, although a number of domestic insurance companies also participate on a pooling basis. While products liability policies offered by excess and surplus lines insurers sometimes follow the ISO standard language, most policy provisions are much more restrictive in scope. Nonstandard forms, for example, sometimes cover only products exposures which are specifically scheduled on the policy, and then only for claims stemming from those products that are manufactured, sold, handled, or distributed by a firm during the policy term. In other words, coverage depends both on when the accident occurs and when the product was manufactured or sold. Product exposures existing before policy inception are not covered. Nonstandard policies also are commonly written on an accident rather than an occurrence basis, and are subject to a variety of exclusions, including the exclusion of claims for punitive damages, for products which are known to violate statutes and ordinances, and for claims stemming from expressed warranties, whether written or not.[1]

When the need for products liability coverage arises on special exposures and a sufficient number of buyers are demanding it, some specialty insurers will tailor special coverages. An example is products failure insurance. This is designed for certain manufacturers whose products might fail to perform as expected.

Commercial excess liability and umbrella liability policies, which basically are nonstandard in nature, also provide products liability insurance.[2] Coverage under these policies usually is handled in one of two ways: (1) as excess over the primary, underlying limits of a policy; or (2) as excess over a high deductible when no underlying insurance applies.

Because the provisions of nonstandard forms lack uniformity, the bulk of this chapter dwells upon the scope of standard coverage provisions.

Scope of Standard Coverage

Since the CGL policy is the primary means for providing products liability coverage, its provisions will be discussed here, along with the significant differences from provisions of other standard liability policies.

The CGL policy, comprising a policy jacket and the CGL coverage part, contains certain provisions that must be understood in determining the scope of coverage. The essential provisions of the policy jacket include the definitions of the terms "products hazard," "named insured's products," "occurrence," and "policy territory." Each of those defined terms often appears in boldface type in both the policy jacket and the coverage part. Thus, whenever a boldface term appears within the provisions of the CGL coverage part, one need only refer to the definition of that term in the policy jacket in order to determine the scope or the intent of the provision. The provisions of the CGL coverage part which are of special importance include the insuring agreement, the exclusions, the persons insured section, and limits of liability provision.

Products Hazard The term "products hazard" is defined in the policy jacket as including bodily injury or property damage arising from (1) the named insured's products, or (2) reliance upon a representation or a warranty that is made at any time with respect to products. It is a further requirement that bodily injury or property damage not only must occur away from owned or rented premises of the named insured, but also after physical possession of those products is relinquished to others.

While the meaning of the term "named insured's products" is of obvious importance in determining the true scope of the term "products hazard," note for the moment the two conditions that generally must be met before a loss is considered to be one of products liability. First, bodily injury or property damage stemming from a product (which either is defective or does not serve the purpose for which it was warranted or represented by the named insured) must occur *away* from the owned or rented premises of the named insured. And, second, the product must be in the physical possession of one other than the named insured at the time of injury. Both of those conditions must be met. One or the other will not do. For example, if a person purchases a product and sustains an injury from its use at any location other than the seller's owned or rented premises, the loss is one of products liability insurance. But if a person is injured while handling a product on the store premises, the loss is the subject of premises and operations liability coverage.

However, only one of the two conditions is applicable when food, beverages, and other kindred products are sold for consumption on business premises. Restaurants, confectionary stores, and caterers, for example, may have as much (or more) exposure to products liability on their premises as they do away from the premises. Since the rate for premises and operations coverage does not contemplate the products liability exposure of businesses which sell products for consumption on their premises, an endorsement, which must be attached to the liability policies of those businesses, redefines the term "products hazard" to include injury or damage occurring on premises of the products seller. The effect of the endorsement is to extend the scope of the products hazard (and, hence, create the need for products liability insurance) to *any* location on or off premises, provided physical possession of the product, at the time of injury, had been relinquished by the seller.

When the purchaser of a CGL or an SMP policy does not desire products liability insurance (which cannot be excluded from such policies as storekeepers liability, druggists liability, garage liability, or the businessowners' package), one of two exclusions must be attached signifying that intent. The choice of those two exclusions depends on the type of business operation.

When a business such as a hardware store does not sell its products for use or for consumption on its premises, the appropriate endorsement excludes bodily injury or property damage loss from the scope of the products hazard, as defined in the policy jacket. The effect of the exclusion is to preclude coverage of products liability losses occurring away from premises of the named insured after possession of its products has been relinquished to others.

If a business such as a restaurant sells some or all of its products for use or consumption on its premises, an entirely different exclusionary endorsement is used. The appropriate endorsement excludes bodily injury or property damage loss arising out of (1) the named insured's products, as defined in the policy jacket, or (2) reliance upon a representation or warranty made by the named insured if loss occurs after physical possession of such products has been relinquished to others. It makes no difference whether loss occurs on premises owned or rented to the named insured or elsewhere; the loss is excluded.

Certain businesses with an insignificant amount of products liability exposure do not need to purchase products liability insurance, since they receive the protection by endorsement without additional charge. Examples of businesses in this category are engravers, funeral directors, theatres (other than drive-ins), electronic data processing centers, tanneries, and publishers. The necessary endorsement states that the term "products hazard" does not encompass bodily injury or property damage arising from any products which are connected with the named insured's premises and operations manual classification. Though bodily injury or property damage claims stemming from products of these businesses are not considered to be within the products hazard per se, such claims are covered under premises and operations coverage. However, it is a requirement that the premises and operations of the business be specifically listed in the endorsement, so that the insurer will not automatically cover other products liability exposures which require a separate charge for products liability insurance. An illustration of how the endorsement operates is a tannery which also operates a retail outlet for its hide and leather goods. Since the tannery classification includes products liability insurance as part of the premises and operations coverage, that operation must be described in the special endorsement. The retail store of the tannery, on the other hand, is not listed in the special endorsement, because separate products liability insurance is required for that latter exposure. If the tannery elects not to purchase products liability insurance on its retail store operations, the tannery will then only have products liability insurance for its tannery operations.

Named Insured's Products The policy jacket definition of "named insured's products" is important because it describes the exposures that are the subject of the products hazard, as well as those exposures that are not within that hazard. The "named insured's products" are goods or products manufactured, sold, handled, or distributed either by the named insured or by others who are trading under the insured's name. The term also includes any containers of products other than vehicles. Excluded from the purview of the term, however, are vending machines or other property (exclusive of containers) that, instead of being sold, merely are rented or situated at various locations for the use of others.

Several additional points are particularly noteworthy about the definition of "named insured's products." It refers to goods or products manufactured, sold, handled, or distributed, and not to the performance of operations, such as the completion of work or service by the named insured. A firm hired solely to perform a service, such as the installation of a heating system that the owner purchased from a wholesaler or a retailer, does not require products liability insurance. Such businesses require completed operations coverage, which deals with losses following the completion of work or service. A firm that both sells and installs heating equipment needs both products liability and completed operations insurance. (Completed operations insurance is discussed later in this chapter.)

Such containers of goods or products as bottles, cardboard cartons to hold bottles, cans, jars, boxes, oil drums, propane tanks or cylinders, and wood crates also are considered to be subjects of products liability insurance. This stands to reason, since containers, as devices used to hold products, also are goods or products themselves, and are capable of producing harm. For example, a court held that steel bands and straps keeping steel coils in place on a skid, which came apart and injured a person, were considered to be a container. Since the claimant did not have products liability insurance, the insurer was not liable for the resulting injury.[3] And, in another case, a court denied recovery for damage to a textile machine when the cables placed around that machine broke. In spite of the argument that the cables were used only for lifting purposes, the court held that the cables constituted a container within the custom of the trade.[4]

Furthermore, containers may still be the subject of products liability insurance even though they remain the property of the manufacturer, distributor, or retailer. Returnable beverage bottles and refillable propane gas cyclinders are examples. As previously mentioned, one of the keys to most products liability exposures is that injury or damage occurs after *physical* possession of goods or products has been relinquished by the named insured. Legal title to goods or products does not have to pass. Nor does ownership of such products necessarily have to be relinquished by the named insured as a prerequisite of any products liability exposure. Returnable fuel oil drums are as much a product liability exposure, for example, as the oil contained in them.

Note also that vehicles are not considered to be containers for purposes of the term "named insured's products." The rationale for specifically exempting vehicles, as containers, is to preclude products liability insurance from covering exposures that are more appropriately handled under other forms of liability coverage. While tank trucks and tank cars operated on rails are common examples of exposures that are intended to be outside the realm of any products liability exposure dealing with containers, the term "vehicle" can constitute a broad range of subjects.

In fact, when the term "vehicle" is considered in its ordinary and popular sense, it is a broader term than either motor vehicle or automobile. Based upon case law over the years, the term "vehicle" has been considered to include a bulldozer, a self-propelled crane, an oil derrick while being moved over land, objects being towed by a motor-driven vehicle, and a tractor used in road construction. A cable attached to a motor vehicle, on the other hand, has sometimes been held to be a vehicle, but other times it has not. Hoists and cargo upon a truck both have been held not to be vehicles because of their nonvehicular nature.[5] Since the term "vehicle" is not defined in the policy jacket or in the coverage part, its meaning—in terms of what may or may not be a container—ultimately is a question of fact for a court to decide.

Vending machines, as goods or products manufactured, sold,

handled, or distributed by an entity, come within the meaning of the term "named insured's products" and, hence, are appropriately within the scope of the term "products hazard." However, when the owner retains the vending machines following their purchase from the manufacturer or the distributor, and either rents them to others or places them at various locations for the convenience of patrons, the machines are outside the meaning of the term "named insured's products." Products liability insurance, therefore, is not necessary. But these vending machines sometimes produce exposures to loss by their very existence. The machines may malfunction, for example, and may cause fire or water damage to the premises in which they are located. Or, vending machines may be responsible for the injury of a person when they are situated in places that hinder the thoroughfare of premises. Such exposures to loss, dealing with the existence hazard of vending machines, are the subject of premises and operations insurance.

Nevertheless, the contents dispensed by vending machines are considered to be a products liability exposure, whether injury or damage arises on or away from premises owned or rented to the named insured. So, when products liability insurance is obtained for the contents of any vending machines, the products hazard must be redefined, like it is for restaurants and similar businesses. The definition must be extended to include damage arising from a product on premises of the named insured, as well as away from premises. When products liability insurance is not obtained for the contents of such vending machines, the same procedure must be followed as would apply to a restaurant that does not obtain products liability insurance. Thus, an exclusion must be attached to the policy so that no coverage applies for injury or damage arising from the named insured's products (vended from those machines) either on premises owned or rented to the named insured, or elsewhere.

Finally, the term "named insured's products" does not encompass liability exposures of businesses that rent or lease their property, exclusive of containers, to others. Businesses in this category are covered against injury or damage arising from such rented or leased property under their premises and operations coverage, subject to a separate premium charge in some cases. If rental of property is incidental to a business, e.g., a hardware store that handles wallpaper and paints and also rents a wallpaper removing machine to its customers, no additional charge is required.[6] But when a business's principal function is to rent or lease equipment or appliances, such as lawn mowers, lawn rollers, ladders, post hole diggers, floor polishers and sanders, refrigerators, stoves, and machines—on a short or long term basis—a separate premium charge is necessary either at policy inception or, if the operation arises during the policy period, upon audit at expiration of the policy period.

Insuring Agreements The insuring agreements of the CGL, SMP liability, storekeepers liability, and garage liability coverage parts contain no reference to products liability coverage. They merely recite the insurer's promise to pay damages on behalf of the insured who is legally obligated to pay them to another because of bodily injury or property damage, covered by the policy, caused by an occurrence. The fact that specific reference to products liability is lacking in those insuring agreements means that all such losses involving the named insured's products, as defined, are covered—except those losses specifically not covered under the exclusions section of those coverage parts.

On the other hand, neither the OL&T nor the M&C coverage parts is designed to include products liability insurance, except when those coverages are written with the SMP policy. Yet, the OL&T insuring agreement resembles the insuring agreement of the storekeepers liability, and the M&C insuring agreement is identical to that of the CGL coverage part. To preclude products liability insurance under both the OL&T and M&C coverage parts, each such coverage part contains a specific exclusion of bodily injury and property damage stemming from losses within the products hazard, as defined in the policy jacket.

The druggists liability coverage part defines the scope of products liability insurance within its respective insuring agreements. The druggists liability form agrees to pay damages because of bodily injury or property damage arising from goods or products, including drugs, medicines, and containers which are prepared, sold, handled, or distributed by the named insured at or from its premises after physical possession has been relinquished to others. Products liability insurance, therefore, applies to drugs and medicines dispensed by a pharmacist and to all other merchandise that the store may handle, such as cosmetics, toys, and gardening supplies. When a CGL coverage part is attached to the druggists liability coverage part in order to provide an entity with premises liability insurance, an exclusion of products liability must be attached to the CGL coverage part, since products liability coverage already is being provided under the druggists form.[7]

Time Period of Coverage Products liability insurance under all applicable standard coverage parts applies to *bodily injury or property damage that arises during the policy period*. This time of coverage provision is made clear under the respective definitions of bodily injury and property damage in the policy jacket. It makes little difference when a product is manufactured, prepared, sold, handled, or distributed, so long as coverage is in force at the time of bodily injury or property damage. For example, assume a product is manufactured in 1979 when a firm does not have products liability insurance. The product is sold in 1980 when that firm had products liability insurance with Insurer A, and the product ultimately causes bodily injury to the purchaser in 1981 when that firm's insurance is with Insurer B. Since Insurer B is providing products liability insurance at the time of bodily injury, Insurer B is the one required to respond to this loss—even though the bodily injury is attributable to an allegedly defective product that was manufactured two years earlier. And, if it is not until 1982 before the firm learns of the loss and notifies its insurer, the policy that applied in 1981 governs coverage, because that is the period in which the bodily injury occurred. However, if that firm were to go out of business and cancel all insurance in 1981, prior to the bodily injury loss, it would be without protection of products liability insurance, since coverage was not in force at the time of the bodily injury.

Claims-Made Basis of Coverage. Of increasing use in independently-filed policies, as well as most policies of excess and surplus lines insurers, is liability insurance written on a claims-made basis, instead of an occurrence basis. Products liability insurance written on a claims-made basis applies only to those covered *claims that are made and reported by the insured during the policy period*, regardless of when bodily injury or property damage arises from any of the named insured's products. Thus, unless a claim is made while a policy is in force, no coverage applies.

Compared to the occurrence basis, the claims-made basis is said to have distinct advantages to insurers and insureds, as follows.

ADVANTAGES TO INSURERS. The major advantage accruing to insurers issuing claims-made policies lies in the area of pricing (rate making). At the end of the policy year, an insurer not only is aware of all products liability claims made against an insured during that period, but also is able to estimate how much it will take to settle the unpaid claims. Policies written on an occurrence basis, on the other hand, merely require that bodily injury or property damage stemming from a product must occur during the policy period. There usually is a delay (so-called "long tail") between the period of injury or damage and the time when incurred losses ultimately are reported to the insurer. The longer this delay in reporting incurred losses, the longer it takes an occurrence-basis insurer to determine and compile its final loss payments and match them to the years in which they were incurred. In contrast, the claims-made basis permits the insurer to determine its claim costs at the end of each policy year, thus enabling the insurer to determine, with more accuracy, just how much rates should be adjusted for subsequent policy periods. Under the occurrence basis, the insurer may have to wait many years before it knows what its total losses were for a previous period, because of the lag in the reporting of losses actually incurred in the previous period. In the meantime, the rates charged are necessarily crude, since it has become increasingly difficult to estimate the incurred but not reported (IBNR) losses (in the products liability area, especially).

ADVANTAGES TO INSUREDS. The claims-made basis may not be as advantageous to insureds as to insurers. It is argued that the claims-made basis permits more equitable premiums for insureds by more closely reflecting the insurance costs during the current policy period. However, if the experience for the class worsens each year, rates may increase much more rapidly than would be the case when insurance is written on an occurrence basis, because of the lag time in compiling statistics. The other advantage commonly cited for the claims-made basis is that an insured is better able to assess the adequacy of coverage limits (limits of liability) when the coverage applies to claims made during the current policy period. An insured of a policy written on an occurrence basis also knows how much coverage is available in the event of loss. However, the limit of liability that is chosen by the insured in a previous period may not be sufficient when bodily injury or property damage arises from a product in a subsequent policy period, though it is a moot point if firms are buying the maximum limits available to them.

DISADVANTAGE. The one distinct disadvantage of the claims-made policy is that it makes it difficult for an insured to switch coverage from a claims-made basis to an occurrence basis. By way of illustration, suppose a manufacturer has a claims-made policy covering its products liability insurance for the period December 31, 1979, to December 31, 1980. During the latter part of 1980, the firm is bought out by another firm which has its products liability insurance written on an occurrence basis. If the buying firm wants to consolidate its coverage along with the seller's coverage on an occurrence basis effective January 1, 1981, losses incurred by the seller during 1980 but not reported until 1981 would not be covered. First, the buyer's occurrence policy only applies to bodily injury or property damage losses which occur during the policy period, i.e., during the period January 1, 1981, to January 1, 1982. Hence, any claim made against the seller for injury or damage prior to that period is not covered under the buyer's occurrence policy. Second, the claims-made policy only applies to claims of bodily injury or property damage which are made during the policy period. If claim is made during a subsequent period after the claims-made policy has been replaced, the firm is without protection.

Territorial Scope of Coverage Whether written on an occurrence or a claims-made basis, bodily injury or property damage from a product must occur within the policy territory. To determine what the territory encompasses, one must refer to the definition of the term "policy territory" in the policy jacket.

The territorial scope of products liability insurance includes the entire world, in the case of a formal lawsuit, provided (1) the *original suit* for damages is made within the United States, its territories or possessions, or Canada, and (2) the product was sold for use or for consumption within the United States.

The phrase "original suit" is important in several respects. For example, if one purchases a product within the United States and subsequently is injured by that product while in a foreign country, the entity liable for that product may have protection under its products liability insurance of the CGL policy, *if* the original suit for damages is brought by that person within the United States, its territories or possessions, or Canada. But if an original suit is instituted by that person in a foreign country and a second lawsuit is brought within the United States or Canada as a formality required by law in recognition of the foreign court's judgment, an entity has no protection under its products liability insurance.

A mere products liability *claim*, on the other hand, is considered to be within the scope of coverage, even though such claim is made in a foreign country (as long as the product was sold for use or consumption in the U.S.). The insurer is obligated to investigate and to settle any such claim wherever it arises. But if a claim culminates in a formal lawsuit, such suit must then be made within the policy territory as defined in the policy; otherwise, the products coverage of the CGL policy will not apply.

Since most standard forms of products liability insurance apply only to goods or products sold for use or for consumption within the United States, its territories or possessions, or Canada, such insurance is not suited to firms that manufacture, sell, handle, or distribute goods or products for purposes of export. Standard forms of products liability insurance apply to losses involving exported products only when bodily injury or property damage occurs (1) within the policy territory, as defined, or (2) upon international waters or in airspace in the course of travel or transportation between the United States, its territories or possessions, Canada, or between the continental United States and Hawaii or Alaska. Note that products liability insurance also applies to bodily injury or property damage on offshore towers situated in international waters, regardless of their location. No coverage applies, however, when bodily injury or property damage occurs (from exported products) while in foreign countries, or during the course of travel or transportation between foreign countries, between the United States and a foreign country, or between Canada and a foreign country. Thus, a firm that customarily sells goods for export or produces tailor-made products for foreign customers, such as customized machinery, may require additional protection.

Many insurers offer a package of coverage extensions for use with the CGL policy (the ISO version or independently filed contracts) which includes products liability insurance on a true worldwide basis, i.e., even when products are sold for export to foreign countries. However, virtually all of the packaged extensions still require that the original suit for any bodily injury or property damage stemming from a product be brought within the United States, its territories or possessions, or Canada.

When firms cannot accept the original suit restriction of standard products liability forms, they can purchase foreign products liability insurance which contains no restrictions as to locations of original suits. Or, if firms can live with the implications of large deductibles, they may be able to obtain products liability insurance for foreign exposures, without restriction to original suits, under some of the nonstandard umbrella liability policies.[8]

Exclusions: Rationale   Only three exclusions of an unmodified CGL policy (i.e., one written without any endorsements modifying its basic coverage provisions) deal primarily with products liability and completed operations insurance: (1) failure to perform exclusion; (2) exclusion of damage to the named insured's products; and (3) sistership exclusion. Only the sistership exclusion can be removed for an additional premium. The three exclusions preclude coverage for (1) loss of use of undamaged tangible property of others stemming from products which do not serve the purpose for which they were intended, whether the products are produced by one firm or with the components of several firms; (2) damage to products, including their loss of use; and (3) the costs of withdrawing, inspecting, repairing, or replacing products which are known or suspected of being defective.

Unfortunately, some insureds are not aware of the exclusions or their underlying purpose until losses are denied by insurers. (Courts sometimes also fail to comprehend the real meaning of those exclusions. The net result is that suits involving defense and settlement awards often are decided against insurers in cases where the insurers felt coverage had been excluded.) Yet, were it not for these exclusions, insurers virtually would be guarantors of product workmanship, rather than providers of insurance. So, the impact of those exclusions can cause burdensome financial consequences, unless steps are taken by entities to prevent or control them. Products liability insurance nevertheless serves a useful purpose in protecting insureds against the consequences of their legal liability when products manufactured, sold, handled, or distributed by them cause bodily injury or property damage to others.

Failure to Perform. The failure to perform exclusion, which forms a part of all commercial liability policies, is unusual in its application. It deals solely with loss of use of *undamaged* tangible property which results from failure of a product to perform as the named insured warrants or represents. This exclusion is not applicable when a product of the named insured causes physical damage to tangible property of others, including its loss of use following such damage. The exclusion also does not apply when failure of a product causes bodily injury.

As an example of a loss that would be excluded by the failure to perform exclusion, consider the manufacturer that sells a steam turbine with the guarantee that such unit will produce a specified level of power within a certain period. The turbine fails to produce power to expected levels, thereby causing its owner to lose the use of certain machinery which is dependent upon that power, as well as causing corresponding losses of production and revenue. Since these results constitute loss of use of undamaged tangible property, as well as loss of intangibles, they are excluded under the liability policy and must be borne by the manufacturer of that steam turbine.

But, if the aforementioned steam turbine were to suddenly and accidentally break apart or its electric generator were to suddenly and accidentally burn out while being used by its owner, the manufacturer would have liability protection against the owner's loss of use of tangible property, other than the turbine.[9] Such other property could even include the owner's entire premises, if loss were serious enough to cause its temporary unoccupancy. Coverage applies because the failure to perform exclusion makes exception to loss of use of other tangible property resulting from sudden and accidental damage or destruction to the named insured's products. The only prerequisite, and it is an important one, is that someone other than the named insured must be using that product at the time of loss. For example, if the purchaser of a turbine were to be operating the turbine and the turbine's failure to perform were to cause fire damage to the owner's premises, including temporary interruption of business and/or bodily injuries, the manufacturer of the turbine would have protection for any such resulting liability under its products liability insurance. But damage to the turbine, being the named insured's product, is excluded.

The net effect of the failure to perform exclusion is to prevent insurers from covering exposures of the type normally considered to be part of the costs of producing products. It stands to reason that when a product does not function properly, the burden of any loss of use stemming from that product should fall upon its maker or assembler, who is the best judge of that product and its capabilities, and who has certain responsibilities to make that product workable as warranted or represented.

Figure 4-1

Scope of the Failure to Perform Exclusion

Not Covered	Covered
Loss of use of undamaged tangible property of others resulting from failure of the product	Physical damage to tangible property of others, other than the product
Loss of use of the product stemming from its failure to perform	Loss of use of tangible property of others, other than the product, only when damage to the product is sudden and accidental
	Bodily injury to others resulting from failure of the product to perform

Figure 4-1 summarizes the preceding discussion of the failure to perform exclusion.

Damage to the Named Insured's Products. As previously mentioned, no liability coverage applies under any commercial liability policy for damage confined to the named insured's product. It does not matter whether that product is physically damaged or is merely rendered useless because it does not work. The exclusion of damage to the named insured's products makes this quite clear. Its purpose also is understandable. It prevents an insurer from having to pay for the repair or the replacement of a product which is incorrectly designed or is defectively produced.

Two aspects of this exclusion are commonly misunderstood. First, when damage arises out of a portion of a product and such damage makes the remaining part of the product useless, the exclusion applies to the whole product, not just to the part from which the damage arises. Second, damage to a product arising from any part of such product is excluded, whether the underlying cause is attributable to the work of a manufacturer, an assembler, or a supplier of any component.

For purposes of illustration, assume Alpha Manufacturing Company is under contract to produce electric generators that Baker Manufacturing Company uses in its steam turbines. One of Alpha's electric generators is defective, and it burns out and causes damage (physical injury or loss of use) to the remaining part of the steam turbine while in the possession of a utility company. Baker Company, in this circumstance, would be without products liability coverage under its products liability insurance for damage confined to the electric generator and to the turbine, because both are considered to be Baker

Company's products. (While Baker Company initially may be responsible for repairing or replacing the electric generator or the entire unit, depending upon the resulting loss to its product, it has a right of recourse against Alpha Company whose defective component is the proximate cause of loss.) Alpha Company has responsibility for the costs of repairing or replacing its defective component, without benefit of insurance, because that component is considered to be its product. Products liability insurance of Alpha Company, on the other hand, should respond for the payment of damage to Baker Company's steam turbine, since that turbine is not Alpha Company's product; i.e., the turbine was not manufactured, sold, handled, or distributed by Alpha Company.

If damage to the generator and to the steam turbine were sudden and accidental, however, Baker Company at least would have protection under its products liability insurance (for loss of use of other undamaged tangible property sustained by the utility company) under the exception of the failure to perform exclusion. Adjustments between the insurers of the Alpha and Baker Companies would then be required, depending upon the proximate cause of that loss. But, damage to the product itself is still excluded from insurance coverage.

Suppose, however, that Alpha's defective component were to make the entire turbine inoperable. The electric generator, in other words, does not burn out and the turbine does not break down, but the entire unit simply does not work. Baker Company, again, would have no coverage for its own product because of the exclusion of damage (including loss of use) to named insured's products. It also would have no liability protection for loss of use of the utility company's undamaged tangible property because of the failure to perform exclusion. Alpha Company more than likely will have to assume the costs of repairing or replacing its defective component, because that component is considered to be its product and, therefore, excluded under its products liability coverage. It also will have to assume those costs representing loss of use of undamaged tangible property of the utility company for two reasons: (1) such loss is not covered under the failure to perform exclusion; and (2) the loss was caused by its product.

While damage (physical injury or loss of use) to the named insured's products is excluded whether products are made by one entity or several, coverage does apply to bodily injury and to other property damage, including loss of use of any tangible property arising out of those products. So, for example, if the defective steam turbine were to damage other property of the utility company, that damage and any loss of use of such property stemming from that damage is the subject of coverage under Baker Company's products liability insurance. The steam turbine, being the product of Baker Company, is excluded.

While the above illustrations deal with relatively clear-cut situations involving component products that are clearly distinguishable, many losses are much more complicated. For example, finding the exact source of food poisoning can be an extremely difficult and costly matter, particularly if the product comprises many ingredients supplied by several entities. Bodily injury by food poisoning is covered, of course, if it ultimately is determined that the product contained botulism or some other harmful, foreign substance. But the producer's loss of use of that product and the costs of withdrawing that food product from the market and destroying it are not covered.[10] Yet, the task of determining which ingredient of an entity is responsible for this kind of loss sometimes is difficult, if not impossible. All entities involved, therefore, may be required to share in the bodily injury liability settlement, as well as for the loss of use and the destruction of the food product, even though only one entity actually may have caused the loss.

Another point about the exclusion of damage to named insured's products, or any exclusion for that matter, is that it cannot be treated in isolation. It has an important effect on other exclusionary provisions, which affect it in turn. No better example depicts this than the previous illustrations of loss involving the exclusion of damage to named insured's products and the failure to perform exclusion. It is not unusual, furthermore, to see losses of entities affected by the interaction of several exclusions. Understanding the exclusions and their applications, therefore, is an important criterion in determining whether the insurance as written is suitable for the liability exposures confronting the buyer.

Figure 4-2 summarizes the preceding discussion of the exclusion of damage to the named insured's products.

Sistership Liability Exclusion. The so-called sistership liability exclusion is another important provision that affects products liability insurance. It is directed at the costs incurred by an entity for the withdrawal, inspection, repair, or replacement of its products, including their loss of use, when its products must be withdrawn from the market or from use, because they are either known to be or suspected of being defective.[11]

Product recalls are common today. Manufacturers and distributors of automobiles, foodstuffs, drugs, toys, and so on must recall their goods or products from the market, or from use by consumers, because they are suspected of being unsafe. It is not unusual, for example, to read or to hear about automobile manufacturers recalling thousands of their vehicles of a certain make, model, and year in order to make adjustments or modifications. Some of these product defects are discovered by manufacturers, distributors, government agencies, or

Figure 4-2

Scope of the Exclusion of Damage to the Named Insured's Products

Not Covered	Covered
Loss of use of the named insured's product because of physical damage arising from any part of the product made by the named insured or by others	Bodily injury to others arising from physical damage to the named insured's product and arising from any part of the product made by the named insured or by others
Physical damage to the named insured's product arising from the insured's portion of the product or from the component of another firm	Property damage of others, including loss of use of such other property, arising from physical damage to the named insured's product and arising from any part of the product made by the named insured or by others

The following are losses which would be excluded or covered from the standpoint of the component maker's portion of the named insured's product:

Not Covered	Covered
Loss of use of the component maker's product because of physical damage arising from its portion of the product	Loss of use of another's product because of physical damage arising out of the component maker's part
Physical damage to the component maker's portion of the product arising from that product	Physical damage to another's product arising from a defect of the component maker's product

consumer groups, while others are not discovered until someone is injured. The general concern of manufacturers and distributors of products no doubt has something to do with these product withdrawals. The age of consumerism and the corresponding willingness of the public to sue producers of products for any type of loss, however, also play an important role in these withdrawals of products. Many of these product recall campaigns are also spurred by the Consumer Product Safety Act and the National Highway Traffic and Motor Vehicle Safety Act of 1966, among others.

Damages claimed for product recalls or withdrawals are not covered under the basic provisions of products liability insurance for at least two reasons. First, product recalls involve extraordinary costs that are not contemplated in the basic rate structure of products liability insurance. This is understandable, since considerable expense can be incurred by a producer of products in communicating its recall campaign to its wholesalers, retailers, and to the general public across the nation or in several states. A producer also must pay for transporting costs of recalled products, and costs for inspecting and repairing products. If the products are instead destroyed, the producer not only loses the value of those products, in terms of raw stock, labor, and sales value, but also incurs costs of replacing recalled products with new ones. Damages claimed for loss of use of recalled products by consumers also can be costly. Such damages, of course, will depend upon the type and usage of the product. It is doubtful, for example, that a consumer of canned goods, purchased for future consumption, would be able to argue that it sustained any loss of use. But a firm whose fleet of defective automobiles is recalled may have a justifiable claim for loss of use.

The second reason damages for product recalls are not covered under the basic provisions of products liability insurance is that separate insurance is available for this exposure. Details of that protection, commonly referred to as products recapture or recall insurance, are discussed later in these pages.

Several points about the sistership liability exclusion are especially noteworthy from the standpoint of understanding its scope. One of these is that the exclusion applies whether damages are claimed for the withdrawal of products from the market, or for loss of use of products before or after they are marketed. A manufacturer of canned goods, for example, has no coverage for the expenses it incurs in withdrawing spoiled goods from its wholesalers or retailers, or from the possession of consumers. It also is without coverage for the costs of inspecting and testing the contents of those withdrawn products, as well as any products that are ready for shipment to the market. And, of course, the definition of occurrence will preclude coverage for the intentional destruction of spoiled canned goods by the producer, including their loss of use.

Another aspect of the sistership exclusion is that it applies to the withdrawal of products which are produced by one entity, as well as situations involving several producers of component products. While the former situation involving a product of one producer should not present any difficulties, the latter situation can become complicated. In either case, the intent of the exclusion is to preclude coverage for the costs of withdrawing, inspecting, repairing, replacing the named insured's products, either as a direct expense of the entity which initiates the withdrawal, or as a liability of another entity whose component is responsible for the known or suspected defective condition of the whole product.

For example, assume that several of Alpha Company's electric generators are suspected of causing Baker Company's steam turbines to produce insufficient levels of power. Baker Company therefore decides to withdraw certain generators from use for purposes of inspecting and repairing them, if necessary. The expenses incurred by Baker Company in withdrawing the generators from use are not covered because of the exclusion in question. The expenses that Baker Company will seek to recover from Alpha Company for these purposes are also not covered by Alpha Company's products liability insurance because they represent damages for which Alpha Company is liable. The sistership liability exclusion refers to "damages claimed for the withdrawal . . . of the named insured's products . . . or of any property forming a part of those products. . . ." It does not matter, therefore, whether the damages for withdrawal expenses are claimed by Baker Company, as an incurred expense, or by Alpha Company, as its liability. The exclusion applies in both instances. (While that is the intent of the sistership liability exclusion, most courts, thus far, have refused to interpret the provision that way. Courts agree that damages are excluded for the firm that does the actual withdrawing, but they do not agree that the liability of a manufacturer whose component is the underlying cause for such withdrawal is excluded.)[12]

Note, furthermore, that damages claimed against Baker Company for loss of use of undamaged tangible property by the owners of those generators and turbines also are excluded by the failure to perform exclusion. And, the exclusion of damage to named insured's products will prevent Baker Company from claiming protection under its policy for loss of use claims imposed by owners of those turbines. The products liability insurance of Alpha Company, furthermore, will not respond for the payment of any loss of use claims sustained by customers of Baker Company who are unable to use their turbines, because of the failure to perform exclusion. Alpha Company also will have to assume the costs of repairing or replacing any defective electric generators that are withdrawn from the market, because of the exclusion of damage to named insured's products. If Baker Company also were to sue Alpha Company for loss of its goodwill, Alpha Company would be without protection, because goodwill is considered to be an intangible, and property damage liability insurance deals strictly with tangible property.

Note, finally, that if an entity does not take reasonable steps to withdraw its products from the market or from use following a series of similar losses to its product, it may be without future protection for its liability to others. This is because the definition of "occurrence" does not include bodily injury or property damage that either is expected or intended from the standpoint of the insured. The sistership liability exclusion is summarized in Figure 4-3.

The sistership liability exclusion applies only to the CGL and garage liability policies. The garage liability policy commonly is written in

Figure 4-3

Scope of the Sistership Exclusion

Not Covered

Expenses incurred by a manufacturer in withdrawing its goods from the market, including costs incurred in inspecting and testing the withdrawn products.

A manufacturer's loss of use of products which had to be destroyed because the products were defective.

Damages for which a component maker is liable because its component damages the product of another firm and the latter firm incurs expenses in withdrawing the product from the market to inspect, test, and/or destroy it.

---

conjunction with the CGL policy, when an entity also is involved in another unrelated business venture, along with a dealership or a garage. Were it not for the sistership liability exclusion in the garage liability policy, the opportunity would exist for an insured under that policy, written in combination with the CGL policy, to maintain that coverage applies for its products withdrawals because of an ambiguity; namely, the CGL policy provisions exclude products withdrawals, but the garage liability provisions do not. The sistership liability exclusion of the garage liability policy is necessary to avoid such ambiguities.

Neither the storekeepers liability policy nor the druggists liability policy contains the sistership exclusion. The exclusion is not necessary because manufacturers of merchandise, not retailers, commonly initiate the withdrawal of goods from the market. However, the storekeepers liability policy is subject to a products exclusion that is not found in other liability policies. It excludes losses within the products hazard, as that term is defined in the policy jacket, when bodily injury or property damage arise out of (1) gas used for heat or power (other than gas used in nonrefillable aerosol containers); or (2) heating or cooking appliances (other than portable camp stoves or blow torches) operated by gas or liquid fuel. The rationale of the exclusion is understandable. The storekeepers liability policy is a package of coverages for smaller size retail businesses. So, when a store sells gas for heat or power, or heating appliances, it must obtain some other type of liability policy. The package premium for all coverages, in fact, does not contemplate the excluded exposures. Moreover, the exclusion cannot be deleted for an additional premium. The only way for a buyer to avoid it is to purchase the CGL policy.

Contractual Liability—Product Warranties Excepted. The contractual liability exclusion of the CGL (and all other standard commercial liability policies) excepts warranties dealing with the fitness or quality of the named insured's products. The purpose of that exception is to make warranties of the named insured's products the subject of products liability insurance, rather than contractual liability insurance.[13] When this exception is considered in light of products liability losses, there should be coverage for bodily injury or property damage of others resulting from an insured's breach of warranty—unless damages are confined to the named insured's products.

It is important to note, however, that liability assumed under contract for loss stemming from products is the subject of contractual liability insurance, not products liability insurance. For example, if a retailer knowingly or unknowingly agrees to hold harmless a wholesaler for any injury or damage stemming from the wholesaler's products, the exposure facing that retailer, in effect, is liability assumed under contract, rather than liability assumed under any warranty of products.

Limits of Liability The limits of liability provisions vary somewhat among policies that provide products liability insurance. For this reason, provisions of the CGL policy dealing with limits of liability are discussed first, followed by the differences as they apply to the storekeepers liability, garage liability, druggists liability, SMP, and businessowners' policies.

Comprehensive General Liability Policy. The provisions of the CGL policy concerning limits of liability contain a preamble to the effect that, regardless of the number of insureds, the number of persons who sustain bodily injury or property damage, or the number of claims or suits brought against the insured, the insurer's liability is subject to the limits which are stated in the policy declarations. This means that the applicable limit is not increased just because more than one insured may be involved in a loss. Nor does the limit apply separately to more than one injured person or claimant. Firms should take this into consideration when they determine their limits of liability, because it is not uncommon to have numerous claimants in any one loss, particularly with respect to injuries caused by food products.

Under the CGL, the products liability limits are divided into two limits for bodily injury liability and two for property damage liability coverage. One limit applies to any one occurrence involving bodily injuries and another limit applies, on an aggregate basis, for all bodily injury losses during the policy period. Two sets of limits also apply in the same way to property damage liability coverage.

Limits Applying to Bodily Injury Liability Coverage. Bodily injury liability coverage is subject to an occurrence limit and an annual aggregate limit. The occurrence limit is stated to be the insurer's total liability for all damages, in any one occurrence, because of bodily injury sustained by one or more persons. If the occurrence limit is $100,000, and three persons are awarded damages of $50,000 each, the insurer would be required to pay only $100,000, and the insured would have to pay the remainder.

Of importance here is the meaning of occurrence. As defined in the policy jacket, occurrence means continuous or repeated exposures to conditions that result in bodily injury or in property damage. But another provision of the CGL coverage part, under the limits of liability section, states that for purposes of determining the limits of liability, all bodily injury and/or property damage arising out of continuous or repeated exposures to essentially the same general conditions are considered as arising out of one occurrence.

The underlying intent of those two provisions is to prevent the pyramiding of limits when injury or damage losses are of a prolonged nature. For example, suppose spoiled canned food is shipped for sale in a three-state area. Several persons sustain illnesses and make claims against the manufacturer. Though the manufacturer makes every effort to withdraw its products from the market, its warnings go unnoticed. Then, in the following policy period, additional persons become ill after consuming the product which they purchased some months earlier. Since all of these bodily injury claims stem from the same canned food, all claims made against that manufacturer are considered to be one occurrence even though injuries are sustained by persons throughout two policy periods. The occurrence limit applying in the former policy period, when injuries first became manifest, therefore applies to all subsequent injuries, regardless of when they occur.

Bodily injury liability losses stemming from products also are subject to an annual aggregate limit. For a three-year policy, the aggregate limit applies separately to each annual period. This aggregate serves as a loss limit precluding any further coverage to an insured when one or more separate occurrences, during the policy period, equal or exceed that aggregate amount. Assume, for example, that an insured has bodily injury liability limits of $100,000 per occurrence and $300,000 aggregate. If the insured sustains two or more separate occurrences during the policy period amounting to damages of $200,000, it has only $100,000 of products liability coverage remaining for the policy period. If the insured, on the other hand, were to sustain three or more separate occurrences during the policy period and the total insured damages amounted to $300,000 or more, its coverage for the remainder of the policy period would be exhausted, even though the per occurrence limit is not reduced by loss. The insured, in this situation, would be forced to obtain additional products liability insurance (or go without it).

LIMITS APPLYING TO PROPERTY DAMAGE LIABILITY COVERAGE. The occurrence and aggregate limits of property damage liability coverage for products liability insurance apply in the same manner as they do for bodily injury liability coverage. In some cases, the CGL may also be written with a comprehensive single limit applying to both bodily injury and property damage.

Storekeepers Liability Policy. The provision of the storekeepers liability policy dealing with limits of liability contains the same preamble for avoiding cumulative limits as is found in the CGL policy. The storekeepers liability policy also provides that all bodily injury and property damage losses arising out of continuous or repeated exposures to substantially the same conditions are to be considered as arising out of one occurrence. But the storekeepers liability policy, unlike the CGL policy, consists of a single limit on an occurrence basis for both bodily injury liability and property damage liability coverages.

Garage Liability Policy. The limits of liability provisions of the garage liability policy are identical to those of the CGL policy, except for one addition. The limits are not increased by the number of automobiles that may be covered by the policy.

Bodily injury liability limits are on a per person and on an occurrence basis. The per person limit is the maximum payable for all damages sustained by one person in one occurrence. The occurrence limit, on the other hand, is the maximum that applies when two or more persons sustain injuries in any one occurrence. Property damage liability coverage of the garage liability policy is subject to an occurrence limit which applies in the same way as bodily injury liability coverage does.

Druggists Liability Policy. The limits of liability provisions of the druggists liability policy state that, regardless of the number of insureds, the insurer's liability is subject to the applicable limits stated in the policy. Two sets of limits apply to products liability losses. The first limit applies for each claim against the insured. This limit serves essentially the same purpose as the per person limit of the garage liability policy. So, for example, if two persons sustain illnesses because of a product sold by the insured, the per claim limit applies separately to each such claimant. The second limit is on an aggregate basis and it applies for all claims during the policy period. Once the aggregate limit is reached, protection of that policy is considered to be exhausted. This is important, particularly since one or more claims or suits resulting from one incident can exhaust the aggregate limit. The aggregate limit, however, applies separately to each insured retail drugstore, including the store designated in the policy declarations, any store which the insured discontinues operating, and any stores acquired during the policy period.

Special Multi-Peril Package. The application of limits dealing with the products hazard of SMP form MP-200 is similar to that in the conventional CGL policy. However, because a comprehensive single limit is used, there is only a single per occurrence limit applicable to both bodily injury and property damage.

Businessowners Package Policy. Limits of liability are applied in a manner similar to those in the CGL policy. However, in the businessowners policy the per occurrence limit is also the aggregate limit.

Vendors' Liability Protection Wholesalers and retailers can become directly involved in claims and suits brought by purchasers and users of their goods and products. It is not unusual, furthermore, for vendors to be held liable for bodily injuries or property damages stemming from the merchandise they sell. For those reasons, vendors sometimes are reluctant to handle merchandise, unless manufacturers not only show proof of products liability insurance, but also add vendors to their policies as additional insureds. By doing so, vendors are provided with defense coverage, and, if any judgments are awarded, they are paid by manufacturers' insurers.

The one standard method that presently exists, for adding a vendor as an additional insured on a manufacturer's policy of products liability insurance, is to use the limited form vendors endorsement. When this endorsement is used, for an additional premium paid by the manufacturer, the "persons insured" provision of the manufacturer's products liability insurance is amended to include the designated vendor, as an insured. The vendor-insured so designated is covered only against the distribution or sale of the named insured's (manufacturer's) products in the regular course of the vendor's business, and the coverage provided is subject to a number of exclusions. The following exposures are *not* covered under the endorsement:

1. Any express (not implied) warranty that is unauthorized by the manufacturer. This provision protects the manufacturer from losses when an overzealous vendor states something about the product's use which is not true, just to make a sale.
2. Any act of the vendor which changes the condition of the product. This provision relieves the manufacturer of responsibility for bodily injury or property damage when an otherwise good product is made defective through fault of the vendor.
3. Any failure to maintain the product in merchantable condition, or any failure of the vendor to make such inspections, adjustments, tests, or servicing as it has agreed to undertake. The rationale for this stipulation is the same as that applying in 2.

4. Any bodily injury or property damage arising out of products that are labeled or relabeled, or used as containers for any other ingredient or substance by the vendor. This proviso, like the others which apply, also prevents the manufacturer from being held responsible for acts or omissions beyond its control.

5. Bodily injury or property damage that occurs from a product on the vendor's premises. Technically, a product that causes injury or damage to others on a vendor's premises is the subject of premises and operations coverage, rather than products liability coverage. This exclusion, therefore, prevents the manufacturer's policy from extending coverage outside the customary realm of products liability insurance.

At one time, a broad form vendors endorsement also was available. Though it has been withdrawn from use by ISO, some insurers still use it with discretion. The broad form contains some of the same exclusions and limitations as the limited form. However, the broad form provides vendors with protection against bodily injury and property damage claims arising out of demonstration, installation, service, and repair operations of products that occur away from premises of such vendors. Coverage also applies when losses result from repacking if the purpose for doing so is to inspect, demonstrate, or test a manufacturer's product.

Figure 4-4 summarizes the uses and advantages of the various standard liability policies providing products liability coverage.

Nonstandard Coverages

Businesses face some exposures from products liability losses which are beyond the scope of standard insurance coverage. Nonstandard forms have been developed to provide insurance for some of these exposures. This section contains a discussion of a few of these nonstandard coverages—products recall or recapture insurance, product failure insurance, and ripping and tearing coverage.

Products Recall or Recapture Insurance Products recall or recapture insurance is a nonstandard form of coverage made available by a few insurers. It is designed to cover certain costs of withdrawing products from the market or from use because they are known to be or suspected of being defective. This coverage therefore closes part of the gap in liability policies which is created by the sistership liability exclusion.

The provisions of product recall policies vary somewhat from one insurer to another. Some cover only expenses for the withdrawal of products which have potential to cause bodily injury liability losses.

Figure 4-4

Uses and Advantages of Policies Providing Products Liability Cover

Since a variety of standard (and nonstandard) liability policies are available to provide products liability insurance, it is sometimes difficult to determine the policy which is best suited for a particular situation. The following summarizes the uses and advantages of standard policies and coverage parts which provide products liability insurance.

Policy or Coverage Part	Uses	Advantages
1. Special Multi-Peril Package and Businessowners Package Policies	Combine all or most of a firm's insurance portfolio, including products coverage, in one policy	Products liability for known and unknown exposures are covered subject to a package discount
2. Comprehensive General Liability Policy	Recommended for all firms whose insurance coverages cannot be packaged, other than businesses that qualify for garage liability, storekeepers, and druggists liability	Products liability for known and unknown exposures is automatically included, unless that coverage is excluded by endorsement
3. Separate Products Liability Coverage Part	Recommended for firms which must obtain products liability cover from an insurer other than the one which provides other liability coverages	Provides a means for obtaining products liability coverage somewhat broader than the CGL, because the coverage part does not contain any exclusion of automobiles, aircraft, and watercraft
4. Storekeepers Liability	Recommended for certain stores that qualify; policy packages liability, including products coverage, for one fixed premium	Products liability cannot be excluded and premium is not subject to adjustment based upon sales
5. Garage Liability Policy	Designed for automobile and equipment dealers, repair shops, and parking lot operators	Products liability is a built-in feature of coverage and no additional premium is required; products applies to autos and accessories, as well as incidental operations
6. Druggists Liability Policy	Designed for drug stores	Products liability coverage is provided for drugs, medicines, and any type of goods and sundries handled by drug stores

Others also cover expenses for the withdrawal of products with potential to cause property damage losses as well. Note, however, that if products do actually cause bodily injury or property damage, coverage does not respond for the withdrawal expenses of the product that produced the injury or damage. Almost all such policies carry both a mandatory deductible and a participation clause, with varying percentages, the latter of which requires an insured to share in every loss over the deductible. For example, if an insured sustains a $20,000 loss in the form of withdrawal expenses for certain products and it has a $5,000 deductible and a 20% participation, the insurer will pay $12,000 of the loss.

Several prerequisites must be fulfilled by manufacturers before they can qualify for this insurance. They must supply information concerning the territorial scope of their products and the names of their vendors, including those that may repack goods under another name. Prospective insureds also must supply insurers with detailed plans for the organized withdrawal of their products from the market or from use by purchasers. Because of these requirements and the high costs of the insurance, many manufacturers forgo its purchase and handle the exposure with various noninsurance techniques.

Product Failure Insurance Product failure insurance, an innovation of Stewart, Smith, Inc., a member of the Stewart Wrightson insurance group, is designed to close the coverage gap created by the failure to perform exclusion of standard and some nonstandard liability policies. Coverage, in other words, is directed at loss of use claims involving a customer's undamaged tangible property when a manufacturer's product fails to perform. The failure, to be covered, must stem from a mistake or a deficiency in design, formula, plan, specification, advertising material, or printed instructions prepared by the manufacturer.

This insurance is available to manufacturers of products, other than those that produce products to buyers' specifications, and to experimental and prototype products that have not been tried, tested, and approved by the manufacturer. Whatever limits ultimately are purchased, the policy is subject to a minimum deductible of $100,000. The deductible, furthermore, serves as a mandatory retention limit. This means it cannot be deleted or covered under some other form of insurance. The reason for the deductible is to force a certain degree of loss prevention incentive upon insureds. Insureds, it is believed, will have to be more loss-prevention conscious when they must retain a substantial amount of the loss.

Ripping and Tearing Coverage Ripping and tearing coverage, designed and marketed by Wesley H. Heston and Company, an affiliate of the Crump Companies, is a unique form of products liability insurance aimed at producers and suppliers of concrete products. Its purpose is to indemnify those firms for their expenses in the following situations: (1) for removing defective, prestressed concrete beams, concrete blocks, or poured concrete from structures or buildings; (2) for replacing forms, reinforcements, piping, and wiring that are destroyed during the course of removing defective concrete products; and (3) for returning the structure or building to the condition that existed prior to the installation of concrete products.

The condition precedent to coverage is that the concrete products are defective. The term "defective" is defined in the coverage form to mean a concrete product which does not meet the contract specifications of strength following its testing by an accredited independent testing agency. Since "strength" is the criterion for defective materials, no coverage applies for expenses in removing concrete products that are of a different shade than that specified in the contract.

This coverage form, which is attached to an M&C policy, contains five exclusions. No coverage applies (1) as the result of any express warranty unauthorized by the named insured; (2) to any property damage or expenses arising out of any physical or chemical change in the product made intentionally by or at the direction of any person at or after delivery of the product to the work site; (3) for expenses or damages incurred by or on behalf of the named insured without written approval of the insurer; (4) for property damage resulting from the erroneous ordering or delivering of concrete products; and (5) to loss arising out of mechanical breakdown of the named insured's equipment.

This coverage is available on a primary basis over a mandatory, minimum deductible of $1,000. The deductible, however, can be increased.

COMPLETED OPERATIONS LIABILITY INSURANCE

Forms Available

Completed operations insurance, like products liability insurance, is available under both standard and nonstandard forms. The common standard forms are the CGL, garage liability, special multi-peril package, and businessowners' package policies.[14] The nonstandard forms include manuscript policies, independently-filed policies of insurers, forms offered by excess and surplus lines carriers, commercial liability excess, and commercial umbrella liability policies.

Standard and Nonstandard Forms The CGL policy deals with completed operations insurance in the same way as it deals with products liability insurance. When completed operations insurance is not desired by or is unavailable to a firm, it must be excluded by endorsement.

The garage liability policy automatically includes completed operations insurance, too. The completed operations coverage cannot be deleted from the garage liability form. (An OL&T or an M&C may be used for some types of garage exposures where completed operations coverage is not provided.) Coverage in the garage liability policy applies against exposures resulting from defective work to automobiles and their equipment, and from defective work on other property considered to be necessary or incidental to the operations of an automobile sales agency, repair shop, service station, storage garage, or public parking place.

The SMP and businessowners' package policies also include completed operations insurance in the same way as they handle products liability insurance.

Although the coverage characteristics of nonstandard forms are too diverse to describe, the forms nonetheless are an important part of the market for completed operations insurance and other coverages. Commercial excess liability policies include coverage for completed operations, but only when the coverage is also provided by underlying policies. Commercial umbrella liability policies, on the other hand, almost always provide completed operations insurance, whether or not the coverage is provided by underlying policies. However, most insurers would not knowingly issue an umbrella to cover completed operations unless underlying coverage was in force.

Scope of Standard Coverage

Since the standard CGL policy is the principal means for providing completed operations insurance, the subsequent comments are based upon its provisions. Significant differences between the coverage provisions of the CGL policy and other standard liability policies will be noted.

Although all policy provisions are important, those that are especially important in determining the scope of completed operations insurance are the policy jacket definitions of completed operations hazard, bodily injury, and property damage.

Completed Operations Hazard The term "completed operations hazard," as it appears in the definition section of the policy jacket, is described in two parts. The first part defines the characteristics of operations included within the hazard, as well as the time periods operations are deemed to be completed. The second part deals with operations that are not considered to be within the scope of the completed operations hazard.

Completed operations hazard is defined to include bodily injury and property damage arising out of (1) operations, including materials, parts, or equipment which are furnished in connection with such operations; and (2) reliance upon a representation or a warranty made at any time with respect to those operations. It is a further stipulation that bodily injury or property damage must occur after operations have been completed or abandoned, and the operations must have been away from a premises owned or rented to the named insured.

The completed operations hazard, like the products hazard, makes loss contingent upon two criteria. First, bodily injury or property damage must arise (1) from work improperly completed, (2) from the use of defective or improper materials, parts, or equipment, or (3) from a completed operation properly performed or free of defects that nevertheless fails to serve its purpose as warranted or represented by the named insured. Second, bodily injury or property damage must arise from operations which have been completed or abandoned at premises other than those owned or rented to the named insured. Both of those criteria must be met. Otherwise, loss is not within the completed operations hazard.

Suppose, for example, part of a building under construction collapses because of a contractor's negligent act or omission and an adjoining building is damaged by falling debris. The resulting damage to that adjoining building is considered to be within the operations in progress hazard of premises and operations insurance, not completed operations insurance.[15] However, if that structure were to partially collapse following its completion, the resulting damage to the adjoining building is the subject of completed operations insurance, even though the underlying cause of that loss was created while operations were still in progress. It does not matter when a defect is created. What matters, instead, is when bodily injury or property damage occurs.[16] The CGL policy, including completed operations insurance, of course, must be in force at the time of injury or damage, because the terms "bodily injury" and "property damage," as defined in the policy jacket, only apply to losses which occur during the policy period. This is something that is not always understood until it is too late. Singsaas v. Diederich, 238 NW (2d) 878, is one example of what can happen when bodily injury results from completed operations of a firm that goes out of business and cancels its policy. This firm originally carried completed operations insurance for the period 1971 to 1974. However, it went out of business and canceled its insurance in July of 1972. Claims were subsequently made against it for injuries sustained by a person in August of 1972 and stemming from work the firm had negligently performed in December of 1971. Since that firm did not have a policy in force at the time of bodily injury, it was without protection. And, in Deodato v. Hartford Insurance Co., 1976 C.C.H. (Fire and Casualty) 360, a construction firm found itself without protection when a roof it had constructed was damaged nine months after its policy lapsed for nonpayment of premium.

Location of loss also is important. For example, if a person is injured by a premises defect after work is completed by the *owner* of the premises, the bodily injury is the subject of premises and operations insurance, because work was performed by the named insured at its own premises. But, when a person is injured by a premises defect at someone else's premises following completion of work by a contracting firm, the resulting bodily injury is the subject of completed operations insurance.

Completed Operations Hazard Versus Products Hazard. Some characteristics of the completed operations hazard are so similar to those of the products hazard that their precise differences sometimes are difficult to detect. Both hazards impose somewhat similar criteria for losses to be covered. Products must be physically relinquished, operations must be completed, and losses emanating from both must occur away from premises owned by or rented to the named insured. Manual classifications and general rules of both hazards also are contained in the product liability manual of ISO.

In spite of these similarities, there is a distinct difference between the two hazards. The products hazard involves losses resulting from goods or products that are manufactured, sold, handled, or distributed by a firm. Such goods or products, furthermore, either are defective or they do not serve their purposes as warranted or represented by the seller. An appliance store that sells but does not install gas ranges needs products liability insurance in the event that bodily injury or property damage emanates from the gas ranges, its products. The completed operations hazard, on the other hand, includes situations in which a firm is engaged in rendering services, rather than being in the business of manufacturing, selling, distributing, or handling goods or products. Such work or service either is performed incorrectly or it simply fails to serve its purposes as warranted or represented by the one who completes the operation. An excavation contractor, for example, furnishes its services in terms of labor and equipment to perform its work under contract. No product is involved. The result of its services, say, is an open trench that may or may not be shored, depending upon its depth.

There are numerous occasions, however, when contractors must physically handle products and even supply them in order to perform their services. A carpenter sometimes recommends and supplies lumber, an electrician supplies wiring and other components, a mason supplies bricks and mortar, a plumber supplies the piping, and the heating contractor supplies the equipment to be installed. The primary exposures of these contractors are concerned with the manner in which work is performed. But if their work results in losses because of defects in lumber, wiring, bricks, pipes, or heating equipment (materials, parts or equipment furnished with such work), those losses still are the subject of the completed operations hazard, rather than the products hazard. This is because the contractors deal in services, not with the manufacture, sale or distribution of products. The matter of defective products used in any work ultimately must be settled, usually by subrogation, between the insurers of those contractors and the manufacturers or distributors of the allegedly defective products.

On the other hand, an appliance store that sells and installs its products needs both products liability and completed operations insurance. The former coverage will protect the store in the event bodily injury or property damage arises from a defective product it has sold, or from failure of its product to serve its purpose as warranted or represented at the time of sale. The latter coverage protects that store against bodily injury or property damage arising from the manner in which work was performed in installing its product.

Time of Completion. The time at which an operation is considered to be completed is important because it can determine whether premises and operations coverage or completed operations coverage is applicable. Thus, when loss occurs after an operation is completed or abandoned and away from premises owned or rented to the named insured, it comes within the scope of the completed operations hazard. Completed operations insurance is therefore the appropriate form of protection. But when a loss occurs while an operation is still in progress, it is the subject of the premises and operations hazard. Premises and operations insurance is therefore the appropriate form of protection.

To avoid any argument in determining precisely when a particular operation is deemed completed, the definition of "completed operations hazard" lists three time periods, and specifies that an operation is considered to be completed by whichever of the following three periods occurs first:

1. when all operations to be performed by or on behalf of the named insured under contract are completed;
2. when all operations to be performed by or on behalf of the named insured at the site of operations are completed; or

3. when the portion of work out of which injury or damage arises has been put to its intended use by anyone other than another contractor or subcontractor who is engaged in performing operations at the same project.

Each of those time periods requires additional comment, because they are not always as clear as they sometimes first appear.

TIME PERIOD (1). The provision of time period (1) requires that all operations to be performed under contract must be completed, whether the work is performed in whole or in part by the named insured or by someone else (such as a subcontractor) on behalf of the named insured. When a subcontractor performs all or part of the work under contract, it needs completed operations insurance just as much as the general contractor. If loss should occur from the subcontractor's completed work, and suit is brought against the general contractor, the latter would be protected under its completed operations insurance, if loss is not otherwise excluded. The subcontractor also would be protected under its completed operations insurance if the general contractor's insurer should decide to seek reimbursement of its damages from the subcontractor through subrogation.[17]

If certain work is only partially done and the one performing it intends to return at a later date to finish it, such work as is already performed is not deemed to be completed. For example, suppose an electrical subcontractor is hired to do the wiring and other related work on a newly constructed one-story building. The contractor does the rough work, but is unable to install the switches, plugs and light fixtures until the walls and ceilings are finished. If someone on the work site, such as a carpenter, should sustain injury from an electrical shock, or if a fire should start from within the circuit breaker box before work is fully completed, loss is the subject of the premises and operations hazard of that electrical subcontractor's CGL policy, rather than the completed operations hazard.[18]

TIME PERIOD (2). The provision of time period (2) specifies that, regardless of all operations to be performed under contract by or on behalf of the named insured, work is considered to be completed as soon as all work that has to be done at the site of operations is finished. Work under this second category usually involves the performance of two or more like operations at different sites. For example, each utility pole removed by a contractor is considered to be a completed operation at each site no matter how many such poles must be removed under contract. Or, each sewer line laid and connected to a newly constructed dwelling is considered to be a completed operation at that site, even though such work must be performed on a whole tract of new dwellings. Each newly constructed and completed story of a high-rise building could conceivably be considered as a separate site of operations. Much depends on how the term "site of operations" is interpreted, because it is not defined in the policy provisions.

As each utility pole is removed, each sewer line is laid and connected, and each story of a building is finished, contractors will need completed operations insurance against any bodily injury or property damage arising from such completed work. They also will need premises and operations insurance against any bodily injury or property damage stemming from operations while the poles are being removed, the sewer pipes are being laid and connected, and work is being performed on the upper levels of a building.

TIME PERIOD (3). The provision concerning time period (3) considers operations to be completed when some portion of work, out of which bodily injury or property damage arises, has been put to its intended use by anyone other than another contractor or subcontractor who is performing operations on the same project. Occupancy or use of work for its intended purpose therefore takes precedence, even though the work in question has not been officially inspected and accepted.

Thus, if a boiler is put to use by its owner before work on the entire heating system is completed and the boiler causes bodily injury or property damage, loss is considered to be the subject of completed operations insurance. The same results are intended to apply when bodily injury or property damage arises from a portion of a newly constructed highway that the public is permitted to use before it is officially opened, and from a building that is partially occupied before it is fully completed. However, when the boiler, the highway, or the partially completed building is being used by other contractors on the same project, the operation is not considered to be completed.

As explicit as the provision of time period (3) may appear, it nonetheless is a source of argument for at least two reasons. First, it is not work used by others that is the controlling factor. It is work that is put to its *intended* use by others. Second, bodily injury or property damage must arise out of that portion of the work which has been put to its intended use by others.

An actual case that illustrates how problems can arise with this provision is Whitten Oil, Inc. v. Fireman's Insurance Co., 293 A. 2d 757. The contracting firm, which did not have completed operations insurance, was hired to replace two underground gas tanks at a marina. It replaced those tanks, but postponed the installation of air separation lines which were required for commercial operation of the pumps. The contracting firm decided that the gas pumps would not be used commercially during the winter, and it would be more convenient to install those lines in the spring. During the period of the contracting firm's absence, the marina pumped gas from those tanks for its own personal use.

In late spring of the following year, before the contracting firm had returned to complete its work, a fire occurred at the marina. The fire allegedly was caused by the contracting firm's failure to remove filler pipes running from the replaced tanks. The insurer denied the loss because operations were considered to have been completed within the terms of time period (3). The New Hampshire supreme court did not agree. In spite of the fact that the owner pumped gas for its own use, the court held that the work was not completed prior to the fire, since the pumps had not been completely installed for their intended, commercial use. The key factor, therefore, is the application of the phrase "intended use" to the circumstances in question.

Completed Operations Requiring Service, Maintenance, or Repair Work. Another important provision of the term "completed operations hazard" deals with operations that require continuous service or maintenance, as well as repair work. The relevant provision states that any operation requiring further service or maintenance work, *or* correction, repair, or replacement because of any defect or deficiency, but which otherwise is complete, is considered to be completed.

Were it not for this provision, firms under a continuing obligation to service, maintain, and repair work would never need completed operations insurance. Firms simply could maintain that operations requiring further service or repair work would be considered still in progress (and covered under premises and operations insurance). In fact, many courts have upheld this reasoning in earlier policy provisions not containing the provision in question.

The conjunction "or" of that provision separates service and maintenance work from correction, repair, or replacement work. This means that service or maintenance work does not have to be made necessary because of any defect or deficiency. Operations concerning correction, repair, or replacement work, instead, must be necessitated by a defect or a deficiency. In either case, however, operations are deemed to be completed at the earliest of the three time periods previously mentioned. For example, assume a firm installs an elevator and promises to inspect and service it periodically, as well as to repair it when necessary. As soon as the elevator is installed and accepted by its owner, it is considered to be a completed operation, unless one of the other time periods occurs first. The fact that the elevator must be inspected and serviced periodically or repaired has no affect on such operation. It still is completed. The elevator firm, of course, needs premises and operations insurance as protection against any bodily injury or property damage that may result while it is inspecting, servicing, or repairing the elevator. However, if the elevator should subsequently malfunction, fall, and injure its passengers because of the way it was installed or because of neglect in servicing it properly, loss is considered to be within the scope of completed operations insurance.[19]

Operations Not Within the Scope of Completed Operations Hazard. Bodily injury or property damage arising out of the following operations are not within the scope of the term "completed operations hazard," unless otherwise excepted:

1. operations in connection with the transportation of property, unless bodily injury or property damage arises out of a condition in or on a vehicle created by its loading or unloading;
2. the existence of tools, uninstalled equipment, or abandoned or unused materials; or
3. operations for which the classification stated in the policy or in the company's manual specifies "including completed operations."

OPERATIONS IN CONNECTION WITH THE TRANSPORTATION OF PROPERTY. To comprehend the full scope of this first condition, dealing with operations in connection with the transportation of property, and the exception dealing with conditions on vehicles created by their loading and unloading, one first must understand the scope of the CGL policy exclusions concerning automobiles, aircraft, and watercraft.[20]

Briefly, these exclusions remove coverage under the CGL policy for bodily injury or property damage arising from the ownership, maintenance, operation, use, loading, or unloading of any automobile, aircraft, or watercraft that is owned, operated by, rented, or loaned to any insured. By exception, therefore, the CGL policy covers bodily injury or property damage stemming from any automobile, aircraft or watercraft that is not owned, not operated by, not rented, nor loaned to any insured. An example of a covered exposure within the meaning of that exception is the automobile, aircraft, or watercraft of an independent contractor.

In light of that exception, the CGL policy applies to bodily injury or property damage stemming from operations in connection with the transportation of an entity's property on vehicles of others. For example, if, following an accident, an entity is brought into suit along with the independent trucker of its goods, the entity has protection under its CGL policy, even though the operations of loading that vehicle have been completed. Since this type of loss is not considered to be within the scope of the completed operations hazard, it therefore is the subject of coverage under the premises and operations. What is not insured by one coverage nevertheless can be insured by another coverage, unless the exposure is specifically excluded.[21]

However, if bodily injury or property damage arises out of a condition in or on a vehicle created by its loading or unloading, loss is the subject of coverage under the completed operations hazard. The vehicle, of course, must be one that is not owned, not operated by, not rented, nor loaned to any insured. And, in line with the definition of completed operations hazard, bodily injury or property damage must occur away from premises owned by or rented to the insured. The exposures in question are those allegedly caused by an insured, or by a person for whom the insured is responsible, who improperly loads or unloads cargo and causes dangerous conditions that result in bodily injury or property damage to others.

As an example of a loss caused by a condition in a vehicle created by its loading, consider the employee who improperly loads cargo onto a vehicle of another and the cargo subsequently shifts during transportation, causing the vehicle to go out of control or overturn. In Lee and Palmer, Inc. v. Employers Commercial Union Ins. Co., 461 F. 2d 257, one of the few court decisions dealing with this provision, it was held that the operations of lashing and securing cargo are not considered to be part of the loading or unloading process. The insured was in the business of lashing and securing cargo aboard ships. The insured, therefore, had nothing to do with stevedoring services nor with the actual transportation, placement, or carrying of goods from land conveyances to ships. Damage to the cargo arose as the result of the insured's negligence in securing it.

The insurer denied the claim, for two reasons. It maintained, first of all, that the property damage arose out of a condition in or on a vehicle created by the loading or unloading process. The insurer argued, secondly, that the loss was excluded under the watercraft exclusion; that is, property damage arising from the ownership, maintenance, operation, use, loading, or unloading of any watercraft is excluded. The United States district court for the southern district of New York did not agree with the insurer. The specialized lashing and securing of cargo, from the court's viewpoint, was not considered to be a loading or unloading operation within the meaning of the completed operations hazard. The lasher's work commenced after the cargo had been hoisted and placed upon the ship. The court also decided that the ship was not a vehicle within the context of the policy language. The exclusion dealing with watercraft was inapplicable, therefore, and the loss was covered under the lasher's premises and operations insurance, as property damage arising out of operations in connection with the transportation of property.

An example of a loss caused by a condition in a vehicle created by its unloading is the insured who improperly unloads cargo and causes some of the oil or chemicals to spill on the truck's surface. This condition either causes someone to slip and fall causing injuries, or it causes a fire that destroys the vehicle and, perhaps, surrounding property.

It should be noted at this point that there are marked differences among the coverages dealing with operations in connection with the transportation of property, the completed operations coverage of the CGL policy, and the separate completed operations and products liability coverage part. If an entity with the latter coverage part does not have premises and operations insurance under some other policy, it is without protection if bodily injury or property damage arises from operations in connection with the transportation of property on vehicles of others. Such exposure is the subject of premises and operations insurance, rather than completed operations insurance. The entity with the CGL policy is better protected in this respect. However, the separate coverage part does not contain exclusions of automobiles, aircraft, and watercraft. Coverage therefore applies to bodily injury or property damage arising out of hazardous conditions caused by loading or unloading of both owned *and* nonowned vehicles. The completed operations hazard of the CGL policy, on the other hand, only applies to losses stemming from such conditions which exist on nonowned vehicles. Such conditions which exist on owned vehicles must be handled under the comprehensive automobile liability policy.

EXISTENCE OF TOOLS, UNINSTALLED EQUIPMENT, OR ABANDONED OR UNUSED MATERIALS. Bodily injury or property damage arising from the existence of tools, uninstalled equipment, or abandoned or unused materials is the subject of premises and operations insurance rather than completed operations insurance. This is the case even though such tools, equipment, or unused materials were used or were intended to be used in performing operations which have since been completed or abandoned away from premises owned or rented to the insured.

MANUAL CLASSIFICATIONS AUTOMATICALLY INCLUDING COMPLETED OPERATIONS. For some classifications in the OL&T and M&C manuals, there is no separate premium charge for completed operations insurance; the coverage is automatically included along with an entity's premises and operations insurance. Among such OL&T classifications are churches, clubs that have no buildings or premises of their own, convalescent and nursing homes, electronic data processing centers, and self-service laundries and dry cleaners. Examples of such M&C classifications are cleaning and renovating outside surfaces of buildings, detective and patrol agencies, engineers and architects who do consulting but no actual construction work, engravers, oil or gas lease operators of natural gas, geophysical exploration, and car washes.

Since the policy provisions govern the terms of coverage between the insured and the insurer, it is necessary that the policy terms state specifically that operations classified in the policy declarations, policy schedule, or manual as including completed operations are not subject to the completed operations hazard, as defined. Through this provision, the policy is stating, in effect, that the completed operations hazard, as a separate, ratable exposure, does not apply to OL&T and M&C classifications that include completed operations. Instead, the completed operations hazard, as included within those classifications, applies as a combined, ratable exposure of premises and operations insurance. This means the insured has completed operations insurance without having to purchase it for an additional premium. So, for example, if a club assists in building a park and playground and someone is injured because of work performed by it, the club has protection under its premises and operations insurance, even though such work has been completed. The only requirement, of course, is that the club have insurance at the time of the injury or damage.

Insuring Agreements The insuring agreements of the CGL, garage liability, SMP, and businessowners' policies contain no reference to completed operations coverage. They merely recite the insurer's promise to pay on behalf of the insured who is legally obligated to pay damages caused by an occurrence. Because specific reference to completed work is lacking in those insuring agreements, all losses stemming from an insured's completed operations, as defined, are covered, except those losses specifically not covered under the exclusions section of these policies.

Neither the OL&T nor the M&C policies, on the other hand, are designed to provide completed operations insurance, except when written in conjunction with the SMP policy. To preclude completed operations insurance under both the OL&T and the M&C policies, each contains a specific exclusion of bodily injury or property damage stemming from losses within the completed operations hazard, as that term is defined in the policy jacket. Nevertheless, entities whose OL&T and M&C classifications include completed operations automatically do receive completed operations insurance, because such classifications are not considered to be within the scope of the term, "completed operations hazard," as defined.

Broad Form Property Damage Coverage Endorsement Firms that perform work or services, rather than produce or sell products, such as construction contractors, repairers of automobiles and machinery, and installers of property, can obtain somewhat broader protection against their property damage liability exposures under the CGL, SMP, and garage liability policies by obtaining the broad form property damage coverage endorsement.[22] This coverage partially modifies the care, custody, or control exclusion and the injury to work performed exclusion. The former exclusion deals with property damage to property in the care, custody, or control of the insured, as explained in Chapter 2, and the latter exclusion, discussed more fully later in these pages, deals with property damage to work performed by or on behalf of the insured.

Two such broad form property damage coverage endorsements are available. One deals with operations that are still in progress and the other one includes coverage after operations are completed. However, the latter coverage endorsement only can be written when a firm has a policy which already includes completed operations insurance. For example, a firm which has an M&C policy can only obtain the endorsement that provides broad form property damage coverage for operations in progress, unless its manual classification automatically includes completed operations. On the other hand, a firm which has a CGL policy that does not otherwise exclude completed operations coverage has the option of purchasing either endorsement.

The broad form property damage endorsement replaces the care, custody, or control exclusion in its entirety and amends portions of the injury to work performed exclusion. But this does not mean that coverage applies for damage to property in the insured's care, custody, or control, or to work performed by or on behalf of the insured. To the contrary, broad form property damage coverage still excludes property damage to property owned by, occupied by, or rented to the insured. It also excludes property damage to property in the custody of the insured which is to be installed, erected, or used in construction by the insured. Note, however, that if the property in the custody of the insured is to be installed, erected, or used in construction by someone other than the insured, coverage applies if the property is damaged. Furthermore, property damage to tools and equipment is excluded while being used by the insured in performing operations. This means that coverage applies while those tools or equipment are not being used by the insured at the time they are damaged.

The interesting thing about this endorsement is that coverage is not stated affirmatively. Coverage, instead, is inferred from the exclusions. The situation dealing with tools and equipment is one example, and others are mentioned subsequently.

Property on Which Work Is Being Performed. The primary advantages of the broad form property damage endorsement are the coverages the insured receives while work is in progress, for property that is not on premises owned by or rented to the insured. Such coverage comes about indirectly as exceptions to an exclusion.

The exclusion states that no coverage applies for damage to property not on premises owned by or rented to the insured in any of the following three situations. Property damage liability coverage does not apply to property damage to:

1. That particular part of any property upon which operations are being performed by or on behalf of the insured at the time of property damage arising out of such operations. The key words are "particular part." Thus, no coverage applies to that particular part of any work that is damaged while work is being performed on it. But, by inference, coverage *does* apply for damage to other work performed by or on behalf of the insured which results from damage to that particular part of work upon which operations are being performed. An example is the general contractor who hires a subcontractor to erect steel beams in constructing a bridge. While employees of the subcontractor are positioning one of the beams, it accidentally slips, falls, and bends so that it is no longer usable. At the time it fell, it also damaged other steel beams that already had been erected. The general contractor and subcontractor would have no liability protection for damage to that particular part of any work (the falling beam) upon which operations were being performed by the subcontractor on behalf of the general contractor. But both have coverage for the other beams that are damaged as a consequence of that incident, because operations were not being performed on them at the time of the accident.

   Damage to work involving separate, identifiable parts, such as the steel beams erected and being erected, presents no problems. But when work is being performed on one unit from which damage arises, it may be difficult to determine from what particular part damage arises. An actual situation is the case of Vinsant Electrical Contractors v. Aetna Casualty and Surety Co., 1976 C.C.H. (Fire and Casualty) 1179, a case in which the contractor was installing two circuit breakers in a switchboard composed of wires, switches, breakers, conductors, and buss bars. While working on that switchboard, an employee inadvertently dropped a socket wrench which came in contact with the buss bars, producing a short and causing the entire switchboard to burn up. The loss was denied by the insurer because of the exclusion in question. The Tennessee supreme court agreed with the insurer. Its reasoning was that the property being worked on, though composed of many parts, was a single item of property and, therefore, "that particular part" of property upon which operations were being performed. So, even this coverage endorsement does not necessarily provide broader coverage in all instances. Much depends upon the nature of work being performed.

2. That particular part of any property out of which property damage arises. This second situation excludes coverage only for the separate, identifiable part of work out of which damage arises. For example, an employee of a firm is working on the steam turbine's electric generator. The generator suddenly burns out and also damages the steam turbine. The electric generator, being that particular part of any property out of which property damage arises, is excluded, but damage to the steam turbine is covered. This second situation could nevertheless cause problems to an insured unless that particular part of any property out of which damage arises is separate and identifiable from other damaged property. The previous example involving the switchboard could conceivably work to the disadvantage of an insured under this second situation as well.

3. That particular part of any property necessitating restoration, repair, or replacement because of faulty workmanship by or on behalf of the insured. This third situation does not require property to be physically damaged, but only that work be performed so improperly that it has to be redone. The painter who uses the wrong shade of paint, the plumber who places pipes in areas not designated in work plans, the elevator installer who installs a unit that does not perform properly following its installation are examples of situations that are not covered by this provision. In each case, the insured must redo work at its own expense.

Broad Form Property Damage, Including Completed Operations Coverage. When an entity purchases the broad form property damage coverage endorsement with completed operations, an exclusion applies to property damage arising out of completed work performed by that entity, as the named insured, as well as out of any parts, materials, or equipment furnished with that completed work. The named insured, on the other hand, has coverage for damage to (1) its work when it is performed on its behalf, such as when a subcontractor is hired to do it, and (2) work of others caused by work of the named insured.

Assume, for example, that the named insured, a general contractor, constructs a dwelling which is accepted by its owner. Six months later, fire destroys that house because of faulty construction of the fireplace. The insured contractor is not covered for this damage to the fireplace and to the dwelling because it was work performed by the named insured. However, if the fireplace were constructed by a subcontractor, the general contractor has coverage for damage to that fireplace and to the remainder of the dwelling, since the exclusion applies only to work performed by the named insured.

Broad Form Property Damage Coverage Without Completed Operations. When an insured has completed operations insurance under its CGL policy, but does not desire completed operations coverage in conjunction with its broad form property damage coverage, two coverages are absent in comparison with broad form property damage coverage written to include completed operations. First, the insured only receives protection while its operations are in progress. Second, damage to work performed by or on behalf of the insured is excluded. In contrast, when completed operations coverage applies, damage to work is excluded only when it is performed by that entity. The only significant difference, therefore, is that coverage written without completed operations still excludes damage to property performed "on behalf of the insured."

Exclusions: Rationale Several of the same exclusions of the CGL policy (without the addition of endorsements modifying its basic coverage provisions) which directly affect products liability also affect completed operations. These are the failure to perform exclusion, the contractual liability exclusion dealing with warranties of products and of work, and the sistership liability exclusion. A number of other exclusions affect only completed operations. Those mentioned previously are the exclusions of automobiles, aircraft, and watercraft owned, operated by, rented, or loaned to the insured, and the exclusion of property in the care, custody, or control of the insured. Others that require mention include the premises alienated exclusion and the injury to work performed exclusion which is the counterpart to the products liability exclusion of damage to the named insured's products.

Failure to Perform Exclusion. When the failure to perform exclusion applies to work performed by or on behalf of the insured, the result is much the same as when that exclusion applies to an insured's products. Thus, if someone sustains loss of use of otherwise undamaged tangible property because work performed on that property fails to serve its purpose as warranted or represented, the loss is excluded.

An example is the automobile garage mechanic who rebuilds an engine on a stock car. When the stock car is put into use at the race site, it does not perform properly. Each time the driver attempts to accelerate the car, the motor cuts out. The owner and its sponsor not only sustain loss of use of that car, but also the entry fee for the race. Loss of the stock car's use is excluded because of the failure to perform exclusion, and loss of the entry fee is not covered because it is not considered to be tangible property.

If, on the other hand, the motor were to suddenly and accidentally blow up in the race pit while the driver is preparing for the start of the race, the automobile garage that rebuilt the motor would have liability protection against any bodily injury and property damage, other than to the motor and other work it performed. Such other property damage could include the remainder of the stock car not worked on, damage to equipment in the pit, and even physical damage and loss of use of the pit itself. Coverage applies because the failure to perform exclusion makes exception to loss of use of other tangible property resulting from sudden and accidental damage or destruction to work performed by or on behalf of the insured.[23]

The net result of the failure to perform exclusion, therefore, is the same as when it applies to an insured's products. The exclusion, in essence, prevents an insurer from having to pay for rebuilding, replacing, or repairing tangible property because of its faulty workmanship when the one performing that work expressly or impliedly guarantees that the work will fulfill its purpose.

Premises Alienated Exclusion. The purpose of the premises alienated exclusion is to prevent coverage for physical injury to, or loss of use of, premises alienated (sold) by an entity when property damage arises out of those premises. This exposure can arise in a number of ways. One is when an entity sells property on which an obscure defect is known to exist and the seller unintentionally fails to inform the buyer of its existence. If, after property is transferred to its new owner, the building sustains damage because of an undisclosed defect, the seller has no protection. The effect of this exclusion, therefore, is to keep the policy from covering the obligation of the seller to make any repairs to alienated premises or to pay for removing any dangerous condition in those premises.

However, any bodily injury or damage to property, other than property alienated, is covered. So, if the buyer of a building or an occupant were to sustain bodily injuries because of a premises defect which should have been taken care of before its sale, the seller is protected. Or, if concealed, defective electrical wiring were to cause fire damage to the alienated premises, as well as to adjoining premises, the seller would be protected only for damage to the adjoining premises.

The coverages granted by exception to the premises alienated exclusion at one time were available under former liability policy editions for an additional premium. The coverage was known then as grantors protective liability insurance. Under present standard commercial liability policies, coverage automatically applies. In fact, coverage applies by exception to the premises alienated exclusion, even when an entity has only premises and operations insurance. However, there are certain restrictions, depending upon the policy.

The OL&T policy, which neither provides products liability nor completed operations insurance, contains the premises alienated exclusion. The coverages granted by exception to that exclusion therefore apply. But, from the standpoint of premises coverage, the OL&T policy only applies to bodily injury or to property damage arising out of the ownership, maintenance, or use of the insured premises. The term "insured premises" is defined in that policy to include premises alienated by the named insured, if possession has been relinquished to others, other than premises constructed for sale. So, the only coverage granted to the named insured is when premises are sold by an entity for some reason other than for conducting a business of building and selling property. If an entity desires coverage for that latter exposure, it should obtain either the CGL policy or some other policy that includes completed operations insurance.

The M&C policy also does not include products liability or completed operations insurance. However, the M&C policy, unlike the OL&T, does not contain a definition of insured premises. The same result is obtained as with the OL&T policy, because the M&C policy excludes bodily injury or property damage included within the completed operations hazard and the products hazard.

The CGL, SMP, businessowners, and garage liability policies on the other hand, contain the premises alienated exclusion, but without any restrictions on premises constructed for sale. The apparent reason for this is that all such policies automatically include completed operations insurance. Of course, if completed operations insurance is excluded under the CGL and SMP policies (it cannot be deleted from the garage liability and businessowners policies), coverage will not apply to alienated premises that were constructed for sale, because of essentially the same exclusion that applies to the M&C policy. And, while coverage applies without restriction to the garage liability policy, the activity of one in the garage business also being in the business of constructing and selling premises seems remote. Coverage also is unrestricted in the businessowners policy but is practically defeated because entities involved in the construction business are ineligible for that policy.

Note, finally, that since bodily injury and property damage, as defined in the policy jacket which applies to all standard policies, must occur during the policy period, an entity must have a policy in effect at the time of such injury or damage for any alienated premises coverage to be applicable.

Injury to Work Performed Exclusion. The injury to work performed exclusion, which forms a part of standard and nonstandard commercial liability policies, including most umbrella liability and umbrella excess liability policies, is a common source of argument because its purpose and scope are often misunderstood. The exclusion is designed to preclude coverage for property damage to work performed by or on behalf of the named insured, including its resulting loss of use, when damage arises out of work, out of any portion of such work, or out of materials, parts, or equipment furnished in connection with that work. The purpose of the exclusion is to prevent an insurer from having to pay for replacing, repairing or otherwise redoing faulty work of the named insured. A number of points about that exclusion are important in understanding its full scope.

First, work partially or fully completed can be damaged or destroyed, resulting also in its loss of use. For example, if a roof leaks or collapses after being built, and the building owner must totally or partially vacate the top floor until the roof is repaired or replaced, the cost to redo the work is excluded, as well as any loss of use to that portion of the building that must be vacated. However, any other tangible property of that building owner that is damaged or destroyed as the result of injury or destruction to the roof is covered, as well as any loss of use of such other property. Damage to work also can come about through its loss of use in circumstances when work, instead of being physically damaged or destroyed, simply fails to serve its purpose. An example here would be a heating firm that services and replaces parts on a boiler in preparing it for the heating season. On the day that it is put into use, the boiler fails to work because of something the heating firm did or failed to do. The cost of servicing and making the boiler functional is excluded. The failure to perform exclusion also could apply in this situation if the owner or occupant temporarily loses the use of the building until the boiler is repaired and the building is heated.

Second, the injury to work performed exclusion not only applies after work is completed, but also during the actual performance of work. At least this is the intent, because the exclusion forms a part of the OL&T and M&C policies and neither policy provides completed operations insurance. And, in the one court case dealing with that point, Southwest Forest Industries v. Pole Buildings, Inc., 1973 C.C.H. (Fire & Casualty) 643, the U.S. Court of Appeals for the ninth circuit held this exclusion applicable to operations in progress and to completed operations. Note, however, that the care, custody, or control exclusion could possibly serve the same purpose as the injury to work performed exclusion while operations are still in progress. Or, if the former exclusion does not fit or apply to a certain loss situation, the latter exclusion should then operate to preclude coverage.

A third point about the injury to work performed exclusion is that it applies to work performed by the named insured, as well as work performed on its behalf. So, if an independent contractor performs faulty work, the injury to work performed exclusion will serve to deny coverage to the general contractor for whom such work was performed. The independent contractor also will be without coverage under its own liability policy, because that exclusion applies to work performed by the named insured which, in this case, is the independent contractor.[24]

Finally, this exclusion not only applies to property damage arising out of the work, but also applies to any portion of the work perfomed by or on behalf of the named insured, as well as from any materials, parts, or equipment furnished with that work. This is an extremely important part of the exclusion, and the part that is most frequently misunderstood. Its net effect is to exclude the particular part of any work that causes damage, as well as any portion of the work performed that is adversely affected by that damage. An illustration should help to clarify just how all-encompassing this portion of the exclusion actually is.

Assume a contracting firm was hired to build a one-family dwelling on a concrete slab. Part of its work involved placing pipes for steam heat on impacted soil and pouring concrete over them in constructing the slab. Because a coupling on one of the pipes is defective, steam ultimately escapes, condenses, and causes leakage into the dwelling. The contracting firm not only is required to tear up a large portion of the slab and retrieve and replace the defective coupling, but also is required to replace the concrete slab. All costs incurred by that contracting firm in performing that work are excluded. The injury to work performed exclusion precludes coverage for property damage to work performed by or on behalf of the named insured (installing the piping and constructing the concrete slab) when damage arises out of any portion of the work, or out of materials, parts, or equipment furnished in connection with that work (defective coupling). The only coverage that firm may have is for property damage to the dwelling owner's carpeting by water leakage, provided the carpeting was not supplied and installed by that contracting firm. As for the defective coupling and the damages caused by it, the contracting firm's only recourse is against the distributor or the manufacturer of that coupling. Note, furthermore, that this exclusion remains unaffected (i.e., it still applies) even if the piping work and the concrete slab work were subcontracted to others, since work performed on behalf of the named insured also is excluded.[25]

Suppose the condensation remains undetected and the water eventually causes the ground to sink, the slab to crack, and the dwelling to tip to the point that it becomes uninhabitable. The contracting firm therefore is required to raze the dwelling and to rebuild it. The exclusion in question will preclude coverage for all damages, including loss of use of the dwelling, for two reasons. First, the entire dwelling is considered to be work performed by that contracting firm, and physical injury or destruction to work performed is excluded, even though the underlying cause of loss is the defective coupling. And, second, loss of use of the dwelling by its owner also is not covered, since the definition of property damage includes any resulting loss of use. So, when damage to property is covered, any resulting loss of use also is covered. But, when damage to property is excluded, any resulting loss of use also is excluded. There can be no coverage for loss of use, therefore, when the subject of damage to property is excluded.

Many firms find it difficult to believe that all work performed is excluded, rather than only the work out of which damage arises.[26] This is not at all surprising, because the financial consequences can be overwhelming. Yet, based upon the court decisions rendered thus far, the majority uphold the intent of that exclusion.[27]

Sistership Liability Exclusion. The sistership liability exclusion also applies to work completed by or for the named insured, as well as to any property of which such work forms a part. In fact, its application is identical to that involving products. The potential exposures involving the withdrawal of materials, parts, or equipment can be costly, particularly when they already form a part of the completed work. Examples include removing defective concrete blocks that already form a part of a building, removing defective wall paneling that is known to blister, and retrieving defective couplings used on piping, even if it involves tearing up concrete to secure them.

Contractual Liability—Warranties of Work Performed Excepted. The first provision of the CGL policy that affects completed operations insurance is the exception, under the exclusion of contractually assumed liability, of warranties that work performed by or on behalf of the named insured will be done in a workmanlike manner. The purpose of that exception is to make warranties of the named insured's work, or work performed on its behalf the subject of completed operations insurance, rather than contractual liability insurance.[28] When this exception is considered in light of losses dealing with the performance of work, there should be coverage for bodily injury or property damage of others resulting from an insured's breach of warranty concerning its work, unless damages are confined to the insured's work product. Take, for example, the roofer that constructs a new roof on a dwelling and guarantees its work for two years. Six months after that work is performed, the roof develops a leak, and property within the dwelling is damaged. This loss is the subject of completed operations insurance, not contractual liability insurance. But the only loss covered is damage to property of that dwelling by leakage (other than the roof), because the roof is considered to be work performed by the roofer.[29]

On the other hand, liability assumed under contract for loss stemming from work performed by the insured is the subject of contractual liability insurance, rather than completed operations insurance. For example, if a subcontractor agrees to hold harmless a general contractor for bodily injury or property damage stemming from work performed by the subcontractor, the exposure facing that subcontractor, in effect, is liability assumed under contract, rather than liability assumed under any warranty of work performance.

Most of the major exclusions directed at completed operations exposures are similar in intent to products liability exclusions. Figure 4-5 summarizes the types of completed operations losses which are excluded in the CGL, a well as the types of losses which are excepted and, therefore, covered.

Limits of Liability The application of completed operations liability limits on all standard liability policies is identical to that of products liability, so it is not necessary to repeat it here. However, the property damage occurrence limit of the garage liability policy contains a $100 deductible that applies to any property damage to an automobile resulting from work completed on it, or on any part of it, by or on behalf of the named insured. Damage to any work on an automobile, in other words, is not covered because of the injury to work performed exclusion. But any other portion of an automobile that is damaged as the result of such faulty work is covered, subject to the deductible. The following are illustrations of losses involving the application of that deductible.

Assume an automobile repair shop employee removes a generator from a customer's automobile and asks a specialist of another repair shop to rebuild that generator. Work is performed improperly. After the generator is placed into the automobile, and its owner is operating it, the generator produces an electrical surge that burns out the generator, melts the electrical wiring, and causes fire damage to the interior of the automobile. Because of the injury to work performed exclusion, damage to the generator—being work completed by or on behalf of the named insured—is excluded. But all other damage to that automobile, including its loss of use, is covered, subject to the $100 deductible.

To further clarify, suppose a person purchases a used automobile from a franchised dealer. The automobile has a defective master brake cylinder which could have been detected by the seller through normal inspection. Before the automobile is relinquished by the dealer, the owner requests an oil and filter change. An employee changes the filter and the oil but fails to replace the plug in the crankcase. As that automobile is being operated on an expressway, its owner applies the brakes and they fail, causing the owner to go off the road and to strike a guardrail. The automobile sustains heavy damages upon impact and its owner sustains injuries. When the automobile is being inspected by an adjuster of an insurance company, it is noticed that the oil plug is missing and that the engine and its parts were ruined from lack of oil. In

Figure 4-5

Summary of Completed Operations Liability Exclusions

Failure to Perform Exclusion

Not Covered	Covered
Loss of use of undamaged property of others because work performed on property fails to serve its purpose	Sudden and accidental physical injury to tangible property of others, other than property on which work was performed
Loss of use of completed work stemming from its physical injury or failure to perform	Bodily injury to others resulting from failure of the completed work to perform its purpose

Premises Alienated Exclusion

Not Covered	Covered
Physical injury to or loss of use of premises alienated (sold) when property damage arises from the alienated premises	Bodily injury; also property damage, other than property alienated

Injury to Work Performed Exclusion

Not Covered	Covered
Physical damage to work performed (during or following completion) by or on behalf of the named insured, when damage arises out of the work, materials, parts, or equipment furnished with such work	Property damage of others, including loss of use of such other property arising from physical injury to work performed by or on behalf of the named insured or out of materials, parts, or equipment furnished with such work
Loss of use of work performed by or on behalf of the named insured because of physical injury arising from the work or out of any materials, parts, or equipment furnished with such work	Bodily injury to others arising from physical injury to work performed by or on behalf of the named insured or out of materials, parts, or equipment furnished with such work

Sistership Exclusion
Not Covered

Expenses incurred by a contractor in removing and replacing defective work or materials from a job which is completed or partially completed

A contractor's loss of use of work which had to be replaced because the work or materials were defective

Damages for which a subcontractor is liable because its faulty work damages the entire work of others at the job site and the subcontractor incurs expenses in removing and replacing the faulty work fully or partially completed a loss situation such as this, the franchised dealer has protection under its garage liability policy for injuries to the automobile owner, damages to the automobile engine caused by the lack of oil, and damages to the guardrail. Nothing else is covered. In the crankcase loss, the crankcase and its loss of oil are considered to be items of work completed by the named insured and therefore subject to the injury to work performed exclusion. The oil plug and oil would not be replaced. On the other hand, the ruined engine resulting from the failure to replace the plug is covered, subject to the $100 deductible. Damage to the remaining part of the automobile from impact with the guardrail, resulting from its defective master brake cylinder, is not covered because of the exclusion dealing with damage to named insured's products. This exclusion states that insurance does not apply to property damage to any of the named insured's products (the automobile), if property damage results from a condition existing in such product or any part (the defective master brake cylinder) at the time the product is relinquished to the purchaser.

Admittedly, the $100 deductible in this situation is of little significance, considering the other losses that must be assumed by that franchised dealer. However, in the normal course of events, the deductible serves two useful purposes. First of all, it reduces the frequency of small claims that otherwise might apply if the deductible were not applicable. Second, the deductible makes entities conscious of the fact that proper performance of work is essential in avoiding the assumption of that deductible amount. In addition, the limits of liability provision of the garage liability policy requires that repairs made by the named insured are to be adjusted on the basis of actual cost of its labor and materials. Some insurers will delete that deductible for an additional premium.

Other Policy Provisions: Rationale It should be readily apparent from the discussions of completed operations and products liability insurance, as well as from the subject matter of the preceding chapters, that coverages, exclusions, and policy conditions do not stand alone. They relate to one another in varying degrees, depending upon the circumstances. In fact, it is only through the interaction of various provisions that one can determine whether, and to what extent, coverage applies. The previous examples dealing with completed operations insurance certainly illustrate this.

The conditions of various liability policies are important because they are the ground rules by which insurers and insureds must abide. An insured, for example, must understand that the premium at policy inception for completed operations insurance is provisional, and that it only is at the expiration of the policy and upon audit that the final premium is determined. An insured is obligated to cooperate with the insurer by maintaining proper records and by permitting an auditor to review them. The unwillingness of an insured to produce its records may lead to cancellation of coverage by the insurer.

An insured also has certain duties in the event of loss or suit. When an insured voluntarily makes any payment or assumes any obligation for loss, the insured ultimately will have to assume these expenses. It is a condition of the policy that any such voluntary actions are at the insured's own cost.

The insurer, on the other hand, agrees to provide the insured with a certain number of days advance notice if the policy is to be canceled. The insurer also promises that the insurance automatically is assigned to a legal representative of an individual, as named insured, who dies.

Policy Territory. The territorial scope of completed operations insurance is not nearly as broad as it is for products liability insurance. In fact, the primary difference between those two coverages is that completed operations insurance is not worldwide in scope. Exposures are covered within the United States, its territories and possessions, Canada, and in international waters and airspace. International waters are especially important to the entity that builds all or portions of offshore oil towers.

The reason completed operations insurance is not worldwide is that firms that build in foreign countries need to obtain special liability insurance. However, firms do receive a certain amount of protection under umbrella liability policies, but only over large deductibles.

Nonstandard Coverages

Nonstandard coverage innovations of completed operations exposures are not as prevalent as with products exposures. One probable reason is that, in terms of magnitude, completed operations are capable of producing greater loss exposures to the work and to other property potentially affected by that work than products, in many cases. Another reason may be that the opportunities for implementing various loss prevention and control devices are more difficult at work sites than at places of product manufacture. Price and demand also have something to do with the lack of innovations, because unique coverages frequently are devised, if a demand exists for them. But, unless their prices, deductibles, and other conditions precedent to coverage are reasonable, those coverages will not be sold. Two types of nonstandard coverage—structural defects coverage and insurance for injury to completed work—are discussed as follows.

Structural Defects Coverage   One of the few nonstandard forms of protection with which some insurers and home builders' associations are experimenting is coverage dealing with structural defects of dwellings. Those involved are offering buyers of used homes in certain select areas protection for a limited duration in the event the dwellings are determined to be structurally unsound, or to contain defective electrical, plumbing, and heating systems.

Those experimenting with this coverage obviously are proceeding with caution. One reason is that used homes, having been lived in for any number of years, are less apt to produce as many defects as newly built homes, aside from normal wear and tear, settling, and cracking. This does not necessarily hold true with electrical, plumbing, and heating systems, but this protection is not offered unless the homes are fully inspected first. Also, the market here deals with dwellings rather than commercial buildings, because the potential magnitude of loss emanating from commercial buildings obviously is greater. And, finally, the duration of protection is being limited to periods of one year or less.

Whether this type of protection ever will be widespread remains to be seen. But, considering the number of insurers that have entered and then left this market over the years, it appears unlikely that a definite market will continue to exist.

Insurance for Injury to Completed Work[30]   One of the rare occasions when insurance protection is given for loss within the injury to work performed exclusion is the insurance program available to members of the Mechanical Contractors Association of America. This coverage, designed by R. B. Jones, Inc., and its affiliate, Illinois R.B. Jones, Inc., provides member contractors with liability protection for injury to work performed by them, following its completion.

Coverage, however, is contingent on loss or damage that (1) arises from completed work on or after the retroactive date of the policy, which generally is considered to be the first inception date of coverage; (2) occurs within five years of completion; and (3) is reported during the policy period, and no other valid and collectible insurance is available to the insured.

Not covered under this insurance program is damage to property owned by, rented to, or leased to the insured; insolvency or bankruptcy of the insured or any other firm or organization; dishonest, fraudulent, criminal, or knowingly wrongful acts or omissions committed intentionally by or at the direction of any insured; and property damage arising out of any professional services performed by or for the insured. This coverage also is subject to a deductible on a per-claim basis.

NONINSURANCE TECHNIQUES FOR HANDLING PRODUCTS LIABILITY EXPOSURES

The first task of risk managers is to identify and analyze the firm's loss exposures. Having done so, they should then determine whether some other technique(s)—avoidance, control, transfer, or retention— may be appropriate as substitutes or complements to insurance. Certainly, with the types of exclusions commonly found in products liability insurance policies, various combinations of noninsurance techniques will be essential. Products liability insurance is not enough— it should be used along with other techniques.

From the standpoint of manufacture, distribution, and sale of goods or products, virtually all of the noninsurance techniques are being used to some degree, in part because of the product liability crisis and the difficulty of obtaining insurance at an affordable price.[31] But most firms continue to rely upon insurance, and some do so without giving sufficient attention to loss control and other noninsurance techniques, which is undoubtedly one of the reasons why products liability insurance is so expensive today. As one corporate insurance director stated in reference to products liability:

> Insuring potential loss is not the answer, because insurance adds premiums to existing costs. And, after losses are paid, the loss expenses are transferred to other insureds, frequently doing nothing to root out the underlying causes of losses. Further, the exposures seem so catastrophic in nature that it is doubtful that adequate coverage can be obtained at a reasonable cost.[32]

Also, some products liability exposures are not insurable at any price. They must be retained unless they can be avoided in the first place.

Avoidance of Products Exposures

Avoidance, as a noninsurance technique, can take one of two forms. One is where a firm never creates the exposure. For example, a pharmaceutical firm decides against the production of a new drug product because of the potentially severe repercussions that can result from claims and suits and the unavailability of adequate insurance. Another example is the firm that decides against expanding into an unrelated field, such as the production of paints or toys, because high loss frequency, large court judgments, and sharp increases in insurance premiums would be likely. The approach of never creating an exposure was, until the 1970s, seldom practiced because most losses could be covered by insurance at reasonable prices. Today, the public is more claims conscious, courts are more generous with judgments, federal agencies are more stringent in upholding the laws to protect the public, liability of product producers and sellers is nearly absolute, and liability insurance, as an aid to handling products loss exposures, is becoming very costly.

The second form of avoidance is where a firm already has an exposure and decides to eliminate it. An actual situation in the early 1970s involved the makers of certain diet soft drinks containing cyclamates as a sugar substitute. Following a series of tests by a federal agency over a long period, it was determined that the consumption of cyclamates in very large quantities could be a cause of cancer. The Federal Food and Drug Adminstration therefore halted the production of diet soft drinks containing cyclamates. The avoidance of that exposure, though federally imposed, was eventually overcome when soft drink manufacturers substituted saccharin for cyclamates.

Products liability exposures sometimes present so serious a threat that a firm has no other choice than to avoid them altogether by going out of business. Havir Manufacturing Company, a builder of punch presses, is believed to be one of the first to take that approach voluntarily. That firm had seventy-five employees and annual sales between $2 and $3 million based upon production of about 1,000 punch presses annually. Two major problems confronted Havir. First, it was being sued by individuals who were operating some of its 25,000 punch presses that were sold prior to 1969. In fact, some of the lawsuits against it involved punch presses that were thirty years old. Havir's second problem was that its products liability insurance became too expensive to purchase. Its bids for insurance had an annual average price of $150,000 for $500,000 coverage and a minimum deductible of $5,000. The company executives decided that since matters would get worse before they would improve, the only alternative was to liquidate the business.[33]

Control of Products Exposures

Loss control is an indispensable technique, whatever the exposure. Control most frequently takes the form of measures which are aimed at reducing the frequency and/or the severity of losses. However, separation and combination can be viewed as forms of control. Separation involves the division of loss exposures into smaller, more manageable units. Decentralizing the operations of a manufacturer is an example. By keeping the operations separated, it may be easier to pinpont areas of high loss frequency or severity and take corrective measures. Combination, as a form of control, involves the combining of many units of exposure to enhance the predictability of losses. For instance, a manufacturer may be able to acquire or consolidate with another manufacturer in order to maintain an operation that is large enough to predict its losses more accurately.

Products liability loss control measures are viewed as positive approaches to minimizing the financial impact of loss costs of the products themselves. Firms should exercise special precautions to see that their products are free from defects and reasonably safe for their intended purposes. By implementing workable standards and control measures, firms may be able to reduce their products liability loss exposures, and, hence, their insurance costs. Taking positive steps to reduce or control losses also should help in the defense of suits which arise from product injury or damage.

Company Policy and the Role of Management and Personnel No products loss control program, however carefully structured, will produce results, unless it has the backing of top management and personnel at all levels. One of the first requirements, many experts believe, is to establish a written policy on the objectives of the loss control program. All personnel should be made to understand their role in maintaining the quality of products.

In order to assure a properly coordinated loss control program, many firms are establishing products reliability or safety committees that include top management personnel from research, production, sales, industrial relations, legal services, purchasing, engineering, and risk management. It is the committee's function and responsibility to develop the corporate policy on loss control and see to it that line and staff responsibilities are carefully communicated and executed. Each committee member usually is directly involved in the production of a safe product from the time it is first researched and designed to the time when the product is ready for sale.[34]

Since motivation also is an essential characteristic of a workable loss control program, it has been suggested that a program be related "in terms of profits and bonuses for management personnel and wages and jobs for the work force," because this is language everyone understands. Complementing this approach, an internal cost control program also is advisable, so that employees know what their efforts are doing to reduce losses. Each department and division can then be rewarded or penalized, depending upon its successes or failures.[35]

Implementing Effective Loss Control Measures Effective loss control is an expensive and a complicated undertaking involving every facet of the manufacturing process. As Figure 4-6 shows, products liability suits arise from all phases of the manufacturing process, and loss control measures should form an integral part of design and engineering functions, manufacturing and assembly, including materials and components, advertising and sales literature, warranties, packaging, instruction manuals, and sales, service, and parts.

While this discussion deals with loss control measures of manufacturers, some of the measures also can apply to wholesale distributors, dealers, and retailers that package or assemble goods, such as heavy equipment dealers and bicycle shops.

Design and Engineering. Since the function of design and engineering primarily is devoted to the planning, designing, and testing of new products, it is considered to be one of the more crucial of all functions in the manufacturing process. It stands to reason that if a product is improperly designed or inadequately tested, it is seldom possible to prevent an exposure to loss, even though the product is manufactured and assembled according to all specifications of the design plan.

In planning and designing a product a manufacturer should keep in mind that a safe product is not one which it believes to be safe, but what the average consumer believes to be safe. Manufacturers, some have suggested, practically have to make their products "idiot proof" to avoid any complications following the sale of their products.[36]

It is nearly impossible to anticipate all the possible uses and abuses to which products may be subjected, particularly durable goods with use expectancies of many years. It is also difficult to design and produce a competitively priced product that will meet the standards of safety of the future. Consider the example of the punch presses that were sold as long as thirty years ago. Though the presses were properly designed and manufactured by the then existing standards, the manufacturers of those old machines are now being held legally accountable for injuries to machine operators because the machines did not have the safety controls on them that are currently required.

This particular trend runs counter to the customary precautions that manufacturers have been following for years. Industrial products have been designed according to the specific standards of government or industry; or, when specific standards were lacking, manufacturers, to be safe, were required to search out unwritten standards referred to as "customs of the industry." In some cases, standards had to be disregarded altogether because they were not keeping pace with technological changes. Manufacturers in these situations have been required to design economically feasible products corresponding to the "current state of technological knowledge." Yet, in spite of all the care exercised by manufacturers, they are still being held liable for injury stemming from their products from a variety of causes, including negligence of the product users.[37]

Figure 4-6

Where Product Liability Suits Arise*

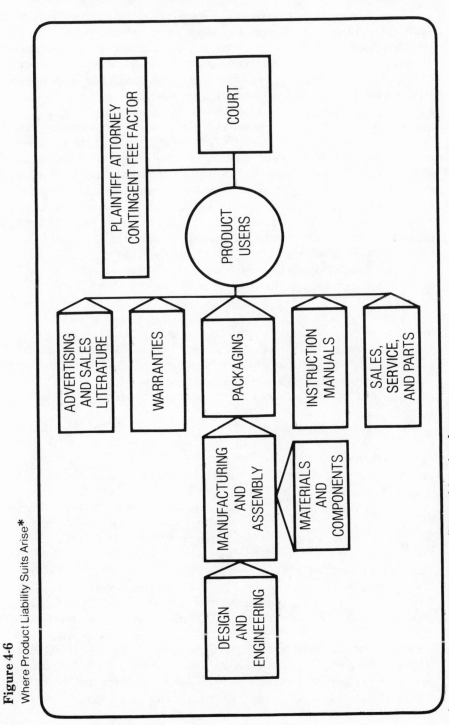

Manufacturing and Assembly, Including Materials and Components. Following the design and testing of what a manufacturer considers to be a safe, reasonably priced, and usable product, the next crucial step in the production process involves the actual manufacturing of the product, usually with raw stock or component parts supplied by others. This is a crucial stage, because an otherwise properly designed and tested product still can produce adverse exposures when it is improperly manufactured or incorrectly assembled.

It is impractical to provide any detailed discussion on the elements of the manufacturing process. However, the following points commonly are considered to be fundamental to the average exposure: (1) quality control on incoming goods, (2) proper storage of materials and component parts, (3) spot checks during the manufacturing process, (4) need for records on critical parts, (5) control of rejects or reworked items (large amounts of reject materials along the assembly line should be an indication that something is inherently wrong with the system), (6) full testing before shipment, (7) proper marking of products or containers, and (8) the need for modifications of products and the effects of such modifications.[38]

The importance of properly handling, inspecting, and testing raw materials of others that are transformed into a finished product, or component parts of others that are assembled as part of a complete product cannot be overemphasized. Exposures to loss from materials and components confront many manufacturers, since many do not desire to produce a product in its entirety and some would be incapable of doing so.

The average American-made automobile, for example, consists of over 7,000 parts, ranging from the frame, engine block, fuel tank, and sheet metal pieces to the nuts, bolts, and rivets. While any one of those parts may be faulty or may malfunction, it has been stated that approximately 2,000 parts of an automobile may relate to the cause of accidents and to injuries.[39] Producers of automobiles, as well as of other products that use components in order to assemble the complete product should be just as careful about handling components as they are about handling products or parts of their own manufacture.

Furthermore, the overwhelming weight of case law clearly shows that a manufacturer can be held accountable for damages stemming from the components of others. The rule is that if a defective component is incorporated into a product of another manufacturer and the defect could have been discovered by conducting reasonable tests and inspections, the manufacturer of the ultimate product can be held liable if the inspections or tests were not performed or were performed negligently. The manufacturer can be held liable for damages in tort, by breach of warranty and, in some states, by strict liability in tort.[40]

Advertising and Sales Literature. A firm whose product is properly planned, designed, tested, manufactured, and assembled, can still face tremendous exposures to loss when its advertising or sales literature is misleading or lacks sufficient warning or instructions. It is for this reason that sales literature and advertising should be coordinated with the engineering, legal staff, or products safety committee to see that all material clearly represents the use and capabilities of the product.

As difficult as it often is to sway consumers in a competitive marketplace, manufacturers must be extremely careful not to make statements in their advertising that are exaggerated or untrue. Costly losses have all but eliminated the practice of manufacturers describing their products in such absolute terms as "safe" and "foolproof." The misuses of advertising seals of approval also have caused difficulties. In his testimony before the National Commission on Product Safety, Irving D. Gaines, a Milwaukee attorney, said about advertising seals:

> The public is lulled into a sense of security by these so-called "seals of approval." The consumers of this nation would be appalled to learn that most anyone who contracts with *Good Housekeeping* and *Parents' Magazine* for a stipulated amount of annual advertising in their publications can usually obtain the "seals of approval" for their product in the same package.[41]

Many products, particularly durables, cannot be designed and produced to withstand all unforeseeable or even foreseeable abuses, nor can they be built to operate without the exercise of some special precautions. It therefore is important that sales literature, advertising and warranties be made to communicate precisely what products can and cannot do, and what must be done to operate or use them safely. The advertising division of manufacturers should make this point clear to all of its personnel, to its outside advertising firms, and to all of its distributors and retailers.

Warranties. Since the various kinds of warranties and their nature were discussed in Chapter 3, it is not necessary to dwell on their ramifications here. It is important to note that when statements in advertising and in sales literature are held to be warranties, the results can be damaging to manufacturers. Thus, care in the wording and use of warranties is an important element in any products loss control program.

Packaging. Product packaging provides a double-barreled exposure. A package is both used as a container for a product and considered to be a product itself. Paper product containers usually do not present too many problems. But packaging takes in a wide spectrum of uses, including containers for liquids, flammables, and heavy expensive machinery. What all of this means is that the design, production, and advertising of packaging is just as important as the requirements of any other product. If a package is defective or not suitable for its intended purposes as designed or advertised, the package can give rise to a products liability loss.

Instruction Manuals, Sales, Service, and Parts. Instruction manuals may relate to the installation, operation, maintenance, service, or repair of products. Their purpose is to assist persons in learning about the product, how it is made, how it works, and what to look for and to avoid. To this end, there are several basic points that should be considered in preparing such manuals.

1. What may appear clear to the technical writer of the manual may not necessarily be clearly understood by others. Terminology and language, therefore, should be used with the consumer in mind.
2. Reference should be made to standards and codes which govern the installation and operation of the product.
3. Instructions should emphasize the critical and/or procedural steps that are important in minimizing start-up or final operation failures.
4. Appropriate warnings may be neecessary when materials are flammable or hazardous.
5. Pictures and photos may be necessary to illustrate the product with proper guards and an operator wearing protective gear.[42]

Since the function of product service affects completed operations loss exposures, a considerable amount of competence is required of service personnel; and, of course, there should be a good rapport between such personnel and the manufacturer. Since those who install or service products usually are the first to know whether a product is not functioning properly, they should be the first to notify the manufacturer. In fact, early identification of product difficulties will not only control the size of problems but also will reduce the expenses that usually accompany them. Training, competence, and a direct line of communication between service personnel and the manufacturer therefore is considered necessary.[43]

Record Keeping. Maintaining records is a key factor in any loss control program, whether an entity produces the whole product or only a component and regardless of how sophisticated its loss control program may be. To be effective, records normally should be kept on all materials that go into the product, including the components of others, and on the quality control standards of the entire manufacturing process, from research, design, and testing to sales and service. It also is vital that these records be maintained for at least the anticipated use expectancy of the product.

Records are essential in any loss control program, for at least three reasons:

1. They can be used in locating the division or department and the source of the production process that consistently causes the production of poor-quality products that have to be rejected or recalled, or that cause a frequency of similar losses. Records, for example, may show that the component of a supplier was not properly tested before being used, or that proper quality control standards were not maintained as required during the production process. Without records, it may be impossible to determine problem areas, or possible only at considerable expense.
2. They can facilitate the systematic withdrawal of products from the market or from use when they are known or suspected of being defective or unreasonably dangerous.
3. Records also can serve as post-loss measures in aiding firms with the defense of lawsuits. In the majority of cases, manufacturers do not learn about their products liability losses until they are served with a summons and a complaint. When this happens, manufacturers must move quickly to produce detailed records which will enable their attorneys to prepare their cases. The more comprehensive the records, the easier it is for manufacturers to support their arguments. Many manufacturers have won cases with records by illustrating that it was not their product which caused injury or damage but negligence of the user.

Product Recall Programs. Since a producer of products can control but not entirely eliminate its exposures to loss without going out of business, the potential always exists for actual or threatened claims or suits. And, while a firm's loss control program may be effective in locating and correcting the source of problems, a firm cannot afford to ignore the further threat of loss from products which are in use. What an entity needs to complement its loss control program, therefore, is an organized system of communicating and, if necessary, of recalling its products from the market or from use. This system must be so structured that notice of a defective or unreasonably unsafe product can be given to distributors, retailers, and customers as promptly as possible. It also must be organized to facilitate, if necessary, the prompt, orderly withdrawal, inspection, repair, or replacement of products that are known to be or suspected of being harmful.

Organizing and maintaining an effective product recall program can be an expensive proposition. Yet, if the initiative is not taken to implement such a program, the repercussions can be far-reaching, whether a firm handles its products loss exposures with a funded retention program and/or with products liability insurance. Furthermore, the whole purpose of a loss control program is defeated if measures are not taken to prevent or reduce losses from exposures that are known to exist. Consumers also can lose confidence in a firm that does not seem to care enough about the safety of its own products. If a product comes within the jurisdiction of the Consumer Product Safety Act, a firm also faces serious penalties for any failure to comply with the commission's requirements dealing with the notification and the withdrawal of products.

Manufacturers realize that product recalls can be damaging to their image, if only by the implication that something is wrong with their quality control standards. But, in one study on the subject of product recalls, the two authors, George Fisk and Rajan Chandran, maintained that recalls can be viewed as an opportunity rather than a threat, for the following reasons:

> First, the ability to show that a product safety problem is being handled professionally can be proof that quality control systems work to protect the customer even after the product is sold. Service after sale offers many unexploited opportunities for extending customer loyalty. An excellent example is American Motors "Buyer Protection Plan": the company recalls and repairs manufacturing defects at company expense—even providing the customer, in some cases, with a replacement car and lodging expenses for the duration of the repairs. These services, highlighted in creative advertisement, have not only helped AMC's image but have enlarged its market share as well.
>
> Second, a product traceability and recall system, along with good quality control procedures, can provide a good-faith legal defense in many product liability cases.
>
> Third, a product traceability and recall system can also help a manufacturer understand his distribution system better. For instance, recall strategies offer an opportunity to devise a reverse and backward channel of distribution for recycling wastes—a goal of many ecologists.
>
> Fourth, a system can enable the manufacturer to keep in touch with the consumer. Companies expend great effort and skill to determine what customers will buy, but they rarely find out whether customers are harmed by the product after purchase. For example, no effort has been made to recall "clogs" (high platform shoes), despite repeated warnings by leading doctors about their hazards and news reports of broken and twisted ankles.
>
> Fifth, a product traceability system can supplement a test program under direct factory control. The findings of a test program, in conjunction with field usage studies, can be valuable in developing better products in the long run.[44]

In spite of those suggested measures which possibly can produce opportunities for manufacturers, it has been argued that

> ... recall campaigns, contrary to the expectations of some writers, will not allow the manufacturer of a defective product, that may be unreasonably dangerous, to shift the risk of loss on a large scale simply by notifying consumers that their products have been recalled. The law has created a duty to recall that will in many instances prevent the manufacturer from shifting responsibility for his defective products to someone else.[45]

Fisk and Chandran also maintain that since speed is of the essence in recalling products, a firm should have a "predetermined structure and procedures" that can be implemented the moment the need arises to recall products. They suggest eight steps to consider in organizing a program to handle product recalls:

> 1. The first step is to set up an emergency recall organization. With advance planning, the trace and recall organization can go into action immediately.

> A vice president for product safety, who acts as the emergency coordinator, can head the organization. Regardless of the chief officer's title, the aim is to assign traceability and recall responsibility to a single individual who can begin notification and put the recall machinery into effect. The heads of the following departments—all part of the emergency organization—report to him: marketing (sales manager and salesmen), shipping and transportation, advertising and public affairs, manufacturing, finance and accounting, legal affairs, research and development, quality control, and consumer affairs. Each department should have specific responsibilities to fulfill.

> The organization should ensure that all members understand procedures and are properly trained to handle emergencies. They should review all systems involved and stage "mock recalls" to test communication within, and operation of, the system.

> 2. Upon discovering that a product is unsafe, a company must inform the CPSC [Consumer Product Safety Commission] immediately. Sometimes manufacturers fail to report cases because they fear litigation, but as ... mentioned earlier, such notification is required by law.

> 3. When informing the CPSC, dealers, or the public, specific notices are best. News releases should identify the product item, brand name, trademark, stores where the product is sold, and other relevant information.

> All forms of media, including personal letters in foreign languages to countries in which the product has been sold, should be used to disseminate warnings about the defective product.

> Ambiguous letters or news releases that do not spell out the product defect clearly may lull dealers and the public into a false sense of

security. This is one of the main reasons product owners have been unwilling to cooperate with manufacturers in having products repaired—even at the manufacturer's expense. In such cases, the CPSC has come down hard on these manufacturers and has requested changes in wording of letters or news releases.

Another strategy is to educate consumers through advertisements to report defects in products immediately. Providing a telephone number (either in instruction booklets or, in some cases, directly on packages or labels) that dealers and consumers can call in the case of safety-related problems also is advisable. The CPSC itself lists a number so that all potentially hazardous products can be reported to it anytime.

4. Manufacturer-dealer relations can be strengthened by telling all middlemen about imminent recalls. Since middlemen are usually the pivot between the public and manufacturers in a recall situation, their understanding and cooperation are crucial. Organizations that fail to extend this normal channel courtesy have had confused and angry middlemen on their hands. It is also advisable to inform key accounts with whom the manufacturer has direct dealings.

In a recall, middlemen will need clear instructions about product disposal. If they should return the product to the manufacturer, strategic collection points will facilitate efficient transportation for safe return. Well-defined control procedures can be instituted to prevent accidental reintroduction of recalled items as safe products. If items are to be destroyed that contain safely salvageable materials, another set of controls might be applied. If the items are to be repaired, the emergency organization can make sure that dealers have either replacement parts or the personnel to repair or replace them before announcing the recall. In this way, the entire system can be ready when the rush begins.

5. Resources permitting, retailers might be encouraged to establish their own testing laboratories to conduct extended usage studies in their areas. Sears and Penney's have such laboratories and they occasionally find defects overlooked by a manufacturer's quality control laboratories.

6. A product traceability system should also include up-to-date field reporting by salesmen. Accurate performance data about usage patterns and extended use characteristics are essential for prompt action. Analysis of salesmen's reports will also indicate potential problems which can lead to design changes. Obtaining this information requires careful preplanning, however.

Perhaps salesmen can be rewarded for reporting all product-related accidents to their supervisors. Often salesmen forget or tend to overlook accidents because they are not in the position to judge whether the mishaps result from peculiar circumstances or product defects and how serious a particular situation may be.

In the case of emergency recalls, a company might seek the help of its competitors and their salesmen through industry trade associations.

Although rarely required, such help can be used, if mutually agreed upon in trade meetings.

7. The legal and financial departments should continually review the need for documenting evidence of product-related accidents. They may also consider implications of court decisions and new legislation.

8. It may be advisable to arrange for product recall insurance for both the manufacturer and the distributors, regardless of fault. Some companies have group programs available to all their distributors, so that they may buy insurance at cheaper rates.[46]

Whether a product has to be recalled depends upon a number of factors. At Sears, Roebuck & Company, the product safety committee assesses the seriousness of the exposure and decides whether the product should be recalled, replaced or repaired. If the potential exposure to the public is minimal, a "stop shipment order" may be sufficient. If, on the other hand, the exposure is minimal but additional sales could increase the exposure, a "stop selling order" may be issued. If the ultimate decision is to recall products, the action taken will depend on the procedures of "advance planning, speed and accuracy."[47]

Record keeping, mentioned earlier, is also an essential part of any product recall program. One reason is that records can help identify the particular batch or serialized group of products that need to be recalled, repaired or replaced, as well as the distributors and the geographical areas of sale. As a product is designed, produced, tested, coded, and shipped, records should be made and retained at all stages. Depending upon the product, sales invoices of distributors and retailers may be useful in identifying buyers of that product. Otherwise, other media will have to be used to put consumers on notice. The second reason recordkeeping is important is that it is a prerequisite to purchasing products recall insurance.

Space does not permit an in-depth exploration of all facets of loss control. Moreover, the levels of exposures that can be controlled, the mechanisms required to control them, and the costs of actually implementing controls are variables that differ for each firm. Some firms can afford safety committees, a staff of loss prevention engineers, a full-time risk manager, and all types of sophisticated measures to handle their product liability exposures. Others must do the best they can with available resources, including the services provided by insurance companies.

Regardless of the intensity of loss control efforts, losses still will occur. Accordingly, firms should have the foresight to determine how the losses should be handled by yet other techniques.

Noninsurance Transfer of Products Exposures

Manufacturers, distributors, and retailers sometimes find the technique of noninsurance transfer helpful in dealing with some or all of their products liability loss exposures. This technique can be employed in one of two ways. First, the activity that produces a particular exposure can be transferred to another entity. And, second, the financial consequences of an exposure, rather than the activity that produces the exposure, can be transferred to another.[48]

An example of the first method, involving the transfer of an activity-producing exposure, is the manufacturer of a particular component or ingredient that discontinues its production and hires another firm to produce the product instead. Or, faced with too great a products liability loss exposure and no economically feasible means to handle it, a firm may decide to transfer its production exposure entirely by selling out to another firm. Note the distinction here between the noninsurance techniques of transfer and avoidance. In a transfer, the activity, its loss exposure, and potential financial consequences continue to exist. The only difference is that the exposure now confronts the entity that accepts the transfer of that activity. With avoidance, the exposure either is not created in the first place, or is eliminated in its entirety.

An example of the second method of transfer, involving only the financial consequences of an activity-producing exposure, is the wholesale distributor or retailer that contractually transfers its potential financial loss, from a product it handles or sells, to the manufacturer of that product. The vendors liability insurance form and the purchase order agreement are two of the more common tools for effecting this type of transfer.

The vendors form, as mentioned earlier, is purchased by the manufacturer for the benefit of wholesalers and retailers which handle and sell its products. If a wholesaler or a retailer is confronted with a loss that is covered under the terms of the vendors form, the manufacturer's products liability insurer will protect such vendor as an additional insured. When a manufacturer handles its products liability loss exposures by means of retention, comparable arrangements can be made for protecting its vendors. In either case, the wholesaler or the retailer still is involved in the activity-producing exposure of handling and selling products, but at least part of any financial consequences stemming from that exposure are transferred to the manufacturer.

Under a purchase order agreement, a manufacturer agrees to hold harmless its distributors in the event of loss stemming from the manufacturer's products. The activity-producing exposure still remains with the wholesaler or the retailer, but the financial consequences of that exposure are transferred to the manufacturer to the extent of the contractual assumption. The manufacturer can protect itself, in turn, by the purchase of contractual liability insurance.

Retention of Products Exposures

As noted earlier, many firms rely upon insurance to handle most of their products liability loss exposures. Even so, retention necessarily plays an important role, because some products liability loss exposures are uninsurable at any price, whereas others are insurable only at a price that management feels is prohibitive.

A survey on business attitudes toward risk management conducted by Hogue and Olson involved 1,143 businesses in construction, manufacturing, transportation, wholesale, retail, and service organizations. The survey shows that entities are willing to absorb some of their uninsured losses without establishing reserves, for the following reasons:

1. Sixty-four percent stated that if reserves were set aside, investments in other business activities would have to be avoided.
2. Sixty-one percent maintained that loss costs can be absorbed with working capital.
3. Twenty-three percent stated that contributions that are made to reserves are not tax deductible.
4. Only nine percent gave the reason that generally accepted accounting principles do not permit the deduction of contributions to such reserves for stockholder reporting purposes. The survey also notes that only the larger firms are apt to give this last reason, and those firms only account for four percent of the entities represented in this survey.[49]

Although this survey was not confined to businesses confronted with products liability loss exposures, it is reasonable to infer that among firms which elect or are forced to retain products liability losses, many would not do so with funds set aside in advance.

Whether firms can *safely* use the technique of total retention for handling products liability exposures is open to question. If there is no other reasonable alternative, many firms will attempt it. Total retention might even force some firms to practice better loss control and manufacture safer products. Furthermore, there has been a general trend, during the past several years, toward the greater use of retention.

As a result, many insurers and independent firms now offer to design retention programs, as well as to provide loss control and general administrative services. Eventually, it may become somewhat easier for firms to implement the retention of products liability losses.

However, in spite of the pressures created by the unaffordable price of products liability insurance and the growing availability of outside assistance to administer formal retention programs, the dangers of totally retaining products liability losses should be carefully considered. If a firm does not have sufficient working capital or cash flow to pay the losses which occur, the firm could easily become bankrupt overnight. Advance funding could help soften the impact of losses, but, for reasons mentioned earlier, many firms prefer not to fund for losses in advance. There is also the inescapable fact that products liability verdicts or settlements, individually or collectively, can be virtually unlimited in amount. Thus, even if a firm wanted to fund for losses in advance, there can be no real assurance that the fund would turn out to be adequate. Partial retention would be a far superior alternative, assuming some sort of excess insurance is available to the firm. If excess insurance is not available or is not available at a reasonable price, the executives of the firm face a real dilemma. They should at least understand that the entire business is at stake.

NONINSURANCE TECHNIQUES FOR HANDLING COMPLETED OPERATIONS EXPOSURES

With some notable exceptions, noninsurance techniques do not seem to be very widely used for handling completed operations exposures. One probable reason is that most completed operations exposures can be transferred to insurers at costs that are still regarded as being reasonable in light of other alternatives. Also, many construction and service-oriented firms are small and they cannot or will not implement control measures.

Of course, there are some construction firms that are large enough to hire full-time risk managers and loss control engineers. But most small and medium-sized firms rely upon agents, brokers, consultants, and insurance companies for expertise and direction.

The fact that a firm does not have its own risk manager does not obviate the need to analyze and implement various techniques. These functions still need to be performed by someone, if only to increase the efficiency of the business, and to preserve the future market for its insurance protection.

Avoidance of Completed Operations Exposures

Avoidance, in terms of not creating an exposure in the first place, is not something that is practiced, because construction and service organizations usually have little control over the creation of completed operations exposures. Their only choice is to accept the work to be completed and the exposures that follow, or to reject the work. When rejected, the exposure ultimately will continue to exist to the entity eventually found to perform that work. The only possible exception is when the owner of the project also is the construction firm. If the exposure to be completed and to be sold is too severe, the entire project may be terminated before work commences, thereby avoiding the exposure altogether.

The second approach to avoidance, whereby an entity must eliminate its exposures because of difficulties, particularly financial in nature, is quite common. Many construction firms are forced to liquidate following completion of their work in spite of their insurance protection, because of severe losses involving the uninsured exposure of faulty work. By liquidating and filing bankruptcy, all outstanding completed operations exposures to loss are avoided. Another contracting firm might buy out the troubled entity, in these circumstances, but that would mean that the buyer also must assume the outstanding completed operations exposures which may not be wise.

Control of Completed Operations Exposures

The techniques of control are somewhat less manageable with completed operations exposures than they are with products liability exposures. This is partially because the work or service environment usually varies significantly from one job to the next. This does not mean that control techniques should be ignored. They should be used, even if work or service is performed by well-trained personnel. Firms that ignore control measures may find insurance protection difficult to obtain at at affordable price, and they may not be able to absorb uninsured losses, particularly when there is an unusual frequency or severity of losses.

Although most construction and service firms do not have to be concerned about many of the specific control techniques which are necessary for manufacturers of products, it may be necessary for the larger firms, at least, to practice comparable control measures when they perform design and engineering work on projects.

Noninsurance Transfer of Completed Operations Exposures

Construction firms often employ the technique of noninsurance transfer in dealing with completed operations exposures. Furthermore, this technique involves the same two forms of transfer that apply to products liability exposures. Thus, entities can transfer the activity-producing exposure of completed operations or the financial consequences of a completed operations exposure (or sometimes both).

In regard to the transfer of an activity-producing exposure, a frequent one is the general contracting firm that subcontracts portions of a work project to others such as those involved in plumbing, electrical, and masonry work. Another less common one, but nevertheless important, is the contracting firm that decides to sell out because one of the principals is in ill health.

General contractors frequently require that they be held harmless for completed operations exposures performed by others. Quite frequently, both forms of transfer can be effected under one contract, when a general contractor not only subcontracts the work activity but also requires that it be held harmless for any subsequent loss involving completed operations performed by others.[50]

Retention of Completed Operations Exposures

Since the basic principles of retention also apply to entities of completed operations exposures, it is not necessary to repeat them here. It is important to repeat that this technique must be employed by all entities confronted with completed operations exposures to loss, regardless of size, because not all such exposures can be transferred by insurance or handled by other techniques.

Regardless of the type or extent of retention, firms should do everything conceivably possible to reduce or control the amount of their losses. Every dollar of loss that must be borne means that one less dollar can be used for some other business purpose.

Chapter Notes

1. Bernard J. Daenzer, "Market Availability of Products Liability," *Excess and Surplus Lines Manual* (March 1976), pp. 8-10.
2. These two policies are discussed in Chapter 2.
3. Whittaker Corporation v. Michigan Mutual Liability Co., 1975 C.C.H. (Fire and Casualty) 817.
4. Lewis Card & Co. v. Liberty Mutual Ins. Co., 193 SE 2d 856.
5. 65 ALR (3d) 824.
6. Sun Ins. Co. of New York v. Hammanne Center, 306 A. 2d 786, held that the rental of a wallpaper machine was incidental to the business of a hardware store under the premises and operations coverage of its OL&T policy. This case also bears out some of the problems of determining when an operation is or is not incidental to a business.
7. If an OL&T coverage part were attached to the druggists liability form instead of the CGL coverage part, an exclusion of products liability would not be necessary, because the OL&T coverage part does not include products liability insurance. The only disadvantage of the OL&T coverage part is that its coverage is restricted to the ownership, maintenance or use of the insured's premises and to operations which are necessary or incidental to such business covered by that form. The OL&T coverage part therefore can handicap the druggist firm that desires to expand its operations into other unrelated business activities during the policy year. The CGL coverage part, on the other hand, permits other unrelated exposures during the policy period.
8. Umbrella liability policies are discussed in more detail in Chapter 2.
9. Liability of the named insured for damage to the steam turbine is not covered under products liability insurance, because of the exclusion of property damage to named insured's products. This exclusion is discussed later. It therefore is up to the owner of that turbine to settle with the manufacturer on the matter of damage to its turbine. However, if the owner has boiler and machinery insurance covering the turbine against breakdown or burnout, the matter of having to settle loss with the manufacturer of the turbine can be avoided. The owner, instead, can receive its settlement from the insurer of the boiler and machinery policy. It would then be up to the insurer to seek reimbursement of damages.
10. Loss of use of a product by its manufacturer, assembler, or vendor is not covered, because the exclusion of damage to named insured's products precludes it. On the other hand, the costs of withdrawing and/or destroying food products are not covered, because of the so-called sistership liability exclusion. That exclusion is explained in detail later.
11. The derivation of the term "sistership liability" is interesting. As explained by Norman Nachman, of ISO, in his 1972 study entitled *Products Liability Insurance*, "sistership liability" is terminology used by aircraft liability

insurers to signify the liability for damages that usually follows the withdrawal, inspection, repair, replacement or loss of use of aircraft, because of known or suspected defects. When one aircraft, for example, has a suspected defective condition because of its design or a production error, all like aircraft of the same manufacturer—all sister ships—also are grounded until they are fully inspected. Sistership liability therefore is an appropriate term for all kinds of products of manufacturers that must be withdrawn from the market or from use when they are known or suspected of being defective.

12. Examples are Gulf Insurance Co. v. Parker Products, Inc., 498 SW 2d 676; and Thomas J. Lipton, Inc. v. Liberty Mutual Insurance Co., 34 NYS 2d 356.

13. In fact, the definition of "contractual liability" of both the designated contracts and blanket contractual coverage parts specifically precludes any assumption of liability dealing with the fitness or quality of the named insured's products. The definition of "products hazard," on the other hand, includes bodily injury and property damage arising out of the reliance upon a representation or warranty made with respect to the named insured's products.

14. The storekeepers liability policy includes completed operations insurance as a built-in feature. However, this policy is not viewed as being a common, standard method for providing completed operations insurance for at least two reasons. First, only certain types of retailers can qualify for that package policy, and the ones that do qualify seldom have completed operations exposures. Second, an exclusion applies to any bodily injury or property damage arising out of the installation, servicing or repairing of heating or cooking appliances operated by gas or liquid fuel. Stores with that exposure, therefore, must obtain some other type of coverage, such as the CGL or the SMP policies.

15. The contractor responsible for that damage should have protection against its liability for damage to the adjoining building. But protection may or may not apply against damage to the structure under construction. Much depends upon the circumstances, and whether the CGL policy consists of more than the basic coverage provisions. If the contractor is doing all of the work and has a standard CGL policy with basic coverages, its protection against damage to the structure under construction should be precluded by two exclusions. The first is the exclusion of property in the care, custody, or control of the insured. The second, discussed more fully later, is the injury to work performed exclusion. Briefly, that exclusion applies to property damage to work performed by or on behalf of the insured, whether property damage arises out of the work, or out of materials, parts, or equipment which is furnished in such work. If that contractor has broad form property damage coverage (this also is discussed later) protection even may apply against damage to work performed by that contractor, other than damage to the particular property on which the contractor was working at the time of loss. When, on the other hand, that contractor is among several who are performing different work at the site of operations, protection should apply against damage to work performed by others, provided the damaged property is not in the care, custody, or control of the negligent contractor.

16. While the cause and result of bodily injury usually are simultaneous, it not always is possible to pinpoint the exact time at which property damage arises. An actual case in point is Villere v. Mook, 266 So. 2d 468. This involved a contractor who installed a lavatory and vanity that leaked for an unknown period before damage to property became evident after work was completed. The insurer denied coverage because the contractor did not have completed operations insurance. The court, however, upheld coverage for the contractor, because the insurer could not prove when the leakage actually commenced, i.e., while operations were in progress or after work actually was completed.

17. That subcontractor, however, only has protection against damage to work performed by others. Damage to its work thus far performed is not covered under the basic coverage provisions of the CGL policy because of the injury to work performed exclusion. That exclusion is discussed later in these pages.

18. Only fire damage to work of others is covered, and not damage to work thus far performed by the electrical subcontractor, because of the injury to work performed exclusion. If the general contractor should be brought into suit, because the electrical subcontractor was hired and was performing work on its behalf, the general contractor should be protected under its owners and contractors protective liability insurance of its CGL policy. The subject of owners and contractors protective liability insurance is discussed in Chapter 5.

19. The only loss subject to coverage of completed operations insurance, however, is injury to the passengers and to property of the building owner—other than the elevator. The elevator damage and any additional work required to repair or replace the elevator in a workable condition, being work performed by the named insured, are excluded by the injury to work performed exclusion. Note also that the elevator maintenance company might treat this exposure with a noninsurance transfer in the form of a hold harmless clause in its elevator maintenance contract with the building owner. The building owner's assumed liability would be covered by the building owner's premises and operations insurance as an incidental contract.

20. The exclusions of the CGL policy dealing with automobiles, aircraft, and watercraft are discussed in more detail in Chapter 2.

21. For example, it is the completed operations hazard of the CGL policy that encompasses loss arising from the erroneous delivery of liquid products into the wrong receptable or at the wrong address, if bodily injury or property damage occurs *after* such delivery is completed or abandoned. It does not matter whether that liquid product was delivered in a vehicle owned by the insured. There are two reasons for this. First, such loss has nothing to do with the vehicle or its operation, since it already has left the site of operations before the loss occurred. And, second, the completed operations hazard does not exclude such losses. In fact, the completed operations hazard is the proper means of covering those types of losses, because the comprehensive automobile liability policy, endorsed with the erroneous delivery of liquid products exclusion, precludes such losses after delivery has

been completed or abandoned. However, if bodily injury or property damage occurs before such delivery operations are completed, coverage is the subject of the comprehensive automobile liability policy, as an element of loading and unloading coverage. The subject of the CAL policy and the erroneous delivery of liquid products exclusions are discussed in more depth in Chapter 9.

22. This coverage is not suited to entities whose operations primarily are on their own premises. The reason is, one of the exclusions of the coverage endorsement applies to property while on premises owned or rented to the insured for purposes of having operations performed on such property by or on behalf of the insured. One of the few occasions when coverage may be useful to those entities is when some work is subcontracted to others.

23. Liability for physical damage to equipment and to the racing pit is covered under the completed operations coverage of that automobile repair shop's garage liability policy.

24. When the broad form property damage coverage endorsement is attached to the CGL policy, however, and both the endorsement and the policy include completed operations insurance, the injury to work performed exclusion applies only to work performed by the named insured. The named insured therefore is protected in a situation when damage arises out of completed, faulty work that was performed on its behalf.

25. However, if that contracting firm has broad form property damage coverage, including completed operations, and it uses subcontractors for that work, it would have protection, because property damage arising from completed work performed on behalf of the named insured is not excluded.

26. One probable reason may stem from the fact that until 1966, when liability policy provisions were revised substantially, the provision, which is presently known as the injury to work performed exclusion, often was held to be ambiguous. The ISO, then known as the National Bureau of Casualty Underwriters, stated that damage to all work performed was intended to be excluded, including work adversely affected by that damage. The courts in the majority of cases took the opposite view, holding that the exclusion only applied to the work out of which the damage arose. Damage to other work performed, therefore, was held to be covered. Some people who have not kept up with the changes in policy revisions are under the impression that the exclusion still applies that way.

27. Those who are interested in discussions of numerous court decisions upholding the intent of the injury to work performed exclusion are referred to *The F. C. & S. Bulletins, Casualty and Surety Volume*, pp. Public Liability Pri-1 to 8.

28. Warranties of the named insured's work are commonly thought of as being the subject of completed operations insurance, because most losses involve that coverage. However, losses involving warranties of work also can apply while operations are still in progress.

29. If the roofer had a maintenance bond that guaranteed the workmanship of the roof for one or two years, the roofer would still be required to redo faulty work from its own financial resources, because that bond merely guarantees that the roofer will make good any faulty work. If the roofer is

unable to correct the faulty work, the surety will then be required to pay for having the work done by someone else. The surety, however, still has a right of subrogation against the roofer to the extent of its payment under that bond. The subject of maintenance bonds is discussed in Chapter 13.

30. Wallace L. Clapp, Jr., *Specialty Coverage Market Reports*, October, 1976. This monthly publication, which is the source of information regarding that insurance program, is an excellent means for keeping informed on nonstandard coverage developments.

31. Paul R. Merrion, "No Nationwide Product Crisis, Reports Task Force," *Business Insurance*, Dec. 27, 1976, p. 1. This article reported that the Interagency Task Force on products liability, chaired by the Under Secretary of Commerce, conducted a three month study and reported the following conclusions to the Economic Policy Board: (1) While there is no widespread crisis, a number of small businesses are experiencing difficulties in choosing between the purchase of products liability insurance and going without that insurance altogether. (2) For the most part, the problem is one of affordability rather than availability. (3) Although premiums have increased between 100% and 500%, the increase in some cases has been as high as 1000%. However, most of the increased cost of products liability insurance is being passed onto consumers in the form of increased prices of goods.

32. Norman Hoffman, "Record Keeping To Reduce the Product Liability Risk," *Business Insurance*, Oct. 25, 1971, p. 33.

33. Susan Alt, "Product Liability Costs Force Machine Builder To Liquidate Company," *Business Insurance*, Oct. 25, 1975, pp. 1, 2.

34. Gerald L. Maatman, "Interpret Product Safety As Profit, Bonus," *Business Insurance*, Dec. 8, 1969, pp. 26, 34.

35. Ibid.

36. Paul C. Nelson, "Manufacturing Irregularities Often Crux of Product Cases: Attorney," *Business Insurance*, June 30, 1975, p. 3.

37. *Products Liability Reports*, Commerce Clearing House, Inc., 1971, p. 4733.

38. *Products Liability Loss Prevention Manual*, Chicago: Alliance of American Insurers [formerly American Mutual Insurance Alliance], August, 1976), pp. 11, 12.

39. Dennis D. Skogen, "Product Liability Claims Related To Automobile Accidents," p. 1.

40. 3 A.L.R. (3rd.) 1016.

41. "Product Safety Hearing Examines Seals, Advertising Claims," *Business Insurance*, March 17, 1969, p. 12.

42. *Products Liability Loss Prevention Manual*, pp. 20-22, 24-25.

43. Ibid.

44. George Fisk and Rajan Chandran, "How to Trace and Recall Products," *Harvard Business Review*, Nov.-Dec. 1975, p. 91.

45. David L. Ramp, "The Impact of Recall Campaigns On Products Liability," *Insurance Counsel Journal*, Jan. 1977, pp. 83-96.

46. Fisk and Chandran, pp. 94-95.

47. "Recordkeeping Key To Product Recall Program," *Business Insurance*, June 30, 1975, p. 3.

48. C. Arthur Williams, Jr. and Richard M. Heins, *Risk Management and Insurance*, 3rd. ed. (New York: McGraw-Hill, Inc., 1976), p. 189.
49. Michael E. Hogue and Douglas G. Olson, *Business Attitudes Toward Risk Management, Insurance and Related Social Issues* (Philadelphia: University of Pennsylvania Press, 1976), p. 98.
50. The subject of hold harmless agreements is discussed in depth in Chapter 5.

CHAPTER 5

Contractual and Protective Liability Exposures and Their Treatment

INTRODUCTION

Most of the past few chapters of this text have dealt with an entity's liability exposures arising out of its own acts or omissions. Business enterprises, too, may be legally liable for the acts or omissions of other entities. This chapter will first discuss the exposures arising out of liability assumed under contract—contractual liability—and insurance and noninsurance techniques that may be used to treat those exposures. Secondly, the chapter will analyze those loss exposures arising out of the acts of independent contractors—"protective liability"—and techniques for treating those exposures.

CONTRACTUAL LIABILITY EXPOSURES

The parties to a commercial transaction can often foresee the possibility that one or more of the parties involved could be held liable for bodily injury or property damage that may result in connection with the transaction. The parties to such a transaction often reach agreement as to which party will bear the exposure to loss and pay any damages for which either of the parties to the transaction might become liable. For example, the parties to the sale of a potentially dangerous product, or the parties to a construction contract, may decide that only one of them should bear the burden of any injuries, and will specify this in the sales agreement or contract. Municipalities ordinarily require an indemnity agreement before they will issue to a property owner a permit to build a vault under a sidewalk area—thus the property owner bears the exposure to loss. Such contractual indemnity provisions generally have no effect on the right of the injured person to sue either or both of the parties to the contract, and to obtain a judgment against either or both. They merely determine who shall be the bearer of the cost between those sued parties. Thus, the efficacy of such agreements is ultimately dependent on the ability of the indemnitor to pay.

As a general rule, the courts will enforce an agreement to transfer the exposure to liability loss, if it shifts the cost of ordinary negligence to a party that is voluntarily assuming the exposure. Usually, such provisions or agreements either *indemnify* the other party following a loss, or *exempt* a party from liability with respect to a certain matter. There are strong arguments both for and against such provisions, and the balance between these arguments has led to exceptions from the general rule permitting transfer of liability loss exposures. Specifically, the rule has been qualified in various ways, both by statute and by the courts, for reasons of "public policy."

Transfer of Liability Loss Exposures—Statutes and Decisions

Statutory limitations on transfers of liability loss exposures vary from state to state. In several states, statutes prohibit provisions indemnifying a party against its own negligence in a construction contract. The basic public policy underlying these statutes reflects a concern that indemnity agreements may encourage negligence. In other words, the legislators are concerned that a party who does not have to bear the cost of negligence will not be sufficiently careful. Another public policy often underlying the statutes is the desire to place the burden of loss on the party most able to bear the cost.

There are several kinds of *indemnity* agreements which the courts have been especially hesitant to uphold, particularly those involving (1) contracts of adhesion, (2) contracts with public carriers, and (3) employment contracts.

Contracts of Adhesion Contracts of adhesion are contracts in which one party drafts the instrument and the other party merely accepts it as written. The parties to such a contract almost invariably have unequal bargaining power. Where the courts fear that a party has been forced by an inferior bargaining position to assume liability for the stronger party's negligence, they will be extremely reluctant to uphold the contract. A disclaimer of liability printed in small type on the reverse side of a job order is a good example of a contract of adhesion unlikely to be upheld by the courts.

Contracts with Public Carriers It is also generally held that those engaged in public service may not properly bargain against liability for harm caused by their negligence in the performance of their public duties. A common carrier, for example, may not attempt to *exempt* itself from liability for the negligence of itself or its servants, because of a belief that such provisions would lower the standard of care. (The Interstate Commerce Commission does permit carriers to *limit* the dollar amount of their liability exposure for property damage, as discussed later in this chapter.)

Employment Contracts   In an employment contract, an employer may not attempt to exempt itself from liability for injury to its employees. This rule recognizes the courts' reluctance to lessen the employer's duty to keep the job area safe for its employees.

Other Considerations   In addition to these specific exceptions, contractual shifting of liability is restricted to liability for ordinary negligence. A party may not, as a general rule, exempt itself from liability for gross negligence or willful or wanton misconduct, or for the results of criminal conduct. Again, the concern is that such an indemnity would encourage reckless action.

While many indemnity agreements are considered contrary to public policy, this is counteracted by the basic right of freedom of contract. Courts encourage parties to make their own bargain and to allocate loss exposures in whatever manner makes sense to the parties involved. Courts are reluctant to make decisions about factors which are best judged by the parties to a contract at its inception.

Transfer of liability loss exposures theoretically will follow economic benefits, if the contract results from positions of equality in negotiation. Therefore, one reason for shifting liability may be that one party is unable to bear the cost if a contingency should occur, whereas the other party may be in a better position to pay for a loss. For example, a small company may not have the funds to pay large judgments or settlements which frequently result from the use of a defective product.

Liability loss exposures may also be transferred to budget costs—shifting of liability can serve the useful economic function of spreading costs. Most such transfers are imposed by one party on another because of *unequal bargaining positions*. A business generally will not be willing to assume the liability of another business unless (1) it had been in an inferior bargaining position and had to assume the liability in order to obtain or retain the other party's business, or (2) it was able to exact concessions which were worth more than the costs of contractual liability insurance or the anticipated costs of retaining the exposure.

Forms of Contracts

Contractual liability provisions may take various forms. The provisions may be tailored so that one party will assume liability for all or only a certain portion of a potential liability arising from a certain situation. For example, subcontractor S might agree to indemnify the general contractor for any liability the general contractor might incur for losses caused by S's own negligence. Thus, if an injured party recovers from the general contractor for injuries sustained as a result of S's negligence, the general contractor may, under its contract with S, be reimbursed.

Agreements are often broader than the contractual provisions discussed above. For example, an agreement could cover nearly all injuries arising out of a particular situation, including those resulting from the sole negligence of the indemnitee. Thus, if subcontractor S had executed such a broad agreement, it could be liable for a party's injuries whether they were caused by either S's or the general contractor's negligence.

A hold harmless or save harmless provision may not only indemnify a party for liability arising out of that party's sole negligence, but in some states may also involve the duty of the indemnitor to defend the indemnitee. If subcontractor S had executed an agreement of this type, S might be required to both defend and indemnify the general contractor, even for losses caused by the sole negligence of the general contractor.

Examples of Contracts and Agreements Which May Involve Tort Liability Assumptions

Liability loss exposures are often transferred in connection with construction contracts, purchase order and sales agreements, incidental agreements, and surety agreements.

Construction Contracts Construction contracts frequently include agreements by a party (usually the contractor) to indemnify another party (usually the owner) against tort liability resulting from a class or classes of occurrences specified in the contract. An example of a limited assumption of liability is the following portion of an indemnity provision which was at issue in the case of Continental Casualty Company v. Municipality of Metropolitan Seattle, 405 P. 2d 581 (Wash. 1965):

The contractor [General Construction] covenants...that he will indemnify [Metro]...from any loss, damage, costs, charge or expense whether...to persons or property to which [Metro]...may have been put...by reason of any act, action, neglect, omission or default on the part of [General Construction]....

In case any suit...shall be brought against [Metro]...on account of...any act, action, neglect, omission or default of [General Construction]...[General Construction] hereby covenants...to assume the defense thereof...and to pay any and all costs, charges, attorneys' fees and other expenses and any and all judgments that may be incurred by or obtained against [Metro]....

Assumptions such as the preceding may be valuable in limiting costs for protection against liability connected with construction projects, because they make unnecessary the purchase of full insurance by *both* parties. The purpose of these indemnity clauses was well stated by the New Jersey court in Buscaglia v. Owens-Corning Fiberglas, 172 A. 2d 703, 707 (N.J. 1961):

Indemnity clauses of construction contracts are to be viewed realistically as efforts by business men to allocate as between them the cost or expense of the risk of accidents apt to arise out of construction projects on a fairly predictable basis, rather than upon the generally debatable and indeterminate criteria as to whose negligence, if any, the accident was caused by, and to what degree....

Courts will uphold contractual assumptions of tort liability in construction contracts which are reasonable attempts to predict and allocate the costs of possible accidents associated with a construction project, especially where the assuming party assumes liability for actions, negligence or omissions connected with its own activities. Courts will also uphold intermediate assumptions, wherein the assuming party undertakes to hold the other party harmless for its partial or contributing negligence. In the Buscaglia case, an indemnity agreement provided that the contractor would hold the owner harmless from liability for accidents "occasioned by" the work being performed under the contract. The court found that the owner's negligence causally contributed to the accident, but that the indemnity provision was nevertheless effective to indemnify the owner against liability. The court reached this conclusion "in the light of the purpose and function which the clause was to play in regulating the allocation of costs and expenses as between [the owner and the contractor]." 172 A. 2d at 708.

Common Law. Under the common law, even a broad assumption of tort liability in a construction contract was effective and enforceable (and still is, where there has been no intervening statute).[1] Courts look to the language of the indemnity agreement, and have indemnified a solely negligent party when that obligation was within the scope of the indemnification agreement. The common law viewed broad indemnification agreements in construction contracts as part of a bargain between equally powerful parties, and therefore not in violation of public policy.

Statutes. As noted previously, the common law has been preempted in some states by enactment of statutes relating to the assumption of tort liability for another's negligence in the context of construction contracts. For example, a statute enacted in Illinois in 1971 voids indemnity agreements in construction contracts which hold a party harmless for its own negligence. The statute reads as follows:

> With respect to contracts or agreements, either public or private, for the construction, alteration, repair or maintenance of a building, structure, highway, bridge, viaducts or other work dealing with construction, or for any moving, demolition or excavation connected therewith, every convenant, promise or agreement to indemnify or hold harmless another person from that person's own negligence is void as against public policy and wholly unenforceable. *Ill. Rev. Stat.*, ch. 29 §61 (1975)

Similar statutes have been enacted in several other states.

The enforceability of a construction contract indemnification agreement which seeks to hold harmless a party for its own negligence is likely to vary from state to state. Therefore, an evaluation of the exposures in any particular situation must be based upon a knowledge of the law(s) which pertain(s) in the jurisdiction involved. Note that, if an agreement is unenforceable, any insurer which agreed to insure the assuming party for contractual liability would not be required to pay under the insurance contract, and liability would rest with the negligent party, despite the attempted assumption. This is a key point that will be reemphasized when contractual liability insurance is discussed later in this chapter.

Purchase Order and Sales Agreements Purchase order agreements and sales agreements generally involve the same considerations in evaluating the effectiveness and enforceability of tort liability assumptions. In addition, there are problems unique to such agreements.

First, a purchase order or sales agreement may include an assumption of tort liability as a result of the superior bargaining position of one party. When one party forces a shifting of liability to avoid having to bear any loss exposures, and when there are no economically or socially desirable advantages resulting from the assumption of liability, courts will usually try to avoid giving effect to the liability assumption agreement.

Second, purchase order and sales agreements also involve the possibility that a liability assumption will not come to the attention of the assuming party. Suppose, for example, it has been printed in small type on the back of the purchase order or sales agreement. If the entity assuming the burden is not aware of it, the provision usually will not be enforced.

The "Battle of the Forms." A contract for the sale of goods often will be embodied in two separate writings—a purchase order prepared by the purchaser and a sales document prepared by the seller. It is often the case that these writings include differing provisions, including inconsistencies as to which party may bear tort liability relating to manufacture or use of the goods which are the subject of the contract. Thus, a question arises, in view of the variation in terms, as to whether a contract has been formed and, if so, *which* terms are part of the contract. This has been described as "the battle of the forms."

Under the Uniform Commercial Code (UCC), when the parties have knowledge or skill peculiar to the practices or goods involved in a transaction, the seller's use of a form which includes terms additional to or different from terms included in the purchaser's purchase order may not prevent formation of a contract.[2] For example, if the seller's sales document contains a provision (not included in the purchaser's document) whereby the purchaser agrees to hold the manufacturer harmless for personal injury resulting from the purchaser's failure to install or properly assemble the product, that term would become a part of the final contract between the parties, *except* in one of the following three circumstances:

(a) the offer expressly limits acceptance to the terms of the offer;
(b) they materially alter it; or
(c) notification of objection to them has already been given or is given within a reasonable time after notice of them is received. UCC §2-207(2)

Thus, if the original purchase order states that the purchaser wants a contract to be formed only on the precise terms included in that order, the inclusion of additional terms may result in the failure to form a contract. Also, if additional or different terms materially alter the contract, no contract may have been formed. The question as to what constitutes a material alteration is a question of fact based on all the surrounding circumstances and the customs of the trade. For example, it is likely that a term in a seller's sales form shifting liability to the purchaser for negligence in the manufacture of a product would constitute a material alteration, and therefore would prevent a contract from being formed.

There is an important exception to the above UCC rules. If the conduct of both parties recognizes the existence of a contract, the UCC will hold a contract to have been established, *despite* the existence of material alterations in the seller's form or the other two circumstances which otherwise could lead to a finding that no contract has been created. In such a case, the terms of the particular contract will "consist of those terms on which the writings of the parties agree," plus those general provisions of the UCC which are needed to provide the essential terms of the agreement. UCC §2-207(3)

In summary, there is substantial uncertainty as to whether, in a contract for the sale of goods, an attempt by one party to shift tort liability to the other party will be effective. Such an attempt may result in one of the following: (1) there may be a failure to form a contract; (2) the shift may become a term of the contract; (3) if the liability shift materially alters the contract, but the parties nonetheless carry out the other terms of the contract, it will not be considered a part of the final agreement because the parties did not agree on that term; or, (4) even if it becomes part of the contract, it may be unenforceable as contrary to public policy.

Incidental Contracts Most general liability insurance policies do not cover the insured's contractual assumption of another's liability, unless the coverage is purchased for an additional premium. However, as noted in Chapter 2, nearly all general liability policies provide automatic coverage for liability an insured may assume under so-called incidental contracts. Therefore, it is desirable to consider separately the exposures which may be created by incidental contracts. These incidental contracts include:

1. lease of the premises;
2. easement agreement, except in connection with construction or demolition operations on or adjacent to a railroad;
3. undertaking to indemnify a municipality when required by municipal ordinance, except in connection with work for the municipality;
4. railroad sidetrack agreement; and
5. elevator or escalator maintenance agreement.

These incidental agreements or contracts basically represent ordinary situations which occur most commonly and, for the most part, are well defined over a long period of judicial precedent.[3] In any case, incidental contracts frequently contain liability assumption provisions, and the following discussion concerns the extent to which such provisions are enforceable at law. (Since insurance against incidental contracts is covered by most premises and operations liability policies, treatment of these exposures has already been discussed in Chapter 2.)

Lease of Premises. In leases, clauses limiting the liability of either party are usually upheld against challenges based on public policy. As a general rule, exculpatory provisions which do not violate public policy can effectively shift liability from lessor to lessee, or vice versa. However, a contrary result may be reached if there is a substantial disparity of bargaining power between the parties, particularly where the assuming party (usually the lessee) assumes liability for the negligence of the lessor.[4]

It is important to determine whether the legislature in a given state has acted to limit the ability of lessors to exculpate themselves from liability for their own negligence. For example, the following Illinois statute makes void and unenforceable certain agreements exempting lessors from liability:

> Every covenant, agreement, or understanding in connection with or collateral to any lease of real property, exempting the lessor from liability for damages or injuries to person or property caused by or resulting from the negligence of the lessor, his agents, servants or employees, in the operation or maintenance of the demised premises or the real property containing the demised premises shall be deemed to be void as against public policy and wholly unenforceable. *Ill. Rev. Stat.*, ch. 80 §91 (1975)

Significantly, this Illinois statute limits only the lessor, and it applies only to liability resulting from the lessor's own negligence (and the negligence of the lessor's agents and employees). It does not limit the lessor's ability to exempt itself from liability for damages or injuries resulting from the negligence of the lessee or other parties.

Easement Agreements. Easement agreements are entered into to allow one party the use of another's property for a specified purpose, or to limit the owner's use of his or her own property for the benefit of the other party. The easements with regard to which an indemnification agreement would be covered by the CGL policy would include, for example, use of another's driveway for access to a garage, emergency use by a city of a private alley, or use of a pathway across another's empty lot. In such a case, the party using the other's property would agree to indemnify the owner of the burdened property. Such an indemnity agreement generally is enforceable; however, it probably would not be enforceable, even if so specifically provided, if the sole or primary negligence of the owner of the burdened property caused the loss.

Municipal Indemnification. Many activities by private contractors introduce a possibility of damage or injury to nearby property and people. Often, municipalities are involved in such activities because the contractor is using public property or is disrupting public utilities, or because the city has chosen to regulate the activity. In other instances, the contractor may be working for the city, a situation which is not automatically covered by insurance, since the CGL policy specifically excludes coverage of indemnification liability in such circumstances.

Sometimes an indemnification agreement will be made between a municipality and a contractor, even though no ordinance requires such an agreement.[5] In those cases, liability is not covered under the standard CGL policy. However, when a municipal ordinance requires a contractor to indemnify the municipality, resulting liability will be covered under the contractor's CGL policy.

Municipalities frequently require indemnification for a number of activities. For example, Chicago has ordinances covering sidewalk and driveway builders (§33-47), fireworks display contractors (§125-29), roofers (§165-4), wrecking contractors (§43-20), and many others. Some of these ordinances require an indemnification bond in a specified amount, while others are more broadly drafted to require the contractor to make provision for large potential indemnification liability.

While in most cases indemnification required by ordinance would be clearly enforceable, some indemnification ordinances are so broadly drafted that they do not exclude indemnification for any loss incurred in connection with a given activity, regardless of causation. It would appear that a serious question exists as to the obligation of a contractor to indemnify, if the municipality itself is *solely* negligent. See De Vries v. City of Austin, 110 N.W. 2d 529 (Minn. 1961), and General Heating, supra at 555 (Miller dissent), where it was stated that:

> It is a general rule that an indemnity agreement does not protect the indemnitee from the consequences of his own independent negligence unless its language expressly provides for such indemnity. The intent to provide it must clearly and unequivocally appear.... 301 F. 2d at 555.

Thus, if the ordinance is ambiguous in that it fails to expressly provide for indemnification when the indemnitee is solely negligent, and no separate contractual agreement so provides, the indemnitor may not be obligated to indemnify.

Sidetrack Agreements. Another incidental agreement customarily containing a hold harmless provision is the agreement between a railroad and a private business for the construction and operation of a spur track or sidetrack from the railroad's main line to a factory or warehouse. In such agreements it is customary for the company desiring the spur track to indemnify or hold harmless the railroad from liability for personal injury or property damage resulting from the operation, maintenance or construction of the track.

In the usual sidetrack situation, the track will be constructed on land not owned by the railroad, and the service provided the company will be one which the railroad is not normally required to provide as part of its duty as a carrier. Hence, the railroad is in a strong position to attach such conditions as it sees fit in providing the special service. In addition, in the usual situation, the parties to the agreement are of relatively equal sophistication and have comparable bargaining power. Therefore, hold harmless or indemnification provisions in sidetrack agreements are generally enforceable, since they are not contrary to public policy.

Unlike the property lease situation, it is much more likely that a court would uphold a sidetrack provision indemnifying the railroad from liability for loss caused by its own negligence, if such were the intent of the parties as indicated in the contract. However, liability for willful or wanton acts could not be transferred.

Elevator-Escalator Maintenance. Building owners frequently enter into maintenance agreements with independent contractors to inspect and to maintain elevators in efficient and safe working condition. The maintenance agreement often requires the elevator owner or lessee to hold the maintenance company harmless in the event claims for personal injury or property damage are filed against the company.

Enforceability of the hold harmless provision, and therefore insurance company liability under the CGL policy, is not in doubt when the negligence causing injury or property damage was that of the elevator owner or lessee. This will often be the case, because the landlord usually has a better day-to-day knowledge of the condition of the elevators, particularly since tenants are more likely to report any problems to the landlord rather than to the maintenance company. If the landlord fails to act to remedy a known problem, particularly if the problem is serious or has persisted for a substantial time, and the maintenance company is sued for resultant injury or damage, the indemnification provision is clearly enforceable.

Even if the injury or damage is caused by the equal negligence of both parties, the indemnification provision will most likely be enforced in favor of the maintenance company. However, if the maintenance company's negligence is the immediate cause of the injury, or is substantially greater than the owner's or lessee's, there is serious doubt as to the enforceability of the hold harmless provision. For example, in Meltzer v. Temple Estates, 116 N.Y.S. 2d 546 (N.Y. 1952), the court refused to require indemnification where the party to be indemnified was more negligent than the indemnitor, and the indemnitee's negligence was the immediate cause of the injury.

Surety Agreements In general terms, a surety is one who is *primarily liable* for the debt or obligation of another.[6] A surety agreement thus involves three parties: (1) the *surety*, who is liable for (2) his or her *principal* (the debtor or obligor), who in turn is obligated to (3) the *obligee* or creditor. The liability of a surety is measured by and is strictly limited to that assumed by the terms of the surety agreement or "bond." (Corporate suretyship will be discussed in detail in Chapter 13.) In certain instances, however, surety agreements may involve the assumption of tort liability, and it is this aspect which will be reviewed here, under the headings of public officials and employees, public contracts, and private contracts.

Public Officials and Employees. The common indemnity statute for tort liability of state or local government employees or officials requires them to furnish a surety bond for the payment of judgments for damages caused by their negligence while engaged in the performance of governmental duties.[7] These statutes typically waive the governmental immunity of public employees for such torts, and require parties injured by such employees to file a notice of claim with the state or local governmental unit, and bring suit within a specific period of time. Often, however, the governmental body is permitted by statute to provide a defense for the employee.

Supporting these statutes is the theory that the indemnification of public employees against loss for torts committed in the performance of their official duties will encourage those employees to use their initiative and carry out fully the letter of the law, without fear of incurring liability. These statutes are also supported on the ground that they provide a source of monetary recovery for the general public against the negligence of public officials, who often would not otherwise have the personal resources to compensate injured parties. In accordance with these statutory policies, recovery is not permitted if the employee was guilty of willful and wanton misconduct, or if the injured party was contributorily negligent. It is also generally held that there is no right to recover punitive damages under these indemnity statutes.

Public Contracts. Duties arising under public bonds are determined by the statute defining the duty or are implied from the statute pertaining to the public office. The duties may not be modified between the obligor [principal] and obligee.[8]

Contractors who work on construction projects funded by public monies are often required by either federal or state statutes to furnish a contractor's bond. Unless the bond specifically covers claims for injuries to person or property caused by the negligence of the contractor in the performance of the contract, such tort claims generally are not considered to be part of the obligation covered by the contractor's bond, and the surety generally would not be held liable for such injury or damage.

Private Contracts. In contrast to the bonds of public officers or bonds for public projects, the terms of bonds given to secure the performance of private contracts are determined by the parties themselves. In some cases, however, a statute may require that a certain kind of bond be made to secure the performance of the contract. One example of a private bond is a bond given to secure "the faithful performance of duty" of a person employed in a position of trust. Such a bond operates as a security against all loss resulting from misconduct or the lack of care of the principal in fulfilling the duties of the position of trust.

So-called bonds of general indemnity encompass not only honesty in the performance of duty, but also the exercise of the reasonable skill and care expected under the contract of employment. For example, even though a bonded employee may be scrupulously faithful and honest, a surety will be liable under a bond of general indemnity if a loss occurs through the negligence of the employee. If the bond limits the surety's liability to the losses caused by the principal's "fraud or dishonesty," however, the surety would not be liable for mere negligence or a mistake of judgment by the bonded employee, but only for affirmative acts of fraud.

Builders are often required to obtain surety bonds to secure the performance of construction contracts. These performance or payment bonds are designed to ensure that a building is completed in the fashion and at the time agreed upon, and that the building owner or obligee on the bond will not be burdened by the claims of third persons who furnish labor and materials. Unless specifically provided, these bonds do not provide indemnity for liability to employees or other persons caused by the contractor's negligence. Some performance bonds, however, contain a provision that obligates the contractor to save the owner harmless for losses, liability, injuries, or damages arising out of the performance of the contractor's work under the building contract. In some instances, a performance bond will contain a specific agreement by a contractor to indemnify the owner against loss or liability on account of injuries to third persons (in connection with the contract work) which are caused by or result from the owner's negligence. These bonds have been found valid and will be enforced by the courts.[9]

Liability Assumed by Law

Strict Liability   In addition to contracts and agreements in which tort liability may be assumed by one party, there are also numerous instances in which a particular type of relationship between private parties may result in tort liability being imposed by law. Because the sources of this type of liability are myriad and vary among jurisdictions, the following discussion will focus on only a few illustrative applications of the principle.

Many of the statutory applications of the principle of imposition of tort liability by law are based on the concept of strict liability. This concept holds that in some cases a party should be held liable for injuries caused to another, even though no affirmative act of wrongdoing is charged, and even though that party has not acted unreasonably or without due care.

Workers' Compensation   Perhaps the most prevalent application of this principle is in the workers' compensation acts. The theory behind these acts is that the burden of industrial accidents should fall upon the employer, because the employer is in a better position to prevent loss and to bear the burden by shifting it to the public at large by means of purchasing insurance coverage and/or the pricing of goods. Under workers' compensation statutes (which are the subject of Chapter 6) the employer assumes liability for job-connected injuries or diseases of employees, without regard to the negligence of either itself or the injured employee.

Food Laws   As another example, many food laws make the seller of defective food liable to an injured purchaser, even though all reasonable precautions were taken.

"Dram Shop" or Civil Liability Acts   In many states, these acts impose strict liability upon establishments that sell alcoholic beverages when the sale results in harm to third persons because of the intoxication of the buyer. This liability is seen as a loss exposure which must be assumed by all persons who engage in the business.[10] Most such establishments transfer that loss exposure by purchasing appropriate dram shop insurance.

"Factory Acts," "Scaffold Acts," Etc.   Similarly, there are a number of so-called factory acts, scaffold acts, and the like that impose liability upon employers and others in order to protect employees. For example, the Illinois Structural Work Act,[11] commonly known as the "Scaffold Act," creates a general standard of safety for certain structural devices and provides a cause of action against persons "having charge of the work" for injuries occurring from violations of its safety standards.[12] In order to increase safety in construction work and facilitate actions by an employee against those responsible for dangerous working conditions, the act eliminates the common-law defenses of assumption of risk and contributory negligence.

Similar policy considerations on the federal level are reflected in statutes such as the Federal Safety Appliance Act,[13] which requires trains involved in interstate commerce to be equipped with certain safety devices. The act also holds railroads responsible, even without proof of negligence, for a deficiency which injures employees or others likely to suffer harm.

In addition to the statutory applications of the principle of the imposition of tort liability by law, decisional case law has in recent years begun to rapidly expand the type of circumstances under which this principle will apply. As discussed in Chapter 3, the most prevalent example of this expansion is in connection with sellers of products, who in many jurisdictions may be held strictly liable for defects which cause harm to the purchaser. This is commonly known, in products liability terms, as the doctrine of strict liability.

Note that, while the transfer of loss exposures in many of the above examples is accomplished through the acquisition of appropriate insurance (for example, workers' compensation insurance), the exposures are not usually within the scope of contractual liability insurance.

Circumstances When Tort Liability Cannot Be Assumed or Delegated Under Contract

As discussed earlier in this chapter, contractual provisions are often used to shift tort liability from one party to another in order to place the cost on the party with the greatest ability to prevent a loss. Thus, parties often agree in advance that there shall be no obligation to take precautions and hence no liability for negligence, or that one party shall assume the burden of loss for any negligence. However, such exculpatory clauses will not be allowed to exempt persons from negligence liability for harm willfully inflicted, or caused by gross or wanton negligence. In addition, under certain circumstances, the courts will hold exculpatory agreements void as against public policy. And statutory enactments have already expressed the public view that tort liability cannot be assumed or delegated under certain types of contracts.

Public Policy Whether or not a contract providing for exemption from liability for negligence is deemed void as a matter of public policy depends on a number of considerations. No clear-cut rule can be deduced from the opinions of the courts. On one hand, some courts seek to discourage negligent behavior and broadly hold that one cannot by contract avoid liability for negligence. On the other hand, many other courts emphasize the freedom of parties to contract as they wish; they condition the validity of exculpatory contracts, in any particular case, on the relations of the parties, the presence or absence of equality of bargaining power, and other circumstances. Thus, courts may strike down exculpatory provisions, under certain circumstances, in order to protect those in need of goods and services from those who have a far superior bargaining position. A prime example, mentioned earlier, is when exculpatory provisions are invalidated because they are really contracts of adhesion.

Public Servants The area in which courts most often impose restrictions on people's freedom to contract for exculpatory provisions is where contracts are entered into by public servants for the performance of public duties for compensation.[14] In accordance with this rule, for example, it is held that common carriers, i.e., those that hold themselves out to transport persons or goods of all who choose to employ them, may not exempt themselves from liability for negligence in the performance of their duties.

Common Carriers. It has been mentioned that, while common carriers may not completely exempt themselves from their tort liability, they may contractually limit the amount for which they shall be liable in case of harm to property caused by their negligence (provided they have complied with all federal and state statutory and regulatory provisions). Common carriers must also offer to render the public service at a reasonable rate without such a limitation, and the public must be given a choice between the two forms of liability and the two rates. In most instances, this limitation will take the form of a maximum valuation amount of property that the carrier transports, commonly known as the shipper's "declared value."

Others Performing a Public Duty. In addition to common carriers, there are numerous other categories of contracting parties who are considered to be performing a public duty. Such parties are also barred from benefiting from a clause exculpating them from their own negligence. For example, public utilities such as gas, electric power and telegraph companies have been regarded, with respect to customers, as having such a monopolistic position that they will not be allowed to exempt themselves from liability for their own negligence.

Common carriers and others performing a public service are not the only parties that will not be permitted to benefit from a contract exculpating them from their own negligence. In the precedent-setting opinion of Tunkl v. Regents of University of California,[15] the Supreme Court of California held invalid a contractual clause exempting a charity hospital from tort liability, even though the hospital had no duty to serve the public. The hospital was a nonprofit, research-oriented organization that admitted only the types of patients whose study and treatment would aid the development of a research and medical education program. In order to be admitted as a patient, Tunkl had to sign a "release" exempting the hospital "from any and all liability for the negligent or wrongful acts or omissions of its employees if the hospital has used due care in selecting its employees." Tunkl subsequently brought a lawsuit for damages for the injuries allegedly caused by the negligence of two hospital physicians. The court found that the hospital's contract with the patient affected the public interest. The hospital offered services to a selected portion of the public. The price of admission was the acceptance of a clause waiving the hospital's negligence. The court found that Tunkl, and other patients in his position, did not really acquiesce in the contractual shifting of tort liability, because as charity patients they had no choice but to enter into this contract of adhesion if they desired medical attention.

In addition to contracts which exempt a person from willful or negligent action, agreements to commit a tort or to injure third persons will also be held illegal as against public policy. This rule also encompasses agreements made for the purpose of defrauding a third person, agreements to place false and deceptive labels on goods in order to deceive purchasers, and agreements that would involve the breach of a contract with a third person.[16]

Similarly, a contract to indemnify against the consequences of illegal or tortious action will also be held invalid because of its tendency to promote illegal acts. The validity of such a contract depends upon whether the party who performs the illegal action is acting in good faith and without knowledge of the illegality. For example, an agreement to indemnify a publisher against the consequences of publishing libelous material is generally invalid. However, where it is not anticipated that any material in a book will be libelous and an exculpatory clause is inserted into the contract or publication merely as a backstop against unforeseen liability, the contract will be enforced.[17]

While the courts have generally upheld contracts that shift tort liability from one contracting party to another, with the numerous exceptions noted above, they often indicate their distaste for these contracts by construing them so strictly as to make the exculpatory clauses inapplicable to the particular facts of any given case. Thus, courts often require that an exculpatory provision in a contract be expressed in clear and unequivocal language to be valid and effective. If the exculpating language is not absolutely clear, the courts may indulge in the presumption that the parties never intended to contractually shift the consequences of their own negligence from one party to another.

CONTRACTUAL LIABILITY INSURANCE

Contractual liability insurance is designed to provide protection for business firms and other entities to whom legal liability of others is transferred under contracts or agreements. In such agreements, the party transferring the liability is the *transferor*. The party to whom the liability has been transferred is the *transferee*. The transferee will indemnify the transferor for any loss within the scope of the contract. Thus, the transferee is sometimes referred to as the *indemnitor*, and the transferor is sometimes called the *indemnitee*.

(Both sets of terms—transferor-transferee, and indemnitee-indemnitor—will be used in this text. The terms transferor and transferee are more comfortable in any discussion of noninsurance transfers of loss exposures. Indemnitee and indemnitor seem more appropriate in any discussion of indemnification following a loss—indeed, the term indemnitee is unavoidable because it is part of the policy language of contractual liability insurance. Note that, when contractual liability exposures are transferred, the transferor is the indemnitee, and the transferee is the indemnitor.)

Insurable contractual assumptions can range from agreements which hold a transferor harmless for legal actions stemming from a transferee's tort or negligence to agreements which hold a transferor harmless for all tort actions, including those attributable to the sole negligence of the transferor.

Those who contractually assume liability of others can handle the resulting exposure in several different ways. Many transferees elect to treat the exposure by transferring it to insurance companies, either because the transferees are financially unable to assume the consequences of those agreements or because they are required by transferors to obtain insurance and show proof to that effect.

The mere fact that contractual liability insurance is purchased does not in itself mean that all possible consequences of contractual assumptions are covered. What is covered depends upon the insuring agreements, exclusions, conditions, and other such policy provisions. State laws also play an important role in determining what is and what may be covered, just as they do with other forms of insurance and suretyship. Both transferors and transferees are often under the mistaken impression that the entire assumption, as agreed upon, is covered by insurance. But certain types of loss may be excluded, and others may be beyond the scope of the terms "contractual liability," or "bodily injury," or "property damage," as they are defined in the policy. Furthermore, certain types of contractual assumptions have been declared void under the applicable statutes of some states. And, even in the absence of statute, a court of law may hold the terms of a contract to be in violation of public policy. In such instances, despite the contract, the transferor has not transferred the exposure.

Coverage for liability assumed under contracts or agreements is handled under most commercial liability forms in one of two ways, depending upon the contractual assumption in question. If the subject matter of the contract comes within the category previously referred to as "incidental contracts," coverage is automatically provided under premises and operations policies without additional charge. If insurance is desired for any other form of contractual undertaking, it must be provided under separate coverage parts that are written in conjunction with commercial liability policies. Two such coverage parts are available. One handles *specific* insurance on an individual contract basis. The other deals with *blanket* insurance on all written contracts, or all contracts of a specified type. Both coverage parts contain insuring agreements, exclusions, and special provisions applicable to their respective coverages. However, in order to form a complete policy, the desired coverage part must either be attached to the standard policy jacket which contains general definitions and conditions that are common to commercial liability provisions, or, as is more common, the coverage part may form a part of the CGL policy (which consists of the comprehensive general liability coverage part and the standard policy jacket).

Exposures Covered

Insurance Services Office (ISO) has developed two standard coverage parts for handling contractual assumptions, other than incidental contracts. One, which is titled "Contractual Liability Insurance (Designated Contracts Only)," covers only such written contracts as are specifically identified and designated (along with the appropriate premium charge) in the schedule of the coverage part. Thus, if an entity enters into a hold harmless agreement and that agreement is not identified and designated on its policy, it will have no coverage for losses stemming from that particular agreement.

The other coverage part, entitled "Contractual Liability Insurance (Blanket Coverage)," is an advisory form that insurers may adopt for use. It covers all written contractual assumptions of the type agreed upon by the two parties and by the insurer.

In addition to the two standard forms used strictly for contractual assumptions, ISO provides yet another method for obtaining contractual liability coverage. The form is referred to as a broad form comprehensive general liability endorsement, and it consists of ten coverage extensions, including blanket contractual liability insurance for both written and oral agreements. (This form was discussed briefly in Chapter 2. Comparable versions also are available under independently filed forms of many insurers.) However, unless otherwise stated, the provisions discussed hereafter are those of the ISO standard form.

Designated Contracts Basis To determine the scope and nature of exposures covered on a designated contracts basis, it is especially important to examine the insuring agreements, the special definitions of terms, the parties who are considered insureds and, of course, the exclusions.

The insurer, under the insuring agreement of this particular coverage part, agrees to "pay on behalf of the insured all sums which the *insured*, by reason of *contractual liability* assumed by him under a contract designated in the schedule for this insurance, shall become *legally obligated* to pay as damages because of *bodily injury* or *property damage* to which this insurance applies caused by an *occurrence*. . . ." Each of the terms italicized in the above insuring agreement must be carefully analyzed to determine the scope of coverage.

The party to whom coverage applies must come within the definition of *insured*. If the named insured (as named in the policy declarations) is an individual and is designated in the declarations as such, he or she is an insured. Should the named insured be designated as a partnership or a joint venture, the firm itself is an insured, along with any partners or joint venturers to the extent of their liability. If the named insured is a corporation, the corporation so designated is an insured, as are any of its executive officers, directors or stockholders while acting within the scope of their duties. Other persons or organizations can be added as insureds by endorsement. The rules of the contractual liability manual specify those who can be added and whether there will be an additional premium charge.

For coverage to apply, the insured must be *legally obligated* to pay for the damages sought by the claimant. The obligation must be legally enforceable. It is not enough for the insured merely to feel a sense of duty, obligation or responsibility to a claimant.

It is important to note that the full protection of the policy will apply only when the event giving rise to the loss is covered and when the insured is legally obligated to pay the damages. Contractual liability insurance will not respond in every case where a contract is involved. Some losses are outside the scope of contractual liability insurance, and must be retained or insured under another form of insurance. As mentioned earlier in this chapter, it may happen that although a loss was within the scope of policy coverage, the contract involved is not legally enforceable. Then, since the insured has no obligation to pay, the insurer has no obligation to pay on behalf of the insured. In such a case, the insurer would, in accordance with policy terms (as discussed later), defend the insured until the insured was cleared of any liability.

It is important to remember that the only contractual liability covered under this form is that assumed by the insured under a contract that is designated in the schedule of the coverage part. Also vital is the type of contractual undertaking that is designated. The schedule of this coverage part, for example, may specify the location at which work is to be performed, as well as the names of principals who are involved in that undertaking. The schedule will show the code number, for statistical purposes, corresponding to the proper manual classification of the contract which applies. And it will show the total cost of the specific project, the rates for bodily injury and property damage that apply per $100 of such project cost as designated, the premium, and any minimum premiums that may apply.

Because the insurance coverage applies only to the particular contracts which are both designated and described in the schedule, no coverage would apply even if an entity were to enter into another contract of the same type unless it, too, is designated in the schedule, along with other information describing the project and the appropriate premium.

It is important to understand the meaning of the term *contractual liability*, which appears in the insuring agreement. The term is defined in the additional definitions section of the coverage part as follows:

> "Contractual liability" means liability expressly assumed under a written contract or agreement; provided, however, that contractual liability shall not be construed as including liability under a warranty of the fitness or quality of the named insured's products or a warranty that work performed by or on behalf of the named insured will be done in a workmanlike manner.

It is quite clear from this provision that liability must be *expressly* assumed *in writing*. An assumption of liability that may be *implied* in a written contract is not intended to be covered, nor is a contract that is made *orally* between the parties. The definition, furthermore, makes it clear that any warranty—expressed, implied, written, or oral—dealing with (1) an entity's products (those manufactured, sold, handled, or distributed by it or by others trading under that entity's name), or (2) work performed by or on behalf of an entity, is not the subject of contractual liability. Coverage for these two exceptions may be obtained under products and completed operations insurance, as discussed in Chapter 4.

The terms *bodily injury* and *property damage* are defined in the standard policy jacket to which all coverage parts must be attached. Losses resulting from such things as mental anguish, humiliation, invasion of privacy, or slander are not encompassed by the definition of bodily injury.

Occurrence, which also is defined in the standard policy jacket, includes any adverse condition that continues over a long period and eventually results in bodily injury or in property damage. An important criterion of occurrence, however, is that the resulting injury or damage must be something that was neither expected nor intended from the standpoint of the insured.

The designated contracts coverage part contains a provision

concerning defense coverage that is identical to other coverage parts with the exception of provisions relating to arbitration proceedings. The insurer of contractual liability will provide defense not only in a suit, but also in an arbitration proceeding to which an insured must submit or to which the insured has submitted with the insurer's consent. The insurer is entitled to exercise all of the insured's rights in the choice of arbitrators and in the conduct of any such proceeding.

Blanket Contractual Basis Most of the previous discussion of contractual liability insurance on a designated contracts basis also applies to coverage written on a blanket basis. The only significant difference between the two bases (other than certain exclusions discussed later) lies in the descriptive wording of the insuring agreements. The ISO advisory blanket form can deal with all liability assumed by the insured under any written contract, or it can deal with any written contract except those specifically stated to be inapplicable. For example, in the former case the declarations might read: "Blanket all written agreements," whereas the declarations in the latter case might read: "Blanket all written agreements, other than special hauling permits."

Technically, if contractual liability insurance is to be written on a blanket basis, it would be ideal to cover all written and oral agreements without exception. Some insurers provide coverage on that basis under their own contractual liability forms. Other insurers utilize either the ISO form or their own version of the broad form liability coverage endorsement in conjunction with the CGL policy. But, before providing coverage for all written and oral contracts most insurers will consider the type of operation, the expertise and loss experience of a firm, the premium volume it generates, and the other coverages that are provided. And, while some insurers will not require copies of the agreements made by their insureds, except when the policy is being audited for premium purposes, other insurers are somewhat more stringent in their demands. They not only will insist upon obtaining copies of contractual agreements, but also will require notice from their insureds of any contractual undertaking within the policy period.

Exposures Excluded—Rationale

As with many other types of insurance, contractual liability coverage is limited by certain exclusions. The following discussion will describe the exposures that are excluded or limited, along with their rationale—as they apply to the standard provisions of the designated contracts coverage part. Those exclusions and limitations that apply to the advisory blanket contractual liability coverage part then will be noted to the extent that they differ.

Designated Contracts Basis

Professional Liability. Insurance under the designated contracts coverage part does not apply to bodily injury or to property damage arising out of the rendering of or the failure to render professional services by the insured (transferee) or its indemnitee (transferor) when either or both are architects, engineers or surveyors. Illustrative of the losses so excluded would be those which stem from the preparation or approval of maps, plans, opinions, reports, surveys, designs or specifications, as well as any losses arising from supervisory, inspection, or engineering services. The purpose of this exclusion is to avoid providing coverage for exposures which insurers prefer to cover, if at all, under professional liability insurance forms with appropriate premiums.

War. Also commonly excluded under this and other forms of liability insurance are bodily injury or property damage losses due to war, whether declared or not, civil war, insurrection, rebellion or revolution, or to any act or condition incident to these exposures. The rationale for this exclusion is twofold: (1) such losses have unmanageable catastrophic potential; and (2) they are fundamental in nature and basically unpreventable and uncontrollable. Coverage for these exposures is available, and is particularly of interest to those whose operations extend into foreign countries, but the cost may be prohibitive.

Liquor Liability. An enterprise with no known connection to the liquor business could conceivably become involved with an uninsured liquor liability exposure through a contractual assumption. A store owner, for example, may sign a hold harmless agreement, in favor of a liquor dealer, under the terms of which the store owner agrees to assume the dealer's liability under statute or at common law. To prevent this transfer of liability *by those who should purchase separate liquor liability insurance*, the contractual liability coverage part excludes certain exposures of indemnitees that could implicate their indemnitors under contract.

Excluded is the situation where an indemnitee may be held liable for bodily injury or property damage resulting because it is engaged in the business of manufacturing, distributing, or selling alcoholic beverages, or simply in a circumstance of serving such beverages—at a company picnic, for example. To be excluded, the liability of the indemnitee (transferor) must stem from its selling, serving or giving such beverages (1) in violation of any statute, e.g., dram shop act, (2) in violation of any ordinance or regulation, e.g., alcoholic beverage control laws, (3) to a minor, (4) to a person under the influence of alcohol, or (5) in situations when such alcohol causes or contributes to the intoxication of any person. To illustrate how the coverage of the contractual liability form is limited by this exclusion, consider the following situation. Company A desires to hold a picnic for its employees and their families. A engages B, a wholesale distributor of alcoholic beverages, to dispense beverages at the picnic. As a condition precedent to the undertaking, A signs a contract agreeing to hold B harmless from any liability that could result from serving such beverages. A member of an employee's family becomes intoxicated and causes an automobile accident after the picnic. As a result, a suit is brought against B. Because B (the indemnitee) is engaged in the liquor business, neither B (an indemnitee who seeks protection under its contractual agreement), nor A (who accepted such an agreement) is protected *under contractual liability insurance*. B, of course, still can maintain a right of action against A under the terms of the contract and wholly apart from insurance. Or B may have liquor liability insurance that would protect itself in this suit.

It is possible that A would have protection under its CGL policy if the injured party brought a suit against A. Such protection comes about as an exception to an exclusion. This exclusion, in essence, holds that no coverage applies to those that are *in the business of* manufacturing, selling or serving any alcoholic beverages. So, if A is not in the liquor business, the coverage may still apply depending on the circumstances of the case.

The second of the excluded liquor liability exposures pertains to situations where an indemnitee may be held liable as an owner or a lessor of premises which are used in whole or in part for a liquor business. For example, an owner or a lessor of premises used as a liquor store may attempt to transfer its potential liability stemming from violation of any statute, ordinance or regulation dealing with that type of business, to the operator of such store. However, the store operator's contractual liability insurance would not provide coverage in such a situation. Everyone who is subject to possible suit arising out of the liquor business should purchase liquor liability insurance—contractual liability insurance is not intended to serve as a substitute.

Workers' Compensation. An exclusion, under the designated contracts part, prevents coverage for any obligation for which an employer or its insurer may be held liable to employees under workers' compensation, unemployment compensation, or compulsory temporary disability laws. However, coverage does apply for the assumption of any liability to compensate or to pay a *third party* for a work-related injury. Agreements involving the latter types of contractual assumptions are common. Owners of projects often require general contractors to assume third-party liability, and general contractors often require subcontractors to do likewise, because an owner (or a general contractor, as the case may be) is otherwise open to suit by an injured employee of another who is involved in the project, particularly when an owner contributes to the injurious exposure in some way. To avoid adverse judgment against it and the inconvenience of being confronted with a costly and time-consuming suit, an owner will require the general contractor and subcontractors to enter into an agreement which obligates them to handle such matters without involving the owner. It is important to note, however, that if the allegations of an employee are based upon a warranty that work performed by the employer was unworkmanlike, the employer will have no coverage under its contractual liability insurance. Such warranties specifically are outside the definition of contractual liability. Thus, in such a situation, the employer would have to rely upon its own employers' liability insurance.

Third-Party Beneficiaries. An exclusion unique to contractual liability insurance precludes coverage for any obligation to third-party beneficiaries, e.g., the public at large, when losses arise out of work performed for a public authority. However, this exclusion does not apply if legal action is instituted by the public authority or by any person or organization which is directly engaged in the public project. The net effect of this exclusion is that coverage will apply for liability assumed under a written contract of the type covered if (1) a public authority brings suit against the indemnitor in a public project, or (2) a person or organization involved in the project brings suit against the indemnitor. But coverage does not apply to a suit against the indemnitor of a public project by a person or organization which is not directly involved in such project. (Note, however, that a third-party suit is covered against the indemnitor of a *private* work project because that exposure is not specifically precluded.)

The purpose of the third-party beneficiary exclusion is to avoid the multitude of claims that might otherwise be initiated by members of the public who are entitled to the protection of their health and safety in public projects. Nonetheless, special types of license and permit bonds are available (and sometimes required) to guarantee that the one performing the work will indemnify the public for losses sustained during public work projects. (These bonds are discussed in Chapter 13.)

Other Exclusions. Many of the same exposures excluded under the provisions of commercial liability policies, such as the CGL form, also apply to the contractual liability coverage part. One such excluded exposure is damage to property in the insured's care, custody, or control. Liability assumed for such damage is best covered under an appropriate form of bailee coverage, often written as inland marine insurance. Another exposure commonly excluded is property damage to premises alienated (sold) by an entity. But any liability assumed for damage to other property caused by a condition of alienated premises is covered. Suppose, for example, a building is sold and the purchaser is not informed of certain hazardous conditions that are not clearly visible, such as faulty electrical wiring. If fire subsequently were to damage or destroy the building, the seller of the building would have no contractual liability insurance protection if suit were brought against him or her. But if the fire spread to and damaged an adjoining building, the seller would be protected for any liability that may have been contractually assumed by that person. The rationale of this exclusion is to avoid paying for losses confined to the condition of premises which should have been made known by the seller (indemnitor).

Furthermore, no coverage applies for the assumption of any bodily injury or property damage losses within the so-called contamination or pollution exclusion, unless the event giving rise to injury or to damage is sudden and accidental. Exposures of this nature are excluded for a variety of reasons, discussed fully in Chapter 11.

Another exposure not covered is liability assumed under any agreement for bodily injury or property damage arising out of the ownership, maintenance, operation, use, loading or unloading of any mobile equipment while being used in any type of racing, speed, or demolition contest. This type of an exposure simply is too hazardous for most insurers to accept. In fact, the same exclusion applies under the provisions of other liability coverage parts. Some forms of liability insurance for such activities are obtainable in the specialty lines market.

The assumption of liability for loss of use of tangible property which is not physically injured or destroyed is excluded in two situations. The first is when loss of use results from a delay in or lack of performance by or on behalf of an entity of any contract or agreement. Such agreements, which are fairly common in the construction business, are excluded from contractual liability insurance because the exposures, by their very nature, are more appropriately handled with suretyship instruments such as performance bonds. The second situation is when loss of use results from the failure of a firm's products, or work performed by it or on its behalf, to meet the level of performance, quality, fitness, or durability that may be warranted or represented by such firm. As noted earlier, the definition of contractual liability does not encompass warranties pertaining to the performance of work or products. The reason for this exclusion is to place the responsibility for any loss of use of products or work upon those who had control over their production in the first place.

Additionally, it is not the intent of contractual liability insurance to guarantee the workmanship that goes into products or into various kinds of work. However, coverage does apply, *when assumed under written contract*, to any loss of use of *other* tangible property resulting from sudden and accidental physical injury to, or destruction of, a firm's products or work. For example, damage to a boiler which explodes because it was negligently installed by a heating contractor is not covered, whether such liability is assumed or not. But loss of use of the building, resulting from that explosion, is covered.

Three additional exposures concerning products and the performance of work were discussed in more depth in Chapter 4. Briefly, they relate to property damage to a firm's products or to work performed by it or on its behalf. Coverage of damage to products or work is virtually unavailable, because it would involve guaranteeing faulty products or faulty workmanship. The third excluded exposure involves damages claimed for the withdrawal, inspection, or loss of use of products or work because of any known or suspected defect, when such liability is assumed under any written contract. This exclusion also appears in most other liability coverage parts. Those who desire to cover that exposure can do so by purchasing products recall insurance.

Finally, exposures involving the assumption of property damage within the explosion, collapse, or underground property damage hazards (so-called xcu hazards or exclusions) are not covered, unless a transferee is willing to pay extra to remove the exclusions. The xcu exposures present hazards which require additional premiums. It is doubtful, however, whether a court of law would enforce the assumption of another's liability for work within the explosion hazard. As discussed earlier, it has been held that one who engages another to perform hazardous work may not escape liability when an injury results, not from the manner of doing the work, but from the very performance of such work.[18] For example, a firm which hires another to perform blasting work may not pass along liability to the one actually performing that work.

All of these exclusions and limits are contained in the standard provisions of the coverage part for designated contracts. Other exclusions may be added depending upon the nature of the contract(s) being assumed and the type of operation. For example, an exclusion may possibly be added if work is to be performed on or near railroad property, or on or near maritime vessels.

Blanket Contractual Basis In view of the fact that blanket contractual liability insurance is based on advisory forms, some of the exclusions used will vary somewhat among insurers. Most blanket contractual coverage parts do contain a number of the same exclusions, nonetheless, and it is these common exclusions that will be described.

Generally, all of the exclusions, limits and exceptions contained in the standard coverage part for designated contracts are also contained in blanket contractual coverage parts. However, the blanket contractual coverage part commonly contains three additional exclusions which do not form a part of the designated contracts coverage part.

One of the exclusions stipulates that insurance does not apply to liability assumed by any indemnitor under any *incidental contracts*. The fact that the blanket contractual coverage part usually covers *all* written contracts (and sometimes oral contracts) makes this exclusion necessary. Its purpose is to avoid the overlapping coverage which otherwise would result because coverage for liability assumed under incidental contracts is automatically included under most commercial liability policies. The other two exclusions apply to extra hazardous exposures which require an additional premium as a prerequisite to deleting them. Specifically, the two exclusions apply to bodily injury or property damage arising out of (1) construction, maintenance, or repair of *watercraft* or their loading and unloading, and (2) operations within fifty feet of any *railroad property*, affecting any railroad bridge or trestle, tracks, road beds, tunnel, underpass, or crossing. The latter exclusion involves exposures which are the subject of railroad protective liability insurance, discussed later in this chapter.

Other Provisions—Rationale

Both the blanket contractual and the designated contracts coverage parts contain additional provisions which further define the extent of coverage, its territorial scope, the application of policy limits, the method of calculating the premium, and the persons and firms which are considered to be insureds under the coverage parts. Though most such provisions, which are identical to those applying to other liability coverage parts, have been noted previously, the provisions pertaining to policy territory and persons insured deserve additional comments.

Policy Territory The insurance under both coverage parts in question applies only to bodily injury or to property damage which occurs within the policy territory. To determine what is encompassed by that term, one must refer to the definition of policy territory in the standard policy jacket. Insofar as contractual liability insurance is concerned, the term "policy territory" means (1) the United States of America, its territories or possessions, or Canada, and (2) international waters or air space, provided injury or damage does not occur in the course of travel or transportation to or from any other country, state, or nation. Thus, if a construction contracting firm were to accept some type of temporary work assignment in a foreign country, or in Puerto Rico, which is neither a territory nor a possession of the United States, it may be without protection in that country, or commonwealth, even though the type of loss would otherwise be covered under its liability policy. A firm such as this would have to obtain additional coverage for that foreign exposure. (If the firm has an umbrella liability policy, its contractual liability protection will more than likely be on a worldwide basis, subject to a "self-insured" retention.)

Persons Insured Although the persons insured provisions of the two contractual liability coverage parts list those who automatically are included as insureds, two limitations should not be overlooked. First, insurance does not apply to injury or damage arising out of the conduct of any partnership or joint venture of which the insured is a partner or a member, unless the joint venture is specifically designated and covered. Because contracting firms often enter into these types of arrangements, it would be well for them to keep this limitation in mind.

Furthermore, employees are seldom automatically covered as additional insureds. But, because they, too, can be held personally liable for any acts or omissions arising out of and during the course of their employment, they should be specifically added as additional insureds. It is important to note, however, that adding them as additional insureds for general liability coverages is not sufficient to protect them in situations involving contractual liability exposures. They must be added as additional insureds under the contractual liability coverage parts as well. However, regardless of the number of insureds named in the policy, the number of persons that sustain injury or damage, or the number of claims made or suits brought, the limit of liability provision makes it quite clear that the limits applying to bodily injury and to property damage are the maximum in any one occurrence. Were it not for the occurrence limitation, the limits for both coverages could conceivably be made to apply to each person against whom claim is made. The net effect would be to make the limits apply on a cumulative basis.

NONINSURANCE TECHNIQUES FOR HANDLING CONTRACTUAL LIABILITY EXPOSURES

When an organization assumes the liability of others under contract, it may become responsible for loss caused solely or partially by those over whom it has little or no control. This lack of control makes for an exposure much more difficult to treat than the exposure to loss caused by the acts or omissions of employees or agents over whom some control is exercised.

Insurance is not the only way to treat contractual liability exposures, even though many of those who transfer their loss exposures to others under contract require some evidence that the transferee has purchased contractual liability insurance. Contractual liability insurance, as provided by insurers under standard and nonstandard forms, seldom will cover all loss exposures. Even blanket contractual liability insurance will still exclude the types of loss situations mentioned earlier.

Loss Control

Actually, whether insurance applies or not, effective handling of contractual liability exposures involves a number of techniques. One of these techniques is preventive in nature. It involves determining not only what is to be assumed under existing contract or contracts under consideration, but also estimating what loss exposures probably will be assumed in the foreseeable future. Granted, this is not an easy task, especially since it must be done before some of the contracts are accepted and signed. Yet, of all the problems arising from contractual agreements, many stem from the fact that indemnitors seldom question the terms of contracts they sign, or do not take the time to consult competent legal counsel to interpret such contracts. Many indemnitors simply agree to the contract terms for fear of losing the job in question. When a questionable loss arises and a court is called upon to interpret the terms of the contract, the court may hold the indemnitor (transferee) responsible for substantially more than the indemnitor thought possible.

By determining contractual responsibilities and implementing certain measures of loss prevention and control before problems arise, indemnitors may go a long way in reducing their losses. Nevertheless, once an indemnitor agrees to assume losses of another, some types of losses may be nearly impossible to prevent, especially when the assumption of liability encompasses acts and omissions of those over whom an indemnitor has no control. A project owner, for example, may cause injury to some third party in a circumstance that has no direct relationship to the performance of the contractor's work. The obligation of the contractor to defend the project owner in this instance may appear to be somewhat unreasonable, particularly when the contractor has all it can do to handle its own affairs. Yet, if the contract between the owner and the contractor clearly and unequivocally makes losses of this nature the obligation of the contractor, the court may uphold it. Of course, some courts have declared such agreements to be against public policy. But the danger is that no one can tell in advance how a court may rule. For this reason, if no other, the parties to a contract should understand its terms.

Contractual liability problems are not necessarily confined to relationships between general contractors and owners of projects. Many also arise when general contractors shift their potential liability to subcontractors who are involved in the same project. Some general contractors even may stipulate contractual terms for subcontractors that are broader in scope than the terms imposed by owners upon general contractors. A subcontractor, for example, may be held responsible, under contract, for any losses caused by the concurrent or even the sole negligence of the general contractor. Or, a general contractor who has agreed to be responsible for any loss caused by the owner may attempt to transfer such obligation onto the subcontractor.

Contractual liability exposures can sometimes be reduced by amending the terms of the contract(s) involved. Whether the terms of any hold harmless agreement can or should be amended in order to reduce any future problems depends upon the specific situation. As was pointed out earlier, a complex and ambiguously worded contract may be interpreted by a court in a way which is detrimental to either party to the contract. Likewise, a loss that exceeds the scope of any contractual liability insurance can place additional burdens upon both parties, particularly when the party that assumes the contract terms is financially unable to handle the defense and the settlement of any such uninsured loss.

So, if a prospective indemnitor feels that a particular contract assumption provision is too much to handle, it is better to act on it early while the terms still stand a chance to be altered, instead of being forced to react when the harsh terms are enforced later. The possibility of amending the contract depends in part on the relative bargaining power of the parties involved. If the terms of a contract cannot be amended to more suitable conditions, the prospective indemnitor must then make a thorough assessment of the exposures involved to determine whether contract terms can be met if it ever becomes necessary. Of course, the economic profits to be gained under the contract must also be weighed against the probability of a loss because of the contract.

Avoidance

Avoidance, as a method of handling contractual liability exposures, is sometimes the only feasible avenue to follow, especially when alternative methods are unacceptable or unavailable. Indeed, based upon the numerous court decisions which have been adverse to indemnitors, avoidance of contractual liability should be utilized more than it is.

Of course, a contractor who insists on avoiding all contractual assumption provisions might lose some lucrative contracts to competitors who would accept such provisions. In many cases, it would be foolish for the contractor to lose such contracts, since insurance for the losses to be assumed is available at an attractive price (and the premiums can be included as a cost in the contractor's bid, directly or indirectly).

Retention

Today, insurance is probably the leading method of handling exposures arising out of contractual assumptions that cannot be avoided, particularly those relating to construction contracts. Based upon what has been said about the nature and scope of assumptions under many construction contracts, this is understandable. But the financial consequences of some contractual agreements can be consciously retained without presenting any undue hardships. In fact, the use of insurance sometimes can amount to little more than a wasted expenditure because so little is being transferred to an insurer.

Sellers of goods or services, for example, often agree to hold purchasers harmless, under certain types of purchase order agreements, against any statutory violations in the production of products or common-law liability for injury. Sellers often do this voluntarily in order to retain their clientele. If these sellers were to attempt to transfer the loss exposure to an insurer, it could amount to a waste of premium expenditures because sellers cannot transfer their obligation to obey the law.

Some exposures arising out of agreements relating to construction work can even be retained safely by transferees (or need not be specifically insured), particularly those contracts sometimes classified as "limited forms." Under limited form contracts, a transferee usually agrees to nothing more than to hold a transferor harmless for any liability stemming from the transferee's negligence. Bringing this into perspective, the contractor is simply agreeing to handle the project owner's defense and indemnify him for any vicarious liability which might be imposed on the owner in the event the owner is sued because an act or an omission of the contractor results in injury or in property damage to others. (As discussed elsewhere in this chapter, a contractor can [or sometimes is required to] obtain an owners and contractors protective liability [OCP] policy in the name of the entity for whom work is to be performed. This will provide the entity with defense coverage in the event it is brought into a suit involving the contractor.)

One could speculate, nevertheless, that if any assumption under a written contract of the limited type is not specifically covered by insurance, an insurer could deny any claim involving work subject to that contract under the contractor's CGL policy, because of the contractual liability exclusion in the CGL. Insurers, in fact, have attempted this on a number of occasions. However, the consensus of the courts seems to be that an insurer cannot deny defense to an insured under such circumstances, particularly when an insured would have had protection under its policy in absence of such an agreement. Even though the contractor's defense and obligation to pay any damages are covered under the contractor's CGL, this still leaves the indemnitee without proper protection in the event of suit. But *perhaps* the defense costs of the indemnitee are something that the indemnitor can satisfactorily retain, even though defense can be costly. If not, it may be more economical for the indemnitor to obtain protective liability insurance (discussed later) for the indemnitee.

Those entities that already handle many of their loss exposures under a formal retention program likely will also retain their contractual liability exposures. But, of course, the final decision depends upon the reason retention was chosen as a risk management device. The advantages and disadvantages of retaining loss exposures have been discussed in CPCU 1 and elsewhere in this course.

Selecting Among Risk Management Alternatives

If a contractor can delete (or amend) the provisions under which contractual liability is assumed without losing the business, such avoidance or control probably is the best way of handling the exposure. If the contractor may lose business by insisting a contract be amended, he can try to insure the assumed exposures. If insurance is not available (or is available only at a price which is unacceptable to the contractor), retention must be considered.

If retention would be unwise or impossible, and if insurance is unavailable or unaffordable, the best alternative may be to avoid the contract altogether. Any such decision is difficult, and the avoidance of a loss exposure must be weighed against the chance of a profit from the contract. Although it is never an easy decision to forgo a potentially profitable contract, just such a decision could have helped many contractors avoid bankruptcy.

WRAP-UP APPROACHES

The wrap-up approach introduces a method of handling the insurance needs of a number of entities. Because of its effect on the contractual liabilities of the various parties involved in a construction project, it is appropriate to discuss this approach at this point.

An owner of a project, or whoever is in charge, will sometimes arrange the insurance for a construction project in such a way that all interests involved, such as the owner, general contractor, subcontractors, architect, engineer, and surveyors, are combined and insured on one policy with one insurer. This type of an arrangement is referred to as a "wrap-up program." Such programs are permissible only in a few states. Their availability depends upon the cost of the project, and they are restricted to work at one location (except when they involve such things as highway construction). Wrap-up programs also must have a definite completion date. Examples of some of the larger multimillion-dollar projects which have been handled under these programs are the Bay Area Rapid Transit system (BART) in San Francisco, and the John Hancock building in Chicago.

Wrap-up programs do not necessarily eliminate the need for contractual assumptions. Their principal purpose is to maximize efficiency by providing better insurance protection for all parties involved at lower total insurance costs. These programs, furthermore, make it possible not only to reduce the administrative details that go with paper work, but also to facilitate the handling of claims. In addition, when one insurer administers the program of loss prevention and control, all involved need only abide by one set of standards, rather than the number of different standards which normally apply when many insurers are involved in such projects.

While wrap-up programs sometimes attract strong support, they also attract strong opposition, even though they appear to eliminate some of the inefficiencies that otherwise can exist if all involved are represented by their own insurers. Perhaps the leading argument against them is that normally no one other than the manager of such programs realizes a reduction in costs. It is from the mechanics of a plan, rather than cost-savings, that benefits for others are derived. Two such plans are available: (1) the designated carrier plan, and (2) the ex-insurance plan.

Designated Carrier Plan

Under the designated carrier plan, each person or organization involved in the project is required to purchase the coverages specified through the producer and the insurer designated by the party managing the project. While each entity involved has the responsibility for paying the premiums on its coverages, any dividends and other savings go to the project manager. But, because insurance is purchased on an individual basis, the plan produces little or no rate reduction. The designated carrier approach nonetheless permits centralization of various control measures, such as loss prevention and control, as well as claims handling.

Ex-Insurance Plan

The ex-insurance plan requires the *project manager* to arrange and to pay for insurance to cover all interests through one insurer. The term "ex-insurance" is derived from the fact that everyone's bid excludes the cost of insurance that otherwise would normally be included. And, because the project manager is purchasing all coverages from one insurer, a better opportunity exists for obtaining rate advantages.

In the usual course of events, it is not necessary for the one who is managing a wrap-up program to decide immediately which of the two plans to use. Instead, specifications can be drawn so that all potential participants must submit their bid proposals with and without the inclusion of their insurance costs. In that way, the review of bids on both bases can determine which of the plans is more advantageous to the project manager.

Workers' compensation coverage is not always permitted in wrap-up programs under state law. Even when the use of workers' compensation insurance is permissible, the manager may not wish to incorporate its use in a program, in which case each participant with employees must make its own arrangements to cover that exposure. Whatever coverages may be required, it is important that participants exclude the exposures insured under a wrap-up program from their regular insurance portfolio to avoid duplicate coverage and premium costs.

Whether contractual liability insurance (or proof of a satisfactory retention program) will be required of wrap-up participants is a matter left to the discretion of the project owner or manager. The ideal situation, at least among all participants of a wrap-up program, is to avoid the use of hold harmless agreements, or to at least avoid agreements that impose obligations which are broader in scope than what normally are the responsibilities of those who are involved in the project. After all, a wrap-up program is supposed to eliminate some of the problems that otherwise could apply if insurance matters were to be handled on an individual basis. Nonetheless, broad hold harmless agreements are often required by project owners to avoid any possibility of implicating the owners in time-consuming lawsuits. Yet, whether these hold harmless agreements solve anything really depends upon the nature and efficacy of the agreements, how the insurance matters are handled and, of course, on the nature of the losses which occur.

When all required insurance (including workers' compensation) is handled by one insurer, it is doubtful whether the use of hold harmless agreements will serve any purpose in transferring loss exposures, since the wrap-up insurer would be required to provide protection to whomever may be involved in a loss covered by policy terms. However, if workers' compensation insurance were to be written wholly apart from a wrap-up program, the insurer of the wrap-up program might have the opportunity to recoup some of its losses, particularly losses involving third-party-over actions. Third-party-over actions, which are so prevalent today, come about when an employee of a contractor, after collecting benefits under his or her employer's workers' compensation policy, sues the project owner and perhaps other subcontractors for their contributory negligence in causing the compensable injury.

Third-party-over actions are discussed more fully in Chapter 7. However, the following example will illustrate the potential for complex claim situations even when a wrap-up is involved.

Wrap-Up Program Examples

For purposes of illustration, assume that the job specifications of project owner O, under a wrap-up, prohibit hold harmless agreements and require the wrap-up of all insurance coverages except workers' compensation. In other words, one insurer handles all coverages for everyone involved in the project, with the exception of workers' compensation insurance. E, an employee of subcontractor SC, is injured on the job when he falls into an unguarded pit. The negligence is allegedly attributable partially to O and partially to SC.

E collects benefits under the workers' compensation policy of SC, normally the exclusive remedy against employers. But, realizing that the benefits are insufficient, E sues O, who was partially negligent, for a larger settlement. The CGL policy of the wrap-up program should serve to protect O for this loss. But, say SC is implicated because of its partial negligence. Because SC is not protected under the CGL policy (employee suits against employers are excluded in order to make workers' compensation the exclusive remedy), SC must look to its workers' compensation insurer for protection under employers' liability insurance. This is the proper procedure, in fact, because employers' liability coverage is intended to include such third-party-over actions, provided liability is not assumed under any contract. Since no liability was assumed by SC under contract, in this case its employers' liability coverage applies to the third-party-over action.

Essentially the same situation works out differently when the insurer also provides contractual liability insurance against hold harmless agreements required of everyone by the project owner. Using the same set of circumstances as the previous illustration, here is what can happen following suit brought by subcontractor SC's employee E against project owner O.

Because SC agreed to hold O harmless against any tort losses, however caused, it is up to the insurer of contractual liability insurance under the wrap-up program to defend O in this action. If SC were to become involved, SC could not look to its workers' compensation insurer for protection, because employers' liability insurance does not respond when liability of an employer is assumed under any contract or agreement. Contractual liability insurance does, and it is up to the insurer to provide coverage to protect SC as well.

Going one step further, assume that the defense of both O and SC is denied for any reason by the insurer. Quite obviously SC would be required to defend O from SC's own financial resources. Thus, SC can be held responsible for the defense of O and the payment of any judgment, independently of any workers' compensation settlement. If SC for some reason were financially incapable of defending O, it is then up to O to protect itself, since no policy will be available to provide the necessary protection.

These examples illustrate some of the problems that can arise with wrap-up programs, whether or not they involve hold harmless agreements. Of course, there are other loss situations under wrap-up programs, with or without the use of hold harmless agreements, that can work to the advantage of all parties involved. Because the relationships of parties involved in a wrap-up can become complex, careful planning and execution is essential.

CONSTRUCTION MANAGEMENT[19]

Construction management is a very simple concept that appears to be coming into vogue as a means of maximizing the efficiency of everyone who is involved in a large nonresidential construction project. Space does not permit a lengthy description of this interesting development. But, briefly, the project owner, who may not be well versed in all the technicalities of construction work, can hire a construction manager to handle the entire function, as illustrated in Figure 5-1. The person or organization which serves as construction manager then selects the architect and engineers, along with the

Figure 5-1

Construction Management—A Changing Order of Responsibilities*

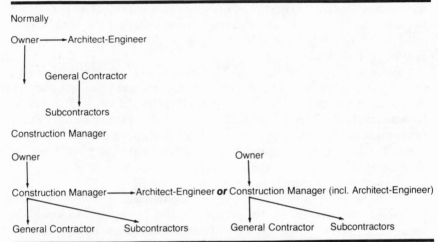

*Reprinted with permission from *FC&S Bulletins*, Management and Sales Section Surveys (Cincinnati: National Underwriter Company), p. CM-2.

general contractor and all subcontractors. Sometimes the construction manager also performs the function of architect and engineer, depending upon its professional expertise. Thus, the project owner is saved from the anguish that commonly goes with having to hire and monitor all of those people.

Proponents of the approach believe that by utilizing a competent construction manager, who is an agent of the owner, many of the usual problems can be minimized. The construction manager can provide the leadership and control considered essential if the owner, architect, engineer, and general contractor are to work together effectively toward one common goal. The construction management concept may alter the traditional relationships of the parties involved and the need for contractual liability insurance.[20]

PROTECTIVE LIABILITY EXPOSURES

Thus far, this text has provided a detailed analysis of the liability loss exposures arising out of premises and operations, products and completed operations, and liability assumed under contract. An additional loss exposure will be discussed in the remaining pages of this chapter, under the headings "Protective Liability Exposures" and "Protective Liability Insurance."

Vicarious Liability

Vicarious liability may result from employer-employee relationships, principal-agent relationships, or relationships with an independent contractor. The "protective liability exposure" arises out of an
entity's *vicarious liability* for the acts of an independent contractor. The
following example will clarify the type of loss exposure involved.
Contractor *A* employed subcontractor *B* to perform the plumbing work
in *A*'s construction project. *A* presumed that any negligence by *B* would
result in a claim against *B*, and that *A* would not be implicated.
Therefore, *A* did not recognize that a new exposure had developed, and
made no preparation to treat the exposure. However, when a claim
developed because one of *B*'s plumbers negligently dropped a pipe on
the head of a passerby, the claimant sued both *A* and *B*. (Although *A*
was not actually doing the plumbing work, it was alleged that *A* was
vicariously liable for the acts of *B*.) Because *A* had not recognized that
he was exposed to loss arising out of the acts of independent contractors,
and had not made plans to treat the exposure, *A* was faced with the cost
of defending himself in the suit. If the courts found *A* responsible for
any liability in this case, *A* would also have been responsible for paying
the damages.

The term "protective liability" is derived from the name of the
insurance policies that provide coverage against this exposure by
"protecting" a building owner or contractor against third-party claims
arising from hiring independent contractors. This is an exposure which
many of the insurance policies previously discussed do not cover, or
cover only at an additional premium—a point discussed in greater detail
later in this chapter.

The principle of vicarious liability describes situations where one
party will be held liable for the negligent acts of a second party—even
though the first party is otherwise free from all fault, did nothing to aid
or encourage the second party's negligence, played no part in it, or even
possibly did everything possible to prevent it.

Torts Committed by Employees Although not normally considered a part of the protective liability exposure per se, vicarious liability
is commonly illustrated by noting that an employer is often liable for
the negligent acts of an employee committed in the course of the
employment. This rule is justified based on the desire to allocate loss
exposures so that the burden is placed upon an employer who engages in
a for-profit enterprise that will possibly involve harm to others through
the torts of employees. The rationale is that the employer is better able
than are innocent injured third parties in such a situation to absorb the

losses caused by the torts of the employees. Loss exposures are allocated by distributing the costs of those losses to the public at large through prices which reflect the cost of the losses and any insurance acquired to protect against them.[21]

Torts Committed by Agents Other Than "Servants" Traditionally, a "servant" is defined as a person who is employed to perform services in the affairs of another; or whose physical conduct in the performance of the service is controlled, or is subject to a right of control, by the other.[22] Since an agent who is not a servant is not subject to any right of control by his or her employer over the details of his or her physical conduct, the responsibility for the agent's conduct ordinarily rests upon the agent alone and the principal or employer is not liable for the torts which the agent may commit.[23] Nonetheless, under exceptions to this rule, liability of the principal can result from the tortious conduct of a nonservant agent.

A principal who expressly or impliedly authorizes or ratifies the tortious acts of his or her agent will be held liable for those acts. This is particularly true when a tort such as fraud or deceit occurs in the course of a transaction between an agent and an injured person. However, it must appear that the representations made either were within the actual or apparent authority of the agent, or were of a kind normally expected by the employer in connection with the transaction, or that the agent has been placed by the principal in a position which enabled him or her to commit the fraud, while apparently acting within his authority.[24]

Torts Committed by Independent Contractors As a general rule, a party is not vicariously liable for the torts of its independent contractor. There is a distinction between this rule and the master-servant rule. This is most often explained by the observation that, because the party has no right to control the manner in which an independent contractor does his or her work, it is to be regarded as the contractor's own enterprise. The contractor, rather than the party, is the proper person to be charged with the responsibility of preventing and distributing the risk.[25]

Exceptions. The "general rule" relating to vicarious liability and the acts of independent contractors is, however, nearly swallowed up by no less than twenty-one recognized exceptions to the general rule. These can be boiled down into three generalized groupings—negligence of the employer, nondelegable duties, and inherently dangerous activities.

NEGLIGENCE OF THE EMPLOYER. The employment of an independent contractor will not insulate the employer from vicarious liability for acts of the contractor where the employer fails to take reasonable precautions where there is a foreseeable chance of harm to others. It is the employer's duty, for instance, to exercise reasonable care to select a competent and careful contractor with the proper equipment for the job involved.[26]

The employer is also required to exercise reasonable care for the protection of others to the extent that he or she furnishes equipment for the work[27] or retains control over any part of it. If the work is done on the employer's own land, he or she will be required to exercise reasonable care to prevent activities or avoid conditions which could lead to the injury of those outside the land or those who enter it as invitees.[28]

NONDELEGABLE DUTIES. There are many duties that relate to the safety of others that either by statute, contract or the development of common law cannot be delegated by an employer to an independent contractor. It is not easy to formulate a general standard for determining which duties are nondelegable. However, the courts have generally found such duties to be of a nondelegable character upon a determination that the responsibility to the community is so important that the employer should not be permitted to transfer it to another.[29] Included in these duties are the responsibility to provide employees with a safe place of work[30] and the retention of responsibility for injuries to those on or outside the owner's land or buildings, if the owner retains possession during the progress of repairs or other work performed by a contractor.[31]

INHERENTLY DANGEROUS ACTIVITIES. This set of exceptions to the general rule recognizes that there are certain activities where a peculiar chance of injury to others exists in the very nature of the work undertaken by the independent contractor, unless special precautions are taken. The title of this category is descriptive not only of the types of exposure involved, but also of the policy reasons behind the imputation of negligence to the employer. If the employer engages in an enterprise which could lead to a foreseeably heightened exposure to innocent third parties, the courts are reluctant to shift the area of exposure away from the employer. Examples of such work include demolition of buildings,[32] the construction of a dam,[33] and excavations in or near a public highway.[34]

The Joint and Several Vicarious Liability of an Employer

The vicarious liability of an employer for the tortious acts of agents or independent contractors is called "joint and several." A liability is said to be joint and several when the injured party may sue one or more of the responsible parties separately for the injuries suffered, or all of them together, at the injured party's option. Essentially, therefore, the term refers to a situation where the injured party may look to any one or all of the legally responsible parties and seek recovery for the entire amount of the injury suffered.[35]

The vicarious liability of an employer, in itself, does not relieve agents and independent contractors from personal responsibility for their own torts.[36]

No agreement generally entered into by an employer (with either his or her agent or independent contractor) which attempts to secure an exemption from liability for harm caused by the negligence of the agent or contractor is binding on an injured third party. These types of contracts usually have been held to be illegal on public policy grounds.[37]

Examples of Torts Imputed to Others

Independent Contractors Company *A* sells pianos on the installment plan. It employs company *B*, a collecting agent, to collect the unpaid installments on the pianos. Company *A* knows that company *B*'s employees are rough and violent and prone to quarreling with the customers of its clients. Company *A* instructs company *B* to collect *C*'s unpaid installments. Company *B* sends *D*, one of its employees, to do so. *D* gets into an argument with *C* and, in the course of the argument, unjustifiably knocks *C* down and seriously harms him. *A* is liable to *C*.[38]

A second example of imputed liability involves the situation where *A* employs *B*, an independent contractor, to erect a building upon land abutting a public highway. The contract entrusts the work to *B*, and contains a clause requiring the contractor to erect a sufficient fence around the necessary excavations. The contract also contains a clause by which *B* assumes all liability for any harm caused by his work. *B* digs the excavation, but fails to erect a fence. In consequence, *C*, while walking along the highway at night, falls into the excavation and is hurt. *A* is liable to *C*.[39]

Agents *B*, an agent of *A*, while acting within the scope of his apparent authority, showed *C*, a prospective purchaser, two lots and told him those were the two lots *C* was buying. *B* gave *C* a receipt purporting to correctly describe the lots. *B*, however, negligently permitted a mistake in description to be carried into the formal contract of sale. When *C* learned of this mistake made by *B*, *C* elected not to rescind the contract, but to affirm it for the purchase of the lots he had not intended to buy. *C* is not precluded from suing *A* for any damages he could prove, and *A* will be held liable to *C*.[40]

A second illustration is represented by a situation where *A* owned certain farmland. *B*, who was an agricultural agent and the manager of *A*'s land, made false representations to *C*, a farmer seeking to lease certain farmland, to the effect that A's land had sufficient water for irrigation. When C leased A's farmland and C's crops suffered from the lack of sufficient water, C sued A for rescission of the lease and damages resulting from the lack of sufficient water. Because B knew that his representations to C were false and because such representations were within the scope of his authority as the agent for A, A is liable to C for damages resulting from those false representations.[41]

Partners In general, both the individual partners and the partnership entity itself are liable to third persons for injuries resulting from tortious acts of a partner while acting within the general scope of the partnership business.[42]

A and B were partners who owned and operated a steamer. B was also the captain of the ship owned by the partnership. When the ship was wrecked, resulting in the death of C, B was found to have negligently operated the steamer, causing the fatal wreck. A is also liable to C's survivors for the negligence of his partner, B.[43]

Joint Venturers A "joint venture" (or joint enterprise) is in the nature of a partnership, but is a broader and more inclusive term. A joint venture includes both partnerships and less formal arrangements for cooperation for a more limited period of time and a more limited purpose. Nonetheless, the tortious acts of a single joint venturer can be imputed to the other joint venturers according to the same principles regarding the vicarious liability of innocent partners for tortious acts committed by their negligent partners.

PROTECTIVE LIABILITY INSURANCE

Protective liability insurance is designed to provide an insured with protection in the event it becomes implicated in a legal action because of (1) a loss allegedly caused by an independent contractor hired by the insured, or (2) an act or an omission of the insured in supervising the activities of an independent contractor.

Many persons find the need for this insurance difficult to comprehend, because the one performing the work is ordinarily thought to be the party responsible for any resulting injury or damage to others. It is essentially true that the one causing injury or damage to others ordinarily is responsible. However, those who hire independent contractors can also become involved, because of the exceptions to the general rule of immunity which have just been noted. In fact, what may be even more startling to some is that a hold harmless agreement signed by an independent contractor usually will not be upheld by the courts, if a loss involves a situation within one of the exceptions. This is why protective liability insurance usually is recommended even when there is a hold harmless agreement. If a hold harmless agreement is not enforceable, the indemnitee can then rely upon its protective liability insurance.

An actual situation illustrating the need for protective liability insurance in spite of a hold harmless agreement is the case of Sites v. Atlas Powder Co., 133 N.E. (2nd.) 671. An oil company engaged a construction firm and a powder company to erect a pipeline. The oil company imposed a contract stipulating that the two firms were independent contractors and that they would hold the oil company harmless from any damages. In a suit by the owner of property due to damages by blasting, the oil company was held directly liable, despite its defense that the work was performed by independent contractors. The court held that the operation (blasting) was inherently dangerous, and a party could not relieve itself of such responsibility. The court added that the principal can delegate such work, but it cannot delegate its responsibility.

It is common practice today to name virtually all possible parties as codefendants of a legal action. Thus, protective liability insurance can serve a useful purpose even when the potential liability of a particular defendant appears to be remote. Though eventually absolved of any liability for damages per se, the defendant is at least provided defense coverage by its liability insurer. And defense costs alone can be very large indeed.

The term "protective liability" is not the only name used for the coverages to be discussed here. Such coverages are frequently referred to as "independent contractor coverage," "structural alterations coverage," or "owners and contractors protective" (OCP), depending on the set of circumstances.

OCP insurance serves the same purpose for both owners and contractors. However, "owners protective" commonly is considered to protect the entity that undertakes hazardous projects (such as structural alterations that change the size or the shape of a building, new construction, or demolition) or hires an independent contractor to perform the entire work (for example, the store owner who decides to construct an addition onto the store, or who hires an independent contractor to do it). "Contractors protective," on the other hand, is considered to protect the entity that is directly involved in a given project, but hires an independent contractor to perform some of the work. An example is the general contractor of a building project who hires a subcontractor to install the heating plant. In either instance, OCP coverage applies only while operations are in progress. Once operations are completed, losses thereafter become the subject of completed operations insurance.

Policies Providing
Owners and Contractors Protective Liability Coverage

Protective liability coverage is available under various insurance contracts—comprehensive general liability (CGL), storekeepers (SK), owners, landlords, and tenants (OL&T), garage liability (GL), and manufacturers and contractors (M&C). In addition, separate owners and contractors protective (OCP) coverage parts are available.

Comprehensive General Liability The CGL policy provides full owners and contractors protective liability insurance, whether the insured performs the work or an independent contractor performs it. Thus, if an insured decides to enlarge its building and plans on assisting an independent contractor in performing the work, the insured should have protection for a loss not otherwise excluded. However, an additional premium will be required when the policy is audited because of the additional exposure.

Storekeepers Liability Policy (SK) The storekeepers liability policy (SK) is comparable to the CGL policy, except that no protection applies with respect to demolition operations. So, if that type of exposure arises, separate coverage must be obtained before the commencement of work.

OL&T, garage liability, and M&C forms provide only limited coverage, but each of these contracts can be amended to provide the broader coverage.

Owners, Landlords, and Tenants (OL&T) The OL&T policy covers losses dealing with the ownership, maintenance, or use of the insured premises, as well as all operations necessary or incidental to them. However, the policy excludes losses stemming from any structural alterations which involve moving or changing the size or shape of a building or structure. New construction and demolition operations are likewise excluded. The exclusion applies whether work is performed by the insured or by an independent contractor. Any other type of work performed on premises by or on behalf of the insured is covered. In order to obtain broader coverage under the OL&T policy, it is necessary to delete the exclusion just mentioned and amend the coverage part to read "Coverage for Designated Premises and Related Operations in Progress *Including* Structural Alterations, New Construction and Demolition." Appropriate references to independent contractor coverage also must be inserted in various provisions of the OL&T policy so amended.

Garage Liability (GL) The coverage and excluded exposures of the garage liability policy are comparable to those of the OL&T policy, with two exceptions. The exclusion of liability for structural alterations, new construction, and demolition operations applies when work is performed by an independent contractor, or when loss arises out of omissions or supervisory acts of the insured in connection with work of that nature. Thus, when the insured performs that type of work, the exclusion does not apply. However, there is coverage even for the excluded exposure, provided the insurer is notified of such undertaking within thirty days after the operation commences.

Manufacturers and Contractors (M&C) The M&C policy excludes losses resulting from operations performed for the insured by an independent contractor (as well as losses arising out of the omissions or supervisory acts of the insured in connection with all operations) with two exceptions—the policy covers losses which occur in the course of (1) maintenance and repairs at premises owned by or rented to the named insured, or (2) structural alterations at those premises which do not involve changing the size of or moving buildings or structures. Coverage for the independent contractor exposure can be added by taking two steps. The exclusion must be deleted, and the coverage part must be amended to read "Operations in Progress *Including* Operations of Independent Contractors." Like the OL&T policy, appropriate references to independent contractor coverage also must be inserted in the declarations on this form.

Separate OCP Coverage Part Another common method of providing OCP insurance protection is by way of a separate coverage part designated as "Owners and Contractors Protective Liability Insurance, Coverage for Operations of Designated Contractor." The separate coverage part is not intended for use on an existing liability policy. Instead, it must be issued as a separate policy, which simply involves attaching the coverage part to the standard policy jacket. Its use, furthermore, is restricted to situations where a general contractor purchases the coverage in the name of the project owner for whom work is being done, or when a subcontractor purchases it in the name of the general contractor in a given project.

Reasons for Purchasing OCP Coverage

Many people, particularly those who must purchase OCP coverage on behalf of others, question its need, especially when those for whom work is to be performed already have protection under their own CGL policies, or when those who are to perform the work have contractual liability insurance. Although the coverage seems superfluous in those situations when the owner or the general contractor already has a CGL policy, its purchase is nevertheless considered sound practice, for economic reasons and to avoid inter-company disputes between insurers.

Economic Reasons It has just been noted that many policies automatically provide OCP coverage, with an appropriate premium for the OCP exposure charged either when the policy is written or collectible at audit. This insurance expense can be avoided by a project owner if the owner requires the general contractor to purchase insurance in the owner's name. (Or a general contractor may avoid the insurance charge for this exposure by requiring such a purchase by a subcontractor.)

Avoiding Inter-Company Disputes Defense is one of the most important parts of OCP coverage, since plaintiffs generally name as codefendants every party even remotely involved with a loss. If an owner and general contractor (or contractor and subcontractor) have different insurers, both insurers will likely be involved in defense. If one or more parties is found liable for the loss, further litigation may result between insurers attempting to allocate responsibility for the loss. Such inter-company disputes among insurers are eliminated when OCP coverage is purchased by the contractor for the owner, because only one insurer is involved with a covered loss affecting both parties.

Owners and Contractors Protective Liability Policy

Coverage Provisions The insurer of owners and contractors protective insurance written to cover a designated contractor agrees to pay, on behalf of the entity named in the policy as the insured, all damages because of bodily injury or property damage caused by an occurrence, and arising out of (1) operations performed for the named insured by the contractor designated in the policy declarations at the designated work site, or (2) acts or omissions of the named insured in connection with its general supervision of such operations that are being performed by the designated contractor.

The primary reason for owners and contractors protective liability insurance is found in (1) above. When any operation performed for the insured by an independent contractor results in a loss, the latter is usually held solely responsible. But all parties involved are commonly named as codefendants in a legal action. If this should happen, the insured at least has defense coverage. The contractor, on the other hand, will have to rely upon its own premises and operations insurance (or retain the loss).

The second coverage is needed because those for whom work is being performed usually reserve the right to check on its progress, and to see that the work is being done according to specifications. And, it is because of an insured's acts or omissions in connection with such functions that some losses are actually or allegedly caused. However, it sometimes is a difficult matter to pinpoint whether the act or omission in question is within the scope of an insured's general supervision of work. Complicating matters is an exclusion of bodily injury or property damage arising out of any act or omission of the named insured or employees, other than the general supervision of work, and the absence of any definition for the term "general supervision." The net result is that many losses involve questions of fact for the courts to answer.

An actual case that illustrates the complexity of these situations is Union Electric Co. v. Pacific Indemnity Co., 425 S.W. (2nd.) 87. An employee of a tree-trimming contractor doing work for the utility was severely burned when he came into contact with an uninsulated high voltage circuit. Under the terms of the agreement with the contractor, the utility was required to designate areas where trees were to be cut and trimmed, and it was required to inspect the progress of such work. The injured employee filed suit against the utility and charged it with negligence in inadequately maintaining uninsulated wires and failing to warn of their presence.

The utility's liability policy provided coverage for claims stemming from (1) operations performed for the insured by independent contractors, and (2) general supervision by the insured of operations performed for it by independent contractors. The utility's insurer refused to provide defense, because the insured failed to show that it "generally supervised" the work performed by the tree-trimming contractor. After having settled the claim with the contractor, the utility sought reimbursement from its insurer. The lower court held in favor of the utility, because the utility in no way controlled the work of the independent contractor, but only acted in a supervisory capacity within the terms of the policy.

On appeal, the insurer contended that the tree-trimming contractor alone controlled the work being performed under contract and that there was no evidence (to which the court also agreed) to show that the utility supervised the method, manner or means by which the contractor performed the work. The insurer therefore maintained that its policy did not obligate it to provide defense.

The ultimate question before the court of appeal, which affirmed the lower court's decision, was whether the negligence of the utility in failing to warn of a dangerous condition could be considered as failure of the utility to generally supervise operations performed on its behalf by independent contractors. The court held that the inherently dangerous nature of the wires created a primary, nondelegable duty upon the utility to take measures commensurate with that dangerous condition. And, since the term "general supervision" is not defined in the policy, the court stated that a liberal definition of that term would encompass the supervisory duties of the utility in the designated areas, as well as the utility's omission to warn of any danger. After reviewing a number of dictionary definitions of the term, the court concluded that "general supervision" encompasses work only to the extent necessary to see that it is being performed properly. The court stated, furthermore, that the term does not encompass control or supervision over the method, manner or means of carrying out such work. If the utility had exercised such control, it would have destroyed the independent contractor relationship and would have nullified the utility's coverage.

Another exclusion that is peculiar to OCP insurance deals with bodily injury or property damage which occurs following either of two circumstances. The first part of the exclusion applies to any loss that arises after completion of all work (other than service, maintenance and repairs) on the project to be performed by or on behalf of the named insured. The purpose of this part of the exclusion is to make it clear that the coverage applies only while work is in progress. Any work which is completed, except in the following circumstance, is the subject of completed operations insurance. The second part of the exclusion applies to any loss occurring after that portion of the designated contractor's work is put to its intended use by any one other than another contractor who is engaged in operations on that same project. The purpose of this part of the exclusion is the same as the former one. However, coverage still applies to the contractor whose work is completed, if operations still are being conducted at the site by other contractors. Once the entire project is completed by all contractors, however, coverage terminates under this insurance.

Most of the other exclusions applying to owners and contractors protective liability insurance are common to other liability policies. Excluded are liability assumed by the insured under any contract or agreement, other than an incidental contract; any obligation for which the insured or his or her insurer may be liable under workers' compensation or similar law; bodily injury to any employee of the insured arising out of and during the course of his or her employment, or to any obligation of the insured to indemnify another because of such injury; and property damage to that property in the insured's care, custody or control.

Also excluded is bodily injury or property damage due to war, civil war, insurrection, rebellion, or revolution; any mobile equipment being used in any prearranged racing contest; or the use of snowmobiles. The contamination or pollution exclusion also applies, as well as the so-called business risk exclusion, which excludes loss of use of tangible property which has not been destroyed.

Additional Interests When an owners and contractors protective liability policy is issued in the name of the owner or the prime contractor, other interests may be added for additional charges. Among those who can be added are architects, engineers or surveyors. However, coverage does not apply for losses arising out of professional services they perform on behalf of the insured, including (1) the preparation or approval of maps, plans, opinions, reports, surveys, designs, specifications, and (2) supervisory, inspection, or engineering services.

Since employees can be held personally liable for their acts or omissions during the performance of any work for their employers, they, too, can be added as additional insureds on policies of their employers.

Instead of having to incur the extra expense of purchasing a separate owners and contractors protective liability policy for an owner or general contractor, it also is permissible to add such person or entity as an additional insured on the CGL policy of the contractor. (However, a subcontractor normally cannot be added as an additional insured on the policy of a general contractor.) Nothing is changed by adding others on an existing policy as additional insureds insofar as the coverage provisions are concerned and there may be some premiums saved. However, it should be noted that, when one policy is intended to cover several parties, the limit of liability that applies on the one policy must be shared by all interests. Thus, in the event of a loss involving both the contractor and the owner, the limit of liability of the contractor's CGL policy would be the maximum that applies for all interests. Whether these limits are adequate will depend upon the loss. It therefore is important that this alternative and its premium savings be compared to the method of obtaining two separate policies: one for the owner or the contractor for whom work is to be performed, and one for the contractor who is to perform that work.

Principal's Protective Liability Insurance

Thus far, the discussion of protective liability insurance has centered on insurance against the vicarious liability exposures of owners and contractors engaged in construction operations, who may become liable for acts of independent contractors. Another type of vicarious liability exposure arises out of a different type of independent contractor relationship. Newspaper publishers have such an exposure in connection with the newspaper carriers who serve as independent contractors. Action could be brought against the newspaper alleging damages caused *by* their independent contractor. It is also possible that the newspaper could be held liable for injuries *to* their carrier. Other firms are faced with similar liability exposures because of their use of independent contractors—for example general insurance agents or real estate agents who hire solicitors and sub-agents, or distributors of products who engage door-to-door canvassers who sell and make delivery of the product. The latter category would include persons selling vacuum cleaners, encyclopedias, brushes, or cosmetics, as long as they are, in fact, independent contractors, rather than employees.

It has been mentioned that principals *generally* are not held to be responsible for torts which are committed by others, such as agents and independent contractors. However, there are enough exceptions to the preceding rule to make it uncertain, at any given time, whether or not the torts of persons can be imputed to others. Especially troublesome in this regard is the question whether a person's status is one of an employee or an independent contractor. It is said that the matter of control over a person is the primary criterion in establishing a person's status. But how much control is necessary before a person becomes an employee may depend upon the circumstances. These uncertainties generate a need for protection against a loss exposure, and principals can protect themselves by purchasing principal's protective liability insurance.

Principal's protective liability insurance offers a two-part coverage. The first coverage part is designed to protect a principal in the event an independent contractor or an employee of such contractor sustains bodily injury while performing work on behalf of the principal. Although the claimant must prove that the principal is liable for the damages, the latter does receive defense protection while the issue is being decided—provided of course, the complaint alleges the type of act or omission which is otherwise covered by the policy.

To qualify for principal's protective liability insurance, the principal must normally show proof that he or she has a workers' compensation policy in force. The rationale for this latter requirement is to make workers' compensation insurance applicable in the event that (1) it ultimately is determined that the injured person is an *employee* of the principal and is not an independent contractor, or (2) an independent contractor does not carry workers' compensation on its employee(s) and the state law therefore requires the principal to be liable for compensation to such employee(s). This first coverage (injury to workers), therefore, is intended to apply only when workers' compensation insurance is not a factor.

The second coverage part is intended to protect the principal against his or her vicarious liability which stems from bodily injury or property damage caused by the act or omission of an independent contractor or an employee of the latter during the course of the contractor's employment for the principal. Not covered is any liability stemming from the use of the principal's owned or hired motor vehicles; liability assumed under any contract or agreement; and liability for any obligation for which the principal may be held liable under any workers' compensation law. This coverage is similar in concept to the coverage which is provided by owners and contractors protective liability insurance, except that principal's protective liability coverage relates more to service-type exposures, rather than construction, demolition and building repair work.

Railroad Protective Liability Insurance

When any kind of construction work involves a railroad right-of-way (highway or bridge construction are common examples) it is nearly universal practice for the railroad to insist upon rather sweeping protection for itself. This protection not only encompasses freedom from liability to the public, but also involves obligations of the railroad's own employees and its own rolling stock. And, unless the railroads are given this protection, they will not grant the easement rights which are necessary if work is to commence on or near that property.

Such requirements are usually met with railroad protective liability insurance. Such insurance can be obtained by the railroad, but paid for by either the contractors involved in the project or the public authority for whom work is being performed. The policy names the railroad as the named insured and it covers the railroad against bodily injury and property damage losses sustained by almost anyone at the designated work site. The railroad, in other words, is given protection whether loss involves members of the public or employees of the general contractor or subcontractors. The insurance also provides first-party coverage for any physical damage to rolling stock of railroads, as well as their contents and equipment. Though the limits demanded usually are extremely high, the coverage must be obtained before permission will be granted by the railroads to commence any work.

In lieu of a railroad protective liability insurance policy per se, a railroad sometimes will accept the contractor's proof that the obligations of the railroad, as assumed by the contractor, are covered by other insurance or by a formal retention program. Yet, in spite of the fact that the contractor may have blanket contractual liability insurance, coverage still may be insufficient for this purpose, even when it is provided for "all written contracts without exception." As noted earlier, the standard blanket contractual coverage part contains an exclusion of injury or damage involving work on or near railroad property (although the exclusion can often be deleted for an additional premium).

Work projects involving railroads have been and continue to be troublesome in at least two ways. The first is the difficulty of obtaining a meeting of the minds among all those who are involved in a work project affecting railroad right-of-ways. Sometimes railroads have been known to be unrealistic in their demands. The other problem is that of obtaining the necessary types and limits of insurance demanded by railroads. Yet, the railroads' demand for complete protection is understandable. After all, they seldom benefit from such projects (the building of highways, in fact, poses direct competition for railroads) and, yet, they can become involved in large lawsuits because of such projects.

NONINSURANCE TECHNIQUES FOR HANDLING PROTECTIVE LIABILITY EXPOSURES

Before a firm can handle protective liability exposures in a way that will avoid any undue financial burdens, it must not only understand the reasons exposures exist, but also the ways by which losses can result. This is not always easy to do. In fact, most persons find this subject difficult because the legal ramifications of principal-independent contractor relationships are complex. Many people understand the general rule of law that independent contractors are held solely responsible for whatever losses may result from their acts or omissions. However, few seem to understand the ways in which that rule of immunity may be nullified, and this is where much of the problem dealing with protective liability exposures lies.

Yet, in spite of the potential problems of protective liability exposures, it is likely to be an exceptional situation when noninsurance techniques are singled out to handle such exposures when the exposures have been identified. There is still sufficient, reasonably priced insurance available, in most instances, to protect persons and firms in the event they are held to be vicariously liable for the torts of others.

Nearly every liability policy for commercial enterprises and entities, for example, automatically provides some form of protective liability insurance. And, if the protection provided by policies is not broad enough to handle the exposures (for example, the limited coverages provided by the OL&T and M&C forms), it usually can be broadened by endorsement. Also, if a loss results from an independent contractor's act or omission which is deemed by law to be nondelegable, the principal can then look to its premises and operations liability insurance (which is a basic coverage of almost all liability policies) for protection. Principals also can obtain extra protection against their protective or premises and operations liability losses under umbrella liability and excess liability policies.

Despite the foregoing measures of protection which undoubtedly are relied upon by many firms today, it is (or should be) a well-known fact that liability policies, no matter how comprehensive, do not cover all loss exposures. When exposures cannot be avoided or insured, there may be times when the noninsurance technique of retention will have to be relied upon as a method of handling some of the exposures to loss.

Any discussion of noninsurance transfers in this regard takes an interesting twist because the protective liability exposure is often the *product* of a noninsurance transfer. A hold harmless agreement, for example, may be intended to shift the consequences of loss to another person or firm which is in a better position to prevent loss, or the transfer may be effected simply as a means to escape any resulting liability. Aside from the possibility that the obligation being transferred may be nondelegable, it may be to the indemnitee's advantage to aid the indemnitor, whenever possible, with whatever loss prevention measures may be within the indemnitee's control. If for no other reason, that type of assistance may help to strengthen the work arrangement and to prevent or at least control the kind of claims for which the arrangement was purposely created, i.e., to reduce the chances of any claim adversely affecting the transferor (indemnitee).

Not all persons or firms have transfer of liability in mind when they hire others to perform work or services on their behalf, nor are some of those persons or firms in any position to assist in loss control as, for example, the building owner who hires an experienced contractor to make certain difficult repairs. On the other hand, some owners and contractors of projects voluntarily impose stringent loss control measures which can affect everyone on a project. (The wrap-up arrangements mentioned earlier sometimes involve circumstances whereby the owner or general contractor engages loss control and engineering experts to enforce safety in all phases of the work, instead of allowing each subcontractor to rely upon its own loss control expertise. This approach is likely to enhance safer conditions or produce more uniformity than if several different loss prevention people are involved at one work project.) Sometimes owners or contractors of projects are legally required to implement certain loss control measures to provide safe places of employment, such as the requirements of the Occupational Safety and Health Act (OSHA). Whether voluntary or mandatory, loss control can go a long way toward directly or indirectly preventing losses stemming from protective liability exposures, as well as from premises and operations and workers' compensation exposures.

Another possible approach for handling protective liability exposures (an approach which involves a type of loss control) may be for principals to make special efforts to hire only competent persons or firms. When an experienced and knowledgeable person is engaged to perform a service, there is less likelihood of an error, other things being equal, than if an inexperienced person were hired instead. It is the employer's duty to exercise reasonable care to select competent and careful people who have safe and proper equipment for performing their work.

If a given type of work, such as blasting near a heavily populated area, is so inherently dangerous that the work cannot be transferred, the exposure cannot be safely retained or effectively controlled and the firm has no in-house expertise to handle the project, the only other alternative may be avoidance. Avoidance should be seriously considered when the chance of a serious loss more than outweighs the opportunities for profit. What is of extreme importance, however, is that a firm recognize the circumstances under which protective liability exposures can and cannot be transferred. For example, a firm which hires a contractor to perform blasting work and requires a hold harmless agreement as an additional measure of protection, may likely find itself confronted with a situation when there is no alternative but to retain the loss exposure, unless the firm (indemnitee) is fortunate enough to be carrying operations liability insurance for the blasting exposure.

Despite the fact that protective liability insurance may be the most common way to handle protective liability loss exposures, the foregoing remarks illustrate that there are many noninsurance techniques for handling those exposures which can be used in lieu of or to complement the insurance.

Chapter Notes

1. See White v. Morris Handler Company, 7 Ill. App. 3d 191 (1972).
2. Article 2, the "Sales" article, has been adopted (with minor modifications in some states) in every state except Louisiana.
3. Georgia Chapter CPCU, *The Hold Harmless Agreement* (Cincinnati: The National Underwriter Co., 1973), p. 89.
4. See Strench v. Charles Ap. Co., 1 Ill. App. 3d 57, 273 N.E. 2d 19 (1971).
5. See General Heating Engineering Co. v. District of Columbia, 301 F. 2d 549 (D.C. Cir. 1962).
6. A guarantor, on the other hand, is only *secondarily liable*, and his or her liability is contingent on the default of his or her principal. Unlike a surety, a guarantor only becomes absolutely liable when the principal's default occurs and the guarantor is notified of it.
7. Arthur Adelbert Stearns, *The Law of Suretyship* (Cincinnati: W.H. Anderson Co., 1951), p. 8.1.
8. See Annotation, "Validity and Construction of Statute Authorizing or Requiring Governmental Unit to Indemnify Public Officer or Employee for Liability Arising out of Performance of Public Duties," 71 A.L.R. 3d 90 (1976).
9. Annotation, "Building Contractor's Liability, Upon Bond or Other Agreement to Indemnify Owner, for Injury or Death of Third Persons Resulting from Owner's Negligence," 27 A.L.R. 3d 663 (1969).
10. See Ill. Rev. Stat., Ch. 43, Section 135 (1975); Klopp v. Protective Order of Elks, 309 Ill. App. 145, 33 N.E. 2d 161 (1941).
11. Ill. Rev. Stat., Ch. 48, Sections 60-69 (1975).
12. While an injured worker cannot sue his or her employer in Illinois due to the Illinois Workmen's Compensation Act, Ill. Rev. Stat., Ch. 48, Sections 138.5(a), 138.11 (1975), the worker may proceed against contractors, owners, and other parties "having charge of the work" for damages under the Structural Work Act.
13. 45 U.S.C. 1 et seq. (1975).
14. See Annotation, 175 A.L.R. 8 (1948).
15. 60 Cal. 2d 92, 32 Cal. Rptr. 33, 383 P. 2d 441 (1963).
16. John D. Calamari and Joseph M. Perillo, *Law of Contracts*, 365 (St. Paul: West Publishing Co., 1971).
17. Samuel Williston, *A Treatise on the Law of Contracts*, 1749A at 133, 3rd ed. Walter H. E. Jaeger, ed. (Mount Kisco, NY: Baker, Voorhees & Co., 1972).
18. Blount v. Tow Fong, 138 Atl. 52.
19. Thomas F. Sheehan, "Construction Management, Opportunity for Profit or Financial Disaster," *F.C.& S. Bulletins*, Management and Sales, pp. Surveys Cm-1 to 9.
20. It might also be noted that specialty insurance is available to cover construction management professional liability. Further information on this

can be found in the *F.C.& S. Bulletins*, Management and Sales Section, Surveys Cm-7.

21. William L. Prosser, *Handbook of the Law of Torts*, 4th ed. (St. Paul: West Publishing Co., 1971), p. 459.
22. *Restatement of Agency*, 2d 220 (1).
23. *Restatement of Agency*, 2d 250.
24. Ibid. at 251-262.
25. Prosser, p. 468.
26. Kuhn v. P. J. Carlin Construction Co., 278 N.Y.S. 635 (1935).
27. Lamb v. South Unit Jehovah's Witnesses, 232 Minn. 259, 5 N.W. 2d 403 (1950).
28. Stickel v. Riverview Sharpshooters' Park Co., 250 Ill. 452, 95 N.E. 445 (1911).
29. Prosser, p. 484.
30. Myers v. Little Church by the Side of the Road, 37 Wash. 2d 897, 227 P. 2d 165 (1951).
31. Lineweaver v. John Wanamaker, Inc., 299 Pa. 45, 149 A. 91 (1930).
32. Bonczkiewicz v. Merberg Wrecking Corp., 148 Conn. 573, 172 A. 2d 917 (1961).
33. Trump v. Bluefield Waterworks & Imp. Co., 99 W.Va. 425, 129 S.E. 309 (1925).
34. Campus v. McElligott, 122 Conn. 14, 187 A. 29 (1936).
35. Harry Campbell Black, *Black's Law Dictionary*, 4th ed. (St. Paul: West Publishing Co., 1968), p. 972.
36. *Restatement of Torts*, 2d, 384, 403, and 404.
37. *Restatement of Torts*, 2d 575 and Arthur Linton Corbin, *Corbin on Contracts*, 1472 (St. Paul: West Publishing Co., 1962), pp. 591-596.
38. *Restatement of Torts*, 2d, 411.
39. Ibid. at 416.
40. Eamol v. Big Bear Land & Water Co., 98 Cal. 2d 370, 220 P. 2d 408 (1950).
41. Fowler v. Uezzell, 94 Idaho 951, 500 P. 2d 852 (1972).
42. *Corpus Juris Secundum*, "Partnership," 168 (Brooklyn: American Law Book Co., and St. Paul: West Publishing Co., 1946).
43. Morrison v. Coombs, 23 F. Supp. 852 (D. Me. 1938).

CHAPTER 6

Employers' Liability and Workers' Compensation Exposures

GENERAL NATURE OF EMPLOYERS' EXPOSURES

When an employee sustains a job-connected accident resulting in bodily injury or suffers an occupational disease in the course of employment, the employer is subject to liability. The employer's legal responsibility may be imposed by the common law or it may be a liability created by an applicable compensation statute. Hence, claims made by employees may result in a court-imposed money judgment or an award of benefits prescribed in a statute. In either case, the dollar amounts recovered by the employee or the employee's dependents may be substantial.

Employers' liability and workers' compensation exposures are linked to the relationship between an "employer" and an "employee." An *employer* is one who engages the services of another under a contract of hire requiring the payment of wages, salary, or commission. The employer fixes the hours of employment, provides the tools with which to do the work, and defines and supervises the methods and means of doing the work. An employer could be a corporation, a partnership, or an individual. However, as a general rule, an employer's legal obligations for occupational injury or disease extend only to its employees, not to independent contractors.

An *employee* is one who acts for another under a contract of hire for wages or other forms of remuneration, subject to the terms, conditions, hours, and rules promulgated by the employer. The employer has the right to control and direct the activities of the employee who performs the services, not only as to the result to be accomplished, but also the methods and means by which the result is obtained.

The matter of control of activities of the employee is one of the distinguishing features of the employer-employee relationship. Absent the control of the hours of work, the methods of doing the work, the supplying of necessary tools and other machinery to accomplish the work in return for the payment of wages or salary, the relationship is not that of employer and employee.

The payment of salary or wages does not necessarily have to be in money, but can be the equivalent thereof, such as room and board, the use of an apartment with utilities, or the use of farmland for agricultural purposes. In addition, payment for the employee's services may be made on a commission basis, or the employee may receive a nominal amount of money with the balance being received in tips and other emoluments. The method of payment will not affect the relationship, as long as the other elements, noted above, are present.

An *independent contractor* is not an employee. He or she, in the exercise of an independent employment, represents the principal only as to the results to be accomplished and is not subject to the control of the principal as to the methods and means of doing the work. The independent contractor determines the hours of work, directs and controls the work, and may employ assistants when necessary. The principal will set the specifications for the work to be done and may also require that the work be accomplished on or about a certain date. The principal may also require that the work be done in a workmanlike manner, and the payment for the work may be dependent upon a strict adherence to the specifications and upon the completion by a certain specified date. For example, suppose a principal contracts with an individual to do some plumbing work on the principal's premises. The plumber furnishes the tools, fixes the hours to devote to the task, and is responsible to the principal only as to the successful accomplishment of the job. In such a situation the principal is not responsible, as an employer per se, for any occupational injuries the plumber may sustain.[1] Of course, since the plumber and the plumber's employees are classed as business invitees, the firm which contracted with the plumber may be liable in tort to the plumber or the employees, under the same circumstances and to the same extent that the firm may be liable to any member of the public. Such liability does not arise from any employer-employee relationship, but because of the firm's exposures as an owner or occupier of the premises. (The latter exposures were discussed in Chapter 2 of this text.)

Thus, the right of control as to the mode and method of doing the work is the principal consideration in determining whether one engaged is an independent contractor or an employee. One who represents another as to the result to be accomplished and exercises his or her own judgment as to the methods and means to accomplish the result is an independent contractor. On the other hand, one who is subject to the control and direction of the principal as to the methods and means of doing the work is an employee or servant. The following examples might serve to clarify how these general principles are applied.

In the moving industry, it is the general practice for the moving company to engage the services of a driver and a van which is usually owned by the driver. The driver delivers goods exclusively for the moving company and has the name of the company painted and displayed on the van. The driver is subject to the control and direction of the moving company. He or she is therefore an employee, even though the commission contemplates not only his or her own work but also the use of the van.[2]

On the other hand, where the individual does a piece of work for the principal and is permitted to decide how and when the work will be performed, the individual is an independent contractor. In addition, even though the principal provides some of its own workers to assist the individual, the individual is still an independent contractor. For example, in one case the individual contracted to paint smokestacks, furnishing his own tools and equipment, with no control being exercised by the principal as to the time of the beginning of the work or the methods to be employed in accomplishing it. He was held to be an independent contractor, even though the principal supplied the paint and furnished him with a helper.[3]

The determination of the question as to whether an individual is an independent contractor or an employee is not free from difficulty. Each situation will be determined by the specific facts. Generally, however, the answer to the question will turn on (1) the intention of the parties, and (2) control by the principal of the hours of work, as well as the methods and means of accomplishing the work. For example, a newspaper carrier is not under the control of the newspaper. Usually he or she pays for the newspapers and collects the money from the customers. The newspaper has no control over when and where the newspapers are delivered. The carrier is therefore an independent contractor and not an employee. However, some states have by statute (workers' compensation) defined a newspaper carrier as an employee who, as such, is entitled to all of the benefits of the law.

In some states, caddies have been held to be employees of the country club, not employees of the individual members who employ them, in spite of the fact that their only recompense was derived solely from payments by the members who utilize their services, and no salary or other remuneration was paid by the club. On the other hand, baby-sitters have been held to be independent contractors and, in some states, the workers' compensation laws specifically exclude them from coverage.

Corporate officers pose some special problems of interpretation. A corporation has been defined as an artificial person, created by statute, which can act only through agents. The agents in charge of the corporate enterprise consist of the corporate officers and the board of directors. The problem therefore arises as to whether a corporate officer is an employer or an employee. Unquestionably, when the individual is acting as an officer of the corporation and directing the management of the corporation, he or she is in fact an employer. On the other hand, in many small corporations, the officers also do the work of employees, in addition to their corporate duties. In deciding the question, the courts have adopted the "dual capacity doctrine," which in essence holds that when the individual is acting as a corporate officer, he or she is not an employee. When the individual is engaged in nonexecutive type of work for the corporation, he or she is an employee and, thus, is entitled to the benefits of the workers' compensation law.

The dual capacity doctrine has been under attack for some time, on the theory that regardless of the nature of the work performed by a corporate officer, he or she is nevertheless an employee. Finally, in Mine Service Co. v. Green, 265 SW 2d 944 (Kentucky), the court held that the dual capacity doctrine involved an artificial distinction. In that case, the president of the corporation was killed while driving to a convention to represent the corporation in an executive capacity. The court recognized the corporation as a separate entity and gave the corporate officer employee status, since he was actually employed by the corporate entity.[4] Some vestiges of the dual capacity doctrine still remain, although the latest pronouncements of the courts suggest that it is on the wane. In fact, in at least one state (Kentucky) the workers' compensation statute now includes corporate executive officers in its definition of covered employees.

Individual proprietors and partners in a partnership are not employees, and therefore are not entitled to workers' compensation benefits under most statutes.

EMPLOYERS' LIABILITY EXPOSURES
AT COMMON LAW

Originally, the courts applied common-law tort concepts to the disposition of occupational injury and disease claims by an employee against an employer. Except where the common law has been modified by statute, the same basic principles are applied to cases of this type today. The employer is bound to exercise a high degree of care for the safety of the person of the employee. The failure on the part of the employer to exercise such care as the circumstances require constitutes negligence. Where such negligence is the proximate cause of an employee's injury, the employer is answerable in damages. Conversely, if there is no failure on the part of the employer to meet the duty of care and an injury to an employee occurs, there can be no recovery by the employee, regardless of how serious the injuries happen to be. In all cases, the burden of establishing the negligence of the employer is on the employee. Unless the employee can sustain that burden, the employee may not recover under common law.

Statutory Modifications

As will be discussed more fully later in the chapter, employers' liability statutes and workers' compensation laws have been enacted which change the applicable common law in some areas and in certain employments. If the law specifically alters the common law, the courts will give effect to the legislation. On the other hand, the courts will strictly construe laws which change or amend current common-law rules, and unless the language of the statute clearly indicates that the legislative intent is to change the common law, the courts will continue to apply the law as it existed prior to the legislation. Therefore, in the absence of legislation which has been construed to change the common law, the employers' liability exposure will continue to be based on negligence concepts.

It should be emphasized that the legislature has the power to change any rule of law adopted by the courts by means of properly written legislation, and the courts are bound to give effect to the will of the legislature as expressed in the legislation. However, the courts are jealous of their jurisdiction. They will not construe legislation as effecting a change in the existing decisions and rules of law, unless the legislation specifically manifests an intent on the part of the legislature to change the existing rule of law. To be effective, the legislation must be precise and must exhibit a legislative intent to change the existing law. The courts will construe the legislation as affecting only such changes as are specifically required by the language of the statute and nothing more. For example, under some workers' compensation statutes, a minor is deemed to be *sui juris* (legally capable) for the purpose of making a claim for compensation benefits. However, the courts will not construe this legislation as making the minor *sui juris* for all purposes. Should the minor bring a tort action against a defendant, he or she must bring the action through a guardian. Likewise, even though the minor is *sui juris* in compensation matters, it does not mean that he or she is *sui juris* for the purpose of defending a tort action brought against him or her. Again, the appointment of a guardian is required by the courts. In most states, minors are licensed to drive automobiles and, in the operation thereof, the minor is held to the same degree of care as an adult. Even though the minor has the privilege of driving an automobile, it does not mean that he or she is *sui juris* for the purpose of bringing suit for accidents arising out of the operation of the vehicle. The courts construe the driving privilege as a privilege and nothing more. If the legislature intended that the minor driver would acquire other legal rights, they could have said so. The legislature not having said so, the minor obtains the privilege of operating the motor vehicle and nothing more.

Therefore, it must be concluded that any legislation or statute which purports to change the existing common law or the existing rules of law will be strictly construed. As a result, the common law or existing legal rules will apply to all situations not covered by the workers' compensation laws or other statutes.

Elements of Negligence Liability

In a definitional sense, negligence consists of the failure to exercise that degree of care which the law requires to protect others from unreasonable risks of harm.

Among the legally protected rights recognized by law is the right of safety of person. Others have the duty of exercising reasonable care so as to avoid invading that legally protected right. A breach of this duty may consist of either (1) an act of commission (e.g., careless driving of an automobile); or (2) an omission (e.g., failing to maintain the premises in safe condition). A possible defendant is not a guarantor of the safety of all others with whom he or she comes in contact, but a defendant's conduct will be judged by the "reasonably prudent person" standard in a court of law. If the defendant's conduct is equal to what the reasonably prudent person would or would not do under the same or similar circumstances, he or she is not negligent, regardless of whether or not an injury is sustained by the plaintiff. On the other hand, if the defendant's conduct falls below the reasonably prudent person standard, he or she is negligent. The essential elements of a cause of action based on negligence consist of the following:

1. a legal duty owed;
2. failure to comply with the standard of care required to meet the duty; and
3. damages as a proximate result.

The plaintiff must allege and prove all three of these elements. If any one element is lacking, there is no cause of action. The same principles are applied to the relationship of employer and employee. The employer has certain duties which are imposed by the common law.

Common-Law Duties of the Employer to Employees

The common law requires that the employer exercise reasonable care for the safety of his or her employees. This general duty of care has been broken down, in the decided cases, into the following specific duties owed by the employer.

Provide a Safe Place to Work This requires that the employer not only provide a physically safe building or area, but also that the employer maintain the premises in reasonably safe condition, provide proper housekeeping, and make periodic inspections at reasonable intervals. What is a "reasonable" interval will depend upon the nature of the work and the frequency of occurrence of unsafe conditions (e.g., those due to debris and other material which might accumulate in the work area). In determining whether or not the employer has met this duty, the reasonably prudent person standard is again applied. The reasonably prudent person will not only make inspections to determine the presence of unsafe conditions, but will also take immediate steps to remedy such conditions, taking precautions against injury during the time of repair. In addition, he or she will comply with all state, county, and city safety requirements, as well as the federal safety standards set forth in the Occupational Safety and Health Act.

The employer's duty to provide a safe place to work is not limited to the premises where the work is to be performed; it could involve other factors which might make it unsafe for the employee. For example, an employer failed in his duty of exercising ordinary care for the safety of an employee where the employer's medical department found that the employee was suffering from a tubercular condition which made it dangerous for the employee to continue to work in the employer's plant. An award in favor of the employee was sustained.[5]

In some municipalities, the local ordinance requires that all door-to-door salespersons and solicitors be licensed. In the absence of such license, they are subject to arrest and imprisonment. In Richards Co. v. Harrison, 262 So. 2d 258 (Florida), the employer failed to apply for and receive such a license, and an employee selling the employer's books was arrested and jailed. In an action against the employer, the employee was awarded damages arising out of his arrest and incarceration. The court held that the failure of the employer to obtain a license was a breach of his duty to provide the employee with a safe place to work.

Provide the Employee with an Adequate Number of Competent Fellow Employees This duty contemplates an obligation on the part of the employer to provide a sufficient number of fellow employees to do the work in safety. The actual number will depend upon the nature of the work and the extent of the hazards involved. The employer also is required to exercise care in the selection of fellow employees. He or she must make inquiry as to their previous work records, observe their actions on the job after they are employed, and dismiss anyone whose job habits might cause injury to another. It should be noted that the employer, under the common law, ordinarily is not responsible for the negligence of a fellow employee who has been selected with reasonable care and whose employment activity did not require dismissal. A person placed in charge of the work is not a fellow employee. Such a person is considered a vice-principal of management and, as such, is responsible for his or her own negligent acts. Such negligent acts are also imputed to the employer under the agency doctrine of *respondeat superior* (let the superior party answer).

Provide Safe Tools and Equipment The employer is required to provide safe appliances and machinery. This means that the machinery should be adequately guarded, properly maintained, and equipped with all normal safety features. It does not mean that the employer is bound to provide the newest and safest machinery possible. It is sufficient if the machinery provided can be used in safety by a competent employee. Also, proper equipment must be provided. This would include goggles for employees engaged in grinding and respirators for those exposed to noxious fumes or injurious dust, such as silica, anthracite, and asbestos.

Warn the Employee of Inherent Dangers This duty obligates the employer to warn the employee of any work-related dangers of which the employer is aware, or which by the exercise of reasonable care the employer could discover, and of which the employee is ignorant. For example, the employer should forewarn employees of the presence or use of beryllium, free silica, or radioactive material, as well as the hazards created by the use of certain chemicals and dyes. The inhalation of beryllium oxide dust can cause pneumonoconiosus (a disease of the lungs), acute pneumonitis (pneumonia), or chronic granulomatosis (nodules of inflammatory tissue in the lungs). Inhalation of silica can cause silicosis (fibrotic deterioration of the lungs).

As to readily apparent dangers, there is no duty to warn, since the employer has a right to assume that the employee, experienced or not, would be aware of the danger and be able to protect himself/herself from it. Accordingly, the employer would be under no common-law duty to warn the employee of the dangers of fire in a smelter, heat in an oven, using a grinding wheel without goggles, lifting unusually heavy objects, or putting a hand in machinery while it is in operation.

Make and Enforce Rules for the Safety of All Employees The employer is required to use reasonable care in devising and enforcing rules for the safety of his or her employees. The rules thus devised must be adequate in the light of the dangers to which the employees are exposed. The greater the danger, the more rigid the rules must be. The rules for the conduct of the employees must be enforced, and the employer may not sanction or tolerate continued violations. Enforcement might even require the discharge of employees who constantly violate the rules. In any event, the failure of the employer to enforce the safety rules, along with an injury to an employee caused by a violation of the rules, will make the employer liable to the injured employee.

Where the process is simple and the dangers, if any, are open and apparent to all, employees would be expected to protect themselves against all such dangers, without having rules which require them to do so, and the employer would not be obligated to make and enforce any rules.

Common-Law Defenses in Negligence Actions

To the employee's cause of action based upon the employer's negligence (i.e., the failure of the employer to meet one or more of the duties imposed), the employer has three common-law defenses (unless abolished or modified by statute). These are the defenses of *assumption of risk, contributory negligence,* and *the negligence of a fellow servant.*

Assumption of Risk The assumption of risk defense contemplates the existence of two elements: (1) the employee's knowledge or awareness of the existence of the risk, with a corresponding appreciation of the extent of the danger, and (2) the employee's voluntary exposure to the danger.

The employee will be charged with the knowledge of the danger when it is open and apparent. If the employee accepts employment under those circumstances, he or she will be exposed voluntarily to the danger, and may not recover for any resulting injury. The same thing is true where the employer has failed to meet a duty imposed upon him or her, such as failing to provide a safe place to work or failing to provide the proper equipment and tools, and the employee is aware of these failures but continues to work. The employee will be held to have assumed the risk of injury. In other words, the employer could use the assumption of risk defense successfully.

On the other hand, the employee cannot be held to have assumed a risk of which he or she was not aware. For example, if, unknown to the employee, radioactive materials were being used in another section of the plant and the employee suffered an injury from exposure to radiation, it cannot be said that the employee assumed this risk, since he or she was not even aware of it in the first place. The same thing would be true when, without warning, the employee's work involves contact with chemicals with which the average person is not familiar. For example, an employee was required to handle aniline dyes. There was no warning given as to the toxic effect of such chemicals when they contact a person's skin. Unaware of the danger, the employee suffered contact dermatitis as a consequence of exposing his skin to the dye. He did not assume the risk of this injury, and the employer would not be successful in using the assumption of risk defense.

The only major exception to the application of these rules involves a situation where the machinery with which the employee is required to work is defective and unsafe. When the employee has protested to the employer and the employer has promised to make the necessary repairs to correct the defective condition, some cases have held that the employee's actions in continuing to work do not constitute an assumption of risk, at least not until it becomes apparent that the employer has no intention of making repairs.

Contributory Negligence At common law all persons are required to exercise care for their own safety. If an employee fails to exercise such care, he or she will be deemed contributorily negligent, even though the negligence of the employer also was a contributing cause of the injury. The common-law rule is that if the employee's contributory negligence is responsible to any degree in the causation of the accident, the employee is barred from recovery. Thus, at common law, a momentary lapse or forgetfulness on the part of the employee (in exercising care for his or her own safety) will defeat recovery, even though the negligence of the employer contributed to a greater degree to the causation or the extent of the injury. For example, the employer supplied the employee with a truck with defective brakes. The employee knew that the brakes were defective, but managed to control the vehicle by pumping the brake pedal. An accident occurred in which the employee was injured. His disregard of his own safety by continuing to drive a vehicle with defective brakes constitutes contributory negligence.

In some states, this common-law rule has been modified by legislation which adopts the rule of comparative negligence. In such states, the contributory negligence of the employee will not defeat recovery, but may be taken into account by the jury in reducing the amount of recovery.

A few courts regard assumption of risk as merely another form of contributory negligence. However, the Restatement Torts (Second), Section 496, defines assumption of risk as follows:

> A plaintiff who voluntarily assumes a risk of harm arising from the negligent or reckless conduct of the defendant cannot recover for such harm.

Certain comparative negligence statutes do not eliminate the defense of assumption of risk. If the statute does not specifically include the defense of assumption of risk under its definition of contributory negligence, then the defense is still available to the defendant. For example, in Anderson v. Cooper, 391 P. 2d 86 (1964), the Kansas court denied recovery, even though Kansas has a comparative negligence statute. In that case the plaintiff sought damages for injuries received from a defective ensilage cutter. The defendant claimed that the plaintiff had worked with the machine for several weeks and had known of its defects. In a later case in Kansas, the court recognized the viability of the defense of assumption of risk, but limited it to master-servant relationships. Smith v. Blakey, 515 P. 2d 1062 (1973). The courts of Oklahoma (Okla. Stat. Ann. tit. 23, Sec. 12) and Arkansas (Bugh v. Webb, 328 SW 2d 579) also retain the defense of assumption of risk.

Some courts have held that the defenses of contributory negligence and assumption of risk often overlap and that the same set of facts may involve both. As a result, some courts have merged these two defenses into one and have applied both under comparative negligence statutes or decisions. In Nga Li v. Yellow Cab Co., 532 P. 2d 1226, the California Supreme Court expressed the policy of such a merger:

> We think it clear that the adoption of a system of comparative negligence should entail the merger of the defense of assumption of risk into the general scheme of assessment of liability in proportion to fault in those particular cases in which the form of assumption of risk is no more than a variant of contributory negligence.

The decision by the Wisconsin Supreme Court in Netzel v. State Sand & Gravel, 186 NW 2d 258, is to the same effect, holding that the plaintiff's unreasonable assumption of risk did not bar his recovery but reduced his recovery in proportion to his fault. In that case, the plaintiff was burned by skin contact with defective concrete. He knew from experience as a concrete worker that exposure of the skin by contact with concrete would cause severe burns. The court took this into consideration in apportioning damages. Thus, assumption of risk was considered to be a form of contributory negligence.

The court in Washington (Lyons v. Redding Construction Co., 515 P.

2d 821) abrogated entirely the defense of assumption of risk and merged it with contributory negligence as one type of defense. In addition, the New York comparative negligence statute (N.Y. CPLR 1411) provides: "the culpable conduct attributable to the claimant or to the decedent, including contributory negligence or assumption of risk, shall not bar recovery."

Therefore, the viability of the defenses of contributory negligence and assumption of risk will depend upon the provisions of the various comparative negligence statutes and the decisions of the courts which interpret them. In many states, the question is still an open one.

Negligence of a Fellow Employee It may be a complete defense for the employer if the injury is caused *solely* by the negligence of a fellow employee. This is an exception to the general rule that the negligence of an employee acting within the course and scope of his or her employment may be imputed to the employer under the doctrine of *respondeat superior*. The rule has been subject to criticism by text writers and some courts for this reason. However, the courts still apply the rule in the absence of legislation.

A fellow employee is defined as an employee of the same rank as the injured employee. A supervisor, therefore, is not usually a fellow employee. The theory is that since the supervisor is an agent of management, his or her negligence should be imputed to the employer. Some courts have gone beyond this point and have held that the fellow employee defense does not apply to any management employee who would be deemed a "vice-principal" of the employer. Vice-principal employees would consist of those who are responsible for meeting the duties of the employer to provide a safe place to work, select competent fellow employees, and warn employees as to the inherent dangers of the work. In addition to these exceptions, some courts have held that an employee of another department is not a fellow employee.

In general, the courts have not been too happy with the fellow employee defense. They grudgingly apply it only where it is absolutely necessary to do so. If they can find some excuse to deny its application, they will.

Statutory and Judicial Modifications of Common-Law Defenses

A number of states have enacted so-called employers' liability statutes which include various provisions relating to the common-law defenses of the employer. Some have eliminated entirely or effectively reduced the least popular defense of the negligence of a fellow employee. Others have abrogated the defense of assumption of risk.

As to the defense of contributory negligence, a number of states have replaced it by the enactment of comparative negligence statutes, and the courts in some states have adopted the comparative negligence principle by decision. Comparative negligence adopts the principle that the contributory negligence of the plaintiff shall not be a complete defense, but the negligence of the plaintiff may be taken into account in reducing the amount of the recovery. (It might be added, parenthetically, that these statutes and decisions are not restricted to matters involving employer and employee.)

There are two forms of comparative negligence statutes; namely, the "modified form" and the "pure form." Under both forms the jury is required to bring in a verdict indicating the percentage of negligence, if any, applied to both the plaintiff and defendant. Under the modified form, if the plaintiff's negligence equals or exceeds the amount of negligence allocated to the defendant, the plaintiff may not recover. Under the pure form, the plaintiff may recover, regardless of the percentage allocated to his negligence or that of the defendant. For example, if the plaintiff's damages amounted to $10,000 and the percentage of negligence ascribed to him or her is 40 percent, the plaintiff would receive a verdict of $6,000, $4,000 representing the deduction taken for his or her contributory negligence of 40 percent. On the other hand, if the plaintiff's negligence was adjudged to be 60 percent, under the pure form he or she would receive a verdict of $4,000. Under the modified form, he or she would get nothing.

It must be emphasized, however, that regardless of whether or not some or all of the employer's defenses have been abrogated, or whether or not the case is governed by the comparative negligence principle, the employee may not recover at common law unless he or she can establish that the employer has failed to meet one or more of the duties which the common law imposed.

When the employee does make out a prima facie case and does receive the verdict, his or her measure of damages may include the following:

1. out-of-pocket expenses for medical, surgical, and hospital services, nursing, ambulance, convalescent home, or nursing home, if necessary;
2. loss of wages during disability;
3. disability due to permanency;
4. pain and suffering;
5. loss of the enjoyment of life, temporary or permanent;

6. value of a lost opportunity, if one was present at the time of the accident or subsequent thereto; and/or

7. loss of consortium by the spouse.

Thus, the employee who does receive the favorable verdict is entitled to any or all of these elements of damage.

Death Claims The common law did not recognize that a dead person had any legal rights. He or she could not sue or be sued, and his or her legal existence ended with death. Therefore, where the employee suffered an accident which resulted in death, there was no action which could be taken against the employer, even though the injury and death was caused through the negligence of the employer. There was no recognition given to the damages suffered by those who were dependent upon the deceased for their support. Thus, such persons had no legal remedy and in many cases were forced to join other destitute persons on the public charity rolls. As a consequence, public pressure demanded that the British Parliament enact legislation which would allow a recovery against the wrongdoer. The response came in the form of the Fatal Accidents Act of 1846, which is more commonly referred to as Lord Campbell's Act.

This new act created a new cause of action which could be brought for and in behalf of the dependents of the deceased against the tortfeasor where the death was caused by his or her wrongful act, neglect, or default. The purpose of the legislation was to create a means whereby the dependents would be able to recover an amount equal to the pecuniary loss which they had sustained as a result of the death. There was no recovery for mental anguish or bereavement, and the recovery was limited solely to the pecuniary loss which the dependents had suffered.

In the United States, all of the states have passed wrongful death statutes, the majority of which are similar to Lord Campbell's Act. Other states base the amount of the recovery on the degree of culpability of the defendant's conduct, or on the loss sustained by the estate of the deceased.

WORKERS' COMPENSATION STATUTES

The common-law system of compensating injured employees seemed to work quite well when the hazards of industry were minimal and the incidence of injury was quite small. However, with the coming of high-speed machinery, the development of assembly-line techniques, and the ever-increasing line of sophisticated products, the frequency of industrial injuries and diseases increased sharply. Since recoveries of compensation for industrial injuries were restricted by the common law to only those cases in which the employee could establish the employer's negligence as the cause of the accident, the number of uncompensated injuries became so large that it posed serious social problems. Ultimately, the problem reached the legislatures, which were confronted with the problem of finding some means of compensating injured workers and their families.

The legislatures ultimately addressed the problem by enacting workers' compensation legislation. Workers' compensation is a system of law whereby when an employee sustains a work-related injury, the employer is obligated to pay him or her certain benefits during the period of disability which is causally related to the injury sustained.

The system originated in Germany during the 1880s and was later adopted in England. It finally found its way to the United States, where the first workers' compensation law was enacted in Wisconsin in 1911. The first states to follow Wisconsin's lead were the highly industrialized states where industrial accidents were more numerous, but ultimately all other states followed. At the present time, all states and the District of Columbia have enacted workers' compensation legislation.

Under the typical workers' compensation law, the injured worker is entitled to receive weekly payments of indemnity payable in the same manner and at the same intervals as wages during his or her period of disability. In the case of permanent injury, such as the loss by severance or the loss of use of certain members, the injured person is entitled to additional payments of indemnity as set forth in the statute. In addition, the employer is obligated to pay for the reasonable cost of medical, surgical, hospital, and nursing services which the nature of the injury and the process of recovery may require. In the case of death resulting from the injury, payments of indemnity are required to be made to the deceased worker's dependents.

The advocates of this type of legislation argued that the cost of the product should include the "blood of the workers" and that this cost should be passed on to the consumers in the form of increased prices for products and services. The opponents argued that the legislation was unconstitutional, in the sense that it deprived the employer of property without due process of law, since it required the employer to make these payments regardless of whether he or she was negligent or not. After much litigation and some amendments being made to the state constitutions, the Supreme Court of the United States decided that workers' compensation legislation is not violative of the Federal Constitution nor any of the various state constitutions, and is therefore constitutional.

State Statutes

Mindful of the constitutional objections, the state legislatures declared the public policy of the state to include the passage of a workers' compensation system which would be applicable to accidents and some occupational diseases suffered by workers in hazardous industries (as defined in the statute), with the employer being liable for the payments of the benefits set forth in the statute. Thus, the statutes imposed a form of absolute or strict liability upon employers.

In order to avert a possible attack on the constitutionality of the legislation, some of the earlier statutes provided for an election on the part of the employee as to whether he or she would be bound by the provisions of the workers' compensation law or would retain the common-law rights. The rejection of the provisions of the workers' compensation law was required to be made prior to the occurrence of the accident. Some laws contained a presumption under which the employee was presumed to have accepted the compensation act in the absence of a rejection filed with the employer prior to accident. A number of states have retained these provisions.

As to the employer, some state legislation provides that the employer may reject the act, and in the case of such rejection, the employer is usually deprived of certain defenses to common-law actions, such as the defense of contributory negligence, assumption of risk, and the negligence of a fellow employee. The underlying principle here is to provide an inducement to the employer to accept the workers' compensation act.

As to industries not defined as hazardous in the act, and as to injuries or diseases not specifically covered by the act, the common-law or employers' liability exposures still remain. This follows the common-law rule that any statute in derogation of (contrary to) the common law is to be strictly construed. Thus, where the workers' compensation statute changes the rights and liabilities of the parties, it will be construed as changing only those relationships and those situations covered by the act and no others. The statute changes the common law only as to the specific situations stated in the statute, and then only to the extent that the statute says it does.

Nature of State Statutes Today, all workers' compensation statutes cover most public and private employments, whether or not they are "hazardous" in the earlier sense of the term. Some include within the scope of their coverage civilian volunteers, such as volunteer fire fighters, auxiliary police officers, and civil defense workers. Some of the earlier statutes covered only employments carried on for pecuniary gain. Such a provision would eliminate all public employees, such as police officers, fire fighters, and sanitation workers, as well as those employed by a charity, since these are not profit-making enterprises. Some laws have retained this provision.

Most state workers' compensation laws specifically exclude domestic servants and farm workers from the operation of the law. Therefore, such employees retain their common-law rights in their entirety. However, in Gallegos v. Glaser Crandell Co., 202 NW 2d 786 (Dec. 21, 1972), the Michigan Supreme Court held that an agricultural exclusion in the workers' compensation act is an arbitrary and unreasonable classification in violation of the equal protection clauses of the United States and the Michigan constitutions, and that a compensation claim by an agricultural worker, employed on a piece-work basis, must be sustained.

The effect of a compensation statute as to the employee is to take away his or her common-law rights against the employer and to substitute in their place a remedy which requires the employer to pay a weekly benefit during disability or, in the case of death, a weekly benefit to dependents. The right to compensation is the employee's exclusive remedy (except, in states which permit it, where the employee has rejected the act prior to an accident). The effect of the workers' compensation law is to relieve the employer of the duty to respond in damages which otherwise might have been imposed for his or her failure to meet the common-law duties to the employee. The statutes require that weekly payments be made promptly, as wages, with the first payment being due usually at the end of the second week of disability. At common law, the injured worker would be subject to the usual delays of litigation, and would receive no money unless and until the case was tried or settled.

Types of Benefits Provided The employer is obligated to pay compensation for disability or death, and also medical expenses. The payment of indemnity is designed to take the place of wages, but in no case will it equal or exceed the amount of wages which the claimant received while working. The statutes provide for a percentage of the average weekly wages (usually 66⅔ percent). The theory is that the reduced amount will provide some incentive for the injured to return to work as soon as possible after disability ceases.

The amount of compensation is further limited by a maximum rate which is set forth in the statute. The maximum rate differs state by state, and in some states the duty of establishing the maximum rate is delegated to a state official who will follow a formula directed by the legislature. This formula is usually based on the average wages earned in the state during the preceding year. Thus, in such states the maximum rate of compensation will change at the end of each calendar year.

Compensation is payable for disability, or the inability to work due to injury. The disability may be total or partial, and either of these conditions may be temporary or permanent, as described below.

Temporary Total Disability. This means that the quality of disablement is such that the injured employee is expected to recover but is unable to do any work for a limited period of time. For such period, the maximum rate of compensation applies in all states.

Temporary Partial Disability. This means that the injured employee can do some work, but cannot work at full capacity and command the same earnings as when working at his or her regular job. For this type of disability, he or she is entitled to receive a percentage of the difference between the amount which is now being earned and the wages previously earned. It is contemplated that the employee will eventually return to regular work at the usual wages.

Permanent Partial Disability. Where the claimant has sustained an injury from which he or she will never recover, but which injury only partially affects earning capacity, payments of permanent partial disability compensation will be made. The employee may be able to do his or her old job, but the permanent condition usually will reduce efficiency and will in the future reduce his or her ability to compete in the labor market. For example, if the employee sustained the amputation of one finger, he or she may be able to continue working as a carpenter or an electrician, but the employee's future employability will not be the same as that of a person who has sustained no injury. Permanent partial disability compensation payments are designed to pay for the effect of the injury on the employee's future earning capacity. Such payments are made in accordance with the provisions of the particular statute. Most states divide injuries of this type into two groups: (1) schedule injuries, and (2) nonschedule injuries.

SCHEDULE INJURIES. With few exceptions, most compensation laws provide that where there has been a permanent injury to certain members of the body, either by amputation or loss of use; or loss of vision, total or partial; or loss of hearing, total or partial, the amount of disability compensation will be fixed by a specific schedule which will set forth the amount of compensation payments the injured person will receive. Most schedules refer to a number of weeks of disability compensation which will be paid to the claimant, whether he or she is working or not. Thus, under a schedule payment, the amount is fixed by statute, without reference to the actual influence the injury has on the employee's earning capacity.

NONSCHEDULE INJURIES. States which do not estimate permanent injuries on the basis of the body as a whole, in addition to the schedule, compensate permanent injuries on the basis of the actual loss of earning capacity, awarding compensation benefits on the same basis and by the same computation used in determining temporary partial compensation. In most states, cases in this category can be settled by means of a lump sum payment which is agreed upon by the parties and approved by the hearing officer.

Permanent Total Disability. As the name implies, this type of disability means that the injured person is totally disabled (not able to do any kind of work) and that this condition will continue for the balance of his or her lifetime. It will not improve under treatment or rehabilitation. In some statutes, the payment of benefits will continue for the remainder of the injured person's lifetime, while in others the maximum payment is set forth in the statute, either by limiting the payment to a number of weeks of compensation benefits or a dollar amount.

Compensation for Death. When the injured worker dies as a result of the accident or as a result of the injuries sustained, the dependents of such worker are entitled to receive (1) the reasonable value of the funeral expenses, and (2) payments of the compensation benefits set forth in the statute for the benefit of the persons defined in the statute as dependents. In the more generous states, payments to the surviving spouse continue indefinitely with a lump sum (usually the equivalent of two years' benefits) payable on remarriage. Other states limit the period during which this type of compensation will be paid to a number of weeks (e.g., 400-500) from the date of death. In addition, other dependents, as defined in the particular statute, usually include the dependent children, and the benefits are paid only during their minority. Legally adopted children also come within this category. In some states, if there is no surviving wife or child (or dependent husband), then an award of compensation is made for the support of grandchildren or brothers and sisters under the age of eighteen years. Also, where there are no persons entitled to compensation for the death benefits, some states require a payment to a vocational rehabilitation fund or some similar fund. The amount of the payment is set forth in the statute.

Other Compensation Benefits. In addition to the foregoing classes of disability, some statutes provide for a payment to be made in the case of serious facial or body disfigurement, the theory being that the injured person, because of the scarring, would have a harder time finding employment.

Medical Benefits. In addition to the payment of compensation benefits, the injured worker is entitled to such payments for medical, surgical, and hospital services as the nature of the injury and the process of recovery require, including necessary dental care and treatment. Some states allow the injured worker to select a personal physician or dentist, while others require that the employer supply the medical attention through its own physician.[6] As to what constitutes "medical" treatment, all states are in agreement that services rendered by a duly licensed physician come within this classification. Some states by statute also include treatment rendered by an osteopath, a chiropractor, or a religious reader.

Most states require the payment of medical expenses without any upper-dollar limit, while others limit the period of time within which the employer is liable for medical attention and/or impose a dollar maximum. Most states also provide that the employer is liable for the payment for eyeglasses and glass eyes, as well as for the furnishing of prosthetic devices, such as an artificial arm, hand, or leg.

Accidents Covered The compensation statutes change the common-law rules with respect only to accidents which "arise out of and in the course of employment." The incident must be an accident in the sense that it is an event which takes place without one's foresight or expectation, a fortuitous event which takes place without any intent of injury to the injured worker or another. It also must arise out of the work which the injured was employed to do, and it must be in the course of such work. If the incident does not meet these criteria, the workers' compensation statute has no application. Each of these elements will now be considered in turn.

Accident. In construing the provisions of the workers' compensation acts, the courts generally have regarded the legislation as remedial, in the sense that it was to correct the inequities of the common law and provide a statutory remedy for industrial injuries. As a result, they have adopted a very liberal attitude with regard to factual situations. The general rule is that if the situation was "accidental" from the standpoint of the injured person, it is within the compensation act. For example, an employee has lifted heavy objects for several years. On one occasion the employee lifts a heavy object in the same manner as has been done previously, but this time the employee sustains a strained back or a hernia. As to the employee, this is an accident, and the courts will so construe it, even though the factual situation did not indicate any departure from the employee's usual action in doing the lifting.

Unusual conditions of the employment may expose the employee to a risk of injury. Where these conditions produce a deleterious condition on the body, the resulting condition is regarded as accidentally sustained. For example, heat prostration is an accidental injury, if the employment exposes the employee to the risk of such an injury. Those who suffer heat prostration while working at a blast furnace, or those whose employment exposes them to the sun's rays on a hot day, can qualify as being the victims of an accidental injury. On the other hand, if the employee is exposed to the same weather conditions which are endured by the general public, then any result of the weather, including heat prostration, would not be considered as an accidental injury. To be an accident, the exposure must be greater than that to which the general public is exposed. It is only where the employment increases the risk of heat prostration or similar conditions, because of conditions peculiar to the employment, that the resulting physical ailment is considered to be an accident.

The same reasoning is applied to other conditions which produce harmful physical results to the body, such as freezing and sudden chilling. If the condition to which the employee was exposed is the same as that to which the general public is exposed, there is no accidental injury. But where there is a special hazard of the employment which exposes the employee to a greater risk of injury, then the resulting injury is an accident.

An accident is not always the result of a physical impact. It can come about as a result of a mental injury. In Klimas v. Trans-Caribbean Airways, 10 N. Y. 2d 209, the court held that "undue" anxiety, strain, and mental stress are frequently more devastating than physical injury. Therefore, where it was claimed that the employee's death from a heart attack was induced by emotional stress without physical impact, the facts supported the conclusion that the deceased had sustained an accident within the meaning of the compensation act.[7]

There are different shades of opinion among the courts as to exactly what type of accident is compensable under the various compensation acts. This is due primarily to the particular wording of the applicable legislation. Some acts refer to accidents, while others refer to personal injuries or accidental injuries.

Arising Out of the Employment. In order to be compensable, the injury must occur as a consequence of exposure to a hazard which is peculiar to the employment, not a hazard which is common to the general public. For example, while an employee is at work the ceiling falls on him. Since his work required him to be at the plant, the falling ceiling was one of the exposures peculiar to the occupation. The same thing would be true if the employee were injured by a machine which he is operating, or even if he hit his own hand with a hammer. These are hazards of the employment.

The employee is also covered while entering or leaving the premises. This includes the usual entrance ways on the employer's property, as well as lobbies, elevators, and stairs in the building in which the employer's premises are located, whether the employer owns the building or not. Parking lots, whether owned by the employer or not, but furnished by the employer for the employees' use, are considered part of the employer's premises for the purposes of determining whether the employee is on the premises or not. The use of bathroom facilities or washing up are both considered as arising out of the employment. If an employee goes out to lunch or for a coffee break off the premises, he or she is entitled to an egress and ingress to the premises. While on the premises, whether going or returning, the employee is within the scope of employment. Once the employee is outside of the premises, however, the exposures are personal. Should the employee be injured during this period, the accident does not arise out of the employment.

In some cases, the employer may provide a lunchroom where the employees may eat either their own food, food purchased from the employer, or food which is supplied by the employer; or, the employer may permit the employees to eat their lunches in their work areas. Should an employee be injured during such lunch periods, the question of whether the accident arose out of the employment will depend upon whether the hazard to which the employee was exposed was one which the employment exposed the employee or one which was entirely personal. For example, suppose an employee brought her own lunch and was eating it in her work area or in the lunchroom. If the building caught fire and the employee was burned, the injury occurred as a result of a hazard to which the employment exposed her. On the other hand, if the employee, while eating lunch which the employee supplied, swallowed a chicken bone, or the food contained some deleterious substance which made the employee ill, the injury was not one which the employee received because of the employment. Instead, such an accident involved a personal exposure. However, if the employer either sold or provided the food for lunch and it contained some harmful substance which made the employee ill, then the accident did arise out of the employment.

Ordinarily, where an employee is employed at a fixed place, he or she is not within the scope of the employment when traveling between home and the place of work. Since the employee is in the scope of employment only after he or she reaches the employer's premises, accidents which occur while en route are not compensable.

However, where the employer provides the transportation, either by bus or private car, the employee is in the scope of employment upon entering the vehicle. Where the employee is required to travel as part of his or her work, the hazards of travel are those of the employer, and accidents which occur while the employee is traveling come within the scope of employment. The accident does not arise out of the employment if it occurs when the employee has substantially deviated from the normal travel route for purposes of his or her own. The employee is then outside the scope of employment during the entire period of deviation, and does not return to employment until returning to the normal route.

Some employers supply "company" cars to their outside representatives. While using the company car on the business of the employer, the employee is in the course of employment. Some employers require that the automobile be returned to the company garage at the end of the business day. After returning the car, the employee is not in the course of employment while returning home. However, some employers require that the employee garage the company car at home. In such a case, the employee is still in the course of employment both while returning the car home and while on the way to the office or the first appointment the next day. If the employee uses the company car on personal business, he or she is not within the scope of employment while so doing.

Where the employee is given living quarters on the premises of the employer, or where the employee is on call twenty-four hours a day and the employer provides accommodations, if the employee is injured because of an unsafe condition on the premises, the accident arises out of the employment, whether the employee is actually engaged in work or not. For example, in Giliotti v. Hoffman Catering Co., 246 N. Y. 279, a chef was required to sleep on the premises and was subject to call at all hours. The premises were destroyed by fire and the chef suffered fatal burns. At the time of the fire, the chef was asleep. It was held that the accident arose out of the employment and compensation was awarded.

On the other hand, where accommodations are furnished by the employer and the accident arises out of some personal act, even though it occurs on the premises, the accident does not arise out of the employment. In Pisko v. Mintz, 262 N. Y. 176, the claimant, a janitor required to sleep on the premises, was burned by a fire which was caused by a lighted cigarette while he was smoking in bed. It was held that the accident did not arise out of the employment; hence, compensation was denied.

Where the employment requires the employee to reside in a zone of special danger, any accidental injury arising therefrom is compensable, regardless of whether the employee was at work at the time. For example, in Lewis v. Knappen Tippetts Eng. Co., 304 N. Y. 461, an engineer assigned by a New York firm to Israel was shot and killed by Arabs while on a sightseeing trip. Compensation was awarded to his widow.[8]

In some cases, where the employment is in a remote area, compensation has been denied, especially where the employer provided adequate recreational facilities for remote-area employees. Under such circumstances, independent recreational jaunts are not within the scope of the employment.[9]

Course of Employment. An accident is said to be "in the course of employment" when it occurs when the employee is at his or her place of work, during the hours that he or she is expected to be there and engaged in doing the task he or she was employed to do. This would not necessarily mean that the employee would have to be at the employer's office or plant at the time. The employee could be traveling to or from a customer's premises, or doing work at other work places designated by the employer. The phrase refers to the usual hours of work, but includes overtime which the employee was required to perform or which was undertaken voluntarily for the benefit of the employer. Some courts have suggested that the two tests of "arising out of" and "in the course of" should not be kept in separate compartments, but should be merged into a single concept of work connection. In other words, if the accidental injury or death is connected with any of the incidents of one's employment, then the injury or death would arise out of and be in the course of such employment.

Injuries Covered. In order to be compensable, the accident must result in bodily injury. No compensation is payable for property damage which is the result of the accident. Thus, accidental damage to clothing, an artificial leg or arm, a glass eye, or false teeth is not recoverable.

Let us now summarize what has been discussed thus far about the nature of accidents and injuries covered by the typical state workers' compensation statute. To qualify for the payment of compensation benefits, the employee must not only have sustained an injury to the physical or mental structure of the body but also must meet the other tests of compensability; namely, the employee must have sustained an "accident" which "arose out of and in the course of his employment." The final two qualifications have to do with the cause-effect relationship and the extent to which preexisting conditions may be compensable.

Causal Relationship. The injury for which a compensation claim is made must be the proximate result of the accident which the employee sustained. If there is no such causal relationship, the employee may not recover. For example, an employee cut his finger. Two days later he had an attack of appendicitis. There is no causal connection between the finger injury and the appendix condition. On the other hand, if the employee sustained a cut finger and several days later the lacerated finger became infected, there is a connection between the infection and the original injury, and thus the disability caused by the infection is compensable.

Aggravation of a Previous Condition. It has been observed that "industry takes the employee as it finds him." That is to say, if the employee is suffering from a preexisting condition and sustains an injury which aggravates this condition, the employer nevertheless is fully liable for the ensuing disability, even though the period of disability might not have been so prolonged if the employee had not been suffering from this other condition. For example, assume that the employee was suffering from tertiary syphilis and sustained a deep laceration of the arm and hand. The presence of syphilis in the blood stream prevented complete healing of the wound. While there is no responsibility on the part of the employer for the syphilitic condition, the employer is liable for the increased disability, and in some cases it would be to the advantage of the employer to pay for the anti-syphilitic treatment in order to reduce the period of disability. Syphilis is a blood stream disease which has the effect of reducing the healing properties of the blood. Thus, one affected by the disease will be disabled for a longer period of time than one who is not, unless the syphilitic condition is under control. The same thing would be true in the case of a person suffering from diabetes mellitus. The employer would have no responsibility for the causation or the aggravation of the diabetes, but in order to terminate the present disability for which the employer is responsible, the employer might be persuaded to assume the cost of the medication necessary to keep the diabetes under control.

Consequential Accidents. It sometimes happens that because of the existence of a compensable injury, the employee sustains another and further injury, either to the injured area or another. If there is a direct chain of causation from the original injury to the second injury, then the employer is responsible also for the second injury. For example, an employee sustains a fractured leg and must use crutches. The crutches slip out from under the employee and cause a fall which fractures the other leg. Under these circumstances, the employer is responsible for the second fracture, as well as the first. In another case, the injured employee goes to a drugstore in order to fill a prescription made necessary by the injury. The employee is struck by a motor vehicle while crossing the street. There was no direct chain of causation from the original injury to the second accident. Therefore, the employer is not answerable for the second injury, since the cause itself was remote from the happening of the first accident.

Major Variations Among State Laws When the concept of workers' compensation was first introduced, the laws were bitterly opposed by industry. The handling and costs of employees' claims under common-law rules had been satisfactory from the standpoint of many employers. Statutory workers' compensation would cost employers a great deal more money. When their attacks on the compensation statutes on constitutional grounds failed, the employers' groups convinced the legislators to lessen the financial impact of the compensation laws by keeping the benefits at relatively low levels. Though some states have increased benefits, particularly in recent years, most have retained limits on the level of compensation and the period of time during which compensation benefits are payable. And there are still significant variations among the state laws in terms of the level of compensation, the coverage of disease, the employments covered, and other specific provisions. Thus, all that will be attempted here is a brief summary or overview of some of the salient features of state workers' compensation statutes generally.

Benefit Levels. As noted previously, most states now have no upper limit applicable to the payment of medical expenses. However, in most states the rate of compensation payable for disability, partial or total, is limited to a percentage of the employee's average weekly wage, up to a weekly dollar maximum provided for in the statute. The weekly dollar maximum was initially fixed at a time when there was little inflation and was considered to be fair at the time. In most states, the legislatures have not seen fit to reevaluate the dollar maximum in the light of changing costs of living. In some states the legislatures have provided for a sliding scale based on the average weekly wage earned by all employees in the state who are subject to the unemployment compensation law. This maximum figure will fluctuate each year as a new calculation is made.

The period for which compensation for disability, partial or total, is payable likewise differs by state. In some states the maximum period for temporary total disability is as little as 200 weeks, as opposed to states in which the compensation is payable without limit for the entire period of disability. Other states limit the payment of compensation for disability to 650, 500, or 450 weeks.

Compensation for death likewise is subject to variations. In the more generous states these benefits are payable to the widow until she dies or remarries and to the children until they reach the age of eighteen. One state even provides for a payment of two years' compensation in a lump sum payable to the widow if she remarries. Other states limit the period for which death benefits are payable to 500 weeks. In addition, funeral expenses are payable, subject to the maximum provided for in the law, usually from $750 to $1,000.

Coverage of Disease. In most states there is coverage for "occupational disease," which is usually defined as a disease which is peculiar to the occupation, not a disease to which the general public is exposed. Most states have a list of the particular diseases which are covered, whereas the other states cover any and all occupational diseases. In states where the particular occupational disease is not covered by the statute, the employee retains his or her common-law rights and may exercise them by bringing a tort action against the employer.

Rehabilitation. Generally speaking, the employer has no direct responsibility for rehabilitation costs. Some states have maintained rehabilitation programs, and the employer indirectly bears the costs in various ways. In some states there is a tax on awards which is paid to the rehabilitation program. In other states, all penalties are so payable, and in still others a payment is required to the vocational rehabilitation fund in all death cases in which there are no dependents.

Elective Versus Compulsory Laws. When compensation laws were first introduced, there was some concern that they might be unconstitutional in the sense that they deprived the employer of property without due process of law. Therefore, the first laws were "elective," which meant that the employer could voluntarily be brought within the terms of the act. The advantage to the employer was that if he or she did elect to come under the act, the right to compensation was the sole remedy of the employee in the event of an industrial accident or disease. The employee, in some states, had an opportunity to reject the act prior to accident, but failure to file a rejection with the employer prior to accident would raise a presumption that the employee had accepted the act. It normally would be to the advantage of the employee to accept the act, for the reason that he or she was certain of receiving compensation benefits in the event of an accident. In addition, the elective laws typically provide that if the employer rejects the act, he or she will be deprived of the defenses of contributory negligence, assumption of risk, and the negligence of a fellow employee in any litigation brought by the employee. These provisions are still in effect in New Jersey, South Carolina, and Texas.

Under "compulsory" laws, unless the type of employment is specifically excluded, statutory compensation is mandatory. Neither the employer nor the employee has the right to reject the act. Compulsory laws also specify that all employers subject to the act must carry compensation insurance (or a formal retention program, where permitted). Failing to do so will subject the employer to penalties provided in the statute and in addition, will restore the employee's common-law rights, if he or she chooses to assert them. If not, the employee may claim the statutory compensation benefits, which will then be assessed against the employer.

Employees Excluded. Under almost all compensation statutes, whether elective or compulsory, domestic servants and farm laborers are excluded from the benefits of the law. However, as noted earlier, the Michigan Supreme Court in Gallegos v. Glaser Crandell Co., 202 NW 2d 786, in construing the agricultural exclusion of the Michigan Act, held that the exclusion was unconstitutional in that it denied to agricultural workers equal protection of the laws. Therefore, at least in Michigan, agricultural workers are entitled to the full benefits of the workers' compensation act. Whether or not other states will follow Michigan is an open question. Some laws further define domestic and farm workers as to include "baby-sitters, cleaning persons, harvest help and similar part-time or transient help." Other employees excluded are casual employees not employed in the usual course of the employer's business, as well as employees of charities. A casual employee has been defined as a worker whose employment is not regular, periodic, or recurring and for whom the occasion for employment arises by chance or is purely accidental. The test is the nature of the work or whether the employment is necessary to carry out the employer's business in the usual way. For example, the employer hires a carpenter to do some alteration work, on a daily basis and under the control of the employer. When the alteration is completed the employment ceases. The carpenter is a casual employee.

Employer and Employments Excluded. As in most other respects, the state laws differ concerning the types of employments excluded. Some states include only employments carried on for pecuniary gain. This would exclude charities, voluntary hospitals, municipal and state employees, and all volunteers such as civil defense workers, auxiliary police officers, volunteer fire fighters, forest-fire wardens, and forest-fire fighters. In addition, employers who regularly employ fewer than a specified number of employees are excluded in some states. Family members may be classified as employees even though they work for a proprietorship, partnership, or corporation in which the family has the sole interest or a substantial interest, provided that they meet the usual tests of employment.

Some states have defined hazardous employment to include all employers having three or more employees, so that such employers would automatically come within the scope of the compensation statute, regardless of the kind and type of business involved, with the exception of charities. Other states include within the definition of employments covered by the compensation law all state and municipal employees, as well as those employed by charitable corporations (including the Red Cross).

Privilege of Voluntary Compensation. In many states the employer may voluntarily provide compensation benefits for employees who do not come within the scope of the compensation law coverage. These might include domestic servants, farm laborers, those employed exclusively in a foreign country, or those employed in an area of federal jurisdiction, such as interstate railroads or vessels.

Some states have specific provisions for such action on the part of the employer. These provide that the employer may secure insurance and give notice to the employees by means of a sign, conspicuously posted in the work area, which advises the employees of the employer's action. The absence of an election by the employee that he or she will not be bound by the compensation benefits in the event of an accident will be deemed to be an acceptance of the compensation benefits in lieu of all other rights which the employee may have against the employer. Thus, in those states where the employer has secured compensation insurance and has given notice of this action to the employees, the measure of damages in the case of an accident will be the provisions of the compensation law. Any rights which the employer otherwise may have had at common law are abrogated.

In states which do not have the aforementioned provisions (most do not), there is no way that the employer can deprive the employee of his or her common-law rights. The employer can purchase voluntary compensation, but if the employee presses his or her common-law claim, the existence of this insurance will have no influence on the result. Under this type of insurance, the insurer agrees that in the event of an accident arising out of the employment, it will offer the compensation value of the case in return for a general release. The insuring agreement further provides that the filing of any suit for damages shall be deemed to be a rejection of such voluntary compensation (whether offered or not) and that the insurer would have no further obligation under the voluntary insurance agreement. This creates a problem for the injured worker, especially in cases where the injuries are serious. He or she can accept the compensation value and give a release, which will effectively terminate the claim.

On the other hand, an injured worker may bring suit for damages against the employer. In doing so, however, he or she loses any rights which may have existed under the voluntary compensation insurance because, by filing suit, an irrevocable election has been made. Voluntary compensation benefits will be paid to the employee regardless of liability, if he or she desires them, whereas if suit is filed, the employee must take the chance of being able to establish the negligence of the employer.

Voluntary compensation insurance is sometimes utilized by the operators of small interstate railroads to avoid litigation. Their employees are entitled to the provisions of the Federal Employees Liability Act (FELA), which enables railroad employees to bring suit against the employer and recover based on the employer's negligence. The acceptance of voluntary compensation benefits in return for a release of all claims will preclude the bringing of a lawsuit and will terminate the claim. Employers of sailors on vessels sailing in navigable waters also utilize the voluntary compensation device. Sailors have a right to sue the vessel for injuries caused by the negligence of the owner. If the sailor accepts the compensation benefits, the lawsuit is avoided. The system of voluntary compensation is most frequently used in cases involving employees whose work is exclusively outside of the country. Since they do no work in any particular state, they are not subject to the compensation laws. They might possibly have some cause of action against the employer under the laws of the country in which they are working. To avoid any such conflicts, the employer and employee agree, as part of the contract of hire, that the provisions of the compensation law of the state agreed upon shall be the measure of damages between the employer and employee in the event of a work-connected injury. This type of procedure is legally sound and is not in violation of any state or federal laws.

Administration of Compensation Laws. In the majority of states, the compensation statute creates a quasi-judicial body, variously called the Industrial Accident Commission or the Workers' Compensation Board, whose duty it is to administer the law, and more importantly to hear and determine claims and disputes. Appeals may be taken to the courts from any decision of such a body. In a few states, the claims are heard and determined by the courts, like any other type of lawsuit. In those states, the administration of the law is usually undertaken by the insurance commissioner.

Security for Compensation. The methods of securing the payment of compensation benefits differ depending on the type of law in force within the particular state, but they may be described under the headings of (1) monopolistic state funds, (2) competitive state funds and private insurance, (3) private insurance only, and (4) retention. The descriptions here will be brief, since insurance and retention arrangements are discussed fully in Chapter 7.

MONOPOLISTIC STATE FUNDS. In the majority of these states the security for the payment of compensation is maintained by the state and the premiums are collected by the state. Generally, no private or substitute benefit plans are approved. However, in Ohio, Washington, and West Virginia, the employer has the option of providing "self-insurance" by establishing a retention program and depositing a bond and other securities with the state.

COMPETITIVE STATE FUNDS AND PRIVATE INSURANCE. Compensation is secured by obtaining a policy of compensation insurance from either the state fund or a private insurance carrier authorized to provide such insurance.

PRIVATE INSURANCE ONLY. In all of the states where there is no monopolistic state-managed compensation insurance program, insurance may be provided by any authorized insurance company.

RETENTION. In most of the states, with the exception of some of the monopolistic states, the employer may qualify as a "self-insurer." Some states require the deposit of securities or a bond, whereas others require only a financial statement indicating the employer's financial ability to pay the compensation benefits. The employer who retains the exposure may purchase excess workers' compenstion insurance, over and above a "self-insured retention," or such excess coverage may be required by the state in question.

Extraterritoriality. Under most compensation laws, either by statutory provision or by judicial interpretation, where the contract of hire is made within the state and the employee does some work in the state, the compensation law of the state of hire can be applied to accidents employees may have in another state, in a foreign country, or on the high seas. The theory is that where a contract of hire is made for work in the state, one of the incidents of the contract is the employee's right to compensation under the state law.

Where the contract of hire is made in the state for work to be performed exclusively outside the state, it cannot be said that the contract was made in contemplation of the compensation benefits provided by the state law. The location of the place of contract will not subject either party to the jurisdiction of the state compensation act. In such a case, the parties intended by implication that the state in which the work is to be performed would have jurisdiction. In the case of work to be performed in a foreign country, the law of that country will prevail, unless the parties have agreed to other terms in the contract of employment.

Some states limit the extraterritorial effect of their compensation laws by applying the law only to accidents which occur within a certain time after the employee leaves the state. Such time periods may be as little as ninety days or as much as one year. As to states which do not have such provisions, the period of time is unlimited. In applying the limited time periods, the time runs against each absence and is not cumulative. For example, if the employee works in another state for a period of thirty days and then returns to the state for one day and leaves again, the time period on his second absence begins to run on the day he leaves and runs for the full statutory limit. The prior thirty-day absence is not counted.

Third-Party Claims. Where the employee is injured by the negligence of a third party, he or she has a choice of remedies. The employee may (1) sue the third party and reject his or her compensation remedy, (2) accept compensation and forgo his or her remedy against the third party, or (3) accept compensation and also sue the third party.

SUE THE THIRD PARTY. If the employee selects the alternative of suing the third party, the employee must bring the action at his or her own expense (although the fee of the plaintiff's attorney, under the usual contingent fee arrangement, would be payable only in the event of a recovery). If unsuccessful, the employee may enter his or her claim for compensation at that time. The fact that he or she did sue the third party will not affect the right to statutory compensation, even though the compensation claim will be deferred pending the outcome of the third-party action.

ACCEPT COMPENSATION. The employee may decide to accept compensation and take no interest in pursuing his or her remedy against the third party. However, the employer or the employer's insurer is subrogated to the rights of the employee against the third party and may bring an action at its own expense (in the name of the employee) against the third party. In the event of a recovery, the employer will first reimburse itself for the compensation and medical payments made (or for which it is liable), together with the costs of the action. Where the insurer recovers more than its expenditures in the third-party action, any excess will be paid to the employee on a percentage basis. For example, Section 29, subd. 2 of the New York Workmen's Compensation Law reads in part as follows:

> If such injured employee, or in the case of death, his dependents, has taken compensation under this chapter but has failed to commence action against such other within the time limited therefor by subdivision one, such failure shall operate as an assignment of the cause of action against such other to the state for the benefit of the state insurance fund, if compensation be payable therefrom, and otherwise to the person, association, corporation or insurance carrier liable for the payment of such compensation.

> If such fund, person, association, corporation or carrier, as such an assignee, recovers from such other, either by judgment, settlement or otherwise, a sum in excess of the total amount of compensation awarded to such injured employee or his dependents, and the expenses for medical treatment paid by it, together the reasonable and necessary expenditures incurred in effecting such recovery, it shall forthwith pay to such injured employee or his dependents, as the case may be, two-thirds of such excess, and to the extent of two-thirds of any such excess such recovery shall be deemed for the benefit of such employee or his dependents.

Obviously, unless the action is brought in the name of the injured person or his or her dependents, there can be no excess over the amount of the insurer's payments. Should the insurer bring the action, the measure of damages would be limited to the amount of money for which the insurer is liable and nothing more. Should the action be brought in the name of the injured employee or his or her dependents, then evidence of the actual damages suffered by such persons may be admitted in evidence.

ACCEPT COMPENSATION AND SUE THE THIRD PARTY.   If the employee chooses this alternative, the employer or the employer's insurer has a lien on the proceeds of the employee's recovery to the extent of the compensation and medical payments made. The employer or the insurer may intervene in the employee's suit as a party plaintiff. In the event of recovery, most state laws provide that the employer's lien attaches only to the employee's net recovery after the payment of costs and attorney's fees has been made.

If this third alternative is chosen, the law provides that the employee must begin the third-party suit within a certain period of time, usually six months but in no case more than a year after the first payment of compensation. This is for the purpose of protecting the employer's subrogation rights, since if the employee does not begin the suit promptly, the statute of limitations may be applied to the entire claim. The provision further states that if the employee does not begin the suit within the time set forth, the employer automatically takes over subrogation rights.

National Commission on State Workmen's Compensation Laws   In 1971 Congress directed its attention to the conditions of the American worker and the question of whether the various compensation statutes adequately meet the problems they were designed to solve. In its declaration of policy, Congress made the following findings:

A. The vast majority of American workers and their families' full protection requires an adequate, prompt, and equitable system of workers' compensation, as well as an effective program of occupational health and safety regulation.

B. In recent years serious questions have been raised concerning the fairness of present workers' compensation laws in the light of the growth of the economy, the changing nature of the labor force, increases in medical knowledge, changes in the hazards associated with various types of employment, new technology creating new risks to health and safety, and increases in the general level of wages and the cost of living.

By means of an Act of Congress (P.L. 91-596), the National Commission on State Workmen's Compensation Laws was created effective April 28, 1971. This presidentially appointed commission rendered its report in July, 1972. It found that the protection furnished by the fifty state-administered programs was "neither adequate nor equitable." The report offered a number of specific recommendations for the states to use in reshaping their own programs, particularly as regards the amount of benefits to be paid and the bringing of all employments within the scope of the compensation laws. It also urged that the states be given a reasonable opportunity to comply with these recommendations before the enactment of any mandatory federal standards.

Faced with the prospect of federal legislation, many of the states amended their current laws so as to comply with some or all of the recommendations of the Commission. These recommendations have received serious consideration in all states, but not all have amended their statutes so as to comply strictly with the recommendations. Major Commission recommendations and the extent of state compliance follow.

Compulsory Compensation Laws. The Commission recommended that all compensation laws be made compulsory for all employees, including those engaged in agricultural or domestic pursuits. Prior to 1972, the date of the report, six states (Florida, Georgia, Iowa, Nebraska, Oregon, and South Dakota) had enacted compulsory compensation legislation rather than elective coverage, which brought to thirty-four the number of states with compulsory compensation laws. After the end of 1972, six more states (Alabama, Kentucky, Montana, New Mexico, Tennessee, and Vermont) adopted the compulsory form of compensation statute and repealed their former elective provisions.

Removal of Limits on Medical Expense Benefits. The Commission recommended removal of any limitations on the amount or duration of medical expense benefits. Such limitations have now been removed in all but a few states (some having done so prior to the issuance of the Commission's report).

Coverage for All Occupations. The Commission report recommended that all occupations be covered, regardless of whether they are hazardous or not, including coverage for all farm or agricultural workers and domestic servants. Concerning the coverage of farm workers, the response by the states has not been very great. Prior to 1972, some twenty-five states extended some coverage to some farm workers, but did not cover all of them. In an attempt to comply with the report, Iowa, Montana, and Virginia extended their compensation coverage to some or all agricultural workers. Many laws exempted employees of nonprofit, charitable, or religious institutions from the operation of the compensation law. There is no evidence that any changes are contemplated in this particular area. A few states still restrict the compensation coverage to employees in hazardous occupations, as variously defined in the statutes.

Removal of Numerical Limitations. Twenty-two states exempted from their compensation law those employers with less than a specified number of employees. The range prior to 1972 was from fewer than two employees in two states to fewer than ten employees in another state.

The typical exemption referred to employers with less than three employees. The Commission's recommendation was that all employers with one or more employees should be subject to the compensation law. Since the report, seven states (Arizona, Florida, Kentucky, Maine, Ohio, Texas, and Vermont) have removed all numerical exemptions. Two others have reduced their exemptions (Georgia and Virginia). Even in the jurisdictions with no numerical exemptions, there are still restrictions as to the type of employment covered, the primary exemptions being agricultural employment, domestic service, and casual labor.

OSHA and Workers' Compensation Of relevance to the workers' compensation exposure is the Occupational Safety and Health Act of 1970 (OSHA), 29 USCA 651, which authorizes the Secretary of Labor to promulgate and establish federal standards which promote occupational safety and health. It further provides for inspections and citations for the violation of the regulations created by the Secretary of Labor. This amounts to a delegation of the law-making power of Congress to a federal agency.

OSHA further provides for penalties for the violation of such regulations. One who willfully and repeatedly violates the conditions (i.e., does not comply) is liable for a fine of $10,000. If the violation is not of a serious nature, the fine can be as low as $1,000. The failure to correct a violation within a reasonable time will also prompt a penalty of $1,000. The liablity of the employer under OSHA is not currently insurable, but many insurance companies do have loss control departments which are familiar with the regulations and are available to their insureds.

Proposed Federal Legislation The National Commission on State Workmen's Compensation Laws recommended in its report to Congress that "the States' primary responsibility for the program should be conserved." However, inspired by the apparent success of OSHA, the Senate Labor Committee has conducted hearings in many states to determine whether or not federal legislation in the area of workers' compensation is necessary. Under consideration is the National Workmen's Compensation Standards Act (Williams-Javits Bill, S20008) which, if passed, would (1) require each state compensation law to meet twenty-one benefit and coverage standards, and (2) authorize the Secretary of Labor to promulgate additional standards which he or she may deem necessary. Failure of the state to so legislate would authorize the Secretary of Labor to require that employers provide workers' compensation benefits equal to those provided by the Longshoremen's and Harbor Workers' Act.

As previously noted, the states have made efforts to comply with the recommendations of the National Commission. In fact, it has been estimated that some 600 amendments have been passed to improve the quality of workers' compensation and the amount of benefits to be paid. Traditionally, the subject of workers' compensation has been within the jurisdiction of the states. The kinds and types of employment in some states are different from others, and the legislative response to the will of the state citizens would also seem to differ state by state. The proposed federal legislation would seem to place all employments and employees under a single standard.

Existing Federal Statutes As a result of the Revolutionary War, each of the thirteen colonies became an independent nation with all the attributes of sovereignty. Previously, the colonies had been bound together by an alliance under the Articles of Confederation and, realizing the advantages of a united effort in the matter of self-preservation, it was thought desirable to continue some sort of an alliance which would provide the means of meeting common problems. They agreed to create a central or federal government to which each sovereign state would voluntarily transfer certain rights and attributes of sovereignty. The document by means of which all this was accomplished is the Constitution of the United States. The rights transferred by the states are fully set forth in that document. Any rights not specifically delegated to the federal government are still retained by the states. Certain powers granted to Congress, such as the regulation of interstate commerce, can be exercised only by the passage of legislation. Where Congress has not legislated, the rule is that the states may exercise the power unless and until it is displaced by Congressional legislation. Where Congress has legislated, it is said that Congress has "preempted" the field and the states may not exercise that particular power as long as the Congressional legislation is in force. For example, in 1908 Congress passed the Federal Employers' Liability Act, to be discussed later, which provided a means of recovery for personal injury or death sustained by employees of an interstate carrier by railroad. This was an exercise of the interstate commerce power. The states could not thereafter exercise legislative jurisdiction over such employees. However, since Congress did not legislate with respect to other employees engaged in interstate commerce, such employees remained subject to state laws. When the workers' compensation laws were passed, these employees came within the scope of such laws. Thus, interstate bus drivers and interstate truck drivers are subject to the workers' compensation laws of the states.

The Constitution also created a federal judiciary under Article III, which provides in part as follows:

Section I. The judicial Power of the United States shall be vested in one Supreme Court, and in such inferior Courts as the Congress may from time to time ordain and establish.

Section II. The judicial Power shall extend . . . to all Cases of admiralty and maritime jurisdiction. . . .

This direct grant of power to the federal judiciary means that the states have divested themselves of all legislative and judicial power with respect to cases of admiralty and maritime cognizance. Statutes passed by the states can have no effect on the admiralty and maritime jurisdiction of the federal judiciary. In other words, having given away the power to exercise jurisdiction in the maritime area, there is no way that the states can get it back short of a constitutional amendment. This grant of power to the federal judiciary differs from the powers which were delegated to Congress by the Constitution. Congressional powers may be exercised by Congress as it sees fit. If the power is not exercised, it still may be exercised by the states. Here, however, the states have divested themselves of all jurisdiction with respect to cases of admiralty and maritime jurisdiction, and cannot thereafter assume any jurisdiction or legislate in that area, in the absence of a constitutional amendment.

Admiralty and maritime cases refer to the jurisdiction exercised over commerce and navigation on water. The mere fact that a transaction has some relationship to the water does not necessarily make it a maritime transaction. For example, the work of a longshoreman loading or unloading a vessel used for commerce on water is a maritime contract of employment. On the other hand, a messenger who goes aboard the same vessel to deliver a package or a message is not engaged in maritime employment, even though the injury might have been sustained on the vessel. The work of the person must have some direct relationship with navigation and commerce on water in order to bring it within maritime jurisdiction. To further illustrate the fine line of distinction between maritime and nonmaritime cases, a contract to build a vessel is nonmaritime and the contract is construed by land law. The reason for this is that the vessel may never be finished and may never become an instrument of commerce on water. Once the vessel is commissioned and is used for the purpose of commerce, it is then an instrument of commerce, and any employment furthering that purpose is considered maritime in nature. Navy vessels, such as aircraft carriers and battleships, are not instruments of commerce on water and, as such, are not subject to the maritime jurisdiction of the United States. They are, of course, subject to the directives and discipline ordered by the President as Commander-in-Chief of the Navy.

A vessel which has been withdrawn from navigation and is no

longer an instrument of commerce on water is not subject to admiralty and maritime jurisdiction. For example, following World War II, a number of old victory ships, used for the storage of surplus grain, were moored in the Hudson River. Such ships are subject to local state jurisdiction and are not within the scope of federal admiralty jurisdiction. Therefore, a watchman on one of the ships who was injured came within the scope of the New York Workmen's Compensation Act and was not accorded any of the rights of a sailor.

The traditional area of maritime jurisdiction was limited to the high seas and territorial waters within the ebb and flow of the tide. In the United States, by Act of Congress in 1845, the navigable waters of the United States were defined as including any body of water which is used or capable of being used for navigation and commerce between different states or from one state to the open sea. Maritime jurisdiction will not apply to any body of water, whether a lake or a river and regardless of size, which is entirely located within one state. To bring it within federal maritime jurisdiction, the waterway must be a connecting link between two or more states or between one state and the open sea.

As to employees, it must be emphasized that the federal admiralty and maritime jurisdiction applies only to maritime employees injured on navigable waters. The state workers' compensation acts apply to nonmaritime employees injured on navigable waters, as well as to all injuries which occur on land, whether sustained by a maritime worker or otherwise. (But see 1972 amendment to the Longshoremen's and Harbor Workers' Act in the following section.) Therefore, a maritime employee who is injured on land is subject to the state workers' compenstion act. Since a pier or dock is considered to be an extension of the land, accidents which occur there are land accidents. For example, in Isthmian S. S. Co. v. Olivari, 202 Fed. 2d 492, an employee of a watchman's service, injured through the shipowner's fault while on the pier watching cargo, came within the workers' compensation law of the state and had no cause of action against the shipowner cognizable in admiralty.

Conversely, where a maritime employee is injured on a vessel then lying in navigable waters, the federal admiralty and maritime jurisdiction is paramount. The state workers' compensation act can have no application. For example, in Southern Pacific Co. v. Jensen, 244 U. S. 205, a claim was made under the New York Workmen's Compensation Act for the death of a longshoreman which occurred in the hold of a vessel then lying in navigable waters. Compensation was awarded, but the Supreme Court of the United States held that the New York statute was inapplicable, pointing out that any state legislation to the extent that it deals with matters of admiralty jurisdiction is invalid.

At the time of the Jensen decision, there was no federal workers' compensation statute applicable to longshoremen. The accident which Jensen sustained was due solely to his own negligence. As a consequence, his widow had no assertable cause of action against the ship or its owners. She was thus left without a recovery. If the accident had occurred on the pier some twenty feet from where the accident actually happened, the widow would have recovered death benefits under the New York Workmen's Compensation Act. There was indignation in labor circles that a mere twenty feet would be the only reason that the widow was denied a recovery.

U.S. Longshoremen's and Harbor Workers' Compensation Act   As a result of the public reaction to the Jensen decision, in 1927, Congress passed the Longshoremen's and Harbor Workers' Compensation Act (33 USCA 901-950), which in essence provided for the payment of compensation and medical benefits with respect to the disability or death of an employee employed in maritime employment. The Act specifically excluded from its operation a master or member of the crew of any vessel, or any person engaged by the master to load or unload a vessel under eighteen tons net. Also excluded are officers or employees of the United States or any agency thereof, or of any state or foreign government, or any political subdivision thereof. Under Section 903 of the Act (as amended in 1972), the scope of the coverage of the Act is defined as follows:

> Compensation shall be payable under this Chapter in respect of disability or death of an employee, but only if the disability or death results from an injury occurring upon navigable waters of the United States (including any adjoining pier, wharf, drydock, terminal, building way, marine railway or other adjoining area customarily used by an employer in loading, unloading, repairing or building a vessel). No compensation shall be payable in respect of the disability or death of:
>
> (1) a master or member of the crew of any vessel, or any person engaged by the master to load, unload or repair any small vessel under 18 tons net; or
>
> (2) an officer or employee of the United States or any agency thereof or of any state or foreign government, or any political subdivision thereof.

Under the 1972 amendment, the act purports to assume jurisdiction over an area of state jurisdiction, such as the pier, wharf, drydock, terminal, and other adjoining area. The state did divest itself of jurisdiction with respect to cases of admiralty and maritime jurisdiction. It did not cede jurisdiction over any part of the state territory. Whether or not the Supreme Court will decide that the present statute is within the constitutional grant of power to the federal government is an open question at this time. In any case, the employer is currently exposed to a possible liability under the Longshoremen's and Harbor Workers' Compensation Act, as well as under the state workers' compensation act.

The rate of compensation payable under the Longshoremen's and Harbor Workers' Compensation Act is two-thirds of the average weekly wage, subject to a weekly dollar maximum. For accidents occurring prior to September 30, 1975, the average weekly wage upon which the compensation rate is based shall not exceed 175 percent of national average weekly wage as determined by the Secretary of Labor. For accidents occurring after September 30, 1975, the maximum average weekly wage shall not exceed 200 percent of the national average. Security for the payment of these compensation benefits is compulsory and may be obtained by the purchase of insurance from a private insurance carrier authorized by state or federal law and approved by the United States Employees Compensation Commissioner, though self-insurance is permitted.

Through the Outer Continental Shelf Lands Act, the Longshoremen's and Harbor Workers' Compensation Act also applies to employees on offshore drilling platforms, except masters and members of the crew of vessels.[10] In fact, this same Act, with some modifications, is applicable to employees (other than government employees) in the District of Columbia.

Defense Base Act   Under Public Law 208, Congress has applied the benefits of the Longshoremen's and Harbor Workers' Compensation Act to civilian employees at any military, air, or naval bases acquired by the United States (after January 1, 1940) from foreign governments and also to public works contracts outside of the United States. The benefits are payable in U. S. currency.

The types of employees who will benefit by this legislation include employees of government contractors, civilian employees of post exchanges, ships service stores, and other military installations, as well as employees of contractors engaged in public works projects. As to the employers of such personnel, the previously discussed insurance or self-insurance requirements of the Act are applicable.

Federal Employees Compensation Act   This Act (5 USCA 751 et seq.) provides for a system of workers' compensation for civilian employees of the United States government. It does not apply to members of the armed services. The Act is administered by the United States, which retains the exposure, and there is no provision for the purchase of private insurance. Where a third party other than the United States is liable for the injuries sustained by the employee, the Secretary of Labor may require the employee to assign his cause of action to the United States, in which case the action may be brought in the name of the injured person or in the name of the United States.

Federal Employers' Liability Act This Act (usually abbreviated to FELA) was passed by Congress in 1908, long before most state workers' compensation statutes came into existence. It creates a cause of action by the employee or his or her personal representative for injury or death caused by the negligence of the railroad. Since the rule of comparative negligence is adopted, the contributory negligence of the employee shall not defeat the cause of action, but may be taken into account by the jury in reducing the amount of damages awarded. It must be emphasized that this Act applies only to employees of an interstate carrier by railroad. It normally does not apply to employees who are not employed by an interstate railroad, even though their employers might be engaged in the furtherance of the interstate function of the railroad or may be engaged in interstate commerce themselves. Thus, the Act would not apply to employees of the Pullman Company, postal employees, truckers who deliver freight to and from the railroad depot, or contractors who are engaged in the construction or repair of the roadbed, signal devices, grade crossings, or the inspection of railroad equipment. It likewise does not apply to other interstate carriers, such as bus lines and long-haul trucking corporations. Since Congress has never legislated with respect to these latter employees, state compensation laws apply to them. It sometimes happens that an intrastate railroad connects with an interstate railroad carrier by means of a siding or interchange carrier and thus becomes an instrument of interstate commerce. In such a case, for the purposes of FELA, the intrastate carrier is regarded as being in interstate commerce and, thus, its employees are subject to the Act.

Because of the application of the comparative negligence doctrine, most claims under FELA result in a recovery. In addition, since the injuries are usually serious, the juries customarily bring in substantial verdicts. With the introduction of workers' compensation laws, the railroad unions and their members showed little interest in substituting the compensation remedy for the substantial verdict potential of FELA. As a result, railroad employees get more favorable treatment in the case of accidents than is generally accorded to other employees.

Rights of Sailors In a legal sense, sailors are among the best protected class of employees. Some of the rights and benefits came into existence thousands of years ago and are still enforceable today. Others came into existence as a result of judicial fiat and gained their authority from the repeated holding of the courts in acknowledging their validity. Still others have come into existence as a result of modern statutes.

A sailor who is injured or taken ill in the service of the ship is entitled to enforce the following rights against the vessel or its owner:

(1) wages, transportation, maintenance, and cure; (2) damages under the General Maritime Law; and (3) damages under the Jones Act.

Wages, Transportation, Maintenance, and Cure. This is one of the ancient rights given to sailors and is considered one of the elements of the contract of hire, whether the articles of employment mention them or not. A sailor who falls sick in the service of the ship is entitled to (1) wages to the end of the voyage; (2) transportation back to his homeport, either in the same ship or another ship of similar accommodation; (3) maintenance, which means food and quarters to the end of the voyage and payments to cover expenses during the period of medical treatment; and (4) cure, which means medical attention and other similar services which extend beyond the end of the voyage and which are required either to cure the condition or bring it to a point where it is pronounced permanent or incurable.

General Maritime Law. This is generally referred to as the common law of the sea. While unwritten in the sense of a statute, it derives its authority from court decisions allowing recoveries. Under this system, the sailor is entitled to damages from the vessel for any injury or illness brought about by the unseaworthiness of the ship. In general, there is an implied warranty of seaworthiness arising out of the relationship of the vessel and the sailor. The guarantee warrants not only the physical structure of the ship and its ability to withstand the ordinary perils of the sea, but also that it is properly loaded, the cargo is properly stowed, that it has been provided with a competent master, a sufficient number of competent officers and sailors, and that it has all the requisite appurtenances and equipment, such as ballast, cables, anchors, cordage, sails, and lights, all in good condition, as well as food, water, fuel, and other necessary and proper stores and implements for the voyage. If the vessel lacks any of these items, it is unseaworthy. If the sailor is injured as a consequence of an unseaworthy condition, he or she may bring an action for damages against the vessel.

In admiralty, the vessel is charged with the responsibility of responding to the rights of sailors, be they referable to wages, transportation, maintenance and cure or for the recovery of damages for bodily injury due to unseaworthiness. This liability is imposed on the vessel itself and not on the master or the owner personally. In order to recover, the sailor will initiate action by means of a writ of attachment (called a libel) against the vessel. This writ is served by a United States Marshal and is physically attached to the vessel, with the marshal taking possession thereof. The plaintiff-seaman is referred to in admiralty as the "libellant." The owner enters the litigation as the "ship's claimant" and usually offers a bond in order to release the attachment. The case then proceeds as any other lawsuit.

Under the General Maritime Law, there is no recovery for wrongful death. The damages to be claimed are only those items which accrue to the seaman alone.

The Jones Act. The Merchant Marine Act of 1920 (46 USCA 688), which is commonly referred to as the Jones Act, merely applies to sailors employed on American vessels the same system and the same type of remedy granted to railroad employees. The Act reads as follows:

> Any seaman who shall suffer personal injury in the course of his employment may, at his election, maintain an action for damages at law with the right of trial by jury, and in such action all statutes of the United States modifying or extending the common law right or remedy in cases of personal injury to railway employees shall apply; and in the case of death of any seaman as a result of any such personal injury, the personal representative of such seaman may maintain an action for damages at law with the right of trial by jury, and in such action all statutes of the United States conferring or regulating a right of action for death in the case of railway employees, shall be applicable. Jurisdiction in such actions shall be under the court of the district in which the defendant employer resides or in which his principal office is located.

As noted earlier, the sailor is entitled to wages, transportation, maintenance, and cure in all cases where he falls sick or is injured in the service of the ship. These rights are part of the contract of hire and the sailor is entitled to enforce them, regardless of how the injury or illness was acquired, with the exception that there would be no recovery if the illness or injury came about because of the sailor's own misconduct. (Misconduct might consist of participation in a mutiny or disobedience of orders.) In addition, the sailor may bring an action against the vessel owner for personal injuries which were brought about by the unseaworthy condition of the vessel. With the passage of the Jones Act, the sailor may elect to bring an action against the owners based on their negligent operation of the ship and, in the case of death, the sailor's personal representative may bring action for wrongful death. Thus, the Jones Act enables the sailor to bring action directly against the owners for bodily injury and, in addition, creates a cause of action for wrongful death. It thereby amends the General Maritime Law by permitting a direct action against the owners and by creating an action for wrongful death which never existed before.

Conflicts of Compensation Laws Where the employee is hired in one state, does all work in that state, and is injured in that state, there are no jurisdictional questions involved. The employee only has a claim under the state workers' compensation act. Where the employee is hired in one state, does some work in that state, and then is injured in another state where his or her work is required, the general rule is that the employee has a choice of jurisdictions and may make a claim in either state. Usually he or she will choose the state which gives the greater benefits, but the employer may be exposed to liability in either state, depending upon where the employee brings the claim. Where the contract of employment is made in one state for work exclusively outside of the state and the employee does no work in the state of hire, the workers' compensation law of the state of hire has no application. Where the employee is hired in one state and does some work within the area of federal jurisdiction, the employer may have a liability under either the state or federal jurisdiction.

State Versus State. Where the employee sustains a compensable injury in a state other than the state of hire, he or she may make a claim in either state. The employee cannot file claims in both states and effect a double recovery—a decision must be made as to which state law will be invoked. Problems arise when, after receiving an award in one state, the claimant discovers that he or she would have been entitled to greater benefits in the other state, be it the state of hire or the state of the accident. The claimant then brings an action in the second state and asks for an award for the difference between the amount awarded and the total amount that would have been received if a claim had been made in the second state. The restatement on Conflict of Laws (Sec. 403) suggests the following rule to handle such a situation:

> Award already had under the workers' compensation act of another state will not bar a proceeding under an applicable act, unless the act where the award was made was designed to preclude the recovery of an award under any other act, but the amount paid under the prior award in one state will be credited on the second award.

The question of whether or not the employee may recover a second award will depend upon the provisions of the law under which he or she received the first award. If that law gave the award the status of a judgment of a court of law, the second state must, under the Constitution of the United States, give full faith and credit to such award as a final judgment, i.e., the second state may not disturb the initial finding. On the other hand, if the award is only a judgment of a compensation commission and it does not under the law in which it was obtained constitute a judgment of a court of law, the second state may make an award for the deficiency between the amount actually received and the amount to which the employee would have been entitled if he or she had brought the claim under the law of the second state. Under these latter circumstances, the employer could have a possible compensation liability, in two states, for one accident.

State Versus Federal. The primary area in which the state jurisdiction comes into conflict with federal authority is in the case of maritime employees who are injured on land. As to members of a crew, federal jurisdiction is exclusive, regardless of where the accident occurred. For example, in Rudolph v. Industrial Marine Service, 210 SW 2d 30 (Tennessee), the death of an employee of a riverboat, who was killed when struck by a train while on land in the performance of work assigned by his employer in the service of the ship, was held to be not covered by the state workers' compensation, since the exclusive remedy was under the Jones Act. Likewise, maritime workers (other than members of the crew) who are injured on a vessel lying in navigable waters are exclusively covered under federal law, and the workers' compensation law of the state has no application.[11] As to maritime workers injured on land, the federal longshoremen's and harbor workers' legislation applies to the dock or pier and all other areas used for the purpose of loading and unloading vessels. As to other areas not within this definition, it would appear that the longshoreman would be entitled to state workers' compensation benefits. Unfortunately, the federal legislation passed in 1972 is so new that there is not yet a definitive answer to this jurisdictional problem. In any case, employers should protect themselves by insurance or other means to meet claims under either the federal or state act.

Another troublesome area is where state and federal authority seem to overlap and the injured employee has the choice of whether to bring the claim under the state or federal act. This area is frequently referred to as the "local concern doctrine" or the "twilight zone." For example, the following employments have been held to be maritime but of such a nature as to involve only the local area and to have no particular relationship to navigation and commerce on water: (1) a carpenter injured while working on a ship which had been launched but not yet completed; (2) a diver employed by a shipbuilding company to remove obstrutions in the course of a river near its base of operations; (3) logging operations employees; and (4) employees aboard a dredger engaged in digging new channels or improving the shore. In each of these cases, claims made under the state workers' compensation act were sustained. It is possible that if the claims were made under the federal longshoremen's act the claims would be sustained. Thus, in these types of cases, the employer has a possible liability under either the state or federal compensation act.

As to railroad employees, since the Supreme Court has held that it is beyond the power of the state to interfere with the application of the Federal Employers' Liability Act, such employees are not affected by the workers' compensation act.

CURRENT STATUS OF EMPLOYERS' LIABILITY AND WORKERS' COMPENSATION EXPOSURES

Originally, employers were deemed liable under common law for injuries to employees, but certain defenses were available. The workers' compensation concept has now been adopted in all of the states. Workers are covered for accidents which arise out of and in the course of employment, as well as for such occupational diseases which are included in the statute.

Scope of Employers' Exposures

Unfortunately, not all employments are covered under the various workers' compensation statutes. Most laws exclude farm workers and domestic servants from the coverage. The latest figure from the Bureau of Labor Statistics indicates that 84.4 percent of the total work force of approximately 76 million employees come within the scope of the compensation acts. As to the other workers not so covered, the common-law rights are still in existence and the employer is exposed to tort liability. Therefore, it is essential that the employer also be fully protected against this contingency.

Illustrations of the Exposure

Under the common-law system, the extent of the employer's liability is unlimited, since the amount of damages to be assessed against him or her is what the court or jury will award. Under the workers' compensation statutes, the employer's liability is limited to the benefits set forth in the act itself. In an effort to convey the full scope of the employer's exposure, the following are offered as illustrations of losses which frequently occur.

Liability Under the Statute for Occupational Injury or Disease The employer is liable for the full benefits prescribed by the applicable compensation act(s) for accidents arising out of and in the course of employment and for compensable occupational diseases. The legislature may increase the benefits of the act at any time, and the increased benefits must be paid to the employee when the accident or occupational disease occurs after the effective date of the increase. Thus, the liability of the employer for statutory compensation benefits is at the will of the legislature. In addition, the legislature may enlarge the scope of the act to include employments which were previously excluded. Under most state statutes covering occupational diseases, the date of disablement is considered to be the date of the accident for the purpose of determining the benefits to which the employee is entitled.

Liability to Loaned Employees It sometimes happens that one employer will "loan" one employee to another employer, usually for the purpose of doing some special job, with the understanding that the employee will remain on the first employer's payroll and will return to the first employer when the assignment is completed. In this situation, the first employer is referred to as the "general employer" and the borrowing employer is called the "special employer."

Because the need for temporary employees has increased in recent years, a number of firms have entered the business of furnishing temporary help, including clerical, construction, and trucking employees. It is estimated that temporary employees constitute upwards of 2 percent of the work force, and there is every indication that this percentage will increase. Therefore, it becomes necessary to determine the compensation responsibility between the lending and the borrowing employers, as well as the tort liability exposure of the borrowing employer. This latter exposure is important in some cases, since the chance of injury to a temporary employee is often greater, due to unfamiliarity with the work and the conditions under which it is to be performed. Where there is no provision in the applicable workers' compensation act, the cases produce some confusion. Sometimes, where the relationship is that of general and special employer, both employers are jointly and severally liable for compensation to an injured employee. The compensation commission may find either or both employers liable. Usually one employer is selected and the employer found liable is the one who exercises the greater control.[12]

Many of the court cases involving loaned employees place the responsibility for workers' compensation on the special or borrowing employer. The theory behind this allocation of responsibility is that the special employer has the right to control and direct the work of the employee, even though such employee is not on their payroll. For example, in Galloway's case, 237 NE 2d 663 (Mass.), the employee registered with the Certified Business Employment Service as a clerk typist and was sent by Certified to Sylvania Electric Products. The conditions of the work, its nature, and the efforts expended by her were subject to the direction of employees of Sylvania, even though her employment was temporary. At the end of each week of employment, she furnished Certified with an account of the number of hours she worked so that they could bill Sylvania. Certified charged Sylvania $2.60 per hour for her work and Certified paid her $2.00 per hour. She sustained an injury while so working. Emphasizing Sylvania's direction and control, the court concluded that Sylvania was the employer liable for compensation.

Some states have specific provisions in their workers' compensation statutes which place the compensation responsibility on either the lending employer or the borrowing employer, or in some cases on both. For example, in D'Andrea v. Manpower, Inc. of Providence, 249 A 2d 896 (Rhode Island), an eighteen-year-old employee was hired by Manpower and was sent to another employer with a work slip. Under the Rhode Island statute, the court held that the general employer was responsible for the compensation benefits and further held that Manpower was such a general employer. Hence, Manpower was liable for the compensation benefits. On the other hand, the Illinois statute imposes the primary liability for compensation on the borrowing employer.[13]

It often happens that the firm engaged in furnishing temporary help will advertise that the loaned employees would be covered under the compensation policies held by the lending employer. This can be misleading. If the borrowing employer is held to be responsible for the compensation benefits, the borrower alone will have to respond. The mere fact that another party to the transaction carried some sort of insurance will not insulate the borrowing employer from responsibility. In states where the borrowing employer is not responsible for the payment of compensation, there always exists the possibility that the loaned employee may bring a tort action for personal injuries against the borrowing employer. In relation to the borrowing employer, the employee is a business invitee. In any case, most of these actions which have been brought have been unsuccessful due to the difficulties confronting the employee in establishing proof of negligence. The borrowing employer, however, is exposed to the expense of defending the lawsuit.

In the trucking industry it is customary for a truck owner to lease both truck and driver to a delivery company. The truck driver remains on the payroll of the trucking company with reimbursement from the delivery company. The driver is subject to the orders and control of the delivery company. This involves the relationship of special and general employer, and the compensation liability is imposed in accordance with the law of the state of the accident, or the state which otherwise has jurisdiction.

The principle of special and general employers should not be confused with dual employment. It is possible for an employee to work for two employers at the same time and in the same place. For example, a watchman was employed by two companies to watch two buildings which were owned separately. His wages were paid on a proportionate basis by each company. The liability for compensation was apportioned against both companies.[14]

Contractor and Subcontractor The legislatures recognized that an employer could easily circumvent the operation of the compensation law by employing an uninsured subcontractor who would borrow as many employees as may be needed without involving the principal contractor. Therefore, a provision was added to some of the laws which in essence makes the principal contractor liable for the payment of compensation benefits to employees of an uninsured subcontractor. The typical provision further provides that in the event of the payment of any compensation benefits by the principal contractor, he or she is entitled to reimbursement from the uninsured subcontractor for the payments so made. Thus, the employee of the subcontractor is assured of the payment of benefits, regardless of whether the subcontractor-employer is insured. Because of this provision, the general contractor usually requires that the subcontractor submit a certificate of compensation insurance and, in addition, requires an agreement on the part of the compensation insurer to give notice to the general contractor in the event of cancellation.

Substitute Benefit Schemes All compensation laws forbid the substitution of any scheme whereby benefits other than compensation benefits are to be paid. Unless the employee rejects the act in a state which permits it, the employee may not waive his or her rights to compensation benefits *in advance of injury*. Nor may an employee, prior to injury, waive his or her right to sue for damages. The usual statutory provision is as follows:

> No agreement, composition or release of damages made before the happening of an accident shall be valid or shall bar a claim for damages or a claim for compensation for the injury resulting therefrom, and any such agreement is declared against public policy. The receipt of benefits from any association, society or fund to which the employee shall have been a contributor shall not bar the recovery of damages by action at law or the recovery of compensation under this chapter.

This means that the employer may not make an agreement with the employee to waive statutory compensation and substitute different methods of payment.

Clearly, after the injury, the employee may elect whatever methods of collection of compensation or damages which are open, and may waive one cause of action in favor of another. But the statute forbids any agreements in advance of the happening of the accident.

Suits by Employees or Prospective Employees There are a number of situations wherein the employer might be exposed to liability as a consequence of litigation brought by employees or those seeking employment. Among the possible causes of action are the following.

Employees and Employments Not Covered. If the occupation in which the employee was working at the time of the accident is excluded from the operation of a compensation statute, either because of the nature of the occupation (such as domestic servants and farm laborers) or because of the number of employees employed, the employee's common-law rights against the employer are unaffected by the compensation law. The employee still retains the right to bring action against his or her employer based upon the failure of the employer to meet any one of the common-law duties imposed.

In most states where the compensation statute is elective and the employer rejects it, the nonassenting employer is deprived of some or all common-law defenses. If the employee can establish the negligence of the employer, he or she is certain of recovery. However, it must be emphasized that even though the employer is shorn of common-law defenses, the burden is still on the employee to establish the employer's negligence.

Disease Not Covered by the Statute. Most statutes do not cover all occupational diseases, but only those diseases which are described in the statute. Regarding the diseases which are not covered under the statute, the employee may bring action at law against the employer, subject to the common-law defenses which the employer may interpose.

Assault by the Employer. The compulsory state compensation laws provide that in the case of an "accident," the covered employee's claim for statutory compensation benefits is his or her exclusive remedy. An assault and battery is not really an accident, in the sense that it is an intentional act on the part of the perpetrator.[15] But it could be considered as an accident to the injured employee. Therefore, the injured employee has the choice of making a claim under the compensation act, in which case compensation benefits would be the sole and exclusive remedy, or bringing a tort action against the employer. Clearly, the tort action, which may include a recovery for pain and suffering or other intangibles, may result in a greater amount of damages.

In Smith v. Lannert, 429 SW 2d 8 (Missouri), a supervisory employee spanked a female employee. The court found that since the supervisory employee's act was within the scope of his employment, the employer was vicariously liable, in tort, for the supervisor's assault on the plaintiff. False imprisonment or wrongful detention take on all the attributes of assault and are similarly treated. For example, in Skelton v. W. T. Grant Company, 331 Fed. 2d 593, the employee was detained one and one-half hours against her will in an attempt to extort her confession to a theft of merchandise. In the subsequent suit, the court allowed a recovery and held that the exclusive provisions of the compensation act were not applicable. Also, in Moore v. Federal Dept. Stores, Inc., 190 NW 2d 262 (Michigan), it was held that the employee's injury, consisting of humiliation, embarrassment, and deprivation of personal liberty due to false imprisonment, was not in contemplation of the compensation act, and the employee's action at common law was not barred.

Thus, an intentional injury inflicted by the employer upon the employee will expose the employer to tort liability. The compensation law will not insulate him or her from this responsibility.

Retaliatory Discharge of Employee. While an employee generally may be discharged at any time, if it can be established that the employee was discharged solely because a compensation claim was filed against the employer, the employee has a cause of action in tort against the employer. The theory behind this is that public policy demands that the employee be able to file a claim for compensation without any fear of reprisal or the loss of the job. In addition, the law creates a duty on the part of the employer to compensate the employee for work-related injuries, either through insurance or other means. Clearly, if the employer was allowed to penalize the employee who filed a claim, the purpose of the compensation law would be thwarted and the employee would be deprived of the provisions of an act intended for his or her benefit. In Frampton v. Central Indiana Gas Co., 297 NE 2d 425 (Indiana) the employee injured her arm in the course of her employment. The employer paid her full salary during the four months she was unable to work, as well as her medical bills. Some nineteen months later she filed a claim for permanent partial disability compensation. After her return to work, she had performed capably and well. Upon learning from the insurer that the employee had been awarded permanent partial disability compensation based on a 30 percent loss of use of her arm, the employer discharged her without any reason being given. She brought action against the employer and sought actual and punitive damages. Her claim was upheld by the Indiana Supreme Court.

Employer's Physician. Where the employer has a physician on the payroll for the purpose of making pre-employment examinations, as well as treating employees, the physician is the agent of the employer. The employer is responsible (under the doctrine of *respondeat superior*) for the physician's wrongful acts, if committed in the scope of his or her employment. Should the physician misdiagnose or fail to discover the presence of an illness, the employee so treated may have a cause of action against both the physican and the employer as his or her principal. Since this would not be an "accident" arising out of the employment in a way which would involve the compensation act, the employee could pursue his or her remedy at common law. Another type of wrongful act which may be committed is where the physician recommends that a certain employee be discharged because of some preexisting or after-acquired condition which may be aggravated in the event of an injury. If discharged for that reason, the employee may have a cause of action against both the physician and the employer.

Malpractice of Treating Physician. Where the employer engages a physician to treat injured employees, whether the treatment is rendered in the employer's plant or at the physician's office, generally the physician is an independent contractor over which the employer has no control as to the methods and means of doing the work. Accordingly, the employer is not vicariously liable for the physician's malpractice, since the physician is not an agent but an independent contractor. The employee, however, may assert a cause of action against the physician as a third party, in which case the employee's recovery would be based on the injury caused by the physician's malpractice only. The physician would not be responsible for the original injury. If the employee fails to bring a third-party action against the physician, in some states the employer is subrogated to the employee's right of action. It should be emphasized that where the physician's malpractice has aggravated the injury or caused a prolongation of disability, the employer is still liable for the compensation benefits. In addition, where the physician's malpractice has resulted in a greater permanent injury than would otherwise be the case, the employer is still responsible for the entire injury. But where the employee has recovered from the physician as a third party, the employer would be entitled to credit for the amount recovered as against the compensation benefits due.

Suits by Third Parties Not only is the employer liable for the payment of statutory compensation benefits to the employee, there are some cases in which the employer is also liable to third parties who may have suffered damage as a result of the employer's negligence.

Spouses for Loss of Consortium. As part of the marriage contract, the common law recognized that the husband was entitled to the "services" of his wife. These services consist of sex, society, and other services. Sex is the right of the husband to have sexual relations with his wife. Society means that he is entitled to her companionship, and other services have to do with the performance of household chores such as cooking, cleaning, and other duties necessary for the proper maintenance of the home. Collectively, these "services" are referred to as consortium. Any wrongful interference with these rights of the husband, because of an injury to his wife, would give the husband a cause of action against the wrongdoer who caused the injury. The husband is obligated to provide for the care and comfort of his wife in the case of illness or injury. Where the husband has been injured due to the wrongful act of another and the wife has been deprived of his services, the common law never recognized that she would have a cause of action. One reason may be that in the old common-law days the wife had no status to sue or be sued. She was regarded as a "superior servant" of her husband and he exercised some sort of guardianship over her rights. She could sue or be sued only in the name of her husband. Therefore, it is understandable why no claims for loss of services were asserted where the husband sustained injury.

With the turn of the century there came some awareness of the legal status of women. All states passed statutes which "emancipated" married women from the dominance of their husbands in legal matters. Now, the married woman may sue or be sued, just as if she were a single woman, and she no longer requires her husband to join with her in any litigation.

In Hitaffer v. Argonne, 183 Fed. 2d 811, the plaintiff's husband was injured while at work, the injury having been caused by the negligence of his employer. He filed a claim for workers' compensation and received his benefits regularly. The plaintiff-wife brought action against the employer for damages for the loss of her husband's services. The Circuit Court of Appeals for the District of Columbia, recognizing the inconsistency of allowing the husband to recover for loss of services where his wife was injured and yet denying the same rights to the wife where the husband was injured, modified the common law and allowed the wife to recover damages.

At first the courts rejected the Hitaffer decision, but with the present thinking in the area of equality of rights between the sexes, the trend is definitely to the adoption of Hitaffer. At the present time, the courts of the following states have recognized the wife's right to bring an action for the negligent loss of her husband's consortium:

Alaska	Kentucky
Arizona	Maryland
Arkansas	Massachusetts
Colorado	Michigan
Delaware	Minnesota
Florida	Missouri
Georgia	Montana
Hawaii	Nebraska
Idaho	Nevada
Illinois	New Hampshire
Indiana	New Jersey
Iowa	New York

Ohio

Oregon

Pennsylvania

Rhode Island

South Dakota

Wisconsin

Wyoming

Not all of these cases do involve claims for loss of consortium arising from compensation claims by the husband. However, since the courts of these states are committed to the Hitaffer dictum, they would undoubtedly apply the same rule to cases arising out of compensation accidents. In Witty v. Daw Drug Co., 326 N.Y.S. 2d 885, the wife's right to recover for loss of consortium was held to be independent, nonderivative, and not barred by the husband's inability to recover from the tortfeasor by virtue of the exclusive provisions of the workers' compensation law.

It would appear that where the wife is injured through the negligence of her employer, the husband would have the same right to assert a claim for loss of her services. It should be emphasized that in cases of this nature it is incumbent upon the plaintiff to establish that the injury to the spouse was caused by the negligence of the employer. If negligence cannot be established, there is no assertable cause of action.

Suits by Third Parties. Under certain circumstances, the employer may be held to be answerable in damages to a third party if the employer's negligence contributed to the liability imposed on the third party. This somewhat complicated situation can be best illustrated by referring to an actual case. In Westchester Gas Co. v. Westchester Small Estates Corp., 15 NE 2d 567 (New York), the employer was engaged in building a housing development. In the course of this work the employer caused a rupture in the gas main in the street, which he repaired. The employer's watchman, who normally slept in one of the houses nearing completion, was asphyxiated by illuminating gas and was found dead. His dependents filed suit against the gas company, alleging that the gas company was negligent in not discovering the leaking gas main. Judgment was entered against the gas company, which it paid. The gas company instituted suit against the employer on the theory that the employer-contractor's negligence in breaking the gas main and improperly repairing it created a liability to the dead man's dependents. The employer contended that its only liability to the employee's dependents was set up in the compensation law, which was the exclusive remedy. The court held that the contractor-employer had a duty of care with respect to the gas main and the repair thereof. Since this was an independent duty which it owed to the gas company, the court held that the contractor-employer was liable for damages to the gas company (i.e., the third party).

In Dole v. Dow Chemical Co., 30 NY 2d 143, Dow, a manufacturer of chemicals, produced methyl bromide, a penetrating and poisonous fumigant used for the control of storage insects and mites. It was labelled by Dow as poisonous, dangerous, and highly volatile. The employer (Urban Milling Co.) used it to fumigate a grain storage bin and shortly thereafter it directed the plaintiff's husband, its employee, to enter the fumigated bin and clean it. In so doing, he was exposed to the poison and died as a result. In the action brought against Dow Chemical Co., the defendant impleaded by third-party complaint the employer, Urban Milling Co., alleging that Urban was negligent in failing to take proper precautions in fumigating with methyl bromide; in using untrained personnel for this work; in failing to follow instructions on the label and the literature available to it; and in failing to test the premises after fumigation and to properly aerate it afterward. The complaint further asked for damages from the employer, if it was found that Dow is liable to the plaintiff.

This parallels the Westchester case, supra, except that the employer here was brought in on a third-party complaint rather than a separate suit. In any case, the court upheld the third party complaint as constituting a proper cause of action. In both of these cases neither plaintiff could have sued the employer directly, since their only remedy would be under the compensation law, but by taking a circuitous route, the employer ultimately became liable for the damages. In summary, even though the compensation law provides that it is the exclusive remedy as between the employer and employee, there are some situations where the employer could be held liable for damages for injuries sustained by employees due to the employer's negligence.

Penalties There are a number of penalties which may be imposed upon the employer for violation of various laws, some of which require a fine or license revocation and others of which involve the payment of increased compensation benefits by the employer.

Illegally Employed Minors. The labor laws of the various states set forth the kind and types of work which may be done by minors (e.g., under the age of sixteen or eighteen, as the law may state). All forbid the employer to allow the minor to work on any machinery with moving parts. In case of a violation, the employer is subject to fine or imprisonment. If the minor is injured while so employed, the compensation law also provides for penalties against the employer. Some states provide for double indemnity, which means that the same award that is made against the insurer is also made against the employer. This not only includes awards for temporary total and permanent disability but also death benefits as well. The law further provides that the employer alone, not the insurer, shall be liable for this extra compensation or death benefit, which is over and above the usual amount provided by law for disability or death. A typical provision of this type is as follows:

> If the injured employee at the tme of the accident or compensable occupational disease is a minor under 14 years of age employed in violation of labor law or minor between 14 and 18 years of age employed, permitted or suffered to work without an employment certificate or special permit, if required by law, or at an occupation prohibited at the minor's age by law, a compensation or death benefit shall be payable to the employee or his dependents which shall be double the amount payable under this Chapter.

Other states permit minors who are employed in violation of the law and who are injured to bring an action at law against the employer or claim compensation. In the event that the law action is elected, the employer is not entitled to interpose any of the common-law defenses.

Discrimination Against Employees. Most compensation acts contain a provision protecting the employee against discharge or discrimination because he or she either filed a claim, testified in support of another employee's claim, or was about to so testify. Violators of the provision would incur criminal penalties in the form of a fine or imprisonment. In addition, the employee is entitled to restoration of his or her former job status. Usually the employer alone is responsible for the penalties imposed by this provision. A typical provision (New Jersey) reads as follows:

> It shall be unlawful for any employer or his duly authorized agent to discharge or in any manner discriminate against an employee as to his employment because such employee has claimed or attempted to claim workmen's compensation benefits from such employer, or because he has testified, or is about to testify, in any proceeding under this chapter to which this act is a supplement. For any violation of this act, the employer or agent shall be punished by a fine of not less than $100.00 nor more than $1,000.00 or imprisonment for not more than 60 days or both. Any employee so discriminated against shall be restored to his employment and shall be compensated by his employer for any loss of wages arising out of such discrimination, provided, if such employee shall cease to be qualified to perform the duties of his employment he shall not be entitled to such restoration and compensation.

> The employer alone and not his insurance carrier shall be liable for any penalty under this act.

The provisions of this act do not preclude the possibility of a suit against the employer by the employee for wrongful discharge or other damages which he may have sustained.

Employment of Females. Until the adoption of equal rights legislation, most states had statutes which set forth the hours during which females could be employed and the ages of employment. The usual provision was that females from sixteen to twenty-one years of age could not work after 10 P.M. and before 6 A.M. Those over twenty-one could not be employed after midnight or before 6 A.M. Violation of these rules would result in a fine or other penalty, including the suspension of the license of the business which it requires to operate. Employees engaged in interstate commerce were not affected by state laws. Since the adoption of equal rights legislation, it is questionable whether any such laws could be enforced.

Safe Place to Work Laws. Many states have labor statutes which require that all manufacturing plants and other places to which the law applies be so constructed, equipped, arranged, operated, and conducted as to provide reasonable and adequate protection to the lives, health, and safety of all persons employed therein or lawfully frequenting such places. All machinery, equipment, and devices in such places are to be so placed, operated, guarded, and lighted as to provide reasonable and adequate protection to all such persons. The laws also provide for a board which shall have the duty of promulgating additional rules to carry the law into effect, as well as the duty of providing for periodic inspections. Machinery found to be defective by the inspector may not be used until the defect is corrected. These laws parallel the Occupational Safety and Health Act and are enforced in connection therewith. Penalties are imposed for violation of the board rules and, in extreme cases, the employer may be enjoined from operating.

Failure to File Accident Reports. Most state compensation laws require that the employer make an immediate report of any employee accidents to the Industrial Accident Board or similar body. Failure to do so will subject the employer to a fine set forth in the statute, usually from $10 to $50 per violation.

Failure to Secure Workers' Compensation Insurance. In states where workers' compensation insurance is required, the failure of the employer to secure such insurance and keep it in force will subject the employer to a penalty, usually in the form of a fine up to $1,000 and, in some cases, to imprisonment. When the employer is a corporation, the president, secretary, and treasurer thereof who are actively engaged in the corporate business are liable for the failure to secure compensation insurance.

A Final Note. If the foregoing review has been convincing, it should have at least conveyed the immense and formidable scope of employers' liability and workers' compensation exposures. Fortunately, there are some effective methods to deal with such exposures, and these methods, including insurance, will be discussed in the next chapter.

Chapter Notes

1. However, as will be discussed later, the compensation statutes of some states obligate the principal-contractor to pay compensation benefits to the *employees* of an uninsured subcontractor. But the principal is entitled to reimbursement from the subcontractor for any such payments.
2. See Caicco v. Toto Brothers, Inc., 62 N. J. 305, wherein the owner and operator of a dump truck, who hauled exclusively for one person who controlled the time and place of the work, was held to be an employee.
3. In Johnson v. Ashville Hosiery Co., 153 SE 591, the court defined an independent contractor as follows:

   One who exercises an independent employment and contracts to do a piece of work according to his own judgment and methods, and without being subject to his employer except as to the results of the work, and who has the right to employ and direct the action of the workmen, independently of such employer and freed from any superior authority in him to say how the specified work shall be done, or what the laborers shall do as it progresses.

4. Another interesting problem is where the corporate officer owns all of the outstanding stock. It can be argued that since such an officer is the alter ego of the corporation, he cannot be employed by himself. There are no cases directly on this point, although there are many where the corporate officer was a principal stockholder. In these latter cases, the dual capacity doctrine was applied.
5. See Union Carbon & Carbide Corporation, 237 Fed. 2d 229 (Tenn.).
6. In states where the employer is required to render medical attention, the insurer usually supplies the employer with a list or panel of physicians to whom the patients are to be referred. It is to the advantage of the insurer to provide the best medical treatment obtainable, since doing so may reduce the period of disability and in some cases reduce the degree of permanence. In the few states where medical treatment is limited to a period of time or to a dollar amount, it is sometimes to the advantage of the insurer to render treatment beyond the statutory limit, in order to reduce the period of disability or the amount which the insurer might be ultimately required to pay for the permanent condition. On the other hand, if the treatment is merely palliative and will not effect a cure or a reduction in the ultimate permanency, most insurers will stand on the statutory limit, i.e., they will not provide medical treatment beyond that point.
7. See also Wolfe v. Lindsay et al., (NY, 1975), 330 NE 2d 603.
8. Other areas which have been held to expose the employee to a special danger are Guam (O'Leary v. Brown-Pacific-Maxon, 340 U.S. 504); Grand Turk Island (O'Keeffe v. Pan American World Airways, 338 Fed. 2d 309); San Salvador (Pan American World Airways, 335 Fed. 2d 70); Hawaii (Liberty

Mutual Ins. Co. v. Gray, 137 Fed. 2d 926); and South Korea (O'Keefe v. Smith, Hinchman & Grylls Associates, 85 Sup. Ct. 1012).

9. See Arabian Am. Oil Co. v. Ind. Acc. Comm'n., 94 Cal. App. 2d 388, 210 Pac. 2d 732 (Saudi Arabia), and Brown-Pacific-Maxon, Inc. v. Pillsbury, 132 Fed. Supp. 421 (California).

10. See Outer Continental Shelf Lands Act, 43 USCA 1333.

11. See Southern Pacific Co. v. Jensen, 244 U. S. 205.

12. For example, in Ettlinger v. State Ins. Fund, 206 NYS 2d 739, an employee of Office Temporaries was assigned to work for the Oxford Paper Company and, while so engaged, was injured on the latter's premises. The employment company (Office Temporaries) which paid the employee's wages and had the right to assign and discharge employees was held liable for the employee's compensation benefits. In another New York case, Meyer v. Tops Temporary Personnel, 144 NYS 2d 775, the court reached the same result. The employee worked for Tops and was sent out as a temporary office helper. Tops paid his wages but the Manufacturers Safety Deposit Company instructed him on how to perform his duties. Tops was held liable for workers' compensation.

13. See Albert Mojonnier, Inc. v. Industrial Commission, 242 NE 2d 184.

14. See Hunt v. Regent Development Company, 143 NE 2d 892 (New York).

15. For example, in Readinger v. Gottschall, 191 A. 2d 694 (Penna.) the employer and his wife physically ejected the dismissed employee from the premises. The court held that these facts did not constitute an accident covered by the workers' compensation law.

CHAPTER 7

Treatment of Employers' Liability and Workers' Compensation Exposures

INTRODUCTION

The current system of workers' compensation is significantly different from the system that first appeared in the early 1900s as one of the earlier forms of social insurance in the United States. Today, the majority of state laws are compulsory, encompass many additional classes of private and public employments, and provide broader coverages, along with higher benefits.

While some of the improvements stem from traditional socio-economic pressures, most are attributable to the efforts of the National Commission on State Workmen's Compensation Laws. This commission, which was authorized by the Occupational Safety and Health Act of 1970 and made up of representatives from business and labor, surveyed the system which was then considered by many to be inadequate. Following its study, the commission produced eighty recommendations for improvement, nineteen of which were considered to be essential, and indicated that if states did not take the initiative to improve their laws, federal legislation would be enacted to replace the entire system.

In spite of changes over the years, the compensation system's underlying purpose—to serve both humanitarian and economic roles in society—remains virtually unchanged. The workers' compensation system has two primary objectives in its humanitarian role. One is to prevent human injuries, disabilities, and deaths through the maintenance of safe working conditions. The other is to assist the disabled so that they may eventually return to their jobs through the aid of physical and vocational rehabilitation. By providing safe places to work, accidents can be prevented and workers can continue to earn a living uninterrupted by the affliction of pain and suffering that accompanies injuries and diseases. Families can continue to rely upon the support and the affection of their bread-winners through continued employment. Employers can benefit from the uninterrupted productivity of their employees and can minimize the costs that go along with providing benefits, whether through insurance or retention programs. Society also benefits from not having to support the disabled and from the continued productivity of human resources.

Unfortunately, not all accidents and diseases can be prevented. When they occur, workers' compensation insurance, in its economic role, serves to provide certain benefits to assist in the financial hardships that always follow injuries, disabilities, and deaths. For example, workers' compensation insurance now provides virtually unlimited medical and hospital care benefits to work accident victims. It also provides disability income to replace part of the earnings that are lost when work-related injuries or diseases result in temporary total disability, permanent total disability, or death. Since the underlying concept of workers' compensation is to assist the disabled to return to their jobs, or at least to some form of gainful employment, various physical and vocational rehabilitation benefits are also made available.

WORKERS' COMPENSATION AND EMPLOYERS' LIABILITY INSURANCE

Nature and Scope of Insurance Coverage

The standard workers' compensation and employers' liability policy is a combination of two separate coverages that serve both employees and employers in situations involving occupational disability and death.

The first of these coverages, workers' compensation, is governed entirely by the applicable statutes. Its purpose is to alleviate some of the financial hardships of employees who sustain work related injuries, sicknesses, or deaths, as well as the hardships of their dependents, by providing varying degrees of benefits prescribed by law. This coverage also benefits employers because insurance companies and state funds, in taking over the obligations of insured employers, pay almost everything that is required by law to settle claims of employees.

The second coverage, referred to as employers' liability, is for the benefit of employers. While there are a number of uses for this coverage, its primary purpose is to protect employers from suits brought against them by or on behalf of their employees who are victims of work related incidents, separate and distinct from any claim for workers' compensation benefits. This protection is much like that provided under a comprehensive general liability policy, in that it also provides employers with defense coverage. The standard policy is designed in such a way that employers' liability coverage does not overlap with general liability protection.

In those jurisdictions where employees are permitted to purchase compensation insurance from private insurers, coverage for both workers' compensation and employers' liability exposures is provided under one policy. An interesting feature of this policy is that it contains uniform provisions, even though workers' compensation benefits vary by jurisdiction. It is possible to use the same policy for basic coverages in various states, without endorsements, because the compensation laws of states control the conditions of coverage, rather than the policy provisions. The compensation laws are read into the policy provisions in determining the scope of coverage.

Workers' Compensation Coverage Under the basic workers' compensation coverage the insurer simply agrees to pay promptly, when due, all compensation and other benefits required of the employer, as the insured, by the workers' compensation law that applies. The policy refers to workers' compensation laws as the compensation and any occupational disease laws of the state(s) designated in the policy declarations, and it defines "state" as any state or territory in the United States of America and the District of Columbia. Note that since the policy deals specifically in terms of state laws, no automatic protection is provided against claims involving employees who are subject to federal compensation laws, such as the Federal Employees Act and U.S. Longshoremen's and Harbor Workers' Compensation Act. (Coverage for these exposures will be discussed later.)

No limits apply to the workers' compensation section of the policy, such as those of a fire policy or a general liability policy, because none are permitted by law. The insurer, instead, is required to assume whatever liability is prescribed for its insured by the statute in question, except for any punitive or exemplary damages that may be assessed against an employer. The absence of policy limits does not mean that benefits are unlimited. The kind and the extent of any benefits that may be payable depend upon the nature of the disability and upon the state law that controls. Benefits, as a whole, have increased over the years, particularly since the recommendations of the National Commission on State Workmen's Compensation Laws in 1972, but the statutes still prescribe dollar and other limits on most types of benefits.

How promptly an insurer is obligated to pay compensation benefits also depends upon which state law and what type of benefit is applicable. Generally, most state laws require that expenses for both medical and hospital care be paid immediately. But when it comes to disability income benefits, most state laws specify that a waiting period must elapse before income benefits become payable. This period ranges from two to seven days. However, if the disability continues for a certain number of days or weeks, most laws of states provide that disability income benefits must be paid retroactively to the date of injury or disease. It should be reemphasized that it is the law of the state in question, and not the policy provisions, that dictate when an insurer must begin providing benefits to employees.

Since the policy restricts protection to that required by the state law or laws listed in the declarations, it is important that the policy declarations designate the state or the states where all business locations or operations, involving employee work exposures, are or may be maintained. (Other procedures must be followed in obtaining workers' compensation insurance for exposures that exist in any jurisdictions with monopolistic funds, as will be discussed later.)

As brought out in Chapter 6, most state laws are extraterritorial. An employee hired by an employer in state A may be injured on business in state B. That employee, depending on the laws and/or circumstances, might file a claim under the compensation laws of either state A or state B. If the declarations of the employer's policy listed only state A, there would be no insurance coverage for a claim filed under the laws of state B. The broad form all states endorsement, discussed later in this chapter, can be added to the policy in situations where extraterritorial exposures exist.

Employers' Liability Coverage Statutory workers' compensation benefits are usually considered to be the exclusive remedy to those covered employees who sustain occupational injuries and diseases. Employees cannot reject the statutory benefits after an injury and decide to sue their employers with the idea of possibly obtaining higher awards at common law. Nor can employees accept the benefits and decide later to sue their employers for additional money damages. Yet, there may be a need for additional protection. Employers, for example, may not elect to come under the laws, if laws are not compulsory, or they may not be subject to the laws because of numerical exemptions. There may be times, too, when the injury, disease, or death of a victim does not meet the criteria for coverage or, in some cases, the workers' compensation act specifically permits (or is interpreted as permitting) suits against employers by third parties, such as dependents of an employee. Employers also can be involved in "third-party-over" actions, as they often are called, particularly in cases involving products liability claims.

Briefly, a third-party-over action arises when an injured employee sues and recovers from a negligent third party. The third party, in turn, sues the employer for at least partial recovery based upon contributory negligence of the employer. For example, an employee is injured by a machine which the employer, with knowledge of a safety defect, allows to be operated. The employee sues the manufacturer of that machine, rather than accepting the compensation benefits of his or her employer, in order to obtain a higher judgment. The manufacturer then sues the employer on the basis that the employer was partially negligent in permitting the machine to be operated in an unsafe condition.

Were it not for the availability of employers' liability coverage, any one of these circumstances could produce serious gaps that could jeopardize the protection of employers, especially since these exposures are not covered under general liability policy provisions.

Employers' liability coverage provides employers, as insureds, with protection when suits are made against them for work-related incidents that are not compensable under workers' compensation coverage. Although the basic amount of liability coverage is usually $100,000, it can be increased at the option of the insured. The coverage applies not only to operations in states designated in the policy, but also to operations necessary or incidental thereto. Coverage also applies on a worldwide basis, with respect to employees who are citizens or residents of the United States and Canada, if they are involved in the same type of operations as described in the policy declarations.

The insuring clause of employers' liability coverage is best understood by examining each of the several aspects that collectively determine its scope.

Legal Liability. No payment will be made on behalf of the employer, unless the employer is reasonably believed to be, or is ultimately determined to be, legally liable for the damages claimed.

Damages. The damages which the insurer will pay because of bodily injury or death include those for care and loss of services—such as loss of consortium—and those assessed against employers in third-party-over actions.

Bodily Injury by Accident or Disease. The policy applies only to bodily injury caused by accident during the policy period, or to bodily injury by disease if the last day of the last exposure which causes or aggravates the disease occurs during the policy period and while the employee is in the employment of an insured. The insurer whose policy was in force on the date of the last exposure is liable for the entire claim, provided written notice of claim is made to the employer within thirty-six months after expiration of the policy. The policy also covers death claims, regardless of when the deaths occur, so long as the deaths resulted from an accidental bodily injury or a disease which was covered.

Note that employers' liability coverage applies to claims of *bodily injury by disease*, while statutory workers' compensation coverage sometimes concerns itself only with claims of *occupational disease*. The fact that employers' liability coverage applies to claims by disease means that employers are protected for suits even though the contraction of a disease is not peculiar to employment. Pneumonia, or a staph infection that is contracted because of alleged failure to maintain a sanitary place of employment are examples. Occupational disease, on the other hand, is commonly thought of as one that is caused by conditions peculiar to one's employment. Silicosis resulting from exposure to silica dust and asbestosis resulting from asbestos fibers are examples.

However, the difference between bodily injury by disease and occupational disease is no longer as significant as it once was, because the majority of state laws have been amended over the years so that the definition of "occupational" disease now includes most types of diseases. But if there is some question of coverage under workers' compensation, the employer still has some degree of protection under employers' liability coverage. The insurer at least is required to defend such claims against employers, and to pay any judgments, up to the policy limits.

In addition, the policy defines the terms "bodily injury by accident," and "bodily injury by disease," primarily to avoid any argument that an injury is attributable to both an accident and a disease. The two terms are mutually exclusive. The policy also specifies that assault and battery is considered an accident, unless it is committed by or at the direction of the insured-employer.

Where Coverage Applies. Coverage applies to injuries by accident or disease, including resulting death, whether they are sustained within the United States, its territories or possessions, Canada, or elsewhere. Coverage, in other words, may be worldwide. The territory wherein injury or death is sustained nonetheless does have an effect on the scope of coverage.

Coverage applies, first of all, to any employee of the insured when injury or death arises out of and in the course of his or her employment and occurs either during operations in a state designated in the policy, or during operations that are necessary or incidental to such operations, while within the United States, its territories or possessions, or in Canada. Whether an operation is "necessary or incidental" to the operation(s) specified in the policy could very well be a question of fact. The employer, in any event, at least receives defense coverage until it is determined whether the employer is legally liable.

Coverage also applies to claims by an employee who is a citizen or a resident of the United States or Canada but who has sustained injuries while *temporarily* outside of the United States, its territories or possessions, or Canada. However, claims by foreign nationals or American citizens who are permanently employed in a foreign country do not come within the scope of this coverage. Employers in these situations should make other arrangements to insure or otherwise handle those exposures, depending upon the circumstances. Employees, for example, may have to be covered under the workers' compensation acts of foreign countries. Or, an employer may be required to purchase foreign voluntary compensation coverage, either under a separate policy or by endorsement to an existing policy (as discussed later).

Suits against employers stemming from foreign operations must be brought within the United States or Canada. Any suit brought in or any judgment rendered by a court outside of the United States, its territories, possessions, or Canada is outside the realm of employers' liability coverage.

Application of Policy Limits. Employers' liability coverage, unlike workers' compensation coverage, is subject to a minimum liability limit of $100,000 in most jurisdictions. This limit, however, can be increased to as high as $500,000 or $1 million. (Still higher limits may be obtained under umbrella liability or excess liability policies.) Whatever the limit, it applies in two ways.

First, the limit applies to all claims for *bodily injury* (or death) in any one *accident*. This limit is the maximum that would apply whether one employee or several employees were injured in the same accident. The limit would also apply if there were more than one claim arising out of a single injury to one employee. This could happen if the employee were to sue and the employee's spouse were to institute another claim for loss of consortium.

Second, the limit applies to all claims because of *bodily injury* by *disease* in each state. In the majority of cases, this aggregate limit applies for one year in each state covered.

Defense, Settlement, and Supplementary Payments The provisions of the workers' compensation and employers' liability policy concerning defense, settlement, and supplementary payments are similar to those of most other liability policies. The insurer agrees to:

1. Defend the insured employer in any proceeding seeking benefits, or in any suit seeking damages, even if the proceeding or suit is groundless, false, or fraudulent. This does not mean that the insurer must defend every suit made against an employer. If the allegations or the details of the claim are outside the scope of employers' liability coverage, the insurer can still refuse to defend its insured-employer.

2. Pay premiums on bonds to release attachments or premiums for appeal bonds, without any obligation to apply for or furnish such bonds. Court bonds such as these are not always easy to procure, particularly by defendants in court proceedings, which is probably the reason why insurers do not want to be obligated to apply for or furnish them.

3. Pay all expenses incurred by the insurer, and all costs taxed against the employer, in any proceeding or suit.

4. Pay all interest that has accrued after entry of judgment and until the insurer has paid, tendered, or deposited such part of the judgment in court as does not exceed the limit of liability that applies under employers' liability coverage. The interest on a judgment can involve a substantial sum, especially when an insurer decides to appeal an award and loses the appeal some years later.

5. Reimburse the employer for all reasonable expenses—other than loss of earnings—incurred at the insurer's request. What is meant by the word "reasonable" is uncertain. It would appear that if the expenses are incurred specifically at the request of the insurer, it would be difficult for the insurer to deny the reimbursement of some of them on the basis that they are unreasonable. The word "reasonable" may be there as a safeguard in the event of some misunderstanding by the insured concerning permission to incur expenses.

The amounts incurred in any one or all of these provisions concerning defense, settlement, and supplementary payments are payable by the insurer in addition to the amounts payable under workers' compensation coverage, or in addition to the applicable limit of liability under employers' liability coverage.

Exclusions and Their Rationale

The workers' compensation and employers' liability policy contains six exclusions. Two of them apply to both workers' compensation and employers' liability; the other four deal solely with employers' liability coverage.

Other Insurance or "Self-Insurance" The first exclusion which applies to both coverages stipulates that operations at or from any locations not described in the policy—emanating from operations of states listed in the policy declarations—are nevertheless covered, unless the insured has other insurance under the workers' compensation law for such operations or the insured is a qualified self-insurer. The intent of this exclusion is to avoid overlapping coverage. On occasion, firms, for business reasons, will buy their insurance from more than one producer and/or more than one insurer. It is thus not impossible for a firm simultaneously to have in existence two or more workers' compensation policies which cover separate operations within a state or in different states.

Domestic or. Farm Employment   The other exclusion which applies to both coverage sections precludes any coverage for domestic employment, or farm or agricultural employment, unless persons in those categories are required to be covered, or are voluntarily covered. As more states comply with the recommendations of the National Commission on State Workmen's Compensation Laws, this exclusion, particularly with respect to farm and to agricultural employment, will be unnecessary. In fact, the laws in a majority of jurisdictions have been amended to include this class of employment either on a compulsory basis without exception or within certain guidelines, such as when the payroll in these categories exceeds a certain amount.

Contractual Liability   The first of the four exclusions that apply solely to employers' liability coverge specifies that liability assumed by the insured (employer) under any contract or agreement is not covered. Liability assumed under any contract or agreement, including the assumption of any liability to compensate or to pay a third party for a work-related injury (other than one that the insured or its insurer is obligated to cover under workers' compensation insurance) is the subject of coverage under contractual liability insurance.

Agreements dealing with the assumption of liability of third parties are not uncommon. General contractors often are required to enter into such agreements with owners of work projects. And subcontractors also enter into assumption of liability agreements with general contractors, often as a condition to obtaining the jobs. An owner of a work project is open to suit by an injured employee of a contractor (or subcontractor), particularly when an owner contributes to the injurious exposure in some way. To avoid adverse judgments and the inconvenience of being confronted with suits, owners frequently require contractors to agree, under contract, that contractors will handle and settle the entire matter without involving owners, whether owners are negligent or not. Since agreements such as these also may be covered under contractual liability insurance, it is unnecessary to duplicate coverage under employers' liability coverage.

However, employers' liability coverage, as an exception to the exclusion, does extend to liability under any warranty that work performed by or on behalf of the insured will be done in a workmanlike manner. Such liability coverage does not come within the scope of

Figure 7-1

Workers' Compensation Loss Involving Contractual Agreement

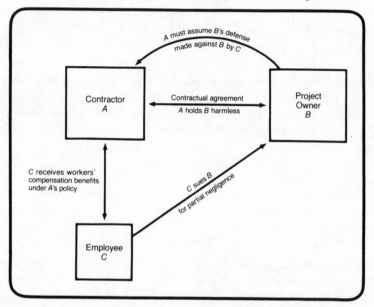

contractual liability under the general liability policy. To avoid any gap in protection, employers' liability insurance covers this exposure.

For a further illustration, refer to Figure 7-1. Assume that A, the contractor, enters into a contractual agreement with B, the project owner, assuming any liability attributable to the acts or omissions of the project owner. C, an employee of the contractor, is subsequently injured because of B's negligence. C collects benefits under A's workers' compensation insurance, and then decides to sue B. B submits the claim to their general liability insurer. If a settlement is made with C, B's insurer then has a right of subrogation against A, who agreed to assume B's liability. A would then be obligated to pay whatever damages were paid by B's insurer. If the allegations of the claim were based upon a warranty that work performed by A was unworkmanlike, A would be given protection under employers' liability coverage. Otherwise, A's contractual liability coverage would apply.

If the project owner, B, did not have a liability policy, it would have been necessary for the owner to request defense from the contractor's insurer. In a case such as this, the insurer would be obligated to defend its insured and the project owner in the claim brought against them by the employee.

Situations such as these can become quite involved. It behooves those who enter into contractual agreements, therefore, to proceed with caution, because there may be occasions when either one or both of the parties involved can be without the protection they sought in the first place.

Punitive or Exemplary Damages Workers' compensation laws require employers personally to assume any punitive or exemplary damages that are assessed against them for violations of law. Under employers' liability coverage, employers are denied coverage for any punitive or exemplary damages because of injury to a person who is employed in violation of law (minimum age or other such laws) with the knowledge or acquiescence of the insured or any executive officer.

Timing of Claim or Suit Another exclusion applying only to employers' liability coverage deals with the time period within which any claim or suit must be brought against an insured in the event of injury or death by disease. This exclusion serves to bar any protection for the employer, unless a claim is made or a suit is brought by an employee within thirty-six months of the policy expiration. Were it not for this cutoff period, an insurer could experience difficulties in establishing whether it rightfully is the insurer for the benefit being sought.

Workers' Compensation Exclusion The final exclusion concerning employers' liability coverage precludes any possibility that employers' liability will cover an exposure that rightfully is the subject of coverage under any workers' compensation or occupational disease law, as well as any unemployment compensation or disability benefits law, or similar law.

Policy Conditions

The workers' compensation and employers' liability policy contains a number of conditions that concern the duties and the obligations of both parties.

Premium Provisions of this condition handle such matters as deposit premiums, audits, and premium adjustments. Workers' compensation premiums are usually based on the employer's payroll in each applicable rating classification. Because it is impossible to determine, at the time the policy is issued, what the payroll for the policy term will be, an advance or deposit premium is collected when the policy is issued. The final premium is calculated according to the exposures which actually existed during the policy period. The insured is required to keep and furnish records that will enable the insurer to compute the earned premium. The compensation manual, which contains the rules, classifications, and rates, is considered to be an integral part of the policy (although the courts do not always support this condition). So, for example, if an insurable exposure should arise during the policy period, it is covered subject to rates and rules of the manual that apply at the time.

Long-Term Policy   When a policy is written for a term longer than one year, it is agreed by both parties that all provisions, including premiums, apply as though separate annual policies were in existence. Thus, if rates are changed, the premium for periods after the first year may be revised.

Partnership or Joint Venture as Insured   If the named insured is a partnership or a joint venture, the insurance applies to each partner or member of such partnership or joint venture, but only while such persons are acting within the scope of their duties for the named insured. If a partner is engaged in some other business as an individual or as a member of another partnership, no automatic coverage applies to that partner in the other business affair. The same is true with individuals involved in joint ventures. The effect of this condition is to keep the policy from covering business functions which are (or should be) insured under other policies.

Inspection and Audit   The insured agrees to permit the insurer and any rating organization having jurisdiction to inspect the premises and operations covered by the policy. Insurance company inspections are highly important in workers' compensation insurance, not only for providing insurers with underwriting information, but also in connection with insurer loss control activities. The inspection and audit condition contains the statement that any such inspections will not constitute an undertaking by the insurer to determine or to warrant that the premises or operations are safe or in compliance with law. This qualifying statement is considered necessary to preclude the possibility that the insurer could be held liable for unsafe working conditions that might result from failure to perform an inspection, or from an inadequate inspection.

Under this condition, the insured also agrees to permit the insurer to examine all payroll records and other reports that may be necessary in determining the amount of remuneration that applies for rating purposes. Usually a premium auditor hired by the insurance company will examine the insured's records, after the conclusion of the policy term, to determine the actual earned premium, based on the actual payroll during the policy period. This condition clearly gives the insurer the right to make such an audit.

Notice of Injury When injury occurs, the insured agrees to notify its insurer or agent as soon as practicable. Such notice also must contain enough particulars of the claim to identify the circumstances and the parties involved.

Notice of Claim or Suit If a claim, suit or other proceeding is actually brought against the insured, the insured agrees to forward particulars to the insurer immediately.

Assistance and Cooperation of the Insured This condition is virtually identical to the ones in most other property-liability insurance policies. The insured agrees to cooperate with the insurer in securing evidence, in attending trials and hearings, and in effecting settlements.

Statutory Provisions for Workers' Compensation Coverage The insurer agrees, under this condition, to be directly and primarily liable to any person who is entitled to workers' compensation benefits under law, even though an insured is insolvent. In addition, it is agreed that all provisions of applicable compensation laws apply just as if they were written into the policy. However, this policy specifically excludes the payment of any punitive or exemplary damages. There are occasions when insurers will pay such damages as part of an entire judgment rendered against its insured. When this occurs, the insured is obligated to reimburse the insurer for any amount in excess of those regularly permitted by law.

Limits of Liability for Employers' Liability Coverage The provision has been previously discussed in detail.

Action Against the Company for Employers' Liability Coverage The insured may not sue the insurer unless the insured complies with all the provisions of the policy.

Other Insurance We have already noted that there may be occasions when an employer will have more than one workers' compensation and employers' liability policy covering its exposures at different locations within a state or interstate. If a claim arises whereby two or more policies might apply, each will be called upon to contribute, pro rata, to the payment of loss.

Subrogation In the event of any claim payment, the insurer is subrogated to all the insured's rights of recovery, as well as to the rights of other persons who receive benefits, against other persons or organizations. Furthermore, the insured must do nothing that would prejudice these rights. This condition is growing in importance. It has become increasingly common for insurers to exercise their rights of subrogation, particularly in cases involving employee injuries caused by unsafe machinery. Insurers of workers' compensation insurance, for example, pay benefits to injured employees, as imposed by law, and then seek to recover their payments by suing manufacturers of unsafe machinery. The increased use of subrogation in such situations has increased the number of losses ultimately borne by products liability insurers.

Changes Policy provisions can be amended only by endorsement.

Assignment Assignment of interest is possible only with the written consent of the insurer. For example, if Bob operates a janitorial service and sells his business to Mary, he cannot assign coverage under his workers' compensation policy to Mary, unless he has his insurer's written consent. This is a common provision in property-liability policies. The insurer has an opportunity to determine whether the moral and morale hazards associated with a given insured are acceptable. Barring this condition, an insurer might find coverage under his or her policy assigned to some party it does not choose to insure. (Special consideration is granted in case of death of an insured.)

Cancellation The policy can be canceled by the insured at any time simply by mailing to the insurer a written notice which states when the coverage is to be terminated. The insurer, on the other hand, can cancel the policy only when the insured is given at least ten days notice—unless the law of an applicable state specifies some other period.

Terms of the Policy Conformed to Statute Any terms of the policy which conflict with the provisions of the worker's compensation laws are automatically considered to be amended to conform to such laws.

Declarations All information on the declarations page should be complete and accurate, because the insured agrees that the declarations page contains statements which are the insured's agreement and representations.

Other Coverages

While the basic protection provided by the workers' compensation and employers' liability policy is sufficient for many businesses and organizations, others have operations which require protection of a broader scope. For this reason, a variety of endorsements are available to tailor protection more closely to the needs of entities. Most such endorsements initially may be added without cost to the insured. But if the anticipated exposure develops during the policy period, an additional charge is made following an audit of the employer's records. Methods commonly used to broaden the scope of protection include the broad form all states endorsement, the voluntary compensation endorsement, the various policies dealing with monopolistic funds, and the stopgap coverage.

Broad Form All States Endorsement   It has previously been mentioned that most state compensation laws provide that there will be some extraterritorial coverage, although there is a great deal of variation in the ways extraterritorial coverage applies. An unendorsed workers' compensation policy provides coverage only under the laws of the state(s) listed in the declarations. If an employee injured in another state files a claim under the laws of the state listed in the declarations, coverage applies. However, if the claim is filed under the laws of a state not listed in the declarations, there will be no coverage for that claim. It behooves employers to be sure that their workers' compensation policies specify all states where operations can be anticipated. However, this is not always feasible, particularly for a firm with a number of employees who travel on business. The broad form all states endorsement provides a solution to this problem. First of all, it provides workers' compensation and employers' liability insurance automatically in all states not listed in the declarations (except monopolistic fund states) just as if the state in question were designated in the policy.

Second, there may be circumstances where some states do not recognize the broad form all states endorsement as the equivalent of an actual policy written for a particular state. When these conflicts arise, this endorsement will reimburse the employer for any claims paid.

The broad form all states endorsement does not cover any fines or penalties imposed upon the insured for failing to comply with the requirements of any state compensation law. The endorsement is optional, but there is no additional charge.

Even with the broad form all states endorsement, the workers' compensation policy provides coverage only with regard to employees who are compulsorily subject to coverage of state compensation laws. Not all employees or employment groups are subject to coverage on a mandatory basis, although there is a trend in that direction. The National Commission on State Workmen's Compensation Laws recommended the discontinuance of numerical exemptions, and special employee exemptions (such as farm and agricultural workers). Until that recommendation is followed by all jurisdictions, there will continue to be a need for voluntary compensation coverage.

Voluntary Compensation Endorsement   The principal purpose of the voluntary compensation endorsement is to extend workers' compensation benefits to employees who are not eligible for mandatory coverage under a state law. When the voluntary compensation endorsement is added to the basic policy, it does for the employee groups named therein what a workers' compensation policy would have done in a particular state, if it had been required for that group, with two important exceptions.

First, an injured employee not covered by compulsory compensation laws can refuse to accept the compensation benefits and proceed against the employer under a common-law action. Then the voluntary compensation endorsement would not apply, since it covers only statutory benefits. The employer is given protection under its employers' liability coverage, of course, if the claim concerns itself with an injury that arises out of and during the course of employment of the person in question. But, if it subsequently is determined that the injury in question did not arise out of and during the course of that person's employment, the common-law suit against the employer would be covered instead under general liability policy provisions. General liability policy provisions exclude bodily injury to any employee of the insured only when such injury arises out of and during that person's employment.

When an employee does decide to accept the statutory benefits, the employee is required to release the employer and the voluntary compensation insurer from further liability. In the event an injured employee or the estate of a decedent has a right of action against a third party whose negligence contributed in some way to the harmful event, it is a requirement of this endorsement that the employee or the estate assign its claim to the insurer. The insurer may then subrogate against the third party. Should the insurer recover any amount in excess of its initial settlement and subsequent subrogation costs, the excess is payable to the employee (or to the employee's estate).

The second way in which voluntary compensation coverage differs from regular workers' compensation is that the former applies only to claims involving bodily injury by accident. Coverage against bodily injury by disease, including death resulting therefrom, is not provided under basic voluntary compensation. However, disease coverage can be specifically added. The basic limits of liability for this coverage are $5,000/10,000. There is greater potential for claims under voluntary coverage because employees have the option of refusing compensation benefits and pursuing their remedy in suit against their employers. They can select whichever course of action offers the greatest potential settlement. Those who are subject to compulsory workers' compensation benefits, on the other hand, do not have that option.

The voluntary compensation endorsement is commonly attached to a workers' compensation and employers' liability policy providing statutory coverage. It also can be used on a policy strictly to provide voluntary compensation coverage. When the endorsement is added, covered employees need not be named individually. They may be designated by generic groupings such as "all executives," "all agricultural workers," "all employees," or "all employees except...." The endorsement also requires designation of the state of operations and the designated workers' compensation law that applies.

If an employee sustains injuries arising out of and during the course of his or her employment and the injury occurs in some state other than that designated in the endorsement, the employer may still be protected. However, the operations must be necessary or incidental to those of the state listed in the endorsement, and the employee must be willing to accept the benefits of the state which is designated in the endorsement. Otherwise, to be protected, an employer must also have the broad form all states endorsement.

The voluntary compensation endorsement, like statutory coverage, still contains a possible gap for claims arising in states with monopolistic funds. Whether there is a gap depends upon the nature of the claim and the requirements of the state(s) in question.

Monopolistic State Funds—Insurance Requirements Neither the standard workers' compensation and employers' liability policy nor other optional coverage provisions automatically extend coverage into the monopolistic states, thus adding to the complexities of an already complicated system of protection. Yet the methods of obtaining proper protection through these funds are anything but complicated. In fact, the extraterritorial application of other states' coverages sometimes is sufficient for protecting employees and employers whose operations extend into one or more of the six states with monopolistic funds. A synopsis of the general requirements in each of the six states follows to illustrate some of the criteria that may be imposed upon outsiders.[1]

Nevada. Employers that have employees who are not residents of Nevada may be exempt from the law of that state while temporarily working there, by filing proof of insurance with the Industrial Commission. This filing is acceptable only if the employer is domiciled in a state which has a reciprocal agreement with Nevada. If the nonresident employer and its nonresident employees are from a state that does not have a reciprocal agreement, workers' compensation insurance must be purchased from the Nevada state fund, assuming that the employer's business is one which comes within a statutory category calling for compulsory insurance. Also, if a nonresident employer hires employees from within the state of Nevada and the employment comes within a compulsory coverage category, that employer must obtain insurance from the fund without exception.

North Dakota. The requirements of North Dakota are virtually identical to those of Nevada. The chief differences concern themselves with which states have reciprocal agreements, and the specific categories of employments that come within the scope of compulsory coverage.

Ohio. Nonresident employees who are covered by workers' compensation insurance in their own states are exempt from the provisions of the Ohio act for a maximum period of ninety days. After that period, the employer must purchase insurance for its employees from the Ohio fund. However, any nonresident employer that hires employees from within the state of Ohio for work in that state must purchase coverage from the fund. Whether coverage is required through the fund for resident employees who will be working out of state depends upon the duration of work in other states.

Washington. Employers of employees who are not residents of the state of Washington may be exempt from the law of the state of Washington if the work is of a temporary nature and Washington has a reciprocal agreement with the home state of such employees. (The term "temporary" is not defined in the law.) In these cases, employers are required to submit a certificate to the state specifying that certain named employees will be working in Washington for a period and that they are covered under the workers' compensation laws of their home state. Employers in states which do not have reciprocal agreements with the state of Washington must obtain insurance from the fund, just as they must do if they hire resident employees of this state.

West Virginia. Although workers' compensation insurance is compulsory in West Virginia for most employments, there are no restrictions or prerequisites for an out-of-state employer that has nonresident employees in this state. Nonresident employers of nonresident employees and/or *temporary* resident employees may work in this state without first having to purchase insurance from the state fund or having to show proof of insurance. However, the nonresident employer is not precluded from electing to come within the workers' compensation coverage of West Virginia.

Wyoming. Any employer that uses nonresident employees is exempt from the provisions of the Wyoming law, while such employees are temporarily within this state and the employer has insurance from some other state covering those employees. (A temporary work certificate is required which expires after six months. A new certificate must then be filed or workers' compensation insurance must then be purchased from the state fund.) However, like some of the other states, the extraterritorial provisions of Wyoming apply only to states which reciprocate.

Although the foregoing synopsis is incomplete and oversimplified, it should suffice as a basis for making some general observations. For example, nonresident employers that enter a monopolistic fund state with nonresident employees may still be in compliance with such state law if their existing policy provides acceptable extraterritorial coverage. This holds true even though the scope of the workers' compensation and employers' liability policy (as well as the broad form all states coverage provisions) falls short of applying in monopolistic states. The key for protection hinges on whether the employment is considered to be compulsory in that monopolistic state and whether there is a reciprocal agreement between the employer's state and the monopolistic state in question.

There are areas of these laws that can present difficult problems unless they first are identified, analyzed, and solved promptly. One such problem would be avoidable if a broad form all states endorsement permitted coverage in monopolistic states. This problem involves the nonresident employee in a monopolistic fund state who seeks the benefits of the state fund because they are better than those of the employee's state of domicile. The employer of a state which has a reciprocal agreement with a monopolistic state only has protection for such a situation if the employee seeks the benefits of the home state. It therefore is necessary for the nonresident employer to compare the benefits offered between the home state and the monopolistic state. If the latter state has better benefits, an employer may find it necessary to purchase insurance from the fund.

On the other hand, an employer that is domiciled in a monopolistic state may have to purchase other insurance if business is extended interstate, in spite of any reciprocal agreements the home state may have with other states.

Another problem is that monopolistic state funds do not complement their workers' compensation coverage with employers' liability coverage. This can present some difficulties to employers domiciled in monopolistic states that operate interstate. Recall that there are some special uses for employers' liability insurance beyond that which may be available under other liability insurance. Depending upon the provisions of monopolistic state laws, it may be necessary for employers to purchase stopgap coverage.

Stopgap Coverage It is the purpose of stopgap coverage to provide a business or other organization with employers' liability insurance when that protection is not otherwise available with a workers' compensation policy. Monopolistic state funds, as previously explained, do not offer employers' liability protection along with workers' compensation benefits. Yet, there are circumstances when an employee who is subject to workers' compensation benefits may be precluded from collecting them, or where the employee has the right to reject the benefits and file a common-law action against the employer.

Moreover, employers may be confronted with third-party-over actions of the type previously discussed.

Stopgap coverage usually can be purchased as an addition to some form of general liability insurance. The wording and the provisions of stopgap coverage are essentially identical to those of employers' liability insurance under the standard workers' compensation and employers' liability policy.

Coverage for Other Exposures

All fifty states, the District of Columbia, Guam, Puerto Rico, and the Canadian provinces have workers' compensation laws, and a large percentage of the work force is subject to compensation benefits. As each of the jurisdictions within the United States continues to improve its laws in accordance with the standards set by the National Commission on State Workmen's Compensation Laws or otherwise, additional workers will have the benefit of the compulsory provisions of those laws. Yet, state workers' compensation laws do not apply to everyone. Persons who are employed by federal institutions or who work upon federal lands or waterways, including federal projects abroad, must obtain protection under other laws. Thus, we will now direct our attention to some of the laws and coverages which are available for persons outside the scope of state compensation laws.

U.S. Longshoremen's and Harbor Workers' Compensation Act The Longshoremen's and Harbor Workers' Compensation Act was discussed in Chapter 6 of this text. The purpose of the act is to provide benefits to such persons as are engaged in maritime, longshoring, stevedoring, harbor work, ship repairing and building who are outside the scope of state compensation laws.

Coverage for this act is provided by using the standard workers' compensation and employers' liability policy with a Longshoremen's and Harbor Workers' Compensation Act endorsement. The endorsement amends the definition of the term "workers' compensation law," as it applies in the standard policy, to include reference to the act. The act is then read into the policy coverage, just as is done for coverage subject to state compensation acts.

Coverage under the workers' compensation section of the policy, with the aforementioned endorsement attached, still applies without limit, while the employers' liability section of coverage is subject to a minimum limit of $100,000. This latter coverage provision is needed by employers for essentially the same reasons it is needed by employers who are subject to state laws.

As noted in Chapter 6, the Defense Base Act and the Outer Continental Shelf Lands Act extend the benefits of the Longshoremen's and Harbor Workers' Compensation Act to additional workers. Again, coverage may be provided by endorsement to the standard workers' compensation and employers' liability policy.

Yacht owners receive protection under the Longshoremen's and Harbor Workers' Compensation Act by purchasing protection and indemnity coverage (P & I) as part of a yacht policy. P & I, considered an ocean marine insurance coverage, is discussed in CPCU 3. P & I is not restricted to employers' liability protection. It also serves to protect vessel owners and charterers for suits alleging their negligence and resulting in bodily injury to persons (such as passengers) and in property damage (to docks, wharves, bridges, and so on).

Although the Longshoremen's and Harbor Workers' Compensation Act applies to persons engaged in maritime employment, it specifically excludes maritime coverage for masters and members of crews of vessels, because they are the subject of protection under the Merchant Marine Act of 1920, also commonly referred to as the Jones Act.

Jones Act The purpose of the Jones Act, discussed in Chapter 6, is to permit masters and members of crews (sailors) of vessels who sustain illnesses or injuries to maintain right of actions directly against their employers when there is reason to believe that such illnesses or injuries are the result of their employers' negligence.

Employers subject to the Jones Act can obtain protection in one of two ways. Employers, first of all, can purchase protection and indemnity insurance, commonly referred to as P & I, which is an ocean marine coverage. The second way by which employers can obtain a certain degree of protection is to amend their standard workers' compensation and employers' liability policy by endorsement. The endorsement in question is entitled "Amendments to Coverage B Endorsement— Maritime (Masters or Members of the Crews of Vessels)." The insurer agrees to provide employers' liability coverage in the event of bodily injury by accident or disease, including death which results from either, at any time, and sustained by any person employed as a master or a member of the crew of any vessel of the insured. Since the standard workers' compensation and employers' liability policy does not encompass such exposures, the endorsement amends the territorial scope. Coverage not only applies within the continental United States of America, Alaska, Hawaii, or Canada, but also upon a vessel "plying" directly between ports of such areas, or upon vessels that are engaged in offshore operations from any port described in the endorsement.

An exclusion applies for any liability of the insured to provide employees with wages, transportation, maintenance, and cure. Furthermore, this insurance does not apply if the insured has other coverage available to handle claims, such as a protection and indemnity or other similar policy, except in cases involving deductible or other-insurance clauses.

The limits of liability condition dealing with employers' liability coverage in the standard policy also is amended by this endorsement. Instead of the usual limit of $100,000, the endorsement is subject to minimum limits of $5,000 for any one employee who sustains bodily injury by accident or by disease, and to $10,000 for all damages sustained by two or more employees. The other standard provisions dealing with these limits, however, remain unchanged. The rationale for these lower minimum limits is that the potential for third-party suits is greater for this maritime exposure than others because suits against employers are the only avenues open to employees for recovery of damages. Those eligible for workers' compensation benefits, for example, are less likely to sue than those who must sue to recover damages.

Federal Employees Compensation Act The purpose of the Federal Employees Compensation Act is to provide a program of compensation benefits for certain federal employees who are not given protection under other acts. This act was discussed in Chapter 6. As noted, the act is administered by the United States as a self-insurer, and there is no provision for the purchase of private insurance.

Foreign Voluntary Compensation Coverage The underlying purpose for foreign voluntary compensation coverage is to extend workers' compensation benefits to nationals of the United States who are hired or assigned by their employers to work indefinitely outside the country, and who are outside the jurisdiction of any compulsory workers' compensation or similar act.

Generally, the insurers under this coverage, which can be added by endorsement to the standard workers' compensation and employers' liability policy, agree voluntarily to pay covered employees the benefits provided under the Defense Bases Act. This act, as previously mentioned, extends to covered employees such benefits as are provided under the U.S. Longshoremen's and Harbor Workers' Compensation Act. The appropriate titles and sections of both acts are therefore recited in the endorsement that provides this voluntary coverage.

When an employee is covered under any other foreign workers' compensation act or law and the employer is paying the premiums, the voluntary coverage insurer is only obligated to pay the difference, if any, between the benefits provided by the Defense Bases Act and the benefits payable under the foreign act in question. Most other provisions applicable to this foreign voluntary compensation coverage correspond to the voluntary compensation coverage endorsement described earlier. Even the limits are the same, but there are differences between the two coverages. Foreign voluntary compensation coverage, for example, includes a so-called repatriation expense agreement under the employers' liability section (for an additional premium, in most instances). An employer usually underwrites the travel expenses of its employees to and from the foreign country of employment. But travel expenses of an injured or disabled person or the remains of a deceased person can be more expensive than those for a healthy person. Also, an emergency trip could be more expensive than a trip scheduled in advance. When repatriation expense coverage applies, the insurer pays only for those costs which exceed normal outlays for returning an employee or a deceased employee to the United States. The maximum limit is $5,000 for any one employee or body.

Finally, the insurer is not liable under foreign voluntary compensation coverage for any consequence, whether direct or indirect, of war, invasion, act of foreign enemy, hostilities, civil war, rebellion, revolution, insurrection or military or usurped power.

Coverage Relationships—Overlaps

The opportunity for Americans to obtain various forms of economic security in the event of injury or disability continues to have unprecedented growth during the twentieth century. Through the combination of private and public programs, people are now able to secure protection under individual and group health plans offered by private enterprise, and under a variety of social insurance programs provided primarily by the government. Millions of persons purchase individual health insurance to supplement their coverage under group health plans, which are made available to them as part of employee benefit package programs, and whatever protection may be available to them under social insurance programs.

The result of all this insurance is that at times benefits will inevitably be duplicated. However, duplication is not necessarily something that must be entirely avoided. The pace at which medical and hospital care costs are rising, for example, almost requires that people seek secondary sources for the payment of those potential costs. But, on the other hand, when the duplication concerns itself with disability income benefits, it is usually undesirable (from a public policy point of view) for total benefits to exceed the amounts actually earned prior to disability. The reason is clear. There would be no economic incentive for persons collecting duplicate disability income to return to their jobs, or to participate in any programs of rehabilitation. Such circumstances could foster malingering.

Treatment of Workers' Compensation Claims Under Private Plans The income replacement benefits of the workers' compensation system are designed to limit coverage to amounts that are less than the actual earnings of workers. But, because of the availability of other similar benefits under private and public health plans, an additional safeguard is required to uphold that intent. The workers' compensation policy, for example, contains an "other insurance" clause which attempts to limit the payment of benefits to a pro rata amount when an insured has other workers' compensation insurance that also applies. Other potential coverage overlaps under private plans will be discussed as follows.

Medical Expense and Disability Income Insurance. Medical expense and disability income insurance may be written on either a group basis or on an individual basis, as discussed in CPCU 2. These types of insurance, like workers' compensation, provide coverage for accident, disease, and disability. However, coverage under such private plans usually applies twenty-four hours a day, unless limited by other policy conditions. Unlike workers' compensation, coverage is not limited to employment-related accidents or diseases.

There is no provision in the workers' compensation policy that modifies coverage to allow for insurance under a private plan of this type. However, duplicate coverage is minimized or eliminated by the coordination of benefits provisions of many medical expense and disability income policies.

Because of the wide variation in policy forms, it is difficult to generalize. Some private plans contain no workers' compensation exclusion. Other forms exclude coverage altogether when workers' compensation benefits are payable. Many forms *reduce* the benefits by any amount payable under workers' compensation insurance. For example, assume the workers' compensation statute limits temporary total disability income benefits to $100 per week, and a person has coverage under a private plan to provide short term disability income for $200 per week. If the employee was temporarily disabled in a nonemployment-related accident, the private plan would pay $200 per week. If the disability occurred on the job, the employer's workers' compensation insurance would pay $100 per week, and the private plan would pay $100 per week (the difference between the $100 workers' compensation benefits and the $200 benefits under the private plan).

It is important to realize that workers' compensation insurance does not eliminate the need for individual or group medical expense and disability income insurance. Many exposures are not employment-related. An individual may become ill due to natural causes, or may be involved in an accident away from work. There may be cases where an employment-related loss does not fall within the workers' compensation statute. In other cases, statutory workers' compensation benefits may be inadequate unless supplemented by insurance under a private plan—such as disability income benefits for a person in the upper-income bracket. Of course, children and unemployed adults will not qualify for workers' compensation benefits and can only be covered under private plans. Many private plans contain coordination of benefits provisions to eliminate coverage overlaps; such programs complement or supplement workers' compensation coverage.

Life Insurance. Life insurance plans do not provide for a reduction of benefits when benefits are also payable under workers' compensation insurance, because there is an unlimited insurable interest in one's life.

Automobile Insurance. The potential for a coverage overlap with automobile insurance arises when an employee, in the course of employment, is injured in an automobile accident.

No-Fault Plans. Very little uniformity exists under automobile no-fault insurance plans thus far enacted. However, no-fault plans, in an attempt to avoid the problems of duplicate benefits, usually specify that benefits recoverable under no-fault plans are reduced by the benefits payable under workers' compensation, social security, Medicare, and various other hospitalization plans.

Automobile Medical Payments; Accidental Death and Disability. With respect to automobile insurance purchased by individuals, automobile medical payments insurance and automobile accidental death and accidental disability benefit coverages often do not have offsets against coverages otherwise available under other private and public insurance programs. One possible reason is that the amounts payable under those automobile coverages are not so large as to create any problems, even when people are able to obtain duplicate benefits under other plans.

The automobile medical expense coverage of some policies does have an exclusion eliminating coverage also payable under workers' compensation. Also, many automobile policies permit the medical payments or medical expense insurer to subrogate.

Commercial automobile medical payments coverages exclude coverage for bodily injury to an employee of the named insured if benefits are payable or required to be provided under a workers' compensation law. For this reason, many employers do not purchase automobile medical payments coverage on commercial automobiles which will be driven exclusively by employees on the job.

UNINSURED MOTORISTS. Uninsured motorists insurance provisions specify that they will not inure directly or indirectly to the benefit of any workers' compensation or disability benefits insurer, or to any organization qualifying as a "self insurer" for those coverages. If a claim is compensable under workers' compensation or disability benefits coverage, the insurer of either such coverage is precluded from denying or reducing the amount of its benefits just because of the existence of uninsured motorists coverage. Thus, for a work-related incident, workers' compensation insurance is primary. But if the workers' compensation benefits are insufficient, the injured person can then proceed with an uninsured motorists claim.

General Liability. General liability policies exclude coverage for injury to employees of the insured arising out of their employment, and they also exclude coverage for any loss for which the insured might be held liable under a workers' compensation law. These exclusions are discussed in greater detail in the chapters on general liability insurance.

The workers' compensation exclusions in the general liability policies might not apply if a person is injured in connection with the premises or operations, or products or completed operations, of someone other than the injured person's employer. In such cases, the injured person would have a cause of action against the party causing the injury, and/or against the employer's workers' compensation insurer. Duplicate coverage is eliminated because of the subrogation clause of the workers' compensation policy.

Treatment of Workers' Compensation Claims Under Public Programs

Social Security. Benefits currently available under social security may duplicate those benefits payable under workers' compensation insurance when persons are totally disabled. This duplication came about in 1956 through a liberalization of the Social Security Act. Many consider that development as just another example of government's efforts to broaden the scope of social insurance in this country.

If a person is eligible for both workers' compensation and disability benefits under social security, the latter must be reduced so that a person receives no more than 80 percent of what was considered as that person's average current earnings just prior to the disability.

Before a person can qualify for disability benefits under social security, he or she must (1) be insured as specified under the law, (2) be under age sixty-five, (3) be disabled for twelve months (or be expected to be disabled for twelve months) or have a disability that is expected to result in his or her death, and (4) file an application for disability benefits.

Medicare. "Medicare" is the popular name given to the Hospital Insurance and Supplemental Medical Insurance Program for persons sixty-five and over (and for certain kidney patients and the disabled of any age). Medicare does not duplicate the benefits provided under workers' compensation insurance, because services covered under workers' compensation insurance are specifically excluded under Medicare.

Medicaid. Medicaid, introduced in 1965, provides medical assistance for the needy. This coverage, like Medicare, is not intended to duplicate benefits available under workers' compensation insurance.

NONINSURANCE TECHNIQUES FOR HANDLING EMPLOYERS' LIABILITY AND WORKERS' COMPENSATION EXPOSURES

The workers' compensation exposure is unique among liability coverages. A great majority of employers fall within the scope of state or federal workers' compensation statutes or must be insured under monopolistic funds. Where benefits are provided by statute and the employer has not purchased insurance, the employer is still required to provide statutory benefits and may, in addition, incur a penalty for failing to purchase insurance or establish a retention program that meets statutory requirements. Where workers' compensation benefits are compulsory, there is no practical alternative other than to purchase insurance or establish an approved retention program.

For employers who are not required to provide compulsory workers' compensation benefits, an exposure still exists. An injured employee may institute a common-law action against the employer. Although insurance is not compulsory, this exposure can be covered through voluntary workers' compensation and/or employers' liability insurance.

In short, anyone hiring one or more employees has a workers' compensation and/or employers' liability exposure.

A study published in 1974, involving a cross section of American businesses with ten or more employees, revealed that 75 percent were fully insured on workers' compensation. The rest have varying forms of insurance to be sure they are covered as required by state law.[2] (See Table 7-1.)

Workers' compensation exposures are also unique in that benefits are prescribed by statute, and even the smallest employer has the potential for a high-severity loss. Even if there is only one employee, that employee may suffer a permanent total disability for which sizable

Table 7-1

How Workers' Compensation Is Insured*

	Total Business
Fully insured (no deductible)	75%
Fully self-insured (no insurance)	3
Self-insured with excess-of-loss coverage	3
Self-insured medical expenses with commercially insured income replacement	5
Merely something required by state law (vol.)	6
Not sure	8

*Reprinted with permission from *Businessmen's Attitudes Toward Commercial Insurance*, Louis Harris and Associates and the Department of Insurance, The Wharton School, University of Pennsylvania, 1973, p. 19.

statutory benefits are payable for the remainder of the disabled employee's life.

Claim frequency is higher under workers' compensation insurance than under most other lines of insurance. No matter how safe the working environment, minor injuries can be expected in the form of cut fingers, sprained ankles, slips and falls, and so on. In industries involving more strenuous activities, sprained backs, amputated limbs, and even deaths may occur with a higher frequency. The relatively high frequency of workers' compensation losses makes it difficult for any employer to deny that an exposure exists. There is a consolation of sorts, however, in that loss experience is more predictable in a line of insurance with a high frequency of losses.

Rating will be discussed in detail in CPCU 5. However, it should be noted here that there is a relationship between most employers' loss experience and the cost of insurance. Smaller employers are class-rated, and pay manual rates for their compensation insurance. Larger employers, however, are experience-rated. The workers' compensation premium is modified based on loss experience during the preceding years. When retrospective rating is used, there is an even more direct relationship between loss experience and the ultimate cost of insurance. If a retention program is used to cover this exposure, the relationship between loss costs and the cost of handling the workers' compensation exposure is even more direct. (Retention programs will be discussed in detail later in this chapter.)

Whether insurance is obtained because it is essential, desirable, or simply available, it does not eliminate the exposure. When businesses take an attitude of indifference merely because insurance is available, or when businesses otherwise abuse it, they soon will find insurance too expensive to purchase or too difficult to obtain. A business enterprise, therefore, must take whatever means are necessary to avoid, control, or reduce losses, whether it has insurance or not.

There are incentives that automatically serve to foster loss control to a certain degree. For every work-related incident, employers sustain two types of costs. The first of these represents the settlement costs and the compensation benefits that are paid to workers when due either by the insurer on behalf of the employer or by the employer who retains the exposure. (Workers' compensation insurance, in other words, does for an employer what liability insurance does in protecting a business that causes damage to others. The principal point of departure is that the liability of an employer under workers' compensation is absolute.) But, depending upon the frequency and severity of claims, an employer also sustains a number of other loss costs, as a consequence of work injuries, that are not recoverable under insurance. These are commonly referred to as uninsured costs. Among costs in this latter category are the following:

1. cost of the injured employee's lost time;
2. cost of time lost by other employees who stop work out of curiosity, sympathy, or to assist an injured employee;
3. cost of time lost by supervisors and others in similar positions who assist the injured employee, investigate the accident, prepare accident reports, attend hearings, arrange to have another employee continue the work of the injured person, or hire and train a new employee for the vacated position;
4. cost of the time spent in providing immediate medical assistance to the injured employee;
5. costs stemming from damage to machine, tools, or other property that is affected by an accident;
6. incidental costs emanating from interference with production, and the inability to fill orders or to fulfill the employee's work on time, as well as any loss of profit resulting from the employee's productivity;
7. costs to the employer in continuing the wages of the injured employee in full after his or her return, even though the services of an employee who is not fully recovered may be worth something less than that amount in terms of production.[3]

Placing this into perspective, it was estimated that 245 million days were lost to production during 1976 because of work-related injuries and deaths. Of that total, the actual time lost from disabling injuries (fatalities are included at an average of 150 days per case, and permanent impairments are included at actual days lost) was 45 million days. Even more noteworthy is the fact that the time lost to production by persons who were not injured but who assisted the injured or who were disrupted by accidents out of curiosity, amounted to a total lost time of 200 million days, and resulted in total costs of $7.9 billion. This lost time can never fully be recovered. As a matter of fact, it was estimated that of the 245 million days that were lost to 1976 production, 120 million of them would extend into and affect the production of future years as well.[4]

The point of all this is that for every claim that occurs, an employer will automatically sustain certain losses over and above those identifiable costs covered by workers' compensation insurance or a retention program. How many uninsured costs a business can assume without impairing its financial status obviously depends upon its financial circumstances. Furthermore, if the frequency and/or severity of compensable claims increases, the costs of insurance may become prohibitive or a retention program may become impractical. These costs can be considered costs of doing business and may be passed on to consumers, or they may reduce net income. But, if the business desires to remain competitive and profitable, there will be a limit to such procedures.

Certain financial incentives do exist, therefore, in attempting to reduce both the insured and uninsured costs of work-related accidents and diseases.

Beyond these financial incentives, most employers are genuinely interested in reducing employee injury, disease, and death for the sake of the workers. Insurance alone does not eliminate the financial and social costs of employee injury, disease, and death. Businesses must take an active commitment to avoid, reduce, or otherwise control losses through whatever methods are best suited to the exposures they face.

Avoidance

Businesses may avoid a workers' compensation or employers' liability exposure by (1) never having an exposure, or (2) abandoning an existing exposure.

Small individual proprietorships or partnerships may be able to avoid workers' compensation or employers' liability exposures simply by hiring no employees. While this may be feasible for a one-person insurance office, or for a "Ma and Pa" grocery store, such avoidance is not feasible for a majority of business enterprises. Even such small proprietorships or partnerships might find it desirable to hire an occasional part-time employee for maintenance work or temporary help.

Liability under workers' compensation statutes may be avoided if only those operations are performed which do not fall under the statutes requiring compulsory insurance. A business enterprise might choose to locate in a state where that enterprise's type of operations does not fall within the statute. Or, an enterprise might keep the number of employees and/or the type of business operations to the point where the statute does not apply. Although such methods might make it possible for an employer to avoid providing compulsory workers' compensation benefits, they do not avoid the exposures at common law. These exposures must still be retained or covered with employers' liability insurance.

There may be other times when an entire project will have to be avoided or abandoned because the potential consequences may be detrimental to the health of employees, or workers' compensation insurance may be too expensive or unavailable.

Loss Control

Most workers' compensation and employers' liability exposures cannot be avoided. Even if it is possible to avoid being subject to a workers' compensation law, there is still an exposure to employees or independent contractors. Even the individual proprietorship or partnership with no employees has an interest in preventing, controlling, or reducing the direct and indirect costs that might be incurred if an owner is injured.

The study published in 1974 and referred to earlier indicates the increasing outside pressures felt by businesses in employee safety (see Table 7-2). It is interesting to note that the pressure is felt most heavily by the larger businesses. In all likelihood, pressures have increased since that study because it has become more difficult, in recent years, to obtain workers' compensation insurance, and rates have increased dramatically.

Loss control techniques, as a noninsurance means of dealing with these exposures, are perhaps more important in the field of workers' compensation than in any other field of insurable exposures. More time and effort is spent in the area of employee safety than in any other area of loss control, and yet not all firms have safety programs. The same study mentioned earlier showed that only 38 percent of all businesses had no employee safety programs (see Table 7-3). Although the lack of a safety program is more prevalent in small businesses than in large companies, the 18 percent of large companies who had no such program may be considered substantial.

Effective loss control programs require more than just safety

Table 7-2

Increasing Outside Pressures in Employee Safety Area in the Past Few Years*

	Total Business	Sales Volume		
		Small	Medium	Large
To improve employee safety				
Increasing	61%	57%	66%	74%
Not happened	27	29	24	20
Not applicable (vol.)	12	13	9	5
Not sure	—	1	1	1
To review and assess your risks in protecting employee safety				
Increasing	57%	54%	60%	72%
Not happened	29	29	29	21
Not applicable (vol.)	14	16	11	6
Not sure	—	1	—	1
To warn your employees about the possible hazards or dangers in their work				
Increasing	52%	50%	51%	69%
Not happened	31	30	34	23
Not applicable (vol.)	16	19	14	7
Not sure	1	1	1	1
To assume more liability for employee accidents and health hazards				
Increasing	46%	42%	49%	57%
Not happened	38	39	38	31
Not applicable (vol.)	15	16	13	11
Not sure	1	3	—	1
To take out more comprehensive insurance to cover possible claims by your employees				
Increasing	33%	28%	40%	41%
Not happened	47	48	47	44
Not applicable (vol.)	18	21	12	14
Not sure	2	3	1	1

*Reprinted with permission from *Businessmen's Attitudes Toward Commercial Insurance,* Louis Harris and Associates and the Department of Insurance, The Wharton School, University of Pennsylvania, 1973, p. 10.

Table 7-3

Safety Training and Engineering Programs Undertaken to
Reduce Work Injuries*

	Total Business	Sales Volume		
		Small	Medium	Large
Undertake	53%	46%	57%	78%
Do not undertake	38	43	34	18
Does not apply (vol.)	0	10	8	2
Not sure	—	1	1	2

*Reprinted with permission from *Businessmen's Attitudes Toward Commercial Insurance*, Louis Harris and Associates and the Department of Insurance, The Wharton School, University of Pennsylvania, 1973, p. 11.

slogans and posters. At a minimum, the positive commitment of top management also is required. If both the interest and the motivation for such programs are lacking among executives, both will falter on all other levels as well. Management must communicate its short- and long-term loss control objectives to all levels, and it also must specify the procedures to meet those objectives, as well as the personnel who are to be responsible for seeing that they are fulfilled. Specific procedures obviously will vary depending upon the size and the complexity of operations and the cost of such a program to a firm. However, all safety and loss control programs deal in some form with the physical facilities, as well as with the hiring, training, and supervision of qualified personnel.

Table 7-4 will illustrate the types of safety programs commonly found in American business.

Among the 53 percent of those businesses in Figure 7-2 who had undertaken a program of employee safety training, the top two efforts were "on-the-job safety training" (90 percent of the 53 percent surveyed who had safety programs) and "on-the-job safety supervision" (89 percent). Another 74 percent reported that they "used 'spot-promotion techniques,'" such as circulars, posters, and bulletin boards." However, only 50 percent said they had "safety engineering requiring the re-evaluation of plant and machinery," and only 46 percent had "regular safety seminars for employees."[5]

A key to any program is the use of inspections by plant safety personnel, insurance company or producer representatives, or outside consultants. Their purpose is to verify the implementation of the safety program and enforce standards which are not being observed. How often inspections should be made depends upon the circumstances in each case. Accidents nevertheless will occur, since they cannot be totally

Table 7-4

Employee Safety Programs*

	Total Business
No programs at all	38%
Safety programs do not apply	9
Have safety programs	53
On-the-job safety training	48
On-the-job safety supervision	47
Use of "spot promotion" techniques	39
Safety engineering requiring re-evaluation of plant and machinery	26
Regular safety seminars for employees	24

*Reprinted with permission from *Businessmen's Attitudes Toward Commercial Insurance*, Louis Harris and Associates and the Department of Insurance, The Wharton School, University of Pennsylvania, 1973, p. 12.

eliminated. When they do occur, they must be investigated and analyzed promptly. Adjustments may then be required in order to avoid similar incidents from occurring in the future if at all possible. It is only when everyone is safety-minded, and when everyone consciously seeks to avoid accidents that a program will have the potentials of success.

Beyond the implementation of a written loss control program, safety meetings, posters, safety supervision, and so on, there are many specific actions which can be taken to reduce exposures to employee loss. A complete discussion of workers' compensation and employers' liability loss control techniques is beyond the scope of this text. The following examples are not exhaustive, but serve merely to illustrate the types of measures that can be taken to reduce employee exposure to loss:

- proper machine guarding,
- a requirement that two persons lift heavy material,
- required use of safety glasses, hard hats, safety shoes, and other safety equipment,
- wearing ear protection in high noise areas, or modification of machinery to reduce noise,
- ventilation to reduce toxic vapors in the work area,
- proper shoring of mines,
- fire safety measures, to prevent employee injuries in a fire,
- adequate exits to evacuate employees in an emergency,
- vehicle inspections to decrease auto accidents

- good housekeeping to eliminate tripping hazards,
- a first aid station and/or nurse on the premises,
- use of cleaning chemicals that will not cause dermatitis, and
- preemployment screening to be sure workers are physically capable of the work involved.

Importance of Loss Control Programs   Occupational accidents in 1976 claimed 12,500 lives compared to 13,000 lives in 1975. These accidents also resulted in 2.2 million disabling injuries during 1976, which was unchanged from 1975.[6] When one compares these figures with the occupational accident statistics of 1912, which is when workers' compensation laws were just being enacted, the significance of the figures becomes more readily apparent.

In 1912, for example, an estimated 18,000 to 21,000 workers lost their lives. Yet in 1976, with a work force more than doubled in size and producing more than seven times as much as in 1912, only 12,500 lives were lost to production. (Statistics are unavailable for the period between 1912 and 1932.) But since 1936, when the death rate per 100,000 workers was at its highest for manufacturing firms, and for nonmanufacturing in 1937, death rates have decreased more than 60 percent to the present.[7]

Loss prevention programs certainly can be credited for much of the reduction in occupational accidents over the years. It is a proven fact that formal programs with the solid backing of management can produce results. Furthermore, the impetus for job safety controls certainly exists, considering the fact that most every claim involving workers causes certain uninsured costs that cannot be avoided by the employer.

Examples of individual company accomplishments concerning continuous hours of work without a disabling injury are shown in Table 7-5.

Rehabilitation   Rehabilitation programs, such as those now provided under the compensation laws of many states, also are thought of as means to reduce the seriousness of disabling injuries. They meet that purpose, in part, by providing vocational or physical assistance to the injured so that they can return to some form of gainful employment.

The interests of both disabled employees and their employers generally favor starting rehabilitation as soon as possible. Rehabilitation is considered an integral part of complete medical treatment, but it may go much further and include such things as vocational training, training to drive a specially equipped car, and so on.

Many states include specific rehabilitation provisions in their workers' compensation laws. But rehabilitation is provided in all states, even if unspecified in the law.

Table 7-5

No-Injury Records*

Industry	Company and Plant Location	Hours Worked Without a Disabling Injury
Chemical	E. I. Du Pont de Nemours & Co. Kingston, NC	66,645,399
Aerospace	Hughes Aircraft Company El Segundo, CA	53,163,698
Automobile	General Motors Corp. Wilmington, DE	20,719,687
Sheet Metal	Remington Arms Co. Independence, MO	20,023,455
Construction	E. I. Du Pont de Nemours & Co. Old Hickory, TN	9,165,858

*Reprinted with permission from *Accident Facts 1977* (Chicago: National Safety Council, 1977), p. 38.

Many insurers have been leaders in carrying on rehabilitation for disabled industrial workers, often providing rehabilitation benefits well beyond those specifically required by statute. In some cases this reduces the ultimate loss cost, and thus the severity, of a compensation claim, because rehabilitated workers are able once again to seek gainful employment. More important is the social benefit of making disabled workers able to feel themselves a meaningful part of society.

Implications of the Occupational Safety and Health Act In spite of the overall reduction in occupational deaths and disabilities, there was a period—throughout the 1960s—when the annual rate of approximately 14,000 deaths and 2.2 million disabilities was fairly consistent from year to year. People could not accept this overall record as satisfactory. Even the workers themselves complained about the lack of safety programs. There were some industries, as well as particular firms within industries that were doing remarkably well in reducing and controlling their occupational accidents, but many others were not. Conditions existed in many firms that simply had to be eliminated or improved in order to provide people with truly safe places to work. This was the primary reason why the Occupational Safety and Health Act of 1970 was enacted by Congress.

The primary concern of OSHA, as noted in Chapter 1, is to guarantee every worker in industry a safe place to work. OSHA attempts to ensure that places of employment are relatively free from hazards likely to cause occupational deaths, diseases, and serious injuries. The consequences of noncompliance involve not only stringent penalties, but also shutdowns for violators who refuse to correct certain conditions following warnings by federal inspectors. Since the construction industry had one of the worst records of any major industry group, it became OSHA's initial target. The enforcement of OSHA has now spread into other industries with poor safety records. The mere threat of OSHA, much like the Sword of Damocles, has brought about improvements in the physical hazards of many firms, although more direct action has been necessary with other firms. Some firms have even been forced to shut down their operations because it was too costly to remove certain hazards to comply with OSHA requirements. Many question this sort of action, particularly when it deprives people of their livelihood.

An actual case illustrating the dilemma created by OHSA regulation is the situation involving producers of vinyl chloride. Research indicates a relationship between that chemical and a rare liver cancer known as angosarcoma. OSHA demanded that workers wear protective devices, and that manufacturers control contamination of the air at a level of one part per million concentration. The manufacturers, employing nearly 6,500 workers, argued that such standards were technologically and economically not feasible.[8] Thus, this industry is caught in the middle: the compliance with OSHA regulation is prohibitive, but the consequences of noncompliance are at least equally prohibitive.

OHSA administrators have also been criticized as being overzealous in their desire to warn workers of all possible occupational hazards. For example, one widely publicized OSHA bulletin was written to inform farmers that wet manure is slippery.

OSHA has been criticized for going too far in encroaching on private enterprise. Yet, despite these criticisms, it would be difficult to deny that OSHA has had an effect on employee safety programs. According to one study, 36 percent of the businesses surveyed said they had put in safety programs as a result of OSHA (see Table 7-4). Given the fact that 53 percent of the businesses surveyed had a safety program, the authors of this study concluded that OSHA alone had, at least in part, accounted for over six in ten of all programs then on line. The impact of OSHA has been particularly heavy among businesses in the contracting and heavy manufacturing industries, among the larger

Table 7-6

Employee Safety Programs as a Result of OSHA*

	Have Put In	Not Put In	Not Sure
Total Business	36%	62%	2%
Industry			
Contracting	58%	39%	3%
Heavy manufacturing	45	54	1
Sales Volume			
Small	32%	67%	1%
Medium	41	58	1
Large	53	45	2
Full-time insurance department	59%	36%	5%

*Reprinted with permission from *Businessmen's Attitudes Toward Commercial Insurance*, Louis Harris and Associates and the Department of Insurance, The Wharton School, University of Pennsylvania, 1973, p. 12.

firms, and among those with a full-time insurance department (see Table 7-6).

Businesses with a safety program were also asked directly how much of an influence OSHA had been. No more than 28 percent with a training program were able to say OSHA has "had no influence at all." The remaining 72 percent split, with 35 percent saying OSHA was a minor influence and 37 percent acknowledging that it was a major influence.

As a result of the OSHA legislation and regulations, businesses acknowledging OSHA's influence report many new safety programs, as noted in Table 7-7. Some insurance company loss control representatives feel that the federal law has made it easier for them to obtain compliance with their recommendations from insured firms.

Despite the fact that many safety programs have been instituted as a result of OSHA, many still question OSHA's value. It has not been possible to prove statistically that worker safety has been significantly improved as a result of OSHA. One possible reason for this is that OSHA standards concentrate on physical work hazards, whereas a majority of occupational accidents are not caused by unsafe conditions, but by unsafe acts. The suggestion is made that if job safety is to be improved, primary emphasis must be placed upon the "attitudes, habits, and actions" of workers.[9]

Some have even blamed government safety standards for causing

Table 7-7

Programs Instituted as a Result of OSHA*

	Total Instituted Programs
Safety training classes	33%
Make employees wear safety equipment	16
Have regular safety meetings	16
Displayed safety signs, posters	13
Started first aid programs	12
Improved safety of building	12
Put in safer machinery	11
Put in guards, locks, safety belts	11
Have complied with regulations	10
Pass out safety booklets	7
Become more involved in safety	5
Have regular inspections	5
Fire prevention drills	4
Employ safety consultant	4
Have own safety evaluation	1
Not sure	1

*Reprinted with permission from *Businessmen's Attitudes Toward Commercial Insurance*, Louis Harris and Associates and the Department of Insurance, The Wharton School, University of Pennsylvania, 1973, p. 16. (Base: Instituted safety programs=36%).

workplace accidents. According to one commentator, some businesses have falsely assumed that compliance with "ridiculous" OSHA standards was the way to stop losses, and OSHA has placed too much emphasis on attempting to comply and not enough emphasis on preventing accidents. "OSHA standards have handicapped us in the education of the business community of what safety is all about."[10]

Whether OSHA is making a difference in this nation's occupational accident and disease record is open to serious question. Part of the difficulty in assessing its performance is that OSHA's statistical input and analysis vary considerably from the normal methods that are being promulgated by such organizations as the National Safety Council and the Bureau of Labor Statistics. OSHA's frequency rate, for example, is based upon cases per 100 man-years of work, while other bureaus base their rate on cases per 1,000 man-hours of work. More important, the definitions of occupational injury, illness, and lost workdays, as used by OSHA, also are different from those of other data gathering organizations. It therefore may be years before it will be possible to know definitely just how effective this federal agency really is.

Retention

The use of retention in treating the workers' compensation exposure has increased in popularity over recent years. Several factors contribute to this increase, including restricted markets for workers' compensation insurance and increasing costs of insurance. In many ways, the workers' compensation exposure lends itself to retention, because there is a higher loss frequency for it than for many other loss exposures. With higher frequency comes greater predictability, and predictability is desirable when losses are to be retained.

Whether losses are retained under a retention program depends upon the size of losses and the existence of excess insurance to cover catastrophic losses. Excess insurance is often purchased for losses exceeding a specified amount in any one occurrence or in the aggregate during a one-year period. In some states, on the other hand, one or both forms of excess insurance is/are required when a firm has a workers' compensation retention program.

The way in which funds to pay losses are initially accumulated is discretionary. Some businesses create funds through an initial appropriation of liquid assets. Others attempt to accumulate funds gradually if their expenses in administering a retention program are less than the expenses normally associated with workers' compensation insurance.

Although retention programs are used for a variety of loss exposures, those dealing with workers' compensation are among the more common. The motives for retaining the workers' compensation exposure vary from one firm to another, but many firms institute retention programs in anticipation of lower costs and improved cash flow.

Lower Costs While the benefit levels and, hence, the pure loss costs of workers' compensation are the same whether or not an insurer is involved, firms often can realize savings by reducing or eliminating some of the insurer expenses that are included in insurance rates— general administrative costs, underwriting and inspection costs, acquisition expenses, taxes and other assessments and, of course, a margin for insurer profit. While inspection costs and administrative expenses exist whether or not a firm retains the exposure, it often is argued that acquisition costs, which include commissions of producers, and underwriting expenses are of no value to the insured. With the reduction or elimination of some of these expense loadings that go into insurance rates, many firms believe they can handle the entire function for less money by retaining the exposure.

Cash Flow Businesses can obtain a certain amount of "use value" by controlling their own reserve funds. These funds may be used in the business or otherwise invested until they are needed to pay for incurred losses. This becomes an especially important factor in periods of inflationary spirals when interest rates usually are increased in order to curb borrowing.

Once a retention program for workers' compensation losses is implemented, a firm usually is able to secure a number of "fringe" benefits when the program is efficiently operated. For example, when an employer pays all losses with company funds, it may take a more active interest in preventing losses than if an insurer were to handle the entire program. (The opposite may also be true, since insurers frequently provide extensive loss control services to their insured accounts.)

Furthermore, some feel employees may be less likely to submit minor claims or to inflate their claims when an employer is administering the program than when an insurer does it. The net effect of this is that it helps an employer to decrease an outflow of money when losses are retained. Prompt handling of claims by the employer no doubt will aid employer-employee relations too. Others point out that employee relations problems may be magnified with a retention program if a claim is delayed, mishandled, or denied.

In spite of the advantages of retaining workers' compensation loss exposures, retention is not necessarily the ideal tool for all businesses, even though they may generate large premiums and otherwise qualify. A great deal hinges upon the ability of a firm to prevent, reduce, and control its losses effectively and pay claims. It also is important to be able to predict losses with relative certainty. No retention device would be adequate if either or both of those qualities are lacking. This is especially significant considering that workers' compensation laws hold employers strictly liable to virtually unlimited benefits.

If it is to obtain the lower costs that commonly are cited as one of the primary advantages of retention, a firm must be able to administer its program efficiently. This means that its overall costs and expenses must be substantially lower than those that otherwise would apply if protection were provided by an insurer instead.

Before establishing a retention program, it is not enough to compare the direct cost of insurance with the anticipated direct cost of retention. Accounting and tax implications must also be explored. As discussed in CPCU 1, insurance premiums are tax deductible as a business expense. Under a retention program, only amounts actually paid or unequivocally payable in the future are tax deductible. If a worker was totally and permanently disabled in an industrial accident, the firm may be obligated to pay him or her $200 a week for life. Because the continuation of these payments in future years depends on how long the worker lives, only the amounts actually paid are tax deductible.

There is more to the costs of administering a retention program than simply paying for losses. Firms must allocate and pay such fees as those that may be assessed for supporting state workers' compensation departments or industrial commissions, as well as second injury funds. They must pay taxes, too. But the costs of maintaining loss prevention and claim services which might otherwise be performed by an insurer, and an experienced staff to perform those and other services, are without a doubt the most important factors that must be considered. Then, too, under a retention program, a firm must pay their own defense costs in any hearings and trials. When all of these and other essential costs equal or exceed what it would cost under a program of insurance, the idea of retaining this exposure probably should be abandoned or at least postponed.

State Regulations It is permissible to retain workers' compensation losses under the U.S. Longshoremen's and Harbor Workers' Compensation Act, and under the compensation acts of all other United States jurisdictions, except Guam, Nevada, North Dakota, Puerto Rico, Texas, and Wyoming. But, aside from filing an application as a condition precedent to obtaining a license to establish a retention program, there is little uniformity with the other requirements that must be fulfilled.

Few jurisdictions require filing fees, while many require security deposits based upon the financial status of entities. In this respect, either negotiable securities or surety bonds are acceptable. In Ohio, for example, a $100,000 surety bond or negotiable governmental securities is required. Arkansas also requires a $100,000 surety bond.[11] A variety of assessments are required, such as for the administration of OSHA, for second injury funds, and special tax funds. Virtually all jurisdictions also require annual reports indicating payrolls, losses, expenses and other pertinent data.

Excess insurance requirements also vary considerably. Some states require some form of excess insurance for hazardous operations. Others permit or encourage excess insurance for all firms with a workers' compensation retention program. On the other hand, some jurisdictions leave excess insurance up to the firm's discretion, while a few simply do not permit its use under any circumstance.

Aggregate Excess and Specific Excess Coverage Many firms can retain workers' compensation losses, but few are large enough to retain *all* of their losses. Stockholders, banks, and others with an interest in the financial success of a firm would be unwilling to see it exposed to the potential of a loss that might make it insolvent. It is for these reasons, and in the interest of potential claimants, that many jurisdictions require or encourage firms with a retention program to obtain some form of excess workers' compensation and employers' liability insurance as part of their licensing requirements. This excess insurance may be required by law, even though a firm appears to be financially able to withstand catastrophic losses.

Two forms of excess coverage are available. One is referred to as aggregate excess or stop loss insurance, and the other is called specific excess insurance. Whether one or the other or both are used, they serve to pay for losses over those that are retained. It therefore becomes important for a firm to determine just how much it can afford to retain in any one large loss and/or for all losses that may occur within a one-year period. If a firm retains more than it can afford, this could result in a catastrophic situation. Too little retention, on the other hand, could result in unnecessary expenditures for excess insurance premiums.

Aggregate Excess or Stop Loss Coverage. Under an aggregate excess or stop loss arrangement, a firm is insured for losses that exceed a specified aggregate of all losses incurred within one year. The coverage, moreover, is subject to a maximum dollar limit.

The amount that must be retained by a business depends upon its normal premium. The normal premium is that amount which is derived by multiplying the payroll of all employees subject to the program by the applicable rates. (The rates used are those published by the rating bureau having jurisdiction. These rates cannot reflect any premium discounts, but they normally do take experience modifications into consideration.) The normal premium is then modified by a certain percentage specified by the insurance company. The result is the retained amount, or so-called loss fund.

The maximum amount of aggregate coverage provided by an insurer varies. It depends upon (1) what the insured estimates it may need, (2) the firm's loss experience, and (3) the maximum limits which the insurer feels it can safely provide.

For purposes of illustration, say a firm selects, and the insurer agrees to provide, a maximum limit under excess aggregate coverage of $750,000. Its normal premium is determined to be $150,000, and the percentage of the normal premium specified by the insurer is 100 percent. The retained amount therefore is $150,000. During the policy period of this excess coverage, the firm sustains several losses. It settles those losses by paying compensation and other benefits, as required by law, as well as some legal fees in connection with hearings before a workers' compensation board or an industrial commission. The firm also is held liable and is required to pay a sizable judgment involving a third-party-over action, including the assumption of costs for its defense, and the costs for appealing the decision. If the total of all such sums, during the policy period, exceeds $150,000 (the retained limit), the insurer will indemnify the firm for the difference between that amount and the actual amount of all loss sustained up to the limit of $750,000. This means that, while the firm must assume all losses under $150,000, its total loss outlay stops at $150,000. This is the meaning for the term "stop loss coverage."

It is important to note, furthermore, that certain claims are not insured under any circumstances. These correspond somewhat to the exclusions that regularly apply under a workers' compensation and employers' liability policy. For example, aggregate excess insurance does not cover any payments required of the firm under any workers' compensation law in excess of any benefits regularly provided because of the willful misconduct of the employer, or because a person is employed in violation of the law in full cognizance of the employer or its executive officers. Also, no claims are covered for any liability assumed by the employer under any contract or agreement, nor for any punitive or exemplary damages. If, in the previous illustration, all losses are considered to have cost the employer $300,000, and it is determined that $200,000 of that amount involves excluded losses, the insurer of the excess aggregate insurance would be under no obligation to pay any part of such losses. The reason is that the legitimate losses amounting to $100,000 are within the $150,000 retained limit of the loss fund.

Specific Excess Coverage. Some firms retaining the workers' compensation exposure, particularly those that are able to retain large, single losses, often select specific excess coverage as a backup against their catastrophic losses, rather than or in addition to aggregate excess coverage. Sometimes they have no choice. They may be required to purchase this insurance to qualify to administer a retention program under certain laws of jurisdictions.

Under specific excess insurance, a firm selects a specific amount which it feels it can safely retain in any one occurrence. Many factors must be considered in determining that retention amount, including the level of compensation benefits, the financial strength of the firm, the propensity of management to take risks, and the cost of specific excess insurance with different retention limits. If the insurer agrees that the retained limit, which in effect is a deductible, is the proper amount, the firm then purchases coverage for any loss, in one occurrence, that exceeds the retained amount subject to an overall maximum insurable limit.

For purposes of illustration, say that a firm selects $100,000 as the

Table 7-8

Aggregate Excess Versus Specific Excess

Aggregate Excess		Specific Excess	
$100,000 aggregate retention limit		$100,000 specific retention limit	
$1,000,000 maximum limit		$1,000,000 maximum limit	
Losses		Losses	
	$ 25,000		$ 25,000
	75,000		75,000
	90,000		90,000
	35,000		35,000
Total	$225,000	Total	$225,000
Aggregate retention	100,000		
Amount of excess insurance	$125,000		
		Since none of the losses exceeds the $100,000 per occurrence retention limit, the entire loss must be retained.	

limit it safely can retain in any one loss or occurrence. The insurer also is willing to provide an overall maximum limit of $1 million. If the firm sustains a loss of $75,000 in any one occurrence, it will have to retain the total loss. If it sustains a loss amounting to $200,000, it must retain $100,000 of that amount. The other $100,000 will be paid by the insurance company—if the claim is not otherwise excluded. (The coverage provisions and the exclusions of specific excess insurance generally are the same as those applying to aggregate excess insurance.)

Note the difference between these two coverages from the standpoint of paying arrangements. Table 7-8 shows how a firm would be protected under each coverage arrangement, assuming the same maximum limits, same losses, and the same retained limit, except that one is on an aggregate basis and the other applies per occurrence. The firm that has specific excess coverage should take into consideration the possibility of having to pay every loss that falls short of its retained limit. The specific excess retention limit that ultimately is chosen is not to be considered as the maximum safe overall limit, but only that limit which the firm feels it can safely retain in any one occurrence.

The example in Table 7-8 was not intended to imply that aggregate excess coverage is necessarily better than specific excess coverage. The

Table 7-9

Combination Aggregate Excess and Specific Excess Coverage

Aggregate Excess		Specific Excess
$200,000 aggregate retention limit $1,000,000 maximum limit		$100,000 specific retention limit $1,000,000 maximum limit
	Losses $ 25,000 75,000 90,000 35,000	
Total losses	$225,000	

example serves as an illustration of the way each of these two forms would respond to a series of losses. Given a different series of losses, specific excess coverage might be more advantageous than aggregate excess coverage. Of course, the comparative premium cost must also be considered. Many firms will find it desirable or necessary to purchase both aggregate excess and specific excess coverage.

Combination Aggregate Excess and Specific Excess Coverage. There are occasions when a firm with a retention program desires to buttress its specific excess insurance with an aggregate excess policy. This is especially useful for the firm that has an unusually high frequency of losses which (in total) it may be unable to handle without an undue hardship. With an aggregate excess limit applying over a specific excess limit, such a firm may be able to stop its losses to the point where it will be reimbursed for some of its usual losses in a given period. For example, assume a firm purchased combination aggregate excess and specific excess coverage as shown in Table 7-9. In this illustration, the firm chose to limit its retained limit to $100,000 per occurrence and $200,000 in the aggregate. Although no single loss has exceeded the $100,000 specific retention limit, the aggregate losses have exceeded the aggregate excess limit, and the firm will be indemnified for $25,000 of its total losses during that period. It therefore will have to retain $200,000 of the total losses. And, since the losses have reached that stop loss limit, the firm will be indemnified in full for any additional losses up to $1 million that might have occurred during that same period.

The methods for using excess aggregate and specific excess coverages can be adapted in a variety of ways in the best interests of both risk managers and insurance companies, to the extent that they meet the specifications of any applicable laws.

Role of Managing Service Agents Circumstances may exist when a business entity, faced with a profit squeeze and/or with a steadily increasing premium for its workers' compensation and employers' liability insurance, desires to establish a retention program in order to obtain the common benefits of lower costs and improved cash flow. If it has such qualifications as a high premium volume, a large payroll, a high concentration of employees at one or two locations within a given state or geographical area, and a fairly stable loss record, but it lacks the internal expertise for administering the program, it still is possible for that entity to utilize retention as a risk management technique. All that entity need do is to engage a specialty firm to act as its agent in managing all or part of the administrative services that may be required in operating the program.

If a firm does not have the expertise required for administering all facets of its claims handling, it can retain the services of a specialty firm that will do what is required. If the firm can handle its claims but lacks the capabilities for handling all of the required loss control services, it can hire a firm to perform only those functions. There may be times, however, when a firm with a retention program will need a full range of services. In other cases a firm may be required by an insurer, as a condition precedent to obtaining excess insurance, to hire a managing service agent for all of its internal affairs.

When a full range of services is required, it will be the obligation of the managing service agent (1) to fulfill all of the duties that are required of the firm, as the employer, as may be required under a workers' compensation law; (2) to establish and conduct loss prevention and engineering functions, and the reports that go with it; (3) to provide the insurance company with periodic claim records, showing tabulations on claims, and the amount of payments made and outstanding, along with loss adjustment expenses; (4) to file all notices and reports required by the workers' compensation board or industrial commission; (5) to attend hearings and trials as may be required following claims; and (6) to handle whatever else may be required under any workers' compensation law. When this full range of services is provided, the only obligation of the firm is to provide ample funds so that the managing service agent may pay all of the claims as payment is required. Of course, the firm must also pay the managing service agent for their services.

At one time there were but a few such independent services that functioned as managing service agents. But as insurance companies began losing some of their large accounts to retention programs, they began forming subsidiaries to provide such services in direct competition with the independent firms. In 1974, both the independent firms and the insurance companies were vying for business and government accounts amounting to approximately $1 billion.[12] With the increased interest in retention today, more such firms are entering the field.

The costs of such services are an important factor in many decisions connected with retention programs. The fees charged by managing service agents vary a great deal. Although many base their fees on a fixed percentage of the annual normal workers' compensation premium, there are occasions when the fee is based upon a percentage of incurred losses, on a payroll basis, on a claims frequency basis, or a per diem basis. It all depends upon the agent and the services.

However, unless good service is received, and unless the costs of such services by managing agents are no higher than those of an insurer under a primary workers' compensation and employers' liability policy, subject to any experience rating plan, it may not be to the firm's advantage to retain the exposure. It will depend largely upon how much cash flow a firm can otherwise derive from maintaining its reserve fund. This in itself may be advantageous for a time. But if the firm should determine at some future time that its cash flow is not performing up to expectations, problems will arise if the firm should then decide to abandon its retention program and go back to purchasing insurance. One such problem is that the firm will have to maintain funds until all losses incurred under the retention program have been paid. There may be advantages of retention over insurance provided by an insurer, but all factors must be carefully considered if complications are to be avoided.

There may be fewer benefits in the use of retention than are immediately apparent. The cost of providing for the workers' compensation exposure may be less predictable under a retention program than if insurance is purchased. Many of the costs supposedly saved by not paying insurance premiums are not really saved, because of the increased expenses of a self-administered program and the cost of excess insurance. The expenses of handling the workers' compensation exposure may also be reduced through insurance savings generated by experience or retrospective rating, in which a firm's actual loss experience, if favorable, is reflected in a reduced premium.

Captive Insurance Companies A business forms a captive insurance company for many of the same reasons that it establishes a retention program. However, a captive usually operates on a larger scale, and is somewhat more complex to operate.

A corporation experiencing difficulty in obtaining specific excess coverage over its workers' compensation retained limit, for example, might consider acquiring or forming a captive. The argument for a captive is even stronger if that same corporation is experiencing capacity problems with, say, its products liability exposures. The combination of these problems may prompt the corporation to abandon any plans for retention and, instead, concentrate on forming or buying a captive to handle some or all of its coverage needs.

A captive involves the creation of a subsidiary company (or the purchase of an existing insurer) for the sole purpose of providing the corporation with some or all of its insurance needs. By doing so, it also may obtain some of the other advantages that normally accrue with retention, such as cash flow, lower costs for protection, and certain tax advantages. Of course, as discussed in CPCU 1, there are both advantages and disadvantages to captives, just as there are with retention.

Although there are different kinds of captives that serve specialized needs, it is important to note here that a captive operates much like an insurance company. It needs administrators and expertise in loss control, finance, insurance, and so on. Instead of having to purchase specific excess insurance over its workers' compensation retained limit, or catastrophe limits for its products liability exposures from an insurance company, a captive has its own retention limits to the point where it is safe to do so, and then obtains its excess limits through the medium of reinsurance.

Noninsurance Transfers

Those who are unable to avoid their loss exposures, or who are unable or unwilling to retain them, may be able to transfer their responsibility for them in one of two ways: (1) through the transfer of losses to an insurer which accepts them in exchange for a "sum certain," referred to as the premium, or (2) through a noninsurance transfer, so called because someone other than an insurer accepts the responsibility for losses in exchange for an agreed upon consideration that does not necessarily involve money.

Noninsurance transfers are widely used, contractual liability agreements being among the more common ones, and they usually involve a great deal of latitude. However, there are certain limitations, particularly with respect to those that are contrary to public policy. For example, if work is inherently dangerous, such as blasting operations, the possible liability of a person hiring another to perform that work cannot be transferred to the one who will be performing it.

The responsibility for providing workers' compensation benefits also cannot be transferred. This stands to reason, since compensation laws are for the benefit of those who are injured or killed, and the laws make employers responsible for the payment of such benefits. It therefore would be unconscionable to allow that responsibility to be passed onto others who may be unable to fulfill it, particularly since the amount of benefits that may be payable is uncertain until someone is injured.

To ensure that potential recipients of workers' compensation benefits have an avenue of recovery, the laws of most states impose the obligation of such benefits upon others in some circumstances where an employer does not have insurance or is otherwise unable to compensate its employees. This is especially true in the contracting business.

If a subcontractor does not have workers' compensation insurance, and a subcontractor's employee is injured, the laws of most jurisdictions require the general contractor to provide those benefits. Of course, once the general contractor (or its insurer) makes payment, it normally has a right of action against the uninsured subcontractor who is primarily responsible. In many cases, the subcontractor who did not or could not purchase workers' compensation insurance will be unable to reimburse the general contractor (or its insurer) for the benefits paid.

In most such cases, the general contractor unconsciously assumes the exposure of the subcontractor. More astute general contractors routinely require evidence of insurance from subcontractors to avoid assuming this risk. Because a general contractor utilizing the services of an uninsured subcontractor is exposed to loss in the event of injury to employees of the subcontractor, the general contractor's insurer will charge a premium when the records are audited for any subcontracted operation for which the general contractor is unable to produce evidence that the subcontractor was insured.

This mechanism for consciously or unconsciously increasing the exposure of the general contractor is not really a transfer of the exposure because the subcontractor remains primarily liable.

Chapter Notes

1. The following material relating to the six states relies heavily on *F.C.&S. Bulletins*, Casualty Volume, pp. W.C. C-1 to C-8.
2. This study is entitled *Businessmen's Attitudes Toward Commercial Insurance*. It is a Sentry Insurance national opinion study conducted by Louis Harris and Associates and the Department of Insurance, The Wharton School, University of Pennsylvania and published in 1974. The national sample of businesses surveyed during 1973 was designed to be a representative cross section of the major categories of American business. The survey was limited to those companies with ten or more employees, as it was felt that most owners of companies with fewer than ten employees would not be able to articulate their insurance needs in the areas important to the study.
3. "Accident Cost Control," *Bureau of Labor Standards Bulletin*, 1965, as cited in Insurance Institute of America, *RM 55 Practices in Risk Management, Selected Readings*, 1977 Exam Edition, p. 170.
4. National Safety Council, *Accident Facts*, 1977, p. 25.
5. *Businessmen's Attitudes Toward Commercial Insurance*, p. 12.
6. *Accident Facts*, p. 25.
7. Ibid., pp. 25, 29.
8. Editorial Opinions, "No Easy Way Out for OSHA," *Business Insurance*, 8 July 1974, p. 16.
9. Herbert E. Wolff, "OSHA Not Enough, Loss Control Also Needed," *The National Underwriter Company*, Property and Casualty Edition, 15 August 1975, p. 28.
10. Andre Maisonpierre, as quoted in Jerry Geisel, "Work Comp Costs Climb; Self-Insuring Pools Grow," *Business Insurance*, 12 December 1977, p. 69.
11. Geisel, p. 69.
12. Margaret LeRoux, "Self-Insurance of Work Comp Heats Up Market for Administrative Services," *Business Insurance*, 11 November 1974, p. 78.

Index

C

G

H

I

M

O

S

U

Y